# ADDICTED TO NOISE

Also by Michael Goldberg

Nonfiction
*Wicked Game: The True Story of Guitarist James Calvin Wilsey* (2022)

Fiction
*True Love Scars* (2014)
*The Flowers Lied* (2015)
*Untitled* (2016)

# ADDICTED TO NOISE

## The Music Writings of
## MICHAEL GOLDBERG

Foreword by Greil Marcus

Backbeat Books
ESSEX, CONNECTICUT

An imprint of Globe Pequot, the trade division of
The Rowman & Littlefield Publishing Group, Inc.
4501 Forbes Blvd., Ste. 200
Lanham, MD 20706
www.rowman.com

Distributed by NATIONAL BOOK NETWORK

Copyright © 2023 by Michael Goldberg

All images are from the author's collection or were taken by the author unless otherwise noted.

Front and back cover design by Todd Alcott

Cover design and artwork based on the 1953 original edition of William Burroughs' *Junkie*, which features a painting by Al Rossi on the cover.

*All rights reserved.* No part of this book may be reproduced in any form or by any electronic or mechanical means, including information storage and retrieval systems, without written permission from the publisher, except by a reviewer who may quote passages in a review.

British Library Cataloguing in Publication Information available

**Library of Congress Control Number: 2022934027**

ISBN 978-1-4930-6810-4 (cloth)
ISBN 978-1-4930-6811-1 (epub)

∞™ The paper used in this publication meets the minimum requirements of American National Standard for Information Sciences—Permanence of Paper for Printed Library Materials, ANSI/NISO Z39.48-1992

To my beautiful, soulful wife,
Leslie, the love of my life, who was
there for the wild ride that
resulted in the writings in this book.

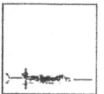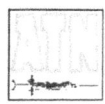

Original *Addicted To Noise* logo, 1994. Design by Frank Kozik

# CONTENTS

Foreword     ix
*Greil Marcus*

Preface     xi
*Michael Goldberg*

| | |
|---|---:|
| John Lee Hooker: Born to Boogie Woogie | 1 |
| Ramblin' Jack Elliott: Driftin', Pickin', & Boltin' Brew | 9 |
| Bob Dylan's Beat Visions (Sonic Poetry) | 13 |
| Punk Lives! | 37 |
| Professor Longhair | 45 |
| Van Morrison Breaks His Silence (Sort Of) | 47 |
| Patti Smith: Return of the "Bad Girl" | 53 |
| Ramones Look Like Hoods, but They're Not | 79 |
| The Clash: Revolution Rock | 83 |
| God Save the Sex Pistols! | 89 |
| An Audience with The Artist Formerly Known as Prince | 93 |
| Muddy Waters | 101 |
| The Hated Flipper | 105 |
| Flipper Interviewed | 108 |
| Prime Time for Crime | 125 |
| Sleater-Kinney: The Band from the End of the World | 131 |
| The New Look Behind KSAN's New Sound | 165 |
| The Sedating of Rock & Roll Radio | 174 |
| Consume the Minimum, Produce the Maximum | 181 |
| James Brown: Prisoner of Love Meets the Prisoners of Hate | 189 |
| James Brown: Wrestling with the Devil | 196 |
| Talking Heads | 209 |
| John Fogerty Looks Back on the Glory Days of Creedence Clearwater Revival | 211 |
| Chris Isaak: The Making of a New Elvis | 219 |
| Townes Van Zandt | 229 |
| Gil Scott-Heron and "'B' Movie" | 230 |
| The Elusive Jolie Holland | 233 |

| | |
|---|---:|
| Tom Waits Interviewed | 237 |
| Michael Jackson: The Making of the "King of Pop" | 243 |
| Devo: Sixties' Idealists or Nazis & Clowns | 255 |
| The Loner: A Conversation with Neil Young | 261 |
| San Francisco: The Sound of Freedom | 265 |
| Flamin' Groovies: Legends Out of Their Own Time | 271 |
| American Music Club: Ready for the American Music Public | 275 |
| AMC's Mark Eitzel Interviewed: Wishing the World Away | 280 |
| Laurie Anderson | 295 |
| Lou Reed's Rock & Roll Heart | 301 |
| Sly Stoned No More | 313 |
| George Clinton: The Return of Dr. Funkenstein | 317 |
| Rick James: Sex, Street Smarts, & Success | 323 |
| Rick James: The Untold Story | 330 |
| The Last Days of Dennis Wilson | 337 |
| Brian Wilson: God Only Knows | 346 |
| Captain Beefheart | 357 |
| Zappa as Reporter, Historian, & Cynic | 359 |
| Zappa Comes Clean | 365 |
| Stevie Wonder: The Timeless World of Wonder | 371 |
| Richard Thompson Shoots Out the Lights | 384 |
| The Second Coming of Robbie Robertson | 389 |
| Inventing (Punk) Rock at the Mabuhay | 399 |
| Eyes: The First Feminist Rock & Roll Band | 407 |
| | |
| Discography | 413 |
| Acknowledgments | 415 |
| Permissions | 416 |

# FOREWORD

I TOOK NOTICE WHEN I first read Michael Goldberg in the *San Francisco Chronicle*. He appeared to be a stringer, a byline appearing occasionally and unpredictably, and then more often, then something to look forward to. It was the late seventies or early eighties. It wasn't that he was covering bands and records others weren't. He brought certain values to his work that were unmistakable and seemingly contradictory.

These were empathy and ambition. This was someone who clearly meant to get his name out there, to make you pay attention, to make you do what I was doing—looking for his name. He was careful with his facts—Goldberg is, I think, a reporter before he's anything else. There was a sense of hurry in his writing—you could get the idea he wrote a lot more than was getting into print. But there was no narcissism in that ambition, no preening, no persona, none of the Wouldn't-You-Like-to-Buy-Me-a-Drink smirk of the likes of Jeff Goldblum's rock critic in the 1977 *Between the Lines*, which was the likes of all too many real-life music writers then, before, and after.

It was clear that this was someone who was interested in what others had to say. Who came first, the listener or the writer? Maybe the writer, because that got him in the door, but after that, he wasn't like the other people the people he was talking to had talked to before. That evidence was there from the first and it's never lessened. In these pages, that might be Brian Wilson or Flipper, Gil Scott-Heron or Van Morrison, Rick James or the Minutemen. Right off, whether these are profiles, interviews, or, as you'll find here, raw Q&As more formal pieces were drawn from, you are hearing questions other people don't ask, an honest curiosity that has nothing to do with a catchy headline or even a pull quote. You can feel the atmosphere: someone has walked into a room with a pencil in his hand—as the words go in perhaps the first song about a music critic, not counting Chuck Berry's aside about the writers at the rhythm reviews—and suddenly people are relaxed. They get the feeling that this person is not Janet Malcolm's reporter: the person no one able to conquer his or her own vanity should ever trust. He isn't after your secrets. He doesn't want to ruin your career to make his. He doesn't care what you think you need to hide. He actually is interested in why and how you make your music and what you think of it. So people open up, very quickly, and, very quickly, as a reader, you're not reading something you've read before.

For me, this stands out most dramatically, in ways that aren't dramatic at all, in the work here on Sleater-Kinney and Robbie Robertson. You can feel inner lights go on: whether eager, as Janet Weiss, Corin Tucker, and Carrie Brownstein are, or ruminative, digging down, as Robertson is, you feel that Goldberg's uncostumed directness ("What do you think gave you, particularly early on, the confidence to believe in yourselves? Where'd it come from?"), which is also an invitation to depth, produces responses that are unfiltered, unguarded, unprotected. You can feel that the people in Goldberg's pages never talked to anyone the way they're talking to him before—not close friends, who wouldn't ask big-deal questions, not other writers, who wouldn't know to.

Questions of success, of career, of what's next, of the-new-album, are a different language here, if they're here at all. "I think that's really crucial that just as soon as I started playing music when I was 18, there were all these people that completely encouraged me and wanted to put out a record even though I had played four shows," Tucker says. "And they were doing that for all these other people in the community too. You were part of something that was encouraging this underground, that you wouldn't have to rehearse for two years before you cut your first LP." In these pages, against that, Robertson speaking in 1987 on why, 11 years before, he, in Goldberg's words, "shut down The Band and walked away," leap out, he and Tucker talking about the same thing from different poles of gravity: "I just had nothing left to say. I would look around, and I would see all these other people who had nothing to say either, but they insisted on making records and I thought, 'I don't want to do that.' I felt like I'd made a hundred records." He talks about why he doesn't want to talk about Richard Manuel of The Band, who had killed himself the year before: "I can't tell other people's stories. It's not right."

The pain of loss in what both people are saying is undeniable, but there's no self-pity, no begging for alms, which is to say admiration: Look what I survived! The absence of cliché, on the part of the interviewer but more so on the part of the person being interviewed, is even more striking—and you can reach the conclusion that Tucker, Robertson, and so many others here don't speak in clichés because they've heard that Goldberg doesn't, and, responding to his empathy, reply in a way that communicates the emotional fact that they want to speak on the same level, as if the usual suspects from any musician-interview aren't good enough for him, and by extension his readers, and by extension your fans, and by extension yourself.

All through these pages, you can hear the people Michael Goldberg is talking to and talking about reach the same conclusion. I can trust this guy, they say. What the hell.

—Greil Marcus
Oakland, California
December 2018

# PREFACE

ON DECEMBER 1, 1984, with the help of some Santa Cruz, California-based programmers, I launched the first internet rock & roll magazine, which I called *Addicted To Noise*. But that is *not* why *Addicted To Noise* is the title of this book. (More on that soon enough.) And this book is not an anthology of articles that were published on the *Addicted To Noise* website, although a half dozen of my *Addicted To Noise* interviews are included here.

Prior to *Addicted To Noise*, or *ATN* as some of us referred to it, I was best known as a senior writer at *Rolling Stone*, where I worked for nearly a decade. Before that, I wrote freelance articles about music, musicians, and the music business for many publications, including *Esquire, DownBeat, New Musical Express, San Francisco Chronicle, Berkeley Barb, Musician, Creem, San Francisco Bay Guardian, In These Times, New West, New Times*, and *New York Rocker*.

This book collects some of my feature stories, profiles, essays, and interviews published, mostly in print but some online, over the course of 47 years, from 1975 to 2022. The earliest is a Q&A that my wife, Leslie (she was my girlfriend at the time), and I did with Frank Zappa in 1975. The most recent are a 2018 consideration of the lasting influence of San Francisco's Mabuhay Gardens punk club and a 2022 essay about Eyes, the first all-woman feminist rock & roll band.

The writings included here are my favorites. I spent a lot of time on some of these stories—from months to as long as a year. In some cases, I had extensive knowledge of my subject long before I began preparing the story included here. I already knew Chris Isaak for five years and had written about him at least two times when I profiled him for the piece in this book. I spent a year, off and on, working on the Robbie Robertson profile and had listened to The Band since their debut, *Music from Big Pink*, was released in 1968. I'd been a fan of Frank Zappa and the Mothers of Invention since 1967, the same year I saw Captain Beefheart and His Magic Band for the first time when they played a set at the KFRC Fantasy Fair and Magic Mountain Music Festival on Mt. Tamalpais in Marin County; I was 13 at the time. When I finally interviewed Lou Reed in the mid-'90s, I had been listening to the Velvet Underground as well as Reed's solo albums for three decades and had read numerous interviews with the famously feisty artist, and the same was true of Neil Young. I first interviewed Patti Smith in 1975, before her debut album, *Horses*, was released, 21 years before the lengthy interview with her that is included in this book.

The artists here might seem to be quite random. I mean what do Professor Longhair, Lou Reed, and Chris Isaak have in common? Or Gil Scott-Heron, Neil Young, and Flipper? Townes Van Zandt, the Flamin' Groovies, and Black Flag? The through line is my love of their music; with few exceptions, these artists matter to me. The other through line is my intense curiosity regarding the creative process and what motivates the musicians I

Cover of the one and only issue of *Hard Road*, 1970.

care about, which are many and quite diverse. So there *are* themes that run though these interviews, which tie them together in unexpected ways.

I guess you could say that what most unifies all the musicians included in this book is me. I wanted to talk to and write about all of them, and I was lucky enough to have that opportunity, sometimes more than once. For that I am to this day grateful. I don't take it for granted. It was a gift.

There are many, many artists whose music I love that aren't in this book because either I never had the opportunity to write about them, or I'm not happy with the results from when I did write about them—too many to list here. But I do want to draw attention to two bands that you may not be aware of. Clover were originally a four piece country-rock band with Alex Call, a soulful singer, writer, and rhythm guitarist; John McFee, an amazing pedal steel player and lead guitarist; John Ciambotti, an excellent bassist; and Mitch Howie, a solid drummer. They are best known for backing Elvis Costello for his debut, *My Aim Is True*, but only two of them played on it and what they should be known for are their two excellent early '70s albums, *Clover* and *Forty-Niner*, which are what led Elvis to ask them to play on his album. Clover added additional members including Huey Lewis (before he became a star), but it's those two albums they made as a quartet that are worth seeking out. Their version of "Stealin'" on *Clover* and "Mr. Moon" on *Forty-Niner* are transcendent. The other band is Stoneground, which included former Beau Brummels singer Sal Valentino and four terrific women singers, Lydia Moreno, Lynne Hughes, Annie Sampson, and Deirdre LaPorte. Stoneground recorded three strong albums in 1971 and 1972. I recommend *Stoneground* and *Family Album*.

Some background: I was born in Oakland, California, and grew up across the highway from Mill Valley, in a suburban house my dad built in the early '50s. I was a rabid reader of books, loved movies, loved *Mad* magazine and Marvel comics, and by the age of 13, was taking photos of rock stars including Janis Joplin and Jim Morrison. The Beatles were the first rock band that excited me, but soon I was digging the Stones, the Yardbirds, the 13th Floor Elevators, and Love.

I read rock reviews in the *San Francisco Chronicle* starting when I was 12 or so and recall being mesmerized by a cover story in *Ramparts* about Bob Dylan by Ralph J. Gleason. Soon after the first issue of *Rolling Stone* was published in 1967, I knew I was going to write about rock music. I wanted into that rock & roll world I was reading about, and it seemed like the guys (it was mostly guys at the time) writing in *Rolling Stone* had access to that world. And I wanted to write! I wanted to share my perspective on music and musicians with others who love music, and I wanted to be the best writer I could be, so that I could adequately communicate what I saw and heard and felt and experienced.

At 17, with some friends, I published one issue of a Bay Area rock magazine we called *Hard Road* after an album by the British bluesman John Mayall; the cover story was an interview with Jerry Garcia. I had met Garcia at my friend Tom Donahue Jr.'s house (yes, the son of Tom "Big Daddy" Donahue, the man who created underground free-form rock radio) and when I asked Garcia if he would let me and my *Hard Road* cofounder interview him, he said yes and, amazingly, gave us the address of his house in Larkspur. Yeah, I had chutzpah.

That interview with Jerry Garcia contains one quote that has stayed with me. At that time, the summer of 1970, the Sixties weren't really over yet. Young people, myself included, really thought a revolution was at hand, that the values of the counterculture would replace those of "the establishment." One of us asked Jerry Garcia this question: "Do you agree with some of the people that rock music is a manifestation of revolution?"

"It isn't that to me," he said, "but I could see that someone could think that it is, yeah. I agree that there are people that say that, yeah. Well I think that the whole thing about what revolutions are is all completely different. I mean the unfortunate thing about the revolution that's going on now is that there's a lot of people that are still stickin' to like an old-line revolutionary tack. Which has been shown to be a miserable failure and it's like I think that the revolution that's going to make some sort of dent or some change, is already over, it's already happened in principle and the waves of it are now moving away from ground zero at the rate of about, you know, a mile every four years *(he chuckled)* or something like that. You know it's going real slow but eventually the whole world will be a different place. As a result of things that have already happened. It's already gone, it's already passed and the rest of it is like telling everybody who missed it that it's already happened. A friend of mine says that it's a cleanup action. Mop up action. And I'm inclined to agree with that."

What Garcia was saying was that a philosophical change had occurred in the mid-'60s, and some people understood that, got it when it happened, and were living their lives with different values—values of love and empathy and community, not consumerism, everyone for themselves, and the almighty dollar rules. Valuing creativity and staying true to one's beliefs, rather than pursuing money as the be all end all. Or at least that's how I interpreted what he said. I thought music, art, writing, film, and photography were the most import things in the world, and writing and photography were what gave my life meaning. Maybe what Garcia said that day helped me pursue what mattered to me, writing about music and musicians (and photographing them) at a time when almost no one thought you could make a living as a rock critic.

While attending the University of California, Santa Cruz, I wrote reviews for the college paper, *City On a Hill Press*, and soon wrote features and reviews for the local underground paper, *Sundaz!* I broke into the "big time" in 1975. I was a copyboy at the *San Francisco Chronicle*, so I knew *Chronicle* art critic Tom Albright. I also knew Paul Krassner, editor of *The Realist*, whom I had interviewed for *Sundaz!* and who in 1973 had lived down a dirt road from me just above the beach, between Santa Cruz and Watsonville. In 1975 my then-girlfriend and soon-to-be-wife Leslie Robinson and I went to a show by the great New Orleans combo, The Meters, at the Boarding House in San Francisco, and afterward I spoke to their manager and got his phone number. The band was going to return to the Bay Area, and I got it into my head that Leslie and I could write a story about The Meters for Francis Ford Coppola's *City of San Francisco* magazine. I didn't even talk to the band; instead, I interviewed the manager over the phone. Leslie and I wrote the article and then I wrote a letter to the arts editor at Coppola's magazine, telling her that Albright and Krassner both thought this article might be right for *City of San Francisco*. Our article on The Meters was published, and so began our professional careers as journalists.

I learned how to report stories and write profiles, features, and essays by closely studying articles I liked, and by doing 100s of interviews, writing 100s of stories, and working with a number of great editors. For nearly 10 years, I had one or two stories in nearly every issue of *Rolling Stone*.

I was young when I wrote some of these articles, and at times I was rather overenthusiastic, as when, for instance, I wrote that the music and lyrics of the Clash were "as rich as anything that Bob Dylan or the Rolling Stones created in the '60s." I no longer think that is true, though I still love the music and lyrics of the Clash.

At the beginning of most of the articles, essays, and interviews here, I have added a newly written introduction, some short, some a bit longer, to provide context of one sort or another. You might notice that I took more than 20 of the photographs in this book; for a time, until I was hired by *Rolling Stone*, I would interview the artist or band *and* photograph them. Once I was working for *Rolling Stone*, that was no longer practical.

Please note that from one piece of writing to another, there are some inconsistencies of style. You will find "Seventies" in one piece and "'70s" in another. The writings here, for the most part, are reproduced just as they were originally published. Exceptions are where something was factually wrong, or if a word was misspelled—that kind of thing.

But about the title of this book. My relationship to rock, going back to when I was 10 years old and first heard the Beatles as I watched the *Ed Sullivan Show* in February 1964, has been akin to a junkie and the drug to which they are addicted. When I first came up with the name *Addicted To Noise* for that internet magazine I was starting, I was under the mistaken impression that in the mid-'50s Frank Sinatra had criticized rock & roll as "noise," but though in 1957 Sinatra trashed the music as "the most brutal, ugly, desperate, vicious form of expression it has been my misfortune to hear," I can't find evidence today that he ever called it "noise." Still, I think Addicted To Noise captures the spirit of rebellion kids felt in the '50s and '60s, listening to what was then a new kind of music. To my dad, rock was noise, and I was addicted to it. I still am.

—Michael Goldberg
El Cerrito, California
January 2022

John Lee Hooker won four Grammys, and was honored with a Grammy Lifetime Achievement Award.
© Robert Knight

# JOHN LEE HOOKER: BORN TO BOOGIE WOOGIE

*I was lucky to meet three of the great bluesmen of all time: Professor Longhair, Muddy Waters, and John Lee Hooker. All three have since left the planet. The blues came of age and flourished a time long gone. Once the blues sounded brand new, as brand new as rock & roll in the '50s or punk in mid-'70s, but by the time I first heard this great American music as a teenager, the blues was an art form of the past, the '20s and '30s right up into the late '30s and '40s when T-Bone Walker, John Lee Hooker, and Muddy Waters took the sounds of the Delta and plugged them in, and on into the '50s and early '60s. Originally a music made by and for Blacks, since at least the mid-'60s and perhaps a bit earlier, the blues has been fetishized for the most part by white men: academics, critics, and collectors. For most teenagers and 20-somethings today, the blues is as ancient and irrelevant as the writings of Homer. That is unfortunate. I met John Lee Hooker late in his life. He was riding high, with two homes, one in Vallejo where I first spent a long afternoon conducting an interview for* Rolling Stone *that was never published, and the other in Redwood City, a suburb south of San Francisco, where I spent another afternoon with him for the story you're about to read. Sadly, Hooker passed away on June 21, 2001; he might have been 88, but you never know, 'cause Hooker could never be pinned down as to what year he was born. Thanks to his comeback hit album, 1989's* The Healer, *Hooker had more than a decade of the good life. I got to see him perform once; it was at the Sweetwater, an incredibly small club in Mill Valley. I sat about 10 feet from Hooker, who I believe was in his late 70s at the time. He was the real deal. If anyone doubted that the blues was still alive, while John Lee Hooker played and sang that night, it was. Alive. (Please note that when this story was originally published, there were lyrics from John Lee Hooker's songs at the top of each section. I have had to remove those because the publishers of those songs wanted to charge me $300 per song to include a few lines. However, I have used the title of each song as the title of a section, and you can easily check out the lyrics if you search for the song using Google.)*

## Crawlin' King Snake

FROM THE OUTSIDE, IT looks like just another of the many middle-class homes lined up along this quiet suburban street in Redwood City. Two-car garage, neatly mowed lawn, beautifully trimmed Christmas tree in the front window. One can almost see Ward Cleaver adjusting his hat as he exits the front door, heading off to work.

But the scene inside is almost surreal. For there in the living room, sitting on the couch opposite the TV set, is the one and only, the legendary Delta bluesman, John Lee Hooker. It's as if Elvis or Robert Johnson or Hank Williams had materialized in the aisles at Kmart.

The King of the Boogie extends a hand in greeting. "We gonna talk some *talk*," says John Lee Hooker with a sly grin. His voice is deep and mellow, like a good glass of Cabernet Sauvignon. He glances over at an attractive young lady named Lynn, who is sharing a couch with his nephew Archie, and his goddaughter, Chris. "Maybe we should go talk in the back room."

"Ah, we've heard it all, John Lee," smiles Lynn.

As always, as he's appeared in every photograph, and on every stage he's graced, John Lee Hooker is dressed to the nines. His outfit—really, it's his trademark after so many years—consists of a shiny, dark-gray suit with a silk kerchief poking out of the breast pocket, a silk shirt, dark-burgundy gangster tie, black socks with red stars all over them, a white fedora, and diamond-studded gold rings glistening off fingers on each hand. This is, after all, the man who John Belushi and Dan Aykroyd based the Blues Brothers on. This is the real Blues Brother.

Hooker asks for a cup of tea and Chris heads off to the kitchen. Years ago he would have been after a slug of whiskey. But unlike many of his peers, Hooker didn't succumb to the excesses of a life as one of the preeminent bluesmen. "Life didn't beat him up," says Bonnie Raitt, who shared a Grammy with Hooker last year for their stunning rerecording of one of Hooker's early hits, "I'm in the Mood." "John Lee quit drinking years ago. That's a big difference between him and a lot of the other bluesmen whose lifestyle encouraged alcoholism. The late hours and endless bad food and cheap hotels and boredom of being on the road encourages a lifestyle that's not so healthy. It must be some kind of destiny, some angels watching over him. Right now he's at the top of his form."

These are good times for John Lee Hooker. His hit album, *The Healer*—which features, in addition to Raitt, a number of other musicians he's influenced, including Santana, Los Lobos, George Thorogood, and Robert Cray—has sold over a million copies, a phenomenal feat for a blues album. Earlier this month, Hooker was inducted into the Rock & Roll Hall of Fame—an honor well overdue—at a prestigious awards banquet at the Waldorf Astoria attended by some of the biggest stars in popular music. The 70-year-old bluesman pops up frequently on MTV and VH-1. The Rolling Stones featured him on their live pay TV broadcast at the end of their Steel Wheels tour; he's even had his own Showtime special. Many of his peers—Muddy Waters, Howlin' Wolf, Sonny Boy Williamson—are dead, and others—Willie Dixon, Albert King, B. B. King—are either resting on their reputations or have gone Vegas. But Hooker has suddenly become hot while remaining true to the classic Delta style he learned as a kid. In fact, he is more popular right now than he has ever been during his lengthy, 40-plus-year career.

"Yeah, I've been trying to figure out why," he says, shaking his head. "To me it's just the greatest thing. I appreciate it, I love it, but I still wonder."

## Boogie Chillen'

ONE NIGHT IN THE 1950s, Sammy Davis Jr. sent a limo to pick up John Lee Hooker and deliver him to a private party to perform for the Rat Pack: Frank Sinatra, Dean Martin, et al. On another occasion, Elvis shut down a club so that Hooker could perform for the King of Rock & Roll and his entourage. "He transcends boundaries," says slide guitarist Roy Rogers, who produced *The Healer* and has toured with Hooker for years. The Stones, Elvis, the Rat Pack. "He's appreciated by all those people and the man on the street. That's the power of his blues."

John Lee Hooker casts an immense shadow across rock & roll. Both Bo Diddley and Carl Perkins, who along with Elvis, Little Richard, and Chuck Berry helped invent rock, were heavily influenced by Hooker's songs, which they heard on the radio years before they started making their own records. "I was on tour with Carl Perkins years ago," recalls Hooker, removing his hat and rubbing his head. "And he said, 'I got this from you, this rock & roll thing.' And I said, 'You've got to be kidding.' And he said, 'No, you started it and you don't know it.'"

When Sam Phillips was getting Sun Records going in Memphis and before the Chess brothers had struck pay dirt with their blues label in Chicago, Hooker was already a star. He hit big in the blues field with "Boogie Chillen'" in 1948, then followed it up with "Hobo Blues," "Crawlin' King Snake," and "I'm in the Mood," which reached the Black Top 5.

Bob Dylan's first important engagement in New York was opening for Hooker at Gerde's Folk City in 1961; the Rolling Stones were Hooker's opening act on a European tour in the early '60s; and even the Beatles were humble in his presence. "I met them when I was living in England in the early '60s," says Hooker. "They said, 'You the talk of the country.' They didn't say the talk of the town. 'You the talk of the country. John Lee Hooker! We love your music.'"

The Doors, the Lovin' Spoonful, Van Morrison, David Bowie, Jimi Hendrix, the Who, Rod Stewart, Stevie Ray Vaughan, Santana, Aerosmith, the Animals, Little Feat—the list goes on and on and on. Nearly 45,000 teenagers showed up for ZZ Top concerts at the Cow Palace last November to hear the Texas boogie band play its rewrites of classic Hooker guitar grooves. "We just consider ourselves proud to be interpreters of the blues," said ZZ Top guitarist Billy Gibbons. "After all, guys like John Lee Hooker—the original guys—are still around." Hooker, naturally, gets a kick out of all this. But he doesn't quite get it. "I ask myself, 'What do I have that everybody wants?' To me, it's just old, funky guitar playing. I don't play no fancy chords, just a driving, funky beat. I guess that's what they want. I'm not a fast player. So many people are doing that. There's no style to them. You hear one, you hear they all sound alike.

"What am I doing that's so different? I just got this rockin', steady beat, very lonely and sad. Sometimes I hear people say of a musician, 'He's a heck of a guitar player.' Well I don't look at the blues like that. I look at it as a thing that's a deep, deep feeling."

Hooker is the consummate bluesman. He has a deep, resonant voice that he has used to sing some of the most powerful blues ever recorded. He sings many of his songs in an almost confessional manner, as if he were confiding his darkest secrets to a close friend. His songs—from early recordings like "Sally May" to recent masterpieces like "Rockin' Chair" and "My Dream"—are simple, poetic representations of what he has seen and the life he has lived. His guitar playing—he tunes his red "Lucille" model Gibson guitar to an open chord—is all feel.

As Hooker is quick to admit, he is not a blues guitarist like B. B. King; he doesn't launch into extended single-note solos. Rather, Hooker's blues is about mood, a mood created by his exquisite voice and intense rhythm guitar work. Unlike most electric guitar players who use a pick when they play, Hooker insists on strumming and picking the notes with his fingers. "I asked him about that one time," says Archie Hooker. "He said to me, 'With a pick you can't feel the strings. You got to feel it. Then you can create your own sound.'"

Hooker is an extremely spare guitar player, treating notes as if they were $100 bills, using only as many as are truly necessary to get the job done. Consequently, when he interrupts his rhythm playing to punctuate a passage with a brief melodic line, the notes he plays inevitably add real meaning to the song.

Hooker can literally get more emotion out of one note than others can ripping through the entire scale. This was particularly apparent when Hooker performed his classic tune "Boogie Chillen'" backed by the Rolling Stones and Eric Clapton for a pay TV special in Atlantic City. Toward the end of the song, Hooker signaled to Clapton to take a solo. The British guitarist deftly delivered a blues solo, technically adequate yet emotionally unsatisfying. Clapton had barely finished before Hooker grabbed a couple of strings on his guitar and just started wanging away at them, creating a sound that was simply transcendent.

Clapton just plays the blues; Hooker *is* the blues. Later, asked if there was anything unusual about playing with the Rolling Stones, Hooker shrugged. "No, just like any other group to me. Just like any other group. Nothing unusual."

## Hobo Blues

DEVIL'S MUSIC. THAT'S WHAT John Lee Hooker's daddy, a Baptist preacher and farmer, called the blues. In Clarksdale, Mississippi, where Hooker grew up, his father wouldn't allow him to listen to blues in the house. Clarksdale was a center for Delta blues. The legendary "crossroads" where Robert Johnson supposedly made a deal with the Devil is in Clarksdale. In addition to Hooker, Muddy Waters and Son House are from Clarksdale, and Charley Patton spent years working at the Dockery Plantation, 42 miles from Clarksdale. Bessie Smith died in a Clarksdale hospital. In those days, the late '30s, and for years to come, the blues was considered crude, vulgar.

Yet Hooker loved the songs he did hear. And when his mother remarried, it was his good fortune that his stepfather, Will Moore, was an accomplished blues guitarist willing to teach the kid what he knew.

His first guitars were crude affairs. "I took a board and put wire on the board, and just played it like that. I learned a lot on that. And rubber on the wall. Old strips of tire rubber. Anything to get a sound. Then my stepfather gave me a guitar; I thought I had everything, the world. I would sleep with it in the bed."

He didn't want to work on his father's farm; he didn't want to go to school; he didn't want to do anything but play that guitar. "I didn't get a good education," says Hooker. "I put music over an education. To get a good education, I would have stayed there. And never would have gotten famous. I wouldn't have become a star. So I have no regrets."

At about age 15, he took off for Memphis. His parents went after him and brought him back to Clarksdale, but they couldn't hold on to him. "I went right back," says Hooker. "I had saw the bright lights in the big city of Memphis. I said, 'I'm not going back.' I ran away again. I didn't stop at Memphis; I went on to Cincinnati. From Cincinnati to Detroit."

Even as a teenager, Hooker had seen the writing on the wall; there wasn't going to be much of a life for him in Clarksdale. "Being a Black man, the odds were against you there," says Hooker. "I had people telling me as a kid, 'Get away.' They told me to go up North. So I took their advice."

Hooker was determined to become a star, just like Blind Lemon Jefferson and Charley Patton and Arthur "Blind" Blake, and the other amazing blues singers he'd listened to on the radio. "I wouldn't let nothing discourage me," he says. "Many people would tell me, 'You ain't gonna be a star, you'll never get nowhere.' They call the guitar a 'starvation box.' Like you gonna starve trying to play music."

By the time he was 18, Hooker was working day jobs for 50 cents an hour in Detroit—he was a janitor, a movie usher, "whatever came along"—and playing house parties and funky clubs at night. His big break came in 1948 when a record store owner, Elmer Barbee, saw him perform and decided to become his manager. Barbee had some crude recording equipment and, over the next few months, set about recording Hooker.

When they had something they liked, they approached producer-record company owner Bernie Besman. Besman, now 78, remembers having some reservations about the Black teenager who showed up at United Sound in Detroit to make his first record. John Lee Hooker had a bad stutter at the time, and Besman doubted that a kid who stuttered could be much of a singer. Nonetheless, he gave Hooker a shot.

During a three-hour session, Besman told Hooker biographer Charles Shaar Murray, he planned to record four songs. Most of the session was devoted to "Sally Mae," "Highway 51," and "Wednesday Evening." "I needed four numbers," Besman said. "I was teed off already that I wasn't going to get four records."

But Besman pressed Hooker for one more, a boogie. They ended up cutting three versions of the song now known as "Boogie Chillen'." (The first two takes were eventually released by Besman as "Johnny Lee's Original Boogie" and "Henry's Swing Club.")

Released on Modern Records on November 3, 1948, "Boogie Chillen'" (backed with "Sally Mae") is a masterpiece that not only made Hooker a star, but was the basis for the boogie guitar groove that thousands of rock musicians have been playing ever since.

"I was working at Copco Steel, in Detroit, when it came out," says Hooker. "That 'Boogie Chillen'' comes tearin' the world up. Everywhere you go they playin' it. You go in department stores, they playin' it. Every time you turn the radio on, they playin' it. Now here I am stuck in the plant. I said, 'Here, take this badge. I ain't working here no more. I gotta go!'"

## When My First Wife Left Me

"MY THIRD WIFE DIVORCED ME in 1970—that's when I came out here. She took the house from me. She said, 'Hit the road, Jack.' I drove all the way out here," says Hooker.

He's digging into a huge plate of take-out Chinese food, moving his body to a recent recording he made with John Hammond Jr., a chilling slow blues number called "Highway 13" that is playing in the other room.

"It was raining and storming, I could hardly see the road," Hooker is singing from the stereo. "Driving down Highway 13."

"I packed my bags, put them in my car and started boogieing," he says, resuming his story. "Drove out here and I've been here ever since. Me and my wife broke up and I just said, 'I'm coming out to California! I'm gonna live in California!'"

He's silent for a time, listening to his song and eating. "Not bad," he says of his dinner. "This pretty good."

The blues life effectively destroyed two of Hooker's three marriages (his first marriage, in 1943, lasted less than a year). "That have an effect on your marriage," he says. "You have to have a good woman to really understand a musician's life. Most of them don't. I can understand it. They lonely there. You out on the road. You home a while, then you gone again and she has to stay there at the house. It takes a really subtle-minded woman to say, 'I'm going to hang in there.'"

"My second and third wives tried to get me to quit playing music," says Hooker. "They went along with it for a while, but then they got jealous and thought I'd be out there with women. They tried to get me to quit and get just a regular job, but I didn't put nothing ahead of my music."

He leans forward: "They put it to me: Either them or my music had to go. So I said, 'Well, it's got to be you then.'"

Asked how many children he has, Hooker at first says, "I've got seven kids." But when asked how many sons and daughters, he corrects himself: "Two sons. I lost track . . . Six girls, two boys that's eight. Yeah, they're all grown up, and some of them have kids. They all love me, and I love them. One's in Chicago, Frances, who I don't see too much. The rest of them are in the area."

Although Hooker's career has risen and fallen numerous times in the more than 40 years since "Boogie Chillen'," he's never been out of work. Just when he seems on the verge of being relegated to the history books, his career has picked up new life. "John Lee has always been relatively successful," says Bonnie Raitt. "He didn't have the big 20-year gap where he was unknown and had to be rediscovered, like a lot of these guys."

In the mid-'60s, after his initial success had faded, he recorded successfully for VJ, the first record company to release recordings by the Beatles in the United States. In the early '60s, his song "Boom Boom" took off in England, where dozens of British Invasion bands idolized him. Back home, he was swept along with the early '60s' folk music boom, playing coffeehouses and folk clubs. Dylan worshiped Hooker, hanging out and partying at the bluesman's hotel room in New York in 1961. "We got to be good friends," says Hooker. "He would go down there every night to the club with me, so finally he got on the stage and played, you know. And he was discovered by Albert Grossman [manager of Dylan, The Band, Janis Joplin, and others], who has passed on now."

Hooker says the parties with Dylan lasted all night long. "Oh, yeah. Drinking wine, beer, whiskey. Women. Most of the time he be playing guitar by himself, with his girlfriend Susan [Suze Rotolo] playing an autoharp. [Hooker may be remembering Rotolo's friend, Janet Kerr, who unlike Suze did play the autoharp.] He stood around playing until daylight. Those days! Every time we see each other, we talk about that. . . . I thought he was tremendous. He had a style unto himself, same as me. Nobody sounds like Bob Dylan; nobody sounds like John Lee Hooker."

Hooker played the Newport Folk Festival in the early '60s, which is how Bonnie Raitt first became familiar with him. Raitt was 14 when she bought a recording of the 1963 Newport Festival and was entranced by Hooker's performances. "As young as I was, there was something really deep and emotional about the way he was singing," she says. "He seemed to go deeper than the other blues people. It was real mournful and real sexy and real dark. Not demonic, but low-down. He really stands alone. For Mississippi Delta blues. . . . I've never heard anybody that low-down. He's so unique."

By the end of the '60s, Hooker's tunes had appeared on albums by the Doors, the Animals, Them, and others. Then he hooked up with the Los Angeles–based blues-rock band Canned Heat, recorded and performed with them, and reached a whole new generation of blues fans.

During the '70s, after moving to the Bay Area, Hooker and Van Morrison frequently shared the same stage. Morrison put Hooker on the bill with him when he could—and recorded with him on the album *Never Get Out of These Blues Alive*.

Hooker spent much of the '80s playing clubs and concert halls; he didn't do much recording because he was sick of all the "cut-throat record companies" run by "crooks" and "biting dogs." But a few years ago, his booking agent, Mike Kappus, took over managing Hooker's career and came up with the idea of recording him with some of the musicians he'd influenced. The result was *The Healer*.

A highlight of the sessions was recording "I'm in the Mood" with Bonnie Raitt; it was recorded live in the studio with Hooker and Raitt playing and singing at the same time. "There was a lot of voltage when we sat down and played together," says Raitt. "And there was a lot of erotic tension between our styles of music. So even though personally we're not hitting on each other, there's a tremendous anima going on. . . . My womanhood and his manhood playing together was really very powerful."

Producer Roy Rogers says that after *The Healer* was recorded, it was shopped around to a number of major labels; they didn't want it. So it was released on the small, Los Angeles–based Chameleon label. With sales of over a million copies, Rogers doesn't think there will be any problem getting a major label to handle the next album, which will feature performances by Van Morrison, Robert Cray, and others.

"You get lonely when you're living by yourself," says Hooker as he finishes up his dinner. "You get lonely for a wife or a woman or whatever. But at least you've got peace of mind most of the time. Which isn't easy when you're married. 'Do this, do that, don't go here, don't go there.' You don't hear that. But sometimes you get lonely. But I'm used to living by myself. I may shack up a little while, but I'll never get married again. I been burned too many times. I'm at the end of the road for getting married. Nothing else left there."

Pushing away his plate, Hooker narrows his eyelids to slits. "I bet my wives regret they didn't stay with me now," he says. He laughs a low, deep laugh. "Now that I'm famous."

*San Francisco Chronicle* and *Examiner, Image* magazine, Sunday, January 27, 1991

Ramblin' Jack Elliott in the dressing room of the Rancho Nicasio, Marin County, 1977.

# RAMBLIN' JACK ELLIOTT: DRIFTIN', PICKIN', & BOLTIN' BREW

*I first met Ramblin' Jack Elliott in 1973 or maybe it was 1974. I was writing for a Santa Cruz underground paper called* Sundaz!, *and I photographed and interviewed him for an advance piece. In 1977, our paths crossed again when I spoke to him for a story that ran in the* Berkeley Barb; *two years later a slightly revised version of the* Barb *story ran in the* San Francisco Chronicle. *Many years later, in 1992, I tried to get Ramblin' Jack to record an album for my short-lived indie label, National Records. At that time, it had been a decade since his previous album, and before that, another decade. My hope was that we could get him to record a new batch of songs, not the same ones he'd been singing since the '60s. I thought we might revive his career. He was in the Bay Area, playing gigs in Berkeley and Point Reyes. I spoke to him after the Berkeley gig, showed him the* Berkeley Barb *article I'd written about him so many years earlier, and introduced the idea of a new album with backing by a rock & roll band. A few nights later, after the Point Reyes gig, I hung out with him at the Old Western Saloon in the small town of Point Reyes Station, and a friend played him a Bob Dylan song on acoustic guitar, "Wanted Man," that we thought he should consider recording for the album. After many beers he was still noncommittal; eventually, a week or so later, he told me he wanted $15,000 up front, if he was going to do an album and he wouldn't agree to do new songs. We never made an album together. Eventually, in 1995, a new album,* South Coast, *was released that earned him a Grammy and helped revive his career, as did a documentary,* The Ballad of Ramblin' Jack, *directed by his daughter, Aiyana Elliott, and the 2006 album,* I Stand Alone, *which had accompaniment from Lucinda Williams, David Hildalgo, Nels Cline, Flea, and DJ Bonebrake. The story that follows is a new revision of the 1979* Chronicle *story, which incorporates some key quotes that were in the* Barb *version.*

THE DRESSING room door was kicked open. Ramblin' Jack Elliott strode in carrying a guitar case in one hand and an open bottle of Dos Equis in the other. He was an hour and a half late.

Straggly brown hair sticking out from under a white cowboy hat, bloodshot eyes, and an unshaven face told the story of 20 hours on the road from Colorado. He cast off a worn denim jacket, grabbed his guitar from the case, and began tuning as a horde of people swarmed around him. The club manager, an out-of-town promoter, a young folk singer, and a waitress closed in. Forcing a grin, Jack Elliott singled out the waitress. "Honey, where can a man get a drink around here?"

The thunder of boots pounding the floor and the roar of "We Want Jack" could be heard through the ceiling. Bolting down a double shot of tequila, Elliott said, "Better get up there."

Ramblin' Jack Elliott sings folk songs and "talkin' blues." He performs with just an acoustic steel string guitar and a harmonica. Since the early '50s, he has been performing songs by Woody Guthrie, Jimmie Rodgers, and others. "I've sung the same 25 songs forever," he says. "I'm too lazy to learn any new ones."

Still, people keep coming back to see Ramblin' Jack Elliott. Maybe it's because of the myth. Ramblin' Jack Elliott is like a piece of the past. With the "Wild West" a mere memory gleaned from a black-and-white TV program, Jack Elliott seems like the real thing: A roving cowboy, a connection to a simpler time.

The world of Ramblin' Jack Elliott is filled with dangerous outlaws, jumped trains, and long nights spent passing a bottle of tequila around a campfire. It's an endless series of romances broken by the line, "I've got to be movin' on." It's a search across America for something almost undefined. A search for the freedom the West once implied.

A funny thing about Ramblin' Jack Elliott: He was born in New York. He's the son of a Brooklyn doctor. His real name is Elliott Charles Adnopoz.

Ramblin' Jack Elliott is a character that Elliott Charles Adnopoz invented when he was 16 years old. But after 25-plus years of pickin' and singin', Elliott Charles Adnopoz is long gone and only Ramblin' Jack Elliott, "a [real-life] legendary character," as David Bromberg, the musician, once wrote, remains. As a kid he hungered for something more than middle-class security. After several frustrating years at college, Jack dropped out to pursue the life of a roving singer in the tradition of Woody Guthrie and the country bluesmen.

"People would laugh their heads off at the idea of a kid from Brooklyn singing cowboy songs," Elliott once told an interviewer from *Sing Out!*, the folk music magazine. "So I invented this Oklahoma thing to keep 'em quiet. Said I was born on a ranch."

Ramblin' Jack headed upstairs and took the stage. The hour-and-a-half wait had soured some of the audience's enthusiasm and good humor. Tension was high. Halfway through Jack's version of "Don't Think Twice It's Alright," a fight broke loose. For the love of a lady a table loaded with beer bottles and glasses crashed to the floor. Before more damage could be done Ramblin' Jack intervened. "Hey, lighten up, save it for later." Hostilities were cooled and Jack finished the song.

The angry vibrations permeating the air subsided as Jack sang and told stories. "You know Woody Guthrie once told me," he said, then paused to take a gulp of Heineken, "about the time he was ridin' this freight train and when it stopped the police would come on board and search it. And Woody was carrying a violin case and every time they would make him open it. You see, they were lookin' for this outlaw who was also carrying a violin case." He strummed his guitar. "And that outlaw was Pretty Boy Floyd and this here song is about him."

When he talks, Jack Elliott has a low drawl. Words roll out of his mouth in a constant but unhurried stream. He tends to ramble, and he likes to put interviewers on almost as much as he likes to drink. "Success means having a new hat for Christmas," he told one reporter.

"Well, do you think you've had a successful life so far," asked the same reporter.

"I'm wearing this American Hat Company hat. I feel very successful," said Elliott, looking off across the room.

Between sets, over a bottle of Wild Turkey, Elliott reminisced about meeting Woody Guthrie. "I was playin' 'round New York city in 1951." Jack paused to grab a chair, pull it over and kick his legs up onto it. "I went to visit Woody when he was sick in the hospital with appendicitis and I sang for him. A month or so later Woody invited me to join a group he was gonna start. I started rehearsing with Woody and moved into the house with him and his family and ended up staying there a year-and-a-half. The group never got started but we had a great time of playing music and ridin' around together.

"One time Cisco Houston came to visit Woody. We all drove down by the harbor where the ships come in. As we drove Woody and Cisco began singing a song together, harmonizing like in the old days and I was in heaven. It was one of the finest moments of my life. They sang a song called, 'A Picture from Life's Other Side.'"

Ramblin' Jack Elliott spent eight years playing the drifting picker role in the United States and Europe before he found success. In 1959, he triumphed in the US after a highly praised gig at Gerde's Folk City in New York. During the first half of the '60s, he recorded a half dozen albums and became involved in the burgeoning Greenwich Village folk scene along with Dave Van Ronk, Phil Ochs, and, of course, Bob Dylan.

"I'd gone off to Europe, singing on street corners, in cafes, nightclubs, television," Elliott says. "Sang to Princess Margaret. I came back and found this kid, Bob Dylan, who was starting to sing. When I met him he was only 19 but I knew right away he was gonna go on and be a star. I knew that all along. I wanted that for him because the first time I met him I thought, well, here's the first guy I ever seen that is trying to sound like Woody and Cisco and Leadbelly. At that time all we had was like the Kingston Trio, Burl Ives and Harry Belafonte. It was all so posh. Nobody was digging the real folk sound."

Bob Dylan may have been Elliott's biggest fan. Dylan used to trail around after him, imitating Ramblin' Jack Elliott's style of walking, talking, and singing.

"If he imitated me, so what," Elliott says. "Well how did Woody [Guthrie] feel about me imitating him? Woody was my idol and so I imitated him for five years. Took me another five to stop imitating him. Woody once said, 'Jack Elliott sounds more like me than I do.'"

Jack values his friendship with Dylan. "I love Dylan's singing. He's gone on, he's 'modulated' and 'mellodated' and changed and everything and maybe there's still a little bit of me left in there. There's still a little Woody in me too. And I even imitate Bob Dylan somewhat. And we all learn from each other."

In recent years, Ramblin' Jack Elliott's life hasn't been so successful. In some ways, the myth he invented for himself turned out to be too much to live up to. Acting out, on a 24-hour-a-day basis, the role of Last American Cowboy isn't easy: all that two-fisted drinking and the endless days on the road and the nights sleeping in the back of pick-up trucks or on borrowed floors.

Ramblin' Jack Elliott hasn't recorded an album in over 10 years. Sometimes, he arrives late for gigs. Sometimes, he's too drunk by the time he takes the stage to put in a truly great performance.

Still, for Jack Elliott, it's too late to turn back. He's 47 and traveling from gig to gig is all he knows.

There was a young folk singer sitting quietly in the backstage dressing room. He was listening to Ramblin' Jack Elliott's every word with the same kind of awe that must have been on Jack Elliott's own face when he listened to Woody Guthrie tell tales in the '50s.

Finally, the kid mustered enough courage to blurt, "Hey, Jack, what advice would you give a picker?"

Ramblin' Jack Elliott looked frustrated and tired. He took another slug of beer. "Be a truck driver, get a job on a ranch, I don't know. I don't know how you do it. I just do it by habit. You dig, like when this thing is over, you're gonna look for me, but you won't find me. I'm gonna be gone. I'm gonna be in my truck driving over the hill to some quiet place where I can lay my head down."

*Berkeley Barb*, March 4–16, 1977, *San Francisco Chronicle*, July 15, 1979

# BOB DYLAN'S BEAT VISIONS (SONIC POETRY)

*I first heard "Like a Rolling Stone" in 1965 on the car radio as my mother drove us somewhere. That was all it took; I have been obsessed with Bob Dylan ever since. So in late 2016, when I got the opportunity to write about the influence of Jack Kerouac, one of my favorite writers, on my favorite musician, I took it and ran with it, learning much that I'd not previously known about Dylan despite having read many of the books written about him over the years, and countless magazine interviews and profiles. I spent six months researching and writing the essay that follows, which first appeared in the 2018 book* Kerouac on Record *(Bloomsbury Academic). I regret never having the chance to interview Dylan. I did have one encounter with him. It was in 1986, at a party following a performance at Live Aid in Philadelphia that Dylan did accompanied by Keith Richards and Ron Wood. This was a very private party. No press. Just rock stars, their managers, other celebrities, and a few others who worked for the rock stars. A manager I knew brought me in. Now this was when* Miami Vice *was still on the air and popular, and so Don Johnson being in the room was a big deal. I wrote a cover story about Live Aid for* Rolling Stone, *starting my story like this: "It was superstar heaven. Keith Richards was laughing and talking with Jimmy Page. A bodyguard handed Bob Dylan a beer. Across the room Jack Nicholson and Neil Young chatted. Andy Taylor, guitarist for Duran Duran and the Power Station, took a hit off a joint and screamed out, 'Don,' then gave* Miami Vice *star Don Johnson a hug. 'We gonna get high!'" At one point I approached Dylan. This was my moment, my chance to say something to Bob Dylan. What I wanted was to elicit something from him that I could use in my story, and so I said, "That was great, man! How was it, you know, performing with Keith and Ron?" Dylan looked at me, said something about how he couldn't hear when he was onstage and wasn't at all happy with his short set. And that was it. He moved on, and I did too.*

JACK KEROUAC NEVER GOT a Nobel Prize in Literature, but Bob Dylan did. Oh yeah, Bob got one, finally, later, way later, 2016 later. When the prize was announced, it was hard not to think of Kerouac, one of those who, as Dylan put it, "left the rest of everything in the dust," hard not to think of the other Beat writers who so profoundly influenced Dylan and each deserved their own Nobel Prize. Poet/publisher Lawrence Ferlinghetti, whose "I Am Waiting" is echoed in "It's Alright Ma (I'm Only Bleeding)," and William S. Burroughs, whose extreme imagery was reimagined in Dylan's mid-1960s songs, and Allen Ginsberg, whose "Kaddish" Bob said he dug so much, and whose "Howl" helped Dylan birth "Like a Rolling Stone."

The prize was awarded to Dylan "for having created new poetic expressions within the great American song tradition." Yeah, but that kinda sold him short. The real Big Bang theory: Dylan made a new *kind* of poetry, a sonic poetry that took the lightning flash images of Beat writing and merged them with the raw, wild sounds of primal rock & roll. A new kind of poetry that you could hear on the radio or at a concert hall. Poetry freed

Bob Dylan at the Warfield Theater, San Francisco, 1978.

from the page. "My songs are pictures," Dylan said in early 1966, at the very peak of his creative powers, "and the band makes the sound of the pictures."[1]

In this essay I'll talk about how Dylan came to create that sonic poetry and the profound influence the Beat writers, and in particular Jack Kerouac, had on Dylan. Much has been made, over the many decades since Dylan first appeared on our radar in the early 1960s, of the influence of Woody Guthrie, and how Dylan journeyed to New York in 1961, and then went to Greystone Psychiatric Hospital in New Jersey to visit and sing to Guthrie, who was suffering from Huntington's Disease, a fatal, degenerative nerve disorder. Dylan himself, who was very closemouthed about influences when interviewed in the 1960s, made a point of playing up his connection to Guthrie, writing "Song to Woody" in February 1961, and a poem, "Last Thoughts on Woody Guthrie," which he read at his April 12, 1963, concert at New York's Town Hall.[2] But in terms of Dylan's breakthroughs in songwriting, it was the work of Kerouac and some of the other Beat writers that provided much of the inspiration (and in some cases the actual phrases) that resulted in Dylan's most groundbreaking songs. The focus here will be on the words, not the music. Others have written about how Dylan and various studio musicians forged the music, and anyway, there's simply not space for me to discuss that aspect of Dylan's creative process.

Dylan had many influences, and it would be simplistic (and wrong) to only credit the Beats. A huge trove of songs, poems, novels, films, theatrical productions, and paintings, as well as lived experience, reside behind the hundreds of songs Dylan wrote during the past five-plus decades. But in terms of his WOW! POP! BLAM! CRASH! recordings, mostly made in 1965 and 1966, the Beats were the heart of the matter.

## Voice of a Generation Redux

*I always had the feeling that his true love of the [Beat] period were the works of Jack Kerouac.*

—David Amram, musician, composer and friend
of both Jack Kerouac and Bob Dylan[3]

IT'S NOT SURPRISING THAT DYLAN identified with Kerouac. Both men grew up at a serious distance from the sophistication and power center that is New York City—Dylan at a literal remove in Hibbing, Minnesota; Kerouac at a kind of worldview remove in Lowell, Massachusetts. Both moved to New York City and lived there for decades. In their youth both felt like outsiders: Kerouac because his parents were French Canadian, because he spoke French, not English, until he was five or six, and because he was Catholic; Dylan because he was Jewish. Both were populists. Kerouac wrote of hanging around skid row when he arrived in a town or city and expressed his compassion for the common man in his novels; as a teenager in 1958 Dylan wrote a paper analyzing John Steinbeck's *Grapes of Wrath*, a novel about the plight of a poor family during the Great Depression, for a time idolized and imitated Woody Guthrie of "This Land Is Your Land" fame, and later wrote songs about hobos, immigrants, refugees, oppressed Blacks, and other social injustice. Kerouac, as the writer/photographer John Cohen, who knew and photographed him, wrote, "found his artistic persona as a trouble-raiser and provocateur within literary intellectual circles";[4] Dylan did the same within the worlds of folk and rock music, as well as "literary intellectual circles." Both were seen as the voice of a generation, and both struggled with the aftermath of that kind of fame.

Robert Allen Zimmerman was born in Duluth, Minnesota, on May 24, 1941. As a kid, Dylan felt like an outsider even at home. In an interview for Martin Scorsese's 2005 Dylan documentary, *No Direction Home*, Dylan spoke of discovering that the big radio he and his family sat around listening to also had a phonograph, and on it one day he found a gospel recording, Bill Monroe's "Drifting Too Far from the Shore." "The sound of the record made me feel like I was somebody else," Dylan said. "That I was maybe not even born to the right parents or something." In August of 1949 Kerouac wrote in his journal, "Some people are just made to wish they were other than what they are, only so they may wish and wish and wish. This is my star."[5]

As outsiders, Kerouac and Dylan rebelled against their white privilege and the materialism that dominated American society; both, as young men, were on a search for authenticity. "He [Kerouac] was an outsider, he was on the streets, and everyone reading his book [*On the Road*] was an insider, sitting by their fire, and the idea of the outsider as being the originator was interesting to Kerouac and was interesting to Bob," filmmaker D.A. Pennebaker, a friend of Kerouac's who made the Dylan documentary *Don't Look Back* in 1965 and also filmed Dylan's 1966 tour of England, told me during a March 2017 interview. (Pennebaker died in August 2019; he was 94 years old.) "It still is. He [Dylan] still thinks he's an outsider who has worked his way in."

Pennebaker, who told me he'd read all of Kerouac's books, noted other reasons that Dylan related to Kerouac. "I think the fact that he [Kerouac] was able to thumb his nose at the rules," Pennebaker said. "He was besetting the world of writing as it existed. And he was getting away with it. Also, his writing appeals to Dylan because it has a kind of poetic and musical quality, and Dylan responded to that. The whole thing of sleeping on the beach and the waves, that's the kind of thing Dylan liked."

## "I'm a Poet, and I Know It. Hope I Don't Blow It"

> *Remember, Bob Dylan's a poet, man. So when he writes, it's a poet writing, and when he talks, it's a poet talking.*
> —Bob Neuwirth, Dylan's friend and former road manager

"I'M A POET, AND I know it. Hope I don't blow it," Dylan said in 1964's "I Shall Be Free No. 10." "My poems are written in a rhythm of unpoetic distortion," Dylan wrote in the liner notes to 1965's *Bringing It All Back Home*. He told the Canadian Broadcast Corporation's (CBC) Martin Bronstein in February 1966, "For a while I did consider myself a poet. [Now] I don't like to consider myself a poet because it puts you in a category with a lot of funny people."

Beat poet Michael McClure, a friend of both Kerouac and Dylan who died on May 4, 2020, wrote in a 1974 article for *Rolling Stone*:

> By the time I met Bob [1965], his poetry was important to me in the way that Kerouac's writing was. It was not something to imitate or be influenced by; it was the expression of a unique individual and his feelings and perceptions.

There is no way to second-guess poetry or to predict poetry or to convince a poet that the very best songs in the world are poetry if they are not. Bob Dylan is a poet; whether he has cherubs in his hair and fairy wings, or feet of clay, he is a poet. Those other people called "rock poets," "song poets," "folk poets," or whatever the rock critic is calling them this week, will be better off if they are appreciated as songwriters.[6]

Dylan's first book, 1971's *Tarantula*,[7] is the work of a poet captivated by the Beat writers, as are his liner notes for *The Times They Are a-Changin'*, *Another Side of Bob Dylan*, *Bringing It All Back Home*, and *Highway 61 Revisited*.

"He was a poet first," Lawrence Ferlinghetti told me in February of 2017. "He wanted to be a published poet. But luckily he had a guitar and he knew how to make it into music. His early songs [in the 1960s] were long surrealist poems."

At Hibbing High School, a grand building completed in 1923 at a cost of a then astounding $4 million in Hibbing, Minnesota, the town where Robert Zimmerman spent more than a decade of his youth, there is, as Greil Marcus noted, poetry on the walls—quotes from Tennyson's "Oenone." Dylan's high school English teacher was the late B. J. Rolfzen, who another Hibbing teacher, Aaron Brown, described as a "gentle man who loved poetry, and preached poetry almost like a religion." Teenage Robert Zimmerman sat in the front row of Rolfzen's class (room 204) for two years as Rolfzen lectured about Shakespeare, Keats, Shelley, Byron, Wordsworth, Frost, William Carlos Williams, and others. Zimmerman considered Rolfzen, now deceased, a mentor and in the years following his success as Bob Dylan, the rock star spoke to Rolfzen during at least two of his infrequent visits to Hibbing.

Zimmerman had a rock & roll band when he was in high school, but even before then he wrote poetry. He told CBC's Martin Bronstein that he started writing poems when he was eight or nine "about the flowers and my mother and stuff like that." One of his teenage poems that survives, "Bad Poem," was written in 1956 (and exhibited in the Experience Music Project's traveling exhibition *Bob Dylan's American Journey, 1956–1966*, which was at various museums from 2004 to 2008).[8] The handwritten poem reads in part:

> Waiting in the house, was Raatsi on the bed "I'm gonna pin Boutang's arm,"
> Melvin, then said "A noise outside! and Raatsi's face had gleem [sic]" Ah ha, it was Dale coming on his machine

"It's really like a Bob Dylan song," John Cohen told me. Cohen, who died in September 2019, in addition to being a photographer and writer, was a filmmaker and member of the New Lost City Ramblers; he photographed Kerouac in 1959, and became friends with Dylan and photographed him in 1962 before Dylan's first album, *Bob Dylan*, was released. "So this ['Bad Poem'] is from 1956. What he was messing around with in terms of language in '56. Whew! It's a wonderful missing link, well a link, and it's so early, '56. It's wild."

## "I Came Out of the Wilderness and Just Naturally Fell in with the Beat Scene"

*Was Bob Dylan influenced by the Beats? Well, yeah. Was he influenced by Robert Frank photographs and films, yeah. Bob, you know, he's like a sponge. He's influenced by everybody.*

—Bob Neuwirth

BY THE TIME HE ARRIVED in Minneapolis in September 1959, Robert Allen Zimmerman had traded his electric guitar in for a double-O Martin acoustic like the one Woody Guthrie used, had learned from bluesman Jesse Fuller in Denver to play the harmonica using a neck holder, and had begun calling himself Bob Dylan. It was another poet, Dylan Thomas, from whom Zimmerman borrowed his new last name, as he finally admitted, after decades of denying it, in his 2004 memoir *Chronicles: Volume One*. In Minneapolis, he became truly obsessed with Woody Guthrie and immersed himself in the music of other folk artists including Odetta and Elizabeth Cotten.

Dylan was in Minneapolis to attend the University of Minnesota, but his true education came in the bohemian cafes of Dinkytown, a three-block area centered at the intersection of Fourth Street and Fourteenth Avenues. "I came out of the wilderness and just naturally fell in with the Beat scene, the bohemian, bebop crowd, it was all pretty connected . . . ," Dylan told writer Cameron Crowe during an interview for the liner notes included in the 1985 *Biograph* boxed set. "I had already decided that society, as it was, was pretty phony and I didn't want to be part of that. . . ."

"It [the Beat scene] was Jack Kerouac, Ginsberg, Corso and Ferlinghetti—*Gasoline, Coney Island of the Mind* . . . Oh man, it was wild—*I saw the best minds of my generation destroyed by madness*—that said more to me than any of the stuff I'd been raised on," Dylan continued. "*On the Road*, Dean Moriarty, it made perfect sense to me . . . Anyway, I got in at the tail end of that and it was magic . . . It had just as big an impact on me as Elvis Presley."

Among the books Dylan read while hanging around Dinkytown were Ferlinghetti's *A Coney Island of the Mind*,[9] Burroughs' *Naked Lunch*,[10] Ginsberg's *Howl & Other Poems*,[11] and two by Kerouac, *On the Road*[12] and *Mexico City Blues*.[13] Later, according to Kerouac biographer Dennis McNally, a friend gave Dylan copies of *Doctor Sax* and *Big Sur*, and in his memoir, *Chronicles*, Dylan references *The Subterraneans*.

According to Ginsberg, Dylan told him, "Someone handed me *Mexico City Blues* in St. Paul [Minnesota] in 1959, and it blew my mind. It was the first poetry that spoke my own language."

Ginsberg told McNally that when Dylan read an article in the February 9, 1959, issue of *Time* magazine, "Fried Shoes," about a reading Ginsberg and Corso did in Chicago, Dylan realized there were "other people out there like me."

## "Talkin' New York"

"I SUPPOSE WHAT I WAS looking for was what I read about in *On the Road*—looking for the great city, looking for the speed, the sound of it, looking for what Allen Ginsberg called the 'hydrogen jukebox world,'" Dylan recalled in *Chronicles*.

"Maybe I'd lived in it all my life, I didn't know, but nobody ever called it that. Lawrence Ferlinghetti, one of the other Beat poets, had called it "The kiss proof world of plastic toilet seats, Tampax and taxis" [actually, Ferlinghetti wrote, 'a kissproof world of plastic toiletseats, Tampax and taxis']. That was okay, too, but the Gregory Corso poem 'Bomb' was more to the point and touched the spirit of the times better—a wasted world and totally mechanized—a lot of hustle and bustle—a lot of shelves to clean, boxes to stack. I wasn't going to pin my hopes on that. Creatively you couldn't do much with it. I had already landed in a parallel universe, anyway, with more archaic principles and values; one where actions and virtues were old style and judgmental things came falling out on their heads. A culture with outlaw women, super thugs, demon lovers and gospel truths . . . streets and valleys, rich peaty swamps, with landowners and oilmen, Stagger Lees, Pretty Pollys and John Henrys—an invisible world that towered overhead with walls of gleaming corridors. It was all there and it was clear—ideal and God-fearing—but you had to go find it. It didn't come served on a paper plate."[14]

Less than a year and a half after arriving in Minneapolis, in January of 1961, Bob Dylan got a ride to New York and quickly made his presence known. He met and hung out with Guthrie and got to know numerous musicians including Dave Van Ronk, Ramblin' Jack Elliott, and the New Lost City Ramblers (who included John Cohen); he played Greenwich Village clubs, eventually landing a primo two-week gig (that began on April 11, 1961) opening for bluesman John Lee Hooker at Gerde's Folk City.

Both before and after he got to New York, Dylan read many other poets in addition to the Beats. His early-'60s girlfriend Suze Rotolo wrote in her 2008 memoir, *A Freewheelin' Time*, that she introduced Dylan to the poetry of Jean Nicolas Arthur Rimbaud. Dave Van Ronk told Dylan biographer Robert Shelton that when he brought up the French Symbolist poets Dylan feigned ignorance; but Van Ronk said he found a well "thumbed through" book of translations of poems by the French Symbolists on Dylan's shelf (likely *An Anchor Anthology of French Poetry*,[15] published in 1958, which is currently included in the "Books" section of Dylan's official website). "I think he probably knew Rimbaud backward and forward before I even mentioned him," Van Ronk said, and, in *Chronicles*, Dylan wrote about Rimbaud, noting that when he read one of Rimbaud's letters, "*Je est un autre*" ("I is someone else") the "bells went off."

The Symbolists were, of course, a major influence on the Beats. "I met Jack on the sidewalk outside my loft and told him how I liked his book, *On the Road*, and added that it reminded me of Woody Guthrie's writing," John Cohen wrote in his book of photographs, *There Is No Eye*. "There was a resemblance between their rambling sentences, free grammar, and the long list of places and titles that evoked images of America . . . Jack was indignant. 'Woody Guthrie's just a folk singer. I'm a poet, like Rimbaud and Verlaine.'"

Dylan also read the 15th-century French poet François Villon, and he wrote in his memoir that after he got to New York he read long poems, including Lord Byron's "Don Juan" and Samuel Taylor Coleridge's "Kubla Khan." "I began cramming my brain with all kinds of deep poems," Dylan wrote.

Dylan dug the ultracool monologist and comedian Lord Buckley, whose hip wordplay and controversial raps anticipated the Beats. Buckley, a cult figure who began performing in the 1930s, made his first recordings in the early '50s, but his albums continued to be released throughout the 1960s (following his death in October 1960). A 1961 live recording by Dylan of "Black Cross" (a poem by Joseph S. Newman that appeared as a Buckley monologue on the 1959 album *Way Out Humor*, describing the lynching of a Black man, which has been described as one of Buckley's "signature pieces") was included on *Great White Wonder*, the Dylan bootleg, and Dylan also performed "Black Cross" at the Gaslight Café on October 15, 1962.[16] In the cover photo for *Bringing It All Back Home*, the album *The Best of Lord Buckley* sits on the fireplace mantel. In *Chronicles*, Dylan described Buckley as "the hippest bebop preacher," and wrote, "With stretched out words, Buckley had a magical way of speaking. Everybody, including me, was influenced by him in one way or another."

Sometime in 1961, Lawrence Ferlinghetti, whose book *Starting From San Francisco* was published that year by New Directions Press, finished up his business at New Directions Press (then with offices on the 11th floor of 333 Sixth Avenue), took one of the two elevators in the old building down to the lobby, and there he saw this kid who he later [after Dylan's success] realized was Bob Dylan. "He was hangin' around the elevator with his guitar in the building where New Directions was," Ferlinghetti, who died in February 2021 at age 101, told me. "And as I walked past him, he says, 'How do you git up there?' So he wanted to be published as a poet first. New Directions in those days was the ivory tower for poets."

Neither man—Ferlinghetti nor, Ferlinghetti believes, Dylan—recognized the other that day. Dylan was already a fan of Ferlinghetti's poetry. In addition to *A Coney Island of the Mind* (also published by New Directions), Dylan had read Ferlinghetti's first poetry collection, *Pictures of the Gone World* (which is included in *A Coney Island of the Mind*). Ferlinghetti's poems influenced Dylan. "It's Alright Ma (I'm Only Bleeding)" is the stepchild of Ferlinghetti's "I Am Waiting,"[17] a poem that includes such lines as:

and I am waiting
to see God on television
piped onto church altars
if only they can find the right channel

and:

and I am waiting
for the human crowd
to wander off a cliff somewhere
clutching its atomic umbrella

Numerous poems in *A Coney Island of the Mind* name-drop high-profile personages from history and fiction, something Dylan would soon do in such songs as "I Shall Be Free," in which he mentions President Kennedy, Anita Ekberg, Brigitte Bardot, Sophia Loren, Ernest Borgine, Willy Mays, Yul Brynner, Charles de Gaulle, and Robert Louis Stevenson.

"He [Ferlinghetti] is the Beat poet whose work most noticeably includes constant allusions to others' texts and titles—a feature we recognize as characteristic in Dylan's 1960s' poetry, in 'Tarantula' and throughout his songs," Dylan authority Michael Gray wrote in his *The Bob Dylan Encyclopedia*.

## "So Throw a Match on It"

ON JULY 29, 1961, SUZE Rotolo, 17 at the time and active in the civil rights movement, met Bob Dylan at an all-day folk festival held at the Riverside Church in Manhattan. They soon became a couple, and as Rotolo recounts in her memoir, she took Dylan to the Museum of Modern Art, turning him on to her favorite paintings. They saw plays together, including the Living Theater's *The Brig* and LeRoi Jones' *Dutchman*, and art house films. In late 1962 or early 1963, Dylan and Rotolo viewed photographer Robert Frank and Alfred Leslie's *Pull My Daisy*. Filmed in 1959 (the year Frank's initially controversial book of black-and-white photographs, *The Americans*,[18] was published in the United States by Grove Press with an introduction by Kerouac) and premiered in November of that same year, *Pull My Daisy* was based on the third act of Kerouac's play, *Beat Generation*,[19] and featured an improvised narration by Kerouac; actors included Ginsberg, Corso, and Amram, who scored the film and became a friend of Dylan in the 1960s. In his book *Like a Rolling Stone: Bob Dylan at the Crossroads*,[20] Greil Marcus writes that Dylan's voice in "Visions of Johanna" and "Desolation Row" is "partly Jack Kerouac's voice in his narration for [the] life among-the-beatniks movie *Pull My Daisy*. 'Look at all those cars out there,' Kerouac says. 'Nothing there but a million screaming ninety-year-old men being run over by gasoline trucks. So throw a match on it.'"

On September 26, 1961, Dylan began a series of shows opening for the Greenbriar Boys at Gerde's, and on September 29, Robert Shelton's now-famous review of Dylan ran in the *New York Times*. The next day, Dylan played harp on a Carolyn Hester (then married to novelist Richard Fariña) session being produced by legendary Columbia Records A&R man/producer John Hammond (Billie Holiday, Charlie Christian, Aretha Franklin), who signed Dylan in October. (Hammond oversaw the 1961 release of Robert Johnson's mid-1930s recordings, on LP for the first time, as *King of the Delta Blues Singers*; that album's cover is also among the many cultural artifacts in the photo on the cover of *Bringing It All Back Home*. Dylan wrote in his memoir that when Johnson started singing—Hammond gave Dylan an advance acetate of the Johnson album—"he seemed like a guy who could have sprung from the head of Zeus in full armor." Dylan also wrote, "Johnson's words made my nerves quiver like piano wires.")

Dylan already understood that you could take an existing song and fuck with it and end up with a new song. This was the folk tradition. Robert Johnson, for instance, had turned two of Skip James' songs, "Devil Got My Woman" and "22-20," into "Hellhound on My Trail" and "32-20." Typically, new words were layered on existing melodies. But Dylan would take a postmodern approach, combining his own words with words and phrases he picked up from films, magazine and newspaper articles, and books, utilizing them as raw materials to tell his own stories.

Dylan's first album, released in 1962, was nearly all covers of blues and folk songs, but there were two originals, "Song to Woody" and "Talkin' New York," and both showed that Dylan was aware of the folk tradition. In the case of "Song to Woody," the old song was Guthrie's "1913 Massacre" (which in turn used a tune likely borrowed from the English folk song "Hear the Nightingale Sing," which goes under a number of names including "One Morning in May" and "The Nightingale"). Dylan's "Talkin' New York" was based on Guthrie's talking blues, and borrows or reworks phases from Guthrie's "Talkin' Subway" and other songs on *Talking Blues*, an album by folklorist John Greenway released on Folkways in 1958; Greenway's version of "Talkin' Subway" includes verses written by Guthrie but never recorded by him.

It wasn't until his second album, *The Freewheelin' Bob Dylan* (1963), which Dylan spent a year, off and on, writing and recording, that we saw the first evidence of Bob Dylan the revolutionary songwriter. "Blowin' in the Wind" gave Dylan songwriting cred when Peter, Paul, and Mary's version reached number 2 on the *Billboard* pop chart in August of 1963. Dylan took the melody for his song from the old spiritual, "No More Auction Block for Me," which musicologist Alan Lomax said originated in Canada and was sung by former slaves who went there after Britain abolished slavery throughout the British Empire in 1833. Dylan likely heard Odetta's version (he was a major fan of the woman whom Martin Luther King Jr. called "the queen of American folk music"), which appeared on her 1960 album, *Odetta at Carnegie Hall*. But it was another song Dylan wrote for the *Freewheelin' Bob Dylan* that was his first step into a whole new dimension of songwriting.

In September of 1962, Dylan was upstairs in what folkie Tom Paxton called a "hang-out room" above the Village Gaslight Café, a club where Beat writers including Ginsberg and Corso had appeared in the late 1950s. By 1962, Beat poetry readings were giving way to folk music performances, and the Gaslight was the premier folk club in the Village (Dylan performed at the club a month later, in October of that year). "Dylan was banging out this long poem on Wavy Gravy's typewriter [Wavy Gravy was still Hugh Romney at the time]," Paxton said. "He [Dylan] showed me the poem and I asked, 'Is this a song?' He said, 'No, it's a poem.' I said, 'All this work and you're not going to add a melody?'" Romney, who has corroborated Paxton's story, was the Gaslight's poetry director at the time (earlier drafts of "A Hard Rain's a-Gonna Fall" were handwritten in a notebook).

John Cohen, who also frequented the hang-out room, told me, "I came back from making my film, *The High Lonesome Sound*, in Kentucky. He [Dylan] showed me the words to 'Hard Rain.' This was as he was writing it. And I said, if you're going to write stuff like that, this isn't Woody Guthrie, this is more like Rimbaud. He claimed he didn't know who I was talking about."

Soon Dylan turned that "poem" into a song.

One of the Beat poets who Dylan admired, Allen Ginsberg, was blown away when he heard the recording of "A Hard Rain" in 1963. "When I got back from India, and got to the West Coast, there's a poet, Charlie Plymell—at a party in Bolinas—played me a record [*The Freewheelin' Bob Dylan*] of this new young folk singer," Ginsberg said during an interview for *No Direction Home*.

"And I heard 'A Hard Rain,' I think. And wept. 'Cause it seemed that the torch had been passed to another generation. From earlier bohemian, or Beat illumination. And self-empowerment . . . There's a very famous saying among the Tibetan Buddhists, if the student is not better than the teacher then the teacher's a failure. And I was really knocked out by the eloquence, particularly, 'I'll know my song well before I start singing,' and, 'where all souls shall reflect it' and 'I'll stand on the mountain where everybody can hear.' It's sort of this biblical prophecy. Poetry is words that are empowered that make your hair stand on end that you recognize instantly as being some form of subjective truth that has an objective reality to it because somebody's realized it. Then you call it poetry later."

Ginsberg also said he thought Dylan's writing was "an answering call or response to the kind of American prophecy that Kerouac had continued from Walt Whitman."

Although based on the old Anglo-Scottish border Child ballad "Lord Randall" (also known as "Lord Randal"), "A Hard Rain" displayed what would mark Dylan as unique among his peers at the time, his ability to write song lyrics that were literature. It is no surprise that Dylan was writing a poem, and only after he'd written several drafts did he transform it into a new kind of song.

As Dylan expert Clinton Heylin wrote in his book *Revolution in the Air: The Songs of Bob Dylan, 1957–1973*, what is also unique about "A Hard Rain" is "the relentless rivulet of images, pouring down on one another in a stream so unending that in the final verse he cannot stop himself from breaking the very bounds of song form itself in order to 'tell it and think it and speak it and breathe it' like it is. Such a freewheelin' verse structure was not something he acquired from either Woody Guthrie or Robert Johnson. It smacked of Ginsberg's 'Howl' or the speed rapping of Kerouac—and it transformed Dylan into a folk modernist."

It was in the winter of 1963 that Dylan met Kerouac's good friend, Allen Ginsberg, who Dylan would describe to Robert Shelton in a March 1966 interview as "holy." They were introduced at a party held in Ted Wilentz's apartment in the Village upstairs from the Eighth Street Bookshop (which Wilentz co-owned with his brother Eli, and where in the early 1950s you could, on occasion, find Kerouac, Corso, and other Beats browsing) and spoke about poetry. It was the beginning of a friendship that would last until Ginsberg died on April 5, 1997. The night after Ginsberg's death, Dylan dedicated his performance of "Desolation Row" to his friend.

David Amram told me in February 2017 that he thinks the initial motivation for Dylan, who never met Kerouac, to become friends with both Ginsberg and himself was their friendships with Kerouac. "After 1959 Jack had bailed out of New York except for an occasional visit," Amram said. "So when Dylan came [to New York] loving Jack's work, I think the only two people who had been part of that [friends of Kerouac] were Allen Ginsberg and myself. I always wondered what interest he could possibly have in what I was doing as a jazz player who wanted to write symphony music and I realized that probably the closest he could get to Jack was through Allen and me."

## "The Great American Road Trip"

IN FEBRUARY 1964, BOB DYLAN literally went on the road, traveling for 20 days across the country in a Ford station wagon. It was what his road manager at the time, Victor Maymudes, called, in reference to Kerouac, "the great American road trip." They were joined by folk singer Paul Clayton and *Daily Mirror* reporter Pete Karman (a friend of Suze Rotolo), who was there, according to Maymudes in his book, *Another Side of Bob Dylan*, "to record the journey south into the dark and dangerous country of America." "I think it was in the back of everybody's mind that this was sort of an *On the Road* redux," Karman told Dylan biographer Howard Sounes.

This Kerouacian journey—in which they picked up a hitchhiking miner and tried unsuccessfully to talk to Hamish Sinclair, secretary and strike leader for the National Committee for Miners in Harlan County, Kentucky; played pool and went bowling in Asheville, North Carolina; and had a brief, awkward conversation with Carl Sandburg at his home in Flat Rock, North Carolina—would be the catalyst for the next stage of Dylan's writing. He worked on two transformative songs in the back seat during the trip, songs that were a piece with his transition to writing Beat influenced picture poems: "Chimes of Freedom" and "Mr. Tambourine Man." And he heard the Beatles on the radio.

"When we were driving through Colorado, we had the radio on and eight of the 10 top songs were Beatles songs. In Colorado! 'I Wanna Hold Your Hand,' all those early ones," Dylan said during a 1971 interview with one of his biographers, Anthony Scaduto. "They were doing things nobody was doing. Their chords were outrageous, just outrageous, and their harmonies made it all valid. . . . But I just kept it to myself that I really dug them. Everybody else thought they were for the teenyboppers, that they were gonna pass right away. But it was obvious to me that they had staying power. I knew they were pointing the direction of where music had to go."

Dylan was also taken with Rimbaud at this time. He told Karman, "Rimbaud's where it's at. That's the kind of stuff means something. That's the kind of writing I'm gonna do." In fact, it would appear that Dylan's "magic swirling ship" in "Mr. Tambourine Man" was inspired by Rimbaud's poem *The Drunken Ship* (included in *An Anchor Anthology of French Poetry*), which includes the line, "Now I, a little lost boat, in swirling debris."

When Dylan and his road buddies arrived in the Bay Area, Karman split, and Bob Neuwirth, a musician and painter who Dylan had met at a folk festival in 1961, joined the entourage before they headed to Carmel, and then on to Los Angeles. For the next few years Neuwirth, who died in May 2022, would be one of Dylan's closest friends as well as his road manager. Before they left the Bay Area, Dylan wanted to make contact with Ferlinghetti. He attempted to visit the poet/publisher but he wasn't at home; Dylan left a note.

Back in New York in March 1964, Dylan rented an electric guitar. A month later, he dropped acid for the first time. Producer Paul Rothchild told Dylan biographer Bob Spitz he was present when Dylan took his first hit of LSD at his manager Albert Grossman's mansion in Woodstock. Although Dylan has denied it, his experiences on acid clearly affected his songwriting (as well as the poetry he wrote for *Tarantula* and his liner notes).

In the months that followed there must have been some contact either between Dylan and Ferlinghetti, or Grossman and Ferlinghetti—in which the possibility of Ferlinghetti's City Lights Books publishing Dylan's writing was discussed. Ferlinghetti told me he had hoped to publish Dylan at that time. In April, the month he dropped acid, Dylan wrote a long 118-line prose-poem letter to Ferlinghetti, which is now part of the City Lights Archive at the University of California, Berkeley, Bancroft Library, in which Dylan expressed the hope that he would get some material to Ferlinghetti "one of these days." The letter reads, in part:

> have t look thru all my pants pockets
> an collect things t send t you.
> as of now I am in the midst of destroyin all I've
> done (I've even crashed my old typewriter t pieces an have burned my pens into little tiny plastic statues)
> I know I will send you something one of these days.
> all I have t do is finish something t send you.
> in any case, if I am poisened [sic] or framed or kilt or ratted on
> I will will will you some edgar lee masters?
> type (bob dylan written) poems of grand embarassment [sic].
> thelonius [sic] monk grand style grand (me upright)
> the world's fair begun down there.
> I'm gone

Dylan didn't write a book for City Lights. Instead, Grossman made a deal for Dylan with the Macmillan Company. As Ferlinghetti told me, there was no way City Lights could compete with Macmillan. Dylan completed *Tarantula* in 1966. It was written in a stream-of-consciousness, at times hallucinogenic, Beat style like the liner notes Dylan had been writing for his albums.

*Tarantula* was to be published in the autumn of 1966, but following Dylan's motorcycle accident he put the book on hold; it wasn't until 1971 that it was published. That year Dylan told *Rolling Stone* publisher Jann Wenner, "Boy, they were hungry for this book. They didn't care what it was. They just wanted . . . people up there were saying, 'Boy, that's the second James Joyce,' and 'Jack Kerouac again' and they were saying 'Homer revisited' . . . and they were all just talking through their heads."

During that summer of 1964, while up in Woodstock, New York, where his manager had a mansion and where Dylan sometimes rented a cabin from the mother of folk singer Peter Yarrow of the group Peter, Paul, and Mary, Dylan wrote a song that broke more new ground, another song that clearly showed the Beat influence, "It's Alright Ma (I'm Only Bleeding)."

The song begins with a rush of images:

Darkness at the break of noon
Shadows even the silver spoon
The handmade blade, the child's balloon
Eclipses both the sun and moon
To understand you know too soon
There is no sense in trying

and later:

Old lady judges watch people in pairs
Limited in sex, they dare
To push fake morals, insult and stare
While money doesn't talk, it swears
Obscenity, who really cares
Propaganda, all is phony

"It's Alright, Ma" appeared on Dylan's first rock album, *Bringing It All Back Home*, released in March of 1965. Most, if not all, of the songs on that album, including "Subterranean Homesick Blues" and "Mr. Tambourine Man," show the influence of the Beats, and Dylan underlines that by including a mention of Ginsberg in his liner notes and a photo of Ginsberg wearing Dylan's top hat on the back cover. Among the many cultural artifacts in the front cover photo is a copy of *GNAOUA*, a one-shot magazine published in 1964 that focused on exorcism and Beat-era poetry (including writing by Ginsberg and Burroughs) edited by the poet Ira Cohen.

One song on *Bringing It All Back Home* has a key line that in an odd way seems influenced by both Kerouac and novelist Nelson Algren, best known for writing 1949's "The Man with the Golden Arm" and 1956's "A Walk on the Wild Side." A film of *The Man with the Golden Arm* starring Frank Sinatra was released in December 1955. It is likely that Dylan saw the film and possibly read one or both of the novels. If he was familiar with Algren's name, a book review of *On the Road*, written by Algen and published in the

*Chicago Sun-Times* on September 2, 1957, would have caught his attention; Dylan was 16 at the time. In the review, Algren wrote, "Man can't live by bread alone even if it's wrapped in cellophane is what really hep cats know—and to prove it put as much drive in *trying to fail as squares do striving to succeed.*" This seems a likely inspiration for Dylan's infamous line from "Love Minus Zero / No Limit": "She knows there's no success like failure, and failure's no success at all."

## "A Hundred-Mile-an-Hour Clip"

THE DOCUMENTARY FILMMAKER D. A. Pennebaker was asked by Albert Grossman to film Dylan's spring 1965 acoustic tour of England. Pennebaker had, in the late 1950s, been given the rights by Kerouac himself to make a film of *On the Road*; he had those rights for about a decade, he said, until the end of the 1960s or early 1970s. Pennebaker had become friends with Kerouac years before the Beat writer wrote *On the Road*.

"Well I had the rights to it [*On the Road*] only because Kerouac wanted me to do it," Pennebaker told me during a March 2017 interview. "I kept telling him I didn't know how to do that kind of film. I said, 'If you guys can put on your wading boots and stand by the highway up at Bear Mountain, I'll stand with you [and film it] and we can ride out to California. 'Cause I don't know how to make a film with actors acting like you guys.' And he said, 'Well you can figure that out. You can get somebody to help you do that.'"

Pennebaker had concluded that he didn't want to make fictional films, and had already made a handful of cinema vérité documentaries. In late 1964 Pennebaker agreed to make the documentary film that became *Don't Look Back*, which in its own way is a kind of homage to Kerouac and *On the Road*.

"I knew there had to be some way to translate Kerouac's particular angst, his fidgety enthusiasm, and love of things around him, people around him, in film terms," Pennebaker told Dylan biographer Bob Spitz. "From watching Dylan's absolute compulsion to somehow evolve from Kerouac, I began to understand how to approach the film [*Don't Look Back*]. Kerouac and Neal Cassady lived a hundred-mile-an-hour clip; Dylan and Neuwirth enjoyed their own fantastic [lifestyle], and in a way, their essences were intertwined."

During the mid-1960s, Dylan and Neuwirth were a kind of Kerouacian pair, getting their own kicks in Manhattan and during Dylan's tours in the US and Europe (when Andy Warhol gave Dylan one of his Double Elvis paintings, Dylan and Neuwirth tied it to the roof of Dylan's Ford station wagon "totally unprotected," according to writers Tony Scherman and David Dalton's book, *Pop: The Genius of Andy Warhol*, and drove up to Woodstock, depositing the canvas at Grossman's mansion), but also, like Kerouac himself, searching for truth in a world where truth is often buried beneath a mountain of lies and misdirection. One gets a good idea of the Dylan–Neuwirth dynamic in *Don't Look Back*, where the duo ceaselessly make fun of Donovan, who had a hit record while Dylan toured England.

"I think Bob always, without voicing it, always considered himself a Kerouac kid," Pennebaker said at the outset of our interview. "Kind of a jail kid that's gotten loose. He would often refer to stuff that Kerouac had done or written."

Writing about Neuwirth in *Chronicles*, Dylan made a Kerouac reference: "Like Kerouac had immortalized Neal Cassady in *On the Road*, somebody should have immortalized Neuwirth. He was that kind of character. He could talk to anybody until they felt like all their intelligence was gone. . . . I got a kick out of everything he did and liked him. . . . We liked pretty much all the same things, even the same songs on the jukebox."

Dylan and Neuwirth, according to Pennebaker, spoke about Kerouac when they were all in England in late April and early May 1965 making *Don't Look Back*. "Dylan would say something [about Kerouac]," Pennebaker said. "Neuwirth knew the book [either *Dharma Bums* or *Desolation Angels*]. Dylan liked that idea, of the mountain time [Kerouac's time as a fire lookout on Desolation Peak in the North Cascade Mountains of Washington state in 1956]. Dylan liked that idea of the mountain and got intrigued by it. So there were mentions of the book."

Dylan appears to have considered making a film of *On the Road*. In a letter to his agent Sterling Lord dated February 29, 1968 (published in *Jack Kerouac: Selected Letters 1957–1969*), Kerouac wrote, "Let me know what develops with Jack Geoghegan [editor-in-chief and president of Coward-McCann, the company that published *Desolation Angels* and *Vanity of Duluoz*] selling Vanity reprint, and with the movie Bob Dylan plan for ROAD."

Dylan himself no longer has any memory of wanting to make a film of *On the Road*, according to his manager. Neither does Sterling Lord. Responding to an email I sent him, Lord wrote, "I do not recall anything about that situation" and in another email, "I do not remember anything Jack Kerouac said about Dylan. I never heard him talk about Dylan."

Kerouac actually did say a few things about Dylan. Kerouac's friend, writer John Clellon Homes, interviewed by Kerouac biographer Dennis McNally, said that at first Kerouac thought Dylan was "another fucking folk singer" but changed his mind and "gruffly conceded" to Holmes, "Well okay, he's good."

## "Writ for My Own Soul's Ear"

*"Like a Rolling Stone" probably owes more to Allen Ginsberg's 1955 "Howl" than to any song.*
—Greil Marcus, *Like a Rolling Stone: Bob Dylan at the Crossroads*

IT IS 1965. ALLEN GINSBERG sits at his desk in his North Beach apartment. On his wall he's tacked his friend Jack Kerouac's "Belief and Technique for Modern Prose," a list of 30 suggestions for getting to the heart of things in one's writing.[21] (And now for a two-paragraph digression but an important digression.)

Kerouac had struggled for several years trying to write his second novel, after *The Town and the City*. Much had been written, but Kerouac wasn't satisfied. Finally, in April 1951, partially inspired by a letter wild man Neal Cassady had written him, and with his notebooks and journals next to the typewriter, he started over and wrote what would become the most famous and influential of Beat novels, *On the Road*, in three intense weeks at his apartment on West 20th Street in the Village, onto a 120-foot "scroll," as Kerouac called it, of tracing (*not* teletype) paper. Typing at breakneck speed, fueled by many cups of black coffee (as well as Benzedrine), Kerouac was like a jazz musician improvising late into the night, letting the facts of his road trips with Cassady blur into the fictional account of Dean Moriarity (Cassady) and Sal Paradise (Kerouac). There were three additional drafts (typed on conventional typing paper, not scrolls) before the book was eventually published by Viking Press on September 5, 1957.

As Ginsberg wrote (quoted in Howard Cunnell's essay for *On the Road: The Original Scroll*), Kerouac had developed a style that was "a long confessional of two buddies telling each other everything that happened, every detail, every cunt-hair in the grass included, every tiny eyeball flick of orange neon flashed past in Chicago in the bus station; all the back of the brain imagery. This required sentences that did not necessarily follow exact classic-type syntactical order but which allowed for interruption with dashes, allowed for the sentences to break in half, take another direction (with parentheses that might go on for paragraphs). It allowed for individual sentences that might not come to their period except after several pages of self reminiscence, of interruption and the piling on of detail, so that what you arrived at was a sort of stream of consciousness visioned around a specific subject (the tale of the road) and a specific view point . . ."[22]

Some of Kerouac's writing suggestions on that sheet tacked to Ginsberg's wall freed Ginsberg to write "Howl," the poem that essentially launched the Beat movement and which was also named by Kerouac, who read early drafts.

As poet, songwriter (for Tim Buckley and others) and Beat expert Larry Beckett noted in his book, *Beat Poetry*,[23] writing about the genesis of "Howl," Ginsberg makes reference to a number of Kerouac's techniques:

1. Scribbled secret notebooks, and wild typewritten pages, for your own joy . . .
4. Be in love with your life . . .
8. Write what you want bottomless from bottom of the mind . . .
24. No fear or shame in the dignity of yr experience, language & knowledge

"I thought I wouldn't write a poem," Ginsberg wrote in *Howl: Original Draft Facsimile*, "but just write what I wanted to without fear, let my imagination go, open secrecy, and scribble magic lines from my real mind—sum up my life—something I wouldn't be able to show anybody, writ for my own soul's ear."

The result was a draft of the first part of "Howl" which begins:

I saw the best minds of my generation
destroyed by madness
starving, mystical, naked,
who dragged themselves through the angry streets at
dawn looking for a negro fix

In 1956 Ferlinghetti published Ginsberg's first book of poetry, *Howl & Other Poems*, which, thanks to an obscenity trial, brought Ginsberg widespread notoriety and brought attention to the Beat scene, which turned into a national fad after *On the Road* was published on September 5, 1957. (Ginsberg, acting as an informal agent for Kerouac and William Burroughs, is credited with helping get Kerouac's first novel, *The Town and the City*, published by Harcourt Brace in 1950.)

"Well the language which they [the Beats] were writing, you could read off the paper, and somehow it would begin some kind of tune in your mind," Dylan told John Cohen during a 1968 interview for *Sing Out!* "I don't really know what it was, but you could see it was possible to do more than that . . . not more . . . something different than what Woody and people like Aunt Molly Jackson and Jim Garland did."

## "Hey, You Dig Something Like Cut-Ups?"

ON MAY 3, 1965, THE DAY Jack Kerouac's 11th novel, *Desolation Angels*,[24] was published, Bob Dylan sat in a room of the Savoy Hotel in London, and with Joan Baez providing harmony vocals, sang Hank Williams' "Lost Highway." Dylan started with the third verse, followed with the fourth and then seemed at a loss before Bob Neuwirth called out to him, "There's another verse, 'I'm a rolling stone.'"

Dylan then sang, "I'm a rolling stone all alone and lost / For a life of sin I have paid the cost."

And that was the moment, Greil Marcus said during a conversation with D. A. Pennebaker about *Don't Look Back* for the November 24, 2015, Blu-ray edition of the film, "when the notion of 'Like a Rolling Stone' first appears."

Dylan wanted to break free of traditional song structures. He told journalist Paul Jay Robbins in March 1965, "I've written some songs which are kind of far out, a long continuation of verses, stuff like that—but I haven't really gotten into writing a completely free song. Hey, you dig something like cut-ups? I mean, like William Burroughs?"

He went on to tell Robbins, who interviewed him for the *Los Angeles Free Press* when Dylan was in Southern California in late March of 1965 playing the Santa Monica Civic Auditorium, that he wrote *Tarantula* because

> there's a lot of stuff in there I can't possibly sing . . . all the collages. I can't sing it because it gets too long or it goes too far out. I can only do it around a few people who would know. Because the majority of the audience—I don't care where they're from, how hip they are—I think it would just get totally lost. Something that had no rhyme, all cut up, no nothing, except something happening, which is words.

Drugs certainly played a part in the next phase of Dylan's songwriting. In a February 1966 interview with Nat Hentoff, Dylan's comments about LSD might explain the anger and desire for revenge expressed in some of his *Highway 61* songs. "I wouldn't advise anybody to use drugs—certainly not the hard drugs; drugs are medicine," Dylan told Hentoff. "But opium and hash and pot—now, those things aren't drugs; they just bend your mind a little. I think *everybody's* mind should be bent once in a while. Not by LSD, though. LSD is medicine—a different kind of medicine. It makes you aware of the universe, so to speak; you realize how foolish *objects* are. But LSD is not for groovy people; it's for mad, hateful people who want revenge. It's for people who usually have heart attacks."

The Beats were decidedly on Dylan's mind during his spring 1965 British acoustic tour. He hung out with Allen Ginsberg, who appears in the short film Pennebaker shot in London for "Subterranean Homesick Blues" (seen at the start of *Don't Look Back*), spoke to a reporter about Burroughs, and repeatedly brought up Kerouac in Pennebaker's presence.

In outtakes for *Don't Look Back* shot in England in late April and the first two weeks of May 1965, Dylan is seen showing a journalist how he attempted to use Burroughs' "cut-up" technique to write a song, but said it hadn't worked for him "because the rhyming scheme sounded so weird."

During Dylan's stay at the Savoy Hotel, he was constantly writing in his room, typing away, as seen in *Don't Look Back*, and described by Marianne Faithfull in her autobiography.

"For a while he had a roll of that waxy English toilet paper in the machine," Faithfull wrote. "It was just the right width for song lyrics, he said. A little bit of *un homage à Kerouac*, too, of course."

Back in the US in June of 1965 (a decade after Ginsberg wrote "Howl") at the cabin in Woodstock that Dylan sometimes rented from Peter Yarrow's mother, Dylan finally did what Kerouac and Ginsberg had done: He put aside the "rules" of traditional songwriting and let words flow in a rush from his subconscious onto the page. The result was the words he would edit into what some believe is his greatest song, "Like a Rolling Stone."

Sometime in early June while he was working on "Like a Rolling Stone," Dylan bought a large 11-room, two-story arts and crafts house called Hi Lo Ha in Byrdcliffe, New York, not far from both Woodstock and Bearsville, where his manager Albert Grossman had the big house in which Dylan had often stayed. Still in Woodstock, he completed the lyrics and set them to music.

With "Like a Rolling Stone" and possibly other new songs written, Dylan called guitarist Michael Bloomfield and asked him to come up to Woodstock to stay with him and wife, Sara, at the new house and learn the songs during the weekend of June 12–13. "And I went to Woodstock, and I didn't even have a guitar case, I just had my Telecaster and Bob picked me up at the bus station and took me to this house where he lived . . . ," Bloomfield told Larry "Ratso" Sloman in November 1975; Sloman quoted him in his 1978 book, *On the Road with Bob Dylan*:

> He taught me these songs, "Like a Rolling Stone" and all those songs from that album and he said, "I don't want you to play any of that B. B. King shit, none of that fucking blues, I want you to play something else," so we fooled around and finally played something he liked, it was very weird, he was playing in weird keys which he always does, all on the black keys of the piano, then he took me over to this big mansion and there was this old guy walking around and I said, "Who's that?" and Bob said "That's Albert." . . . We fucked around there for a few days and then we went to New York to cut the record. . . .

Dylan described the song—recorded with Dylan's producer, Tom Wilson, on June 15 and 16, 1965, at Columbia Studio A in Manhattan (the keeper take was cut on June 16) and released as a single on July 20—as a "breakthrough." And it was! Dylan had made something brand new. He had fused the dense, vivid, and at times, surreal imagery of the Beats' writing to the wildest rock & roll. The result: a kind of sonic poetry.

"Like a Rolling Stone" was Dylan's first pop hit, reaching number 2 on the *Billboard* Hot 100 on September 4, 1965 (the Beatles' "Help" was number 1 that week).

"You have to vomit up everything you know," Dylan told Ginsberg and journalist Ralph J. Gleason just five months later in December 1965, while in San Francisco. "I did that. I vomited it all up and then went out and saw it all again."

Dylan was asked by CBC's Marvin Bronstein, during an interview in Montreal on February 20, 1966, to name the song he remembered being a breakthrough. "Do you mean the most honest and straight thing which I thought I ever put across?" Dylan said. "That reached popularity, you mean . . . If you're talking about what breakthrough is for me, I would have to say, speaking totally, it would be 'Like a Rolling Stone.' I wrote that after I had *quit*. I'd literally quit, singing and playing—I found myself writing this song, this story, this long piece of vomit, twenty pages long, and out of it I took 'Like a Rolling Stone' and made it as a single."

Dylan, in talking about his process to Bronstein and others was, as usual, taking poetic license. He told other interviewers his "long piece of vomit" was ten pages (Jules Siegel) or six pages (Robert Shelton). Whatever.

"And I'd never written anything like that before and it suddenly came to me that that was what I should do," he told Bronstein. "Nobody had ever done that before. . . . Anybody can write a lot of the things I used to write, I just wrote 'em first because nobody else could think of writing them—but that's only because I was hungry. . . . I'm not saying it's ['Like a Rolling Stone'] better than anything else. . . . After writing that I wasn't interested in writing a novel, or a play. I want to write *songs*. Because it was a whole new category."

During his February 1966 interview with Jules Siegel, while talking about "Like a Rolling Stone," Dylan brought up "hatred" and the desire for "revenge," two of the emotions he told Hentoff he associated with LSD, a drug he had taken within the previous two years. "It wasn't called anything, just a rhythm thing on paper all about my steady hatred directed at some point that was honest," Dylan said.

"In the end it wasn't hatred, it was telling someone something they didn't know, telling them they were lucky. Revenge, that's a better word. I had never thought of it as a song, until one day I was at the piano, and on the paper it was singing, 'How does it feel?' in a slow motion pace, in the utmost of slow motion following something. It was like swimming in lava. In your eyesight, you see your victim swimming in lava. Hanging by their arms from a birch tree. Skipping, kicking the tree, hitting a nail with your foot. Seeing someone in the pain they were bound to meet up with. I wrote it. I didn't fail. It was straight."

## "No Rhyme, All Cut-Up, No Nothing, Except Something Happening, Which Is Words"

> *I couldn't have written those songs back then. If I had just come out and sung "Desolation Row" five years ago I probably would have been murdered.*
> —Bob Dylan to Nat Hentoff, autumn 1965, unpublished interview for *Playboy*

FOLLOWING THE MAY 3, 1965 PUBLICATION of *Desolation Angels*, the publisher, Coward-McCann, a subsidiary of G. P. Putnam's Sons, ran full-page ads in the *Sunday Times Book Review*, the daily *New York Times*, the *New York Review of Books*, and elsewhere. If you were in New York, and dug Jack Kerouac, it would have been hard not to know that the "King of the Beats" had a new novel in the stores.

Hi Lo Ha, Dylan said, was where he wrote the rest of *Highway 61 Revisited* in the six weeks between the June 15 and 16 sessions in Manhattan where "Like a Rolling Stone" was recorded, and the late July and early August sessions at which the rest of the *Highway 61 Revisited* album was completed. (Dylan, ever the poet, said that in one interview, but in another with Jann Wenner for *Rolling Stone* he said he wrote the *Highway 61* song "Desolation Row" "in the back of a taxicab" in New York.)

More interesting than where the songs that comprise *Highway 61 Revisited* were written is that just six weeks after *Desolation Angels* was published, Dylan used the book as a major source of raw material for his new songs. "Desolation Row" took the first half of its title from Kerouac's new book, and Dylan seems to have gotten the idea for the song's main theme from Kerouac as well. In *Desolation Angels*, Kerouac writes about "Surrealistic Street,"[25] and describes a wild cast of characters that he sees out on skid row. What is "Desolation Row," as Dylan describes it in his song, if not a dark, at times horrific version of Kerouac's "Surrealistic Street"?

In *Desolation Angels*, Kerouac writes about "the sisters from Arkansas who'd seen their father hanged."[26] Dylan's song begins, "They're selling postcards of the hanging," a reference to the lynching of three Black circus workers on June 15, 1920, in Duluth, Minnesota, the city where Dylan was born; Dylan's father was nine years old in 1920 and lived two blocks from where the hangings occurred. Shockingly, postcards with a photo of the dead men hanging from a tree were later sold there.

There's much more: Dylan slightly reworked four of Kerouac's phrases for his song. Kerouac wrote, "They sin by lifelessness,"[27] that Dylan turned into "Her sin is her lifelessness." "Cabinets with memories in them"[28] became "memories in a trunk." "The perfect image of a priest"[29] became "a perfect image of a priest." "Get his letter"[30] became "received your letter." Historical figures that were in Kerouac's book appear in Dylan's song: Romeo, Einstein, Noah, and the Phantom of the Opera. Kerouac writes about a hunchback; Dylan name-drops the Hunchback of Notre Dame.

And still more: "Completely in a trance"[31] becomes "got him in a trance." "Asking for cigarettes" becomes "bummed a cigarette." Kerouac writes about a "heart attack" and "fornicating machines"; Dylan sings about a "heart-attack machine." "Tell your fortune" becomes "fortune-telling lady." "Blow up" becomes "blow it up." Kerouac writes of a girl "getting upside down ready before her stagedoor mirror"; Dylan sings of the Good Samaritan "getting ready for the show." Kerouac writes "Death is our reward"; Dylan, "Death is quite romantic." Kerouac's "vests and ironed pants" became Dylan's "iron vest."

There are also many duplicated words. "Postcards," "sexless," "painting," "passports," "sailors," "blind," "circus," "restless," "moaning," "riot," "sweeping," "ambulance," "jealous," "monk," "immaculate," "electric," "patients," "peeking," "nurse," "agent," "factory," "sniffing," "kerosene," "castles," "insurance," "escaping," "captain," "fishermen," and "flowers" are in both the book and the song.

Near the end of "Desolation Row," Dylan sings, "I had to rearrange their faces / And give them all another name." This was exactly what Kerouac had done in all of his novels; changing names so the real people his characters were based on wouldn't be identified.

Other songs borrowed from Kerouac as well. In *Desolation Angels*, Kerouac describes a trip he took with his mother to Juarez;[32] Dylan started "Just Like Tom Thumb's Blues" with his narrator in Juarez; and in that same song Dylan borrows a phrase from Kerouac's book: "Housing Project hill."[33] Near the end of *On the Road*, Sal Paradise, Kerouac's narrator, after visiting a Mexican whorehouse with his friend Dean Moriarty, is sick and alone, abandoned by Moriarty; once Sal recovers, he returns to New York. Dylan's narrator in "Just Like Tom Thumb's Blues" is sick and alone in Juarez and has been ground down by his dealings with prostitutes and others, and his friends, who "said they'd stand behind me," are gone; he intends to return to New York. Kerouac writes in *Desolation Angels*, "As Cody wins he really loses, as he loses he really wins,"[34] which seems relevant to Dylan's "Up on Housing Project Hill / It's either fortune or fame / You must pick one or the other / Though neither of them are to be what they claim." Dylan's "fortune or fame" also echoes Kerouac's "poverty and fame." There were other influences in addition to Kerouac. The inclusion of "Tom Thumb" in the title is an obvious reference to Rimbaud's poem "Ma Bohème" ("My Bohemia"),[35] with the line "Little Tom Thumb, I dropped my dreaming rhymes," a poem included in the same book of French Symbolist poetry Dylan likely owned in the early 1960s.

In *Desolation Angels*, Kerouac writes, "I was 24 sitting in my mother's house all day while she worked in the shoe factory";[36] the chorus to "Tombstone Blues" is "Mama's in the fact'ry / She ain't got no shoes." Kerouac writes about a burlesque house skit in which a woman talks of having sex in a graveyard;[37] in "From a Buick 6," Dylan says he has "this graveyard woman." Kerouac mentions both junkyards and angels; Dylan sings about a "junkyard angel."

There is, of course, a long history of repurposing ideas and even words in art and literature; T.S. Eliot in his epic poem "The Waste Land" does just that. Dylan was quite familiar with Eliot, and included him in "Desolation Row," "fighting in the captain's tower" with Ezra Pound. He also named Eliot's two wives, Valerie and Vivien, in 1967's "Too Much of Nothing." "Desolation Row" has been compared to "The Waste Land."

In his book *The Sacred Wood: Essays on Poetry and Criticism*,[38] published in 1920, T.S. Eliot wrote, "Immature poets imitate; mature poets steal; bad poets deface what they take, and good poets make it into something better, or at least something different. The good poet welds his theft into a whole of feeling which is unique, utterly different than that from which it is torn; the bad poet throws it into something which has no cohesion."

"Open up yer ears an' yer influenced," Dylan himself wrote in a prose-poem, "My Life in a Stolen Moment," published in the program for Dylan's April 12, 1963, performance at New York's Town Hall, "an' there's nothing you can do about it."

Dylan's brilliance as an artist has always been his ability to absorb art "like a sponge," as Neuwirth put it, and in the case of the *Highway 61* songs, to take Kerouac's phrases and ideas and words and utilize them to write something only Dylan could write. *Desolation Angels* may have been where Dylan got the idea to sing about the Duluth lynchings, but it took Dylan's genius to turn that idea into such a moving opening line.

*Highway 61 Revisited*, released in 1965, is a masterpiece, but there were more breakthroughs. Without even coming up for air, Dylan would write and record his greatest album, the following year's *Blonde on Blonde*, which contains his greatest song, "Visions of Johanna" (and during the summer of 1967, Dylan and his band members would record the now infamous and revelatory "Basement Tapes"). Tellingly, "Visions of Johanna" (and much of the rest of *Blonde on Blonde*) would also borrow from the dense imagery of Ginsberg and Kerouac and would even draw its title from another Kerouac novel, 1963's *Visions of Gerard*.

That the Beats continued to be on Dylan's mind is evidenced by the photos he had taken by Larry Keenan of himself and Robbie Robertson with Michael McClure and Ginsberg in the alley outside City Lights Books on December 5, 1965. Dylan had planned to use at least one of the photos for the *Blonde on Blonde* album artwork, but changed his mind. (Photos by another photographer who was there, Dale Smith, show Ferlinghetti standing next to Dylan, Ginsberg, and McClure.)

"Visions of Johanna" was such a breakthrough for Dylan because with it he reached his goal of writing a "completely free song." There is no message, only the vague hints of a story, hints that leave the mystery intact. The song captures a state of mind as the narrator recalls being in a particular room at a particular time. It is also a song packed with amazing word images: "the ghost of 'lectricity howls in the bones of her face"; "But Mona Lisa musta had the highway blues / You can tell by the way she smiles"; and "Oh, jewels and binoculars hang from the head of the mule."

Dylan conveys what it was like to be in that room with the heat pipes coughing, music from the country music station playing softly as a surreal scene—word pictures—flash through the narrator's mind. His earlier political songs are transparent; "propaganda songs" as The Minutemen would sing. "Visions of Johanna" is deep. Multilayered, it catches the atmosphere, the moment, what it was to be in that room, thinking those thoughts, feeling those feelings. With that song, just as with Ginsberg's poems and Kerouac's novels, Dylan was not trying to make some big statement, he wasn't trying to fabricate something, he was simply laying out his truth. Art allows us to see through the façade to what's beneath it. That is what the Beats did, and that is what Bob Dylan did (and still does) with "Visions of Johanna" and many of his other songs.

Dylan would, in the years that followed, write some excellent songs. But, as he eventually acknowledged, as time passed, he could no longer write the kind of free, hallucinatory songs he'd written in the 1960s. "To do it, you've got to have power and dominion over the spirits," he wrote in *Chronicles*. "[You had to be able to] see into things, the truth of things—not metaphorically, either, but really see, like seeing into metal and making it melt, see it for what it was and reveal it for what it was with hard words and vicious insight."

## "An Unmarked Grave"

> *Dylan and Ginsberg visiting Jack's grave was an honoring of Jack's importance to them.*
> —John Cohen

IN NOVEMBER OF 1975, ALLEN Ginsberg stood with Bob Dylan at Kerouac's grave at Edson Cemetery in Lowell, Massachusetts. Ginsberg opened Kerouac's book of poetry, *Mexico City Blues*, and read from the 54th Chorus. Dylan then read a line from the 230th Chorus:

The quivering meat of the elephants . . .
Ginsberg finished the line:
. . . of kindness

Then Ginsberg jumped to the last two lines:

Like kissing my kitten in the belly
The softness of our reward.

After that the two of them, Dylan and Ginsberg, made music, Dylan with his Martin, Ginsberg with his harmonium; they played what Sam Shepard described in his book,

*Rolling Thunder Logbook*, as a "slow blues," trading verses, right there at the grave, the grave of Jack Kerouac, right there in Lowell, Massachusetts, where Kerouac was born.

"This gonna happen to you?" Ginsberg had said with a nervous laugh, before the jam session, as they stood looking at the grave, looking at the tombstone that says "Ti Jean, John L. Kerouac, Mar. 12, 1922–Oct. 21, 1969—He Honored Life."

A nervous laugh, as if Ginsberg wasn't so sure he shoulda said what he said. "Nah," Dylan said, "I'm gonna be in an unmarked grave."

*Kerouac on Record: A Literary Soundtrack*, June 2017

# Notes

1. Jonathan Cott, ed., *Bob Dylan, The Essential Interviews* (New York: Wenner Books, 2006), 97. *Playboy* magazine interview published March 1966.
2. Bob Dylan, "Last Thoughts on Woody Guthrie." Accessed March 17, 2017, at https://bobdylan.com/songs/last-thoughts-woody-guthrie/
3. All unattributed quotes are from interviews conducted by the author during January, February, and March 2017.
4. John Cohen, *There Is No Eye: John Cohen Photographs* (New York: Powerhouse Books, 2001), 118.
5. Jack Kerouac, "On the Road again," *The New Yorker*, June 22, 1998, 56.
6. Michael McClure, "The Poet's Poet," *Rolling Stone*, March 14, 1974, 32.
7. Bob Dylan, *Tarantula* (New York: Macmillan, 1971).
8. Robert Zimmerman, "Bad Poem," Accessed March 17, 2017, http://www.bonhams.com/auctions/23878/lot/64/?category=list&length=10&page=7
9. Lawrence Ferlinghetti, *A Coney Island of the Mind* (New York: New Directions Publishing Corporation, 1958).
10. William S. Burroughs, *Naked Lunch* (New York: Grove Press, 1959).
11. Allen Ginsberg, *Howl and Other Poems* (San Francisco: City Lights Books, 1956).
12. Jack Kerouac, *On the Road* (New York: Viking Press, 1957).
13. Jack Kerouac, *Mexico City Blues* (New York: Grove Press, 1959).
14. Bob Dylan, *Chronicles, Volume One* (New York: Simon & Schuster, 2004), 235–236.
15. Republished as *The Anchor Anthology of French Poetry from Nerval to Valery in English Translation*, ed. Angel Flores (New York: Anchor Books, 1958).
16. "Black Cross" by Joseph S. Newman, and Lord Buckley's version, accessed March 17, 2017, at http://keever.us/blackcro.html
17. Ferlinghetti, *A Coney Island of the Mind*, 50.
18. Robert Frank, *The Americans*, intro. Jack Kerouac (SCALO Publishers; original New York: Grove Press, 1959).
19. Jack Kerouac, *Beat Generation* (Cambridge, MA: Oneworld Classics/Da Capo Press, 2005).
20. Greil Marcus, *Like a Rolling Stone: Bob Dylan at the Crossroads* (New York: Public Affairs, 2005).
21. Jack Kerouac, "Belief and Technique for Modern Prose," *Evergreen Review* 2, no. 8 (Spring 1959).
22. Howard Cunnell, *On the Road: The Original Scroll, Jack Kerouac* (New York: Viking, 2007), 22.
23. Larry Beckett, *Beat Poetry* (New York: Beatdom Books, 2012).
24. Jack Kerouac, *Desolation Angels* (New York: Coward-McCann, 1965).
25. Ibid., 116.
26. Ibid., 131.
27. Ibid., 405.
28. Ibid., 67.
29. Ibid., 208.
30. Ibid., 107.
31. Ibid., 134.
32. Ibid., 382.
33. Ibid., 164.
34. Ibid., 187.
35. *The Anchor Anthology of French Poetry*, 106.
36. Kerouac, *Desolation Angels*, 315.
37. Ibid., 118.
38. T.S. Eliot, *The Sacred Wood: Essays on Poetry and Criticism* (London: Methuen, 1920; Kindle version location 1376).

Black Flag at the Mabuhay Gardens, 1981. © Photo by Chester Simpson / Rock-N-RollPhotos.com

# PUNK LIVES!

## They Don't Sound Like the Ramones, and they don't look like the Sex Pistols, but bands like Black Flag, Hüsker Dü, the Minutemen, and the Meat Puppets are keeping the spirit of '77 alive.

*I read about punk before I heard it, which is not exactly true. I'd already dug the Stooges and the MC5 and the New York Dolls, as well as the numerous garage rock bands that preceded punk. But by the mid-'70s, when bands that would be called* punk *started playing CBGBs in New York, I read about them in the now shuttered* Village Voice. *By the time Patti Smith and the Ramones and Television played San Francisco, I was already a fan. The first time I heard records by the next wave of punk, the Sex Pistols and the Clash, I dug them. So by the late '70s and early '80s, when a third (fourth?) wave of punk bands appeared, bands like Flipper, Black Flag, Hüsker Dü, the Minutemen, and the Replacements, I dug them too. And I realized that this new wave of punk bands, who were getting their music out through indie labels including Subterranean and SST and Twin/Tone, needed to be covered in* Rolling Stone, *where I then worked.* Rolling Stone *had mostly ignored these bands, but I convinced my editor that we needed a story. I hung out at SST Records in Redondo Beach, California, met up with The Minutemen and traveled to Las Vegas with Black Flag in their van. Separately I met with the Replacements when they played the I-Beam in San Francisco. I spoke to Hüsker Dü during one of their visits to San Francisco as well, which is where I interviewed Flipper. This story meant a lot to me when I wrote it, and I have learned since that it meant something to many of the people who read it.*

WE ARE IN A WAREHOUSE turned punk-rock dance hall in the shadowy industrial section of Las Vegas, Nevada, across the highway from the gaudy, neon-lit Strip. Here, away from the MGM Grand and Circus-Circus, far from the middle-aged gamblers and the $4.99 buffets, most of Las Vegas' punk-rock fans—all 400 of them—have assembled to see Arizona's highly touted Meat Puppets, a newer outfit called Tom Troccoli's Dog, and Black Flag, perhaps the most infamous punk band since the Sex Pistols.

There are teenage girls in mohawks. There is a boy who has greased and twisted his long hair so 15 spikes rise at odd angles from his head. There are guys trying to be Sid Vicious in their ripped T-shirts, tight black jeans, and black-leather jackets, handcuffs dangling from their belts. Girls flaunt the Bride of Frankenstein look. Someone is wearing an Iggy Pop T-shirt. To wit, nearly everyone here looks as if he or she just stepped out of a punk documentary, circa 1977.

Only something is wrong. It's not punk. Onstage, Tom Troccoli's Dog is in the middle of a psychedelic jam. The drummer has dreadlocks. The guitarist, sporting long, curly brown hair and a Grateful Dead T-shirt, coaxes feedback from his amp. The punks watch, bemused. Some complain about "the hippie music." A few try to slam dance to the languid rhythms. Others sit on the floor, staring at the stage as San Francisco hippies used to do at the Fillmore Auditorium about 20 years ago.

What's going on here? What happened to Loud Fast Rules? Two-chord punk rock? Beat on the brat with a baseball bat?

Primal punk is passé. The best of the American punk rockers have moved on. They have learned how to play their instruments. They have discovered melody, guitar solos, and lyrics that are more than shouted political slogans. Some of them have even discovered the Grateful Dead.

The reinvention of punk rock began a few years ago when Black Flag, at the time a fairly typical punk band, underwent a metamorphosis. Singer Henry Rollins, who used to shave his head, let his hair grow down his back. Slow, heavy-metal dirges and jazzy, psychedelic instrumental jams were integrated into the group's sets, as were intense guitar solos. This caught Black Flag fans off guard. Kids with shaved heads and KILL THE HIPPIES painted on the backs of their leather jackets suddenly discovered that their favorite band now looked like a bunch of hippies. Help!

In Las Vegas, driving in a dusty black van with white rats spray-painted all over it, Henry Rollins, 24, and (soon to be former) Black Flag drummer Bill Stevenson, 21, make fun of the "punkers" and "stylers" who still rigidly conform to the retro-punk look. "We ought to get our hair cut like the cover of *GQ*," says the bearded drummer, laughing. "That would really turn some heads around."

THIS IS THE NEW PUNK ROCK, 1985 style. Or at least one version. For there is a whole new underground now. Punk—in all its obnoxious, rebellious, snotty glory—lives. It may not get much press these days, a full decade after it was practically invented at a club on New York City's Bowery called CBGB's but it's still around.

You can find it in Minneapolis, where the Replacements, drunk out of their minds, sing songs like "Gary's Got a Boner" and "Fuck School." You can find it in San Francisco, where the original punk spirit of anyone-can-do-this lives on in Flipper, a band that, when it's not in the midst of one of its periodic breakups—as it is at the moment—lets members of the audience climb onto the stage and sing. And, naturally, you can find it around Los Angeles, where Black Flag releases albums like *Family Man*, with a cover that pictures a man holding a gun to his own head, while his wife and kids lie slaughtered nearby. The caption on the cover of *Family Man* reads: NOVEMBER 23RD, 1963. "We like to make an impact," says Rollins.

"We're getting away with doing what we like to do," says Ted Falconi, 38, a former art teacher and a guitarist for Flipper. "We're rock's bad boys."

These bands tend to be classified as punk or, in the last few years, as hardcore. But to lump them all in the same category is to ghettoize them. For Black Flag and the others are simply carrying on the most basic of rock & roll traditions. They fit nicely alongside rock's flamboyant rabble-rousers, from Little Richard to the New York Dolls, from the early Elvis to the Doors. These bands are loud, wild, intense, unpredictable, irritating and, of course, controversial. Guaranteed to upset your parents. Most of your friends too. "A rock & roll band needs to get under people's skin," says Paul Westerberg, 25, lead singer of the Replacements. "If it can't, then you ain't worth nothing. You should be able to clear the room at the drop of a hat."

"So what?" you may say. Isn't this just more of the same old adolescent blather punks have been spewing out for years? Yes and no. For one thing, the sound has changed. Though it was the rigid amphetamine thrash of New York's Ramones and, a few years later, a batch of English punk bands that inspired and defined hardcore music in the late Seventies, the music of the neopunk bands is both varied and eclectic. Among their influences you'll find such diverse artists as Hank Williams and Rick James, ZZ Top and José Feliciano. The Meat Puppets play a kind of psychedelic country & western music. Flipper specializes in haunting drone rock. The Replacements mix country and blues with hard rock Rolling Stones–New York Dolls style. The Minutemen's one- and two- minute haikus are set to condensed punk versions of rock, jazz, blues, country, and funk. Hüsker Dü's music is an ear-splitting roar of frenzied power chords and life-is-pain screams.

These groups all have something to say. The Replacements rant about technology that alienates people ("Answering Machine") and the way the video revolution has sold out rock & roll ("Seen Your Video"). Black Flag deals with hypocrisy and guilt ("Slip It In"), indecision ("I Can't Decide"), and jealousy ("Black Coffee"). The Minutemen worry, in one song, about Michael Jackson wasting his power ("A Political Song for Michael Jackson to Sing"), while noting in another how punk rock changed their lives ("History Lesson Part II"). Flipper philosophizes about boredom ("You Nought Me") and pollution ("Love Canal").

The common thread that continues to run through punk is a dissatisfaction with the modern world. How that frustration is articulated varies greatly. The Minutemen advocate political awareness. "Music can inspire people to wake up and say, 'Maybe somebody's lying.' This is the point I'd like to make with my music," says Minutemen bassist Mike Watt, 27. "Make you think about what's expected of you, of your friends. What's expected of you by your boss. Challenge those expectations. And your own expectations. Man, you should challenge your own ideas about the world every day."

Hüsker Dü tends to be more introspective. "I don't write about politics because I'm not an expert," says Bob Mould, Hüsker Dü's 25-year-old singer and guitarist. "Some bands find it very necessary to claim they're politically relevant when in actuality they don't know shit about politics. Not informing people is much better than misinforming people. We're sort of like reporters in a way. Reporters of our own mental state. Reporters of the state of the air. Consciousness. Of the day. We make personal statements."

A common complaint heard from the bands is that they are misunderstood. "The critics equated the abrasiveness of the band and some of the harsh personal realities expressed in our songs as being negative because it wasn't all love and flowers," says Bob Mould. "I think we're trying to say something fairly positive."

Most of these neopunk bands are not signed to major labels. They do not have big-time managers. They do not have much money. Black Flag tours constantly, crisscrossing the country in a beat-up van. The group played over 200 gigs last year. On a good night, Black Flag may earn $1,000, which has to cover a soundman, a couple of roadies who also sell T-shirts, truck rental, and other expenses. On tour the four members of the band somehow exist on $12.50 a day. At home, in LA, they "scavenge" food and lodging. "We are the hungriest band I've ever seen," says Rollins, who grew up in the suburbs around Washington, DC. "I've never seen a band who would go to any lengths to play like we will."

On the road, many of the musicians sleep in their vehicles or on any sofa or floor they are offered. When they are home, they crash in rehearsal halls, low-rent apartments, or even with their parents. "We get in the van and drive to a town, play, stay at a friend's house," says Paul Westerberg. "Wake up when they throw us out. Drive the rest of the day. Play the next night. We get fifteen dollars a day. And when we're home, we don't get nothing. We're way in debt. We have van problems. We own a van, it breaks down, and you know when you play that the gig money goes to pay for the broken-down van. We're used to it."

There are also lifestyle differences between the neopunks and their progenitors. Many of the new bands avoid drugs stronger than marijuana. Some concern themselves with eating healthy food and staying fit. Some don't drink. Black Flag guitarist Greg Ginn, 31, and Flipper singer-bassist Bruce Lose, 26, are vegetarians. Black Flag and Hüsker Dü pride themselves on being "responsible"—a claim Johnny Rotten would never have made for himself.

Unlike the punks of the Seventies, this new generation also has some respect for the hippies and the values they embraced in the Sixties. Around the Black Flag office and rehearsal room, in Redondo Beach, California, one frequently sees long-haired roadies wearing Grateful Dead T-shirts and playing *Aoxomoxoa* or *Workingman's Dead* on their boom boxes. Greg Ginn says one of his dreams is for Black Flag to open for the Grateful Dead. "It seems like a lot of the things that happened in the Sixties—freedom, having an open attitude—are being replaced by a new puritanism," complains Ginn. "It's time to loosen it up. A lot of stuff done in the Sixties was important."

IF YOU SAW HENRY ROLLINS hitchhiking, you wouldn't stop to pick him up. He looks like a psychopathic hippie, part Jim Morrison, part Charles Manson. Real bad news. A BORN TO LOSE kind of guy.

Get close to him—it's downright scary. Eyes that bore right through you. Hair, a tangled mess that falls past his shoulders, down his back. Ragged, ripped clothing. Lots of tattoos: skulls and snakes, ghouls, a spider, a bat. And, etched across his upper back in inch-high letters, Henry Rollins' philosophy of life: SEARCH & DESTROY.

"I think you really got to look at it deeper than surface level," says Rollins. "I mean, the way I look—this is only skin." Perhaps, but Rollins' image—and the way it alienates him from so much of society—in many ways characterizes the relationship between Black Flag and mainstream America. "I guess we offend a lot of people," Rollins has said. "The hair length, the way we look, the way we dress isn't conducive to one-way thinking."

An aura of dark violence hangs in the air around Black Flag, like soot from a turn-of-the-century factory smokestack. Sitting in a hamburger joint down the street from Black Flag's office, Rollins wolfs down a burger and stares at several kids glued to videogames. "Life, for a lot of people, is a very surface-level experience," he says. "I see these lard-assed kids in front of these videogames. You know, as close to any kind of real destruction as they'll ever get is to put a quarter in and blow something up. When I see complacency, I just got to fuck with it. This is such a soft place to live. A lot of places to me are like a big open throat waiting to be cut. You can walk into a lot of these houses and kick the door down and just take it. It's yours. I'm not going to be cutting nothing, because that's not my life. But I'm in favor of something else for me."

Black Flag has been associated—unfairly, its members claim—with punk violence since the late Seventies. People have accused the band with being sexist, racist, and fascist. The group was forced to move out of three LA communities. "Our whole thing has been made out to be brutal, fascistic and violent," says Rollins, who does not drink or use drugs. "Those are three things that we're very much not into at all. We're not violent. We're not evil. We don't like to see anybody hurt at any time. I don't like to see violence at anybody's shows. I've seen more violence at Van Halen [shows] than at any of our gigs."

While Black Flag's music no longer resembles the punk of the past, there are similarities between a late Seventies' Sex Pistols concert and a Black Flag performance. There is a feeling that outbursts of crowd violence are imminent. Sometimes the audience spits at Rollins. Sometimes he jumps right into the crowd, a swelling, moving, slam dancing group of kids. Rollins has been known to punch out a particularly obnoxious and unreasonable heckler who wants to fight and will not let him perform. "My thing is real confrontational," says Rollins of his performances, which have, on occasion, left him with broken bones. "I mean, I don't like to go beat people up, but I like to be real close. Bring it home. If someone wants to touch me, kiss me, hit me, stab me, talk to me, sing with me, they should be able to lean over and do it!"

Perhaps more than anything else, Black Flag wants to shake up its audience. "I find it really distasteful to have a band that plays to me what I want to hear," says Greg Ginn. "That's no kind of expression. We don't play to satisfy an audience. We play what we want them to hear. If you love your audience, you try to bring them something they don't already have. You don't play to their current sensibilities and not give them anything that would threaten them. To me, that shows a total disrespect for an audience."

"IF YOU WORK FOR SST Records you have to be prepared to sleep on the floor," says Jordan Schwartz, 21. That's just what Jordan and Black Flag manager Chuck Dukowski do. They sleep on the floor of the messy office in Redondo Beach, which, along with a cramped, low-ceilinged downstairs rehearsal room, serves as Black Flag's base of operations.

SST is the most important underground record label in America. As the *Los Angeles Times* noted not long ago, "The company [SST] has matured into a showcase for some of the best alternative rock bands in the country." In addition to Black Flag, other acts include the Minutemen, the Meat Puppets, and Hüsker Dü. (In early 1986 SST would sign Sonic Youth and in May release *EVOL*.) In its five-year existence SST has released over 40 recordings, 18 of which are LPs. Last year alone SST released four albums by Black Flag as well as double albums by the Minutemen and by Hüsker Dü and albums by the Meat Puppets, Saccharine Trust, and St. Vitus.

SST is just one of a group of underfinanced, low-budget underground labels—San Francisco's Subterranean and Minneapolis' Twin/Tone are two others—which have been recording bands that the major labels have either overlooked or dismissed as uncommercial. "Me and my friends wanted to record the punk-rock scene," says Steve Tupper, 38, explaining why he formed Subterranean Records in 1979. The label's best-known act is Flipper. "We have this viewpoint of looking at this musical underground, rather than the established or commercial acts—this feeling that there is a real musical underground, and that's where the most interesting stuff is coming from. A lot of the stuff we put out is abrasive. We like to annoy."

Like a handful of English indies—Factory, Mute, and Rough Trade, for example—the American underground labels are not as interested in making money as they are in effecting culture. Which explains why a guy like Steve Tupper worked in a machine shop for several years, pouring all his extra money into Subterranean, recording bands that have absolutely no chance of ever being popular. "Our music is a real alternative to mainstream music," says Tupper. "Why that's important is that society as a whole is totally fucked. What we're looking at is using music to challenge a lot of the assumptions of what constitutes music and what constitutes an acceptable form of entertainment and expression."

SST also began in 1979, when the members of Black Flag realized that if they were going to make records, they would have to do it themselves. The first release, a Black Flag EP called *Nervous Breakdown*, cost $600 to record. Flipper made its now-classic first LP, *Album—Generic Flipper*, for less than $3,000. The Replacements' critically acclaimed album *Let It Be* cost $6,000. Hüsker Dü's two-record set, *Zen Arcade*, cost $3,200, while the Minutemen wrapped up their two-disc masterpiece, *Double Nickels on the Dime,* for $1,500.

To date, nearly 250,000 of Black Flag's albums, EPs, and singles have been sold. The other labels—and bands—have not fared as well. Twin/Tone has sold 42,000 copies of the Replacements' *Let It Be* and another 30,000 of the band's previous releases. Subterranean has sold about 28,000 copies of Flipper's first two albums. Nearly every SST release has more than made back its cost, and the recent Hüsker Dü and Minutemen albums have won both bands voluminous amounts of critical praise.

One problem these labels share concerns independent distribution. "A record store takes one Black Flag album," says Ginn. "If they sell it, they wait until the distributor comes in a week later, then order one more Black Flag album, which they don't get for another week. Meanwhile, people come in looking for the albums, and they're not there. Or they file them in the import section. Or under NEW WAVE. If we were distributed by a major label, we'd be filed in the rock section, which is where a lot of our fans expect to find our records. We're not New Wave."

Even if a record sells well, collecting revenues from the independent distributors is not always easy. "We've grossed almost $300,000 this year," says Chris Osgood, head of distribution at Twin/Tone. "But we've got $133,000 outstanding that I haven't been able to collect from distributors because nobody really wants to pay you until you have the next release. I'm sure that all indie labels have that problem."

One band that is tired of dealing with alternative labels is the Replacements. After considering offers from both CBS and Sire Records—the label Madonna records for—the Replacements recently made a deal with Sire. "If they leave us alone and give us a little push, they're going to have much better results than trying to steer us in directions," says Paul Westerberg. "We're all bullheaded. You know, if anyone tells us what to do, we're real immature about it, and we'll go in the exact opposite direction."

Black Flag tried working with larger labels three and a half years ago in hopes of alleviating its distribution problems. The group signed a distribution deal with Unicorn Records, an LA label that, in turn, had a distribution deal with MCA. But when an MCA executive heard the Black Flag album *Damaged*, he refused to distribute it. He called it "an antiparent record." Then Black Flag and SST got in a protracted legal hassle with Unicorn that kept SST from releasing any Black Flag albums until the end of 1983. So much for major labels.

Of course, neither Warner Bros. nor CBS is exactly jumping to sign Black Flag or any of the bands that record for SST or Subterranean. It's hard to imagine any major label releasing an album like *Family Man* and its violent cover. Or Black Flag's *My War,* the cover of which depicts a smiling hand puppet holding a butcher's knife. And the song "Slip It In" would definitely be considered obscene by the PTA.

Yet even without the push major labels could give them, the neopunk bands will continue, struggling along, keeping the rebel spirit alive. All of the key bands have been together for more than five years—and they plan to stick around. "I think being outside the mainstream music business is good," says Bob Mould. "When you tie yourself down to a major label, you give up all your individual control over things. You become part of a machine. It wouldn't seem right for Hüsker Dü to come out on Polymer Records."

Or, as Bill Stevenson says in Vegas before beginning the all-night drive back to Redondo Beach, "I won't sell my art for money. I've got too much of my soul in this. I'd rather kill myself."

*Rolling Stone*, July 1985

Professor Longhair in his hotel room, San Francisco, 1977.

# PROFESSOR LONGHAIR

Rock and rhythm is what I play. I don't play no blues. I don't play no rock. Rock and rhythm.

**Why he didn't tour:**
I didn't want to travel. I don't like airplanes. Still don't. Me and heights don't agree. I've got a superstitious feeling about it.

**On how he got ripped off over the years:**
A lot of mysterious fellows managed my affairs.

**About the music industry:**
They kill you quick if you don't take cautious steps.

September 1977

Van Morrison at the Old Waldorf, San Francisco, 1978.

# VAN MORRISON BREAKS HIS SILENCE (SORT OF)

### The mystery man says he's no longer interested in the "rock & roll circus."

*Van Morrison can be a real jerk—at least if you're a reporter trying to interview him. There was a long stretch when he wouldn't even talk to journalists. I lucked out. Sort of. Morrison was booked to headline at the Palace of Fine Arts in San Francisco, and there was some concern that the show wouldn't sell out without advance media coverage. So an interview was arranged. I was going to write a story for the* San Francisco Chronicle. *Morrison, as it turned out, lived up to the reputation he had then (and now), but I don't want to give too much away. Over the many years that I've interviewed musicians, most of the interviews went smoothly, and most of the musicians I interviewed were friendly and professional. They wanted the coverage, and I wanted a story. My job was to get them to tell me things they hadn't told other writers. With Morrison, because he spoke to the press so infrequently, I was at an advantage, and as long as I got coherent answers from him, I would have a story. And once I had interviewed him, I knew who else would want that story. It was 1982, and I was occasionally writing for* Rolling Stone *at the time on a freelance basis. This was one of the stories that led to my being hired by* Rolling Stone *a year and a half later, in the fall of 1983. I love how this story begins.*

VAN MORRISON'S BROWN, TWO-STORY, shingled house sits alongside a narrow road that snakes up Mount Tamalpais above the sleepy Marin County town of Mill Valley. From the road, only a mailbox, with a large number that looks as if it were painted by a child, indicates the presence of Morrison's home.

Down a short driveway is a tall, weathered picket fence; a chain-link fence surrounds the rest of the grounds, which are concealed for the most part by shrubbery and trees. Through the gate, one can see the house; a sloping, grass-covered hill to the right of the house ends at a long, rectangular swimming pool. A few chairs and a small stone statue of a young boy stand on the hillside among the grass.

Inside the gate, it's so quiet that the cars occasionally driving past are barely audible and one can hear the whir of hummingbirds flitting from flower to flower. It's the kind of peaceful retreat where a person can sit in the sun by the pool and watch deer leap over the fence and prance across the grass—which is exactly what I'm doing on a chilly winter afternoon, as I wait for Van Morrison. He's more than an hour late for an interview at his own house. It is supposed to be the conclusion of an interview session that had begun, very unexpectedly, a few weeks earlier.

THE MESSAGE THAT HAD BEEN left on my answering machine sometime after midnight was simple and to the point: "Van Morrison will do an interview with you tomorrow." It was a surprising bit of information, since Morrison does not like to talk to the press. During the past three years, he has given virtually no interviews. He has, apparently, regretted most of them, "because what I'm saying, most of the time, is not understood," he would tell me.

Morrison is one of the more mysterious stars of popular music. He rarely tours, preferring to divide his time between his home on Mount Tamalpais, where he lives alone, and Europe. He returns to Ireland, his homeland, for inspiration and frequently visits Copenhagen. Morrison's 11-year-old daughter, Shannon [sic] (he was married in the late Sixties and early Seventies to a woman who called herself Janet Planet), recently spent a few months visiting him. His parents, George and Violet Morrison, have lived in the Bay Area since 1973; they run a record store, Caledonia Records, in northern Marin County.

Morrison, who was born on August 31, 1945, in Belfast, Northern Ireland, began singing when he was 12 and soon learned to accompany himself on guitar, saxophone, and harmonica. He played and sang in numerous bands throughout his youth; dropping out of high school when he was 16 to make a career of music. For several years, he toured Europe in an R&B cover band, the Monarchs, before returning to Belfast when he was 19 and forming Them with some friends.

By 1966, Them were part of the British Invasion, scoring American hits with a series of classic rock tracks, among them "Gloria," "Here Comes the Night," and "Mystic Eyes." When the group broke up in 1967, Morrison moved to America, living first in Boston, then Woodstock, before settling in Marin County about 1971. By then, he had recorded *Astral Weeks*, the album upon which his reputation as an Irish rock & roll mystic rests, and had established himself as a commercially successful solo artist with two Top 10 hits, "Brown-Eyed Girl" and "Domino," and several hit albums.

Only in the San Francisco Bay Area have Morrison's fans had much opportunity to see him perform during the past decade. Over the years, he has appeared periodically—often with only a few days' advance notice—at all kinds of clubs and concert halls, from the Sleeping Lady Cafe (capacity 100) to showcase clubs and halls like the Old Waldorf, the Great American Music Hall, and the Berkeley Community Theater. In October of last year, following the completion of a new album, *Beautiful Vision*, Morrison suddenly booked nine dates around the Bay Area. He gave a varied and inspired series of performances that featured material from his three latest albums (*Into the Music*, *Common One*, and *Beautiful Vision*); a few old favorites ("Gloria" and "Tupelo Honey"); and, on at least one occasion, when he performed at the El Rancho Tropicana Convention Center in Santa Rosa, a batch of R&B tunes, including John Lee Hooker's "C. C. Rider" and Sonny Boy Williamson's "Help Me."

Rumors about Van Morrison abound: He is moody, unpredictable, and eccentric. He has recorded entire albums and then junked them. He's very religious and some kind of mystic. He's hell to work with. Since the media have so little access to Morrison—and since he is so reserved and oblique when interviewed—the mystique just grows.

IT WAS A FEW MINUTES after three in the afternoon when the short, stocky man with the reddish hair, the man some have called "the Belfast Cowboy," showed up for our first interview. No one in the mellow Mill Valley restaurant paid him any mind. Morrison nervously looked about the place. I waved him over to my table. "Would you like to sit here or out in the courtyard?" I asked. A look of confusion passed over his face. "Uh, where do you want to sit?" he mumbled.

Once outside, Morrison seemed distracted and guarded. Seated in the shadows, with soft, recorded jazz playing in the background, he set a well-used notebook down on the small table, removed his glasses, and lit a cigarette. He didn't look like the kind of guy who sells out concert halls and makes hit records. He didn't look like a "truck driver at the end of a cross-country haul," as *Newsweek* magazine once described him. He looked like a rather ordinary, if introspective and overweight, 36-year-old man, casually dressed in black cotton-suede pants, a black wool V-neck sweater worn over a sky-blue sport shirt, and a dull-green suede jacket that stopped at the waist.

Asked why he had consented to an interview after three years of silence, Morrison, whose blue eyes were clear and whose face was sprinkled with a day's growth of beard, said, "I didn't think about it. If I had, I probably wouldn't have done it."

Van Morrison is considered one of the originals of rock & roll, and critics have heaped praise on him over the years. But when his critical acclaim was brought up, Morrison said solemnly, "That could just as easily change tomorrow. The same people who build you up are the same people who put you down. So I don't think about it. It doesn't matter."

In fact, Morrison is not only disenchanted with rock critics, he's disenchanted with rock & roll itself. Today, the man who 16 years ago wrote and recorded the rock standard "Gloria" and who as recently as 1977 told an interviewer, "Basically, at heart, I'm a rocker," no longer wants to be associated in any way with rock & roll.

"Once you say rock & roll, people start to project and relate to you in a certain way," he said. "I'm just so far from that image you wouldn't believe it. If anybody looked at the way I live these days—it's so removed from what people think of. In fact, it's dull and boring. I've got nothing to do with that rock & roll stuff at all. I mean, when I started, when I was a teenager, to me rock & roll was Little Richard, Jerry Lee Lewis, Chuck Berry and people like that. But now, what is rock & roll? It's not music anymore. I did the rock & roll thing fifteen years ago. I've done it!"

Morrison also said he was through touring. "I cut that out because I couldn't do it anymore. I started playing when I was 12. I started touring when I was 15. I made my first record and became successful when I was 18. So I'd had a lot of touring under my belt even before I had any success. But by then I'd already had enough. I'd seen what that was and experienced that."

When asked about his unusual choice of venues for recent performances in the Bay Area (the Japan Center and the Palace of Fine Arts), he explained, "It's a platform for some other way of doing it. The advantage is that it's not a rock & roll joint. So, you don't get that element, that atmosphere, the whole vibration that goes with that."

Morrison's disenchantment with rock may account, in part, for the split between him and his former manager, rock entrepreneur Bill Graham, last year. Things got so strained between Morrison and Graham, who is known for his volatile temperament, that at one point the manager reportedly stormed up to Morrison's Mill Valley home and pounded on the front door; Morrison refused to let him in.

At Bill Graham Presents, Nick Clainos, who works in the management division, refused to acknowledge that there had been any bad feelings between Graham and Morrison; apparently, they have made up. "The split was extremely amiable," said Clainos. "The deal lapsed. That's all. We may work with him again in the future. He's a very special guy to us. We'd do anything for Van Morrison."

The waitress arrived, and Morrison ordered a fruit salad, a cup of coffee, and a glass of orange juice. His hand was shaking slightly as he lit another cigarette. He seemed to tense up a little more with each question; he was suspicious of even the most innocuous ones. He didn't want to talk about his business affairs, his personal life, or his past. "I'm not interested in the past, and the past is inevitably brought up. It's boring to me. It's not where I am, and I don't think about it anymore. What I'm doing is what I'm doing this day, this week."

If Van Morrison is not an easy man to interview, he's a harder man to work for. His current and former business associates fall silent when asked about Morrison. At his record company, Warner Bros., employees stiffen at the sound of Morrison's name. And for good reason. A few years ago, Morrison had a Warner Bros. publicist fired after he referred to Morrison as "unstable," and the remark found its way into print. "I don't think you'll get anyone at this company to talk about Van," said one Warner Bros. staffer.

One man who would talk about Morrison was Ted Templeman, a Warner Bros. staff producer known for his work with the Doobie Brothers and Van Halen. In the early Seventies, Templeman produced three of Morrison's albums—*Tupelo Honey*, *St. Dominic's Preview*, and *It's Too Late to Stop Now*—and he was recently quoted in *BAM*, a regional music newspaper, as saying, "I'd never work with Van Morrison again as long as I live, even if he offered me $2 million in cash. I aged ten years producing three of his albums. He's a marvelous talent, a fantastic singer, but he's fired everyone who's ever worked with him—all his producers, his managers, his attorneys. He's so unpredictable."

When I asked Templeman about his statements, he backed off quite a bit. "I've been very depressed since I said those things," he explained. "They came out wrong. I haven't been able to sleep a lot of nights over this. I'll tell you a funny story. After I did that interview, I completely forgot about it. And I had an idea for me and Jerry Wexler to do a record with Van. I talked to Van about it and he said great, and Wexler was ready to do it. In the meantime, that article came out. Van calls the record company and tells them he never wants to see me again. And I got so depressed I felt like quitting. I would make a record with him for nothing, just to make up for saying those things.

"But I gotta tell you. I did stay up night after night trying to figure out how to keep up with him. What didn't come across was that it was his 'genius' that I was trying to keep up with. I did have a rough time working with Van, but I'm not the only one who would say that. He's an iconoclast, really. It's like J. D. Salinger doesn't do things the way other writers do. I had trouble with Van because he'd change his mind all the time. That's the nature of the guy. But it was his brilliance that I was trying to keep up with. And what I'm saying is that I didn't get that point across. I'm probably the biggest Van Morrison fan of all time."

Some of Van Morrison's other fans include Bruce Springsteen, Bob Seger, Graham Parker, Willy DeVille, and Elvis Costello—singers whose styles were strongly influenced by Morrison. "I've got no reaction to it whatsoever," Morrison said. "I never started out to make impressions on people. If that's what they want to do, that's what they're doing and that's it."

So what *is* he trying to do?

"I'm just channeling what I get," he said. "I get bits and pieces of songs and I try to put them together. I'm just channeling the creativity that's coming through me. That's all I'm doing."

Asked if he is a happy man, Morrison frowned and said, "What does that have to do with anything? I don't want to discuss these things in interviews."

He was silent for several minutes. Still, he remained at the table and asked if there were more questions. His fruit salad arrived, and he idly picked at it. When he didn't want to discuss something or didn't have a ready answer, he simply said, "I can't answer that question."

Morrison tends to make light of his vocation. When I asked if he felt his music was more important than his lyrics, he said, "It's my job. I get paid for making records, for writing songs. I get paid for it, so I do it. It's my job, and I've been doing it for 20 years. And I don't have time to think about these things, you know. I can't. I have other things to do, which is write the songs and make records.

"The thing is, when it gets down to it, it is like most people's jobs," Morrison continued earnestly. "Because when you're working in the studio and you're making an album, you have to be pregnant every year and give birth to material. It's not much different from other jobs. I mean, a recording studio is not different from a factory. It's just a factory for music. And sometimes there are moments when you get off, but it's moments. The rest of it is very hard work. And the environment is not a creative environment."

Consistent with viewing the writing and recording of songs as a job is Morrison's refusal to accept the adulation of his fans. "See, the thing is, I am not my albums or performances," he said in exasperation, near the end of the interview. "That's something I do, but I'm not that."

Morrison said he has no interest in contemporary pop or rock music. "I went through that a long time ago—trends and fads and all that stuff—and saw what it was, you know. It's just a passing show. That's what it is. It's just . . . it's for people who are into fads. It's like, 'Okay, that was good, next. Next, next, next, next.' It's like eating too much because you're hungry. More, more, more, more.

"I'm not interested in popular music. Popular music is not going anywhere. It stopped growing. I think there was a time when it could have gone where jazz has gone. I feel that because of the money that's being made from it and the way it's packaged . . . it's gotten involved in other areas, saying things when, really, nothing is being said. And there's also the isolation, people have cut themselves off because of ego and financial considerations, mainly ego about who's on top and when, not like other artists like poets and painters and noncommercial filmmakers who can't afford to do these things because they don't have the money to do them and they have to stick together to continue the form. And there's a lot of negativity in the record business. A tremendous amount of negativity. It's not a creative medium.

"I think that the music business is a fixed system," said Morrison. "I think that banks are looser than the music business. I think it's very fixed, and it's gotten more so in the last five years."

How does that affect him?

"Well, you always hear people saying that when you reach a certain point, you can do what you want. Which is total rubbish, because the music business is simply based on sales figures. They have to sell a certain number of albums to break even and make money, and that's what the music business is based on. It's not based on music; it's based on sales.

"I have no ideals about this situation at all. Like I said before, I'm doing it for several reasons. One reason is that I'm channeling music, and that's what I get coming through me, and that's what I try and put out the best way I can. I don't have any illusions about what I'm doing in the music business at all, because I know what it is . . . a business. It's a business."

Yet Morrison manages to record what he wants. "Yeah," he said, "but I've had to fight for it. I've had to fight a long time for it, and I'm still fighting for it."

Morrison also claimed he is unfazed by the commercial pressures put on him by his record company. "I'm not concerned with what people think about what I'm doing. I just do the best I can, and if you like it, good. And if you don't like it, good. It's up to you. I just do what I do. Take it or leave it."

But doesn't Morrison care about how people react to his music? Doesn't it please him when his music makes people happy? "Umm. That's a difficult question. I don't think I could answer that."

A cool breeze was blowing through the empty courtyard. Morrison had hardly touched his fruit salad. The tape recorder was clicked off, and Morrison asked if he could listen to the tape of our conversation. As he sat with the first 10 minutes or so of the interview murmuring in the background, he seemed to relax. He said he'd recently been thinking that he would like to get on the other side of the microphone and interview some people. "But not music people," he noted. "I like to read them; I just don't like to do them." Then he smiled.

I WAS SITTING BY MORRISON'S pool, thinking about our previous meeting, when the stillness was broken, the gate swung open, and Morrison appeared. He seemed at ease, casually entering his yard. Then he noticed me, and his body visibly tensed. I walked up to meet him.

"I tried to call you," he mumbled. He was not smiling. "Were you home?" We walked through the gate to the driveway where his silver-gray BMW was parked. "Well, I can't do it today," he announced. He stood there uncomfortably, peering at me through plastic-framed glasses. "Things just came up. I don't know." He shrugged. "Call me next week. Call me Monday," he said. "Uh, I hope this didn't inconvenience you."

I said I'd call on Monday. He nodded. I turned away and walked to my car. I looked back and Morrison and his BMW had vanished. That's the last I saw of Van Morrison.

"I've seen him change his mind five times in one hour," said a former business associate when I related the incident to him. "He's a funny guy."

*Rolling Stone*, February 18, 1982

# PATTI SMITH: RETURN OF THE "BAD GIRL"

Once described as the "wild Mustang of American rock," Patti Smith returns to public life as an older, wiser rock visionary.

*In the winter of 1975, I was just beginning to interview musicians and write about them. I knew almost nothing about writing or interviewing, but luckily I didn't know that. I was full of 20-something bravura. I was going to be a "great writer" (that's how the 22-year-old me thought in those days) and nothing was gonna stop me. I was writing for the* Berkeley Barb *and a slick magazine called* City of San Francisco *that the great Warren Hinckle (of* Ramparts *fame) was editing and movie director Francis Ford Coppola was publishing. Both the* Barb *and* City of San Francisco *were interested in stories on Ms. Smith. A week or so before the interview, I got an advance copy of* Horses, *which had not yet been released. I could not believe how great it was, and that I was going to get to interview this incredible artist. I interviewed Smith for the two stories I was going to write with my future wife Leslie (we were collaborating on articles at the time). I knew a job at* Rolling Stone *was just around the corner. I was right, but I was wrong. There would be a job at* Rolling Stone *for me, but it would be eight more years of freelance writing before I'd be hired. At the time of that interview, Smith had gotten some great write-ups in the* Village Voice; *she'd had books of poetry published and written for* Creem; *she'd written lyrics for the Blue Öyster Cult; and had one single, "Hey Joe"/ "Piss Factory" released on her friend/musical collaborator rock critic/guitarist Lenny Kaye's Mer label. She'd previously played once in the Bay Area, at a Berkeley record store, Rather Ripped. What follows is an extensive interview that onetime* Creem *writer Jaan Uhelszki and I did with Smith in 1996, as she was finally returning to live performance and record making after an absence of 15 years.*

## Introduction by Michael Goldberg
Interview by Michael Goldberg and Jaan Uhelszki

## 1. In the Beginning

SO SCRAWNY SHE ALMOST wasn't there at all, Patti Smith sat in the small dark backstage dressing room, exhausted. She had just completed the second of two high-energy performances at the Boarding House, a now long-defunct San Francisco club, and it was well past midnight. Her brow was covered with sweat; her shirt was soaked. It was the winter of 1975; Smith's debut album, *Horses*, had not yet been released. All the same, her four nights of shows—two performances a night—were sellouts. Already, the word was out about Patti Smith. She was the real deal, the genuine article, the spirit of rock & roll materialized in the form of a woman. In the *Village Voice*, in April of 1975, James Wolcott, noting her "stray-cat cool," wrote that "skinny, schizzy Patti is on her way to becoming the wild mustang of American rock."

Patti Smith in San Francisco, 1978, after "Because the Night" was a hit.

A month earlier, in no less a publication than the *New York Times*, John Rockwell had proclaimed: "Miss Smith has it in her to be as significant an artist as American pop music has produced."

In the dressing room, "skinny, schizzy Patti" was ready to talk. "Rock & roll is higher than art," she told me, the eager young journalist, when she had caught her breath. "It's the only open form that we have left." Smith looked like Keith Richards' kid sister. She was wearing espadrilles with multicolored ribbons that wound around her straight-legged black Levi's and a striped black-and-white crew-neck shirt.

"Every other form—religion, art, politics—has closed people off from each other," she said. "But religion does have a chance of being universal. What I'm interested in is pre-Tower of Babel time."

As she spoke, she autographed a book of her poems that I had brought along. "It's like before the Tower of Babel when they split all our tongues," she continued, gaining momentum. "Everyone talked the same language, everyone had the same rhythm, everyone could communicate telepathically. I'm lookin' to rock & roll to be the new tongue extending."

Despite her exhaustion, she had the look of a woman on a mission. "It's like riding through the tunnel of love," she said, staring right through me. "And the tongue of love taking you there is rock & roll."

## 2. Babel On

TWENTY-ONE YEARS LATER, she stood on the stage at the Warfield Theater in San Francisco. "Oh I was bad." She was reciting one of her early poems, "Ballad of a Bad Boy." "Didn't do what I should / Mama catch me with a lickin' / And tell me to be good."

Oh god was she bad. She swore. She stayed out all night. She shacked up with wild boys like Jim Carroll and the Blue Öyster Cult's Allen Lanier. She sang about the hard stuff—heroin—and looked up to the hard cases like Keith Richards and William Burroughs.

None of which would have mattered if she couldn't deliver the goods. She could. Patti Smith was the first artist in the '70s to not only believe, with her heart and soul, that rock & roll was art, but to deliver on that premise. She took dreamscapes and poetry and slammed them up against the rawest of the raw, the three-chord garage rock of "Gloria" and "Hey Joe" and "Land of 1000 Dances." As Dave Marsh wrote 20 years ago, "Somewhere, Patti firmly believed, there was a place where Rimbaud's intense aesthetic lust met the Ronettes' boyfriend's stud passion."

In 1975, the first time I saw Patti Smith, I felt like I had seen the Messiah. That year, shortly after I saw five of her shows, I wrote that Smith was the most "original and important artist since Bob Dylan." I went on to paraphrase Bruce Springsteen's line about looking for a savior, before gushing: "Patti Smith in the '70s, more so then Dylan in the '60s, is that savior, that human we've waited for, not to lead us (for Patti would be the first to quote Dylan's 'Don't follow leaders') but to hip us to, as she sings in 'Land,' 'the sea of possibilities.'"

Patti Smith raised the stakes. Like Dylan before her, she refused to accept the prescribed limits of rock and pop song subject matter. Nothing was forbidden. She sang about death, sex, drugs, and UFO spirits. All raw material for Smith to write lyrics that can, really, only be described as poetry. And the way she delivered them, stretching words, whining them, shouting them, screaming them—firing them out like bullets from a machine gun. Listen to "Birdland" off *Horses*, listen to the way she delivers the line "I'm not human." Two decades after it was recorded, it will still send chills up and down your spine.

Live, Smith was a revelation. Sure she'd learned from the best: Hendrix, Morrison, Dylan, Jagger, Iggy . . . But she had a presence, a this-is-for-keeps intensity that made you believe that while she was performing, nothing else mattered. In 1975, trying to describe my reaction to one of her shows, I wrote: "I felt as emotionally and physically drained as Patti looked."

## 3. Piss Factory

PATTI SMITH INVENTED HERSELF. Cursed with the most innocuous of last names, she transformed herself into a rock & roll Rimbaud, the first lady of punk, before punk had a name. She grew up poor in Pitman, a town in South Jersey. Dad (Grant Smith) was a factory worker; mom (Bev Smith) a waitress. She was the eldest of four children (one sister, Kimberly, is immortalized in a song on *Horses*). "No matter how bad things were, if we didn't have food, or my father was on strike, my mother was always great in weaving a fantasy world," Smith told me in 1975. "Telling us fantasy stories, or getting us involved in stories."

She grew up tough, and to this day there is a wiry edge to her. You don't cross Patti Smith. "I grew up in a tougher part of Jersey than Bruce Springsteen," she told Dave Marsh at the beginning of 1976. "I wasn't horrified by Altamont, it seemed natural to me. Every high school dance I went to, somebody was stabbed."

Naturally, it was the Rolling Stones [in the mid-'60s], not the Beatles, that made her a rock & roll fan; Bob Dylan who paved the way for Smith to mix up poetry and punk. "The Rolling Stones really changed my life," she told me. "When I saw the Stones on the 'Ed Sullivan Show' it made being white cool again."

About one of her heroes she said, "I only liked Dylan 'cause he was looking cool. Growing up in South Jersey, just about all we listened to was Black music. We were like little animals. We liked Gary U.S. Bonds, anything that was danceable and dirty."

She worked in a factory during and immediately following high school (that experience was the inspiration for a key song on her first single, "Piss Factory"). In that song, she recites, "And I will get out of here . . . / I'm gonna go / I'm gonna get out of here / I'm gonna get out of here / . . . I'm gonna be a big star and I will never return / Never return, no never return / To burn out in this piss factory / And I will travel light / Oh, watch me now."

While in junior college, she got pregnant and had a baby, which she gave up for adoption. In 1967 Smith came to New York and began hanging around Pratt, the Brooklyn art college. It was there that she met Robert Mapplethorpe. The future erotic photographer liked her poetry (she'd started writing after discovering Rimbaud's *Illuminations*). In 1970, after a sojourn in Paris, and a brief return to Pitman, Smith moved into the infamous Chelsea Hotel with Mapplethorpe.

And in 1971, she met a rock critic, who played guitar and worked in a record store, named Lenny Kaye. Soon they were performing together, with Kaye adding guitar accompaniment to Smith's poetry readings. That was also the year Smith had poems published in *Creem* for the first time, including one titled "Autobiography." She cowrote a play, "Cowboy Mouth," with Sam Shepard and penned "Career of Evil" for the Blue Öyster Cult.

By 1974, Smith's first record, a 45 rpm with "Hey Joe" on one side and "Piss Factory" on the other, was released on her friend Lenny Kaye's tiny Mer record label. Smith's band, the Patti Smith Group, ultimately included, in addition to Kaye, pianist Richard Sohl, second guitarist Ivan Kral, and drummer Jay Dee Daugherty. A year later Smith was signed by Clive Davis to Arista Records.

Her first album was produced by former Velvet Underground cofounder John Cale at Electric Ladyland. Drummer Daugherty later described working with Cale as "hell."

Writing in the *Village Voice,* Greil Marcus felt the album didn't quite live up to all the hype. I thought he was wrong then, and all these years later I still think he underestimated the record. Still, Marcus did Smith the ultimate honor when he described it as "an 'art statement.'"

## 4. Crash Landing

JUST BEFORE THE RELEASE OF *Horses,* Smith performed at a club called the Longbranch in Berkeley, California. At the show, between sets, I brought several photos I'd taken of Smith backstage and gave them to her. Smith liked the photos, and she said she really dug the article that my wife Leslie and I had collaborated on for the *Berkeley Barb.* "You're the first people to use the stuff about the Tower of Babel," she said. "That's real important to me."

The next time I saw Patti Smith, in the summer of 1979, a few months before she would drop off the face of the earth for some 17 years, everything had changed. The warm, inspired woman I'd last spoken to had transformed into something else altogether.

She had agreed to a press conference of sorts in her hotel room. Standing in the middle of the room, surrounded by a small audience of fans and journalists, self-described "field-marshal" Smith was holding court. "You," she bellowed at a young woman. "What are you doing here?"

Then, before the startled woman could answer, Smith addressed the rest of us. "One by one, you're gonna tell why you've come. If I don't like your reason, we'll have you leave."

Something was wrong. Smith looked more like a crazy woman than a rock star who had entered the Top 10 with "Because the Night." Her longish hair was a tangle. A man's green leather sports coat, at least four sizes too big, hung from her gaunt body. The tight dirty orange striped pants, stuffed into ankle high moccasins, looked as if they hadn't left her body in days. In fact, she looked like she'd slept in the outfit.

"Let me see those questions," she said to another woman.

"Give me those questions or I'll slap you," she said in a tone that was half humorous, half not-so-humorous. She was reluctantly given the list. "Oh, here's a good one," Smith said sarcastically. "How does the weather affect your creativity?"

Turning to me she snapped, "I've been fighting people like you all my life. You're not my type." Then she added, half-heartedly, "Don't take it personal."

This was a scene straight out of the Bob Dylan documentary, *Don't Look Back,* when Dylan tells a *Time* magazine correspondent, "I know more about what you do, and you don't even have to ask me how or why or anything, just by looking at you than you'll ever know about me."

During a radio interview at the time, it appeared that Smith had developed a God complex. "To do this line of work is tough," she told a KSAN DJ. "Look at Christ—he only lasted 33 years. When you really believe in communication with your creator it's a tough thing to be an earthling."

## 5. Set Me Free

ON SEPTEMBER 10, 1979, PATTI SMITH performed what would be her last live rock & roll performance for nearly 17 years, before 85,000 fans at the Stadium Communale in Florence, Italy. Asked "what snapped," Smith now says, "Well, nothing snapped. Just touring and being parted from Fred [Smith, her late husband, former guitarist for the MC5] became unacceptable, so I ceased to tour . . . I didn't say that I was never going to set foot on a stage or make a statement about it. I just stopped."

"She was definitely in a different space," Smith's guitarist and current coproducer Lenny Kaye said. "I thought maybe we'd take a vacation and come back. But there really wasn't that much left we had to say. There were no songs sitting around waiting to be recorded. After *Wave*, there was nothing. There was not one song idea.

"It seemed like our story was so complete, starting from 200 people at St. Mark's Church in '71 to 85,000 people in Florence," he added. "You couldn't write a better movie."

She became a recluse, living in the Detroit area with Fred Smith. They were married in 1980. They had two children, Jesse and Jackson. Smith said that she continued to write poetry. "I did a lot of studying," she said. "Fred and I both studied."

What else was going on, if anything, remains a mystery. Smith recorded no new music until 1988, when her husband and Jimmy Iovine (he'd produced her biggest hit "Because the Night") coproduced *Dream of Life*. That album, a beautiful work featuring the anthem "People Have the Power," was not a hit. Smith didn't perform live and granted just one interview.

Smith now characterizes *Dream of Life* as her late husband's record. "I think he did a beautiful job, but it was just perhaps a time when people really weren't that interested," she said.

Fred Smith died of a heart attack in November of 1994. Ironically, his death somehow triggered Patti Smith to return to the public arena. She performed at a Fred Smith tribute concert at The Ark in Ann Arbor, Michigan, last year. In July she performed in Central Park and made an unannounced appearance at one of the Lollapalooza 1995 New York shows. Modern-day stars including Courtney Love and members of Sonic Youth stood in awe as Smith performed an incendiary set that included "Dancin' Barefoot." In December she spent a few weeks touring with Bob Dylan. That's when former Television guitarist Tom Verlaine agreed to perform as part of her band. Verlaine subsequently toured in Smith's new band (which also includes Kaye, drummer Jay Dee Daugherty, and bassist Tony Shanahan) when they did a short West Coast tour this past March, and he played the exquisite slide guitar parts when Smith appeared on Roseanne's *Saturday Night Special* last month.

Smith now says her return to live performance has been relatively easy, and not at all what she expected. "I imagined that I had changed quite a bit, becoming a wife and mother and withdrawing from public life for so long that I would be a lot quieter on stage," she said. "I imagined that I would just be sort of straightforward and dignified and somewhat folky. And I was kind of amazed to find that [that's not the case]. I'm still ready to kick a photographer in the face."

## 6. Where Have I Yet to Roam

THERE WAS A CALM IN THE hotel room. No crazy, druggy energy. Just a cool, calm vibe. She is sitting over by the window. Her hair, streaked with grey, is long, beautiful.

She is wearing a loose-fitting cotton shirt, cuffed blue jeans. She's barefoot. Patti Smith, the wild Mustang of American rock, is no more. There's almost a Saint Patti quality about her now. But it's a role that she's not willing to accept. If she ever really had that God complex, she's certainly over it now.

"You're only allowed a small bit of sainthood," she says, flashing a quick smile. "They'll be after me soon enough. . . . The press and everybody, I promise you, will be turning on me soon."

Somehow, I don't think so. Smith's new album, *Gone Again*, is a mature work that hints at a number of directions Smith can take in years to come. While there are powerful rockers like the title track and Smith's edgy version of Dylan's "Wicked Messenger," there are also moody ballads ("Wing") and almost folk pieces ("My Madrigal"). "Musically, it's different because I wrote, I'd say, three-quarters of the music on it," she says.

It's the same old Patti: Slouched in a chair, across town from where I'd last seen her perform, at the Boarding House, in August of 1979; same old Jersey accent; same passion in her voice when she talks about the things that excite her; same cool I-could-care-less brush-off when Jaan Uhelski or I ask about something that bores her.

A leather bomber jacket on the bed. Books. Notes. A raincoat. Somehow, as usual, Smith has managed to take a sterile hotel room and make it feel like an artist lives here.

As we sit, facing each other (yeah, Jaan Uhelszki is here too, yet at times it feels like just Smith and I are alone in the room), I marvel at the fact that defiant rebel Patti Smith will turn 50 this year. Her concerns are no longer those of "the kids" as she used to call her fans.

Jaan and I interviewed Patti in late March of this year in the early afternoon a few hours before she delivered the second of two knockout performances at the Warfield Theater, where she performed a mesmerizing dose of material from *Gone Again*.

**Michael Goldberg:** The first line of your first album was one of the most powerful openings of any rock & roll album. "Jesus died for somebody's sins but not mine / My sins, my own, they belong to me." Can you still relate to that?

**Patti Smith:** Not really. I mean, it's not that I don't relate to it. It's just not a preoccupation of mine. I wrote those lines when I was 20 years old, and I wrote them really because I had such a Christian conscience. I was raised Christian. I was deeply religious as a child. But as I wanted more artistic and personal freedom, I was trying to sort of cut the cord with my . . . you know, I imagined that if I was going to explore, both artistically and personally, [then] if I did anything wrong, I'd take the blame. That was really my idea. I'd take the blame and I didn't want Jesus to have to worry about me. And I didn't want him to be responsible for my choices.

It's a very adolescent anthem. At this point in my life, it's not a preoccupation of mine. I'm not an adolescent, for one thing. And I actually find the idea of someone with the intelligence and the spectral vision of Jesus sort of hovering over me or being in my camp or [my] being part of his camp, comforting. In fact, the last time I did that song was in Florence in 1979 at our last job and the line that I sang then was: "Jesus died for somebody's sins / Why not mine?"

So I guess I had already gone through quite a shift by then. I actually developed a much different take on Jesus actually through Pasolini because I read this interview with Pasolini when he was doing the movie *The Gospel According to Saint Matthew*. And he saw Jesus as a very revolutionary man. A man that came upon the scene, the true outsider, the true rock & roll [N-word], the true person outside society who drew to himself the lepers and the whores and the thieves and helped them reclaim their position in heaven or just their dignity as human beings. So I started finding him a lot more interesting. It's sort of like when you're a kid and the only thing you learned about George Washington is he supposedly never told a lie and chopped down the cherry tree. And then as you progress through life, you find that he was an extremely interesting man with very fine ideas and things. He wasn't just an icon or somebody on a dollar bill. Jesus has become for me someone more than an image on a holy card.

**Goldberg:** Are there a lot of ideas that you articulated in songs in the past that you now see in a different way?

**Smith:** Not necessarily. I don't even see things, I'd say, a lot of things, in a different way. I've just evolved. I haven't really thought that much about it lately because I haven't really spent a lot of time listening to my records so I couldn't really give you any specific thoughts about that. What I have been thinking about being back on the stage after so many years is I am finding out who I am in relationship. . . . *[phone rings]* Hello, yes, uh-huh. Talk to him, don't bug me about this shit. OK? *[hangs up]* Sorry. They want me to pay $100 for cleaning a room, fumigating the smoke out of a room. I don't even smoke. Oh man.

**Goldberg:** You were talking about what you were discovering about performing live again.

**Smith:** I really didn't know what to expect as a performer. I imagined that I had changed quite a bit, becoming a wife and mother and withdrawing from public life for so long that I would be a lot quieter onstage. I imagined that I would just be sort of straightforward and dignified and somewhat folky. And I was kind of amazed to find that [that's not the case]. There's certain things that have changed. I am older. I have less agitated adolescent energy. But in place of that, I have another kind of energy. Different strengths. Instead of a real aggressive sexuality maybe a different kind of sensuality or something. It amuses me to find, right in the middle of the song, I think, yeah, I know that person, I remember this, I still got that and I'm still like ready to kick a photographer in the face. Things haven't changed all that much.

In terms of philosophies, my priorities have shifted. In the '70s, I was very concerned with censorship and things like that. I'm not that concerned with censorship right now. I'm more concerned with more global concerns: the environment, communicable diseases, what we can do to help educate the youth about things like AIDS, about the environment, about nutrition, how we can help people who are HIV-positive or have developed full-blown AIDS, how can we help them, things like that. I don't really give a shit, truthfully, about whether people are allowed to say "fuck" on the radio anymore. I don't really care. They probably are allowed anyway. Those things aren't so important to me. I think that's more youth's games, it's their fight.

But lyrically, I really can't think of anything that I've changed my attitudes about. Except for the fact that perhaps in the '70s, before there were incurable sexual transmittable diseases and things like that. . . . What I'm trying to say is, I feel more responsibility right now about the kind of world I might project. But I don't feel apologetic about the world that I helped project in the '70s. A lot of the landscapes that I helped build within art were riddled with sexual imagery, some drug imagery, but it *was* art. I still feel like art should be an open terrain. I do feel that we have to take a certain amount of responsibility for the kind of lifestyles that we seem to be projecting as romantic for the sake of youth. I try now to remind people, through my writing or if I'm talking in person, that art and life are two different things. In art we can perceive with more abandon. In life we have to be more guarded, be more aware. So those are the kind of things I think about. I think that where art and life merge is in the creative process, in the actual process.

**Goldberg:** That's pretty interesting that you really are separating life from art.

**Smith:** Well, you have to. I mean, I've been everything from a murderess to a rapist to some type of Trojan whore, all kinds of things in my art which I wouldn't do in real life. And I feel that in art, in my writing or in the arenas that I create in my work, that I should be able to slip in and out of different personas, different ages. It's one's imagination, you know, the articulating the deep terrain of the imagination. I'm very AIDS conscious, obviously, because I've lost so many close . . . well, we've all lost a lot of close friends, but I lost my very best friend [Robert Mapplethorpe] to AIDS, so I'm very sensitive to it. And having children of my own who are entering a world that has a fatal communicable disease, I think about these things. My conscience is torn sometimes about projecting sort of a science fiction sexual lifestyle in work, which I don't even do anymore, but I did in the '70s. I don't do it anymore just 'cause I outgrew it. But I did in the '70s. And again, I can't feel apologetic about that. But it does make me think. It does make me . . . I would like, if people are gonna read passages in "Babel" or listen to "Poppies" or certain things that I've done, I wouldn't want those same people to go out into the world and commit the acts that the characters in those pieces do. That's actually cerebral work. It isn't a manifesto for one to go out and completely abandon themselves philosophically and morally to the ravages of the world. I think, if somebody's going to do that, then they will. But I'm not urging them through my art to do that. My work in the '70s was a lot of cerebral voyaging.

**Jaan Uhelszki:** I wanted to ask about your decision to stop doing rock & roll. Why was Florence your last show? Were you aware during that show that it was going to be the last one?
**Smith:** Yeah.

**Uhelszki:** That was the turning point? What snapped?

**Smith:** Well, nothing snapped. Just touring and being parted from Fred became unacceptable, so I ceased to tour. And when I decided to do it, then I did it. I didn't do it with any particular fanfare because I don't believe in that. I really dislike these farewell tours or these comeback tours or one-last-time tour. I don't like that concept so when it was time to disseminate—is that the word?—or disintegrate, I just did it. I didn't want to prolong it or exploit it. That's a classic thing to do, to go out and exploit your farewell to the public. Also, it wasn't a conscious decision that that was the end. It was that at that point in my life, it was a decision. I didn't say that I was never going to set foot on a stage or make a statement about it. I just stopped.

**Uhelszki:** Fred was back in Detroit then.

**Smith:** Well, we were both living in Detroit. I was already living in Detroit, so every time I had to tour, we had to be parted. And like I said, that became unacceptable.

**Uhelszki:** You had enough of being a rock star? Did you want to shed that persona?

**Smith:** I don't think of things really that consciously. I had one directive. I didn't want to be parted from Fred. And I've always considered, even if it's sort of egotistical, I've always considered myself as an artist. Never shed that. I was, I suppose that I could say, I was a rock & roll star briefly. That was something I was honored to have the opportunity to do but I didn't . . . people have written all kinds of things like that. I stopped because I couldn't take the pressure, because I was taking drugs, because I . . . or, whatever their take on it was. But it wasn't any of those. I've never had a drug problem. I've never had any drug dependency problem. And, it wasn't that I was sick of anything. I love my band. I had a great band of some of my closest friends, my brother ran the band and the camaraderie was divine, really.

**Uhelszki:** The priorities shift. You know love is love. I mean, how many times does it come? You've got to go with it.

**Smith:** Well, also you can't . . . I always admired Arthur Rimbaud for that. He was the greatest poet of his time. I don't know what would have happened. I like to imagine he could have taken over the world right from the streets of Paris. But he turned his back on it and he went to Ethiopia and became a coffee trader. I think it takes a lot of courage to shed a complete skin and to move on. But it also makes life infinitely more interesting.

**Uhelszki:** Right. It makes your life. . . . Like with Rimbaud, it makes his life his art.

**Smith:** Also, I appreciate the repetition. The performing, there's a lot of repetition involved. In repetition, sometimes one loses the heart, starts to lose the heart or starts to lose the feel for what one's doing. There could have been some of that involved too. I mean, now I can . . . I couldn't even bear doing certain songs anymore. Now I can come back and do songs that people want to hear. I can do "Land" or "Rock & Roll [N-word]" or "Redondo Beach" with a fresh mouth and actually with some humor or with some, even, desire and give the song some new life, where before I was starting to resent my own work because the repetition of performing the same songs, even though we always tried to make varied shows, was really too much. I've always tried to make performing every night its own creative process. But that is also quite exhausting.

**Uhelszki:** Right. What about writing in those years. I mean, you didn't give up writing, you just gave up performing. Were you still writing a lot of poetry?

**Smith:** Always. Mostly prose. I've written quite a bit in the '80s. I haven't published much of it. Hardly any of it. But I worked quite a bit. I did a lot of studying. Fred and I both studied. Fred got a private pilot's license. He studied aviation. He studied golf. He studied various types of . . . the metaphysical sciences, or what is it? Physics. He studied physics. So we were studying quite a bit. I liked to study different periods of literature. 16th century Japanese literature or. . . . So we studied quite a bit and did some traveling before we had Jackson and Jessie. Went to French Guiana and Surinam [now Suriname] and Devil's Island.

**Uhelszki:** I could see him studying golf. He definitely had that Zen personality.

**Smith:** Yeah. That's exactly how he looked at it, as a Zen study. And, he was quite an athlete as well.

**Uhelszki:** Yeah, he always looked like one.

**Goldberg:** Sure. You talked a little bit about this earlier, but during your first period of performing, you were really seen, I think anyway, as kind of a wild female spirit of rock & roll. And now, on your return, there's kind of a Saint Patti kind of a thing with U2 and R.E.M. and all these bands who obviously were inspired by you and look up to you.

**Smith:** That won't last. *[smiles]* They'll be after me soon enough. You're only allowed a small bit of sainthood. I don't mean those groups, but I mean the press and everybody, I promise you, will be turning on me soon. But I don't mind. I don't really care about all that stuff. I don't think about that kind of thing really. When I started doing things . . . my initial motivation was to pump some blood into the arena of poetry and poetry performance and that sort of fanned out into the arena of rock & roll. I didn't really have any specific intentions for myself. I just wanted to urge and inspire and push and overturn others. I just always figured I was sort of an agitator or a visitor. I didn't really think that I had my own specific role other than that. Like I've often said, I always compared myself or the band more to Paul Revere. I imagined we were like the people that were like telling people to wake up and something was comin', wake up and be ready for it and be a part of it. I didn't necessarily think that it was me or I'd be part of it. I just felt like I wanted to get people agitated and ready. I wanted them to do something, especially after a while in rock & roll because I really perceived that rock & roll was in a down time in the early '70s, that we experienced a great period in the '60s with very strong individuals. Some of these individuals died. Other people sort of were laying low. And, I felt what was happening . . .

we were getting more of a . . . it was becoming more of a corporate glamour . . . what's that word . . . with the big shows?

**Goldberg:** Stadium rock?

**Smith:** Well, you know. They had things like glitter rock and Kiss and David Bowie and all those big shows.

**Goldberg:** Glam rock.

**Smith:** That type of thing where it seemed like the trappings were more important than the actual energy, the actual communication. That might have been presumptuous of me, but that's how I felt. I felt that rock & roll was being taken away from the streets, from its roots, from the people and being more taken over by people with money and more show business or theatrical aims. At that time, that was unacceptable to me, so I was really trying to turn the tables. But in terms of my own identity and all that or where I sit in that or my importance in that, I really couldn't tell you. You'd have to ask other people.

**Goldberg:** But you know what happened was your performances were incredible. I know 'cause I saw a bunch of them when you played the Boarding House here and the Longbranch. The kind of connection that you made with your fans is very strong. There are people who waited the 9, 10 years for *Dream of Life* and who then have been waiting for another album from you. It's a very strong thing that you . . . in terms of your communication.

**Smith:** Well, it might be because I talk to them directly. Not each individual. It's not like I want to get into a thing where a guy starts thinking "she just met me" or a girl thinks. . . . It's not like that. *[laughs]* But I comprehend and feel the fact that there's a human entity, a living entity out there that I'm communicating with. Like when we have a night like last night [Smith performed the first of two nights at the Warfield Theater in San Francisco the night before this interview], to me, I look at performance as a mutual responsibility. We're all there together. They're giving their time. I'm giving my time. And we're creating our own atmosphere, our own night, our own energy. And save the fact that there's certain technological things that have to go right, we're creating our own night. I've always felt that.

I've always felt that. I'm not an entertainer. I know sometimes I'm entertaining, but I'm not an entertainer. I don't sing at people. I don't talk at people. If I can't really feel something . . . for instance, last night I was on a roll but at the end, I was getting kinda tired. We were onstage for over two hours. I was tired. We were doing "Not Fade Away," and I like to improvise or take people on a journey, but I didn't have nothing left. I just didn't. So what could I do but within the song just tell them I don't got nothing left. I even feel like a jerk right now. I feel sort of . . . I'm sort of tired and I feel kind of . . . So we make that part of it. I think everybody feels like that sometimes so they can get into it and sometimes people help me turn it around or we got to live with it. . . . That's part of the night. I used to suffer more when those moments happened in the past. They don't really bother me because I figure, after all the things I've seen in my life, it's not the worst thing in the world to feel like a jerk onstage for five or 10 minutes. I can live with that. My goal, the thing that I really want to do is something that Fred and I talked about. If I could make a good enough living with my records, which I haven't quite been able to do yet, but if people like 'em and I can make a good enough living for me and my kids, I'd like to start, if when I perform, every cent other than if I have to pay lighting people or the sound people or a musician or two, all that money go for others. You know, go towards AIDS hospices or the homeless or whoever needs it, whoever locally needs it the most that you can find. So that when I'm onstage, I'm no longer doing it for personal gain so that I become even more like the people. That's my goal: that I'm not profiting by being onstage. Because if I can go onstage and not be profiting one cent, then I'm just like the person there. We're all sort of the same and we are really making the night together and we're making the night together to benefit another. So if the night is great and fiery, fantastic. If it's beautiful and quiet. . . . No matter what it is, it won't matter. What'll matter is we all had this night together and we made some money to help another. That's my goal. Then I'll feel like I've accomplished something as a performer.

**Goldberg:** If you do that, that will be an absolutely revolutionary thing within the confines of rock & roll, as you know, because no one else has done that.

**Smith:** I don't know why. To me, it seems obvious. I find it amazing that really rich groups. . . There are a lot of really great people out there who are really rich. I don't mean sort of rich, I mean who have maybe $100 million. They're making a lot of money out there and I don't think there's anything wrong with that but they don't need all that money. They don't need it. And I think we should all be doing it, the ones who . . . I mean, I'm not in that position, but if I get in that position, I can't wait. If I never get in that position, maybe somebody else can take the idea and do it. But I think it would be a very liberating thing for any performer. I know it would be liberating for me. And why not? Who needs all that dough? I mean, how many houses can you have? How many cars? How many collector guitars? How many Diego Riveras can you own? And I don't mean give $50,000. . . . I mean, fucking give the money away. If you're going on a tour and you're making $11 million, give $9 million away if you can't bear to give it all. Who needs more than $2 million? Give it away. Not sort of give it away. Not like sign a T-shirt or give them your old motorcycle. I mean the lion's share. But it's just an idea.

**Goldberg:** Working on this album, has it felt different than when you made albums in the past?

**Smith:** Well, working on this album was unique, uniquely difficult because I expected to be working on this album with Fred. So I couldn't even begin to tell you what working on this album was for me personally. But the joyful parts of it of course was working with Lenny again and Jay. The first time we practiced a song and I heard Lenny and Jay playing together, there was a certain familiar thing there that just brought tears to my eyes. But I liked working on the record. I did a lot of wrestling. *[laughs]* Musically, it's different because I wrote, I'd say, three-quarters of the music on it. I don't usually write music. So the music, a lot of it's fairly simple. I don't know. I liked recording it. I guess it's just, like I was talking about performing, got in the studio and a lot of it was familiar again. Some of it was a relearning process. Jeez, I'm not saying too much. You'd better ask me.

**Goldberg:** Did you amaze yourself at all when you listened back to what you'd recorded?

**Smith:** No. I think my voice has gotten stronger. I don't know if it translates completely on the record. But I think a lot of that has come from Fred. I learned a lot about music from Fred. I found new voices. There are certain things on the record . . . the things that amaze me on the record are subtle things, just things that I can do with my voice now for whatever reason because it came out of grieving, because I developed my voice through Fred, whatever. So there are certain things that I found interesting. I'm learning what I can do. I'm learning that I can do things that I didn't know I could do. I'm not saying that they're great or anything or I've become a great singer. It's nothing like that. It's just that I'm able to articulate my ideas vocally in some new ways. For instance, I did that song, it's not on the album, but Oliver Ray wrote that song "Walking Blind" for the *Dead Man Walking* soundtrack and I think the vocal on that is more indicative of the kind of thing I'm talking about. I don't really know what kind of singing it is. It's some weird hillbilly blues crossover. I don't really know what it is. Or, South Jersey blues. I don't really know exactly what kind of singing I'm doing because I wouldn't be presumptuous to call myself a blues singer. But I'm doing something that. . . . Michael Stipe calls it "porch singing." That's how he describes my singing, porch singing, so I guess that's pretty good, you know.

**Goldberg:** Is he on the album?

**Smith:** No. How would he be on the album? His encouragement is within it because he is very encouraging but he's not singing on it or anything. We talked about things like that and I think it would be really nice for us to collaborate sometime. But I felt that, it's my duty. . . . This record was my duty. And I know that perhaps it might have more commercial viability if I had my friends come and join me on a track or two but that's not the goal of this record. This record was really my responsibility to record as Fred and I had planned, so perhaps on another piece of work.

**Goldberg:** Do you feel that the album is a departure from vintage Patti Smith stuff?

**Smith:** I think it's different. I wrote three-quarters of the music, I've never done that before. Again, having Fred's spirit with me, I imagine. I don't know how. Fred taught me how play some acoustic guitar. In the last few months, he was giving me my little guitar lessons, and he taught me enough so I could write my own songs and I did write several of the songs. I really don't know how, I'm in some ways so out of touch with things that I have no idea where it fits, where it sits, what people will think about it. I can only say that it's an honest effort. Every record I [sic] done has been an honest effort. *Dream of Life* was really more Fred's record: It was all of Fred's music, Fred's philosophy, "People Have the Power," Fred's concept, the titles of a lot of the songs were Fred's—even though I wrote all of the lyrics, a lot of the titles and the concepts of the songs were Fred's. The title of the album was Fred's *[laughs]* so it was really Fred's gift to me. He really crafted that record for me. This particular record is really my record with Lenny's touches. But it pretty much reflects myself. I don't know what to say about it. I think one couldn't place it—it doesn't have any particular, you couldn't [say] it's any particular kind of music 'cause I don't really think it sits anywhere. I just think it's something people will like or not. I can't ever promise to give people what they want or what's in current favor. All I can promise them is an honest effort. I don't have filler stuff, I don't just throw stuff together. Everything that I do, I work hard on. Then it's up to the people whether they like it or not. It doesn't have any curse words on it.

**Uhelszki:** Well you have kids, now.

**Smith:** It just happened that way. Actually *Dream of Life* doesn't either. But I think all those things weren't even thought of, they just came out as they did. I'm anxious to do another record. This record really does reflect, Fred's in it, a lot of thoughts about losing Fred, whether abstractly or directly. I had to write that, I had to do that. And then the next record I believe I'll really find out what I'm thinking about.

**Uhelszki:** You have to pay homage to him. Somehow or another you will always be singing a Fred song.

**Smith:** Always. Always. I've always been singing them. I don't think people even realize how long I've been singing Fred songs. From "Because the Night"—all these songs. "Twenty-Fifth Floor," "Dancing Barefoot," and "Frederick." I've written so many songs for him long before people even knew I knew him.

**Uhelszki:** When did you meet him? Weren't you intrigued with him before you met him?

**Smith:** Well, I just met him. I only was [intrigued] from the first time I met him. I didn't know anything about him when I met him. I met him one day, it was March 9, 1976. And we met in front of the radiator in front of that hot dog place, the Coney Island place. Lafayette Coney Island.

**Uhelszki:** I remember you once threw a press party there; I didn't know why at the time.

**Smith:** Lenny introduced me to this guy, and I just looked at this guy. I heard that his name was Smith and my name is Smith. We just looked at each other, and I was completely taken by him. And I had no idea who he was, or anything about him until afterwards, when Lenny told me. I was taken by him from the moment I saw him. Lenny introduced me to him and said, "He's one of the great guitar players." And I said, "Perhaps you'll want to play with us tonight." And then he said, "Maybe so." Then he left and I said to Lenny, "So he's good?" And Lenny said, "The best." And that was the first time I met him. So I was playing with him that night. I had a lot of bravado in those days, you know. I didn't care who came on my stage, I didn't have respect for anybody. But I totally submitted to his reign. He came on the stage and started playing and I remember after a while, I just set my guitar down, and let my guitar feed back, and let him just take over because I had felt that I had met my match, that I had met the better man.

**Uhelszki:** It's such a highly charged love story. Did you feel that you had to take those years off to build the relationship?

**Smith:** I've never regretted, I only regret that he's gone. I don't regret nothing else. I have never ever once—never!—regretted anything. Not from the very beginning. I mean I missed my friends, I missed the camaraderie of the band, I missed certain things, but I never regretted a thing. To me it was—even sometimes it was difficult—it was a privilege to be with him.

**Uhelszki:** And there are your two children.

**Smith:** Yeah, and they're great. I've been pretty lucky in my life, and I've known really good people. The two most important relationships I had was with Robert and Fred. And they're both gone, but I feel magnified by them. I feel like when Mary said my soul is magnified by the Lord. I feel like my soul is magnified by them. And I feel actually still, even in losing them, pretty lucky.

**Uhelszki:** You were going to put a song about Jerry Garcia on your new album?

**Smith:** I didn't. But he [does] permeate the album. When we were recording, the night of the day that he died, that night we recorded a song by Robert Hunter called "All of My Friends," a song that he and Jerry Garcia wrote, I think. And we did record that, not for the album. We recorded it for Jerry; we might use it for a B-side of something, but we just recorded it for him. We did have his picture hanging up in Electric Ladyland through the rest of the recording, and we all said hello to him every day. We ate the Ben and Jerry's Cherry Garcia ice cream that night. And when we are performing, we do "Not Fade Away" in his memory. So we do, he's there spiritually.

**Uhelszki:** Did you have an affinity with Jerry Garcia before he died?

**Smith:** I really think we all owe something to him, many of us have an affinity. We opened for them, and they were wonderful people. Lenny had a deep affinity with the Grateful Dead and with him. My affinity is more through others, but I have a happy affinity with them. Certainly they weren't as pivotal for me as somebody like Bob Dylan, but I have good memories of them and a good feeling for them.

**Uhelszki:** You've spoken about Fred teaching you a lot of things. What'd you teach Fred?

**Smith:** I couldn't presume to answer that really. Thank you for asking though.

**Uhelszki:** That's OK. I hadn't seen Fred for a really long time after I left, you know. He was always an amazing character in my personal history. You were moved by Nirvana and Kurt Cobain. You wrote that song "About a Boy." Did you like their music?

**Smith:** Yeah. And it was typical of me to finally find a band I liked and then their leader should pass away, but that was quite a blow. Because I really didn't know anything about the group. I really liked their music. I was taken with them. I felt a certain kinship with their music and Fred did as well. He really liked them. And so it was quite a blow. Mostly what worried me at the time was I worried about young people and how they would take that. I know how it feels. I know when I was younger, I looked to people to help me get through difficult times. You know, I can't imagine how I would have felt if Bob Dylan would have committed suicide. It would have been . . . Because I believed he had so much vision and so much strength and so much urgency and so much life. When I felt less than that, he spurred me on and I'm certain that many young people looked to Kurt Cobain to help spur them on and [it] must have been quite a blow and quite painful.

**Uhelszki:** It's different than Jim Morrison because it wasn't out and out suicide. Or Jimi Hendrix.

**Smith:** Yeah, none of them are pretty deaths, but Jim Morrison was closest because Jim Morrison did drive himself to death through alcohol and drugs, which was also deeply unfortunate and stupid. But Jimi Hendrix was a pure accident. I don't think he was on that plane at all. And he had lots of plans. Jimi Hendrix built Electric Ladyland studios. I saw him right before he died and I was pretty young, and I was at a party for him in 1971, I think, at Electric Lady and sat on the steps with him. He was talking to me. I was a kid and he was telling me his plans. I was calling him Mr. Hendrix, your studio's really great, what are you going to do? He was really nice to me. He said he had to go to England and do some things and he was going to gather some musicians and he was going to go upstate New York and he was going to start sort of a tribal musical experience with all different musicians from all over the world. He wanted to get into a sort of global rock jazz, not fusion, but a crossover and like a commingling of all these different forces and all these different types of music, more in the Coltrane type of line. So he had a lot of plans, but you can't be stupid, and mixing sleeping pills and alcohol [is] stupid. He had a stupid death.

**Jaan Uhelszki:** I think 1996 is your year.

**Patti Smith:** That's what my mother says. It's curious that you say that. My mother said to me, even with all the difficulties I've had, she took my hand one day, still at the end of '95, and said, "Patricia, I just have a feeling that 1996 is going to be your year."

**Uhelszki:** You've been returning to performing in a cautious manner. You weren't so cautious the first time around.

**Smith:** The first time around I evolved. I didn't have any designs about what I was doing. I had a mission. I felt like I had a mission. My mission started out on my own. And then Lenny became part of this mission. And then we grew as a band. But I never, ever dreamed I'd have a rock & roll band. I never planned it or designed it. My ideas were to first of all, to hopefully inject some revolutionary energy into the world of poetry at the time, which I thought was pompous and dead, around 1970–1971. That was my first mission. Then it developed into, it was developing through a lot of talks I had with Sam Shepard about the state of rock & roll. Which I thought was getting questionable by 1971 or '72. You know, we'd lost Hendrix and Morrison and Janis Joplin. And Bob Dylan and the Rolling Stones were sort of like at a different place. And I just felt like a lot of the direction that rock & roll was taking, was getting corporate, was getting show business, was technical, glamorous, and that the idea of the street and heaven were being lost, and I really felt that someone needed to come and save it. I didn't presume myself to be that person, but I thought that if I, I just felt like, I've said this before, but it was always I used to talk about it with my people. I thought of us sort of like Paul Revere and we were like letting people know the revolution was coming. Or something was coming. I didn't think that we'd be part of it, or anything. I just wanted people to wake up. So I felt we were a wake up call, and I gleaned that the people that would really turn things around would come after us.

**Uhelszki:** How natural was it for you to be with Fred Smith, given the MC5's revolutionary stance and awareness?

**Smith:** Which was something I knew very little about, not having been around for all of that. But Lenny was very conscious of what Fred did and what the MC5 did, and [it] influenced him. Some of Lenny's inspiration and Lenny's rhetoric permeated my ideas, and so Lenny brought with him a lot of different histories that I didn't know about. He brought in the history of the MC5, the history of the Velvet Underground—see because Lenny was part of all these scenes. So Lenny's knowledge and Lenny's belief in those people and what they did also became my knowledge and beliefs.

**Uhelszki:** Like you shared a consciousness, you coopted his stuff. You two are very close. Aren't your birthdays just days apart?

**Smith:** Yeah, I'm December 30, he's December 27. Same year.

**Uhelszki:** Was there a point where you knew you'd be a public person again? Do you have an undeniable urge that has to be satisfied?

**Smith:** I still don't think I really get that. The thing is, Fred and I had a plan. We were going to record this summer. We were going to get some people together, I know who he wanted. He really wanted to become more active again. We had to for various reasons. Because we had things to say, and also for practical reasons. As parents we had to get back to work again because we had to start thinking about Jack and Jesse's future. So we had our game plan, and so I was already primed towards certain things. Fred really wanted me to start performing again. He really felt that it was time. He was watching what was happening. He watched a lot, he started checking out things, he was watching other performers. New female artists and things, and he really felt that I should—I don't know, it was really funny. It was uncharacteristic of him. But for some reason he started feeling that he wanted *[sighs]*, he really felt he wanted me to have what he gleaned as my due. Although no one deserved their due more than Fred, he really wasn't that interested in himself. And at the time, I had no real desire to do that. I really didn't think I was even qualified, or prepared to go to perform in a rock & roll structure anymore. But he was pushing me towards that.

**Uhelszki:** Did you think the first time was a fluke?

**Smith:** Well, I was actually very surprised. I never really understood, it never ceased to amaze me that I was on a stage in the context of a rock & roll band. I wasn't raised with those expectations. There was nothing like that in my early life to ever drive me toward that—the idea of a female having a rock & roll band didn't even exist. I used to daydream—if I ever daydreamed about myself singing—I loved Maria Callas, I used to daydream about being an opera singer. And I sort of liked Joan Baez. But it never occurred to me. I just don't know, I just have a certain energy that kept—that came out in spite of myself. I had no idea about it. I used to think sometimes when I used to live with Robert [Mapplethorpe] and sometimes there was a hippie scene in the late '60s, and people would come over and they'd be playing bongo drums and stuff, and everybody would sing, and I'd wind up doing things like "House of the Rising Sun" and Robert would say to me, "You should be a singer. You should be singing." And I'd [say], "No, I'm not a singer, I don't want to sing, I want to be a painter." And Sam Shepard did the same thing when we wrote a play together and performed. He was pushing me towards that type of performance.

**Uhelszki:** You have a quote about Shepard, where you said that he used to pull things out of you, inspiring you to be better than even you thought possible. I think that's similar to what you do for others.

**Smith:** Well the idea is also that people did that for me, I never really thought, I always felt like I was different than other people, or more of a misfit or alien, but I never really gleaned myself as being special. Other people seemed to pull it out of me, whether it was Robert, or Sam Shepard, or Bob Neuwirth. I've been very lucky in my life to have people, various people perceive something in me that I didn't perceive myself. Which is one reason why I have always tried to do that with others, even if I'm performing. I hope that one of the things [that] will happen within the performance, or with anything I do, is that it'll inspire somebody else to do it. Even to the point where they say, she's—or to trample what I do. I'd rather see somebody completely push me or push my work away and think it was obsolete and then do their own work.

**Uhelszki:** Isn't that what happened with Michael Stipe, that he was a fan and was so inspired by your work that he formed R.E.M.? I've read in interviews where he says that if there hadn't been a Patti Smith, there wouldn't have been an R.E.M.

**Smith:** Well that's really nice of him, I'm sure he would have found a way. I've always felt that if there wasn't a Bob Dylan I don't know if . . . I was equally . . . I don't know [*what, on the verge of revealing something—outside the tightly controlled interview persona? stumbles, uh, and ums a lot, isn't comfortable talking about Stipe, equally isn't comfortable revealing her beginnings. Curious. Second time she has been cagey when Stipe comes up. Why?*], I think you also have to give back what you're given. I've been inspired and influenced by a lot of great people and I think it's important, if you have any gifts at all, you have—if you're given a gift, you have to give of it. One can't hoard it. I think that is one thing Fred and I were really talking about after being pretty reclusive for so long, that we did have a certain responsibility and I often, I deeply encouraged Fred, who was one of the most gifted people I ever knew to share his gifts with others and it's regrettable it didn't happen.

**Uhelszki:** I always felt that he took his gifts for granted, and was very *laissez-faire* about them and didn't ever seem to think what he did was extraordinary at all.

**Smith:** He had a lot of thoughts about that I think. But some people are very comfortable with their gifts, somebody like Robert Mapplethorpe was very comfortable with them and used them daily, worked daily. Other people are plagued by their gifts, and I feel myself I have a little more of a better balance of comfortable plagued-ness, I have a little bit of plagued, I often feel dogged yet most of the time I feel blessed. But in terms of coming back or anything, I really proceeded with the plans Fred and I had. I would have proceeded with an even heavier heart than I did, had it not been for the fact my brother, who spent the last month of his life almost completely doing everything he could to inspire me and make me feel better. He really talked to me. We spent the last couple of days before he died talking about nothing else than me performing again. He wanted me to go back to work. I went home for Thanksgiving after Fred had passed away, and I really felt desolate. But Toddy and I took a drive and Toddy brought the soundtrack of *Natural Born Killers* and he put the tape on in his car, he turned it all the way up, he rolled down the windows and he rode really fast and was singing "Rock and Roll [N-word]" for me. Singing along with it. And he said, "You're gonna be alright, you're gonna go back to work and I'm gonna help you. I'm gonna be there, be with you, and you're gonna be great." He really helped lift up my spirits and even though he passed away a couple of days later, that energy that he injected within me in those few days, I haven't lost. And I really feel like, I really try to keep his good spirits and his energy with me. In fact it was really nice when we were opening up for Bob Dylan. The last night we were in Philadelphia, and it was really a special night. And my brother was born in Philadelphia. We dedicated the set to him, and talked about Philadelphia being the city of Brotherly Love and how my brother really epitomized that. Lenny said he could just imagine my brother sitting up there on the balcony smiling away with a cigarette dangling out of his mouth, watching us, and it was really nice.

**Uhelszki:** I always feel that those you love, who have gone before you, are always with you.

**Smith:** Always. Always. I feel like that he guards over my singing. I feel as much sorrow as I feel. I also let myself feel a certain amount of joy.

**Uhelszki:** Are you going to wait until the kids are grown before full-blown going out on tours?

**Smith:** No, I'm never going to go on tour full-blown, never, ever again because first of all, Jessie won't be out of school for another 10 years, and I don't think I'll be going on full-blown tours when I'm 60 years old. I want to be going to Morocco. I want to have my little keef garden and my notebooks and my books and daydream and write. I don't want to be touring the world.

**Uhelszki:** And that light is so flattering to a 60-year-old.

**Smith:** But I'll do what I can. I pretty much will have to work around the kids' school schedule. Like right now, I have two weeks off. They had two weeks off, so I decided to come here. I targeted San Francisco as our first place because I really felt that this would be where, judging from the past, from letters and support and radio and different things through the year, this is where I really felt people would be the most tolerant and the most supportive while I got my feet back on the ground and shook some of the rust and the dust off. So that's why I chose to come to San Francisco.

**Uhelszki:** Did you take the kids to see Haight-Ashbury?

**Smith:** Jackson went.

**Uhelszki:** Good. Everyone should.

**Smith:** I think Oliver [Ray] took Jackson. In fact, it was funny, I was on the radio yesterday and the DJ, the girl said to me, "Oh, you have a son 13? He's probably in the Haight right now." And Jackson was in the Haight with Oliver, and they were in a tattoo parlor and the radio was on. And Jack heard it, so it was kind of cool.

**Michael Goldberg:** You mentioned Nirvana, but have you paid attention to what's come along in rock?

**Smith:** No, not too much. Well, I've glimpsed. Every once in a while I like a group. I remember I liked Sonic Youth when they came out. My brother was into the Pretenders and I remember hearin' "Chain Gang," that Chrissie Hynde song. I thought that was really good. Just checkin' things out. Then I liked just songs. I wasn't really ready to commit myself anymore to groups and stuff. I had like passed that time. I just liked songs like "Billie Jean" and I liked "Into the Groove." *[Starts to sing]* "Get into the groove. . . ." Madonna. So it's more like that. I'd be into a certain song here or there. I appreciated what Sonic Youth was doing because I felt that we had a certain *Radio Ethiopia* kinship with them. But mostly I just listened to Coltrane and Beethoven and what Fred liked.

**Uhelszki:** He was a Beethoven type of guy 'cause he had moods.

**Smith:** Yeah, he liked Beethoven. I didn't really see too much that I really liked. I just perceived though, that the field was opening and I thought that was good. What people do with that open field, that's their business. But I perceived the field compared to the early '70s or the mid-'70s pretty wide open for whatever, whatever gender persuasion, whatever you're into. I'm sure people feel like they're still suppressed and women feel like they're suppressed. And people think there's . . . *[Smith adopts a very stern voice]* . . . not enough girls in the Rock & Roll Hall of Fame and all that shit. Everybody's always worrying about their gender or their race or their whatever, but I think the field's pretty open and there's a lot of space out there and it's up to the people. If they want more space then they've got to create it. They can't expect the record companies to give it to them or radio stations or MTV or anybody. They're not going to get space from those people. They have to create their own space and they should stop whinin' about it.

**Goldberg:** It seems like right now, meaning the '90s, is a better time for rock & roll and for bands, for edgy music.

**Smith:** It's better for everybody. You go in a record store and they got racks of alternative CDs from record companies you never even heard of. When you did your own little record, your independent record in the '70s, if you had a pal or somebody that could put four in their little slot or something. . . . There just wasn't the outlets. It's a lot more organized. The networks are a lot more organized now. And I think the young people are doing a good job. The young people doing their independent projects. And I also like that a lot of them don't seem to give a shit and don't seem like they care whether they're on a big label or they get successful. They just want to do their thing. And I think that's healthy. Everybody doesn't need to be on a big label. They don't need to make their money that way. They don't need to get rich and famous. It's totally unnecessary. They just have to do their work and communicate their work with others. I mean I don't find anything wrong with making money or anything, but it should never be your prime motivation unless you've got mouths to feed.

**Goldberg:** You did *Dream of Life*, and it seemed like you came out, did that and then went back again. Did you feel like the time wasn't really right then?

**Smith:** Well, Fred and I wanted to do a record for two reasons. We had certain things to say, and as parents, we needed to make a livin'. We did it for practical reasons as well as being work motivated. We had no idea where we sat, but we never did. I don't think . . . Todd Rundgren actually said something interesting about that. He said that, really, what happened technologically—which I wasn't even aware of because I missed a lot of the '80s—is because of technology. . . . People used to go and buy a record, come home, put it on the record player and sit and listen to it, look at the album cover, if there were any lyrics [they'd] read the liner notes, get into it as an experience that you had by yourself or you had with friends and you sat there, listened to it, got to know it, as an object it was important to you, the cover, everything. But now everybody's on the fly. They get their little CDs or micro things or whatever these things are called and they're on their Walkman, they're jogging, they're tapin' it, they're reprogramming it, they're taking off the things they like, they're making their own mixes of 'em. So it's a different world out there and people are perceiving work differently. *Dream of Life* was a very old-fashioned record, I suppose. Fred crafted that whole album. He wrote all of the music. A lot of the concept of the songs were his. It was a very universal album. People keep saying, well, "It's a family record." Well, it's the family of man record, really. I think he did a beautiful job, but it was just perhaps a time when people really weren't that interested, or they didn't think they were interested. I still think that *Dream of Life* will find its time and people will see the compassion and breadth of Fred as a man and a musician through that album. I know that he was hoping that people would take it to their hearts, and I think it did discourage him that people had so little interest in it, especially Detroit, which had almost zero interest in it.

**Uhelszki:** Amazing to me, given that MC5 was such a seminal band, the biggest game in town.

**Smith:** Yeah, they gave him nothing really. It's my one small bitterness. *[laughs]* I didn't care for [Detroit] myself. I don't. I really didn't and don't. But he really deeply loved Detroit.

**Goldberg:** I think you're right about that album. There's certain things where as time goes by, like the Velvet Underground are much more influential and important now so many years later than they were perceived of at the time.

**Smith:** Well, I don't even expect that record to be influential. It wasn't really designed to be influential. It was designed to be more inspirational and perhaps it will find its time in that way.

**Uhelszki:** Has raising two children changed your art?

**Smith:** I think in certain aspects of my work, I don't let it touch because there are certain aspects of my work that have to be beyond all things. But the way I conduct myself has certainly changed. I hopefully conduct myself with more dignity, or more discretion, and I try to do things with a little more sense of responsibility. But sometimes when I'm onstage I still feel the urge to kick a photographer in the face. I haven't totally become like a saint or anything. But I find I marshal my energies more, and I'm more focused and perhaps more tolerant as a human being, more patient, but I still have a rebellious streak. I haven't lost it all.

**Uhelszki:** Are both of your kids musical?

**Smith:** Yeah. Jackson started playing guitar about a year ago. He has Fred's Sadowski guitar. It's a really nice guitar that was made for Fred and Jack plays it every day. He teaches himself and he's got Fred's quickness. I just watch him. He's got Fred's speed. He's got hands more like mine, but he's got Fred's speed. It's interesting. I, like, watch Jackson's hands and it's like watching both of us within his hands.

**Uhelszki:** Is he going to play tonight?

**Smith:** I think he might.

**Uhelszki:** So what'd he say, "Hey mom, I want to go onstage"?

**Smith:** No, no, no.

**Uhelszki:** You guys have been preparing this?

**Smith:** No, not really. Right before I left, I said Jack . . . I just invited him to play a song. I said, if you'd like to, the fellas would. . . . He likes Deep Purple, he likes that "Smoke on the Water" song. . . . So Lenny put it together and he gave him the option if he wanted to play, not with any pressure or design or motivation except to give him a nice experience that he could make of what he will out of it.

**Goldberg:** What did he say afterward or did he say anything?

**Smith:** Nothing. He's a man of few words. He just said, "It's cool."

**Uhelszki:** I can't wait to see him . . . The Dylan tour. How did it come about and did you stay in touch with him after you first met him at the Bottom Line in the '70s?

**Smith:** No I hadn't talked to him in some time. Really, as I gleaned from Bob himself, he really felt that it would be good for me to come back out. He thought that I should come back out, and he said really nice things from onstage. I think that he feels I was a strong influence on things, and he thinks I should be out here—out in the front. He was very encouraging to me. I wasn't really ready to work then, I really didn't have a band. We'd been recording but I wasn't really prepared to do anything. But I was so happy that he asked, that we decided to do it and you know we were a little rusty and rag tag but the people seemed happy and he was happy. My main mission on that small tour—it was only 10 dates—was to crack all the energy, to crack all the atmosphere and get the stage ready for him. So we had our time before him and that was my prime directive was to get the night as magic as possible, so when he hit the stage, 'cause he hits a lot of them, that maybe it would feel a little more special than normal. And I think we did a pretty good job and I know that he was happy.

**Uhelszki:** Did you perform the poem, "dog dream," that you wrote about Dylan's dog having wings?

**Smith:** No, because we had very little time. I did do one of his songs, we did "Wicked Messenger," which we also recorded for the album. Anyway, he's heard the poem before, he knows it. I did "Piss Factory," and I occasionally did a poem. I don't think I did that one, I might have. I really can't remember. I was really concentrating on really doing a positive strong set to set things up for him.

**Uhelszki:** Do you feel easy with him, given that he was such a hero of yours? I remember in an interview you did, you said after you met him, you didn't have much to say, because you'd been having conversations in your head with him for the past 12 years, and you didn't think that you needed to stop.

**Smith:** We didn't talk a lot. I find that I'm still—which I'm hoping in time will change—I still find myself a little school-girlish talking to him. I think we had some fine conversations, and we sang together almost every night. We did "Dark Eyes" together, and I felt that, that for me, was a timeless experience. I feel that we both communicated very well performing together. I really felt that we both took it seriously and performed in a way to support each other and make each other comfortable. And I really felt an extreme amount of dignity and happiness singing with him. I allowed myself to think about how important he's been to me, and what a hero, and to glean a certain amount of joy. But beyond that I felt as two people working, I felt when we were onstage working, I felt very proud. In the end we were two people, both with our own struggles and our gifts, trying to accommodate each other.

**Goldberg:** I always felt watching you perform that a spirit would come through you sometimes. Is that how it feels to you sometimes up there?

**Smith:** Sometimes. It's different than it was before. I was intense in a different way, so it was a more frenzied spirit. I sort of demanded that a spirit enter me. *Demanded it.* Now I just do my work and sometimes feel blessed by just feeling a certain thing, I can't say what it is. I just feel . . . I think the best way. . . . It's hard to articulate it except when I feel it, at least the aspect of it that I like the best, is that I'm 100 percent in the present and feeling what's happening. I noticed that, for instance, when we did the Dylan tour and he asked me to sing a song with him and we did "Dark Eyes" every night, it's not quite exactly the thing you're talking about, but I sort of shifted what you said. That feeling of complete, completely—which is hard for an artist because artists are always back into the past, moving into the future, redesigning every moment that's happening and I've always had that difficulty because I never felt like I relaxed and could feel the present. And I can really say that doing that one song each night with him was almost like drinking the purest water or where I felt completely alive and in the present and grateful to be so. It's a different thing than what you're talking about, but that's the kind of thing I feel more now than before. The thing that I used to feel before was more like a visitation from some—whatever I perceived it to be—angel, demon, muse, the energy of the people even. Because I as a performer am also very affected by the energy out there or I was more when I was younger. Now I control that more or I just choose not to be affected. I do it with humor but sometimes I have my own moments. I'm willing to be sort of a mouthpiece for whatever entity or the energy of the people but only to a certain extent. These days more it's my territory. Even last night, for a while I felt like a mouthpiece or for awhile I felt like I was drawing in their energy and giving it back to them. And then there was a point where I was sort of kidding but when I said I'm no longer interested in your opinion or whatever I said. . . . Were you there last night?

**Uhelszki:** No.

**Smith:** Well there was a moment where people kept—which I encourage—talking to me or yelling things out or asking me to do this or talking to me and I said, "I am no longer interested in your opinion," and they laughed, which is appropriate. But what I was also saying, what was also happening is I was entering this other field where I was completely feeling my own power or my own strengths or my own vulnerabilities. All these things—I wouldn't be so concerned about these things or probably talking about them so much had it not been so long since I performed. So I'm finding it kind of fascinating right now. I'm not sitting around analyzing myself but I am finding certain things really interesting.

**Uhelszki:** Do you think sometimes it was accidental before or serendipitous and now you feel you can call it up easier?

**Smith:** No, I just feel like before, like I said, it was more frenetic, it was more aggressive, it was more demanding. And I felt hollow if I didn't get it or burning if I did. Now it just seems to be a part of me, a part of the pulse of my being that does come and go but when it goes, it's not far. And maybe sometimes I want it to go.

**Goldberg:** In terms of your art, is there something you really want to accomplish this time? You said before the first time it was like sort of Paul Revere, a wake-up call.

**Smith:** Well that was in terms of my role within the arena of rock & roll or performance. As I perceive myself—if I perceive myself as an artist, which I don't even know is the right word, I guess what I really cherish the most is writing. Sometimes all of these things do commingle but in terms of pure writing, that's a whole other thing. I don't look at myself as a Paul Revere in terms of my writing. My writing is a separate quest. In terms of performing at this time, I don't have any particular motivations. I'm here to say hello, here to find out where I'm at, you know, here really to get my strength back, to openly accept encouragement from others. I don't have any real deep motivations right now as a performer because I don't really know what my place is, if I have a place, if I want a place. I tend to feel that rock & roll belongs to youth. And the youth of the world is figuring out what they want to do with rock & roll as a form right now. And it's not my business really. My business, if I have any, is to be a good person and do good work and hopefully be somebody that youth, if they're interested at all in what I'm doing, that they can trust. I feel that they can trust me. I also understand if they find the need to trample me because that's their job. *[laughs]* I don't expect or want any deep respect or love from the youth of the world in terms of, within the rock & roll arena. And if I get it, I'm grateful for that but I don't expect it. But I do expect certain things out of myself. I do expect that when I'm doing things, that my path is clean, and I expect that I should keep monitoring my motivations and what I'm doing and what kind of effect I'm having because—*[long pause]*—because I would only want it to be healthy.

*Addicted To Noise,* June/July 1996

# RAMONES LOOK LIKE HOODS, BUT THEY'RE NOT

*On a fall day in 1976, the Ramones were sitting near the pool at a South of Market motel in San Francisco. It was my first time meeting them. Tommy Ramone, the group's drummer at the time, spoke to me about their lyrics, "They come from our subconscious and well, of course, our influences are basically daily living, movies, conversations, and non sequiturs. Anything ya know, it comes out of nowhere. All of our songs are true stories. Sad but true." With their 1975 debut album,* Ramones, *the group delivered what* Creem's *Gene Sculatti called "The most radical album of the past six years." Nearly 20 years later, in 1995, when I was publisher/editor in chief of* Addicted To Noise, *I became friends with Joey Ramone, who, with the help of writer Jaan Uhelszki, provided us with tour reports and other info. Eventually Joey started calling me. Sadly, I was so busy dealing with the million-odd things that keeping an internet magazine afloat entailed, that I didn't always have time to talk to Joey, who could easily talk for an hour or more about whatever happened to be on his mind at the time. I loved the Ramones' music from the first time I listened to* Ramones. *The group never became as popular as they deserved, and broke up in 1996. Joey died from lymphoma in 2001. A year later Dee Dee died of a heroin overdose, and two years later Johnny died of prostate cancer. The story that follows was written after I interviewed them for the second time, in 1978.*

> *The new art stirs such polar responses because it seems to make an active frontal assault on all our esthetic conventions at every level of form and subject matter.*
> —Professor Alan Solomon in *Art International*

HOLLYWOOD—SOLOMON WAS WRITING in 1963 about the then new "pop" trend in art. But he could easily have been writing in 1978 about the Ramones' rock & roll.

Dee Dee Ramone shakes his head. "It was a nightmare." Dee Dee, who plays bass, is commenting on a recent rock concert that found his rock & roll band, the Ramones, opening for Black Sabbath, a 10-year-old group some refer to as a "heavy metal dinosaur." Specifically, Dee Dee is commenting on Black Sabbath's hard-core fans' physical resistance to the Ramones' "frontal assault" on their "established esthetic conventions."

"We've never seen an audience like that in our lives," continues Dee Dee. "They were all drunk. They all had whiskey bottles that they were waving at us and throwing at us."

Guitarist Johnny Ramone adds, "We had to cut short our set after 20 minutes. They started throwing stuff as soon as we hit the stage. The whole stage was covered with junk. Bottles and everything."

"Ice picks," mumbles vocalist Joey Ramone.

"Someone threw an ice pick?" asks Johnny, horrified, turning to Joey.

Drummer Marky Ramone, who replaced original drummer Tommy Ramone earlier this year, just sits on the couch looking irritated.

"Sick," mumbles Joey.

Two years ago, the Ramones' debut album. *Ramones* (Sire) was released. *Ramones* is a dark, overtly unsentimental, and sarcastic commentary on urban violence, psychopaths,

The Ramones at the Tropicana Motel, Los Angeles, 1978.

terrorists, frustration, and teenage boredom. As critic Gene Sculatti wrote in *Creem*, a rock magazine, "*Ramones* is strikingly different, so brazenly out of touch with prevailing modes as to constitute a bold swipe at the status quo."

"Well, we had to make a statement at the time," explains Johnny Ramone seriously. "Everything was just too long, too boring. Too many indulgent guitar solos. The best way to make a statement was to go completely all out. Just leave out any guitar solos. Put 14 songs (all less than two and one-half minutes in length) on the album when everyone else was putting eight songs on an album. Make the album sound real raw when everyone else was into super production that just sounded plastic." That album also featured terse, almost telegram-like lyrics. Their commentary on the S.L.A., for example, was typically succinct. "Jackie is a punk / Judy is a runt / They both went down to Frisco, joined the S.L.A."

"It was a very revolutionary album for its time," states Johnny, matter of factly.

The four Ramones are sitting in a drab, cheap motel room at the Tropicana on Santa Monica Boulevard. They are using the Tropicana as a base of operations while they act in a film, *Rock & Roll High School*, being produced by Roger Corman, and play concerts on the West Coast.

All four Ramones are 26. They are all from New York. They are all wearing tennis shoes, worn blue jeans, and T-shirts. All but Joey are wearing black leather motorcycle jackets. This is the Ramones' look, and the look is ironic because although the Ramones dress and sneer like hoods, they are all slight, pale, and unmuscular. Sylvester Stallone could probably clobber these guys with one hand tied behind his back. And the Ramones know it. "You talk fast," says Dee Dee, explaining how to avoid fistfights. "You try not to fight. You hurt your body, you can't play."

The Ramones' radical visual, lyrical, and musical approach to rock & roll may not seem so radical in view of the punk and new wave rock & roll that has proliferated during the past few years. Actually, the Ramones are considered the main inspiration behind the Seventies' new wave / punk movement. "When we went over there [to England in 1976] those guys in those groups, the Clash, the Damned, Sex Pistols were standing around out in the alley trying to get into our sound check," Johnny Ramone told critic Lester Bangs earlier this year. "And they didn't even have groups yet."

In the past two years, the Ramones have recorded four albums, *Ramones*, *Ramones Leave Home*, *Rocket to Russia*, and the recent *Road to Ruin*, that have received glowing critical acclaim in publications as diverse as *Rolling Stone* and *People*.

The Ramones are boyhood buddies from Queens. None are brothers. They have all adopted the surname Ramone to emphasize "the unity of our group," says Johnny. They didn't form a rock & roll group until 1974. "There's millions and millions of kids our age," says Dee Dee, "who, when they saw the Beatles and the Rolling Stones on TV, there's nothing else they wanted to do again but be in a group."

"Yeah," affirms Johnny, "the first time you saw the Beatles! But everyone making records had been playing 15 or 20 years and you figure, what chance have I got. That stopped us from doing it for a long time. But we lost our jobs and were on unemployment and so we said, alright, let's just fool around. We started to rehearse, and we wrote some songs. It sounded pretty good. We just had something. It clicked."

*San Francisco Examiner* and *Chronicle Sunday Datebook*, December 24, 1978

Mick Jones (left) and Joe Strummer of the Clash at the Berkeley Community Theater, 1979.

# THE CLASH: REVOLUTION ROCK

*The Clash were pissed. At me. It was 1978 and we were in a small room at the Automatt recording studio in San Francisco, the studio where they were completing work on their second album, Given 'Em Enough Rope. The Clash had not yet performed in the US, and it was hard to get up-to-date info on them. I dug their debut album,* The Clash, *which I'd bought as an import (it wasn't released in the US until July 1979), and I was super excited to be hanging out while they recorded vocals. I'd gotten into the studio via local punk wheeler-dealer Howie Klein, whose friend Sandy Pearlman (of Blue Öyster Cult fame) was producing the group's new songs. Although The Clash was a quartet, only singer/guitarist Joe Strummer and guitarist/vocalist Mick Jones were there; the other two were back in England where most of the recording had already taken place. I had just listened, at a deafening volume, to what sounded while it was playing like the greatest song I'd ever heard, "Safe European Home," and now we—me and these two key members of the Clash—were going to do an interview. Working off info on the back cover of the* Clash, *I had copied down the names of the band members, including drummer Terry Chimes. I don't remember exactly what I said, but it was something about drummer Chimes. Oops. As I quickly learned from the two angry musicians facing me, Chimes was no longer in the Clash. And, as they both made clear, I was an idiot. I was supposed to know these things. Still, I managed to get enough out of them to write a Sunday column for the* San Francisco Chronicle. *And it turned out their anger was more drama than real; that was the first of four interviews the group did with me, the first three being used for this* DownBeat *story. The Clash went on to have US hits with "Should I Stay or Should I Go" and "Rock the Casbah." In 1983 drummer Topper Headon and the Jones were kicked out of the band. Strummer, original bassist Paul Simonon, and some other musicians recorded the terrible album* Cut the Crap, *and in 1986 the band broke up. Strummer died on December 22, 2002, of a congenital heart defect. In 2003,* Rolling Stone *ranked the Clash at number 28 in their list of the 100 Greatest Artists of All Time.*

IT'S AN UGLY VOICE. Gruff, guttural, uncouth, barbaric at times. Joe Strummer can't sing, not like an Al Jarreau or a Joni Mitchell, anyway. Lyrics are shouted out in a harsh nearly unintelligible cockney snarl. At times this voice rips at the ears like an exploding letter bomb. It cries out for justice in an unjust world. It nags at the soul like the memory of those nuns killed in El Salvador, like the memory of Allison Krause gunned down at Kent State by the National Guard. Joe Strummer's voice demands to be heard. Surprisingly, it is.

Strummer is the singer, songwriter, and rhythm guitarist for the Clash, the most popular punk rock band in the world. You've probably heard of the Clash. You've probably read that some rock critics think they're "the greatest rock & roll band in the world," as *Village Voice* critic Robert Christgau announced a few years back. Or maybe you noticed that their LP *London Calling* captured the Rock/Blues Album of the Year in the 1980 *DownBeat* Readers Poll.

But if you've only heard of the Clash, and haven't actually *heard* their music—listened to the five albums and the EP that they've released in the US—you may still be wondering what all the fuss is about. You may still be dismissing the Clash as one of those foul-mouthed punk rock bands that made a lot of media noise—and not much else—in the late '70s.

Dismiss them no longer. If you listen to one rock & roll band during the next year, make it the Clash. You will discover music and lyrics as rich as anything that Bob Dylan or the Rolling Stones created in the '60s, back when rock & roll mattered, back when rock was more than the up-tempo elevator music one mostly hears by bands like Journey on the radio today.

At the beginning of their most recent album, *Combat Rock*, Joe Strummer shouts out: "This is a public service announcement . . . with guitars!" That single line does a good job of summing up the Clash. This is a band that makes rock & roll with a message. For the Clash, the message is as important as the rock & roll and vice versa.

"We're dealing with the power of music here" says lead guitarist/songwriter and occasional vocalist Mick Jones, who is thin and gaunt and wears his black hair short and greased back. Jones looks like a cross between a '50s' rockabilly singer and a '50s' hood—and that seems to be his intent. "Music can sooth furrowed brows and all that stuff," he continues, "and it works and it's true and it really can make you feel better when you have the blues. I have a lot of faith in it. The music, as a really good force."

Those are calm and reasoned words from a member of a band that has a punk reputation for being taciturn, moody, rude, even hostile. Jones, as well as his mates—Strummer, bassist Paul Simonon, and drummer Terry Chimes (the original Clash drummer, who played on their first album, was replaced for four years by Topper Headon but began performing again with the Clash following Headon's heroin bust earlier this year)—can certainly adopt a tough pose. Yet beneath the surface bravado and "punk" attitude that they often present to the public and the media, these are dedicated, courageous musicians. Unlike many other punk bands, the Clash have never trafficked in nihilism, never jabbed a safety pin through their ears, either literally or metaphorically. The Clash have always had more in common politically and idealistically with politically aware hippie rockers and folk singers of the '60s like Country Joe McDonald, Joan Baez, and the young Bob Dylan, than with the other angry young men of punk.

The bottom line for the Clash is a belief in the human spirit, in the ability of men and women to do good. And in all their music, in the 100-plus songs that the Clash have recorded in a five-year period, this positive spirit is clearly felt. The Clash may agree with another punk band that sings "the world's a mess," but despite the darkness, they continue to have hope.

The Clash's songs are infused with a sense of social responsibility. In "Hate & War" they declare that we can't ignore the "hate and war" going on in the world today—that we have to "deal with it." Such a refusal to close their eyes to the atrocities played out day by day around the world, and an insistence on writing about those atrocities in their songs, helps to make the Clash one of the few contemporary rock bands that truly matter.

Often, the Clash use sarcasm to make their point. In "Know Your Rights," on their recent LP, Strummer sings that you have to "know your rights," then declares that we have three rights: (1) not to be killed because killing someone is against the law, unless it's done by a policeman or a member of the aristocracy; (2) the right to have something to eat and money, as long as you don't mind being shamed, scrutinized, or rehabilitated and; (3) the right to say what you want, as long as you don't.

Since 1978, when Jones and Strummer came to San Francisco to record vocals for their second album, *Give 'Em Enough Rope*, I've spoken with them on several occasions.

One overcast afternoon, I met them for the first time. They were wary, antagonistic, and mostly impenetrable. Strummer, a short, stocky man with a rotting, chipped front tooth that added menace to his sneer, slouched in the corner of the small lounge where the interview was to take place. He wore dark glasses and a black motorcycle jacket and had short, oily brown hair.

"So how much ya gonna make on this story anyway," badgered his buddy, Mick Jones who was pumping away on a pinball machine. He looked over at Strummer and they both laughed.

"I don't think we should do this interview," continued the guitarist.

"I don't either," muttered Strummer, turning away.

But they did continue the interview. I discovered later that this was just the Clash's nature. In America for the first time, they were particularly suspicious of Americans, who they thought were not to be trusted. In the Clash's camp, one was always suspect until proven innocent.

During that first interview, asked about the problems occurring in England, Jones snapped, "Not as bad as it is here! That's definite. You've got your Hershey bars and your Dr. Peppers. There's a lot more fucking work to be done here than England. Everyone watching TV. It reminds me of the Roman Empire. And every American I meet is a bullshitter. This place tends to look not very real."

Those impressions of America as a land where the reality of the problems faced by the rest of the world do not often penetrate, came out in the Clash's song "Guns on the Roof (of the World)," in which Strummer sings sarcastically that he wished he was in the US, where you can pretend there are no wars.

When I spoke to Strummer and Jones more recently, they were no more enchanted with the US and the complacency of Americans. The group's personal manager, a young man who calls himself Cosmo Vinyl, said, "Nobody in America wants anything to question or upset what they might personally be. Ted Nugent never gives anyone a hard time. He's just like his fans. He never causes them to think things should be different, that things aren't right."

"I agree with him, really," said Mick Jones. "I get depressed at the thought of 50 million people worshiping Ted Nugent." Then Jones cracked a smile and said in an exaggeratedly proper English accent, "We're only doing what we can to impress upon them that there *is* something better going on. By being here, it can only help."

I've been talking a lot about the politics of the Clash, and politics isn't what *DownBeat* is usually about; *DownBeat* is about contemporary music. But with the Clash, one can't avoid talking about politics. The Clash don't see music as something isolated from the rest of life; they see music as a part of life. For anyone who recently lost his job—or knows someone who lost their job—and happened to hear Gary U.S. Bonds' recent hit, "Out of Work," the ability of music to tie into the rest of one's life should be obvious. Don't think, however, that the Clash's music is inconsequential, just because, as is often the case, interviewers and reviewers spend more time considering why the band called an album *Sandinista!* or what they think of Margaret Thatcher, than discussing the Clash's music.

The Clash make magnificent rock & roll. In concert their music roars along like a train whose brakes have worn out. Huge, raw chunks of guitar noise tumble out of Jones' amplifier, Strummer barks out the lyrics, all the while bashing at his own guitar, as if the fierceness of his strum alone determines its volume. On a good night the Clash are like a team of rock & roll guerrillas. With guitars for weapons, they seem determined to show the world that nothing will stop them, that they will win the good fight and keep the fires of truth burning.

It was in 1976 that the Clash formed, inspired by that other famous punk band, the (now defunct) Sex Pistols. Joe Strummer's previous experience as a musician included "playing to earn a living in subways. . . . I had low overhead. No rent and stuff like that. Squatting in empty buildings. Busking. You play and you have a hat and they like what you play and throw money into the hat." When he got busted by the police, Strummer formed a band, the 101ers. His band became popular on the London pub circuit. Guitarist Mick Jones and bassist Paul Simonon were impressed by Strummer and eventually talked him into joining the new band they were starting, which Simonon wanted to call the Clash.

With the Pistols and the Clash at the forefront, a British punk movement sprang up as a gut response to both ever-worsening conditions in England and to a rock music scene populated by elitist and wealthy superstars who had become complacent and, as Strummer railed in one song, "fat and old." Punk was firmly anti-star. "They [the audience] could be up there as easy as me," says Strummer. "In a way, we were just there. And that was it. You feel lucky. Why you? Instead of him. Why you? Don't know why. Don't ask me the fucking meaning of life 'cause I don't know it."

Yet the Clash now find themselves caught in a bind, treated like stars when they tour America despite everything they can do to prevent it. "I find it humiliating," says Jones. "I try not to be anything other than just a human being. But you can't just say I don't want to sign autographs if there's a hundred people there."

"We feel a bond with our audience, but we hate them too," says Strummer candidly. "Best way to explain it is imagine if you were standing on the dock of the bay and lots of fish come. Ten thousand fish and they all came to look at you and opened their mouths. You know what I mean?"

The Clash recorded their first album, *The Clash*, in 1977. Because the Clash emerged as part of England's punk movement, their rock & roll sophistication was initially overlooked. The rudeness of punk was mistaken for musical inability and ignorance. In the US, the Clash's label initially refused to release their first album because of what one Epic Records executive called "the tin-can sound."

But in fact, when one listens a few times to *The Clash*, one discovers much more than the sound of buzzsaw guitars and sour voices. One finds brilliant vocal arrangements that contrast Strummer's ultra-real, man-of-the-street voice against the chanted background vocals of the rest of the band. One finds inventive, concise revisions of the classic Chuck Berry guitar style, savage, but well placed, rhythm guitar work and, overall, a dramatic return to the high energy style of early rockers like the Who and the Kinks. Only this time, instead of singing about how "You Really Got Me," the songs are about unemployment and injustice, war, and racial tension.

Right from the start the Clash demonstrated a tremendous knowledge of rock music, and an uncanny ability to remake the music into an intense, highly original sound. In a song like "White Riot," which is basically about the need for middle-class whites to rebel against the unchallenging lifestyle that the government endorses, Strummer turns in one of his most embittered vocals as he sings about how the rich are the ones with the power, while everyone else is too scared to rebel against that power. The rest of the band counters with background voices singing about wanting to have a "white riot"—that are obviously derived from the purposely "off" horn sections on Jamaican reggae and ska recordings.

In a rock & roll context, this juxtaposition works perfectly, both in terms of the sound, and as far as getting the message across.

Since making that first album (which some critics have flatly stated is the best rock & roll album—period), the Clash have certainly become better musicians, yet they refuse to let technique replace emotion. With honest, uncompromising lyrics they continue to render the ravaged and decaying modern world like punk Picassos painting their own version of *Guernica*.

The Clash's music often sounds like a violent revolution. At times it is a thunderous roar that filters bits of the Rolling Stones, reggae, the Who, Chuck Berry, rockabilly, marching soldiers, gunfire, and a brawl at some London pub into a crashing wall-of-sound. But there's a mellower side of the Clash too. "Jimmy Jazz," from *London Calling,* is reminiscent of Tom Waits, or even Mose Allison. (The Clash included a version of Allison's "Look Here" on *Sandinista!*) And over the course of their five albums, they have recorded a lot of reggae, from the gutsy "Police and Thieves," to more subtle pieces like "One More Time, One More Dub." The Clash have also fit straightforward rockabilly, gospel, blues, and both classic and modern soul music—funk and rap—into their bag of tricks. "The Magnificent Seven," the group's first rap number, was played by some of the more adventurous Black stations in the US; this greatly pleased the band, who felt that they were connecting directly with an audience that could appreciate their songs about oppression.

"We're not minimalists," says Mick Jones. "Where they [most punk bands] tend to keep themselves in one line, we tend to go out in every line possible—all sorts of sub-tracks." In fact, the Clash's embracing of numerous kinds of international music, and their commitment to keep that music alive in the minds of their fans, is a very important part of what they have accomplished. Particularly now, when American radio is more specialized than ever, when jazz, soul, country & western, reggae, and rock are each isolated and never heard on the same radio show, the Clash continue to demonstrate on each album (since *London Calling*) that music, like people, should not be segregated.

Of course the fact that politics are such a part of what the Clash do begs the question: Can political rock & roll actually accomplish anything? The Clash try to be realistic, if not optimistic. "Maybe it won't change anything," says Mick Jones, "but I still believe in it, as something worth doing. Perhaps we're too ambitious a band. I would say rock & roll can contribute toward some minor change." Then he adds stubbornly, "But it ain't gonna tell the politicians what to do. It ain't gonna save people from wars."

Adds Strummer with finality, "But we'll have a go at it."

*DownBeat,* December 1982

Sid Vicious, Johnny Rotten, and Steve Jones of the Sex Pistols, San Francisco, Winterland, 1978.

# GOD SAVE THE SEX PISTOLS!

The Sex Pistols and their American manager, Rory Johnston, thought it would be hilarious to pull a fast one on the journalist from the Berkeley Barb—that would be me—whom a Warner Bros. Records publicist had arranged to interview the group. When I got to Johnston's suite at a hotel located a few blocks from Winterland, where the Pistols would play their final show before breaking up, I was directed to one of the bedrooms and told to wait for the group. I waited for 10, maybe 15 minutes. Finally, sensing that something was amiss, I left the room only to find Johnston, Pistols' drummer Paul Cook and guitarist Steve Jones, and some crew members exiting the suite. I joined them and though they attempted to ignore me, followed them to a nearby Japanese restaurant and sat down directly across from Cook and Jones at a table some distance from where the manager and crew had joined a group from Warner Bros. I got out my tape recorder, turned it on, and obviously unhappy that their joke had backfired, the two Pistols found themselves reluctantly addressing my questions. That was my upfront and personal introduction to the Sex Pistols.

TALKING WITH THE SEX PISTOLS could not actually be called an interview. Lunching last weekend with drummer Paul Cook and guitarist Steve Jones, I felt that the quiet Japanese restaurant near Japan Town had turned into a shooting gallery. The tense exchange continually threatened to explode. I truly expected a glob of spit in my face or at least an overturned table. But to my surprise, no actual physical attack took place, though verbal punches hurled hysterically.

The punks were joined by their American manager Rory Johnston, several members of the Pistols' road crew, a Warner Brothers publicity person, and several hangers-on for a dinner of tempura, teriyaki chicken, and sake. The American media had reported that the group was crashing in cheap hotels, eating simply, and generally avoiding the high life of most rock stars. The Pistols' San Francisco visit, however, proved to be the exception, for the group was found lodged at a famous flophouse, the Miyako Hotel.

When questioned about their accommodations, Cook and Jones became instantly aggravated, their voices shrill. Jones, who was wearing a police shirt and badge, snapped loudly, jolting the quiet atmosphere of the restaurant, "I don't give a fuck where I stay."

"Why shouldn't we enjoy the good life? It's at Warner Brothers' expense," said Cook, who wore a ripped, sleeveless T-shirt, tight back pants, and dirty white leather shoes. His dirty blond hair was clipped to two inches and stuck out in the punk style that the Pistols borrowed from New York punk Richard Hell. Cook's T-shirt featured a monster face superimposed over a British flag.

"Anyway," he continued. "Who gives a fuck where we're staying?!"

"Who are you to give a fuck?" demanded Jones.

The Pistols are notorious for their "rapport" with the press. Both the English and American press have printed sensational stories documenting the Pistols vomiting in airports, spitting at photographers, and swearing on BBC TV. Some think the antagonistic relationship between the Pistols and press has been carefully nurtured, paying off in front page headlines on both sides of the Atlantic.

I asked Jones how he felt about the press.

"Bunch of cunts," he mumbled, washing down tempura with sake.

"Why?"

"'Cause they ask stupid questions like that one," he sneered.

I took a different tack and asked about their problems with the US State Department. Last month, on the eve of their tour, the Pistols were denied visas. Four US dates had to be canceled. Then, very suddenly, the State Department reversed its decision and allowed the group into the country. "Here's a scoop for you," whispered Cook. "The Mafia made Jimmy Carter let us into the US."

"What's the worst thing that's happened to you in the US," I asked, glancing about, checking out a possible quick exit.

"Getting fucked by a lorry driver. American groupies," snarled Jones.

"What's the best thing that's happened?"

"Getting fucked by American groupies," he popped again.

"Why are you touring the US?"

"To lose money. Our manager manipulated us," said Cook.

"Why do people respond violently to you?"

"People want to get involved. It's better than them just sitting on their asses and doin' nothin'," said Jones.

"What matters to you?"

"Nothin' matters. I don't worry about anything so nothin' matters," said Jones.

As more sake is socked away, the conversation continued to deteriorate. "The *Berkeley Barb* a trendy paper?" asked Cook.

"No."

"Well what are you writing about us for? We're trendy," he said.

"Yea, what kind of paper is the *Berkeley Barb*," demanded Rory Johnston, a short, stocky, pug-faced man wearing a black bondage shirt under a black leather jacket. "Who reads the *Berkeley Barb*?"

"I don't know," I said.

A hanger-on blurted, "Negroes read it."

Laughter.

"It's a hippie paper isn't it. You're a fucking hippie," yelled Johnston.

"And a fuckin' punk poser," snarled Jones, eyeing my leather jacket. "Let's see your shoes, probably platform shoes, that's what hippies wear. Spotting my Earth shoe brand with the "negative heels," Jones screamed, "Health shoes!"

There was more laughter.

If only Carol Burnett had known about these guys.

Clearly the interview was about to end. "How are you punks going to keep from becoming just like the Rolling Stones and the other superstars," I asked, packing up to leave.

Surprisingly Paul Cook adopted a serious tone. "We just aren't like that. We won't change. We've learned what not to do from them."

## Winterland, Saturday, January 14, 1978

THE SEX PISTOLS—Johnny Rotten, vocalist; Steve Jones, guitarist; Sid Vicious, bass; and Paul Cook, drums—appeared onstage shortly after 10 p.m.

Johnny Rotten is the dramatic focal point for the Sex Pistols. At Winterland, Rotten appeared in leather pants and vest, a white shirt and metal rings, safety pins and chains hanging from his belt. Though he rarely moved from the microphone and generally held the mike stand in both hands or stood with arms folded, Rotten was a charismatic figure whose wall-eyed performance sent a frenzied crowd to the throes of punk ecstasy, which manifested in waves of pogoing. (Pogoing is the punk dance and is performed by hopping up and down with legs together while allowing arms and head to thrash wildly.)

Bassist Sid Vicious was the most active Pistol, spitting on the audience and leaping up and down, legs apart, jumping-jack style while he flailed at his bass. Lacking any sophistication or subtlety, Vicious' playing is ideally suited to the raw rock & roll the Pistols excel at.

Drummer Paul Cook rocked with a vengeance but added little visually to the Pistols' performance. Guitarist Steve Jones looked like a head waiter from "Tricia's Wedding," wearing an oversized red sport coat with black velvet collar and ugly leer. His playing alternated between fierce power chording and simple, jagged rock leads.

The Pistols' sound derives from the early Who and the New York Dolls. In fact, several of Jones' lead licks sound like direct imitations of the Dolls. Iggy Pop's defunct Stooges and the Ramones are also major influences. The audience was in the Pistols holster from the first and sang along as the group ran through songs off their debut LP, *Never Mind the Bollocks, Here's the Sex Pistols* (Warner Bros.), including "God Save the Queen," "Bodies," "Liar," "Problems," "EMI," "Holidays in the Sun," and "Anarchy in the U.K." Although the audience threw paper cups, flash cubes, belts, empty half-pint bottles, and umbrellas at the band as they played, the objects were signs of affection, not rejection. The Pistols had been quoted as enjoying violent responses from their audience and the Winterland crowd, the largest they have ever played for, were not going to let the band down.

Encoring with the Stooges' "No Fun," the Pistols ended their 45-minute set, left the stage, and did not return despite wild clapping, yelling, and pounding from the crowd.

Bill Graham held a press party backstage after the show. Hundreds of people milled around a low-ceilinged area with a locker room ambience. The cuisine featured hot dogs with chili, served with beer, wine, and milk.

Members of the Avengers, a San Francisco punk band who performed before the Pistols, were well soused and poured beer and popcorn onto the floor until people were slipping and sliding around the room.

"I hate posers," screamed one Avenger at another punk. At least 15 photographers circled, flashes popping as a mock fight took place.

Finally, Johnny Rotten made his appearance, grabbed a beer, and donned shades as the pack of photographers swarmed to him. Followed by a bodyguard, Rotten walked through the crowd and out of Winterland.

I walked out of the party and was about to leave Winterland when I saw Steve Jones, looking quite smug.

"How you doin'?" he said absently.

I asked him if he were glad that the tour was over.

"Yeah, I am," he smiled. Then suddenly, as if he remembered something, his smile turned to a forced grimace.

"No," he snarled. "I ain't."

*Berkeley Barb*, January 20–26, 1978

# AN AUDIENCE WITH THE ARTIST FORMERLY KNOWN AS PRINCE

**Leading his current band, New Power Generation, The Artist is decidedly "in the house," at the top of his form both in the recording studio and on the stage. But are you up for "the challenge"?**

*I will always regret missing Prince's first appearance in the Bay Area, which took place at The Stone on Broadway in March of 1981. That gig was part of the Dirty Mind Tour. I don't know why I missed that show 'cause I had flipped when I heard the gorgeous pop of "When You Were Mine," and I dug the rest of* Dirty Mind *as well.* Dirty Mind *was the first of a string of amazing albums. Prince had previously recorded two albums, but* Dirty Mind *was the game changer; it was the album that introduced Prince's stripped-down new wave pop sound and his "dirty" lyrics. Later, I saw Prince at the Cow Palace in San Francisco during his* Purple Rain *tour, but oh to have seen him in a club. Too bad. By the time I interviewed Prince in 1998, he was long past the days of effortlessly recording hits, sometimes in one night. But he was still a great artist, and I feel very lucky to have had the chance to hang with him. He died of a drug overdose on April 21, 2016; he was 57. In 2004,* Rolling Stone *ranked Prince number 27 in their list of the 100 Greatest Artists of All Time.*

BURBANK, CALIFORNIA—THE SECURITY GUARD in suit and tie who is watching the closed door to The Artist's upstairs dressing room on *The Tonight Show* set in Burbank, California, is given the nod by The Artist's aide, and opens the door.

I can't believe it. Coming toward me is The Artist—aka Prince—himself, looking even cooler in person than in the countless photos and videos I've seen. He smiles and extends a hand.

I've waited 15 years to interview The Artist Formerly Known as Prince. Back when The Artist was still calling himself Prince, back before he became a superstar thanks to the success of *Purple Rain* (the movie and the album), I was scheduled to speak with him in Los Angeles, on the eve of the release of *1999*.

I was waiting for a cab to pick me up and take me to the airport when the call came. It was Prince's publicist. The interview was off. Prince had arrived in LA the day before, and had met with a *Los Angeles Times* reporter. The experience, the publicist had explained, was so "traumatic" that Prince had canceled all other interviews.

Ouch! So close, I thought. I was dying to speak to the man responsible for *Dirty Mind* and *Controversy*. I had been grooving heavily to his music. Prince was the dude—Sly Stone, James Brown, and John Lennon rolled into one.

Sadly, that 1982 interview was not to be.

And, for many years to come, as his fame increased, the hits came fast and furious and the platinum records piled up, Prince did not speak to the press.

Prince at The Forum in Inglewood, California, during the Purple Rain tour, 1985. © Daniel Gluskoter/dgpics.com

But time heals many wounds, and now, arguably the most talented musician of the past 40 years is shaking my hand and inviting me to sit anywhere I like, to make myself at home in his dressing room.

"I'm brand new," he says, explaining his decision to begin speaking to the media—something he's done only occasionally, but with increasing frequency, in the past few years. "With *Emancipation* [the three-CD set released in 1997] there was so much to talk about. My life has changed. I'm with a group, the New Power Generation, and we have an album [*Newpower Soul*] and I want to promote it."

## "Every Day Is a Happy Day"

BRAND NEW? WITHOUT A DOUBT. At 40, The Artist, born Prince Rogers Nelson on June 7, 1958, in Minneapolis, Minnesota, seems a new man. The key to his current happiness seems to be the freedom he has experienced since parting ways with Warner Bros. Records three years ago.

"I'm not bitter," he says, after taking a seat on the dressing room couch so that he is just a few feet away, facing me.

He introduces two of his bandmates, New Power Generation keyboardist "Mr. Hayes" (Morris Hayes), who is sitting in a corner chair, looking decidedly uptown in a shiny olive-green suit, and drummer Kirk Johnson, a towering man with a shaved head who is dressed casually in a sleeveless black T-shirt and black slacks.

The Artist does not allow the few journalists he does speak with to tape-record their interviews. "That's because taping him creates software that can be used by others," explains his attorney, New York entertainment lawyer Londell McMillan, a few days after the interview. "He's concerned about people using his image, likeness, and voice in ways that it was not originally intended [to be used]."

Prior to this meeting, his current publicist told me that it would be all right to shoot video. But when I tell The Artist that I'm going to get out my camera, he replies that he had not been asked whether he wanted to allow the interview to be videotaped, and therefore, he isn't prepared.

"That won't be possible today," he says, in a polite but firm voice.

Concerned that, without a video or a recording, I will not be able to preserve everything The Artist has to say (the original plan was to run a Q&A), I suggest that he allow me to make an audio tape, so that every word of the interview will be accurate.

"This isn't a deposition," he says, grinning slyly. "Now you don't want to start our relationship on that note, do you?"

Quickly pulling out my notebook, I suggest that we begin.

## The Artist as King

TODAY, THE ARTIST LOOKS LIKE the happy king of funk & roll, like a soulful King Arthur holding court. His clothes (which The Artist himself designs) are custom-made, fantasy rock & roll wear that just about anyone else, star or not, would look silly wearing. Who but The Artist could wear a blue-spangled jumpsuit cut low so his chest is exposed, a midlength purple velvet frock coat with foot-deep white sheepskin cuffs, and the hugest collar anyone has worn since the early '70s heyday of "Superfly"?

His hair is tied in numerous mini-pigtails. A gold three-inch-in-diameter hoop earring dangles from his right ear. A fat ring with row after row of diamonds glistens on a finger of his right hand. A diamond version of the now-legendary morphed male/female symbol hangs from his neck.

And then there's the cane—it's clear, and filled with a translucent liquid in which multicolored stars float.

He wants to clarify, right at the outset, that this is a New Power Generation interview, which is why Mr. Hayes and Johnson are present (the rest of the band consists of singer Marva King, bassist Rhonda Smith, and guitarist Mike Scott).

"I think it's a landmark record for me," he says of *Newpower Soul*. "I allowed other sounds made by other individuals. 'Mad Sex' is a creation of Kirk's." He raises his right hand and gestures in the direction of the drummer. "I let that dictate how I wrote and arranged it. I respect the one, the first."

For the Artist, the New Power Generation is more than a band. "The New Power Generation is like a studio, like an idea," he says. "It's a way of doing things."

"It's really a way of life for him and all of us that believe in the New Power Generation for the new millennium," McMillan says.

While The Artist and his extended family understand, much of the rest of the world doesn't get it yet. The Artist complains that Leno is promoting tonight's appearance as "The Artist and the New Power Generation." "They don't say 'Mick Jagger and the Rolling Stones,'" he notes.

Make no mistake, he clearly understands that it's his fame, his success, that is carrying things. It may be an NPG album that the band's here to promote, but it's The Artist who appears, alone, on the *Newpower Soul* cover. It's The Artist whom Leno wanted on his show. And it's The Artist who dominates the interview.

And why not? The Artist is the only superstar in this room. Certainly, Hayes and Johnson are awesome musicians; they bring plenty to the table, whether performing New Power Generation songs like "Come On" and "The One," or older material written by the man sitting before me (both when he was working as Prince and after the name change). Still, it is The Artist who has written and produced and performed the countless hits— from "I Wanna Be Your Lover" to "When Doves Cry" to "The Most Beautiful Girl in the World"—that have earned him the respect of the music industry and fans the world over.

His bandmates clearly understand this. "It's amazing," Johnson says, explaining what it's like working with The Artist. "I have an idea, some beats. So me and our engineer leave some ideas on the board and when we come back it's a whole new beast."

In 1978, the then 20-year-old Prince's first album, *For You*, was released by Warner Bros. He recorded 17 albums for that company as Prince, and another two as The Artist (15 of the albums went platinum, with *Purple Rain* selling more than 14 million copies; 12 of his singles went gold).

For more than a decade, it seemed a relatively smooth artist/record company relationship, from the outside anyway. But by the early '90s, Prince—who changed his name to a male/female symbol in 1993 (he's also been going by "The Artist" since at least 1995)— became frustrated by Warner Bros.' reluctance to release his music as promptly as he wanted.

He tried to get out of his recording contract. He protested publicly, appearing in photos and on television with the word "slave" scrawled on his face. He did a rare interview, complaining about his situation to *Vibe*. In 1995 he enlisted the help of McMillan. "The idea was to seek someone who could relieve him of the restrictive covenants of the Warner Bros. record contract," McMillan says. "We explored contentious and amiable options to relieve him of the agreement. Fortunately, we were able to find a way to terminate it amicably after much negotiation and effort."

The Artist was released from Warner Bros. in the spring of 1996. "The goal was to help him wipe slave off his face," McMillan says. "Because freedom is very liberating and allows one to be as creative and productive as possible."

"The reputation I gained for being bitter was probably because I had 'slave' written on my face," The Artist tells me. "As you can see *[he smiles, rubs his hand across the side of his face]*, I don't have anything written on my face now. I'm free. Every day is a happy day."

I have come to this interview expecting The Artist to elaborate on how he has set himself up to operate independently of the traditional music business. After all, since leaving Warner Bros., The Artist has started his own record label, NPG Records, and released several albums. The first, *Crystal Ball*, was initially only available by ordering it online or via an 800-number. More than 150,000 copies of the five-CD set—selling for $50 each—were ordered in one of those two ways, according to McMillan, before The Artist made a four CD edition of the album available in record stores. He says that 250,000 copies of *Crystal Ball* have sold to date.

The Artist came in for some criticism from fans for the extended time that elapsed between when orders for *Crystal Ball* were first taken (May 1997) and when the albums were finally shipped (spring 1998).

"[It bothers me that people have said] we're running a bad business," The Artist says. "That's not true. We probably have more satisfied customers than anyone. Thousands of satisfied customers. The newspaper says my name is mud. Excuse me! What's the point? It's so one-sided. It's not proper."

Recently, he decided to let his fans download a new 26-minute song, "The War," off the internet (the single is also being sent to everyone who ordered *Crystal Ball*). He requests that they mail him a $1 donation, a portion of which will go to charity, but it's not required.

When I open the interview by bringing up his autonomy from the biz, The Artist shakes his head. "No," he says flatly. "My intention is never to disassociate from or disenfranchise anyone."

"Not to dis!" Mr. Hayes says.

The Artist nods in agreement. "I have no problem with record companies. Record companies work fine. We're taking a different approach to marketing. We're not cutting into their business. Their business is their business and our business is our business."

He smiles as though he's just told a joke that only he and his bandmates truly understand. "I have good friends in the record business," he continues, looking me straight in the eye. "I still have friends at Warner Bros. [Sony Music Entertainment Executive Vice President] Michele Anthony is a very good friend. My next record will probably be at a major."

"The records we've released [independently], it's an alternative," he says. "We're getting our feet wet."

"Stepping out into uncharted territory," Mr. Hayes says.

## Every Day Is a Good Day

IN THE LATE '80s, The Artist built Paisley Park, the 65,000-square-foot studio complex outside Minneapolis where he now does most of his recording. Paisley Park includes four recording studios, a soundstage, and a rehearsal hall. "Paisley Park is set up so we can do what we do," Mr. Hayes says. "Rehearse, sleep, eat, record. It's outfitted so if he has an idea, you just hit a button and go."

Over the course of the interview, The Artist returns often to the subject of his artistic autonomy. "[Since going independent] I've made a lot more money," The Artist says. Now he's really smiling. "I can say that and feel good. With a lot of money you can resuscitate the careers of Larry Graham and Chaka Khan [both now record for NPG]. People say we're not as successful as before. Well, what is success? We define our success. One hundred thousand copies, when most of the profit goes to us is *[he slaps his leg]* like Nelson Mandela just got free."

He pauses, lets what he's said sink in. "I understand money more now. I don't trip on it. I always have it, and so I don't worry about it. [When you have money] it takes the worry away.

"We look at the criticism: 'He ain't selling like he used to' . . . We don't think in those terms. It's not all about the Benjamins. It's back to the fun of just making music. It's not about the *Billboard* charts."

"Long as people can eat and groove," Hayes says, "it's pretty cool."

## A Free Man

I USED TO THINK OF The Artist as a shy man who only came out of his shell during performances. This was a man who could sing frankly about oral sex and incest, but didn't want to speak to the media.

While he may have been bashful once, there is nothing shy about The Artist *now*. As he sits before me, laughing and cracking jokes, he is a forceful, luminous presence. You can practically see the charisma; star power emanates from him in waves.

For nearly an hour he answers my questions. He never raises his voice. He never appears to get mad. He is calm and comfortable addressing everything from his past career problems to the state of the world, from the creative process to artists that he likes (Björk, D'Angelo, the Tony Rich Band).

"We're just out here having a good time," he says of *The Tonight Show* appearance, not "tripping like we used to. When you do music, it's the freedom you best prosper in."

He recalls that he felt no restrictions when he recorded *Dirty Mind*, one of the greatest rock & roll albums ever made. "*Dirty Mind* was a demo tape," he says. "Recorded in my basement. I had complete freedom [making that album]. You lift the veil and see what's inside. When they [Warner Bros.] first heard it—'Oh boy, we're in trouble now.'"

The problems that The Artist had in the past extended beyond a record deal he couldn't stomach. "I had a group of people making decisions for me. [Saying things like] 'you're too prolific.' What does that mean? Too prolific? That's like too wealthy.

"I used to ride my bike to the record store and I bought every single James Brown put out. He'd have a new single every three months. No one said James Brown was too prolific." He laughs. "I wasn't mad if James Brown put out 'Lickin' Stick.'"

Mr. Hayes says quietly, "Mad if James had skipped putting a record out after three months."

## "The War"

IN JUNE, THE ARTIST had some lyrics he was "messin' with." He brought them into the studio and "we just jammed on it." The result, released in mid-July, just a month after it was recorded, is the 26-minute epic social statement, "The War."

"The War" is an apocalyptic cut that features vocals, guitar, keyboards, and percussion work by The Artist, and the refrain "One! Two! The evolution will be colorized," a reference to social critic and singer Gil Scott-Heron's classic poem/recording, "The Revolution Will Not Be Televised."

"We are about to challenge what you believe / If you do not wish to be challenged, you should leave now," The Artist says over a funky groove. He than asks if the listener loves where they live as much as they love God and then declares that people are running out of what is necessary to keep living: air, water, food, and fertile earth.

"It's self-explanatory," The Artist says when asked to elaborate on the song's lyrics. "It's a challenge. All I can say is, if you accept the challenge, then you can deal with what's inside."

The Artist says that releasing "The War" (which isn't on *Newpower Soul*), so soon after the *Newpower Soul*'s release is another example of the freedom he now enjoys. "In the past [when he was signed to Warner Bros.] they'd have said, 'You can't put out a 26-minute song—it'll kill the album.' We're not tripping on that. We got in it for the funk of it."

He glances at Hayes and Johnson. "Anybody begins a sentence with the word 'but,' we figure that's where their words are coming out of."

The three men laugh.

## "What's That Stuff in the Cane?"

WHAT MANY PEOPLE DON'T seem to understand about The Artist is that while he has a shrewd understanding of the music business, his art has nothing to do with the biz. At one point he says that he wants the conversation off the record for a moment and then explains something to me. In the course of his explanation, he says something that I ask him about once we're back on the record.

He had said that his work reflects "a life that I'm living."

I tell him that when he said this, what struck me was the idea that for 20 years his life has served as the inspiration for the records he has written and produced. In other words, he doesn't go into the studio to write a hit, he goes in to document where he's at.

The Artist turns serious. "It's a record of the event," he says. "Now the biz wants you to put something out [every few years]. I don't do things like they do. I'm an artist and for me that isn't rewarding. I handed you a copy of [the new single] 'The War.' That was recorded a month ago. Not six months ago."

He tells me about a song he once recorded, called "The Rock," inspired by a dance he'd seen kids doing at the clubs. He wanted it released right away, but, he says, Warner Bros. wouldn't release it. By the time it could be released, the moment had long passed, so he rewrote it, and it was finally released as "Let's Work."

Johnson says they sometimes joke about record executives lying on the beach "sippin' their drinks and talking about what you can't do."

"I sold out Wembley Stadium [in London] in a day once," The Artist says. "So when I heard that I said, 'then put another day on sale.' And they [his advisers at the time] said, 'No, you don't want to do that. It might be half full.' So? I'd play a half-full stadium."

"We wouldn't want to turn away people who want to see us perform," Mr. Hayes says.

The subject switches to Love 4 One Another, the children's charity that The Artist and his wife, Mayte, founded in 1996. These days, in each city where he performs, he does something for the underprivileged. "Tithing works," he says. "I wish you'd title this article that, 'tithing works.' You help somebody and you'll get rewards upon rewards. Love life, love life."

As I look at The Artist, I want to tell him how much his music has meant to me. How I've played "When You Were Mine" hundreds of times over the 18 years since *Dirty Mind* was released—literally wearing my vinyl copy out. How I grooved through the years to *Controversy* and *1999*. The ecstasy of listening to *Purple Rain* and *Sign O' the Times*. How cool "Manic Monday" (the song he wrote for the Bangles) is, and "Nothing Compares 2 U," a song he wrote that was a breakthrough hit for Sinéad O'Connor.

I want to be sure he understands the kind of impact he's had on contemporary music, and all the musicians he's influenced and who love his work. And the fans. The millions and millions of music lovers who have danced and loved and grown up to his songs.

Instead, I ask for an autograph, and he politely tells me he doesn't do that.

The audience with The Artist is at an end. He indicates that he's got to prepare for the New Power Generation's *Tonight Show* performance—but that it's possible we'll talk again. He rises from the couch, picks up his cane and leans on it, waiting for me to leave.

"What's that liquid in the cane?" I ask, as I pack up my notebooks.

He raises the cane in the air and rotates it, so that the stars floating in the liquid catch the light and sparkle.

"Sperm," he says, and laughs. "When I'm 75, I can break it out."

*Addicted To Noise*, Summer 1998

# MUDDY WATERS

*Friday the 13th, just before midnight. Muddy Waters, 62, takes his last bow before an almost berserk crowd filling San Francisco's Theater 1839 in the Fillmore District. The folks have turned out to see one of the last surviving elder statesmen of the blues in a rare local appearance. Backstage, it's the usual: a sparse, dingy dressing room. Muddy Waters and his band have been through it 1,000 times before. Champagne, friends, fans, and the occasional amateur musicologist. Laughter. Listening closely, you hear an intense rap and it's always the same: the blues. A young woman wanders in and gives Muddy a hug. Looking uptown in a brown suit and white patent leather shoes, Muddy sports a watch on each wrist. Perched on a wood bench, the kingly Muddy Waters is always the gentlemen, pouring champagne for friends and himself.*

I WAS TRYING TO PLAY the blues and sing the blues when I was three years old. I used to beat on pans and things when I was three years old and sing my little songs. All my life I was trying to play blues. When I was seven years old, I had a harmonica. Nine, I was playing pretty good. Thirteen, I was great. Seventeen, I was playing guitar awfully good.

**Best gig you ever played?**
When I started makin' two dollars and fifty cents a night in Mississippi. That was the best gig I ever had. 'Cause like hey man I was making 50 cents to a dollar. When the man raised me to two dollars and fifty cents, says, "you're good," that's when my buddy got drunk and wouldn't play and I played by myself. He says, "You can have the gig yourself. We give you each a dollar and a quarter so you can have the whole two dollars and fifty cents yourself if you play." That was about 1936. That was good money for me. I loved it 'cause I wasn't makin' but 75 cents for workin' [driving a tractor on a sharecropped plantation].

**In 1944 Waters formed what he claimed was the first electric blues band.**
I'm the first. I mean it happened when I was in Chicago. See I always liked guitar and harp, so we had to electrify the stuff when I got to Chicago. 'Cause playin' in those bars without electricity, you ain't got nothing going, you know? So I had to buy an electric guitar. I got a band together. Little Walter on harp, Jimmy Rogers on guitar. Baby Face Leroy on guitar and drums and me singin' and playin' guitar. That's what started two guitars in a band. 'Cause before that people weren't playing but one guitar in a band. I'm telling you my idea for using a couple of guitar players. It was like if one gets sick, you'd be stuck so that's why I started doing that and I kept going. And what else you want to know, huh?

A lotta young kids comin' up and gettin' my licks and makin' big stars outta themselves and I love that. I'm not jealous. I'm glad they did it. Somebody needed to do it. I couldn't do it. So like the Rolling Stones and all the rest of the kids, Paul Butterfield, they went out and did something. I'm proud of it. Now today some of the kids are making some of my songs, putting them on their albums and that bring in a little change.

Muddy Waters at Theater 1839 in San Francisco, 1977.

**In 1958 Muddy Waters and his band toured England. According to Muddy he turned England on to the electric guitar.**
I did in England. I goes over and I got an amplifier with me, a big Fender amplifier and we had Otis Span's piano miked and the next morning we was in the headlines in the paper with that "screaming guitar and howling piano." When I went back to England a few years later I didn't bring no electric guitar, just an acoustic and they say, "How come you didn't bring no electric guitar?" and I said, "No man, you don't like it over here" and they just laughed because everybody was playing electric guitars then. I turned England on to amplifiers.

Well, hey, I don't have enough money to write home and tell momma about but I got enough to go out to the supermarket and get a couple T-bone steaks about twice a week and that's pretty good for me. Oh, I got a couple of houses, five or six cars, swimming pool, two German shepherds and seven kids. I guess I got seven or eight kids. I got four grandkids, two great grandkids. That's pretty good, isn't it?

**Have you had a happy life?**
Sure, I had happy, and I've had a little sad. My grandmother passed and that one was a sad day. And I had a beautiful uncle pass. Had my daughter that passed, and my wife passed. I've seen a few sad days, but in my life, I think I've had a happy life. I think I've had one of the beautiful lives, more than you would expect. I had it up and down. Let me go to 80 and then I quit.

*Muddy got sick in 1982 and had to stop performing. He died in 1983; he was 70 years old.*

May 1977

From the photo session that produced a press photo used to promote Flipper's first album, *Album—Generic Flipper*, San Francisco, 1982. © VinceAntonPhoto

# THE HATED FLIPPER

*Writing about Flipper for the "Pink Section," which was the term most people used (maybe still use) when talking about the* San Francisco Chronicle's *Sunday Datebook (the entertainment section) because it was printed on pink newsprint, was a challenge. The audience was large (as many as two million people saw the Sunday paper), and you had to assume they knew nothing about the subject you were covering. And you had to assume they had no interest in a little-known punk band called Flipper. My job was to write a general interest story that a reader, if they read my first sentence, wouldn't be able to put down. So, while I personally dug Flipper and still love their debut album,* Album—Generic Flipper, *that was beside the point. Flipper, who had been around for more than three years and were popular on the underground club circuit, were amused that, finally, the* San Francisco Chronicle *wanted to interview them. They didn't understand that the* Chronicle *could care less about them. It was I who wanted to interview them. And though I wrote freelance articles for the Pink Section and was paid a princely sum of $35 per article, I was most decidedly not the* San Francisco Chronicle. *What follows is "The Hated Flipper," the story I wrote about the band, followed by the full text of my interview with them, which has not been previously published. I think you'll find both amusing, whether you have or haven't listened to Flipper. And if you haven't, their recordings can be streamed via Spotify; I highly recommend that you listen to* Album—Generic Flipper, *while reading the story and the interview, or right after. Sadly, Flipper singer/bassist Will Shatter (Russell Wilkerson) died of a heroin overdose in 1987. Singer/bassist Bruce Loose (Bruce Calderwood), who in the early days of the band called himself Bruce Lose, left the band in 2006, after suffering from a back injury. The band was a favorite of Nirvana, including Kurt Cobain, who wore a Flipper T-shirt when Nirvana performed on* Saturday Night Live *on January 11, 1992. Nirvana bassist Krist Novoselic later played in a revamped version of Flipper. With only two original members left, Flipper's most recent performances were at the Bottom of the Hill in October 2015. A few years ago, I bought a Flipper T-shirt like the one Cobain wore and if you run into me in the East Bay, where I live, on the right day, I'll be proudly wearing that Flipper T-shirt.*

MEMBERS OF THE MOST hated punk rock band in San Francisco were ordering another round of drinks in a rather seedy hofbrau in San Francisco's Tenderloin.

A cloud of cigarette smoke rose from the red Formica table as Flipper faced up to its infamy.

"A lot of people think we're a joke," said Steve DePace, the 25-year-old drummer with Flipper's trademark, a mean, ugly fish with sharp teeth, outlined in white on the front of his black T-shirt.

"Some people think we're selling out and some people think we're a joke," grunted 23-year-old vocalist/bassist/songwriter Bruce Lose (born Bruce Calderwood), the Universal Life Church minister who performed the wedding ceremony when Dead Kennedys' leader Jello Biafra was married.

Lose took another slug of his Margarita.

Flipper thinks of itself as "the Grateful Dead of the '80s."

They're also the only punk band that would admit that sensitive folk-poet Leonard Cohen is an influence.

But then Flipper have never quite fit into the punk scene.

For most of their three-year existence, they've found even the hardcore punks (the gang that go in for leather motorcycle jackets and mohawks and chains and engineer boots and slam dancing) less than thrilled with their music.

There are reasons for this. Punk rock, like country music or the blues, has strictly defined rules.

Songs are short, chords are few, instrumental technique is out, and attitude is bad.

But Flipper plays *long* songs. They like to set up a wall-of-sound reminiscent of a tornado ripping apart a small town, set it to a four/four beat, and then let it drone on and on and on, while Lose or singer/songwriter/bassist Will Shatter (born Russell Wilkerson) shout and mumble and talk and slur lyrics. One of their tunes, "Ha Ha Ha," finds them laughing sarcastically for most of the piece.

"I called us the Grateful Dead of the '80s," said Lose, who even admits to liking the Grateful Dead, heresy for a punk. "Not only because we play our songs for a long time, but because of the fact that we jam. We never play the same song in the same way. The arrangement is always different.

"We like to play long sets. We don't even start getting going until we've played for an hour. And I think we're going to keep going for years . . . The Grateful Dead, they've been together 25 years . . . 15 years, something like that. I'd gladly play for that long in this band."

At a recent performance at San Francisco's Elite Club, a concert hall that was once the world famous Fillmore Auditorium, Flipper, which, in addition to Lose, Shatter, and DePace, includes 34-year-old guitarist Ted Falconi, had to follow up an act whose showstopper came when a member of the audience leaped onto the stage, slammed into the lead singer, a frail blonde girl in the Blondie mold, and literally knocked her unconscious; she was carried off the stage.

Flipper managed to make everyone forget about that incident by immediately launching into one of their dirges and then allowing a member of the audience who climbed onto the stage to sing most of the song, while Lose and Shatter stood to the side, sipping beer and smoking cigarettes.

This kind of approach to performance has not been overlooked by members of San Francisco's punk rock establishment.

Howie Klein, president of the new wave record label 415 Records, and a DJ at KUSF, San Francisco's all-new wave rock station, said, when asked what he thought of Flipper's music: "They play music?"

Others laugh derisively when Flipper's name comes up. Still, the band has gained a following in the Bay Area. And, with the recent release of their album, titled simply *Album—Generic Flipper* and packaged like a generic product—solid yellow cover with only the words "Album" and "Generic Flipper" along with a computer pricing code—they have found some of rock's influential and respected critics in their camp.

The band spent a mere $3,000 recording their record; most albums cost between $50,000 and a $100,000 to record.

Rock critic Robert Christgau wrote recently, "I love them, you may hate them, and that's the way Flipper planned it."

In the lead music review in New York's *Village Voice* recently, critic John Piccarella put Flipper with rock greats Elvis, Jerry Lee Lewis, the Beatles, the Stones, the Sex Pistols, and the Clash, and stated: "And they create the most immediate, engaging, powerful rock music since UK 1977. In fact, 'Sex Bomb,' the final cut on their debut *Album*, is probably the noisiest thing with a good beat I've ever heard."

"Sounds good," said DePace, when read those lines. "Another reviewer in another magazine said we took what the Sex Pistols did and carried it further or something."

"I think we've dragged it further into the ground, if anything," said Lose.

"Yea, we took it and buried it," laughed DePace.

Actually, Flipper's response to the recent critical praise is typical of their general approach to life, what someone recently characterized as "laughing while the world burns."

"It's like a carpenter who makes a chair," said Will Shatter, who is 26 years old. "And he works hard and does a good job on it. And then people come up and they go, 'This chair, it's a work of art, oh my God, look at that.' And the carpenter laughs. And then they go, 'Oh, you're not serious!'"

"Or the carpenter makes the chair, and he thinks it's so wonderful and everybody hates it," said Lose. "They say, 'You're a cruddy carpenter' for three years and then all of a sudden, 'He's a great carpenter.' And you keep laughing. 'Cause you know you're just a carpenter."

Flipper wanted to make it clear that they are not interested in fame, or a lot of money. "We just do what we want to do," said Lose.

"Like Ian, our agent, when he finds out that so and so is out in the audience, Robert Christgau or someone, he goes, 'I want you guys to play good, I want you guys to make a set list tonight,'" said DePace.

"And I go, 'OK Ian, all right, sure, f--k you!'" said Lose.

"We just laugh at the guy, he has a nervous breakdown," said DePace.

"Just like we laugh at anyone who's made any demand of us," said Shatter.

"I laughed for two days when I heard you wanted to come and interview us," grinned Lose.

Said Shatter: "We've gone through an almost complete media ban for three years."

A waitress arrived and the punks ordered another round. Then Will Shatter asked, "By the way, can we get our page printed in white?"

*San Francisco Examiner* and *Chronicle Sunday Datebook* ("Pink Section"), June 27, 1982

# FLIPPER INTERVIEWED

**Michael Goldberg:** Why did you call the band Flipper?

**Will Shatter:** Shall we get out our form answer for this one?

**Steve DePace:** The original singer in the band [Ricky Williams] named everything he owned Flipper. All his pets. So we named the band Flipper too. Iguanas, turtles without legs, dogs, parakeets.

**Goldberg:** Do you guys know about that *Village Voice* review? "They create the most immediate, engaging rock music since UK '77."

**DePace:** Sounds good.

**Bruce Loose:** What the hell is UK '77?

**Shatter:** Chelsea, Generation X.

**DePace:** Another reviewer in another magazine said we took what the Sex Pistols did and carried it further or something. Or not.

**Loose:** I think we've dragged it further into the ground, if anything.

**DePace:** Yeah, we took it and buried it.

**Goldberg:** What do you think about getting a review like that?

**Loose:** New York, they seem to have a better idea of what the hell we're doing for some reason. They're able to understand us better than they are out here.

**DePace:** Everybody chooses different things to compare us to. We don't really think in those terms. We don't go out and do something the Sex Pistols did or outdo UK '77. We just do what we do. And people can call it what they wanna call it.

**Shatter:** There's no formula or scheme to what we do. It's just what we do.

**Goldberg:** In contrast to good reviews in New York City and Boston, around here Flipper has had a weird reputation. For years people have laughed at you.

**Shatter:** Like the "Pink Section."

**DePace:** A lot of people who snub us knew us when we started. They were our friends. Then there are always people that have been established in the scene who have never bothered to get to know us, really know what we're doing. They think something weird about us for some reason. A lot of people just think we're a joke.

**Loose:** Well, some people also think we're so totally serious right now that we're not worthy of whatever the ideal was that was set in the first place. Some people think we're selling out and some people think we're still a joke.

**DePace:** I've had several people come up to me and not knowing I'm in the band say, "Well I don't think Flipper will ever make it. Flipper's just a joke." That's just the way some people take it. I don't know why. Maybe it's because we make fun of ourselves a lot, jokingly. And maybe they just think we're a joke.

**Loose:** We are.

**Shatter:** I think people get confused too, because in the very beginning we made fun of the way everything was, the way the whole scene was.

**DePace:** The way rock & roll is.

**Shatter:** The way the clubs work, the way the promoters work, the way the bands work. And we've laughed at it.

**Loose:** Fashion, the whole bit. Like what the bands played, what people wore, how they acted, what their attitude was about, which after a while just turned into—just stupid. Where punk is right now. I don't like it at all. It's moronic, 17-year-olds thinking they are like the next hot shit, just like I thought I was the next hot shit when I was 17.

**Shatter:** They're just like us.

**Loose:** Yeah, but I don't know. I don't like it. It bugs me.

**Goldberg:** Why do people think you sold out? What have you done?

**Loose:** Nothing. We've just kept playing.

**Shatter:** We do interviews like with the Pink Section.

**DePace:** *[laughs]*

**Shatter:** We get compared—now we're in the same league with Romeo Void, or something.

**Loose:** Well, not quite.

**Shatter:** Well, we haven't sold that many records yet, but we do have an album that's gotten good reviews. So that's definitely a sell out. It must have been something really fucked. And doing this interview is totally insane. And it's against every principle we've ever had before.

**Loose:** But that's why we're doing it.

**DePace:** We're living contradictions of ourselves.

**Goldberg:** How serious do you guys take yourselves?

**Shatter:** It depends.

**DePace:** We take our music very seriously, and then on the other hand, we don't.

**Loose:** Well, we take the music seriously, but we don't so much the performance, or the game of rock & roll.

**Will:** Although we do.

**Loose:** We do it anyway.

**DePace:** Like we mess around in rehearsal, and we do songs we think are funny, and sometimes we'll be laughing through the whole thing 'cause it sounds so silly. But on the other hand—

**Shatter:** We work hard on it. We do take it seriously. But we don't take how it's being taken as serious.

**Loose:** Other people's interpretations we don't take seriously. We take ourselves seriously, about what we're doing. But at the same time, while we're doing it, we laugh at ourselves just because it's a foolish little game.

**Shatter:** It's like a carpenter makes a chair and he works hard and does a good job on it. And then these people come up and they go, "This chair, it's a work of art, oh my God, look at that." And the carpenter laughs, and they go, "Oh, you're not serious."

**DePace:** Or an artist who draws a picture and then tears it up.

**Loose:** Or the carpenter makes the chair, and he thinks it's so wonderful and everybody hates it and he gets even more serious about it.

**Shatter:** They say, "You're a cruddy carpenter" for three years, and then all of a sudden, "He's a great carpenter." And you keep laughing 'cause you know, you're just a carpenter. It seems absurd to you that you've just kept doing the same thing and suddenly you start getting acclaim.

**Loose:** It's gotten where it's gotten.

**Goldberg:** How much did *Album—Generic Flipper* cost to make?

**Shatter:** Total cost was 5,000 or 6,000 bucks. Everything from production to the cover.

**Loose:** That's called cheap.

**DePace:** It cost us about $3,000 to produce it. Another $3,000 to press it. We did it ourselves. We didn't hire people to come in and do stuff.

**Shatter:** We did everything by ourselves except stuff we couldn't do.

**Loose:** Except turning the knobs. We had to have an engineer. Took a year of recording.

**Shatter:** Here he is.

**DePace:** This is Ted.

**Ted Falconi:** I'm late.

**DePace:** Certainly are. All the time.

**Goldberg:** In the *New York Rocker* piece, Will, you said, "We test ourselves as much as we test our audience."

**Loose:** He was just trying to make some nice kind of remark that people—some intellectual remark that would make people go: "Why did you say that?"

**Shatter:** God knows what I meant by that.

**Loose:** We push ourselves to the limit.
*(The other guys start scratching heads while Falconi goes into some obscure explanation about fans who come to see them thinking they're a punk rock band.)*

**Falconi:** They come and then it's, "What is this?"

**Loose:** We did a show in DC, and it started out and the audience was real cold, and just stood there. And Steve got up and said, "What's the matter. Haven't you people heard of partying? What are you? All on downs?"

**Loose:** I said, "No Steve, that's not it, they're not on downs."

**Shatter:** We gave them so much attitude, you wouldn't believe it.

**Loose:** We gave them so much crap for being on drugs that finally by the last song they were screaming, "You're boring and nothing." Finally, everyone's dancing on the last song. People going, "Well, maybe we'll listen to them."

**Shatter:** Or we can take a totally enthusiastic crowd and totally lose them.

**Loose:** Bum them out completely.

**Shatter:** We never know where a sets going to go, where it's going to end up. We don't use a set list. It's never planned what song will come when and how we're gonna do the song.

**Loose:** We never play the same song twice the same way. Not even in rehearsal. We play the same song, but it comes out different. The arrangement is always different. It's very free form.

**Falconi:** Some bands have one arrangement for one song, period. And that's the only way they ever play it. No matter what mood they're in, what mood the audience is in. And a lot of times it doesn't work. We try to at least make it work for us.

**Shatter:** We try to leave things open to possibilities.

**Loose:** You just get up onstage and do it. Look at this audience, what do they need? What song do we wanna play. And then we play it and then I go, "Well, that one worked or it didn't." And then we think of another song. And just do it.

**Falconi:** We do songs rather than reproductions of their albums.

**Loose:** People who want to hear the album reproduced, it won't be.

**Falconi:** We've never been accused of doing the same set twice.

**Goldberg:** Does that keep it interesting?

**Shatter:** We have to do it that way.

**Loose:** If I was in a band that rehearsed four times a week the same fucking set, the same fucking thing, the same song, same monologue, same jokes like I see bands do, it would be no fun for me.

**Falconi:** It would be like playing pool with somebody that you knew you could always beat by 50 balls.

**Shatter:** You don't try.

**Falconi:** So what, you could play the game. It's the other way around, when you set yourself up in a situation where you're always playing against the odds. It brings out our little quirks and personality traits, idiosyncrasies and strangenesses. It's fun, we stay on the edge of it. I never like to learn a song too well.

**Loose:** There's something in life called "on the edge." That's where we are, all the time.

**Shatter:** Except we're not here.

**Goldberg:** Here in San Francisco, you've got a bunch of fans.

**Loose:** We've got them everywhere. We went out to New York for just two gigs.

**DePace:** We don't take it for granted when we go onstage here that everyone will love us.

**Falconi:** Or hate us.

**DePace:** That doesn't guarantee that we'll do a real good set. We play here a lot, so we have a lot of the same people coming to see us and they can get bored real easy.

**Falconi:** We're pretty deliberate about what we do.

**Goldberg:** Some people have called you guys the "Grateful Dead of the rock scene." Why do you think that is?

**Shatter:** We called ourselves that first.

**Goldberg:** Why?

**Loose:** It started out, basically, because we used to play really long songs.

**Shatter:** Because it was funny.

**Loose:** I called us the "Grateful Dead of the 1980s," not only because we play our songs for a long time, but because of the fact that we jam, because of the fact that we like to play long sets. I hate it when they give us a 45 minutes set. I hate it.

**DePace:** We don't even start getting going until 45 minutes, an hour. That's when we start kicking in.

**Loose:** And I compared us to that because I think we're going to keep going for years and years and years and I'd like to keep it going that way. And the Grateful Dead, they've been together 25 years, 15 years? I'd gladly play for that long in this band.

**Shatter:** Are we getting points or what?

**DePace:** Did you write that I'm drinking double bourbon?

**Goldberg:** In the song, "Live for the Depression," whom are you talking to?

**Loose:** That was the first song I ever wrote. When I said, "Play in your band and live for fame, 'cause all you're doing is playing their game," I was talking to other people who were in bands and saying what a joke the music industry is. I guess the original line was, it was just a general resentment towards people who are [trying to become] stars.

**Falconi:** Getting into new wave or punk bands to cash in and get their fame. It was just like a general resentment against people trying to hop into bands or the scene for the sake of cashing in.

**Shatter:** People like us.

**Loose:** People like us. I don't know. It's totally contradictory 'cause I'm playing in a band and I'm living for fame. Well not really. No, I'm not. If a big record company grabs you, they say, "We like you for that sound. Keep playing that sound, and we wanna hear more stuff like that, and like that, and like that."

**Falconi:** You get into music and try to formulate your own sound, and no matter what it is, you always have to deal with their game.

**DePace:** A 45-minute temper tantrum.

**Goldberg:** How do you see yourselves dealing with the music business? Would you like to be famous?

**Loose:** When we first started, I was in the band, and it was a joke, and it was fun and it was something to do. And then, Subterranean Records said, "You wanna do a recording?" and we said, "Fine," and it led up to singles, and an album. It's not so much I want to become famous. I'd like to do what I'm doing.

**DePace:** We want to do what we're doing.

**Loose:** If we make money at it, then I don't have to work, then I can support myself through playing which is cool, I don't need that much money to live on, and I could keep writing and do the starving artist crap.

**Shatter:** It's not a matter of fame or not, it's a matter of can we get more access to the studios, and equipment. There's more freedom with it.

**Loose:** There's an artistic endeavor to this.

**Shatter:** The whole thing about being famous is pretty ambiguous. Is Leonard Cohen famous? Is Tom Rapp [the former singer of Pearls Before Swine who went on to record four solo albums, three of which were released in the early '70s, and one in 1999] famous?

**Falconi:** It opens up a credit card to projects. That's all.

**Shatter:** It's all bullshit, this fame shit. Total fucking bullshit.

**DePace:** Another word for fame is popularity.

**Loose:** I would rather be popular and have people like us and come to see us than to live under the title of the elusive fame.

**DePace:** We do what we wanna do. And if people like it, fine, and if more people like it, fine, and if a whole lot more people like it, then I guess we'd be famous. But really it's just expanding your following.

**Shatter:** If it's 100 people or 10,000 people or a million, I'm not going to play different. I'm not going to sing different lyrics.

**DePace:** We don't conform ourselves to what the audience wants or anything. Okay, what can we do to be famous? What kind of pranks can we do with publicity stunts?

**Falconi:** We worry more about what can keep us entertained to keep us all together.

**Goldberg:** How have you managed to stay together for four years?

**Shatter:** Nobody in the band is like after fame or the immediate money thing.

**Loose:** Except maybe Ted.

**Shatter:** Ted is.

**Falconi:** I want to get off the couch.

**Shatter:** He's been living on a couch in our manager's office for a year.

**Falconi:** We make him [the manager] wear all this leather and stud stuff. He keeps in line. None of us are after it that bad that we're gonna go, "Okay you guys, buckle down. There's a lot of critics out there tonight, so you're going to play good, and you're gonna do it really right."

**Loose:** We just do it.

**Shatter:** If someone comes up and says, "Hey there's a lot of critics out there tonight."

**Loose:** Like Ian, our agent, when he finds out there is like so and so and so and so out in the audience.

**DePace:** Robert Christgau's in the audience, you've gotta play good.

**Loose:** Do a good show. He goes, "I want you guys to make a set list tonight." And I go, "OK Ian, alright, sure. Fuck you!"

**DePace:** We just laugh at the guy. He has a nervous breakdown.

**Shatter:** Just like we laugh at anyone who's made any demands on us.

**Loose:** Like I laughed for two days when I heard that you wanted to come and interview us.

**Goldberg:** Why?

**Loose:** 'Cause I thought it was funny. I mean after seeing everything the "Pink Section" has gone through and everything the Bay Area newspapers have gone through with their pro-punk, anti-punk, pro-this, pro-that, what's the next big trend.

**DePace:** I never believed the "Pink Section" would be interested in doing a story on us.

**Loose:** They cover all this shit that's just a flash in the pan. We're PET, punk existential terrorism. Previously exhausted talents.

**Falconi:** The thing about us is, whatever we do, it sounds like Flipper. If we do punk it sounds like Flipper. If we do funk it sounds like Flipper. If we do heavy metal slow stuff . . .

**DePace:** We can't stop other people from categorizing us, but we don't go along with it.

**Loose:** People are funny. If you actually look at them. They've got noses that stick out of their face. They've got these things that stick out of the sides of their face that let them hear audio sounds, and this thing that's got teeth and a tongue in it. I mean humans are funny. The joke of the universe.

**Shatter:** I think the fact that the "Pink Section" is going and doing an article about us is dangerous for the band.

**Loose:** In a sense it is. As long as we go, "it's dangerous," that kind of kills it out. And it's known that it's like crap, then it's fine with me.

**Shatter:** We don't need that. We've gone through an almost complete media ban for three years. If this article gets printed, I think it's very important that it is known that we are not jumping at this. We have not been sitting here drooling for three years.

**Loose:** We accept the fact that you came to talk to us, but we said, we do it on our own terms somewhat. And we want it known, and we want it said. It's like when Christgau came to write a thing, we let them know the same thing. We want it known. You're here to interview us. We got nothing to say, really, except we're doing what we're doing. We're just being what we are.

**Falconi:** Any magazine that approaches us after three years, it really typifies that they aren't in any way relevant to what's happening now. They're three years late.

**Shatter:** We understand the position of the *Chronicle*. It's just really important that our position is known too. We have been around. We don't feel that this interview will make or break us. Because a lot of people will look at this as something . . .

**Loose:** Like when I saw that story on Romeo Void, she's Indian [Native American], and all woman. I said, "What a crock of shit. So much, bullshit."

**Shatter:** We know that we have been ignored for a long time and we're not going to forget that and we're not going to like start bowing down and scraping. That's not what we're doing now.

**Goldberg:** Why do you think it might be dangerous?

**Loose:** Because. It's dangerous, in that once you start talking to the press that's like a real establishment, it's dangerous 'cause you're putting out your ideas. What we do is make music, songs, and that's the idea. And then when you to go talk to a reporter about it, you take that idea and try to translate that into language in conversation to put that idea across. And we leave it up to the reporter to be intelligent enough to pick up on all the variations of the idea that the songs have. And that's dangerous. That leaves you open to so much interpretation. Opinionated bullshit. Even positive reviews of our stuff. They make up all these insane theories about why we're doing it, man. We are not doing it because we are the most sensitive people or because we have gone through the slime and emerged triumphant. We're doing it because we do it and that's what we do and that's it, bottom line. This is not heroic, or anything.

**Shatter:** Can we get our page printed in white?

**Loose:** How did that ever happen? [The *Sunday Datebook* being printed on pink paper.] Somebody was too loaded.

**Falconi:** What about scratch and sniff? We'll put some fish oil into the printer's ink.

**Goldberg:** What do you think "Sex Bomb" is about?

**Loose:** What do you mean, what do we think it's about? We wrote the fucking song. We know what it's about.

**Shatter:** It's a celebration.

**Falconi:** Some people take flowers home to their wife; he takes songs home.

**Loose:** What do people think it's about?

**Goldberg:** What's your conception? It's about sex . . .

**Loose:** Well something like that. It's pretty basic. It's about anybody who's infatuated with any kind of sex object.

**DePace:** Basically, it's about infatuation.

**Loose:** Is it? I think it's about hot mamas in his life. Really good. Like it's about some hot mamas, that can like lay down. It's, I can go, "Baby," I said, "Baby lay down on his bed, take your clothes off and let me take care of you."

**Shatter:** When you have 10,000 people listen to a song, you have 10,000 interpretations.

**Goldberg:** That's why I was asking you what you thought it meant.

**Loose:** He likes his sex bomb, baby. What the song was about to me, was an easy bass line to rip off from somebody else who never made it. That baseline was used in the '50s on a Chubby Checker song and John Cale used it on "Chickenshit" and Jah Wobble used the same bass for a song called "Sea-side Special" on one album and "Today Is the First Day of the . . . ?" on another album. It's just a basic riff.

**DePace:** Somebody said, "It's 'Wild Thing' burnt down to a burnt pot."

**Goldberg:** How old are you guys?

**Falconi:** 34.

**Shatter:** 26.

**Loose:** 23.

**DePace:** 25.

**Goldberg:** Did you all grow up in San Francisco?

**Loose:** Fresno.

**Shatter:** Modesto.

**Falconi:** Outside Philadelphia. Ardmore, Pennsylvania.

**DePace:** San Francisco.

**Goldberg:** What made you guys want to be in a band?

**DePace?** I didn't have a choice. When I was young, I used to beat on tables and beat on anything I could. And then when I was 14, I bought my first drum kit. And the rest is history.

**Loose:** I was hanging out since the Mab [San Francisco's first and central punk club, the Mabuhay Gardens] started and I just got more bored so I started a band. I spent two years waiting. Just hanging out waiting. What actually happened was I was a longhaired Grateful Dead freak and I saw an article in the *Berkeley Barb*. Punk rock is *it* whatever, is going to do whatever and showed these pictures of all these ugly people and I said, "Oh I won't put up with this. I'm gonna be a sheep in wolf's clothing and infiltrate and change everything." And it sucked me up and I'm still being me anyway and I hate punk rock.

**Shatter:** I always liked listening to very good songs and punk rock afforded a way to become part of songwriting, I could make music without knowing anything about music.

**Loose:** That's one thing I appreciated about it. You didn't have to know shit to do something.

**Shatter:** Like I've always admired really good lyrics and I always wanted to be a good lyricist. But I never thought I was a singer.

**Loose:** I made him sing.

**Falconi:** I started playing, accordion.

**Goldberg:** What do you guys think of old-line bands like Journey?

**Loose:** I don't think about them.

**Falconi:** Are they still around? My parents still watch Lawrence Welk. There will always be a crowd of people that are unable to change and need that kind of stuff to calm them out a bit.

**Shatter:** There's Lawrence Welk, there's Journey, there's Romeo Void, Social Unrest, Code of Honor, Dead Kennedys, probably us to some people . . . There's like . . .

**Loose:** What are you saying?

**Shatter:** It's all in the same category. There's a lot of bands that are totally unknown that are in the same category as Journey. They've latched on to a gimmick, a sound, a scene and that's it. And that's as far as they're ever going to go.

**Goldberg:** How long have you been playing?

**Shatter:** Since September 1979.

**Loose:** The original name of the band was going to be Five White Guys With Dicks Bigger Than [N-words]. Print it. Oakland, sorry.

**Shatter:** Bruce came up with "Flipper Rules."

**Goldberg:** Who spray-painted "Flipper Rules" all around the city?

**Shatter:** We did it first and then we stopped. He still does. How many cans of spray paint do you have in your case, Ted?

**Goldberg:** Why package *Album—Generic Flipper* the way you did?

**Shatter:** Someone came up with the idea to market products as generic. And then these drug manufacturers got a hold of Ted told him: "Someday you can have a generic album."

**Falconi:** The whole thing with *Generic* was to provide a product to someone without any kind of advertising.

**Loose:** The next album Will be called *New and Improved Album—Generic Flipper*. The same cover with red lettering saying *New and Improved*.

**Goldberg:** Are you part of the San Francisco hardcore scene?

**Loose:** We *are* the San Francisco hardcore scene. We are the only thing that's left of the San Francisco hardcore scene.

**Falconi:** Hardcore not by style but by commitment to what we do.

**Goldberg:** What do you think about some of these other bands . . .

**Loose:** Some bands I like. I like the Wild Nixons but they broke up now. The thing that disturbs me are the bands that come out of thinking they're doing something new and they're just doing the old 1234 punk style crap. And that's the type of band that disturbs me. To me, it shows it's not trying to do anything new or create anything.

**Falconi:** We couldn't get into some of the clubs because they were worried they'd get graffiti written on the walls.

**Goldberg:** Some of you work other jobs . . .

**Loose:** We don't wanna get into it. Nobody has any regular jobs. We're kind of like illegal aliens. By hook or by crook. A little here and a little there. Odd jobs now and then. Nothing that we do is illegal or in any way out of the ordinary.

**Goldberg:** Leonard Cohen is kind of an odd influence.

**Loose:** That's just him [Shatter].

**Shatter:** He's a very good lyricist.

**Goldberg:** What do you like musically?

**Loose:** Rap, funk, Velvet Underground, classical and experimental and jazz old and new. Coltrane, horn jazz stuff, modern avant-garde, pop, real raunchy rock & roll.

**DePace:** Music that makes me move. Jump up and down and dance. Funk and some hard rock. Many different types.

**Shatter:** I like folk music. Music, you can't dance to. Music you have to listen to and cry into your alcohol. Lou Reed and Leonard Cohen. Tom Rapp.

**Falconi:** Tibetan temple bells music, rock & roll, electronic music.

**Loose:** Except for punk rock. It's so moronic. It's so easy. I hate it. It's so stupid. It's so ludicrous. It still has the same fucking three chord structure.

**Shatter:** After you hear three punk rock songs.

**Falconi:** It's like, pick a word you like and using it in every sentence for a week, and you'd probably never use it again.

**Shatter:** And then you've got to listen to New Romantic and then you gotta listen to Euro-synth, and then you've gotta listen to white funk bass and then sensitive white . . .

**Goldberg:** You guys contrast positive lyrics with negative lyrics.

**Loose:** That's the whole point of it, just to be opposite.

**Shatter:** "Life" is a political song. It's about politics. There are not standards, moralities, alternatives, to live for. There's no cause to live or die for. There is no reason, other than the fact that you're alive.

**Loose:** The thing is, I'll write one song like "Life Is Cheap"—that's the way I felt at the time. I felt like I was dealt a bad hand. But then again, I'll write something like "Ha Ha," that's just a parody of it all. It's moods and emotions.

**Shatter:** I can't see those songs as opposite. 'Cause "Life Is Cheap" is about living, trying to live for all the stupid cruddy reasons you're given.

**Falconi:** You're supposed to own this, and you're supposed to own that. Oh, you're 22, well why don't you have two kids and a credit card.

**Shatter:** And "Life" is saying the same thing. There's no reason to be alive other than to live. No one is born with an -ism or an -ist. They make that shit up and they ruin their lives with it and they ruin everyone else's lives.

**Loose:** Come on, you're the journalist. Where's your snappy questions?

**Goldberg:** Do you wish the human race didn't exist?

**DePace:** No, 'cause then we realize that we're human too.

**Loose:** Would you guys stop using all my lyrics, please. I said it first. Yeah I do. 'Cause I think the planet Earth would be a lot better place without people. But then again, the planet Earth was the only place [for people to live]. The reason I don't like the human race is because of all the boundaries and limitations that people set up for themselves. When I said in that lyric, "Ever wish the human race didn't exist and then realized you're one too." You're sitting around going, "Fuck, this is real stupid, this really sucks." And then all of a sudden you go, "Wait a second. I'm human too. I fall to all the frailties and faults that everyone else does." So you go, "Oh well." But as far as writing these types of lyrics it's to reaffirm in myself, "Hey look, we're all stuck in this shitty situation, and this planet is dying, everything is fucked up, we've got a screwed government, everything costs. It makes me keep going by writing that I hate it.

**Shatter:** Even the things you can't name, you know are wrong about the way we live.

**Falconi:** We're not just anarchists saying everything is bad. We're searching for alternatives.

**Loose:** It's not so much searching for alternatives as much as waking everybody up so that everybody realizes what the hell is going on, so we can all go "Okay, maybe just blow up the world, or maybe try to make it better."

**Falconi:** Try to make it better?

**Loose:** Why not make it worse? Why not get it over with? Either make it better or get it over with. This is purgatory.

**Goldberg:** Someone described Flipper as laughing while the world burns.

**Loose:** That's okay. At least we keep warm.

**Shatter:** If you don't laugh you cry.

**Loose:** If you don't laugh, while the world burns, you're crying while it freezes over. Most people I see writing other songs, they're bitching about it or moaning about it or crying about it, instead of bringing it to the logical absurdity, that it is. And allowing yourself to laugh at that absurdity. Which is like the thing that keeps me going. I'm sitting here, out of my mind, drinking for days on end, sitting in a room covered three feet in dirty clothes, my life's a mess, dollar in my pocket. I just have to look at myself and go, "God, you're blowing chunks to the max dude," and just laugh. Not that we don't take ourselves seriously. The lyrics are serious.

**Loose:** Just bringing it to the logical conclusion, to just show the absurdity of it all. And in that absurdity there is beauty, and there is horror.

**Goldberg:** Would you guys play a Bill Graham show? (The late rock show promoter Bill Graham was seen as an enemy of the punk aesthetic—in the Bay Area most of the punks hated him.)

**Shatter:** I hope not. Just like six months ago I wouldn't do a "Pink Section" interview.

**Loose:** I hope not. I was pissed at Bill Graham for a long time. How he started getting in on the action that had been created and started by this whole movement. But then I just thought: He's just sapping the people who want to be saps anyway. And he's just supporting the sap bands that wanna be sap bands for the sap people for his sap organization to put on shows. So I just said, "Forget it. It doesn't matter."

**Goldberg:** How do you do end up doing the same thing?

**Shatter:** You get sucked into it. We used to go: Once we start to make it, we're not going to make bands play for 5 percent, we're not going to make bands play for free.

**Loose:** And for a while we did split up the money evenly. But after a while you have to be able to depend on it.

**Shatter:** We're just lame as anybody else. We sell ourselves out, we have. You get greedy.

**Loose:** When you become a band, doing this, this interview, and any time we're playing now, we're not selling out because we're admitting it, but we're still doing it. I don't want to sap all the people for their money, but at the same time I wanna make a living. And three years ago, I would have been pissed about it. There's a fine line between the artistic integrity, blah, blah, blah, and selling out. And it's the finest line there is. It's finer than any other line.

**Shatter:** There's no line. We're still selling out. We're kissing off ideals and goals we set up for ourselves years ago.

**Loose:** Like paying every band equally.

**Shatter:** Never forcing a band to open for free or for $25.

**Loose:** Some of the bands aren't worth it.

**Shatter:** None of them are worth it. Are we worth it? No, of course not. Are we worth $2,500 for half an hour, for 45 minutes of crud. Are we worth it? No.

**Goldberg:** What happens a few years down the line?

**Shatter:** We have a history. People have been saying this shit to us for years. "Hey, you guys are really good when Bruce sings but when Will sings it's really a bummer." Or "Will writes better lyrics than Bruce." And, "Wow man, Ted is the best guitar player in the world," or "Ted can't play at all." Or I can't play bass and Steve is the greatest and the worstest. We've all heard that shit. And we all know where we are.

**Loose:** We're together.

**Falconi:** Reading the reviews, it's important to me when I read, they say Flipper really got it together.

**DePace:** Flipper's existence doesn't depend on what people's feelings are for the band. It's just what we feel we like. That's all.

**Loose:** If somebody says we're lousy, we're not gonna break up the next day. Bad reviews are a lot more interesting than good ones that say stuff like: "Lyrics like Lord Byron, man!" It's ridiculous.

**Shatter:** But it's accurate. But it's not.

**DePace:** Through it all, it's funny.

**Goldberg:** Why did you guys change your names? What are your real names?

**Loose:** Steve, Bruce, Will, and Ted.

**Goldberg:** Your last names?

**Loose:** What does it matter?

**Goldberg:** Why change them?

**Loose:** Because that's what you're supposed to do.

**Falconi:** For fun.

**Loose:** Only did it because that's what you're supposed to do.

**Shatter:** It was exciting at the time. You moved to a new place, had a new name, entered a new life. And then like there were no rules, no obligations, no past or history.

June 13, 1982

# PRIME TIME FOR CRIME

*It was in the summer of 1977 that I first heard Crime, one of the first San Francisco punk bands. I saw them at the Mabuhay Gardens, and I thought they were terrible. I liked punk rock. I had dug such proto-punk bands as the MC5 and the Stooges, and later the New York Dolls. In the mid-'70s I liked the Ramones, Richard Hell and the Voidoids, the Sex Pistols, and the Clash. But in 1977 Crime sounded like noise to me and not a good noise. Forty-four years later, I appreciate Crime. My ears and mind have adjusted; I think I understand Crime. "Hot Wire My Heart," recorded in 1976 and later covered by Sonic Youth, now sounds great. I wrote the story that follows in 1978. It no longer totally reflects my take on Crime, but it certainly captures how I viewed them back in the heyday of San Francisco punk rock. Crime singer/guitarist Frankie Fix died in 1996; singer/guitarist Johnny Strike died in 2018.*

SAN FRANCISCO—THE GIRL IN THE black leather jacket with the safety pin through the collar, the tight black jeans, silver pumps, crew cut, and eye shadow successfully duplicating two black eyes, is smashing bottles out on the sidewalk in front of the Mabuhay Gardens. It's after 1 a.m. San Francisco's finest (also sporting crew cuts) come and drag her away. But the broken glass remains.

Inside, the club is near full. Over 300 of the sleaziest of San Francisco's punk aficionados are standing around trying to look cool, draining long-neck bottles of Bud or staring blankly at the empty stage.

Backstage, the four members of Crime, outfitted in police uniforms: black slacks, wide leather belts, and light blue police shirts with police badges attached, are ready to go. A siren starts to wail and nearly everyone in the club rises to their feet. Crime hit the stage, plug into towering Marshall amps and start to play.

Nothing. No sound from the amps.

"James, there's no power!" screams Johnny Strike, the tall pasty guitarist/singer. The crowd is pressing up against the stage, frustrated by Crime's inability to start blasting. Then the sound hits, like a fist landed squarely on an unsuspecting jaw.

Crime play loud. So loud the plate glass window at the opposite end of the club shakes, tables tremble, and people hang onto their drinks. Loudness may be Crime's only musical raison d'être. This band is a literal translation of the concept "minimal." Drummer Hank Rank thumps out a simple Bo Diddley beat that is only adequate in the context of the rest of the band. Bassist Ron the Ripper coaxes a thick rumble from his amp that reminds one of the thunder of a bulldozer rolling over rugged terrain. And the guitar playing of Strike and Frankie Fix make you feel like you've been forcefully held underwater for the full 25 minutes of the set.

What then, is the appeal of Crime? What draws 300–400 fans to their infrequent gigs? The Crime pose.

Crime are pure style. Content becomes irrelevant in the hands of these image jugglers. Onstage, Frankie Fix assumes all manner of rock & roll hero stances: Elvis, Chuck Berry, Gene Vincent, Eddie Cochran, Lou Reed, David Johansen, and on and on. Though the

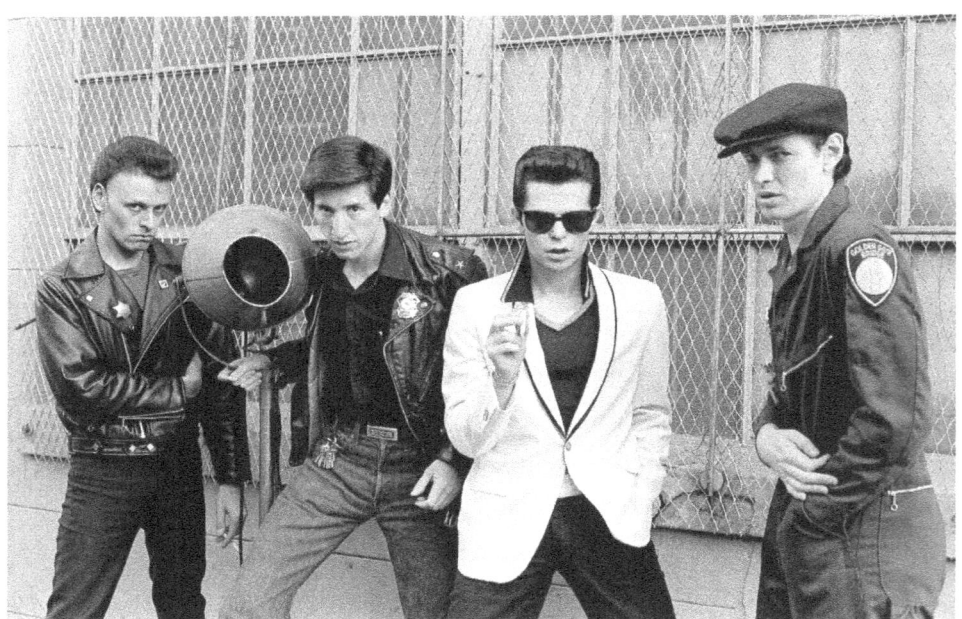
Crime, one of San Francisco's first punk bands, San Francisco, 1977.

rest of the band merely look like escaped cons in police drag, Fix at his best brings to mind every two-bit gangster you ever saw on those late-night "B" movies.

Off stage, however, Crime are at their most potent. Their press photos and publicity posters are the best to come out of the San Francisco new wave scene. Each carries through the Crime concept, portraying the foursome as arrogant rock & roll renegades. Of all the San Francisco new wave bands, only Crime landed a major item in Herb Caen's *San Francisco Chronicle* gossip column (read up and down Northern California) when the Hall of Justice formally requested that the group refrain from impersonating policemen. The group has built its reputation more on what they look like and who they can alienate, than for any real musical worth.

Their song, "Crime Wave," succinctly explains the Crime credo: "We belong to the crime wave / Nobody from your wave / We belong to the other wave / Don't care about new wave / Yea, Yea / We're from the other wave / Don't come around and try to bring us down / We're crime wave rockers with the deadly sound."

At the Mabuhay, as the band plays with a relentless anger, one enthusiast whips a water pistol from his coat pocket and starts squirting Fix. "Keep that shit up and you ain't gonna live," sneers the five-foot-five manic guitarist. The kid in the crowd continues to squirt. Fix jumps off the stage and gives the guy a kick in the chest that doubles him over. Fix remounts the stage and the band launch into "Rockabilly Drugstore," a song about, in Fix's words, "a drug store where people go and hang out and dance and the cops are banging down the door and the cops start dancing and taking drugs." The kid with the pistol recovers and resumes his liquid taunting. Fix is furious. "I'll kill you, asshole," he screams, as he leaps off the stage, throws off his Flying V guitar and leaps on the inciter. The guitar hits the floor and the neck cracks off. Hank Rank pulls Fix off the startled kid. "People got to show a little respect," mutters Fix, grabbing a spare guitar. Crime wrap up their set. No encore.

"We're known for violence and destruction at our shows," says Johnny Strike coolly, in the quiet of Crime's rented rehearsal hall a few days later. "Not that we advocate violence, it just always seems to happen when we play."

"It's alright," adds Frankie Fix, curling his lips to a sneer. Fix looks sleazy, as usual, in a white dinner jacket with the collar turned up, hair greased back Fifties' style, shades, and the ever-present cigarette dangling from his lip. "But we don't like it when they fuck with us."

Though they like to advertise themselves as "San Francisco's First and Only Rock and Roll Band," Crime's actual position in the city is that of most notorious rock & roll band. Their copped costumes have kept them in the news for much of their two-year existence. And Crime earned the wrath of nearly everyone in the San Francisco new wave community earlier this year, when they refused to play a benefit for striking coal mine workers, reportedly saying that "miners are just assholes who drive around in Cadillacs." (The group later amended that statement, according to one newspaper story, claiming that they were actually talking about railroad workers.)

Following that mine workers benefit, the group claimed that they were banned from the Mabuhay (during that three month period they referred to themselves in frequent press releases as "SF's First and Only Rock and Roll Banned") and also claimed they were denied airplay on KSAN's punk show, the Outcaste Hour. They even approached this writer at one point with a convoluted conspiracy theory that involved the Mabuhay, several radio stations, a local record store, and the West Coast editor of this very magazine. All were, they said, conspiring to freeze Crime out of the city. Yet despite these paranoid cries, Crime actually seem to thrive on their alienated stance.

"We stand apart," says Fix, lighting another cigarette as he kicks his feet onto a coffee table and sinks back into the crummy ripped couch that is the only piece of furniture in the stark rehearsal hall.

"We're the out crowd," says Johnny Strike, lounging in a dark blue jumpsuit with shiny police badge attached. "If there's one clique and everybody goes along with it, it gets real boring."

"It's like a fraternity," says Fix.

"We're antagonists," adds Strike. "We're the ones that keep everybody awake. We stick pins in people."

It was just two years ago that Crime made their worldwide debut playing a small San Francisco bar that thought it was getting the latest in disco sounds. "They unplugged us during our fourth song," laughs Fix.

The group went underground, taking up a brief residency at a San Francisco whorehouse, the Bordello, according to Strike. "It was a famous place off Polk Street," Strike recalls. "It was a combination of all different kinds of people from professional hustlers to jet set people to punks. It wasn't just a whorehouse. All kinds of things were going on. There was gambling and drug deals. It was the place to go."

Strike and Fix, who both claim to be 28, are childhood pals from South Philadelphia. Back east, they played in numerous bands together. Most were soul bands, and they are still fervent fans of Sixties soul: the Marvelettes, Supremes, James Brown, Sam & Dave, and the rest. But their band, the White [N-words], was unsuccessful. Three years ago Strike was forced to leave Philly. "I was on special probation," he explained, staring down at his hands. "They were gonna lock me up, so I wanted to get as far away as possible. I was arrested for possession of narcotics."

What kind of narcotics?

"Persian heroin and cocaine. And syringes filled with blood." Strike looks over at Fix and laughs. "It was a joke. We had these syringes filled with blood and we'd go to colleges and high schools and leave them in the bathrooms. The cops loved that."

Once in San Francisco, around 1975, this dynamic duo ran into Ron the Ripper (one-time drummer with the Chosen Few and the Lost and Found, forerunners of the Flamin' Groovies). "See, Ripper had never played bass before joining us," said Fix.

Crime went through an endless series of drummers (including Brittley Black, who went on to drum for the Readymades and who is about to debut a new band on his own, The Next). Finally, Hank Rank showed up. "Hank had never played drums before," said Fix, "But he was into it! He gave us a portfolio that was really well done. Showed pictures of him and explained what he was into. He came down, bought a drum kit, played with us and it was there. We had other guys who came down and said," Fix assumes a hillbilly voice, "You guys are makin' up your own rhythms. I been playin' 15 years and I don't know how to play this stuff. This is crazy! Bye!"

A roadie with some other band walks into the rehearsal hall carrying an amp. "I guess we better continue this elsewhere," says Hank Rank, 23, zipping up his leather jacket. We move out into the cool night air and walk halfway down the alley to a funky bar. Once inside, all eyes turn to stare at the bizarre-looking foursome.

"Let's take that booth," mumbles Fix, pointing to the darkest corner of the bar. When first questioned about their real names, over a year ago, the Crime members were resolutely close-mouthed. Today, they have come around. "We don't see any reason to hide behind phony names," says Strike. "Other bands can do that but not us."

Strike reveals he is Gary John Bassett. Rank is Henry Rosenthal. Ripper, the mostly silent 29-year-old bassist, is really Ron Greco. And Fix was born Marc D'Agostino.

"I'm thinking about changing my name to Frankie Pose," says Fix. "I don't want the record companies to think that I take a lot of drugs. We don't take that much. We're not addicts."

In conversation, the group returns again and again to their look. "It's like James Dean," says Johnny. "He had his pose, but he also broke out of that. We feel the same way. We're known for being unpredictable. We have different looks. We wear Chinese uniforms, rockabilly clothes, tuxedos, detective clothes, gangsters. The police thing is what we're famous for 'cause of Herb Caen. And it shows the authority. We consider ourselves the new authority."

What do you mean new authority?

"The new authority of rock & roll," says Rank.

"The police look is authoritarian," says Fix.

"And it's modern," adds Johnny Strike. "Everybody wears a uniform of some kind. The rock bands have their uniforms, the businessmen have their uniforms. Everybody will wear stylized uniforms in the future."

Crime have released two records during their two years together. Their first, "Hot Wire My Heart" b/w "Baby You're So Repulsive" was a rather primitive and crude effort modeled closely on the New York Dolls sound. The second, "Murder by Guitar"/"Frustration," showed much improvement although, even by the standards of the Ramones' debut album, it left much to be desired. Both records impressed the English rock press and "Baby You're So Repulsive" landed on *Sounds'* alternative chart.

It's been some time since "Murder" was released. The group has been trying to land a record contract. "But it's got to be with a record company who understand our concept," said Rank. Earlier this year, they went into the studio with Elliot Mazer (who produces Neil Young) but were not happy with the tape. An encounter with Lou Reed at a local restaurant recently may lead the former Velvet Underground front man to assume the producer's chair. According to Crime, several record companies including Sire, Radar, Capitol, and Arista have expressed interest.

The band's latest coup, however, was to be the first punk band to play a maximum-security prison. On Labor Day of this year, Crime entered San Quentin and performed for over 500 prisoners. "It was something we had wanted to do for a long time," said Rank. "We knew we'd be playing for a crowd that was really into crime."

As the prison gig approached, Crime almost got cold feet. "As it got closer," said Rank, "things we were hearing got scarier. They said we couldn't wear blue jeans or a work shirt 'cause in the event of a riot, they wouldn't want us to get shot, mistaken for prisoners. Then they told us about the no-hostage rule which is that if you're taken hostage by a prisoner, they will not bargain for your life. If he says he's going to kill you if they won't let him out, they'll say 'Fine, kill this person. We don't care. We're not letting you out.'"

According to the band, the San Quentin gig was not their best. "It was in the daylight," explained Fix, who rarely rises before 5 p.m.

"It was blazing heat," said Rank, "and they had a little speaker for a PA. And imagine, you're looking out there at a mass of 500 people and all I could see were crimes written on their faces: rape, murder, mutilation. All the disgusting side of humanity was sitting there looking at us."

Still one of the top four bands playing the Mabuhay Gardens, Crime see their current underground reputation as merely a precursor to a much more grandiose future. "We want to be the biggest band in the world," said Fix seriously. "Other bands are just content to play a small dive. They don't have as much ambition; they don't have the look. They don't have nothin'! If you've got it and you know you've got it, you'll make it."

"See, the thing is, we're a rock & roll band and we're something different to everybody," says Fix. "Some people call us punks; some people call us rock. We've been called heavy metal?! We've been called a Fifties' rock & roll band."

"They don't know what to call us," says Rank.

"We're even more than rock & roll," says Johnny Strike with finality in his voice. "We're Crime!"

*New York Rocker*, 1978

# SLEATER-KINNEY: THE BAND FROM THE END OF THE WORLD

## Sleater-Kinney speak about independence, freedom, rock & roll, and Courtney Love.

*I learned of Sleater-Kinney from Greil Marcus, who wrote a column about them in* Interview *magazine. Call the Doctor was their first album that I heard. If you've listened to* Call the Doctor, *you know how great it is—more than great. Listening to that album for the first time can make you feel like your life has just changed, and for the better. All the albums they recorded through 2002's* One Beat *are essential. From the mid-'90s into the early 2000s Sleater-Kinney were essential. They mattered like no other band mattered. I first saw them one night at the Bottom of the Hill, a club located in the Potrero Hill district of San Francisco. This was in 1997. The club was crowded but not full. Sleater-Kinney were amazing. The way singers/guitarists Corin Tucker and Carrie Brownstein's voices contrasted, the interplay of their guitars—this was life or death music, which is the music I can't live without, the music I have to hear again and again and again. I flew up to Portland, Oregon, in early 1999 for this interview, and we spoke at a sushi restaurant. It was Tucker, Brownstein, and drummer Janet Weiss. We talked for a long time. They seemed to know that I cared about their music, and they wanted to talk about it. In 2006 they went on an extended hiatus. During that time Brownstein teamed up with comedian Fred Armisen and they created and starred in* Portlandia, *the comedy TV show which won an Emmy; Brownstein also co-founded the band Wild Flag with Mary Timony, Rebecca Cole, and Janet Weiss and they released an album,* Wild Flag, *in 2011. Meanwhile Tucker formed The Corin Tucker Band and released two albums,* 1,000 Years *and* Kill My Blues. *Sleater-Kinney regrouped in 2014 and released* No Cities to Love *the following year;* Live in Paris *was released in 2017.* The Center Won't Hold *came in 2019; drummer Weiss left the group in July of that year, a month before the album was released. Sleater-Kinney currently consists of Tucker and Brownstein. The duo used three different drummers on their 10th studio album,* Path of Wellness, *released in 2021.*

PORTLAND, OREGON—WHEN I WAS IN college in the early '70s, a friend took me to a lesbian bar to see an all-woman band called Eyes months before they were written about in a music column by then-music columnist Ellen Willis, published in, of all places, the *New Yorker.*

People liked to compare Eyes to the Rolling Stones 'cause they had a striking lead singer/songwriter, Alicia Pojanowski, vaguely reminiscent of Mick Jagger, but, as Ellen Willis noted, "she projects an unmistakably female sexuality." I thought they were more like a female version of the New York Dolls than the Stones, raw and punk before the term had been coined to describe certain rock bands.

It was novel then to see a truly great band (any band, really) composed of women. Actually, novel is the wrong word. It was incredibly exciting, maybe even startling. A woman playing lead guitar? A woman drummer?

Sleater-Kinney after being interviewed in Portland, Oregon, 1999. © Charles Peterson.

At a time when feminism was still a new concept, seeing women in roles that had traditionally been occupied by men was a shock. A welcome shock but a shock all the same. In a few years, when punk would break in New York, then England, bands with female musicians would become the norm.

But at the time, it was almost unprecedented.

More than 25 years later, it seems almost wrong to draw attention to the fact that Sleater-Kinney is composed of women. Three young women. And yet after listening to their four albums—*Sleater-Kinney, Call the Doctor, Dig Me Out*, and the brand-new *The Hot Rock*—over and over and over, it seems important.

It's important because these young women—singer/guitarist Corin Tucker and singer/guitarist Carrie Brownstein (drummer Janet Weiss completes the lineup)—are writing songs from a distinctly female point of view (and because they have become role models for other women). Well, actually, that's not really what I want to say. So, I'll try again. The lyrics to Sleater-Kinney songs are written by Tucker and Brownstein. They are unique lyrics written from the perspective of Tucker, a woman, and Brownstein, also a woman.

It's hard to imagine a man writing something so moving as these lines from "Get Up."

"And when the body starts to let go / Let it all go at once / Not piece by piece / But a whole bucket of stars / Dumped into the universe. / Whooh! Watch it go! / Goodbye small hands, good-bye small heart / Good-bye small head / My soul is climbing tree trunks / And swinging from every branch."

I dealt with death last year. Dealt with it very up close.

My mother died. Of breast cancer. She was 70. It didn't happen all at once. It happened over the course of two-and-a-half months. One horrible day after another. There were days when she asked me, over and over, when would it all be over.

So I can certainly relate to the poetry of "Get Up."

And I can relate to "The Size of Our Love," with lyrics written by Brownstein, also from *The Hot Rock*:

*Our love is the size of these tumors inside us / Our love is the size of this hospital room*

Not all of what Sleater-Kinney sing about is that downbeat. The new album also celebrates independence, freedom, and community ("The End of You," "Start Together"). And early Sleater-Kinney songs such as "I Wanna Be Your Joey Ramone" and "It's Not What You Want" are punk-rock anthems.

In the beginning, way back in 1994, Sleater-Kinney sounded something like what you'd get mixing Bikini Kill and the Ramones. They wrote fierce, riot grrrl-style, feminist rants, such as the still mind-blowing "How to Play Dead." Their entire first album lasts about 22 minutes.

At first the group was a side project of Tucker and Brownstein. Tucker, who grew up in North Dakota and Eugene, Oregon, had formed Heavens to Betsy after a literally life-changing experience she had—seeing Bikini Kill perform in early 1991 while attending Evergreen College in Olympia, Washington. Brownstein, who grew up in the suburbs of Seattle and also attended Evergreen, had a similar experience at a Heavens to Betsy show and formed Excuse 17 in 1993.

The two women named the band they formed together (drummer Janet Weiss joined in 1996) after Sleater-Kinney Road, a mile or two north of Olympia, where their former rehearsal space is located.

When I drove to Olympia in late February to attend the opening show of the group's "*The Hot Rock* Tour," I took the Sleater-Kinney Road exit off I-5, expecting to find some cool spot where the band's sound took form. Instead, I found a typical suburban street lined with gas stations, fast-food restaurants, and a discount store or two.

Which makes some sense, because one thing Sleater-Kinney are about is freedom. Tucker and Brownstein sing of escaping boredom, lousy jobs, and crummy lives. By choosing to record for a relatively small independent label, by making all the important decisions about their career, by refusing to compromise to sell more records or attract a bigger audience, Sleater-Kinney have become an important band that stands for something. And playing in a rock band has allowed Tucker, Brownstein, and Weiss to experience real freedom. When I asked Tucker, who often sings with her eyes closed, if she felt free when she was performing onstage, she said, "Yeah, you are in another world and you can do things that you could never do in real life, you know."

In December 1998, shortly after the group completed *The Hot Rock*, I traveled to Portland, Oregon, where the three women now live, to meet with them. I hoped I'd get at the essence of one of the great bands of our time.

**Michael Goldberg:** In the song "The End of You," you sing, "I am not the captain, I am just another fan." What do you mean by that?

**Corin Tucker:** Well, I think that the whole song is about what you get yourself into when you're in a band like this. You realize that the dynamics of it are so crucial to the music, that who we are as people is really intrinsic to the kind of music that we write and the kinds of lives that we lead in the band. You end up realizing that you have to just give up your sense of being more important than anyone else. You have to realize that you're just like anyone else. [I've come to realize] how important they are and how much they're just like us.

**Goldberg:** But it seems like when you're in a band, it almost contradicts that because many people look at band members and idolize them, hang posters of them on their walls. You've even written about that in "I Wanna Be Your Joey Ramone."

**Janet Weiss:** I think all of us, though, were huge music fans when we were younger. We can relate to the kids who come up to us and asked for autographs. That word inspiration . . . I think that we've all had those feelings towards other musicians and still do have those feelings towards other musicians. I think we can relate to that excitement about music and being inspired by music. That's how we're similar to fans.

And we definitely try not to present ourselves as these unobtainable rock stars. We set up our own gear most of the time. We go out after the shows, and we talk to people and we don't just isolate ourselves from the people who listen to the music. I think that the people who listen to the music influence the music as well, in a weird sort of way. Definitely in a live show. But also, like on *Dig Me Out*, I think there were a lot of themes dealing with the relationship between the listener and the person who makes the music and how it's all intertwined and complex.

**Tucker:** This is kind of weird, but that whole song "The End of You," it's about the *Odyssey*. And I was reading that book when I was writing the song and it really inspired me because it's about this person who travels across the world and who has to go through all these adventures and again and again and again is tested. In some ways, what we went through—we went through a really long, hard period of time where we were experiencing this totally different life of being on the road and being in a semi-famous band. It felt to me like we were being tested and tested over and over again. And I think that one of the things that I got from that book is how important Odysseus' relationship with the other people that he's enduring all this with is. Even though he's a leader—he's like this king—he doesn't think that he's better than anyone else and always looks after people. That's something about Greek writing—you always have to remember to be humble and to be kind.

It's really hard when you suddenly hit all these big things and you're offered all these things in music, and it's really easy to not remember that there are other things that are important too.

**Goldberg:** I had another question about that same song, which was—you have the line about: "The first beast will entice us with money and fame / If you listen long enough, you'll forget there's anything else." That sounds a lot like the record business coming around. What was your experience of that?

**Tucker:** Yeah, I think that for us it's been really confusing as to what we want and how— You cannot just be in a band in this world and just play music. It's so much more complicated than that. For us, how are we gonna be able to make a decent living on it and also have enough control over what we're doing. So, looking at major labels and looking at different ways you can do that has been this complicated thing that we've had to work through. And we were approached by every major label. And I think we all learned a lot. We took it seriously and we all thought about it seriously.

**Goldberg:** Why did you decide *not* to go with a major label at that point?

**Carrie Brownstein:** I think mainly we didn't want to be taken out of the context and the community in which our band was fostered and from which we gained inspiration and support. And also, we like to have control over the things we do and to feel like people that are working with us value us for the music that we write and for who we are as people. And I really didn't get that from anybody who we talked to who was in the major-label milieu. I didn't feel like they valued us for anything more than what we could do for them.

**Weiss:** I think the major labels are sort of producing such bad music right now. The full music scene in the major market is not something we want to be part of. And I think we'd be really isolated on a label with a bunch of acts that we don't relate to, we don't like, we don't feel akin to. And I think that would be really hard for us. We'd just be alone in this sea of mediocrity. I think it's better for us to be surrounded by musicians who we admire and play shows with bands who we like and our friends' bands and people who've been supportive to us and who we want to support. I think it's so much more rewarding, and we can be more proud of what we're doing. If we kind of keep it at that level.

**Goldberg:** You brought up before being able to make a decent living. That's a problem for a lot of bands on independent labels.

**Tucker:** I also think the opposite is true, in terms of acts that are on major labels and who [receive] a smaller percentage [for each record sold]. The Artist [aka Prince] moved to his own record label because he was making such a small percentage, not because he even needed the money but for the principle of it. He wasn't making the money for it [that he feels he deserves]. And when you are on an independent label and you're making a much higher percentage [for each record sold], you don't have to sell a million records to make a decent amount of money. So it's definitely a trade-off, and it's really tricky to sell enough records so that you're not in the hole. If you're lucky enough to be somewhere in the middle, then it can work out really well.

**Goldberg:** The title track, "The Hot Rock," is pretty amazing in the way you weave your voices and the guitar parts back and forth throughout it. Can you talk about what inspired that song? And a little bit about the process of how you work?

**Brownstein:** Well, initially, actually, "The Hot Rock" was inspired by the '70s film starring Robert Redford. And it was not initially tied to that, the music that I had written. But when I was coming up with the idea for the song, I wanted to use the idea of stolen merchandise, stolen diamonds, as a metaphor for the lengths that you'll go to in love. And in the search for something genuine and the heartbreak of finding out that it's not genuine, and so that was sort of the metaphor for that song.

Often, when Corin and I sing together, I have to say it's very unrehearsed. I'll say, "Oh, I have this melody; will you sing on part of it?" And suddenly Corin will be singing on the whole song. In terms of the distribution of roles in the band, we don't limit ourselves to any set roles or boundaries. If Corin has a whole melody for the song, she might as well sing with it. And it's not really until we listen to it played back that we realize the intricacies. It's like two interpretations of one theme, practically. I also think that it makes the song more interesting.

Every song doesn't need a verse, and then a big chorus. I think we try to break away from that and use the voices as instruments as much as we can. And that song is, I think, the most remarkable in terms of how the guitars interplay and the voices on top of that. It was really surprising when I heard it back, recorded. 'Cause it's the first time you have a chance to see it happening. It's sort of that visceral—it's not cerebral at all at that level.

**Goldberg:** It's interesting because sometimes, not with every song, but sometimes the different voices, it's almost like different parts of one person.

**Weiss:** It definitely feels like that a lot of times. From just listening to it, sitting in the middle, it's really often like one is talking into the other one's ear, you know. Sort of like feeding this subconscious thought or feeling about something. It's really kind of astounding how it works. And so fragile too. You feel like if anything were out of place, the whole thing would just topple over. Everything's in the right spot at the right time, so it has this really intricate weaving together and structure.

**Brownstein:** To me, songwriting is not about a monologue. It's like a play or something where there's characters and people that interact. You have the set, the background, you have actors playing off one another except that we're not acting. I'd like to think about it as the way that the songs sort of sit in this—they're very multilayered. I think that is much more interesting, the point of interaction and communication [rather] than an oration, just standing up and saying something where it's just one of us speaking. To me, what makes it interesting is the point where they conflict or overlap.

**Weiss:** It's funny, when I was playing "Burn, Don't Freeze" [off *The Hot Rock*], 10 seconds into it, a friend said to me, "This is like two different songs being played at the same time." It's like cubism. It's like two pictures from two different angles, but it's the same thing. And you're seeing them at the same time or hearing them at the same time.

**Brownstein:** There's definitely more of that on this record than any previous record.

**Goldberg:** When did you discover that you could do that and that it worked?

**Brownstein:** For me, it was the song "Call the Doctor" [off Sleater-Kinney's second album, *Call the Doctor*]. I remember Corin was saying the chorus: "I'm no monster / I'm just like you." And I had a melody for that and I started singing it at the same time. And I remember stopping practice actually and we were like, 'Wow, that totally works.' It was definitely the first time that we had two things going at once.

**Goldberg:** So when was that? Where were you when that happened?

**Brownstein:** We were actually still in the practice space near Sleater-Kinney Road. It was during the writing of *Call the Doctor*, which was in the summer of '95. But it was that song. And then later, with "I Wanna Be Your Joey Ramone" and Corin singing the chorus. And I started going "whoa," doing that scream in the background. That was the second time where we were like, "Wow, it sounds great when we do this." And from that point on, it just became a given that there'd be certain songs where one of us would come in at certain points.

**Goldberg:** When you're in the studio, when you're working on stuff, do you still get really amazed at things that happen? Could you give some examples?

**Brownstein:** "Get Up."

**Tucker:** Yeah.

**Brownstein:** "Get Up." How that song came together. The music is very—it's deceptively simple, I should say.

**Tucker:** I remember where we were when we made that.

**Weiss:** Calvin's [K Records head Calvin Johnson] basement.

**Brownstein:** It's deceptively simple, that song. The idea [we had was that] the music [would] be repetitive and that the vocals would be the thing that made this song different.

**Tucker:** That drove it.

**Brownstein:** I think when we heard that song [played] back—

**Weiss:** I had heard the Talking Heads, what is that song? "Once In a Lifetime" [from *Remain in Light*]. I had heard that song on the radio and I was amazed. The music is exactly the same through the whole song and then it goes into the chorus. *[sings]* But it's over the same music. I was like, "Wow, that's so great, to have the vocals and the vocal melodies change the song from verse to chorus." I think we were just messing around with that idea.

**Brownstein:** Yeah, we were really excited, even in the practice space. We were excited when we had that song. Even when we just had the music, we were really excited by the way the three things—there was a really interesting drumbeat and Corin's guitar part was interesting to us.

That's what's fun about being in this band. We are constantly proud of the things that we're producing and excited by the parts that the other people come up with. It never feels old hat. And we don't have a formula, so we don't feel stuck in ruts in terms of, "Oh, this doesn't follow the structure of that one song." We give ourselves a lot of leeway, and it's exciting.

**Tucker:** And we have that leeway because we don't have to write a hit song that's gonna get on the radio.

**Brownstein:** There's no pressure, except from ourselves.

**Tucker:** Yeah. I think that's what's so rewarding about being in this band. We just like playing music. That's what's really rewarding to us. It is writing a song that we're really proud of.

**Goldberg:** I was wondering if there was a different kind of pressure. You've gotten so much acclaim and then you go in to make a new record. Do you feel pressured by the expectations of your fans?

**Brownstein:** No. I think it's more internal for us.

**Weiss:** We put more pressure on ourselves than anyone ever could. The most important thing for us is to make a record that we love and that we think is good. Of course, there's always in the back of your mind, I would love for this to be successful, and I want people to relate to it and love it like we love it. But I think if we didn't love a record, we probably wouldn't put it out. We wouldn't be happy with something until it was what we were shooting for. We're really tight-knit as far as our playing and how we feel about the band. I think it would be really hard for something external to infiltrate that. We have good communication, and we talk about stuff when things get rough and we're pretty open. We all know that we want things to work out and we have the same goals. When you have the same goals, it makes everything much, much easier, although recording was really difficult. It was a really hard record to make. Now we're so proud of it and it turned out so well, I think.

**Goldberg:** Was it hard because you were working with a new producer?

**Brownstein:** Yeah. And it [recording the album] was longer. We're used to just having a really condensed amount of time. In some ways, that's easier. You just get in there and—

**Tucker:** You don't have a choice to do it over a million times. You don't have the time.

**Weiss:** We set goals for ourselves—we want it to sound different, we want it to be a different record, we want to really concentrate on the guitars and the sounds, and I think we had our work cut out for us and got in there. We're just like, "Oh my God, this is hard." At the same time, when you look back on it, it's just worth it. You wouldn't trade that for anything.

**Tucker:** Yeah.

**Goldberg:** Live, you guys are—it's a really fun and exciting experience for people to see you. But at the same time, it seems like in most if not all of the songs, you're really trying to say something about either struggles in personal relationships or about more external things. Can you talk about what you want to convey through the music, what you'd like people to get from the songs?

**Weiss:** That's a tough question.

**Brownstein:** The only way to say what we convey through the music is by listening to the song itself. I can't say what people are getting from the song.

**Weiss:** That's why we make music.

**Tucker:** Yeah. If we could speak it or write it, we would, but we can't.

**Brownstein:** If I could sculpt it or paint it—

**Weiss:** Photograph it.

**Brownstein:** If anything, I just have to say honesty and sincerity. I think whatever comes across live, that is not contrived. And whatever comes across in the record is not contrived. What you receive from that is going to vary from the next person but hopefully it's going to be as powerful and important to you as it is to us. But aside from that, I can't really say.

**Goldberg:** I guess what I mean is historically there have been some artists—Little Richard is an obvious example—where it's almost like the emotion that came through in the records was what came through as opposed to—If you read his lyrics, he wasn't saying a whole lot in his lyrics usually. But with what you guys are doing, the lyrics are really important too. Someone could not understand English and get a lot out of your music but they wouldn't get all of it.

**Weiss:** That's good.

**Tucker:** I think that for us that we just want to do something that on every level is ambitious. I think that we've always really admired music that makes you feel like it relates to you in your life in some way. That's very important. And I think that we try and push ourselves not only with the music but in writing lyrics that seek out different meanings. I think this record, more than any of our other records, it's like looking for a kind of honesty. I really can't explain them except for in the music. It's very much—this band just writes itself. It just happens and we accept that. I think that we're lucky.

**Brownstein:** I think that art and music—I write it because I think it should contrast the coldness of modern society. And I think that's why you don't always have to understand the lyrics. And that's why our live shows are important because it is in such contrast to, often, people's lonely lives and people's technology-driven lives and the drudgery of your job. I think art it should just be in contrast to that. And I think I try to make it as full of life as possible.

**Tucker:** There's so much surrender in this world, to just surrender to the way that things are and surrender to the lack of any honesty or real feelings. I was in this office position the other day and it was so depressing how much people have to make themselves so petty and so small in other parts of the world. They have so little imagination; they have so little room to explore. In music, you can, if you want, if you're able to, you can totally go wherever you want. You can be the kind of person that you really want to be. And that is really precious, I think. And I think that's something that we think about.

**Tucker:** We just like to rock, man. *[laughs]*

**Goldberg:** What about technology? You've had a couple of songs—one on the new record and on the last one. Obviously, there's a really cold, dark side to it but there's also—basically, at this point, you can be 13 or 14 now and you can be like in the smallest little town somewhere and if you can get on the internet, you can find other people. You can find a community of people that is very different than the people where you live. And by the same token, if you wanted to, you could have a band in that town, and you could actually get your music out to people without having to have a record contract and all that. It seems like there's a very positive side along with the negative.

**Tucker:** I think the problem is that there's no group, there's no community that has to do with positiveness. It has to do with what sells, what corporate use can we get out of this technology. Our government is so uninterested in any kind of moral uplifting or cultural uplifting. Anything that has to do with art in technology is something that people have to do in an underground level, which is what I think is good about music and about technology. But I think what technology is used for in this society is for what corporate sales it can yield. I think that's what's so depressing is that we have focused so much on money in this society that we don't have enough community use of technology that can do great things. Now we have ways that anybody can make a film. You can do it in digital video and edit it yourself. You can make a whole movie really cheaply. But we don't have enough concentration on community use of it so that it would be used for that.

**Brownstein:** I think technology, in terms of the internet and computers, is very democratizing in some ways. In terms of people that are anarchists or more subversive have the same voice as . . . They can get their word on the internet. My cynicism comes in terms of the technologizing of human emotions and incorporating computer metaphors for the way we feel and the way we live. And I think that's scary. And it's reflected in our language as it becomes more and more ingrained. And I also think how people are using the internet to form cyber-communities and whatnot and to use loneliness. . . . I hope in real life, in real communities, not just virtual, in cities, that people look at what people are doing on the internet and say, "Oh, people want to be around other people," people want to have a sense of communities and town squares, and make that happen in real life. So that's my only critique of it, is that, well, it's great that it can happen on the computer, but let's change the way our cities work and you know what I'm saying?

**Goldberg:** Yeah, I agree with you. I think it's a little sad that there's a bunch of people sitting alone in rooms staring at monitors instead of being able to be together for real. I think it's really unfortunate. That is part of the dark side of this, of what's happened. On the other hand, someone can get their message out in a way that they never could before.

**Brownstein:** That's what I mean [in saying that] it can be democratizing at the same time, but . . .

**Goldberg:** Obviously, you've received a lot of acclaim for the last two albums. Did that go to your heads? How did you deal with it? Success can sometimes be harder to deal with than failure in the sense that it can throw you off-balance and just be very hard to stay grounded.

**Weiss:** Failure can throw you off-balance too, probably more than anything else. I know so many musicians who have been toiling away for years, good musicians,

**Tucker:** Yeah.

**Weiss:** It's depressing. They work shitty jobs and try to get their records put out. And it's really difficult. Although sometimes doing all the press and doing the interviews and doing the photos can be an intrusion. . . . We know that we're lucky to be able to be doing this and be successful at it and maybe pave the way for other bands like us who are trying to express themselves in a real way and keep control of their images and their lives and their careers.

    I don't think it really went to our heads at all. We still do things the same way. We're trying to be more organized, I think, and make good use of our time and try to get a little bit of help. Other than that, I think it's all taken with a grain of salt. I don't think we put any huge amount of stock in rock magazines. We read them a little cynically. Most people know why. Oftentimes, they're silly and misrepresentative. When you start reading about people you know, you start realizing, "Oh my God, this isn't right at all." So I think that we kind of take it with a grain of salt.

**Tucker:** I think we did make a conscious decision to stay on Kill Rock Stars as a way to keep things to some degree normal, so that we would be able to focus on the music and on playing shows instead of being so famous that we couldn't function as we always have functioned. We do pretty much function as we always have; we just have a little more help. We do realize we're very lucky. I totally agree with Janet. I think for bands it's much more likely that if they don't have any success, it's much harder to keep doing what you're doing. Not having any recognition, I think it's really difficult to keep going. So I think it is really good to have the recognition that we have.

**Goldberg:** Greil Marcus said last year—he was talking about Kim Gordon—and he said she has moments where she becomes free onstage in front of other people and lives a life she couldn't live on the streets or in her apartment. He said, "I think I'm drawn to extremes where what's going on in performances is not going on in that person's everyday life." And he said, "I don't know what Corin Tucker's like in her ordinary life. I mean, if she's like the way she is onstage, I don't know, I can't imagine anyone could stand to be around her, they couldn't keep up, they'd get burned." How is Corin Tucker onstage different from Corin Tucker in ordinary life?

**Brownstein:** Sweatier.

**Tucker:** Perspire more. I think that . . .

**Weiss:** I have an observation.

**Tucker:** OK, Janet, you can answer this question.

**Weiss:** I think the biggest difference, to me, of Corin onstage and Corin in real life is Corin onstage is in her own world, channeling this energy from I don't know where. But Corin in real life is very present and aware of other people around her. *[Looks to Corin.]*

You're aware of other people onstage but you are sort of lost in another character, another world or other parts of yourself. And it's really physical what happens onstage. All your energy is going into this one thing and you're exploding. Real life isn't so much like that at all. I think you're very gentle in real life and very intense onstage.

**Brownstein:** You're a monster onstage. You freak people out. You're just the voice, this big void . . .

**Tucker:** It's very intense, you know. I get used to it and I forget, but what would this be like seeing it for the first time?

**Brownstein:** Yeah, people just think you swallow them whole up there or something. It's so big. Sometimes I look over at you singing. I feel like you're getting sucked into this greater thing. And even when you talk onstage, people are always so weirded out. It just breaks down the difference between your singing and speaking. It's so different. People would prefer I talk, I think. People don't want to hear stories from you. People are always more afraid to talk to Corin than me or Janet for sure 'cause they think she's so intense—tortured and intense. I just see such victory onstage for Corin, you know. Just the height of any, the peak onstage for you. It's *the* most glorious. 'Cause offstage, Corin's just a normal person. It's kind of ethereal and it's pretty amazing. I've seen Corin perform outside of Sleater-Kinney too. But even sometimes when we're . . .

**Tucker:** Karaoke?

**Brownstein:** Yeah, like in karaoke. *[laughs]* Sometimes when Corin and I are just performing onstage, I look over. It's sort of amazing that such a voice can come out of . . .

**Weiss:** Even in practice I'm amazed. Your eyes are shut, and your veins are popping out of your neck. Carrie and I will look at each other—"Oh my God, she's gonna explode."

**Brownstein:** In the chorus of "God Is a Number," Janet and I always look at each other during that part.

**Weiss:** Oh my God, how does she do it?

**Tucker:** I think this is another thing where if I could explain it in words, I wouldn't be singing.

**Brownstein:** It's OK, we'll just explain it for you. That's why you've got to keep us around.

**Goldberg:** When you're onstage, is it really different?

**Tucker:** Obviously yeah.

**Goldberg:** Does it feel free in a way?

**Tucker:** Yeah, you are in another world, and you can do things that you could never do in real life, you know.

**Weiss:** It's also something that it's probably what you're best at. I think for the three of us, I think we all feel like we're really good at that. We're all up there doing this thing that we're good at, at the same time. It is the best freedom. You have so much confidence. There's nothing like it in real life.

**Tucker:** Yeah.

**Weiss:** Nothing like it.

**Brownstein:** There's no physical freedom like it in real life.

**Tucker:** No, there isn't.

**Weiss:** It's real power. How many people feel real power in their life, you know? Very few. And I think that's what people respond to when they come to a live show. "Wow, these people are feeling something." That's kind of life-changing. That's like every night for us.

**Tucker:** Yeah.

**Goldberg:** What does "We're the band from the end of the world" mean?

**Brownstein:** That's your line, Corin.

**Tucker:** Well, Carrie always says "we're banned from the end of the world." And I say "We're the band from the end of the world." 'Cause we are. We're just different.

**Brownstein:** You can't read into that song at all.

**Tucker:** That song is just about fun.

**Brownstein:** I don't know where that line came from. I didn't even know you sang that until we recorded it. Then it was like, "What do you mean we're the band from the end of the world?"

**Tucker:** I just think that we're . . . I don't know.

**Brownstein:** If you're gonna write these lyrics, people are gonna ask you about them. You better come up with some answers.

**Tucker:** There's always no comment.

**Brownstein:** That's your third "no comment." Janet and I aren't having any trouble over here. I explained "The Hot Rock" pretty well.

**Tucker:** You did. That whole song is just about getting wrapped up in all these changes that are happening. I'm so bad at explaining my lyrics. I don't know. I just write them. They make sense to me. And they make sense in the context of the song. The song is about how weird things are.

**Brownstein:** That's good.

**Weiss:** Let's move on.

**Goldberg:** I interviewed Courtney Love earlier this year. Did I send you what she had said?

**Weiss:** She said something about us?

**Corin:** Of course she did.

**Goldberg:** Yeah. This is what she said, and I wanted to get your response to it. She said, "Like all the Sleater-Kinneys and the Babes in Toyland and the L7s, all the people that were like our peers, gone. If they're not gone, they refuse to write hooks. And they could. You listen to Sleater-Kinney. God, these girls have good voices, they have talent, they have a pop sensibility. I hear it, I hear it, where is it? Where is it? Never comes, never comes."

**Brownstein:** Like she would know it if it came!

**Goldberg:** I say, "They still have some time, don't you think?" And then she says, "I don't think they do politically because I think they've been hypnotized, and their souls have been stolen by the males around them . . .

*[They laugh.]*

**Goldberg:** "in their punk-rock scene. Their souls have literally been stolen. They've been told you can't sell out, you can't sell out, you can't be ambitious. You can't just be a fence-sitter. You can't have all this talent, you know. You have talent and then not develop it." And then Melissa [Auf der Maur, Hole's bassist] contradicts her and says, "Well, I think they do have time." And then she says—

**Brownstein:** She sticks up for us.

**Goldberg:** That's basically the gist of it.

**Brownstein:** Well, that's why on the next record, we're gonna have Billy Corgan write half the songs.

*[Laughter.]*

**Tucker:** Our time is up!

**Weiss:** It's not even worth talking about.

**Brownstein:** It's not. I don't wanna fuel her fire. That's her opinion. We have plenty of ambition. Our ambition is to write really good music.

**Weiss:** Our ambition is not to make a million dollars. We wouldn't even know what to do with a million dollars. It's not something we even want to deal with, you know. We don't want to do the things we have to do to make a million dollars. And she does.

**Brownstein:** She's so far removed from our lives. She has no right to say that we've sold our souls to anyone.

**Weiss:** I had this exact same conversation with her. It was just ridiculous. We really aren't speaking the same language. To me, it's about playing music. I'm so proud of the music that I play. And I feel like if she had more of that, maybe she wouldn't be so worried about being ambitious and being accepted.

**Tucker:** Yeah, the sense of power that it seems like she wants has a lot to do with money and has a lot to do with celebrity.

**Weiss:** Like making it in a man's world or whatever.

**Tucker:** We were just talking about what it's like to be singing, that to me is the ultimate power. When I sing, there's *nothing* that can equal that. There's *nothing*. No amount of money can equal that. And if I can't have that, I would be miserable. If I had to in some way be singing a song that didn't give me that, something that didn't equal that, I would be miserable.

**Brownstein:** And to set out to write hooks?

**Weiss:** That's just not our thing.

**Brownstein:** Our sense of validation comes from much more insular and internal sources than external praise. She seems to be searching outward a little more than we are. That's a fundamental difference.

**Goldberg:** It seems like it'd be really hard for you guys to play something you didn't really feel, just because the performances are so intense.

**Weiss:** It wouldn't be worth it.

**Tucker:** Right.

**Weiss:** It wouldn't be worth everything you have to go through to get there, to then get there and have it be music that you didn't totally love. You'd feel like just a sham. All those spent, used-up, old rock stars. They just feel empty 'cause they're liars.

*[Laughter.]*

**Weiss:** They are. They get up and they write hooks. They get up and they play them. It's not meaningful. And eventually they're rich, and so what?

**Brownstein:** Not all rock stars.

**Weiss:** No, just the spent, used-up ones.

*[Laughter.]*

**Weiss:** Those are the ones I'm talking about.

**Tucker:** And I think that in terms of the criticism that we're not ambitious, we want to succeed, obviously.

**Brownstein:** That's bullshit, anyway. It's not like this has just fallen out of the sky. We've been a band for over five years. We work really hard. Because we're on an independent label, we have to work twice as hard as a band on a major label because we're doing half the work ourselves.

**Tucker:** And we're in control of that. And we decide, "Oh, we want to do this for publicity, we want to do this for. . . ." We call the shots. There's no label that has a path drawn for us that we decide is going to make us successful. We decide this is when we're gonna tour, this is who we're gonna tour with, this is what it's gonna look like, this is what our record's gonna look like. We're gonna get these many pressed. And we are the ones who decided we want to make a music video. We pushed our labels into it. And we want to be on commercial radio. We want to sell a lot of records, but we just want to do it on our own terms.

**Goldberg:** Obviously, you can't point to very many successful bands where they have that control. Are you aware of any?

**Weiss:** I'm sure Courtney Love has control over what she does. She probably does, and good for her.

**Brownstein:** There aren't any bands in terms of what Corin's talking about. We're trying to push the envelope.

**Weiss:** Like Fugazi.

**Brownstein:** Yeah, Fugazi sell tons of records. And they don't even do interviews. It's totally based on the fact that they are an amazing live band and write amazing records and tap into a consciousness that is still probably not tapped into too much.

**Goldberg:** One of your best-known songs is "I Wanna Be Your Joey Ramone." You've said in the past that that song was "about the ridiculousness of becoming rock stars and stepping into shoes that are larger than life." You've been put, to some degree, into those larger-than-life shoes. How do you feel now about that song? And can you talk about what was going on when you wrote it?

**Brownstein:** I wrote that song alone in a private space. I wrote the verses and the music. Corin came in with the chorus and the . . . I can't remember if I said Joey Ramone to you. Suddenly she just had this amazing chorus. It was definitely about both of our relationships to music and . . . I wanted Joey Ramone. I felt like he embodies . . . He is the entity, to me, that describes being larger than life and awkward simultaneously in one body, in his physical presence. At the time, it was just this musing. It had nothing to do with our lives at all, just this possibility that . . .

**Tucker:** We felt like we were on the brink of something. Just like that moment when we wrote *Call the Doctor*. No one knew who we were. We had just made this one record in Australia. No one had heard it, but we thought we were amazing. We were like, "Wow, this is different than anything we'd ever seen or experienced." Because we'd been in other bands.

**Brownstein:** I think that my relationship with the song is still very similar except that I . . . It's weirder to sing it. The song just comes up over and over again. It's weird to sing that song when Thurston Moore is watching your show. Or it's weird when Corin is singing something about him in the song or it's weird when I'm saying, "push to the front so you can see" and there are people pushed to the front. It's weird to have written this song that somehow almost predicted where we would be three years later. But I think that that's why that song is still fun to play . . . Because it's about how weirdly exciting and awkward it can be, and that is how I feel when I play music still. It hasn't really changed. I don't feel 100 percent comfortable in the "rock star" shoes or stance or essence. But it's fun, and I'm trying to cope with it. And *Dig Me Out* was a lot about that.

**Tucker:** I think that it is different when we—when we played that song in Central Park in New York City and Thurston Moore was there and Kim Gordon and all these people that we've idolized since we were teenagers. It's just amazing. I just feel like it's really fortunate.

**Goldberg:** Joey Ramone actually expressed the desire to get in touch with you guys to maybe write a song. Did you know about that?

**Tucker:** No. Write a song with him?

**Goldberg:** Yeah.

**Weiss:** Write a song? Who would it be about?

**Brownstein:** I wanna be your . . .

**Tucker:** Ronnie Spector?

**Brownstein:** That's interesting.

**Tucker:** That's the kind of thing that's great about this band. Because we do focus on the music and stuff, we get a lot of respect from musicians, and we get a lot of respect as writers. I think that's really important for a band of all women to be able to . . .

**Weiss:** Unlike some other women who we've discussed in this interview.

**Tucker:** To be, "Oh, we don't want you to do some physical cover [of a magazine] where you're not like, wearing very many clothes. But we want you to write a song because we admire your work." That's really important. That is a lot of power. Joey Ramone is really famous and he's a really respected musician. For him to ask us that, it's important. Ronnie Spector actually knows who we are too and invited us to play with Joey Ramone at her Christmas party. And, unfortunately, we can't go. But just the honor of having someone like that know who we are, it's really great. It's really rewarding.

**Brownstein:** So yeah, if he wants to contact us . . .

**Tucker:** Anytime Joey.

**Goldberg:** Some people have said to me that "A Quarter to 3" is the best song on the album. Can you talk a little bit about what inspired that song and how it came together?

**Tucker:** It's just kind of a love song. I think that one of the things about being in a band is a lot of times you're far away from your friends or from someone that you really care about. That's just what that song's about. I also think that it's frightening for me to write a song like that. It's really pretty, and it's really gentle and vulnerable. I think that everyone has the idea of the Corin Tucker persona as being this really frightening thing. That's something that I did really aspire to as a young woman, trying to get respect. I wanted to be intense and intimidating onstage because I wanted people to take me seriously. So, I think that as we get older and we realize that those kinds of roles and characters and stereotypes actually can hold you back, I think we have to let those go and show other parts of yourself that do happen and that are different than just the angry songs I used to write.

**Goldberg:** Do you feel less angry than you used to?

**Tucker:** Yeah. I think that once you get older, you change. And I think that having the success that we've had in this band has *really* been important to me as a human being, just to feel like I've really had a great life. I've been lucky. And I think that that has just made me a much happier person. Definitely.

**Goldberg:** When *Time* magazine wrote about you guys—a publication that reaches, I don't know, seven million people or something, some huge amount of people . . .

**Brownstein:** And then we sold seven million records, right?

**Weiss:** It reaches seven million 45-year-old men.

**Goldberg:** Here you guys are on a small label, and basically they dissed you. Did that hurt, or did you not care?

**Weiss:** It was fuckin' bullshit!

**Goldberg:** I couldn't comprehend why they would write about you unless they thought—why draw attention to you if they didn't think you were good?

**Weiss:** The funny thing about it is we were in a gas station, we were on tour and we were in a gas station. The guy who came with us to sell our T-shirts was like, "Oh look, here, you're on *Time* magazine." "Oh really? Wow, look, we're on *Time* magazine. What does it say? Oh, God, that's horrible, get back in the car." Then we drove to the next town.

**Brownstein:** We have nothing to do with *Time* magazine. It's so far removed from anything. I don't even read that magazine. I don't respect it.

**Tucker:** That magazine is the most conservative, Republican thing.

**Weiss:** It's terrible.

**Brownstein:** It doesn't reach anybody we want to reach.

**Weiss:** It's like *People* magazine for old men.

**Tucker:** I think that that's part of the grain of salt that you have to look at the press with. Some people are just bitter. With the amount of attention that we get and the amount of acclaim or whatever, some people are just gonna react to that as like, "Oh, they're not so good."

**Brownstein:** Part of the media machine. They just wrote about it because everyone else was.

**Tucker:** Right. Everyone was writing about us at that time.

**Weiss:** It was kind of a phenomenon.

**Tucker:** And so, they had to write about it, but they had to kind of dis it.

**Weiss:** You can't expect them to understand it.

**Brownstein:** We don't write for them anyway. Our music isn't for . . .

**Weiss:** You would hope that your peers would understand it. There are a lot of really good writers out there and hopefully they will convey some of the complexity of your music.

**Brownstein:** Yeah, they simplify it a little bit.

**Weiss:** The *Time* magazine—we just kind of chuckled and kept going.

**Goldberg:** Generally, dealing with things that people write about you, did you have to build up a wall or something?

**Tucker:** Oh yeah. Because if you inhale all the things that people write about you, it's really upsetting. And I think you just have to distance yourself from it. Journalism in general is its own world. It's not my world. And writers do that because they themselves have their identity and their ego is at stake, the way they write. And you have to look at that and realize that that's part of it.

**Brownstein:** No discourse on the music will ever be more important than the music itself. So that's just how I have to think about writing.

**Tucker:** In 20 years, the music will still be there, and what people said about it is gonna be lost.

**Brownstein:** Or separate from it.

**Tucker:** Yeah.

**Goldberg:** What's the "endless race" that you don't wanna get caught up in?

**Brownstein:** I mean in relationship to that song . . .

**Tucker:** Which song?

**Brownstein:** "The End of You." I'm just talking about the endless race, whatever is the norm, whatever pressure [you] feel to conform to certain lifestyles or to what I choose as my job or who I choose to love or who I choose to associate myself with, how we as a band choose to navigate our destiny. Sort of this endless race and constant suggestions and implications by society or friends or parents to do anything. And I'm just saying it's difficult and I would hope that I can make decisions and live my life in ways that aren't just going in this sort of nonstop race, I guess. That's what that line's about. It's just weird. *[laughs]* You've gotten asked harder questions about your lyrics.

**Goldberg:** In one of the things I read, you talked about going to Europe and doing interviews before people had seen you play. People asked a lot of political questions about the band, and then when they actually saw you play, they learned that Sleater-Kinney is also fun. Do you see yourselves as a political band in certain ways? Do you see yourselves as subversive in certain ways?

**Tucker:** I think that we see ourselves first and foremost as musicians. That's our goal. But I think the communities that we have come out of are political and subversive in some ways. The music community that we've come out of is opposed to a corporate lifestyle that values selling a lot of records over actually having the music be worthwhile. Because we've come out of that, that nurtured us as musicians and songwriters. And we've been growing all these years, getting more and more complex and working on it. And I think that's political.

**Brownstein:** A lot of people ask how this new record is political. In a lot of my interviews for Japan, people are looking specifically at the lyrics. But it is political to not be part of a corporation, to be working for an independent label and to be working for yourself. And it's political to be a woman in a band and not to sell your music based on your image, or to be anyone in a band and not sell yourself based on an image. And it's political to sing about—even as a woman talking about the commodification of your lives or the commodification of love or even just singing about sex or love—those things are political in themselves, because often they're not sung about.

**Goldberg:** Or they're romanticized in a way that's completely removed from reality.

**Weiss:** I think to me there's nothing in politics that could equal what you can convey emotionally and spiritually through music. To me, music is so much more powerful than politics could ever be. Politics is such a tiny part of music. But music can make such a difference to people, more so than politics can. Although to some people, politics is the main focus of their life. For us, music is.

**Goldberg:** If a band is saying some meaningful things, and they're playing to an audience that hears those things, and some members of that audience maybe change a little because of that, and maybe change their lives slightly because of what they hear—maybe that's a social impact.

**Weiss:** Yeah. I guess political to me is a smaller meaning than what that is. That to me is bigger.

**Goldberg:** That was really what I wanted to ask about.

**Tucker:** I think that all of us were affected by different bands when we were young. But I think that we were changed by bands that we really admire. For teenagers in America, who can we look up to? Our politicians? Definitely not. No teenagers look up to politicians. A lot of kids look up to musicians. I certainly did. I thought they were the only adults I could trust. They were the only adults that were in any way honest. So, I think that is important. I think that we see that as important and we see young girls who are interested in our music or come to our shows, that they are impacted by three women who are in charge of their own lives. That makes a difference.

**Goldberg:** What do you think gave you, particularly early on, the confidence to believe in yourselves? Where'd it come from?

**Weiss:** That's kind of a complicated question. Obviously, our families must have somehow. I come from a family, there's three sisters, and no one ever told us we couldn't do things, or we weren't smart or we weren't talented. We were always nurtured as capable, smart people.

Unless you're told you can't do something, hopefully you're gonna feel like maybe you can. I didn't have a lot of role models as far as women drummers went. All the drummers in bands were males. I think I just thought, why not? Why not me? I could do this. But I'm not sure where that came from. I think partly it just comes from inside. It's like you as a person making a choice for yourself to do something that you really want to do, and just having the guts to try it. And hopefully getting reinforcements along the way. Like, "Oh, you're good, you could really do this." That's what we mean when we talk about the communities that we grew up in musically, having a lot of reinforcements from other people, and for me, there were some other women drummers in that community. We sort of stuck together and grew up and learned how to play and went through our bad times, as far as music goes, together. I've been in all-women bands since I started playing and it's really supportive in a way, like, "OK, we may suck now but we're gonna get better. We're gonna keep trying," to where now, we don't think that about ourselves. We know that we're good.

**Brownstein:** Do you want answers from all of us?

**Goldberg:** Anything to add to that?

**Brownstein:** Being in Olympia or being in a place where the focus is on your creativity and on your imagination and not on your skill at the beginning. I think that's important not to have the focus be on how many scales you can do on guitar, how many notes you can hit in terms of your voice. If you're hitting the right notes, how many drum fills you can do. That might be your goal when you're a couple of years down the road but when you start out, you want people to be like, "Yeah, you could play a show even though you've only played drums for a week." Or, "Yeah, you should be in a band, even though you can only play one chord on guitar."

**Weiss:** I think we all did that. I think we all just were thrown into performing live and being in bands right when we started playing our instrument. I was on tour within three weeks of playing the drums for the first time. You just don't have time to really stop and think. You go, "OK, I'm gonna do it, I'm gonna try and make my mark and I'm gonna try and make it as much like me as I possibly can," even though obviously we would know that you're not accomplished after a month of playing. Blisters all over your hands. I'm not technically good at this but hopefully I can say something. You're trying to express yourself and hopefully you have people around you who aren't gonna slam you for that, who are gonna nurture you and tell you it's OK.

**Brownstein:** Yeah, and you don't have to have a record out to play a show. You might not even have a full band yet. Sleater-Kinney—just from the fact that we don't have a bass, we never thought that was weird, we never thought that we should wait until we had a proper arrangement. Same with Janet's other band, Quasi. Both these communities—Portland and Olympia—people are able to step outside of the confinements of normality or whatever is considered traditional to express themselves. So, I think we're all lucky to have eventually found ourselves in these communities. I think other people are more isolated. You do have to have the confidence somewhere in you and hopefully that's fostered by other people at some point.

**Tucker:** Yeah, I think that's really crucial that just as soon as I started playing music when I was 18, there were all these people that completely encouraged me and wanted to put out a record even though I had played four shows. And they were doing that for all these other people in the community too. You were part of something that was about encouraging this underground, that you wouldn't have to rehearse for two years before you cut your first LP and all this music-industry crap that just makes sure that no one interesting ever gets anywhere.

**Weiss:** We were lucky that we didn't all start playing music in London where . . .

**Brownstein:** Or in LA.

**Weiss:** . . . where your first show there's 20 journalists there ripping you to shreds. And you have to have your image and your clothes and your band and everything's got to be professional. To me, that's no fun. That takes all the fun out of it and all of the growth process and the festering of your personality coming out in your music. And learning how to really say something with your music is just destroyed. And I think that's why a lot of the music that comes out of London or LA is really generic and really fad-oriented. People aren't expressing themselves. They're just trying to succeed right away. We've all been playing for a while now. We've learned how to express ourselves over all this time.

**Goldberg:** Is there still a musical community here that you feel part of?

**Weiss:** There definitely is, although I was just talking to my friend who is an amazing musician—she was in Calamity Jane and she's been in a million bands—about how a lot of the musicians here right now haven't seen that much success and are regrouping or are in between bands. I think the '90s—'93, '94 in Portland—was an amazing time for music. There were just so many good bands. And all those people who still live here are getting their new bands or trying to muster up the confidence to try it again after having some heartbreak. But you go to a show, there's tons of musicians there who are really interested in what you're doing, and everyone talks and works together, if they can. Have shows where we have our friends play. I think it's real important for us to give bands who are starting out a chance to play a big show and come on tour with us.

**Goldberg:** Will you be able to do that? Bring a band you like on tour?

**Weiss:** Usually we do like maybe five or six shows with different bands, and they're usually people we know and people who we admire. We rarely play with bands that we never heard of. That's like something that we can do and so we use that.

**Goldberg:** When you tour other parts of the US do you still do that?

**Brownstein:** Yeah.

**Goldberg:** What are the things that you would like to achieve as a band?

**Weiss:** Making another good record. Writing the next record.

**Brownstein:** Writing good songs. I think we're gonna have some more travel opportunities. We just licensed our record in Japan, so we'll get to go there. And Australia, maybe South America. Travel is always fun, and it's interesting to see how people relate to your music when there isn't a shared language. I think right now we've so exceeded my expectations in terms of where I thought we would be that I'm very happy with how things are right now. There's not this ultimate, "Oh, when we make it onto this or make it onto that." As long as it's fun and we continue to be inspired by each other and by outside influences, then that's all I can hope for. And hopefully the next record will reach more people than the last one did—that's always a goal, I think. It's hard when you can't just say, "We want to have a number one song." That's not our world. *[laughs]*

**Weiss:** We just think, "Oh, we want to have a successful tour. We want to go to Europe, and we want our record to be well-received." It's kind of organic. There's no big master plan to Sleater-Kinney at all.

**Brownstein:** Yeah, just as long as we're still enjoying it. That's what we hope for.

**Weiss:** Trying to stay healthy and get along and communicate—really important.

**Goldberg:** Would you like to sell a million records?

**Brownstein:** If it can happen the way we want it to.

**Tucker:** If *Kill Rock Stars* could sell a million records, it would be excellent, it would be so great.

**Brownstein:** Like where Janet was talking about the mediocrity of mainstream music, and I think, "Wow, there needs to be a Sleater-Kinney," though I wouldn't want there to be another Sleater-Kinney. I mean, I wouldn't want there to be an imitation of Sleater-Kinney infiltrating the mass market. I feel like there is a need for our music, not only for ourselves but for other people. I think what we do is important, and I would love people to listen to us instead of to Sublime or Green Day, or something. But you have to do it on your own terms, and those terms aren't really available to us the way the industry is set up. So, we'll push and work as hard as we can and hopefully that will reach enough people.

**Tucker:** It's like the song "Get Up." I'm so proud of it. I think it should be a number one song. I think it should be on the radio. But that's because I have my own view of music—that's what it is. I'm saying I wouldn't want to have to write a song different than that in order to get on the radio. I'm really proud of it artistically and I think it should be on the radio.

**Weiss:** When you look at what's on the radio, there's no way they're gonna sandwich us in between the Cherry Poppin' Daddies and—

**Brownstein:** "Zoot Suit Riot."

**Tucker:** We are just intrinsically weird, you know. And it's better to be who you are and not fit in everywhere than to try and fit in everywhere and contort who you are. That's just true about life in general. Maybe that's hard for some people to do but I think that you have a much more interesting life therefore.

**Goldberg:** Before, if you go back to like 1990—I think "Smells Like Teen Spirit" got on the radio maybe '92, the end of '91—but when that happened. . . . Before that happened, radio was totally different, and it really didn't seem like Nirvana would fit. Then suddenly everything shifted for a relatively brief time, and radio was different. Now, radio is right back where . . .

**Tucker:** It totally is.

**Goldberg:** The top 10 albums are so depressing—Celine Dion and Shania Twain.

**Weiss:** It's really depressing.

**Goldberg:** But the fact is that things do change. It doesn't stay the same.

**Tucker:** It's yucky.

**Weiss:** Yeah, you never know when it's gonna change, either. That's why I feel we do what we believe in, and then if things change, they change and that's great. But if they don't change, we still can be proud of it. We don't have to feel like we really tried to get on the radio, when maybe getting on the radio is completely out of the question. It's not something I would even want to try for. If it happened on our terms, that'd be great. And maybe even other bands who are actually singing about something could get on. I don't feel like a goal of ours is to change the way pop culture is. I hope that people can see it and relate to it and realize that what we're doing is really human. But I don't expect that to happen. I think we'd be bummed out all the time if we did.

**Tucker:** Totally.

**Weiss:** Because that's depressing. When you actually start thinking about it like we are now, it is really depressing.

**Goldberg:** There are a lot of people all over the place who relate to what you're doing.

**Brownstein:** Yeah, and that's really rewarding.

**Weiss:** Yeah, and there are a lot of other bands that are doing similar things. They're just not the ones that are on the cover of *Spin* magazine.

**Goldberg:** But they're still doing shows.

**Weiss:** Yeah, and they're vital, and they comprise a music community that we're part of, and we're really happy to be part of it.

**Goldberg:** What's the biggest challenge for you, being in this band?

**Tucker:** I think there are many challenges. That song, "The End of You," is like, "There is always a new challenge." The biggest challenge, I think, is to remain connected to, and to communicate with, each other. When we talk, things are fragile, in a way. . . . It's like this three-legged stool, and if one of the legs drops out, it'll fall over. And I think that we have to always be aware that we have to be honest with each other in order for the music to work. It's not like we could pull it off if someone was disconnected from the group.

**Brownstein:** Also there are other challenges we've talked about in this interview. The industry as a whole, the music industry—those obviously are challenges that we've talked about. I think definitely, though, Corin's right. Our biggest challenges always come on an internal level or personal level. Those are the things that once they fall apart, it's a domino effect that happens after that. We all try to make decisions in our lives to have this be something that is important to us and that has longevity and is fulfilling. But also at the same time to be able to make space so that there's other fulfilling things that can take up in our lives aside from music, which is difficult also.

**Goldberg:** I was going to ask you about the fact that you each are involved in other musical things. Do you feel like that actually adds to Sleater-Kinney, or do you feel that that just happened because it happened?

**Tucker:** Well, I think that all of us love playing music. You realize that if you do only one musical project, in some ways you have your role in that band and that's kind of what your role is. But if you go and do a different musical project, your role is different. And I think it's important for a musician to challenge themselves and to have a more complex musical life. It's good for you to be forced to do different things, I think.

**Brownstein:** And it's fun.

**Tucker:** It's really fun.

**Weiss:** And it makes you appreciate what you have a lot more.

**Tucker:** Yeah.

**Weiss:** I was in Quasi before I was in Sleater-Kinney so it's a little different for me. But nothing makes me appreciate Sleater-Kinney more than being on tour with Quasi for six weeks. I'm like, "Oh, I can't wait to get back." It's really an honor to be able to play with different people. Like I say, you are trying to express yourself and we are all multifaceted people and really different people. And I think that playing with other musicians allows us to express other things about ourselves and learn other things about them and bring it back to this band and be a better player, really. And maybe learn how to communicate in a different way. Kind of keeps you from getting in a rut, I think. Keeps us feeling more excited about the band.

**Brownstein:** It's good to be able to leave and come back to something, no matter what you're doing when you're leaving.

**Tucker:** You don't want to feel trapped.

**Weiss:** Yeah.

**Brownstein:** Whether you're playing in another band or traveling or painting or reading, whatever. It just brings a perspective that you can't have when you're entrenched in something 365 days a year. And I think also your writing becomes really self-referential and you're writing about touring or you're writing about playing guitar. Jesus, that's gonna get old.

**Weiss:** Write a song about bar chords.

**Brownstein:** So it's good for that, if nothing else.

**Weiss:** That's true.

**Goldberg:** Are there things out there that you find of interest right now in music?

**Weiss:** Built to Spill. Always my answer, my stock answer. They're sort of my modern-day heroes, I would say. A band that calls the shots, makes music that's really meaningful and emotional and pertinent—to me, at least. Exciting, moving music. And they're on a major label but they don't do anything they don't want to do. They tour however much they want to. They don't make videos. They obviously aren't into image. It's just the music. It makes me feel good about myself. It's like when you fall in love with someone not because of how they look but because of who they are, which is what you would always hope to do but which rarely ever happens. And it's like you feel good about yourself. "Oh, I love this thing, I love this band, I love these people because of who they are and the music they're making, not because of anything else," which feels really good. I can say more. Belle and Sebastian I've been listening to a lot. Another band from a small, supportive community. Sort of insular, not worried about what anybody thinks, doing their own thing, and everyone else is having to adapt to them and change how they think about what a band is supposed to be, and what a band is supposed to do. They're setting the rules, which I think is really interesting. And of course, I listen to Elliott Smith a lot.

**Tucker:** I think we were talking about a bunch of the records that I like when we were walking over here. I think the PJ Harvey record [*Is This Desire?*] is really one of the most . . .

**Brownstein:** And the Cat Power record [*Moon Pix*].

**Tucker:** Cat Power and Solex [*Solex vs. the Hitmeister*]. Just a lot of women who have made records that are really incredible that I'm really inspired by, that are just testing the limits of what can be done. Solex is amazing. She plays the keyboards. She has all these different characters and voices going on. She's really different.

**Brownstein:** She has these different characters, and every song is named Solex something . . .

**Tucker:** I love the characters.

**Brownstein:** It's like in third person. "Solex All Licketysplit."

**Tucker:** "Solex in a Slipshod Style." I really like the idea of women writing records where they are all these different people. And that's what we were talking about.

**Brownstein:** The PJ Harvey record is like that too.

**Tucker:** Yeah.

**Brownstein:** The scope of that record. It's so big. It's bigger than any other record this year, I think. It's so vast and beautiful.

**Tucker:** It's really one of the only mediums—art is, in general—that you can explore and test the boundaries of identity. I think that's really exciting.

**Goldberg:** Other bands that you're into?

**Tucker:** There's Flinflan, Hovercraft, icu.

**Brownstein:** They're from Olympia.

**Tucker:** They're really amazing.

**Brownstein:** I've been listening to this woman Edith Frost, who's on Drag City. I just heard her new record [*Telescopic*] and then I heard the record before that, *Calling Over Time*, I think it's called, or something like that. And I thought her music was really beautiful, like what Liz Phair should have been. So much more soulful and interesting. What else have I been listening to? I don't know. I definitely clocked a lot of hours with the PJ Harvey record this year, I have to say. I've been listening to a lot of classical music actually. I'm just nerding out. I spend a lot of time at home listening to classical music.

**Tucker:** I like Neutral Milk Hotel a lot and I think they're another band that defy any reason or any kind of normality at all.

**Goldberg:** That record, *In the Aeroplane Over the Sea*, was incredible.

**Tucker:** Yeah, it's really good. They definitely have no idea of what they should be. They get up there with a weird saw and all these weird instruments and stuff. I think that's cool.

**Brownstein:** I listen to that Calexico record a lot. It's called *Black Light*. They're from Tucson, and I really like that record a lot. That's another record—a marriage of a lot of sounds and styles.

**Weiss:** I've been listening to the Pastels a lot.

**Brownstein:** Oh yeah, that's a good record [*Illumination*] too. Their remix record [*Illuminati*] is really good.

**Weiss:** Yeah, it's great.

**Brownstein:** They're a great band.

**Goldberg:** How long do you imagine Sleater-Kinney can go on? Can you see into the future, 10 years from now?

**Weiss:** Let's pick a year now.

**Brownstein:** It's so nice to be able to say that we'll be around for the millennium. It's so easy to say—yeah, through the millennium probably.

**Tucker:** Oh, we're gonna move through into the next century, actually.

**Weiss:** I don't know. It's not really the kind of thing you think about when you're in a band. Like maybe if you're getting married or something, you think about that kind of longevity. But I think we want to be able to make records for as long as we want to, and hopefully that's viable, that we have the resources to do that. If we still really want to do that, I hope we can do it. And I would imagine we could make that happen.

**Brownstein:** We have more songs in us.

**Goldberg:** You see being musicians as what you're gonna do with your lives, right?

**Brownstein:** That's been the hardest thing for me, I think, this last year, is having to see that as my life. It goes against a lot of internal urges and pressures, I think, and external. I mean, I love playing music more than anything but to accept that. . . . To just actually say what you do is, "Oh, I'm an artist," is scary, but it's also great. I'm so lucky to be able to do what I want to do and what inspires me, and not come home from a really horrible job and be so tired that I don't even have the energy to do something creative. Yeah, sure, we see ourselves as musicians. It's hard not to, I guess, at this point.

**Goldberg:** So, whether Sleater-Kinney goes on for years to come or not, one way or the other, you all are going to still be playing music.

**Tucker:** I think Sleater-Kinney will go on for years.

**Brownstein:** Forever.

**Weiss:** As long as I'm alive.

*[Laughter.]*

**Tucker:** I think we'll do other things, like we always do, and hopefully come back to it.

**Weiss:** I'll just wheel myself up to the drums.

*[Laughter.]*

**Goldberg:** Did both of you have to fight against some of the things that you're talking about in terms of just being able to accept doing this?

**Brownstein:** No, not at all.

**Goldberg:** Or was it easier for you to just accept it?

**Tucker:** I knew. I've always known. I wanted it for a really long time. I just think that no matter if I have to make money in a different way, like if I have to work a crappy job, inside I've always thought of myself as . . . Being a singer is like your secret dream. So when you're onstage, it is this secret [you're] sharing with everyone else. That's part of it—it's really important to me. And I would always want to do it.

**Weiss:** *[Laughs.]* I'm just thinking about the drummer's secret. It doesn't sound as alluring.

**Tucker:** At her desk . . .

**Weiss:** It's like what I feel like I was meant to do, for now. That could change eventually.

**Brownstein:** I've always been meant to be on the stage.

**Weiss:** For now, I was born a drummer. I'll be a drummer 'til I die. We're all really different people. We have lots of different ideas about who we are. I think that makes it real interesting and creates tensions that make the music more dynamic.

**Brownstein:** Our next step is to make up shirts that say like, "Drummers don't grow old, they just . . ."—and then it's like a sexual innuendo. That's our next concept.

*[Laughter.]*

**Goldberg:** Are there any of the other songs that we didn't talk about that might be interesting for you to discuss?

**Tucker:** It's so much easier for people to listen to it. It's obviously hard for me to talk about my lyrics and describe them in any other context. Sometimes they really do only make sense in a sonic way. If you're speaking them, it's like, "What does this mean?"

**Weiss:** Like when someone tries to talk about their dreams, you're like, "Oh yeah, that makes a lot of sense." It's so stream-of-consciousness. And I think these two happen to write lyrics that—even when you read them without the music—actually mean something and convey something. It's not completely emotional and it's not completely cerebral. It's like a combination of both. But obviously with the music is the way you're supposed to be experiencing the lyrics.

**Brownstein:** Corin has a voice where she could really be singing, "Oh, this glass is half-empty, we're sitting at the Japanese restaurant," and the way she sings it could make you cry. I tend to intellectualize it a little bit more. And I think to give Corin credit, to give her a break for not being able to explain her lyrics, it is really so much about the delivery. Corin writes amazing lyrics, but it is the essence you get from the song. It's not reading line for line and trying to analyze what everything means. This is what I get when I sit in my room and listen to this song. Or this is what I get when I watch Sleater-Kinney live. You can't look at everything individually and dissect it like that to understand our music.

**Goldberg:** I know. I mean a lot of the questions that I've asked you I'm trying to . . .

**Brownstein:** I'm not criticizing you, I'm just saying in general.

**Goldberg:** I'm fishing around trying to find something that will trigger one of you to say some interesting things about what you're doing, who you are, and what you're about. I could write what I get from all the songs but the whole idea of this is to . . . But I certainly understand if you don't feel like there's any point in trying to explain something that hits someone emotionally when they hear it.

**Brownstein:** I'm just trying to illuminate the difference between—giving Corin a break for not being able to explain cogently.

**Tucker:** We appreciate that you talk about the music.

**Brownstein:** Yeah.

**Tucker:** We appreciate that a lot.

**Brownstein:** Yeah.

**Tucker:** Because that's what we're interested in talking about, trying to talk about. All we can do is try. I think in general this record is really different from the stuff that we've done. And I think that sonically we try to have more layers of sound and different sounds, things sounding different from each other. And I think lyrically, we try to write with different emotions and everything and reflect the sonic differences that we were going through as well.

**Goldberg:** Did that producer challenge you? Did you feel challenged?

**Tucker:** Yeah. I think it was more we knew what we wanted. And we went into it wanting something really different.

**Brownstein:** And the songs dictated it to sound differently anyway.

**Tucker:** Yeah.

**Weiss:** He did challenge us, especially on the takes of the songs. He pushed us in that way.

**Brownstein:** Vocally.

**Weiss:** Vocally. And getting the guitars—working for the extra four hours to get the one guitar to sound the way we knew we wanted it. But when you get in there, you just start to chomp at the bit.

**Tucker:** I think what's true about us is that we're really a live band. We love to play live. And some bands aren't like that, but we really are, so I think in some ways it is difficult for us to record for so long without having any audience.

**Weiss:** And have to play the same song 10 times in a row. It's not something we're used to.

**Tucker:** Yeah, it's hard.

**Weiss:** It was hard, but like I say, it was also really rewarding to listen back to it and be like, "Wow, that's the best we ever played that song." To get us all playing at the same time the same ways without an audience is really tricky.

**Goldberg:** Was most of it all of you playing at the same time?

**Brownstein:** Yeah.

**Goldberg:** Was there very much overdubbing?

**Tucker:** No, most of it was live.

**Goldberg:** Are there any producers or musicians that, at some point, you'd like to work with?

**Brownstein:** I don't know. Especially producers right now, I can't even think. We haven't really started writing new songs for the next record. It's hard to say what would be good for our next batch of tunes.

**Tucker:** We did a lot of guitar stuff on this record. And maybe for our next record we would do something that had even more instruments.

**Weiss:** I'm gonna play steel drums on the next record. *[Laughs.]*

*Addicted To Noise*, February 1999

# THE NEW LOOK BEHIND KSAN'S NEW SOUND

**No longer in "Complete Control," KSAN's disc jockeys spin a format of "Silly Love Songs" as Metromedia attempts to boost the station's ratings with some new faces from Los Angeles.**

*In 1979 I learned that KSAN, the once influential progressive rock radio station, was undergoing disturbing changes. Executives at Metromedia, the company that owned KSAN, were changing the format and firing staff. Sources at the station thought it was a story that needed to be told. I agreed with them and so did my editor at the* San Francisco Bay Guardian. *I had grown up on underground radio, the eclectic approach to radio pioneered by onetime Top 40 DJ Tom Donahue at KMPX in San Francisco before he moved to KSAN. I had met Donahue years earlier when I was friends with one of his sons and had spent time up at their house on Mount Tamalpais. What was happening at KSAN deeply disturbed me. By 1979 KSAN was a far cry from the freewheeling hippie approach to radio, and it was no longer particularly influential. The once free-form progressive format had been replaced by a corporate radio-by-the-numbers approach at numerous other stations around the country. Still, at KSAN the DJs had managed to retain lot of freedom, and they played a lot of great music. As I researched the story and listened to the station, it was clear that those days were gone. Though I didn't know it at the time, the changes at KSAN marked the death of progressive radio.*

THINGS HAD NOT BEEN GOING well for Richard Gossett. For more than a year. KSAN's star disc jockey had been fighting with KSAN management over what made for "good radio." Gossett wanted complete autonomy (a KSAN tradition for its entire existence as a rock station) over his show. Program Director Abby Melamed wanted Gossett to work with the first "format" ever introduced at KSAN. As Gossett told a reporter from the San Rafael *Independent Journal* last December. "For seven years I could walk into the station with anything in my hand and be able to play it. Now it doesn't matter if a new record comes out. It isn't a new record until it's been approved by the programming department."

Put simply, Gossett wanted the freedom to play the Clash's "Complete Control." Abby Melamed wanted him to play Paul McCartney's "Silly Love Songs."

"It was like a collision course," Gossett recalled recently. Last fall, Melamed moved Gossett from the 6 p.m. to 10 p.m. slot, which he had held down for more than seven years, to the 10 p.m. to 2 a.m. shift. "She was slapping his wrists for playing too much new wave," said one disc jockey. Among KSAN jocks, the 10 to 2 slot is known as the "Suicide Shift."

"It turned out to be sort of a contest between Abby and me," said Gossett. "Trying to get me to quit, and I kept saying, 'No, I'm not going to quit. I'm not going to walk out of this place. I'm going to keep doing what I've always done. And if they don't like it, they should fire me.'"

David Moorhead (to the right of the man with the mustache), vice-president of Metromedia, KSAN's corporate owner, meets with members of the press, July 1979.

Melamed began issuing Gossett stiff memos several times a week. "Richard, I've been disappointed in your last two shows," began one memo. "Most importantly, you are not playing enough of the hot material.... Also, why play the Ramones into the Clash at any time—least of all at 10:30 at night."

On July 11 of this year, Richard Gossett showed up at KSAN for his shift. It was a tense time at the station. A week earlier, General Manager Jerry Graham had resigned. On this night, David Moorhead, West Coast vice-president of Metromedia, KSAN's corporate owner, was in town. Moorhead was to replace Graham until a new general manager could be found. There was a good chance Moorhead would be listening to Gossett's show.

Richard Gossett had been drinking that day. "I had a few drinks in the afternoon and at dinner," he said later. "And I drank a few beers during the show, same as I had been doing for years."

It was a Wednesday night. For some time, Gossett had been playing an hour of new records during part of each Wednesday show. For this show, there was a heavy emphasis on new wave artists.

"I have a weird sense of humor," said Gossett. "I'm very extemporaneous. I have been drunk on the air. Obviously, I'm a very loose kind of personality. Banging on goddamn bells and rocking on the board, pounding on stuff. It's a weird kind of radio, that's for sure." Gossett paused a moment. "That night, I was as good as any."

On July 12, Richard Gossett, nine-year veteran of KSAN and the last of the disc jockeys hired by Tom "Big Daddy" Donahue (the man who invented "progressive" or "underground" radio), was fired. The memo that Richard Gossett was given said simply, "You are terminated without cause. Abby Melamed."

Asked why she fired Gossett, Melamed, who was promoted to a newly created position of Operations Manager on July 25, said, "Richard was fired for having a difference of opinion with me as to what he should be doing on the air."

"I think Abby fired him to save her ass," said one KSAN jock. "I would speculate that it was because the big bosses were in town. They might have heard that show. If nothing had been done about it, it would have seemed like leadership at the station was somewhat wanting."

## A Station for the Rest of Us

KSAN WAS RADIO FOR THE rest of us. Flipping to 95 on the FM dial in the late Sixties and early Seventies was like coming home. This was the "real stuff." No hyper sunshine boys hawking pimple goo. This radio was mellow, spacey. Former KSAN Program Director Bonnie Simmons, who worked at the station for eight years, recalled, "You got the feeling that, if you didn't listen to KSAN, you weren't really hip to what was going on." It soothed the soul and blew the mind. As we said in those days, it was "far out."

Now, the station is in the midst of more changes, which the firing of Richard Gossett portended. A major shakeup has been underway for the past month and a half. Judging by the on-the-air sound these days, KSAN has opted out of the role of a radio station willing to try things that are, perhaps, "out there."

The KSAN jocks are currently serving up a steady diet of prefab hit songs and hit groups. A recent typical half-hour featured Ted Nugent, Rod Stewart, Cheap Trick, Led

Zeppelin, Foghat, and the Eagles, slickly spun one after the other, with only minimum on-the-air talk.

"It's a stupid sound," offered one Metromedia executive. "It's geared to a mass audience. It's no longer a sophisticated San Francisco station. It's very energetic and very safe. It's real jive."

Needless to say, perhaps, the disc jockeys have not been happy of late. Tony Kilbert, Norm Winer, Sean Donahue (one of the late Tom Donahue's sons), and Beverly Wilshire—full-time disc jockeys who were working at the station before Gossett was fired—have quit. It's rumored that Glenn Lambert will be leaving. News Director Dave McQueen, who has been with the station for more than nine years, bailed out on August 22. Scoop Nisker's infamous 30-minute *Last News Show* has been dropped. Sales personnel have been departing. New program and music directors have been brought in.

KSAN's listening audience has not remained silent. "The phones are ringing all day long," said a KSAN intern, one of seven who answer the phones at the station. "People are really angry. We've gotten thousands of calls and letters. People say they'll never listen to the station again."

In response to what KSAN management called "rumors" concerning changes at the station, and media and public demands for an explanation, a press conference was called on July 31. More than two dozen representatives of the Bay Area media showed up, from *New West*, KPIX, *Rolling Stone*, both dailies, and *BAM*, as well as the *San Francisco Bay Guardian*. "They expected to hear about the death of a legend," concluded one reporter at the press conference's conclusion.

The man with all the answers was Acting General Manager David Moorhead, best known for the dramatic ratings turnaround he accomplished at Metromedia's KMET-FM in Los Angeles. KMET currently holds the number-one position in LA radio with its mix of familiar rock & roll, current hits, a conservative approach to adding "new music" (new records by unknown or commercially unsuccessful artists), and few disc jockey raps.

A large, beefy man with a black three-piece polyester suit, wide tie, and the look of a bureaucrat, Moorhead gazed over a coffee table at the semicircle of journalists, photographers and a TV crew that filled the conference room. "I feel like I have leprosy," he joked nervously, as he gestured to the empty space on the couch.

Soon reporters began firing questions. "Well, are you going to establish a playlist or allow the jocks to play what they want?" popped one.

"First of all, I am not the program director," replied Moorhead in calm, even tones. "And I learned many years ago that anyone who tries to act as general manager and program a station is a fool."

"What are the problems with KSAN which led Metromedia to bring you in to revamp the station?" asked another reporter.

"KSAN is not attracting, I think, the audience that there is for KSAN," Moorhead answered.

"Look," said a reporter from KPIX, "what people outside this room want to know is, what's it going to sound like? Is it going to sound like House of the Hits Keep Smiling radio? Is it going to sound like it sounded yesterday? Is it going to sound like it did five years ago?"

"It's not going to sound like it sounded yesterday," said Moorhead, "because the station hasn't been doing well yesterday."

"What's it going to sound like?"

"If you could tell me what music's going to sound like in the next year, I could have a shot at it. I can't tell you what kind of music because we haven't had enough time and because we haven't announced a program director yet."

And so it went for nearly an hour. Reporters cleared out of the conference room muttering, "Bullshit."

## Radio Los Angeles

SO, WHAT IS GOING ON at KSAN?

Lots.

Despite the disclaimers, big changes are in the works at KSAN. "Records are just being removed from the air booth," complained one jock. "And they've got a carpentry crew in who are putting in a wall so the main record library can be locked up. Those records are inaccessible to us already. We can't play them on the air." KSAN's record library, across the hall from the broadcast booth, is estimated to contain between 50,000 and 80,000 records and is one of the biggest radio station libraries in the country.

The station sounds a lot like KMET now. The new music director is a man named David Perry, whose last job was as a disc jockey at KMET. The new program director, a woman named Jackie McCauley, has lived in LA for the past few years working in promotion at Warner Bros. Records. The first new disc jockey to be brought in since Moorhead's arrival, Jessica Rhodes, has worked at KMET as a disc jockey. It's rumored that new disc jockeys being brought in to replace Wilshire, Donahue, Kilbert, Winer, and Gossett are also being imported from the Southland.

According to Metromedia management, KSAN has been losing the ratings battle since shortly after Tom Donahue died in 1975. David Moorhead points to the low 1.8 share of the total listening audience, 12 years and over, male and female, which KSAN came up with in the last rating period, July–August 1979.

But former General Manager Jerry Graham, 45, who says he resigned because he "wanted time off, a long vacation," believes that those figures are the wrong ones to use in figuring the station's success or failure. "No station cares about the total listening audience," said Graham. "Every station goes for a more pinpointed audience. KSAN is still the number-one station for males 25 to 34 years old. KSAN has been a financially successful station for the past five or six years. Always making a profit."

One former disc jockey puts the blame on Graham for the station's current state. "Jerry is the one who has the blood on his hands. Jerry Graham sat on his ass and did nothing. Metromedia didn't see anything positive coming out of San Francisco. If he had been just a little bit smarter and jived them and said, 'Leave us alone,' like Donahue did, 'the money's coming in, what are you bitching about?' none of this would have happened."

"The station has been making a profit," KSAN's General Sales Manager David Bramnick confirmed. "KSAN hasn't been losing money, but it's not making enough money in terms of similar stations in our division."

"I can't understand David Bramnick saying something like that," countered David Moorhead when he finally consented to an interview on August 20. "First 26 weeks of the year, the station was in the hole, $13,000 or so. The station has been a disaster area. Anything that's losing money is a problem."

## Breaking the AM Rules

"METROMEDIA IS A REALLY FUNNY company," said Richard Gossett. "Here they take this baby FM thing in 1968. Worked on it. Lost money on it. It took them four years of staying with it to get it to work. It became popular. It worked for a couple of years. They made money on it. They exploited it. And then it's taken them four years to break it right down again."

KSAN was a classical music station at the beginning of 1968. But when a rift between Tom Donahue and the owners of KMPX, the station where Donahue had initially developed the "underground" radio concept, turned into a strike that could not be resolved, Donahue convinced George Duncan, president of Metromedia, to go with his rock format.

"The premise the station was set up on was basically to break every rule that had ever been set up in AM radio," recalled Bonnie Simmons, who left KSAN last summer for a position at Warner Bros. Records as national promotion director of albums. "To take people who were not traditionally disc jockeys, but who were music fans, and turn them into disc jockeys. To be on the radio and play records for your friends. Set up this sort of living room environment. It was all so experimental."

Only on KSAN could you hear 30 minutes of Ravi Shankar segue into live tapes of Big Brother and the Holding Company, followed by four versions of Bob Dylan's "I Shall Be Released," each by a different artist, and then a string of theme-related folk songs. Artists like John Mayall were invited to sit in for hours spinning their favorite obscure discs. The I Ching was thrown and read each morning, and the news sounded a lot more like the *Berkeley Barb* than the *San Francisco Chronicle*.

With Tom Donahue, a renegade from Top 40 radio, as auteur-director of the KSAN script, the station pioneered what became known as "progressive" radio. A larger-than-life figure of Orson Welles-like proportions and intensity, Donahue was a true innovator. "It is not at all outrageous to say that Tom changed the course of American pop music," wrote the late Ralph Gleason, a highly respected music critic, upon Donahue's death in 1975. "He did it by proving that FM radio could play a definite role in exposing all kinds of music to the audience's ears."

KSAN was imitated across the country. "KSAN was a real life force," said Bonnie Simmons. "The lifestyle that we were depicting on the radio was undercover. There was a time when it was the only place in the world where you could tune in and feel that there were other people smoking dope in the world."

Even under Donahue, however, some loose guidelines emerged. "Cautionary words were put out as early as 1973," recalled Simmons. "I remember Donahue beginning to get on people. Play more rock & roll. Stop playing folk music. Stop playing R&B. He never said it that way. It was the percentages he would look at. You were encouraged to start leaning toward a mainstream."

As late as 1977, KSAN was still a leading FM innovator, and the music played on the station was still far from mainstream. When new wave/punk rock came along, KSAN was the first station in the country to play massive doses of often abrasive, controversial, and commercially unproven groups like the Sex Pistols, the Clash, the Ramones, and Elvis Costello.

When Bonnie Simmons resigned as program director, Jerry Graham filled the position with his former secretary, Abby Melamed, who was in charge of promotion for the station at the time. Melamed had no previous music or programming experience at any radio station, including KSAN. Several of the jocks resented her appointment. "She'd make these off-the-wall comments about music," said Richard Gossett. "One time we were discussing the song 'Year of the Cat,' and she said, 'Oh, yeah, I like those songs by Cat Stevens.' And I said, 'Wait a minute. Cat Stevens? That's Al Stewart.' And she said, 'Oh.'"

"A few weeks ago, the *More American Graffiti* soundtrack came into the station," said Glenn Lambert. "Abby picked up a copy. She started laughing and said to me, 'Oh my God, have you ever heard of this? It's called "I Feel Like I'm Fixin' to Die Rag," And she had been programming a rock station in San Francisco?!"

Asked why she thought a number of the disc jockeys were so critical of her, Melamed said simply, "I was their boss."

As program director, Melamed changed the tone of the station, "Abby immediately began exercising rigid control over what records would be added," recalled Lambert. And the memos began circulating to the air staff.

Within the air booth, files with names like "Hot" (20 to 30 current hit albums), "New" (40 to 50 new records Melamed approved), "Watch" (50 to 60 albums that disc jockeys wanted to play), and "Encore" (100 albums, former hits no longer current enough for the "Hot" file) appeared.

Previously, the station had only two files: "Red Dot" and "New." Red Dot were some 1,000 "KSAN classics," records that the jocks had repeatedly played over the years by artists like the Beatles, the Grateful Dead, David Bowie, The Band, Bob Dylan, and the Rolling Stones.

At first, the addition of the new files was merely to "assist" the DJs in programming their shows. By Christmas of 1978, the files had become straitjackets, severely limiting what the jocks could play.

Richard Gossett wasn't the only disc jockey alarmed by Melamed's "format." Beverly Wilshire, Norm Winer, and Glenn Lambert were also vocal. The disc jockeys met among themselves and, as a fairly united force, convinced Graham and Melamed to form a music committee and hold weekly meetings where a pair of disc jockeys would meet with them and discuss new music to be added to the various air booth files.

The meetings were held for most of this year. "Those meetings were basically a joke," said Wilshire, "because they had already made up their minds before we even walked in there as to what they were going to let us add."

The rapport between a number of the jocks and Melamed was continuously strained during this time. Richard Gossett's firing nearly sparked a full-fledged crisis. "The staff were ready to revolt," said Wilshire, "but he didn't want it. He just wanted them to give him his money and get the hell out. So I respected that and calmed them down and said, 'Don't do it.'"

## "A Nonformat Format"

"MOORHEAD'S A SNAKE," SPAT one former KSAN jock. "Did he give any direct answers at the press conference? Never! And he never will. You can't pin him down. He says he has lines you only step over once and you're out. But he'll never tell you what those lines are, because they change from day to day. The man just makes up his own world every morning when he wakes up."

On August 20, David Moorhead was denying that the station had begun aiming for the 18-to-24-year-old audience. "I really haven't made that determination yet," he said.

Sitting in his temporary office, the huge room where the press conference had been held, Moorhead insisted that no format would be in effect at the station. "I hate the word format, 'cause it's really a nonformat format," he said. "Hopefully, it'll go back to being more what it was in 1974."

As he talked, an alarm built into his digital wristwatch beeped every 10 or 15 minutes. "When you're going back over five years and trying to find out what went wrong," continued Moorhead, "you don't do it in three weeks. When I have something to tell you, I'll tell you. But until, don't ask me something I don't know yet."

## A Few Guidelines

WHILE I WAS TALKING WITH DAVID Moorhead, a memo was issued to the KSAN air staff. It read in part:

> To: Air Staff
> From: Jackie McCauley
> Subject: Music Programming
>
> We are still in the process of revamping the studio library. During the interim, please play selections only from albums that are currently in the control room library. General format guidelines for this period are as follows: During each half-hour segment play from the following categories:
>   Current hits—minimum 1, maximum 2
>   New Music (non hit)—minimum 1, maximum 2
>   Cold (previous hit)—minimum 1, maximum 2
>   Other bulk library—minimum 1, maximum 3—with one minimum being easily recognizable by song or group (does not need to be charted song)
>   Also, please take into consideration programming procedures brought out in our previous staff meeting. For example, commercial sets should always be followed by a hit song (current or oldie).
>
> Thank you for your cooperation.
> Jackie.

## "Money Changes Everything"

A WEEK AND A HALF EARLIER, Beverly Wilshire didn't yet know that she would be quitting KSAN. She was in the air booth trying to program a decent show given the format that Abby Melamed had set up. She played songs by Elvis Costello, Moon Martin, Greg Kihn, and the Kinks, "Do I sound more up?" she asked. "They've been complaining that I've been sounding down on my shows for the past few weeks."

"You sound great," offered another DJ who had stopped by. "I just don't know if I'm going to stick around," she said.

She reached over and picked up a single by a group out of Atlanta called the Brains. Richard Gossett had discovered the record. It was obscure; the group had issued it on its own label and printed up a few hundred copies. It was the kind of record that would never again be able to be slipped into the KSAN air booth.

The Brains' little masterpiece, "Money Changes Everything," began playing. While dark guitars murmured ominously and the drums kicked in with military precision, the lead vocalist Tom Gray—a cross between David Byrne of Talking Heads and Ric Ocasek of the Cars—sang.

He sang, in that song "Money Changes Everything," about people who smile and act like they're your friend and promise they'll stand by you forever, but when there's money at stake, suddenly everything changes.

It sounded like an anthem for the Seventies.

*San Francisco Bay Guardian,* August 30, 1979

# THE SEDATING OF ROCK & ROLL RADIO

**The "progressive" stations emerged on the FM dial as an alternative to Top 40 radio. Today, as one promo man puts it, AOR radio is little more than Muzak for teenagers.**

*Four years after I wrote the KSAN story, I wrote this one for* Esquire *magazine. It meant a lot to me to have a story published in* Esquire. *When I was growing up* Esquire *was a big deal, a seriously hip magazine that published the best writers. Writing for* Rolling Stone *and then* Esquire *signaled a coming of age; I had made the big time. Amazingly, by 1983, no one had written about the rise of radio consultants, a handful of men who were determining what was played on 100s of FM rock radio stations. The previous seven years had seen the first serious change in rock music since the mid-'60s, the advent of punk rock. Yet punk wasn't played on commercial rock radio. Subsequently, groups like the Sex Pistols and the Ramones and the Buzzcocks and so many others didn't have a chance to be heard other than on college radio, and the audience for college radio was, for the most part, very small. I wanted to find out what had happened. Why were nearly all the commercial rock radio stations playing either oldies like the Rolling Stones and the Doors or contemporary pabulum like Journey and Styx? And* Esquire *wanted to know too. Although the editor, the late Jim Henke, who hired me at* Rolling Stone *soon after this story was published never confirmed that this story was the one that sealed the deal, I've always thought that was the case.*

LEE ABRAMS DOES NOT HAVE fond memories of the summer of 1981. As the most successful radio consultant in America, Abrams, 29 at the time, was earning close to a half-million dollars a year telling album-oriented radio (AOR) stations—the ones that play cuts from albums in addition to singles—which records they should play. Abrams had come to New York to attend the second annual New Music Seminar, which is a conference held by supporters of New Wave rock, the kind of music seldom heard on stations he consults. For the most part, the attendees were not Lee Abrams' kind of crowd, and the minute he stepped onstage at Private's, the club where the radio panel that he was participating in was taking place, he knew he was in for it.

There were boos; there were catcalls. A beer can was hurled at the stage. When Abrams tried to tell them that it wasn't his fault that the public *liked* the mainstream rock typical of his stations, they shouted "Liar!" When Abrams told them that even he was now bored listening to his own stations, they yelled, "Bullshit!" When he told them there was nothing he could do about the fact that New Wave rock wasn't on the air, they snarled, "You're crazy."

Then Bruce Harris, director of East Coast A&R at Epic, stood up and glared at Abrams: "You and mothers like you are responsible for ruining album radio."

Abrams stared back at Harris. Then he looked around the room. He sat there. He said nothing. Because, in truth, there was really nothing for him to say.

LEE ABRAMS IS A RADIO DOCTOR. He is the guy an AOR station owner or his general manager calls up when his station has been getting bad ratings. To reverse the situation, Abrams may do anything from putting together a TV promotional campaign to replacing staff. But mostly what he does is advise his clients on the particular songs they should put on the air and the frequency that those songs should be played. It is usually enough.

Today Abrams is sitting in a borrowed office at KFOG, a San Francisco station for which he has recently begun consulting. The big desk in front of him is covered with tapes and music magazines and industry tip sheets: thousands of albums are piled on the floor. Grabbing a free moment, he places a call to WKZL, the station he consults for in North Carolina. He opens a scruffy brown leather briefcase and pulls out a piece of paper with notes scribbled all over it. When he's got the station's program director (PD) on the line, he says. "Bump it, I guess," about one record that isn't doing well.

Then Abrams starts tossing out the kind of advice that this station pays him about two thousand dollars a month for. "I think 'Down Under' is a hit. That would be an A. 'Destination Unknown' is probably a hit too. Foghat's doing well for you? Well, add it in P, for two weeks anyway." He's referring to various categories he's created, which indicate how frequently a song should be aired. An A gets played once every five hours; a P gets played every eight hours.

"Did you get that package of themes?" Now he's talking about these old TV themes of *The Beverly Hillbillies, Mr. Ed, The Untouchables,* and *The Twilight Zone* that he's sent to his stations. Abrams thinks this kind of thing elicits an "Oh, wow!" response from his listeners—makes his meticulously programmed stations sound more spontaneous.

"Mickey Mouse's birthday? How about some kind of tribute? By the way, there's an import version of 'Shock the Monkey' in German. That record's getting burned out. Throw in the import version."

Back in the mid-Sixties, "progressive" stations emerged on the FM dial as an alternative to formula Top 40 radio. They quickly moved into the mainstream. Today, as one promo man puts it, AOR radio is little more than Muzak for teenagers. "What started in San Francisco 15 or 16 years ago—free-form radio—certainly doesn't exist anymore," says Joe Smith, former chairman of Elektra/Asylum Records. "And it's the radio consultants and programmers who have changed all that."

What one hears if one tunes in WCOZ in Boston, KLOS in Los Angeles, WQDR in Raleigh, WAPP in New York, or nearly any other AOR station in this country is hits by major stars, past and present. Largely past. The Doors. Led Zeppelin, Jimi Hendrix, and the Beatles are all played often on the stations, prompting one disc jockey to joke that you have to be dead to get air time. And much of the "new music" that is played is by established mainstream rockers, the so-called corporate rock bands like Journey, REO Speedwagon, Styx, and Rush, all of whom share the uniform style of tenors singing over a slick, melodic, high-velocity sound sweetened with whooshing synthesizers.

"You used to travel around the country, and when you went to the Midwest you'd get midwestern food, and when you went down South you'd get southern cooking, and now you travel around the country and you get Denny's all over," says Terre Roche, a member of the Roches, a folk-rock group whose three albums have received great reviews from the critics but negligible airplay on AOR radio. "It's the same premise with these radio stations."

Lee Abrams is not the only AOR radio consultant, but he was the first and is still—with something like 70 stations—the biggest. Abrams was the guy who, at 17, came up with the basic plan that all the others have imitated, a plan that was based on the brilliant if obvious discovery of what Abrams called "the vulnerable Top 40 listener."

"This was the type of person," explains Abrams, "that had just started to get into the sound that was happening then. This person didn't listen to the progressive station, 'cause it was just a little over his head. So he listened to Top 40 but really only liked every third song. He liked it when 'Jumping Jack Flash' came on, but then he'd hear Herb Alpert, then the 1910 Fruit Gum Company, tune out, then hear Santana and like that one. So I thought, that's where the big gap is. There isn't a format that reaches this person."

Abrams verified his hunch with a variety of unorthodox research techniques, among them the "hitchhiking study," in which he hitchhiked around Fort Lauderdale for a week, surreptitiously "observing people switching stations, why they tune in and out of a station." Satisfied, he went through his record collection and those of his friends to compile a list of about 800 songs by "album-oriented artists that would appeal to the 'vulnerable listener.' When I was 18 or 19 it was easy putting the list together," says Abrams. "That's the music I was into anyway. They were the best songs by the best groups. You could instantly hear what sounded right and what didn't. I thought the music should be as commercial as possible without losing the progressive identity." Abrams devised a new radio format from the list and called it Superstars.

The trick of the Superstars system, which is still in use today, is the division of rock artists into a variety of categories based on the artist's popularity. New records deemed suitable for airplay are divided between A, B-1, and P. A records are either hit singles or what Abrams calls "great songs" by album rock artists: the Rolling Stones "Start Me Up" was an A when first released, as was Tom Petty's "Refugee." B-1 records are new albums by extremely popular groups: Led Zeppelin, Jefferson Starship, Journey. These albums include three or four cuts okayed for airplay. A and B-l records are played five times a day. P records, by semipopular artists, are played three times a day. Once a record gets old or, as one program director at an Abrams station says, "is perceived by the public as not current," it is moved into other categories (C-1 or B-2) and gets less airplay. Superstars stations currently play about 700 songs repeatedly during a week, but they tend to be by the same 20 or 30 artists.

Prior to Superstars, disc jockeys at an FM station could play anything they wanted. But at Abrams' stations the disc jockeys use a "How sheet," a piece of paper with the categories printed down the left side. Moving down the list, they first play a cut from the A category, then one from the D-2 category, and so on. The point of all this is to give the station a consistent sound: whether you tune in at 9 a.m. or 4 p.m., you'll hear the same mix of old and new songs.

Another innovation was shifting the emphasis from the song to the artist. "In Top 40 formats, listeners are acquired and retained through the 'Familiarity Principle,'" wrote Abrams in a brochure that explains the format to potential clients. "With Top 40, the familiarity is with the song; with the 'Superstars' format, the familiarity is with the ARTIST." Thus one hears a disc jokey announcing that he's just played the Rolling Stones; he doesn't mention that the cut was "Jumping Jack Flash."

First used at WQDR in Raleigh in 1972, when Abrams was the PD, Superstars was a hit; based on its success, Abrams went into the consulting business. By 1973 he had hooked up with Kent Burkhart, a Top 40 consultant who was looking for a way to pick up more client stations. The two formed Burkhart/Abrams and Superstars took off. As time went on, they found ways to keep in touch with changing tastes: They phoned record stores on a weekly basis to see what was selling locally, kept an eye on the weekly trades, and made note of listener requests. Abrams and Burkhart also passed out questionnaires, attached feedback cards to rock albums, and held focus groups—semi-encounter groups where 20 kids listen to records and talk about what they like and dislike.

With the success of Superstars, free-form radio began to die out slowly, and between 1974 and 1977, dozens of stations were hiring the consultants. "It was like one a month," says Abrams. Usually, when he went up against a free-form station, he won the ratings battle. As one former disc jockey says. "Match a machine against 'whatever happens, man'—the machine wins every time."

FOR A LONG TIME, ABRAMS WAS the only AOR consultant worth talking about. But then, in 1981, a man named John Sebastian came along to throw a monkey wrench into the prevailing methodology. Sebastian decided there was a way to find out *exactly* what the mass audience wants to hear or, maybe more to the point, *doesn't* want to hear. He started using what he termed "call-out" or "passive" research, employing a team of "researchers," usually high school girls, to go through the phone book and make random phone calls in search of, for instance, 20- to 24-year-old males who listen to rock radio. Once one of these males is on the line, the researcher aims to find out which songs will *not* cause him to tune out by playing a series of 30 or so seven-second excerpts from songs. After each excerpt, the man on the phone is asked a few questions: "Have you heard the song? Did you used to like it? Do you like it now?"

Sebastian treated the actives, the kids who phone in to request a favorite song or write the station, as an insignificant percentage of the listening demographic. With the record business in a slump, he also began to ignore sales charts. If fewer people were buying records, he figured those charts weren't accurately portraying what all the radio listeners who weren't buying records really wanted to hear. "We can tell if people like a song or not, not whether people would go out and buy it," he says. "And there's a distinct difference. Everybody doesn't just go out and buy a record 'cause they happen to like it."

"Call-out" allowed John Sebastian to tap into what he saw as the "silent majority" of AOR radio listeners—and it certainly worked. In Boston, one year after he became PD at WCOZ, that station's ratings rose from a 4.1 to a 12.6, the highest rating any AOR station had ever achieved in a Top 25 market. (Just a one-point rise in the Arbitron ratings can mean a million-dollar increase in advertising revenues.) Then he did what any PD who has just won the Super Bowl of radio would do: He started up his own consulting firm.

What Sebastian did in creating his format was take Superstars and tighten it up, make it closer to Top 40 in form, if not content. When he first arrived at WCOZ, he quickly reduced the record library from 5,000 albums to 500. "Prior to his arrival, there was everything," says former WCOZ music director Kate Ingram. "From Bonnie Raitt to the Sex Pistols. Plenty of Black music. As soon as John came in, he took things out right and left." He also even further reduced the disc jockey's freedom. Unlike Abrams, Sebastian provides cards that tell the disc jockey *exactly* what to say on the air. Slogans like, "Playing a wider variety of rock & roll," or "[station's call letters], with one great rock & roll song after another," or "[jock's name], guaranteeing no less than six in a row or we pay you ten thousand, six hundred dollars"—these phrases are repeated three or four times an hour on a Sebastian station 24 hours a day.

Call-out worked to such an extent that two other radio consultants—Jeff Pollack and Dave Hamilton—began to use it. But passive research also has detractors who charge that the method is only effective when used to test old records, such as "Stairway to Heaven" since it's difficult for someone to express an opinion on seven seconds of a song they've never heard before.

Not surprisingly, Abrams is among those critics. "One reason is, sometimes there are records that people like but don't want to hear on the radio. Also, I think it leads you to make real safe conclusions that certainly have their competitive value, but can make a station dull after a while. From what I hear, the Police never tested well. So they [Sebastian's stations] weren't too much behind the Police."

Sebastian counters by claiming that his methods are the most democratic way to program a radio station. "See, as a consulting company, we don't dictate which records are played at all," he says. "While other programmers *subjectively* decide what should be played and what shouldn't be played, we don't. We don't choose to believe we have golden ears."

Of course, Sebastian doesn't really ask people what they like. He asks them to rate the songs he's chosen. If you offer somebody a choice between a Jumbo Jack and a Big Mac, you are offering them a choice but you're still only talking about hamburgers.

Still, the irony of this debate is that though the consultants all claim to use a different combination of research techniques to determine their playlists, they all end up playing the same stuff. A look at the recent Top 20 for each of the top four consulted stations (which is printed each week in an AOR radio tip sheet called *The Friday Morning Quarterback Album Report*) shows the lists have 15 out of 20 bands in common.

RADIO CONSULTANTS HAVE NO shortage of detractors, but their economic success is inarguable. "The appeal of AOR radio used to be very, very small," says John Sebastian. "We have widened that appeal. And now album-oriented rock is one of the most successful formats in the country. It is making money and it is going to survive."

Shelley Grafman, executive vice-president at KSHE in St. Louis, says that his station, which began programming free-form rock in 1967, was taking in between $5,000 and $7,000 a month in the early days. "In those days, if you had receipts for $80,000 or $90,000 a year, you were doing pretty well. There was nothing but losses in terms of economics." Today, a leading AOR station in a Top 20 market may bill as much as three million a year. "When we had the ratings success at WCOZ," says John Sebastian, "they went from charging about $70 a commercial minute to, at times, charging as much as $300 a minute."

Because of their success, consultants are very powerful men. The four most influential—Abrams, Sebastian, Pollack, and Hamilton—directly control the sound of more than 120 rock stations. That's about a third of the stations that count and that doesn't include the influence the consultants have had over others who listen to the consulted stations and imitate their playlists.

The consequence of a system in which, as a former research director at a Sebastian station puts it, "if your new record comes out and all the consultants go on it, you already have over a hundred stations in every market playing that record and it slams through the charts," is a certain oligopoly of taste. "That the record gets played doesn't mean anyone's buying it," says the director, "it doesn't mean anyone really likes it. It just means that a few guys decide to make their stations play that record."

The power of the consultants is such that record companies will sometimes even edit songs at their request. Sebastian, for example, thought the eight-minute live version of Bob Seger's "Let It Rock" was too long, and Capitol Records gladly agreed to press up a shorter version.

But perhaps the most serious consequence of this power has been its influence on the type of rock music many bands now make and the kinds of bands record companies are willing to sign. "When you know something is not in vogue at the radio station, you don't sign the act," says Joe Smith. Many worthwhile acts that do get signed don't get played on AOR. Black musicians, for instance, are seldom programmed by the consultants. And one of the more important kinds of music currently out of vogue with the consultants is Black music. To take just the week of November 19, 1982, one might think that Black musicians had stopped making records: the FMQ "song index," which lists the 100 most-played songs of the week (not including oldies) on AOR radio, includes no songs at all by Black artists. And no Black artists appeared in the individual Top 20 charts that Abrams, Pollack, Sebastian, and Hamilton each provide, either.

The situation is not unique to Black music, however: New Wave, punk, folk—virtually all other forms of pop music have been almost completely excluded from airtime. Given this state of affairs, it is difficult to see how new bands ever get played. Rumors that the consultants take bribes in exchange for advising their stations to play a record are denied as often as they spring up. But all the consultants say that they (or their associates) simply listen to the new rock records and advise their stations to play the stuff that fits their sound. Abrams says that in addition to "gut feeling" he uses sales charts, focus groups, and other soft research techniques. In any case, the type of new music that does make it on the air almost always sounds a lot like the records they're already playing or that are already being played on other stations in the market.

AT THE BEGINNING OF THE EIGHTIES, Lee Abrams started showing up at radio conferences admitting that even he, the man most responsible for the one-sided uniformity in AOR radio, was bored by the format. He said he couldn't listen to his stations anymore.

In a sense, Superstars had become too successful. "I think maybe its success made it look too easy," says Abrams. "Superstars sort of became the standard and everyone sort of felt, 'Well, that's the way to win in AOR.' But that's not necessarily true. It's just one way."

But if Abrams is slightly uncomfortable with the monster he's created, he says he can't really feel guilty about it. "Just came up with the thing, after all: sorry if it worked," and then says, "It's not my fault. It's just like, 'Come on, can't anybody come up with something different?'"

And then somebody did.

In April 1979, a fellow named Rick Carroll became PD at KROQ, a tacky little low rent radio station in LA that played mostly punk and New Wave rock in an extremely loose, free-form format. Like other PDs and consultants, Carroll took the music programming out of the hands of the disc jockeys. But unlike the others, he kept the focus exclusively on New Wave rock & roll. He limited the number of songs and set up an almost Top 40–like rotation. KROQ became known as the station where you could hear the Ramones and Devo, Talking Heads and the Plasmatics, the Sex Pistols and the B-52's, X and Bananarama—in other words, all the stuff that the other AOR stations were ignoring.

Three years after Carroll took the job, KROQ was the number-one rock station in LA, and last July Carroll went into the consulting business. Though he's only got four client stations at the moment, he says 20 others are considering his Top 40-styled, "modern music" format.

To date, the only other consultant who has put a New Wave format into practice is Lee Abrams. Even before KROQ was a hit, Abrams had begun to develop what he calls the Superstars II format, and last October the new format debuted on KFOG in San Francisco. Now Sebastian says he has plans to announce *his* "revolutionary new format" in June. If it's anything like Abrams' program it probably won't be too bad, but even progressive music, when it's packaged like this, has its limits. Abrams calls the format Timeless Rock and that hints at the strategy. For what Abrams is up to is shifting the target from the vulnerable Top 40 listener to what he calls "the weekend hippie," an older listener whose taste in rock was set in the late Sixties and early Seventies, who thinks fondly of Joni Mitchel and the Rolling Stones but can't stomach AC/DC or Styx. So Abrams programs about 30 "modern music" records from the softer side of the New Wave (like Peter Gabriel) along with a selection of compatible mainstream artists (like Tom Petty) and lots of oldies.

Abrams claims he would eventually like to switch many if not all his old-line Superstars stations over to the Timeless Rock format. He also expresses some regret over the death of free form. "I sort of thought the old progressive radio was good," he admits. "The intention was not really to go in and destroy them." The Superstars II format would be closer to that old system, but much of its future hinges on the success of KFOG. "You can't just go into a station that's really successful with Superstars I and say, 'We're going to change.' We got the word from the presidents of these companies: 'Hey, we're very successful; don't go screwing around with it.'"

*Esquire*, April 1983

# CONSUME THE MINIMUM, PRODUCE THE MAXIMUM

**Do you need just one more pretty processor, one more piece of software, one more gearhead gizmo to finally finish the CD, write the hit, get somewhere? Or do you really need to just break the cycle of consumption?**

*I found out about Deck, the program that turned a Macintosh computer into a four-track recording studio, from my friend Jimmy Wilsey, the guitarist who had cofounded Silvertone with Chris Isaak and wrote and played the haunting electric guitar intro and other riffs on "Wicked Game," the recording that made Isaak an international star. Wilsey and producer Erik Jacobsen used Deck when working on the edit of "Wicked Game" that became a hit. After I left* Rolling Stone *in 1993, one of the magazines I wrote freelance articles for was* Wired. Wired *was, at the time, interested in technology that was changing the world and Deck, created by the guys at OSC (Our Stinking Corporation), was one of those technologies. Deck was the basis for Digidesign's ProTools, the multitrack recording program that replaced analog multitrack recording at studios around the world. When I wrote this story, the OSC guys were no longer working with Digidesign. They had chosen to focus on a low-cost multitrack program, called Sessions, that individual musicians could use in their home studios to make recordings. In December 1995, the company was bought by Macromedia, and by the end of 1996, Macromedia had shut OSC down. As much as this story is about the multitrack recording technology that the OSC guys created, it's more about the philosophy that guided them, at least at the time I wrote this story.*

"WOW! SEE THAT GUY over there!"

Walking down the street was a tall man with a stylish haircut and the obligatory black, South-of-Market clothing. I might have been witnessing a rock-star sighting by an excited fan. Only, the awestruck speaker was a rock star himself: Jimmy Wilsey. At the time (1991), he was in Chris Isaak's band and the creator of the memorable guitar intro to the international hit "Wicked Game."

The man he was pointing at wasn't a rock star at all, but rather, the co-owner of a small software company on his way to the MACWORLD Expo in San Francisco. "He's one of the guys who created Deck," explained Wilsey. "He's a heavy dude."

Wilsey and other musicians, both well-known and obscure, have good reason to be impressed. A year earlier, in the summer of 1990, "heavy dude" Josh Rosen and his two partners, programmers Mats Myrberg and John Dalton, formed a company named OSC. Working in concert with Digidesign, a fast-growing developer of digital audio technology, OSC (which stands for Our Stinking Corporation) was primarily responsible for making Mac-based multitrack digital recording possible for the average musician. Earlier this year, the company made it even easier to record with a Mac, releasing Deck II version 2.1, which can turn a Macintosh Quadra 840av (no additional cards or add-on black boxes needed!) into an eight-track digital-recording studio. Cost of the program? Less than $400.

Everyone knows about the phenomenon of desktop publishing. But desktop recording is just now becoming affordable and widespread. Using Deck, the original four-track version of the program, San Francisco's radical art-rock group the Residents recorded *Freak Show*. Deck has also been used by music industry professionals like Columbia Records VP and producer David Kahne (best known for his hits with the Bangles).

Until OSC wrote Deck, multitrack digital recording was not possible on a desktop computer. Digital recording (as well as professional analog recording) had to take place in $200-an-hour recording studios, using costly dedicated multitrack tape recorders. To create a finished master, most artists build a recording track-by-track, with musicians first laying down bass, drums, and rhythm guitar, then adding guitar solos, vocals, keyboards, and whatever else is needed. Because each instrument is on a separate track, when a performance isn't perfect (or if the musician comes up with a new idea) that part of the original recording can be erased and then rerecorded. Stars like Stevie Wonder, Prince, and Trent Reznor have been known to record all the tracks of entire songs, and even albums, through the use of multitrack recording technology.

The introduction of Deck by OSC has changed things. The average musically inclined and financially strapped propeller-head (not just the rock star with a big budget) is truly benefiting from the new software. That's just what the owners of OSC intend.

"Just a year and a half ago, we got calls mostly from more sophisticated people who had grown up with computers," said Rosen one afternoon over drinks at The Slow Club, a San Francisco restaurant just around the corner from OSC's Potrero Avenue offices. "That's changed. Now we also have skateboarders who never learned what MIDI was, but they know the computer well enough to record their garage band."

Rosen smiles. "Which is such a funny idea. They're actually in a garage physically, but instead of stacks of Fender amps, they've got the Mac and a large hard drive."

I first met Rosen and his partners in the spring of 1991, a few months after Wilsey pointed him out to me. At the time, OSC was located in a low-rent Mission District warehouse and garage. The garage, in the back, was where Myrberg hacked code all day. The warehouse, which doubled as living space for Rosen and his girlfriend, contained music and computer equipment: synthesizers, drum machines, samplers, a mixing board, and, of course, a Mac equipped with a four-track Deck setup.

In addition to the original version of Deck, OSC had just released the company's first CD-ROM sound sample compilation, *A Poke in the Ear with a Sharp Stick: Volume 1*, which included such unusual samples as "Martian Ethnic Instruments," "Grungeomat," "Post-Nuclear Holocaust Ambiance," and "The Sounds of Carnage."

Standing in the doorway to the garage, Myrberg, in 1991 sounded like a late '70s punk rocker as he talked about how the new technology that OSC and others were creating was taking the means of music production out of the hands of corporate-funded record companies and allowing the musicians themselves to control their destinies. "Musicians should seize the opportunity that this kind of inexpensive recording equipment allows to make things," he told me. "The control that these bigger entities have been able to exert on musicians is disintegrating. Now, if you could just get around distribution, which the major labels still control, you could completely democratize the production and distribution of music."

Three years later, you need to spend just a little time hanging out at the Internet Underground Music Archive (IUMA) (see *Wired* 2.11, page 146) to get a feel for what Myrberg was imagining. IUMA [which shut down in 2006] is a World Wide Web site with digitized songs by more than 200 mostly unsigned bands. It takes just a couple of minutes to download a 15- or 30-second excerpt of the Whistle Pigs or the Ugly Mugs and then decide if you want to take the time to download the entire song.

Many of the songs are superb. Others are mediocre at best. But there is something truly liberating about the idea of an artist who lives somewhere in Virginia, say, crafting a recording of his or her song in his or her house using a Macintosh-based digital recording studio, then having the finished song put on the Net where it can be downloaded and checked out by a potential audience of millions. In the not-so-distant future it will be possible to download entire albums quickly over the Net.

"Developing technology that helps lots of people create music is a good thing," says Rosen. "People say, 'If more people record music, there's just going to be a lot more crap. But that's missing the point. People stand to gain a lot through demystification of personal artistic expression. Even if you can't make something everyone thinks is good, you gain a lot realizing it is within your grasp to envision something and make it real. Realizing you can write a song means more than answering the question, 'Can they sell it to a million people?'

"Are there pitfalls to the idea that anyone can crank out bad media endlessly?" Rosen continues. "Probably. I find it hard to envision what the dangers are. Other than that in a market-based economy, with too much supply and less demand, music might become devalued, but I suspect it won't. And besides, why shouldn't the creation of music be part of everyone's life?"

"TOOLS ≠ TALENT" is printed in huge letters on an OSC poster (printed on recycled paper). The poster succinctly sums up the group's mind-set, which is radically different from that of your typical software or musical instrument company.

Also included on the poster is the OSC Manifesto, which reads in part: "Does equipment establish the élite? How much 'having' do you have to have?"

Sitting in his messy office, Rosen explains, "Years ago, I had $150,000 of audio equipment, but I couldn't write a song if my life depended on it. I felt burdened. I had it all and it wasn't helping me. I got rid of most of it and found—for me, at least—that it helped me start to create again." Two years ago, OSC moved its offices into a former Pentecostal church ("They were speaking in tongues here, serious," says Rosen), and increased its staff to nine people. Rosen and his partners still get a kick out of puncturing the myth that, somehow, more equipment is all that is keeping Joe Musician from stardom.

Nearly five years after starting OSC, Rosen, 34, still looks like he spends his nights playing industrial rock. "I've noticed some people read the manifesto and go, 'Are these guys selling the idea that they're not trying to sell anything?' To tell you the truth, when I wrote the manifesto stuff, I wanted to create a set of things that I could go to and check when I lost my way—to remind myself what was important. I still go back and look at that during a bad week. It's our positive statement.

"We sell stuff," he continues. "And that's how we survive. At no point did we mean to say there was something inherently bad about owning a business. All we wanted to do was find a way to remain proud of what we were doing based on something other than raw income.

"The key question for us is, how can you be a company, be a commercial entity whose bread and butter comes from selling something, and not get sucked into the fast-growth, high-consumption syndrome that characterizes American business?" This is the dilemma OSC constantly struggles with.

"There's nothing inherently bad about something that grows fast," Rosen adds. "But I think the decision-making cycle of a company compelled to grow quickly—especially when you're funded by venture capitalists who expect a fast return on their investment and aren't really in business for ideological reasons—tends to revolve too much around quarterly growth. Fast growth can be good, but it can lead to cycles of rapid expansion, followed by rapid downsizing. No one wants to be in a position where you have to let people go, or drop development of products you're excited about. It's scary if you get so volatile that at any moment the bottom can fall out. I wanted the ability to make decisions that I felt were based on a longer term, more forward-looking approach.

"On a simple level, we're a bunch of people driven by our interest in the products that we're making. Our knowledge and interest in business for the sake of business was always secondary during the early days of OSC, and it still is."

Rosen continues to work surrounded by music and computer gear. On his left side is his recently purchased PowerPC; a Korg Wavestation is in front of him; a mixing board is to his rear; and videocassette players, amplifiers, and other sound- and video-processing equipment are to his right. There's even some nonhigh-tech stuff, like an old-fashioned electric guitar.

Looking at the Wavestation, which is covered with computer and audio magazines, he laughs, "Is it a desk or a keyboard? Depends on what time of day it is."

Asked why he and his partners named their company Our Stinking Corporation, Rosen smiles again. "We weren't totally comfortable with the idea of forming a company." Why? "Typically, the start-up model is this," he continues. "You start in the garage with two people who are tremendously interested in what they're doing, and five years later there are 700 cubicles, everything's become bureaucratized, and nobody is really personally interested in what's going on."

Rosen shakes his head. "Primarily, we were trying to set up something minimally consumptive, and set up to grow and eat as little as possible. I guess we were trying to create an environment where everybody could stay creative and enjoy what they did and survive—instead of looking at quarterly figures and judging success by growth."

Yet, despite themselves, OSC has grown—at a rate of about 100 percent a year. Last year, OSC grossed about a million dollars, and Rosen predicts the company will gross $1.5 million for 1994. "Making money was never an explicit goal," says Rosen. "But it's implicit. You can't escape that in the world we live in. Ultimately you measure success as a combination of personal satisfaction and cash in the bank."

He grins. "But I don't suspect anybody got into what we're doing for the cash. In the computer industry there's a lot more money in almost every other realm. Look at someone like Mats. He could have made much more money doing telecommunications or larger-scale signal processing work. That's probably still the case."

On another day, Mats Myrberg will tell me this: "I just get off on the technology of music. We were just trying to make a living creating tools and having a fun time doing it. When we first made Deck, we thought, 'Geez, this would be really great, 'cause we could all use it.' We make things that we want to use."

OSC, so far, has managed to avoid the corporate pressures that so often close in on entrepreneurs once the company they've founded begins to grow. In his office, Rosen sits quietly for a moment. Finally, he says, "We ask ourselves, 'How many other companies have started out with a brilliant product, something incredible and have managed to stay driven by actually using the thing they're making?'"

The answer is obvious. "Not a hell of a lot."

It was in 1987 that Rosen decided to move his techno band, R-Complex ("They use that term to describe the reptilian part of your brain," says Rosen; "it's supposedly what makes you want to dance"), from Portland to the San Francisco Bay area. To pay the rent, he got a job at Blank Software, designing Macintosh programs for the Mirage sampler. That's where he met Myrberg, a programmer who had defected from Ensoniq, a company in the synthesizer business.

Myrberg says he was bored at Ensoniq. So he took a job at Blank and what he describes as a more than 50 percent pay cut. "Once they figure out you're good at something, they want you to do that thing over and over and over again," says Myrberg, who is now 34. "I didn't want to write another sequencer and decided it was time to leave."

By 1988, Dalton—who had played in a band and shared a house with Rosen in Oregon—had followed his friend to the Bay Area. Dalton, a musician and hacker, put together a Rube Goldberg recording and sequencing setup at his apartment that made use of two computers and an analog multitrack tape recorder. It was not the most elegant of setups. It was Rosen's frustration with the limitations of Digidesign's "Sound Tools," a program for editing two tracks of audio on a Mac, that led the young men to create what would become OSC's first product. "I wanted to be able to record on the left channel while listening to the right," says Rosen. "I asked Mats, 'Is this possible?' Mats came back to me and said, 'Not only can you play the right while recording on the left, but I can build you a four-track.'"

"One of the things I had always done was write real-time software, which means what it says," says Myrberg. "Things have to happen in real time. And because I had written a lot of code in assembly language—what you had to do to make things happen in real time at that point—I could make a great program for digital recording on the Mac. So then we came up with this prototype, this four-track recorder to mimic a low-fidelity four-track cassette recorder. That was the fall of 1989. It took us, like, eight months to write the program and ship it."

They formed Our Stinking Corporation in 1990; Deck shipped that summer. "We'd all heard the story of The Beatles recording *Sgt. Pepper's* on a four-track recorder," says Myrberg. But the drawback with analog recorders has always been that, as you add more tracks to a piece, you lose sound quality. With Deck, OSC created a product that could record and store music digitally. Digitally recorded music doesn't degrade in quality; you can add multiple tracks without losing or muddying the original tracks.

This was a breakthrough. For the first time ever, Deck let musicians record multiple tracks on a home computer. "The digital musical tools that existed for PCs before Deck were not compositional tools. They were editing and mastering tools," explains Rosen. You still had to go into the studio to record. When Deck hit, it changed the game. Suddenly anyone could generate actual source material. Laying down guitars and singing later or adding drums—whatever you want.

"Today the tools available for the PC are so sophisticated and advanced that there's no professional recording studio that doesn't use some of them," says Rosen. "For me, the greatest moment was the first time I could record a sound on one track and play that back and record the second track. First time I did that, and it came out sounding like a CD, I was ecstatic."

Rosen says sales to date of the various versions of Deck total about 5,000 units. OSC currently handles software design, sound sample creation and editing, packaging, assembly, and shipping from its offices. The company also runs a postproduction house, MetaLanguage, which uses the software OSC develops to work on films and commercials.

The latest product is a piece of software called "Trans-port." In a nutshell, Trans-port converts digital tracks recorded using a high-end digital-recording system in a professional studio to a "Deck session," which can then be taken home and worked on using a Mac and Deck II. The work done at home can then be converted, using Trans-port, back to the format used at the professional studio. "It allows you to take advantage of two things a well-equipped studio offers that your home typically doesn't offer," says Rosen. "One, a great sounding place to record and, two, a well-calibrated place to mix."

The OSC partners typically don't concern themselves with writing software for hardware that doesn't yet exist. Instead, they write software that uses current hardware in a new way. "All you have to do is watch the landscape of computing go by," says Myrberg. "All kinds of opportunities are there."

One afternoon, after Joe Bini, who runs the studio, demos a few rather impressive commercials that were worked on at MetaLanguage, OSC's other co-owner, John Dalton, who is 36, leads me to a small kitchen where, seated at a round table, he starts talking about the future.

"The music studio of the future is just a computer," says Dalton, a soft-spoken man who wears his long brown hair in a ponytail. "You'll do it all in software. Now you can spend $4,000 on a synthesizer, and a year later, you need to buy another synthesizer to get new sounds. In a soft environment you just add another software module." Dalton believes that, ultimately, "open" programs like Deck, which can control, or be controlled by, a number of different MIDI sequencer programs, will take over. "People say that by the turn of the century we'll have supercomputer performance on the desktop for the price of a Mac today. We think a modular software environment is the answer. Trying to make a latch-key proprietary system doesn't work anymore. Look at what happened to Synclavier [an expensive digital recording device that was rendered passé by low-cost Mac-based systems].

"Things are always changing. In a virtual environment, synthesis modules will work together. We are committed to making our stuff work with other people's stuff. We foresee a world where they all hook together."

Such a system will allow a producer to utilize software from numerous companies to add reverb, EQ, distortion, and other DSP processing to the various tracks. Software will also eventually allow for 16 or even more tracks. Already, the open modular concept is partially in place. For example, in putting a Mac-based studio together, one can choose from hard drives made by numerous companies. There are more than a half-dozen MIDI sequencer programs and most are compatible with Deck. You can even choose from a variety of Macs to run recording software on.

"It's not going to be that long before you'll be able to record 16 tracks with your Mac, add digital effects, mix and master, and even create a master CD right at home," says Rosen. "We're very close."

"We have a lot of crazy ideas for things," says Dalton. "New ways to do sound synthesis, a different approach to a sample editing program." Dalton thinks that in many instances, when it comes to creating pop and rock music, "the studio thing is a myth. Look at U2's *Achtung Baby*. If people work within the limitations of what they have, they can do amazing things."

Dalton, Rosen, and Myrberg seem to have an almost religious conviction about following one's own vision. "Our idea was to see if you could have a company that wasn't focused on the business of business, that was more focused on the ideas and the products," says Rosen. "Are we a success? I suppose it depends wholly on what your goals are. What I always come back to asking myself is: Are we happy? Are we proud of what we make? Will we make payroll for the next few months? The answer to all those questions is a resounding yes. A lot of people say, well, those are not very ambitious goals. But they've served us well."

He pauses and looks down at the keyboard for a moment before continuing. "We look at OSC as an experiment. We don't know yet if, in the long run, it'll work or not, but so far it looks pretty good."

*Wired*, December 1, 1994

James Brown, the Godfather of Soul, San Francisco, 1980. Photo by © Chester Simpson / Rock-N-Roll Photos.com

# JAMES BROWN: PRISONER OF LOVE MEETS THE PRISONERS OF HATE

*Oh James Brown! In a way I guess I betrayed you. But in a way you betrayed us all. Not with your music. No, that was a gift. Sure, we paid for it, at least if we wanted a 45 or a vinyl album (or, later, a CD, and still later, an MP3, and later still, the ability to stream it). Yeah, that was one way we paid, but the petty cash was nothing compared to what we got from you. As long as humans survive and as long as there is a way to listen to recorded music, humans will be listening to you. No, it wasn't your music that was the betrayal, it was how you lived your life. And how did I betray you, well that has to do with the two stories that follow. The first, originally written for San Francisco's* Boulevards *magazine and then republished in the* New Musical Express, *was one of the stories I wrote about you that you liked. It was the first story, and it helped me establish a relationship with you. And that meant that when I had other assignments to write stories about you, I could talk to you. The betrayal happened when I wrote my final James Brown story, the one that ran in* Rolling Stone *with a rather horrid painting of you on the cover, which is the second story here. In the many years since that story was published, both before and after your death in 2006, I have sometimes regretted writing that second story. But sometimes I'm glad I wrote it. Speaking the truth is important.*

SAN RAFAEL, CALIFORNIA—THE TENSION inside San Quentin State Prison is so strong I can practically see it. I try my best to remain cool as waves of fear surge through my body. I can't get all the newspaper stories I've read about prison riots and stabbings out of my head.

"If you are taken hostage, we cannot do anything to ensure your release or safety," announces a prison guard as he unlocks the first of three steel jail doors that separate the prisoners of San Quentin from freedom and admits me into the prison.

I feel acute dread as those doors clang loudly and solidly shut behind me. Just the night before, one San Quentin inmate had strangled himself to death in his cell with the cord from his radio.

Today, in late November of 1980, I'm in the company of a one-time criminal who "made good" and is paying a visit to this prison 15 miles north of San Francisco to perform for the inmates. When James Brown, the Godfather of Soul, was 16 years old he was arrested for armed robbery. He spent four years at a work camp in Toccoa, Georgia. It was an experience he has never forgotten.

"It made me realize I wasn't so smart," Brown tells me.

Now, several thousand convicts wait in the prison mess hall, a grim place with grey cement walls. Under the harsh fluorescent lighting, everything looks stark, cold.

Overhead, two armed guards patrol the hall from a catwalk. Light glints off the black metal of their rifles. Below them, a sea of tough Black and Brown faces. The prisoners are all dressed alike: faded denim work shirts, faded denim pants, and black or blue knit wool caps pulled tightly over their heads. There is a large stage at one end of the mess hall. The prisoners face the stage and wait.

They are waiting for Mr. Dynamite, the Godfather of Soul, the Prisoner of Love, the Sex Machine, Mr. Please Please Himself, Soul Brother No. 1—Mr. James Brown.

Mr. James Brown is waiting in his dressing room for his dark, curly hair to dry. The room is small and painted a sickly pale green. Brown sits with his knees spread apart, a large hand resting on each thigh. A stocky man, his perfectly white teeth contrast dramatically against his dark skin. He is wearing a white sweatshirt zipped to the neck and white jeans stuffed into knee-high black suede boots. Several diamond-encrusted gold rings glitter on his fingers.

Behind Brown, a bunch of his stage outfits hang from an electrical pipe. These garish costumes of black, gold, red, silver, purple, and white spandex with glitter and sequins and intricate embroidery look funny in this dingy room. Hair spray, makeup, brushes, and combs scattered around make this makeshift dressing room look like a very funky beauty parlor.

"You're a very strong believer in the American Dream," I say to James Brown. "Do you really believe that if a man works hard, he can become a success?"

"Well didn't I do that?" he asks, almost defensively. "I was a former inmate. I had 8 to 16 years. More than most of the cats have out there."

"So since *you* made it, anyone can make it?"

"Not anyone," says Brown. "You're the one that said that. I think the chance is there for anyone. But anyone can't be a James Brown. But there's something anyone can do. In America, there's something anyone can do if they want to. Everybody can't be a James Brown, but they can go to work. But you got to remember one thing: I went to work before I tried this. I was a janitor when I made 'Please Please Please' [Brown's first hit]. So you got to start somewhere. Most people don't want to start in that place."

I ask Brown how he came to record "Please Please Please," and I set off fireworks.

"Mr. Stallings!" snaps James Brown. "Mr. Stallings!" Brown is calling for his personal manager.

"Sir, don't come here and ask me about the story of my history or my life," shouts Brown, glaring at me. "Please don't do that. That don't make no sense at all. If you want to talk to me, ask me about this show today—Mr. Stallings!"

The contagious tension of this prison has put the highly emotional Brown on edge. Sweat glistens on his immense forehead. He pulls his head out from under the white plastic portable hair dryer. His hair is wrapped around pink and green hair curlers.

"You look out there and you see 99 percent of the people are Black," says Brown angrily. "This is not just a prison. This happens to be a prison with almost all Black people. And I feel sorry for them. I don't want to see any prison, but this prison is as one-sided as the system out there! Now we know we haven't got all Black criminals in the world. What we need to do is see what we can do to our country so it's not so one-sided like that.

"Give those Black kids a hope, give them good education," continues Brown. "Give them heroes. Let them know the true things. Let them know the true things. Let a man like James Brown go all the way to the top rather than trying to put him down. Let people succeed. Give them hope. Those kids don't see no hope. Those Black kids ain't ever seen a Black president and nine times out of ten they won't ever see one. You look out there and see a lot of kids who won't ever have a chance.

"That's why the blues are so popular, gospel. Black people pleading for help and pleading for life. And we got to change that! This country is no better off than it was 25 years ago."

## Mr. Please Please Himself

IF A SINGLE MAN DEFINES Black music, that man is James Brown.

"He hears his sound in a lot of music. And he's proud of it," says Henry Stallings, four days after San Quentin, sitting in a backstage dressing room at The Stone, a San Francisco club as Brown performs to a capacity crowd. "He always say, 'Hey, you know what. I don't know what makes people follow me, but God only knows.' The man knows he's been blessed with a gift the average entertainer don't have. 'Cause he's been current for over 20 years. That's unbelievable."

James Brown is a legend and like many legends, the facts of his life vary depending on who you talk to. Some say Brown was born in Pulaski, Tennessee, on May 3, 1928. Others say it was Macon, Georgia, in 1933. All agree, however, that his family was dirt poor and that he grew up in Augusta, Georgia.

"He didn't have nothin'," says Stallings, who went to elementary school with Brown in Augusta. "He always say that's why he work so hard now. He don't ever want to go back that way. Never, ever again!"

As a kid, Brown reportedly picked cotton, shined shoes, and danced for pennies in front of the Fort Gordon army base.

"He was just one of the kids," Stallings adds. "We played together. He was singing at the talent shows then. At the Lenox Theatre. They used to have talent shows during the week. He used to end up coming out with first place. And he used to sing the national anthem each day at school. That's what they used to have him doing."

And then came the burglaries.

"I think he was snatching hubcaps and batteries. He was stealing, if you want to know the truth." Stallings gives a nervous laugh. "He was caught stealing. So they caught him. I was doing it too, but they didn't ever catch me."

Four years in prison sobered Brown up.

"I believe that's when he changed," says Stallings. "When he went to prison."

When he got out of prison, James Brown wanted to be a professional athlete. He tried his hand at boxing, training with Beau Jack and acting as a sparring partner for Sugar Ray Robinson. Then it was semi-professional baseball. But a leg injury cut short his dreams of making it as a big-league pitcher. "Yea, he had broken his leg," recalled Stallings. "We used to call him Crip after that."

So James Brown turned his attention to music. During the late '40s, Brown learned how to play drums and organ, while working in a number of gospel groups. Eventually he joined the Famous Flames, a rhythm and blues group founded by singer/bandleader Bobby Byrd in 1953.

The Famous Flames were a Black vocal group, like the "5" Royales, the Midnighters, and many others. An early lineup consisted of Bobby Byrd, piano (Byrd still plays in Brown's band); Nafloyd Scott, guitar; Sylvester Keels, vocals; Nashpendle "Nash" Knox, guitar; Ray Scott, bass; Johnny Terry, vocals—and, when he joined in 1954, James Brown on drums and vocals.

It was in 1956 that James Brown and The Famous Flames cut "Please Please Please" for Federal Records, a subsidiary of King Records. At the time, Brown was a janitor.

"I was working 10 hours a day for less than 100 dollars a month," Brown tells me. "I love that song ('Please Please Please') like I love one of my relatives. You know, if it wasn't for that song, I'd still be a janitor."

According to Henry Stallings, Brown's first brush with fame blew his mind.

"'Please Please Please' was the first break in his life," Stallings says. "Getting hold of some bucks, some money—I think he had his fun. He spent a lot of money doing silly things. Like drinking liquor.

"And I think he experienced from his own mistakes. I think he educated himself to a point where if he was going to have anything, he had to start taking care of business."

Part of "taking care of business" meant having the sharpest group in the US. Brown made the Flames wear fancy stage outfits. He rehearsed them until they knew the routines backward and forward and taught them intricate dance steps.

By October 24, 1962, when Brown recorded his first live album, *Live at The Apollo Vol. 1*, he had developed a following all over the country through year-round touring. Although he had to fight with his record company, King Records, to release it, the album reached number 2 on the *Billboard* Pop Album Charts and stayed on the pop charts for an astonishing 66 weeks.

Even so, in the mid-1960s James Brown dissolved the Famous Flames. Since then, he has worked with numerous musicians, and all his bands—The JBs, The New Breed and currently The JBs International—have been superb. Musicians who have served time in Brown's bands include Bootsy Collins, Fred Wesley, and Maceo Parker, all of whom currently play with George Clinton.

Working for James Brown may be the toughest gig of a musician's career. In the '60s, Brown fined his musicians if they showed up late for a gig or missed a note. These days, if they slip up, he fires them.

"He don't allow nobody to drink on his job," says Stallings. "If he catch somebody drinking on his job, they gone. No drugs, no nothing on his job. This man will fire anybody he catch with narcotics. He come around and smell some reefer in this room and everybody in this room is fired. *Everybody*."

## America Is My Home

IN THE LATE '60s, James Brown became such a powerful figure that a day after the assassination of Dr. Martin Luther King Jr., Brown held a free televised concert at the Boston Garden that kept potential rioters inside watching the show. A friend of former vice-president Hubert Humphrey, Brown says today, "I've been very close to most of the presidents. 'Cause I can do so much where they can't. That's been a duty of mine."

Brown recorded a string of political songs including "Say It Loud—I'm Black and I'm Proud," "Don't Be a Drop-Out," and "America Is My Home."

"I've never preached hatred. That's not my bag," Brown tells me. "I've never preached burning or looting. But if I don't gripe, who's going to gripe?

"But I've always supported my country. And even when I identified with the Black revolution, I did it as a human, not as a Black man.

"The only thing worth more than anything to me is to go to Europe and be James Brown the American. And to come back here and be James Brown the Black man—I think that's stupid!

"I lost something before I got home. I lost my identity on the way back. Now you would think you would lose your identity going, but I lose my identity coming back. I want to be James Brown the American."

In the early '70s, James Brown began to slip out of fashion. His records stopped crossing over onto the pop charts, and they were no longer topping the soul charts either. Brown, who had lived in high style at the end of the '60s, flying around the country in a black Learjet he called *Sex Machine*, had to sell the jet along with a mansion with a moat in Queens, New York, and two of his three radio stations. On top of that, Brown locked horns with the IRS, who claim he owes them $2,100,000 for unpaid taxes covering the years 1975–1977.

Some people, including James Brown himself, claim disco was the villain that took his mass audience away from him. He has verbally attacked his record company of 10 years, Polydor—and went on to record his latest album, *Soul Syndrome*, for Henry Stone's TK Records, the independent label responsible for KC and the Sunshine Band's numerous hits. Rumor has it, though, that Brown may soon return to Polydor.

## This Is a Man's Man's Man's World (Part Two)

AT SAN QUENTIN STATE PRISON, James Brown finishes the show with "Papa's Got a Brand New Bag" and "Please Please Please." And then he's gone.

"We want more," chant the prisoners. "We want more."

After five minutes, James Brown reappears onstage, a towel wrapped around his neck, and encores with something that sounds like "Dance Everybody Let's Boogie."

Brown and his band leave the stage for good, and the convicts exit the mess hall. "Anyone who's not a worker get out," shouts a guard. "I don't want my count messed up tonight."

After a half hour, James Brown, Henry Stallings, and I leave the mess hall. We walk beneath a tower from where a guard holding a rifle is surveying the prison grounds.

We walk across a courtyard bordered on two sides by two three-story buildings containing the prisoners' cells.

Suddenly a convict yells from a third-floor cell, "All right JB!"

And James Brown—every inch the Godfather of Soul—smiles, lifts a hand, and offers a regal wave.

*Boulevards/New Musical Express*, April 1981

# JAMES BROWN: WRESTLING WITH THE DEVIL

## The Struggle for the Soul of James Brown

THE GEORGIA JUDGE WHO is about to give James Brown a six-year prison sentence is in a jovial mood as he surveys his courtroom, taking in the television cameras, news photographers, and reporters. "You know they're giving out reports of his progress on the radio," says Judge Gayle B. Hamrick of the Richmond County State Court.

Brown, already serving another six-year sentence at South Carolina's State Park Correctional Center, is being escorted to Hamrick's court in downtown Augusta. The singer is expected to plead guilty to misdemeanor weapons and traffic charges that stem from a now infamous interstate chase that began when he entered an insurance seminar carrying a shotgun last September. It is the same series of events that led to his incarceration in South Carolina.

The judge is talking to a bailiff. "Every few minutes it's 'Hey, we got a report in on James Brown—they just passed us in a police car,'" says Hamrick, smiling.

"Judge, ganna charge admission?" asks the bailiff.

"We're ganna set up three rings out there," Hamrick says.

The courtroom begins to fill. Brown's mother, his aunt, and one of his sons, as well as Danny Ray, his longtime master of ceremonies, and Leon Austin, a childhood friend, find seats. Brown's wife, Adrienne, who is here to plead no contest to her own misdemeanor traffic charges, the result of a 1987 incident, bustles in. "Nothing but a zoo," she says with a frown. "Don't these people got nothing better to do?"

Adrienne Brown's case has already been heard by the time her husband is finally brought into the court a little before 11. Judging by his appearance, no one would know that James Brown has spent the last six weeks in prison. Attired in a three-piece suit and a burgundy silk shirt, a gray silk scarf tied around his neck, he flashes a smile as he greets an acquaintance. But standing before the judge, the singer quickly becomes subdued and somber.

As Brown begins speaking in a low, hoarse voice, reporters strain to catch his statement. "My life has always been a model, and I just don't feel good about it now," says Brown, adding that he is "very sorry" for what happened. "If I had it all to do over again, well, I just wouldn't do it." With his hands clasped behind his back, Brown looks up at Hamrick and says quietly, "I hope this is behind us."

Brown's contrition pays off. After he pleads guilty to the charges, the judge gives him what amounts to a slap on the wrist: a six-year sentence that will run concurrently with his South Carolina term. Brown could be free in August 1991.

Albert "Buddy" Dallas, one of Brown's lawyers, tells the judge that his client is sincere, that he "wants to do good." But three weeks later, Brown is on the telephone, calling from prison, complaining wearily that the police have harassed him for the last two and a half years, expressing disappointment that having served on President Reagan's anti-drug task force for seven years, no one from his administration has stepped in to help.

"I was very much surprised that I didn't get a call from the White House," Brown told *Rolling Stone* in late February. "I think I should get some help. I knew President Carter on a one-on-one basis. I know a lot of the state senators, governors. When they get the message, they going to help me out." Comments like these aren't surprising. Brown recently described himself to one of his former backup singers, Vicki Anderson Byrd, as "the only man who can do anything I want."

Brown thinks he should be released. "Special treatment I'm not looking for," he says. "But I don't think I should be in here. I am not a man who breaks the law. That [the insurance-seminar incident] was something that happened very fast, and I think the policemen just wouldn't accept their responsibility once they shot the car up. Thank God I'm living. Regardless of who did it, I didn't protest against the police, because I didn't want to cause problems. I figured if we could work it out in some other kind of way, if I had to go to jail for 60, 90 days, and then we work it out, I would accept that. If I had actually fought it like it actually happened, we'd have a lot of problems in the state, and I didn't want to see that. I didn't want to have a racial problem. So I took it all on me."

James Brown has always had a tremendous ego, and not without justification. He is arguably the greatest artist in the history of Black music, and his contribution to American popular culture is, simply, immeasurable. His 33 years as a hit-maker dwarf the accomplishments of current stars like Bruce Springsteen, Prince, Michael Jackson, and U2. He invented funk and rap, and his profound influence on music is international in scope. Brown has sat with American presidents and last year even had an audience with the Pope. His words once cooled rioting in Washington, DC, Boston, and Augusta, following the assassination of Dr. Martin Luther King Jr.

According to Joel Whitburn's new book *Top R&B Singles: 1942–1988*, Brown is the most popular Black musician of all time. His recorded legacy—114 charted singles—includes such classics as "Papa's Got a Brand New Bag," "Out of Sight," "(Get Up I Feel Like Being a) Sex Machine," "I Got You (I Feel Good)," "Night Train," "It's a Man's Man's Man's World," and "Say It Loud—I'm Black and I'm Proud."

Brown's fall comes at a time when his influence on the pop scene is as strong as ever. You can see it in the dance steps and music of superstars like Prince and Michael Jackson, Mick Jagger and George Michael, and dozens upon dozens of other entertainers. His own recordings have been sampled to death by Eighties' rappers, like Run-DMC, the Beastie Boys, Eric B. and Rakim, the Fat Boys, Ice T and Public Enemy, which takes its name from an old Brown record. "Everybody samples James Brown," says rapper Melle Mel of Grandmaster Flash and the Furious Five. "You can't make a rap record without using some James Brown."

Or as Brown himself put it with a laugh during his telephone call from prison, "The music out there is only as good as my last record."

But another Brown is now surfacing—one whose bearing is not so regal. Since Brown disappeared behind bars, friends, business associates, and musicians have come forward with horror stories about their days with the man. They say that for 30 years he has been beating women; that he has cheated collaborators out of record royalties. That he threatened musicians with guns; tried to steal their girlfriends; left band members stranded on the road; and got so high on marijuana and PCP that he thought he could "fly like a bird."

"They don't know, sir," counters Brown, who won't talk about his drug use. "My employees tell you, 'Oh, James Brown smokes a little pot.' I won't say nothing about those gentlemen. I'm going to be more man than they were. I'm a clean man."

But what of the PCP that was found in Brown's blood after his arrest? "They can find anything they want to find, don't you know that?" he says. "I'm just the last of the Afro-Americans to have enough intelligence to deal with the business world. And they would like to kick me out, back over into that fast lane. And they're not going to get me to do it."

Despite such denials, Brown's problems are the dark side of the tremendous ego and self-determination that helped a neglected child of poverty to fight his way to the top. But like fellow rocker Jerry Lee Lewis, Brown is a man who has been wrestled to the ground by a host of personal demons.

Some years ago in a fit of rage, James Brown scolded one of his employees by saying, "You know I got the Lord in one hand and the devil in the other, and I can control you. You're nothing without me!"

James Brown might just as well have been shouting at himself.

JAMES BROWN IS A MESS. It is May 6, 1988, and in his plush suite at the Plaza Hotel in New York City, Brown is tripping on PCP, the potent hallucinogen known on the street as angel dust. He is in such bad shape that the hotel doctor must be called to treat him for high blood pressure and hypertension, and his aides are forced to cancel his show at the Lone Star Cafe.

This is almost unheard of: for decades, Brown has been the self-proclaimed "hardest working man in show business."

This also occurs at what should be a time of celebration for James Brown. He is in the midst of a major comeback. In 1986 he was inducted into the Rock & Roll Hall of Fame, and with "Living in America," he made his first appearance on the Top 10 pop charts in 18 years. His latest album, *I'm Real*, is strong on the Black charts. But in the hotel room, there is nothing but misery, "Doc, you just don't understand," says Brown, who is upset by his marital troubles. "You just don't understand."

At the Lone Star, word is brought to Brown's band by his wardrobe mistress, Gertrude Sanders. "Martha, James is really sick," a teary-eyed Sanders tells backup vocalist Martha High. "He's just about gone. I'm scared he's going to die."

A group of Brown associates and employees—including the Reverend Al Sharpton (who is making headlines for his role in the Tawana Brawley debacle), drummer Arthur Dixon, music director Sweet Charles Sherrell, saxophonist Maceo Parker, High and Sanders—head back to the hotel. "You could smell the stuff from the elevator," Sherrell recalls later. "It was heartbreaking. Both of them [Brown and his wife] were just out of it. She could hardly open the door."

Inside, a disheveled Brown sits on the edge of the bed, staring into space. For the next few hours, Brown's visitors try to bring him around by getting him to drink milk, massaging his shoulders, and offering their support. "That was a good show tonight," Brown eventually says. "Wasn't that a good show?"

"Man," says Maceo Parker, "I think you're talking about last night."

"We supposed to work tonight," Brown says.

"He didn't know he'd missed the show," Martha High recalls later. "That's not James Brown. That's out."

LAST YEAR THE SELF-STYLED GODFATHER of Soul continued to make news: In the spring he was arrested after beating up his wife, a one-time "Solid Gold" hair stylist and makeup artist named Adrienne "Alfie" Rodriguez; since then he has been repeatedly busted on drug and weapons offenses. It hasn't helped matters that his wife—also arrested and charged with possession of PCP— told her story to the *National Enquirer*, describing the beatings she had received at her husband's hands in an April 26 article headlined JAMES BROWN TRIED TO KILL ME and let the tabloid photograph her bruises.

Drugs were also tightening their grip. Brown had been smoking reefer spiked with angel dust for years, but he was in command onstage. So band members were shocked when he hit the stage stoned and out of control at both the New Orleans Jazz and Heritage Festival and at the Valley Forge Music Fair, in Philadelphia. In mid-song he would stop the band, stare at the audience and, says Sherrell, "talk about something in left field. It was horrible."

The sad denouement came on Saturday, September 14, 1988, when Brown, high on PCP and carrying a shotgun, entered an insurance seminar taking place in a building adjacent to his Augusta office. According to Geraldine Phillips of Atlanta, who was leading the seminar, Brown wanted to know who had been using his private restroom and began asking her questions. "I thought if I answered one of those questions wrong, he was going to kill me and everybody else," she said later, although it turned out the shotgun didn't work.

The police were called, and a two-state high-speed car chase ensued in which Brown allegedly attempted to run over two policemen who were setting up a roadblock. The police shot out the front tires of Brown's truck, but that didn't stop him. He drove another six miles on the rims, circling back to Augusta before stopping in a ditch. The police said that after they removed him from the truck, he started singing "Georgia" and was doing his "'Good Foot' dance" as they gave him a sobriety test. Released on bail, Brown was in trouble again within 24 hours, when he was arrested for driving under the influence of PCP.

Brown claims the incident happened somewhat differently: that he was just trying to find out why people were using his bathroom without permission and that he stopped for police but that they kicked in his window and shot at his truck. "A man fires 23 rounds of bullets in a truck, two in the gas tank, and then rush me to the hospital and say I am on drugs and I'm going to kill him—they wanted me to plead guilty to that," says Brown. "Worst day of my life."

People close to Brown—his agent, Jack Bart; his attorney Buddy Dallas; his childhood friend Leon Austin—blame Adrienne Brown for the big man's troubles. "She no good for him," says Austin. But artist manager Joyce McCrae, who has known Adrienne Brown since the early Eighties, believes she is as much "a victim of James' problems as James is himself.

"Alfie has been portrayed as the scapegoat, the cause of all of James' problems," says McCrae. "James certainly knew about drugs long before he ever met Alfie. On the few occasions that I sat and listened to her talk, she reminded me of the women I'd seen suffering from battered-wife syndrome on TV talk shows. For her to bear the blame for the downfall and destruction of James is absurd."

"A scapegoat is right," says James Brown. "She is a scapegoat for some people who have taken advantage of her because they don't like the relationship between she and I. They don't like it because we are third-world people. Third-world people are not recognized.

"I'll tell you what got us into this problem," he continues. "Number one, they didn't like the marriage between my wife and I in that small area. Next, they didn't like my wife leaving NBC, coming and staying with me. Some group of people want me to go to New York or Los Angeles. They want James Brown in a big city, think he's more effective with the world. They need my guidance because 85 percent of the business is all James Brown. But I don't want to live in LA. I like coming back home.

"I been a human all my life, but we don't get human rights. Should get them. I don't have to explain myself. You know who explains my problem? Martin Luther King. Kennedy dying for human dignity, human rights, Adam Clayton Powell, James Meredith, Hubert Humphrey. You all want to spend your time trying to make me a drug addict when you should spend your time trying to get me back on the streets so I can help you with the problem."

THERE IS A SMALL PAINTING hanging in James Brown's private office. The painting shows a bull, its back already bloodied, butting its horns into a red matador's cape.

Most stars of Brown's stature are handled by experienced managers based in New York or Los Angeles. Not James Brown. He didn't have a manager, and when he was not on the road, you could often find him in Augusta handling his own business out of a suite of offices in an anonymous-looking executive park near I-20.

On the afternoon following Brown's Augusta court appearance, his wife is sitting at a big desk with an engraved plaque that reads, JAMES BROWN, PRESIDENT. She is on the phone with *USA Today*. "This has been one of the worst days I've had," Adrienne Brown says. "I almost broke down today. I'm ready for the hospital, but I'm trying to keep going."

Brown hangs up. "How much do they want us to take?" she asks. "We're just two people. They had James and I in the same courtroom today! I told God last night I can't take too much more."

Sitting across the desk from Brown is 40-year-old Ray Ferrill, who looks like a low-rent Tom Waits and says he is James Brown's godson. "What we have is a conspiracy to incarceration"; he says and then proceeds—in a rambling monologue—to tie James Brown's problems to Iran, racism, and national security.

Adrienne Brown is exhausted. Her eye shadow is smeared, face puffy. But she is hanging in there, staunchly defending her husband and their marriage. She says his troubles have only helped his career. "This man is so hot right now it's scary," she insists. "There are movie contracts right now they want to negotiate in jail."

Brown pops a diet candy into her mouth. "My husband doesn't take drugs," she says flatly. "They say they want to treat James the same as anybody else. Well, he's not anybody else. And then, what they want to do is come down even harder to show that they're not treating him like anybody else."

"Scapegoat and an example," says Ferrill.

Adrienne Brown says she has also been victimized. "We love each other," she says. "And that's where it's at. This bull of me feeding my husband drugs. You can't make James Brown do anything."

The phone rings, and this time it's Sharpton.

"Hi Rev," she says. "These asshole attorneys made him plead guilty. He got another five years. Well, it's because they figured he'd get a deal. He got no deal. I'm telling you, Rev, we're both doomed people if someone doesn't move on something."

In Adrienne Brown's world, as in her husband's, paranoia runs rampant. She recounts an incident last year in which "a nickel bag of grass" was planted in her husband's coat pocket and insinuates that his lawyer may have had a hand in it. "A month ago, before he went to jail, my husband had his coat hanging here in the office," she says. "We were sitting here in the office—Mr. Dallas, myself, my husband, the people who work here, some reporters. Mr. Dallas says, 'That's a beautiful fur coat—may I see it?' Mr. Dallas walked up to the coat, looked at it, touched it. We went home, and my husband emptied the coat pockets. Do you know what he found? A nickel bag of grass. Now that was put there!"

Adrienne Brown sighs. "Do you understand how we can be set up?" she asks. "These things happen with us. And it's hard for people to believe because it's like a soap opera. But it isn't. It happens to us every day."

Asked about the coat incident, Buddy Dallas recalls "being in the office and asking about the cougar coat." He says, however, that he has had nothing to do with—let alone planting—illegal drugs of any kind.

Adrienne Brown denies she has been beaten by her husband, and she doesn't want to talk about the photograph of her bruises that appeared in the *National Enquirer*. But pressed on the subject, she makes it sound like a publicity stunt. "We sold newspapers," she says. "James couldn't get in those newspapers, no matter all the good he's done. There are many PR schemes that people use."

But at the moment Adrienne Brown is unhappy with the way she and her husband are being portrayed. "Let these animals talk all they want to talk," she says. "As soon as this is over, I'm taking care of them." She pauses a moment. "If this story is wrong, I will hunt you down."

ON THE SATURDAY AFTERNOON before the Augusta trial, Bobby Byrd—a founding and former member of James Brown's Famous Flames and at one time the singer's closest friend—is brooding in the upstairs bedroom of his Atlanta home. Just a few weeks earlier, Byrd, who is in his 50s, suffered a mild stroke when he learned he wouldn't be getting the money—some $25,000 in artist's and writer's royalties—that he claims James Brown owes him.

A spokesman for PolyGram Records, Brown's former record label, says there may be royalties owed to Byrd by Brown. The label currently credits all royalties from James Brown records or productions against monies previously advanced to Brown (Brown's attorney says that figure is about $2 million); it is Brown's responsibility to pay artists like Bobby Byrd who were under his production umbrella.

"Bobby need his name in the paper," says Brown, who denies owing Byrd any money. "Whatever Bobby Byrd did, he did. I know nothing about it. Bobby made a mistake years ago—he quit [Brown's band]. That's his problem. He shouldn't have quit."

"Everything was beautiful when we first started," says Byrd, who cowrote such Brown classics as "Licking Stick—Licking Stick," "(Get Up I Feel Like Being a) Sex Machine." and "Talkin' Loud & Sayin' Nothing." Byrd is thinking of those early years, in the Fifties, when the whole band would pile into a station wagon and head off to gigs.

"We were playing locally up and down the highway, the girls screaming, and that was all that mattered," says Byrd. "Making a few dollars. We all supposed to be together. It was the Famous Flames. Everybody got an equal share of everything. We gonna stick together 'til the very end." Byrd pauses a second. "We thought."

Byrd sips from a can of soda pop. "When it got to the money, then this man changed completely," he says. "It was like the difference in night and day."

"James' head just went bigger and bigger and bigger," says Johnny Terry, another former member of the Famous Flames, during a separate interview.

For years the people who worked for James Brown wouldn't talk about these things. To this day, many of Brown's employees won't say a word against their boss. They include Danny Ray, who has been Brown's master of ceremonies for a quarter-century; wardrobe mistress Gertrude Sanders; the secretaries in Brown's office; and even former members of Brown's band, such as St. Clair Pinckney, who quit last summer after the band was stranded in Rome with no money for nine days. "He's a loving person," insists Sanders, who has been with Brown for decades. "A nice person."

But many others—some no longer on Brown's payroll, some still in his employ—have had it. They are fed up with the world of James Brown, where he is the self-proclaimed king and mere mortals are expected "to bow," as a former band member puts it.

"That goes for the moon and stars and the air outside," says the Reverend Al Sharpton, who once claimed he and Brown were starting a nationwide chain of Groom Me shoeshine parlors, where "unskilled young people" could make a living shining shoes. "That's the way it's always been."

No more. Brown once ruled the recording studio, dictating every note on some of his records, but before he was imprisoned, he was merely showing up to overdub his vocals after hired professionals wrote and produced the tracks. Since the early Seventies, Brown has had major tax problems; he currently owes the government in excess of $9 million. Once considered an astute businessman—whose properties included a booking agency, three radio stations, 17 publishing companies, a record label, a television show, a production company, and a Learjet and who had millions in an Atlanta bank account—Brown no longer even owns the 62-acre Beech Island, South Carolina, ranch where he lives.

JAMES BROWN'S ALMOST SUPERNATURAL ABILITY TO create astounding records from street talk and raw rhythms went hand in hand with an obsession for stardom bordering on the pathological. Abandoned as a four-year-old to the care of relatives and friends, neglected and unloved (he says it was 20 years before he was reunited with his mother), James Brown grew up on the streets of Augusta—the "ill-repute area," he calls it—where he learned how to wheel, deal, gamble, and steal.

"I wanted to be somebody," Brown has said. "To be somebody." He was a tough, street-savvy kid who in addition to working odd jobs—shining shoes, delivering groceries, picking cotton, racking pool balls—put more cash in his pockets by playing dice and directing servicemen from nearby Camp Gordon to the local whorehouses.

"He didn't have nothin'," says Henry Stallings, one of Brown's schoolmates. "He always say that's why he work so hard now. He don't ever want to go back that way. Never, ever again!"

By the time Brown entered the seventh grade, in 1949, he was stealing bicycles, hubcaps, car batteries—anything he could turn into cash. But that came to an end that year, when a night of breaking into cars landed him in Alto Reform School, near Toccoa, Georgia, with a sentence of 8 to 16 years.

"They took me off the street," Brown said this January. "They put me in prison. I thought they were putting me away, but they were saving me. In that prison I found myself."

While serving three and a half years in reform school, Brown met Bobby Byrd during a baseball game between the inmates and some of the local Toccoa kids. Byrd liked Brown and persuaded his mother to intervene in his friend's behalf. The Byrds sponsored Brown and took him into their home.

Byrd also took Brown into his group, the Gospel Starlighters. Before long the members of the group had switched to hard R&B, changing their name to the Famous Flames. In January of 1956, they were signed to King Records, in Cincinnati; four months later "Please, Please, Please" was in the R&B Top 10. By then Brown's ego had already begun to assert itself; at his insistence, the name of the group was soon changed to James Brown and the Famous Flames.

Brown's first taste of fame sent him into hyperdrive. Over the next decade he relentlessly pushed himself, his band, and his business advisers. Along the way he created the baddest rock & roll show the world has ever seen.

Writers have been trying to get the James Brown experience down on paper ever since. "He is in an ecstasy of agony," wrote Doon Arbus in the mid-Sixties. "It is as if he is gripped by demons and poltergeists," wrote Philip Norman of the *London Sunday Times* in the Seventies. "He does a split, erupts in a pirouette, whirls like a dervish, and ends up at the microphone just in time to shriek 'bayba-a-ay' as the band modulates into the introduction to his latest hit," wrote Robert Palmer in the late Seventies, when he was a pop-music critic for the *New York Times*. "James! he was then, shooting out of the wings like a pinball off the spring with a 'pleeeeeeeeese!' that could pop a hairpin at fifty feet," wrote Gerri Hirshey in *Rolling Stone* in 1983.

Any way you put it, Brown was a phenomenon. As Bill Wyman of the Rolling Stones once said—and as one look at the 1965 performance film *The T.A.M.I. Show*, confirms—"You could put Jerry Lee Lewis, Little Richard, Chuck Berry, and Bo Diddley on one side of the stage and James Brown on the other, and you wouldn't even notice the others were up there!"

From the late Fifties through the mid-Seventies, James Brown toured year-round, crisscrossing the country in buses and Cadillacs and later a series of private jets, coming up with ideas for songs in dressing rooms, cutting hits between gigs. Business was done on a cash basis, and Brown carried suitcases full of cash from town to town—as much as $250,000—his employees often passing some of it out to the DJs whom his men hired to "copromote" the shows.

The pace was manic, and Brown gave no quarter. He fined his musicians for infractions ranging from a missed note to a wrinkled stage outfit. "He wanted things to always be razor's edge," says saxophonist Pee Wee Ellis, Brown's arranger during the middle to late Sixties. "He kept people intimidated. Stupid stuff. We had dress-code fines; shoes had to have a certain shine. There were rules about carrying our uniforms."

Brown's passion and obsession made him push harder and harder, fueling a remarkable stream of hit records—17 in a row during one two-year period—that didn't stop until the late Seventies. At a time—the late Fifties and the early Sixties—when record companies typically chose the song, producer, and musicians that would work on a recording session, Brown was a revolutionary. "He insisted on making his records his way," says Alan Leeds, one of Brown's former tour managers who now works for Prince. "He said, 'I'm not going to sound like the Stax sound or the Detroit sound, where everybody has the same studio guys. I got my band, we're gonna play my music, and we're going to play it my way.' And when the record company balked at that, he'd just not record at all. And he'd make them suffer until they needed a James Brown record so badly that they'd take whatever he gave them."

Even disillusioned former sidemen like Ellis and Byrd brighten up as they describe working on the hits. Ellis says that his job was to "act as a translator and a mediator between the bizarre and the guitar, taking the unorthodox ideas of James Brown and making them somewhat conventional but not losing the rawness."

Among the songs Ellis cowrote with Brown was "Cold Sweat," which became a number-seven pop hit in 1967. "He called me into the dressing room and mumbled something, hummed a feeling," says Ellis. "I got on the bus, and by the time we got to Cincinnati (where the studios of King Records were located), we fell off the bus, rehearsed the song for a few minutes, cut it, then got back on the bus and went back to work."

Brown recorded live in the studio. Standing in the middle of the room surrounded by his band, Brown would try out new dance steps even as he laid down a track. Unable to read or write music, Brown would sing each part to the musicians. "He'd take the rhythm section, verbally hum the parts out," says St. Clair Pinckney. "'I want you to play this—dum-da-dum-da-dum-dum. Gimme this kind of beat. Play that for a few minutes. Okay, hold that right there, don't forget nothin'. Hold that groove right there.' Then he'd call the horns in and do the same thing with them. Next thing you know, it's 'Okay, roll the tape.' Most times it was first time down."

Former band members, including Byrd, Ellis, Johnny Terry, and others, complain that Brown didn't always give them full credit for their contributions. They say that Brown would add his name to songs he hadn't written and that instead of paying someone, he might give them a writing credit. Terry claims he wrote "I'll Go Crazy." Both Byrd and Bobby Bennett, another former member of the Famous Flames, say one of Brown's girlfriends, Betty Newsome, actually wrote "It's a Man's Man's Man's World." Although Brown has disputed this, "It's a Man's Man's Man's World"—which for many years was credited solely to Brown—is now also credited to Newsome.

Wherever the songs actually came from, no one denies that Brown made them his own. "It was his energy that gave it the fire," says Bob Patton, who worked for Brown promoting his records and shows. "If you took James away, the band could play the tunes, but they didn't have the spark. He made the engine run. Damn near burn it out sometimes."

Brown could get crazy on the road. In 1968, Bennett was playing cards with Danny Ray in his room at the Ritz in Paris when a furious Brown burst in, a pistol in his hand. "He came in and pointed it at me," says Bennett. "He told me, 'I'm going to kill you. You told my old lady I had another woman on the plane.' He jumped on me. I tried to throw his head out of the 15th-story window. If not for Danny Ray, I'd have driven his head through one of the iron bars they had in the window. Danny was shouting, 'Don't kill him!'"

But Brown saved the worst treatment for his women. "He beat Tammi Terrell terrible," says Bennett. "She was bleeding, shedding blood." Terrell, who died in 1970, was Brown's girlfriend before she became famous as Marvin Gaye's singing partner in the mid-Sixties. "Tammi left him because she didn't want her butt whipped," says Bennett, who also claims he saw Brown kick one pregnant girlfriend down a flight of stairs. Both Bobby Byrd and his wife, Vicki Anderson, say that in the Seventies, Brown abused his wife at the time, Deirdre, "something terrible."

"All the women liked his money and his fame," says Anderson. "They liked being Mrs. James Brown. This is nothing new. The minute he buys you the first thing—if you're his woman—next will come those beatings." Anderson says she has seen Brown repeatedly lure women away from their men with promises of stardom. On a plane flight to London in 1976, Brown even tried to steal his best friend's wife. "He told her that if she left me, she'd have an album and it would be Number One," says Byrd.

"Said he'd make me a millionaire," adds Anderson. "I wasn't going to leave my husband for no hit record."

Brown abruptly ended the prison telephone interview with *Rolling Stone* before he could be asked about abusing his girlfriends and wives over the years, and his lawyer Buddy Dallas said he could not comment because the incidents had occurred before he represented Brown.

SHERIFF CARROL HEATH IS SITTING IN his Aiken, Georgia, office, where a photograph of himself and George Bush is prominently displayed. "About two and a half years ago we started getting the calls," says the sheriff, running a hand across a pale forehead and through thinning white hair. "Either Adrienne, the wife, or her mother. 'James beat up on me.' 'Get someone out there. He's killing her.'"

The sheriff shakes his head. He picks up a phone and asks for a computer printout. The printout shows that Adrienne Lois Brown called the police once in 1984, three times in 1985, once in 1987, and more than half a dozen times in 1988. "On one occasion she said he was going to take her out into the woods and shoot her," Heath says, putting the printout aside. "You know, if a man and woman can't get along, they should part ways."

Captain Jim Whitehurst, a big man who says his nickname around the sheriff's office is Wyatt Earp, steps into the office. In apparent homage to the psychotic villain of *The Night of the Hunter*, Whitehurst has H-A-T-E tattooed on the knuckles of one hand, L-O-V-E on the other. "It's a damn Yankee," says Whitehurst. "I can tell just by looking at you."

Whitehurst is followed by Bill Hartman, an investigator who has been to Brown's ranch. Hartman is wearing a belt with a buckle in the shape of handcuffs. "I went out there the day after the car got shot up," he says, referring to an incident that occurred over the 1988 Easter weekend. "I met her at the hospital. She was beat up real bad. Black-and-blue marks all over her body. Legs, back, side."

Hartman takes a seat. "What was supposed to have happened, they had got into an argument because he wasn't going to take her on this foreign tour," he says. "He went in the house, and first he got her mink coat, throwed it on the ground and shot holes all in it. Then he went back in and got one of these here leather jackets with sable collar and sable cuffs, thrown it on the ground and shot it up."

"Did they have holes in them?" asks the sheriff.

"Sir, I don't know," replies Hartman. "Because before she went to the hospital, she had took them to a furrier to have them fixed. The next-door neighbor told me that the night of the incident she wouldn't even go to the hospital until she took them coats over to that furrier to have them fixed."

"You ever recall going out there and finding the house in disarray and the furniture broken up?" asks the sheriff.

"Just bullet holes," says Hartman, smiling. "Plenty of bullet holes in the house. He took a .22 rifle and went into this walk-in closet and shot down through everything on her side of the closet. Found bullet holes in the bedroom walls"

Whitehurst leans forward in his chair. "Ever shot a monkey?" he asks, idly fingering a bullet he has picked up off the sheriff's desk. "Ever seen anyone shoot a monkey?"

JAMES BROWN IS STANDING IN A SMALL room inside the Law Enforcement Center a few hours after he has received his concurrent sentence. He is smiling, flashing that classic grin, his false teeth glistening. His mother, Susie, her body enveloped in a black fur coat, is seated nearby, staring almost reverently at her son. Seated next to her is Brown's aunt Gerry. "I feel so good," says Brown.

"Yeah, yeah, I'm so happy," interjects his mother.

Brown mentions a Psalm he has been reading; he implies that the spirit has moved him. "At the height of my career, I thought that everything was happening great," he says. "And thank God for it, but the height, the very pinnacle of everything I've ever done in the business, is not 10 percent of what's happened in the last ninety days. See, it's almost a rebirth."

And what has happened?

Brown assumes a thoughtful pose. "I'll tell you," he says, "it's like an omen. As a kid in that prison, I found myself. An omen in my life. The same place I'm at right now. That was the beginning of my life, in 1950. This is the beginning of my life again. An omen. An omen.

"I can't give you the kind of interview I'd like to give you in front of my mother," says Brown. "But, you know, once you be lucky enough to do some of the things I've done in life, there's a lot of stress. Christ went off—he didn't want to be around other people when he was praying. I ain't no Christ, but I at least got to go off and think." He laughs. "If Christ had to do it, what about me?" he asks. "I'm no prophet—I'm just a good person trying to do the right thing. But I got to have that time off."

But what about all the trouble he has been in? What about the drugs? What about the violence?

"Being a victim of different kinds of things going in your system," says Brown. "I've been a victim of that. And to stand here and run my history down would be hard to do, but I'll always be behind telling kids not to use drugs, I'll always be behind drug abuse. I can't stop the pushers, but I can stop the kids from being buyers."

It's time to leave; Brown wants some time alone with his family. But he just can't help himself, and he voices bitterness and resentment over his predicament. "If they catch some sports figure snorting coke or any kind of drugs, you know what they do?" he asks. "Have him sit on the bench and then let him play next week. I can go to some of our highest official wives, they just send them to a clinic. But I'm sure when God wanted Moses, he didn't think of all the people yonder, he thought only of Moses. Maybe if a man is strong enough and people believe in him, maybe they won't take no for an answer. . . ."

Brown flashes that grin again. He is shaking hands, about to turn away. "I thank God that I know what I know," he says. "Everybody help you win. But nobody help you when you lose. So when you get back to winning again, they'll love you again."

Brown's mother and aunt chime in: "That's right, that's right."

"Thank God the Lord gave me something this time to know what I have to do," he says.

"I'm glad to hear you say that," says James Brown's elderly mother. "I was praying for you."

*Rolling Stone*, April 6, 1989

David Byrne of Talking Heads, Old Waldorf, San Francisco, 1978.

# TALKING HEADS

**David Byrne:** I used to do paintings of electric guitars.

**Jerry Harrison:** I started painting when my band [The Modern Lovers] broke up.

**Harrison:** I object to us as "artists who have chosen the medium of music" because I find that distasteful and very unfunky and we don't perform in art galleries.

**Harrison:** The name was chosen so as not to give anyone a preconceived idea about our music.

**Different perspectives in different songs?**

**Byrne:** It's because I feel different ways at different times from day to day.

**Harrison:** They're little statements and feelings he has, rather than trying to get rid of all of them and make up one statement he can always live with.

**Tina Weymouth:** We're a very modern band.

March 1978

John Fogerty said he was "about eight years old" when he decided he wanted to be a rock musician. Photo by Myriam Santos.

# JOHN FOGERTY LOOKS BACK ON THE GLORY DAYS OF CREEDENCE CLEARWATER REVIVAL

*In the late Sixties and early Seventies, Creedence Clearwater Revival scored 14 Top 10 hits. At the time, hit records (and Creedence) weren't considered cool in the San Francisco Bay Area. Underground bands like the Quicksilver Messenger Service, Big Brother and the Holding Company, the Grateful Dead, and Country Joe and the Fish were the cool bands. Still, there was a lot about the band's first album,* Creedence Clearwater Revival, *that I liked. For starters, the first track, a version of Screamin' Jay Hawkins' "I Put a Spell on You," was spellbinding; I hadn't yet heard the original but even later, after I had, John Fogerty's vocal continued to slay me. The whole album is strong, but the standout track for me for many years was "Walk on the Water," in which the singer witnesses a man "from the other side" walking on the water and calling out the singer's name. Later, when I would hear one of the Creedence hits on the radio, I couldn't help but like it. I eventually considered myself a fan of the band that John Fogerty led. I can't say I became friends with John Fogerty, but in the late Eighties after he revived his career with the hit album* Centerfield, *I did establish a relationship in which he trusted me to treat him fairly. I earned that trust when I showed up in court every day during his 1988 trial in San Francisco, a trial that resulted in Fogerty being cleared of the charge by onetime Fantasy Records president Saul Zaentz that in writing the hit song "The Old Man Down the Road," Fogerty had plagiarized his own song, "Run Through the Jungle" (that Fantasy owned the publishing rights to). I was the only reporter there for the whole trial, and Fogerty told me that meant a lot to him. I subsequently interviewed him at least another five times. Whenever we met, Fogerty seemed to relax during our conversations. Fogerty was working on the album that he would call* Blue Moon Swamp *at the time of this interview; that album would be released four years later, in 1997.*

"IN 1968 I ALWAYS USED TO SAY that I wanted to make records they would still play on the radio in 10 years" says former Creedence Clearwater Revival leader John Fogerty as he sits in a LA recording studio where he is working on a forthcoming solo album. Fogerty got his wish and plenty more. This year Credence Clearwater Revival is being inducted into the Rock & Roll Hall of Fame. "It's quite an honor," he says proudly. "I equate Hall of Fame things with baseball, and since I was a little kid, the people in the Baseball Hall of Fame have been my idols. The fact that they now have a Rock & Roll Hall of Fame is pretty cool. Being in the same club, you might say, with Elvis, Booker T. and the MGS and, of course, the Beatles is awesome."

Like the other members of that club, Creedence continues to be a vital influence on generation after generation of rock & rollers. Many of the group's classic songs—including "Proud Mary," "Born on the Bayou," "Fortunate Son," "Green River," and "Run Through the Jungle"—are staples of a number of different rock-radio formats as well as of bar-band repertoires everywhere. U2, Def Leppard, and Bruce Springsteen have all acknowledged a debt to Creedence, covering Fogerty's songs in concert and, in U2's case, on record. Feedback-guitar heroes Sonic Youth even named one of their albums, *Bad Moon Rising*, after a Fogerty composition. "Gee, this is kind of what the Colonel had in mind when he took Elvis off the road, right?" laughs Fogerty, who has only toured once since Creedence broke up in 1972.

"For me personally, it's just neat that it lives on." Fogerty was just 14 when he formed the Blue Velvets, a mostly instrumental band, with two junior-high schoolmates, drummer Doug Clifford and bassist Stu Cock. In 1964, Fogerty's older brother Tom started joining them in the recording studio and by the end of 1965, was performing with them at clubs as the group's rhythm guitarist. Renamed the Golliwogs by a Fantasy Records executive who didn't tell them about the name change until it appeared on their first single, the quartet scored a regional hit with an original song, "Brown-Eyed Girl," which sounded like a slowed-down version of Them's "Gloria."

Like their sappy name, the Golliwogs' singles were uninspired derivations of British Invasion smashes. Realizing a change was needed, the group became Creedence Clearwater Revival in 1967 and started emphasizing a rootsier sound. Creedence scored its first hit in the fall of 1968 with a reworking of Dale Hawkins' "Suzie Q." With the exception of that debut single, Fogerty wrote all of Creedence's 14 hit records. He was also singer, lead guitarist, producer, and arranger of nearly everything that appeared on Creedence's seven studio albums.

Creedence broke up in 1972, after which Fogerty pretty much dropped out of sight. He released an unsuccessful solo album, *John Fogerty*, in 1975, but for most of those years, a variety of music-business problems, some involving Fantasy Records, the company Creedence recorded for, made it impossible for him to create new music. Fogerty finally emerged in 1985 with a Top 10 hit, "The Old Man Down the Road," and the multiplatinum album, *Centerfield*.

Fogerty toured as a solo artist for the first time after the release of the follow-up, *Eye of the Zombie*, but refused to perform any of his old Creedence songs because of his continuing legal battles with Fantasy. More recently, however, Fogerty has started performing the old songs at a handful of special events, including a 1987 benefit for Vietnam vets and a 1991 memorial for Bill Graham.

As anyone who remembers Creedence's heyday will tell you, it's about time.

**Michael Goldberg:** When did you first decide to become a musician?

**John Fogerty:** I remember as early as 1953, when I was about eight years old, that I was going to name my group Johnny Corvette and the Corvettes. I know it was '53 'cause the Corvette was brand new. I had already made a choice: I was thinking about making a career out of music. It was pretty vague. I didn't know if we were singing doo-wop or what, but the imagery of the Corvette—I was pretty psyched on that. And, of course, I was Johnny Corvette. Somehow I was the leader already. Pretty funny.

**Goldberg:** How did you find your singing voice? The difference between how you sounded on those Golliwogs singles and then on the first Creedence recording is startling.

**Fogerty:** I was very self-conscious about my voice. What happened was that me and some other guys went up to Portland, Oregon, of all places, during the summer of 1964. We found a drummer and got a two-week engagement at a club called the Town Mart. At that point, this guy named Mike Burns was the singer. Well, one day I said, "I'm going to sing." And since I was out of my hometown, away from my parents and any of my friends, I kind of just told myself to go ahead and try it, don't be shy. And I had taken a reel-to-reel tape recorder up there. I would record whole sets. Then I'd stay up until sunrise listening to myself. And I heard myself improve. I'd try something like a scream or a hard-edged "Well!" I'd hear myself try to do it on the tape, and the next night I'd go back and try something else. As I used to say, I developed a scream in Portland.

**Goldberg:** The first record you made as Creedence Clearwater Revival was "Suzie Q." Didn't you have a very specific purpose in recording that song?

**Fogerty:** This little underground San Francisco radio station, KMPX [the first progressive-rock station in America], would play all kinds of weird things. I told the other guys that the quickest way we could get on the radio, therefore get more exposure and get this thing going was to specifically go in and record an arrangement of "Suzie Q" that could get played on that station. It's been said that what we were doing seemed very far removed from the rest of San Francisco, but that's not quite true. "'Suzie Q" was designed to fit right in. The eight-minute opus. Feedback. Like [the Paul Butterfield Blues Band's] "East-West." And especially the little effect, the little telephone-box [vocal] in the middle, which is the only part I regret now. It's just funny sounding. But, lo and behold, it worked!

**Goldberg:** So the tape got played?

**Fogerty:** Yeah, they started playing it a lot. That broke the ground for the rest of the stuff.

**Goldberg:** Creedence didn't seem to fit in with the psychedelic lifestyle in San Francisco. Were you guys pretty straight?

**Fogerty:** *[Laughs]* Well, I never inhaled. I was really Mr. Straight. I was scared to death of LSD or any kind of pill. Yeah, I'd smoked some marijuana, and the other guys, I think, were certainly more experimental than me. But I didn't like it as an image. Since I was the leader, I was the guy with the whip saying, "No, we're not going to push this as an image thing." But at the same time, I didn't feel that made us the Osmond Brothers either.

**Goldberg:** As Creedence was experiencing some of its first Top 40 success, The Band came along with its album *Music from Big Pink* and got a lot of media attention. They were one of the first bands on the cover of *Time* magazine.

**Fogerty:** To be really honest, I'd say I was a bit envious. There were a few songs they did that I really loved, like "The Night They Drove Old Dixie Down" and "Up on Cripple Creek." But they got all this validation from the critics. Here I was, a competitive guy trying to make my band the biggest thing in the world, and here these guys [are getting attention] just cause they're from New York or Woodstock or Big Pink or Bob Dylan or whatever. I was definitely envious of all that, which just shows my own pettiness. Because actually it was a great band, and they made good records.

**Goldberg:** What did your brother Tom do in the band? Did he actually play rhythm guitar on the records?

**Fogerty:** Yeah, pretty much. Probably 99 percent of the tracks we did as a quartet are played live with all four guys playing at the same rime. I've heard the rumor over the years that "after they left the studio, John went in and re-recorded all the parts." No. I think the charm of what you hear on those records is four guys really playing.

**Goldberg:** Let's talk about some of your best-known songs. "Proud Mary" was the first of your original songs to become a hit.

**Fogerty:** In the middle of July of '68, I got my honorable discharge from the United States Army after much consternation. I was overjoyed. This envelope containing this little thing that's like a diploma had been sitting on the stairs of my apartment building for a couple of days. It said, "Official Business" or something. Well, I didn't bother to look close at it. Finally, one day I was coming into my apartment, and I look on the stairs, and, "Hey, that's got my name on it!" Well, son of a bitch, I opened it up, and I'm discharged from the army. Holy hallelujah! I actually went out on the little apartment-building lawn and did a couple of cartwheels. At that one moment it was like "Wow, all the troubles of the world have been lifted off my shoulders!"

If it didn't happen within five minutes, certainly within a week and a half I had written "Proud Mary." That one event that led to doing the cartwheels, that's where "Left a good job in the city" comes from. I just felt real good.

Although I didn't recall it at the time when I was doing "Rollin' on the river," there is an old Will Rogers movie about these old paddle wheelers, and I believe at one point they actually sing, "Rolling on the river." I know that buried deep inside me are all these little bits and pieces of Americana. It's deep in my heart, deep in my soul. As I learned in English 101, write about what you know about.

**Goldberg:** What inspired "Born on the Bayou"?

**Fogerty:** I would sit there, kind of look at the blank wall in my little apartment, and I just kind of pictured this story. Now around this same time, because of "Suzie Q" getting played on the underground radio station, we played the Avalon Ballroom, in San Francisco. We were onstage for a two-minute sound check. I started doing this thing with the guitar, and I started screaming into the microphone what would later become a refined melody but at that moment was just noise, and I had Doug and Stu just play along. I just wanted to hear this energy thing. Anyway, that mythical thing that I was dreaming up at night and that burst of energy on the stage at the Avalon came together. "Born on the

Bayou" is almost the Gordian Knot or the key to what happened later. As I was writing it, it occurred to me that there was more power than just this one song. If there was a way to tie it all together on one album, kind of cross-fertilize, cross-relate the songs, you would have a much more interesting and maybe more powerful image. So that's what happened. "Born on the Bayou" sort of relates to "Proud Mary." It certainly relates to "Keep on Chooglin'" and "Graveyard Train."

**Goldberg:** "Green River" also fits right into what critics started calling "bayou rock."

**Fogerty:** "Green River" is really about this place where I used to go as a kid on Putah Creek, near Winters, California. I went there with my family every year until I was 10. Lot of happy memories there. I learned how to swim there. There was a rope hanging from the tree. Certainly dragonflies, bullfrogs. There was a little cabin we would stay in owned by a descendant of Buffalo Bill Cody. That's the reference in the song to Cody Jr. The actual specific reference, "Green River," I got from a soda pop-syrup label. You used to be able to go into a soda fountain, and they had these bottles of flavored syrup. My flavor was called Green River. It was green, lime flavored, and they would empty some out over some ice and pour some of that soda water on it, and you had yourself a Green River.

**Goldberg:** "Fortunate Son" is one of your more political songs.

**Fogerty:** It was written, of course, during the Nixon era, and well, let's say I was very nonsupportive of Mr. Nixon. There just seemed to be this trickle down to the offspring of people like him. I remember you would hear about Tricia Nixon and David Eisenhower. You got the impression that these people got preferential treatment, and the whole idea of being born wealthy or being born powerful seemed to really be coming to the fore in the late-Sixties confrontation of cultures.

**Goldberg:** How did you come up with "Bad Moon Rising"?

**Fogerty:** I got the imagery from an old movie called *The Devil and Daniel Webster*. Basically, Daniel Webster makes a deal with Mr. Scratch, the devil. It was supposed to be apocryphal. At one point in the movie, there was a huge hurricane. Everybody's crops and houses are destroyed. Boom. Right next door is the guy's field who made the deal with the devil, and his corn is still straight up, six feet. That image was in my mind. I went, "Holy mackerel!"

My song wasn't about Mr. Scratch, and it wasn't about the deal. It was about the apocalypse that was going to be visited upon us. It wasn't until the band was learning the song that I realized the dichotomy. Here you got this song with all these hurricanes and blowing and raging ruin and all that, but it's [snaps fingers] "I see a bad moon rising." It's a happy-sounding tune, right? It didn't bother me at the time.

**Goldberg:** "Have You Ever Seen the Rain?" was the last hit the group had before your brother quit Creedence.

**Fogerty:** That song is really about the impending breakup of Creedence. The imagery is, you can have a bright, beautiful, sunny day and it can be raining at the same time. The band was breaking up. I was reacting: "Geez, this is all getting serious right at the time when we should be having a sunny day."

**Goldberg:** Your brother left in January of 1971, reportedly because he felt restricted in Creedence and wanted to write and sing. Was his departure to record a solo album the beginning of the end?

**Fogerty:** No. I think the beginning of the end was almost before the beginning.

**Goldberg:** What do you mean?

**Fogerty:** There was a point at which we had done the first album. Everybody had listened to my advice. I don't think anybody thought too much about it. But in making the second album, *Bayou Country*, we had a real confrontation. Everybody wanted to sing, write, make up their own arrangements, whatever, right? This was after 10 years of struggling. Now we had the spotlight. Andy Warhol's 15 minutes of fame. "Suzie Q" was as big as we'd ever seen. Of course, it really wasn't that big. I looked at it like a stepping-stone. I said to the other guys, "If we blow it, the spotlight's going to move over there to the Eagles or somebody." I didn't want to go back to the carwash.

    I basically said, "This band is going to make the best record it can make and that means I'm going to do things the way I want to do 'em." That sounds very egotistical, but that's what happened, and the other three guys had to swallow and go, "Okay, yeah, that's what we'll do." For the next two years it worked great and then at some point they didn't want to swallow and say, "That's nice," anymore.

**Goldberg:** The seeds were sown before the group really hit big?

**Fogerty:** It was a time bomb.

**Goldberg:** Why did you ultimately give in?

**Fogerty:** Here I had sort of forced my will on them because I thought it was right. Well, in terms of success, it was right. In terms of human condition, I don't know. I just really got beat down. For one thing, I was not popular in my own band. There's an old war movie where the guy says, "When you put on the clothes of the general, you cannot be popular with your men." I gave in 'cause I got tired, and that's what they wanted. Even though I thought it was wrong.

**Goldberg:** How do you account for the lasting impact of Creedence?

**Fogerty:** I tried to make as many of the best type of rock & roll records as we could make. For me, a great rock & roll record must include these elements: First, foremost, it has a great title. No. 2, it has a great sound. No. 3, it should have a great song. In other words, something that really is valid and makes sense and, hopefully, you could sing without hearing the record. And No. 4, the best type of rock & roll record has a great guitar lick in it. I tried like crazy to come up with great guitar hooks to fashion a record around. I'm thinking of the kind of thing that began the song and defined the record. "Born on the Bayou," "Up Around the Bend," "Bad Moon Rising," even though it's just chords, there was a thing to it. "Centerfield." That hook, that guitar thing, is great. Another is "Green River."

I think that's why the stuff is so popular. It's easy to listen to, it's simple to play, it sounds real good in a simple setting. You don't need a lot of equipment. It becomes magical even if you're in a bar in Winnemucca, which, believe me, I have heard.

**Goldberg:** Even Sonic Youth named an album, *Bad Moon Rising*, after one of your songs.

**Fogerty:** I'm aware of the group, but I didn't know about that album. Are they from Seattle? I've never heard them, but I really applaud young bands, like those from Seattle, who find something a little different, but it's full of that garage rock & roll thing, and it's just played to the hilt. That's a musical ingredient I have always valued. Sometimes I lose sight of it, but I'm happy to say I have a strong grip on it now. It's what has always made great rock & roll.

**Goldberg:** Do you keep up much with new music and new bands?

**Fogerty:** To a much lesser degree than while I was in Creedence. Part of that is just lack of time. But when I hear something good, I sure become a fan. I used to hate [Nirvana's] "Smells Like Teen Spirit" first couple of times I heard it. And you make fun of it and delight in squealing like the guy. But the changes, the chords, there's a method to that. It ends up being a riveting piece of music. The Nirvana record has the right spirit. I prefer that to a lot of the slick stuff that comes out with so much hype and gloss.

**Goldberg:** From 1972, when Creedence broke up, until 1987 you didn't perform any Creedence songs publicly, mostly because of problems with the band's old record company, but beginning in '87 you started performing the old hits again. How has that felt?

**Fogerty:** The boy, the child who wrote those songs and the artist who sang them is absolutely thrilled. I'm allowing myself to do that because those are the songs that are identified with me, and if people come to see me, it's really cheating them to not do them. I've had Duane Eddy and some other guys tell me, "John, when they come to see you, they don't want to see 'Your Cheatin' Heart'; they're looking for your songs, the songs you made famous." That's a truth you have to face.

**Goldberg:** How does your new album relate to the sound you created with Creedence?

**Fogerty:** The early Creedence stuff reflected my personality. I made a conscious effort to stop imitating other groups. That was my philosophy in '68. Well, I finally found that inner voice again. And I've been searching for that inner voice even through the experience of *Centerfield*. I knew I hadn't quite discovered that guy. I could see him through the shades. Now I just feel that I have that guy well in hand. This record reflects that person very strongly.

**Goldberg:** So, it's going to be a real rock & roll record?

**Fogerty:** Yeah. Sure. I just think that musically and lyrically it reflects as close to the center as I can get, stripping away all the later influences and things that have happened. This record is much stronger than *Centerfield*. If you were going to bet your life on something, in the old days I would have bet my life on "Born on the Bayou" and "Proud Mary." And at this point this is what I would bet my life on.

*Rolling Stone*, 1993

# CHRIS ISAAK: THE MAKING OF A NEW ELVIS

## Chris Isaak has looks, talent and ambition. But is that enough?

*I was told I should check out Silverstone. They were playing the Berkeley Square on University Avenue. In late 1981 I was researching an article on the San Francisco music scene, and my idea was to find four up-and-coming bands and profile each of them as part of the story. San Francisco had been ground zero for psychedelic rock in the '60s, and had produced some great punk bands in the mid- to late '70s, including the Avengers, the Sleepers, and the Mutants. It was now early in 1982. I had heard a demo tape of a few Silverstone songs, and they were good. Really good. What was also enticing was that Erik Jacobsen, who produced a string of Top 10 hits in the mid-1960s for the Lovin' Spoonful, was working with Silverstone. That night at the B-Square I was blown away. I wrote in the* San Francisco Examiner: *"Earlier that evening, Silverstone had seemed more like Elvis than the Lovin' Spoonful. Wearing black leather motorcycle jackets over red shirts that seemed to glow like embers in a campfire, their hair slicked back like '50s teen idols, Silverstone had blasted into 'Cold Dream,' a song that fuses a classic rock & roll rebel stance to a classic rock & roll melody. 'My mother asked me why I dress like that / I said Mom your boy's just a rockin' cat / Your boy's gone / Rockin' gone,' sang Chris Isaak, who with boyish good looks and mischievous eyes would make a good Huck Finn." The article that follows was published in the* San Francisco Examiner *and* Chronicle Sunday *magazine,* Image, *in 1986. At the time I wrote it, I had already known Isaak for five year, had seen him perform in numerous clubs, and we had become casual acquaintances. More than 30 years since it was written I think this piece stands up remarkably well. It does a good job of explaining where Isaak came from, and what his hopes and dreams were, years before he finally made it. It wasn't until the third album,* Heart Shaped World, *that Isaak scored a hit with "Wicked Game" and became a star. Unfortunately, success caused problems within the band, and in May of 1992, Jimmy Wilsey, whose guitar intro to "Wicked Game" helped make it a hit but who had become addicted to heroin, was fired. Wilsey died of "overall organ failure" in late 2018. Isaak and Jacobsen, who produced seven of Isaak's albums, parted ways in 2002. Isaak's most recent album,* First Comes the Night, *was released in 2015.*

ON A COLD AND windy San Francisco night, a little more than a year ago, Chris Isaak seemed poised on the cusp of rock stardom. This was his night, the night Warner Bros. Records, one of the most powerful record companies in the US, held a party celebrating the release of Isaak's debut album, *Silvertone*.

Several hundred people—the movers and shakers of San Francisco's music scene—were crowded into the Punch Line. To many of those in attendance, Chris Isaak had arrived. His trajectory to the top, reasoned the rock pundits, was inevitable. Fame and fortune would be his. And the scene makers—the ones who could assure you they'd practically

Silvertone, San Francisco, 1982: Jamie Ayres, Jimmy Wilsey, John Silvers, and Chris Isaak.
Photo by © Chester Simpson / Rock-N-RollPhotos.com

discovered him, for Christ's sake, the ones who claimed they'd been there, at the Mabuhay Gardens, oh, four, maybe five years earlier when Isaak was making some of his first tentative public performances, back when absolutely no one had heard of the guy—they were all here to bask in his reflected glory.

There was Joel Selvin, the *San Francisco Chronicle* pop music critic, standing at the bar, talking loudly about how much he liked Isaak's album. And over there hovered Kent Zimmerman of the *Gavin Report*, an influential radio newsletter that program directors across the US use to assemble their play lists. Howie Klein, president of 415 Records and for more than 10 years a rock & roll trend setter, had cornered a San Jose DJ and was earnestly telling him that Isaak's album was "the best record ever recorded in San Francisco." Even a few bona fide celebrities—members of the Forty-Niners defense squad—had made it on down. Isaak took a deep breath. For a guy who still rode the Greyhound bus back home to Stockton every few weeks to have his mom cut his hair and wash his dirty laundry, this was really something.

The new album kept pumping out of the club's sound system. Periodically, the lights dimmed and Isaak's first video, for a song called "Dancin'," lit up a big screen. Each time the lights went back on, the rock VIPs clapped and cheered. Wandering through the crowd, returning the back-slapping and congratulations ("Hey Chris baby, great album!") with a smile and a polite "Thanks" was Chris Isaak himself. As he stopped near the bar, it was easy to see what all the fuss was about.

His is a striking figure, with the handsome face of a 1950s matinee idol. His brown hair was combed back into a great, greasy pompadour. He wore a big, baggy, blue gabardine suit, suspenders, shiny black pointed shoes, a white shirt, and a wide tie covered with about 20 tie clips. As he stood there, shaking hands, rocking back and forth to the sound of his own music, periodically messing with his hair, he was a brash young cross between Elvis and Robert Mitchum.

"It's a real ego trip," said Isaak, gently, staring at an immense blow-up of his face on a poster taped to one wall. "That's what I guess this is meant to do, build me up to other people, which is nice. But I'll tell ya, lookin' at a picture of your face as big as a Volkswagen—that'll do somethin' to ya."

Was all the attention embarrassing?

Isaak thought for a moment. "It's embarrassing that I like it."

## The Album's a "Stiff"

SINCE THAT NIGHT, THERE HAS been a lot more cause for embarrassment. *Interview* magazine displayed a full-page photo of Isaak. The *Washington Post* called his record "one of the most striking debut albums of the year." The *Los Angeles Times* chimed in: "Isaak's eerie debut is a collection of small pop gems." England's terminally hip *The Face* listed Isaak alongside Mickey Rourke, Don Johnson, Rosanna Arquette, Sean Penn, and Madonna in what they called "The Class of '85." Director Jonathan Demme, coming off his celebrated Talking Heads concert film, *Stop Making Sense*, approached Isaak about a starring role in his next movie. A tour of Europe elicited more rave reviews.

In nearly every way, 1985 was a tremendous success for Isaak. Every way, that is, but one: He didn't become a "big star." Though Warner Bros. has, to date, spent between $200,000 and $300,000 on Isaak (the cost of making his album and two videos, promoting and marketing his records, and supporting his tours), the album sold a mere 12,000 copies in the US. In record biz lingo, that's a "stiff."

If Isaak doesn't become a star, it will not be for lack of talent. He is, quite simply, the best rock & roller to come out of San Francisco in at least 20 years. You can say of Isaak what rockabilly great Carl Perkins, the guy who wrote "Blue Suede Shoes," said about Elvis: "The boy had everything. He had the looks, the moves, and the talent. . . . He really was different."

You can hear it in his voice, a deep, lonesome ache that sounds like it contains every sorrow that's ever broken his heart. It's the voice of a country singer, plaintive and sentimental. And it's the voice of a real rock & roller, a cat who can sing, hold notes, and deliver a melody as if his music is the only thing that can truly set him free.

Onstage, Isaak and his band all wear the same baggy suits, white shirts, and wide ties. Their sound and style hearken back to some other time. A time before the complex English Lit rock poetry of Bob Dylan. Before psychedelic drugs turned songs into "experiences." Before punk rock and synthesizers. It's a sound that's raw, rough but right. Four guys playing real instruments: drums, bass, and two guitars. A classic rock & roll combo in the style of Buddy Holly and the Crickets. Or the early Rolling Stones. Or pre–*Sergeant Pepper* Beatles.

The songs, with titles like "The Lonely Ones," "Tears," "Funeral in the Rain," and "Lie to Me," are perfectly crafted rock & roll artifacts. They capture, in the simplest, most concise way, feelings of heartbreak, doubt, and passion. It is a testament to Isaak's considerable talent as a songwriter that in live performance, as the band alternates Isaak originals with rock classics like the Rolling Stones' "Fortune Teller" and Carl Perkins' "Dixie Fried," Isaak's own compositions invariably sound better.

As John Fogerty, the former leader of Creedence Clearwater Revival who made a successful comeback last year, says, "I'm just knocked out by Chris Isaak. It's obvious that he's going to be a big star. That's a dumb phrase, but he really does have the stuff that big stars are made of. To me, he's already like a skyscraper against the landscape."

## One-Room Garage Apartment

HE LIVES IN A ONE-ROOM garage apartment in the Sunset District, a block away from Ocean Beach—the same dark, cramped quarters he's occupied since moving to San Francisco in 1980. When he's not working on his music, he can indulge his other passion: surfing. The afternoon I arrive, Isaak is just back from riding the waves. He hangs up his still-dripping wet suit in the backyard and leads the way into his apartment. "This place may be sloppy," he says, clearing some records off a chair and offering me a seat, "but it's not dirty. No roaches."

Isaak, who is 29, lives alone. Although he has a steady girlfriend, he claims that relationships are difficult for him. "I have a lot of strange ideas about love," he says. "When I tell these ideas to other people, they always kind of look at me like, 'You're joking, aren't you?' Some of them are just old-fashioned ideas, like the notion that getting married means staying together forever and never cheating on your wife. All I see now are single parents. To me that would be tragic. Even though I don't live up to some of my morality, it's still in my head."

Isaak sits down, picks up a small acoustic guitar, and begins to idly strum a country-western melody. He is under a lot of pressure these days. His second album is underway, and he spends five nights a week in the studio. There have been meetings with Jonathan Demme. And there are always interviews. Suddenly he adopts a demented voice. "I should be bigger than Prince. My destiny has been denied. Why has God forsaken me?" He pauses, laughs. "I am bigger than Prince. Hell, I'm six-foot-one-inch; he's only five-foot-something."

Isaak's single bed is in the closet. Most of the small room is taken up by two long clothes racks crammed with vintage clothes: old gabardine suits, Hawaiian shirts, leather jackets, dozens of ties, and vests. Then there are the records: classic disks by Roy Orbison and Elvis, Ricky Nelson and Marty Robbins, the Beatles and Muddy Waters. And two guitars, set out on metal stands: a Gretsch Chet Atkins Nashville and a Sears Silvertone.

"I'd love to sell millions of records," he says dreamily. "But if it happened, I don't know what I would buy. I thought I was going to buy a new wet suit this year, but the one I've got is holding up. There isn't much that I want or need.

"Owning a lot of things can make you a hostage. You have a big house, the government might take it away. You better keep working. But they can't take much away from me. I can get everything I need for about $100. A tape recorder and a guitar, that's it. That's all need to work."

## His Mom Sang "Blue Suede Shoes"

HE WAS BORN CHRISTOPHER Joseph Isaak on June 26, 1956, three months after Elvis scored his first number-one record. Isaak's mother, Dorothy, swears she was singing "Blue Suede Shoes" as she gave birth to her son. "I told the doctor who delivered him, 'Watch out, Dr. Peterson, watch out for your blue suede shoes,' 'cause I knew he was about to make his entrance," she laughs, sitting in a middle-class ranch-style home in Stockton cluttered with ceramic fruit and cups, small figurines, an antique spoon collection, and thousands of other pure Americana knickknacks.

But life at the Isaak residence did not resemble *The Adventures of Ozzie and Harriet*. Chris' parents fashioned themselves beatniks late in the 1950s. "Chris was trained to be creative," says his mother. "I taught him that he had the freedom to express himself."

He was always different. Sipping from a big glass of Pepsi, Dorothy tells one offbeat story after another about her son. Like the time they went to the Santa Cruz boardwalk and a man who sketched caricatures for a buck asked seven-year-old Chris what he wanted to be when he grew up. Chris would have none of that "when you grow up" stuff. "I'm an artist," he said decisively.

Through his older brother Nick, Chris became a big fan of country music. As teenagers, the two would sit in the upstairs hall outside their parents' bedroom singing country weepers like "Letter Edged in Black" and "I Cried" until their mother literally broke down in tears. "We would play those songs to make her cry," he says. "Between me and him it was like tear-jerk city."

As a kid he never had a band, never performed music in public. It wasn't until 1979, living abroad in Japan as part of a University of the Pacific exchange program, that Isaak became a kind of born-again rock & roller. He came across a copy of Elvis' *The Sun*

*Sessions*, a classic collection of songs Presley recorded at Sun Studios in Memphis in 1954. "Hearing that record was a turning point," he says. "That body of work is probably the Rosetta Stone of rock & roll. All of a sudden it clicked: This is what I want to do!"

Returning to the US, Isaak quickly set out to accomplish his dream. He started commuting to San Francisco because "it was the closest city to Stockton." He grew his hair out and started dressing up kind of strange, like "a combination Elvis and Jack Kerouac." He hung out at the Mabuhay Gardens on Broadway, at the time San Francisco's premier punk rock club. "I'd dress up like I wanted people in my band to look. If somebody looked like that, I'd strike up a conversation. 'Do you play an instrument? Do you want to be in a band?' You always lie and say you've got the other guys—never tell them you're the only one. 'You play bass? That's what we need, a bass player!'"

Three months after his first trip to San Francisco, Isaak was one step closer to his goal: He was the leader of a new rockabilly band that he called Silvertone.

## "I'm Gonna Make You a Star!"

THE YEAR WAS 1981 and Erik Jacobsen was at loose ends. More than 15 years previously, Jacobsen had discovered a folk singer named John Sebastian and helped him put together a pop group called the Lovin' Spoonful. Jacobsen produced seven Top 10 hits for the Spoonful. At the time he was all of 25 years old; he traveled around New York in a limousine.

But all that was so long ago. It had been years since Jacobsen had produced a hit. Now he was dejected, halfheartedly searching the Bay Area clubs for an act that would inspire him. And then he discovered Chris Isaak, fronting a rather primitive rockabilly outfit at a San Francisco Art Institute party. "I was reborn," says Jacobsen. "I just loved his spirit. When someone has really got charisma onstage, even if they're a little off or if the band is a little out of tune, the people still watch. The audience found him riveting. So did I."

Jacobsen took Isaak out to lunch the next day. "I wanted to ascertain how deeply committed he was to his career. I asked him, 'What would you do if your band didn't grow fast enough, and you outpaced them?' He said, 'I'd fire anybody in an instant who was holding me back in any way.' That was refreshing to hear."

Soon afterward, Isaak, Jacobsen, and comanager Mark Plummer, a former British rock journalist, entered into a business relationship on a simple handshake. As the two managers spent time with Isaak, they became convinced that they had the "new Elvis" on their hands. "But there are so many things you've got to do right to get where you want in this business," says Jacobsen. There were voice lessons, songwriting sessions, photo sessions, study sessions spent listening to classic pop records and hundreds of hours in low-cost studios. Along the way they fired Silvertone's rhythm section, dropped the rockabilly sound, and replaced Chris' punk-rockabilly look with a more uptown image.

But this was not a case of shrewd managers molding a naive musician into a commercial act. Isaak is centrally involved in all the important decisions being made about his career. "We've been a gang," says the aspiring star. "The three of us have spent a lot of time in Chinese restaurants at four in the morning, plotting strategy."

With Jacobsen and Plummer on board, the next thing Isaak needed was a recording contract. This proved to be no easy task, despite that Jacobsen has had a production deal with Warner Bros. Records since late in the 1960s. Under that arrangement, Warner Bros. finances demo recording sessions for bands he discovers and in return has first option on signing those bands.

Warner Bros. initially expressed an interest in Isaak, based on what Warners' A&R man Michael Ostin called "some very primitive-sounding demos." But the company talent scouts saw Silvertone perform at the I-Beam in San Francisco. "Next day I phoned one of them recalls Jacobsen. "He tells me: 'Frankly Erik, the guy can't sing. He can't write a song. The group is sloppy. Furthermore, I don't see any hope for improvement on any of these fronts.' That was a total pass. We had no deal."

So it was back to the studio. The resulting demo tapes did the trick. Warner Bros. suddenly regained its interest. Early in 1984, Isaak finally made it onto the record company's roster. Following the release of *Silvertone*, Isaak and guitarist James Calvin Wilsey assembled a more proficient band and began rehearsing for a rather offbeat tour. The idea was Plummer's. Since Isaak and his new sidemen had not performed live, Plummer figured he would book them into Nightbreak, a small out-of-the-way club on Haight Street where they could function as the house band for a month or so. Playing four or five nights a week before a live audience would quickly whip the band into shape, reasoned Plummer and attract the attention of the local media. He was right. Joel Selvin of the *Chronicle* was among those who took the bait: "All the pieces fit together like a movie set—the crowd, the club, the band, the sound, the singer," he wrote in a review last spring. "Rather than just gigging, Isaak launched his band in a scene out of *Expresso Bongo*, that '60s British rock film where Cliff Richards is discovered in some dingy cellar of a nightclub." Isaak also played successful "residencies" at the Anti-Club in LA and Danceteria in New York, then went on to tour Europe.

But the bottom line for a recording artist is record sales, and no one was happy with the sluggish performance of Isaak's record. One Warner Bros. executive now complains that Isaak's image is "too '50s," that he needs high-powered management and perhaps even a different producer. Jacobsen and Plummer talk darkly about the pressure they feel to have a hit. "To me, all the pressure that counts comes from myself," says Isaak. "The other people hooting and hollering and wanting this and that—let them make their own album. Sure there's pressure on Erik and all the guys. Everybody wants a hit. But I took the first album very seriously, working as hard as I possibly could. I mean, I'm obsessed with this thing. I've been obsessed since day one."

At Warner Bros., for the moment at least, they still believe in Isaak. "Chris is the kind of artist that we like to bet on," says company president Lenny Waronker. "Somewhere along the line, when you've got somebody that talented, the audience will catch up to him or he'll figure out how to get to them and then you have a career."

## "That Track Shakes Like Hell!"

"IT'S HIT-BOUND. IT'S A platinum smasheroo." The hyperbole clashes with the setting—a funky $30-an-hour South of Market recording studio that one can only reach by a freight elevator. Tonight Erik Jacobsen seems to be trying to convince himself that he's just cut a hit. The song in question is called "You Owe Me Some Kind of Love." It's destined for Isaak's second album.

Isaak, who is standing solemnly behind Jacobsen looking like a pouty high school sophomore in his gray sweatshirt, jeans, and white high-top tennis shoes, just rolls his eyes. One imagines he heard the same superlatives during the production of his first album. That album once seemed "hit-bound" too.

Isaak has been in the studio for three weeks. Until now, things have not gone well. The first two weeks were spent working with Isaak's touring band—drummer Kenney Dale Johnson, bassist Rowland Salley, and guitarist Wilsey—and few of the basic tracks were successful. Now Isaak and Wilsey have brought in seasoned studio pros Prairie Prince of the Tubes and session bassist Chris Solberg to ensure that the rhythm section is rock steady.

Isaak says little about the music. He sits, silently listening; his eyes seem focused on something outside the room. Between takes he picks up an acoustic guitar, sits on the edge of a secondhand couch and strums bits of Beatles tunes. "I don't want to spoil the party, so I'll go," he sings. "I would hate my disappointment to show." He moves on to an old country tune, Hank William's "Lost Highway," but improvises lyrics. "When I pass, all the people say, just an ex-has-been, on the hits highway."

Isaak seems down. In fact, just tonight, after talking it over with his managers, he has reluctantly decided to turn down Jonathan Demme's movie offer. "Too bad the timing on this thing didn't work out," he says, putting the guitar aside.

Plummer says Isaak would have made a cool $75,000 for costarring in Demme's film. "$75,000 seems like a lot now," says Plummer later. "Chris could sure use the money. I could use my cut too. But you can't let that crowd your career. These film offers aren't going to go away. We finish the record, do some videos, play another month in LA and the next time they'll offer half a million." He pauses, smiles, catches himself. "Maybe."

In the studio, Jacobsen tries to keep the mood light. He teases Tom Mallon, the recording engineer, and Wilsey. "We can joke around," says Jacobsen suddenly, "but there is a life and death situation going on here." He says this with exaggerated melodrama, but of course he is serious.

Isaak, Wilsey, and Plummer leave the room, grab Cherry Cokes out of the icebox, and head up to the roof of the building. The air is cold. One can see the freeway, jammed with commuters heading home. "What a life," says Plummer, shaking his head as he watches the headlights inch along.

It's a life that Isaak and the others have chosen to avoid. They rarely rise before noon, don't get to work until two or three, and sometimes don't get to sleep until sunrise. There seems to be an unspoken but shared attitude among them: I live life on my terms and not like the squares.

It's now after midnight and everyone except Isaak who doesn't drink, smoke, or use drugs has had a few beers. Add a little alcohol to a recording session that has lasted more than 10 hours, and things get kind of strange. You start to mistrust your own ears. Bizarre tracks can start sounding like hits; potential hits can sound like duds.

"Turn it up," says Wilsey, tugging at the Giants cap on his head. "You Owe Me Some Kind of Love" is playing again. "Let's see what this thing really sounds like."

The engineer rewinds the tape, jacks up the volume, and lets it roll. Wham! Thunderous rock & roll drums and a twangy, Duane Eddy guitar riff fill the room. Isaak walks to the center of the room, directly between the speakers, and drops to his knees. "You owe me some kind of love," sings Isaak, his voice slightly echoing Roy Orbison. "You owe me some kind of love." Everyone is moving to the beat. "You really came down on the right night," says Plummer later. "This was a real milestone for us. That track shakes like hell!"

Just before 1 a.m., the session ends. Jacobsen and Plummer head off to a bar to drink champagne and celebrate. For now, at least, their heads are filled with visions of platinum smasheroos. Isaak, meanwhile, just heads for his tiny oceanside apartment. Alone.

*San Francisco Examiner* and *Chronicle*, *Image* magazine, April 6, 1986

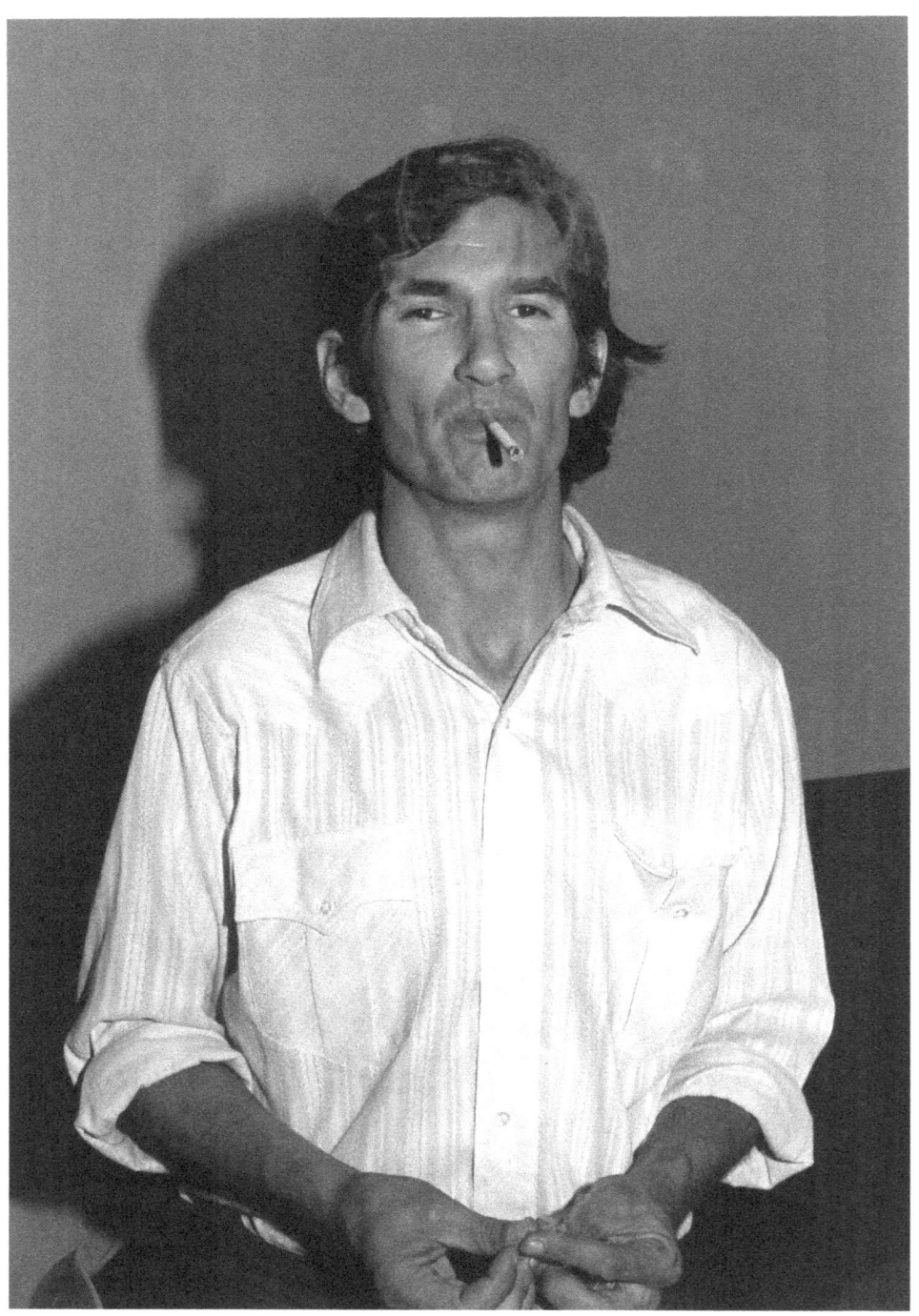
Townes Van Zandt, Great American Music Hall, San Francisco, 1978: "You just have to be willing to starve and blow everything else but folk singing off."

# TOWNES VAN ZANDT

**One writer once said of him, "Townes carried the terror and the sorrow of a sensitive man who has looked into the abyss and seen—the abyss."**

Used to be I was going to solve the world's problems. I was going to keep the sun from burning out by writing a particular song and playing it up towards the sun. Now man, I just go out and play. I figured you could change things in your own brain and a few other brains who are listening at a particular time, but you can't stop the world in its tracks. That's what I became a folk singer for, to alter the course of the universe.

Seeing Elvis on *Ed Sullivan* was the first time I realized that playing the guitar was even something people do for money. Before that I just thought people played guitar for fun and then had a job. Then it snapped, that was his job.

[After high school I] got through all that teenage identity crisis. I just came out of it a folk singer. The folk boom ended about 1966. When I got there, it wasn't like it used to be. Used to be ten folk singers a night, place full seven nights a week. Everybody would get $10 a night. But those places have been gone for years. The prices for folk singers went down. It was hard times in Texas. No money. Playing for $40 or $50 and splitting it among 10 friends and everyone barely getting by. *Tobacco Road*, *Tortilla Flat* type of times.

I never think about what I'm going to write or how I'm going to write it. It's always like—*[Van Zandt made a sound like lightning striking a tree]*—and there's a line. I put it down and whatever it's about, that's what the song is about. It's "here's a line, here's the song." It just appears from the video out of my brain in the finished form. Bukka White said they came from the sky.

When somebody asks me how to do it [be a folk singer], I just tell them, you just have to be willing to starve and blow everything else but folk singing off. I mean if you have to make a decision about how to go about it, forget it. I mean it's supposed to grab you and drag you and give you no choice whatsoever. I resisted for a while just because I didn't know what was going on. I didn't know there was such a thing as being a folk singer. But I didn't resist it for long. Because it's the wild side of life. You're always on that side of life, which is where I'd be anyway. But this way I play the guitar, instead of being 100 percent wild.

**Does he see himself as a tragic figure?**
It might be true. I mean it's just living pretty fast I guess and being semi-crazy. That reputation I got from being in and out of the hospital a few times. Just going loony.

**Does he still go "loony" on occasion?**
Well, days off it happens a lot. If you're playing night after night and all of a sudden you got a day off, nowhere to drive to. So you and the boys get a jug and sit in the room and get blitzed and all a sudden you get crazy.

June 1978

# GIL SCOTT-HERON AND "'B' MOVIE"

*In the late '70s and early '80s I worked for a city magazine in San Francisco called* Boulevards. *I was the managing editor. I was also the only editor, which meant I was responsible for every editorial word that ran in the magazine, as well as for all the art that illustrated the articles. This was not a high-budget operation; it didn't matter. The challenge was to do great work despite the limitations. It was rough going for the publisher, Kevin Jenkins, who was pretty much responsible for getting all the advertising. Eventually,* Boulevards *reached a point where it just couldn't survive, and Jenkins sold it for a bargain basement price to a collective of San Francisco journalists led by the once-great editor, Warren Hinckle* (Ramparts), *who immediately changed the name to the very non-PC* Frisco *(what people who don't live in the Bay Area call the city), and who had the crazy idea that, somehow, in their spare time, Hinckle (then a reporter for the* San Francisco Chronicle*) and his fellow journalists were going to fill a monthly magazine with quality articles. It was during the first few months of operation, while I was still acting as managing editor, that I wrote this piece. It meant a lot to me to talk to Gil Scott-Heron, who authored the great proto-rap number, "The Revolution Will Not Be Televised." Scott-Heron is considered the first rapper. Ronald Reagan was president at the time this article was written. Suffering from both HIV and drug addiction, Scott-Heron died in 2011; he was 62 years old.*

THESE DAYS WHEN GIL Scott-Heron starts talking, Black America listens. In the Bay Area, Scott-Heron's scathing anti-Reagan rap, "'B' Movie," has received 'round the clock airplay on KDIA, the most popular soul station in Northern California. Around the rest of the country, the song has been getting heavy airplay on soul (read Black) stations, though Top 40 pop stations have yet to touch it.

"'B' Movie" makes even the politicized Bob Dylan of the early '60s seem like a wishy-washy liberal. Surrounded by the typical funky dance music of slick soul brothers and sisters singing about romance and sex usually found on Black radio, Scott-Heron's song pops out of the car radio speaker with the shock value of a naked girl running through a Baptist church on Sunday morning.

"Well, the first thing I want to say is, mandate my ass," begins Scott-Heron. Then the sparse accompaniment of an insistent drumbeat and a repeating bass riff begins: "Because it seems as though we've been convinced that 26 percent of the registered voters, not even 26 percent of the American people, but 26 percent of the registered voters, form a mandate, or a landslide. . . ."

"This country wants nostalgia," continues Scott-Heron. "They want to go back as far as they can, even if it's only as far as last week. Not to face now or tomorrow, but to face backwards, and yesterday was the day of our cinema heroes riding to the rescue at the last possible moment. The day of the man in the white hat or the man on the white horse or the man who always came to save America at the last moment. Someone always came to save America at the last moment, especially in B-movies. And when America found itself having a hard time facing the future, they looked for people like John Wayne. But since John Wayne was no longer available, they settled for Ronnie the Ray-gun. And it has placed us in a situation that we can only look at like a B-movie. . . ."

In the course of the 12-minute track, Scott-Heron refers to "Casper the Defensive Weinberger" and "Attila the Haig running around frantically declaring himself in control and in charge." He concludes the song by saying: "As Wall Street goes, so goes the nation, and here is a look at the closing numbers: racism is up, human rights are down, peace is shaky, war items are hot, jobs are down, money is scarce, and common sense is at an all time low in heavy trading. Movies were looking better than ever, and now no one is looking, because we're all starring in a B-movie. And we would've rather had John Wayne. And we would have rather had John Wayne."

That a song of political commentary should get heavy airplay on soul stations across the country at this time is surprising. It brings back memories of the early '70s when Sly Stone's "Family Affair," Marvin Gaye's "What's Goin' On," and Curtis Mayfield's "Freddie's Dead" (and many others) were regularly heard on Top 40 radio. "We felt that it was the kind of song ("'B' Movie") that would wake up people and cause talk among our audience," said Keith Adams, program director at KDIA. The station was playing the album version of "'B' Movie" (included on Scott-Heron's most recent LP, *Reflections*) before his record label, Arista, had even released it as a single. "We only got two negative calls about the record,'" claimed Adams. "One was a gay man who objected to what he thought was a slur towards gays and the other was a Black mother who agreed politically with the song but worried that if her kids heard it, they would start asking her questions. I told her—now this is my personal opinion and doesn't represent the station—that I thought she should be prepared to answer those questions. Most people called and said, 'Right On!' Gil is saying to them what they themselves want to say."

I called Gil Scott-Heron at his home in Virginia and asked him why his song was getting airplay only on soul stations. "I suppose if it has anything to do with who is having the most trouble with Reaganomics or who is receiving the brunt of the current recession, that might have something to do with the response of the various communities," said 32-year-old Scott-Heron, a Black man who speaks and sings with a deep, soulful bass voice. "I think it's still more obvious in our communities that there is a recession and that there has been for the past five or six years, than it is in the community outside of ours. Because we listened to them for a while when they said there was no recession," laughed Scott-Heron.

"We have been aware of Ronald Reagan as long as we have been aware. And the same things that have held true as far as '"B" Movie' is concerned are the same things that have held true throughout his political career. There have been changes and adjustments in the cast of characters, but basically the plot has been the same."

When asked what the current administration has done that makes him most angry, Scott-Heron said, "Oh, we don't have that much time. Well, we just did a 12-minute piece ["'B' Movie"]. After we got through with that 12 minutes, I'm sure there are a few more. You can start there." In fact, Scott-Heron's song changes and grows with each performance. (The lyrics quoted here are from the Arista Records PR transcript.)

"'B' Movie" may have put Scott-Heron in the spotlight, but it's certainly not his first piece of political criticism. Scott-Heron first gained notoriety in the early '70s when he recorded a tough piece of political jazz called "The Revolution Will Not Be Televised" (if you search for it on YouTube, you can give it a listen, and all the lyrics are online as well). The message, which is very sarcastic and is addressed to Scott-Heron's Black brothers, is that the revolution, when it comes, will not be the equivalent of a TV show. Scott-Heron tells his listeners that it will not be possible to escape the revolution via heroin or alcohol while viewing the tube because—and he recites the title of the song. Nor will the revolution be sponsored by various corporations because—and he repeats the title of the song. He tells them there won't be video of police killing Black men on the TV because—and again repeats the title of the song. At the end of the song, he says the revolution will not be a "rerun" because it will be "live." Of course the lyrics are more poetically written than how I paraphrased them.

During the past 12 years, Scott-Heron has written and recorded songs dealing with numerous controversial and timely issues, including bussing, Watergate, unemployment, drug use, racism, and nuclear power. He sets his lyrics to jazz-flavored music that occasionally features reggae rhythms. He's also written love songs and even a rather pretty, though lyrically innocuous song called "A Lovely Day." But it's Scott-Heron's controversial material, of course, that has made him famous among lefties throughout America.

What got Scott-Heron started making political statements set to music? "I just thought it was part of what everybody did," he said. "See, I always thought that people who were writing lyrics had some sort of message that they wanted to deliver, and that if it wasn't going to have a message, it was going to be an instrumental. In other words, people who weren't going to say anything really weren't going to say anything. And it has always been a sort of feeling of mine that there were different sorts of ideas that could be put together to express what you felt. Emotionally, psychologically, politically."

Scott-Heron finds it impossible to avoid political and social issues. "Because they are a part of life," he said. "To ignore a part of life would be rather insensitive and that's not what poets try to do, practice being insensitive. Knowing that social and political issues are a big part of our community and a big part of our lives makes them a big part of the things that our ideas are about. And the best way to try and solve it or bring it in harmony with the rest of your life is to deal with it.

"I would say that Stevie Wonder's 'Happy Birthday' has inspired a lot of people to come out in freezing weather in January in Washington, DC, because they felt it was important for Dr. King to be honored with a national holiday. It seems as though in many instances when ideas of that nature are brought to the attention of the community it works best when it's put in that particular setting [music]."

Though Scott-Heron's songs often are bitter, he is surprisingly optimistic. "Twenty years ago, there were still Black people getting lynched. People being attacked physically and harmed and often killed simply because of what color they are. I like to think that a lot of that has changed and that a lot of those sorts of things will continue to change. Oftentimes, change is not as quick as our outrage. Oftentimes it takes as long to get something straight as it took to get it crooked."

With "'B' Movie" receiving widespread airplay, I wondered if the President was aware of the song. So, I called the White House. "I would doubt that the President has heard it," said Kim Hoggard, assistant to press secretary Larry Speakes. "You can say that he has not heard it. And, we wouldn't have any comment concerning either the song or the response it may be getting."

Gil Scott-Heron was also pretty sure the president hadn't heard his song. "I suspect from time to time that there have been few things that people have said that he's listened to," Scott-Heron said.

*Frisco*, February 1982

# THE ELUSIVE JOLIE HOLLAND

*Initially, in 2003, Jolie Holland pressed up 100 copies of her debut solo album,* Catalpa, *and managed to get it into some San Francisco record stores. I flipped out the first time I played* Catalpa. *I loved it so much, and I immediately wrote the essay that follows for the online magazine,* Neumu, *that I cofounded with Emme Stone in the early 2000s, and for which I was the editor. Holland liked my essay so much she used it as liner notes when she was signed to Anti-Records and they re-released* Catalpa. *I took Jolie out to lunch not long after I wrote the essay and I photographed her. I'm proud that one of those photos (next page) was used on the cover of one of her European CD singles, which includes her wonderful cover of "Delia," a folk song also covered by Blind Willie McTell and Bob Dylan. Jolie and I have remained friends, and she has subsequently recorded many wonderful albums. I like to imagine that this essay helped get her solo career started, but essay or no essay, Jolie's talent would have earned her a record deal.*

YOU HAVE TO STRAIN TO make out some of the words she sings. Even when you turn the volume up, the recording has a slight muffled quality, as if there were a thin wall between you and the singer, whose name is Jolie Holland. As if you were hearing a voice coming at you from the past, all those years between then and now, between her and you. But then you hear those first lines, the ones at the start of "Alley Flowers," a song off her new, debut solo album, *Catalpa*: "Some people say you got a psychedelic presence / Shinin' in the park with a bioluminescence." And you know that this isn't some old-time recording. You've never heard anything quite like this before.

"I'm trying to give people this very spontaneous, from-the-heart sound," Holland said recently.

She sings like a young old-time mountain woman with one foot in the past, one foot in the now. Her voice is comfortable, recognizable, yet different. It's a voice that's sweet and fragile, a voice that understands both hard times and love. When you listen to Holland, you hear a real person singing. At times she just seems to be conveying the story, in the most matter-of-fact manner. For some of *Catalpa*, it's as if a tape recorder had been set up in a room of a San Francisco apartment and Holland simply played her favorite songs, which just might be how some of this wonderful album was made.

Her phrasing is unusual. She sings her words in a way that catches you off guard. With a weird, dull, rhythmic sound that somehow reminds me of an underwater recording of a train moving down the tracks, and a quiet guitar for accompaniment, Holland sings: "Down these streets I see"—*pause*—"you comin'"—*hesitation*—"from afar."

On the Jolie Holland website, she describes her music like this: "New time old time: spooky American fairytales."

Spooky. That's certainly a good way to characterize "Alley Flowers."

When you hear the album's second song, "All the Morning Birds," you might think of Bobby Dylan, back when he was a kid in New York, back before he'd really made it, back when he was still a folk singer. Only this is folk by way of some jazz chanteuse. "By 3 a.m. all the morning birds will be crying," she sings, and as she does, she sweeps you into her

Jolie Holland in Golden Gate Park, San Francisco, 2003.

world. "And that old highway will be sighing and my dreams feel as cold as my bones on the long walk home / And my coat is old and growin' thin / And my feet are numb and stumbling / And it's many the thought of a long lost friend / That comes to me again and again." She ends the song by whistling a brief solo. Imagine! Whistling. And it works.

Holland listened to folk, blues, and jazz when she was younger, drawing on the work of such artists as Leadbelly, Woody Guthrie, Billie Holiday, Dylan, and the numerous artists on Harry Smith's *American Anthology of Folk Music* (as well as such tragic rock icons as Nico and Pink Floyd's Syd Barrett) to come up with her own stripped-down modern folk music.

Her music feels at one with some of Dylan and The Band's "Basement Tapes" recordings. You can imagine her sitting on the steps of a rundown Southern farmhouse, singing her songs to some friends and family. There's mystery here. There's an elusive quality to these recordings, and you'll play them again and again. More is encoded—in Holland's voice, the words (often hers, sometimes penned by others), the sparse music—than you can get at. So you keep listening, trying to get to the soul of it all. "Well, I feel like an old hobo—I'm sad, lonesome and blue," she sings during "The Littlest Birds." "I was fair as a summer's day / Now the summer days are through / You pass through places / And places pass through you / But you carry them with you on the soles of your traveling shoes."

Holland grew up in Houston, Texas, and wrote her first song at age six. She plays guitar, violin, and ukulele. As a teenager she performed onstage, according to her bio, which goes on to recount: "She figured out how to play some Syd Barrett songs, abandoned the concept of going to college to hit the road in 1994, and bummed around between Austin, Texas, and New Orleans among visual artists, musicians, circus performers, puppeteers, etc."

Holland headed west in 1997, eventually landing in San Francisco. Before long she was in Vancouver cofounding the Be Good Tanyas. She split before the group's debut, *Blue Horse*, was released in 2001. She appears on that album, singing on a few songs including "The Littlest Birds," which she re-recorded for *Catalpa*. Of the Be Good Tanyas' debut, England's *Q* wrote in 2001, "If you buy one country album this year you should make it The Be Good Tanyas'."

Holland had felt constrained by the demands of a group. "There were too many cooks in the kitchen—something had to change," she recently told the *S.F. Weekly*'s Dan Strachota.

She returned to San Francisco, where she now lives, and put together Little Boris and the Shoes, which performs once a month at San Francisco's Rite Spot. Holland recorded *Catalpa*, her first solo album, with the band, which includes Chris Arnold (musical saw, percussion), Dave Mihaly (drums, bells), and Brian Miller (electric guitar). She's released it on her own label (it can be ordered from her website). I bought my copy at Amoeba Records; it cost me $10. You really have to wonder when a DIY artist like Holland can sell her album for $10, while the majors are selling theirs for nearly double that.

There's a color photo of Holland on the cover of the album. It's out of focus and the contrast is so extreme that her face appears white and part of it blends into the white background. She's looking down, looking away, wearing a red dress, playing a red accordion.

You get this sense of someone who's only half there. Or maybe someone who's moving so fast that she's already on to something new. One can imagine her, like Dylan, morphing quickly from album to album, changing her music, her attitude, her persona. For someone who could make as unique and striking a debut as *Catalpa*, just about anything is possible.

*Neumu*, February 24, 2003

# TOM WAITS INTERVIEWED

*It was in the spring of 1977 at Zellerbach Auditorium on the UC Berkeley campus where I first met and interviewed Tom Waits. In addition to asking questions, that day I photographed Tom Waits, who was 27. From the article that my journalist wife Leslie Goldberg and I cowrote for the* Berkeley Barb:

> Backstage, after the gig. Squatting in the dressing room, reeling and bopping and drinking brown liquid of unknown origins from a plastic bottle, Tom Waits meets the Press. . . . Tonight his ensemble does lack some of his customary flair and jaunty sense of style. The shiny black suit is clean. The narrow brown tie has but one stain and only his scruffy, black pointed boots look as through they might have pulled time in a trash can. . . . [He] scratches the stubble on his chin, spits. . . . Waits leaps up, stretches his legs, lights another Viceroy and surveys several trays of soggy sandwiches, carrots, and yogurt dip. "Only in Berkeley," laughs Waits, pulling a pile of sprouts out of an avocado and Swiss cheese sandwich. "Only in Berkeley would they give you an organic spread." Tossing the sandwich onto the floor he takes another swig from the plastic bottle.

*That was the vibe as I interviewed Tom Waits all those years ago.*

**Michael Goldberg:** What's the appeal of the sleazebag scene?

**Tom Waits:** An appeal is what comes after a sentence. Ha Ha. What comes after a sentence. It's a little joke. What's the appeal of diners? Ah, it's just around me all the time. I mean I'm really not any different than anybody else. I mean as far as what's American, I mean it's hard to avoid.

**Goldberg:** Well a lot of people seem to avoid it. I mean the newspapers don't exactly put it on the front page. You have to go down to Mission Street [in San Francisco] or the Tenderloin to seek it out.

**Waits:** Seek out what specifically?

**Goldberg:** You're dealing with a certain part of the American culture that's not generally dealt with. A lot of people who are losers, who couldn't deal with the American economic system and have ended up living a financially meager existence.

**Waits:** Well, I don't just sing about that!

**Goldberg:** Well, your image goes with that. Is it true that you live at the Hollywood Tropicana Hotel?

Tom Waits squatting in a dressing room at Zellerbach Auditorium, Berkeley, 1977.

**Waits:** Yeah, I never should have made that public. I get a lot of real strange guests now that I made that public. But it sounded like a good idea at the time. I write about things that are important to me, things I see around me. Give a certain amount of dignity to the things that I find interesting to write about. I'm kind of like a curator or a private detective. I sleep with one eye open. I don't know what you want me to say.

**Goldberg:** Well, how did you end up writing about these things?

**Waits:** There's a lot of money in it. You know what I mean? What do you mean specifically? Pick out something specific that I can talk about. You got a certain image about me already I'm sure that is so far beyond my ability to evaluate anyhow. So, if you'll just tell me about something specific then I can discuss that. Got a song or a story?

**Goldberg:** What about "The Heart of Saturday Night"?

**Waits:** Okay. I was in a car, wrote it in a car driving around Los Angeles about a Saturday. Simple as that.

**Goldberg:** What's your highest value? What's most important to you?

**Waits:** Right at this moment? Well right now what I'm really most concerned about is 12 hours of sleep. That's right now, that's the most valuable to me. Bermuda shorts, recreational vehicles, fried chicken, the Empire State Building, Rodney Dangerfield, pointed shoes.

**Goldberg:** Does it give you a lot of satisfaction to write songs?

**Waits:** Yeah!?! Yeah, it gives me a great deal of satisfaction to finish an album, do all the writing for it, it's the most challenging thing I've ever done and also the most rewarding.

**Goldberg:** Over your four albums you've moved from a straight pop song type thing to . . .

**Waits:** More stylized . . .

**Goldberg:** To the jazz thing you're doing now with spontaneous, stream-of-consciousness sounding lyrics.

**Waits:** Puddle of consciousness.

**Goldberg:** How did that progression occur?

**Waits:** I compete with myself every time that I write. Try to outdo myself. I'm constantly trying to get closer to the bone I guess. Cut away the gristle. I'm my own worst critic. So, I'm real hard on myself as a writer and subsequently, each album, I'm trying to cover new turf and write better songs for Christ sake.

**Goldberg:** How do you write your songs?

**Waits:** First I get entirely naked and then I inject marinated herring and wine sauce right into my jugular vein, and I have to be in Great Neck or Shaker Heights will do but I actually prefer being in Great Neck like in the back of a real estate office at night when they're closed. And I get under one of those metal desks and all of a sudden, I don't know, I black out and when I come to I have all these cameras around my neck and a funny hat with dumb slogans on it and the album is under way. That's how I wrote the last album. This one I'm going to try a new approach.

**Goldberg:** How do you stay in touch with the street life you sing about?

**Waits:** It's very time consuming being out here. And also performing is very insulating, which I don't like. It puts a lot of governors on my normal itinerary. I have very little time to be out on my own recognizance. There's always somebody pulling on my coat, phones ringing, or I gotta go here or I gotta go there, I gotta get up for the show, and then afterwards I gotta go back to the hotel and I gotta watch *The Rifleman* and then *Leave It to Beaver*, *Sunrise Semester*, and then *Farm Report* and *Give Us This Day* and then I have to get up and I have to get in a cab. I mean my whole day is eaten and I get what's left over. When I get home it's different.

**Goldberg:** How is it different?

**Waits:** Well, I'm going to have this whole summer off. This whole thing won't be around me, this pomp and circumcision. I won't have to do it. Won't be around me. Press and all that shit.

**Goldberg:** What's your nonperforming life like?

**Waits:** Probably very much like your own. I brush my teeth. I don't usually even admit that. I have certain things I have to do just like everybody else to get through the day.

**Goldberg:** I guess what I want to know is, when you have a vacation, what do you do for fun?

**Waits:** Well, I have a summer home in Monte Carlo, it's not much, $150,000, and I have a little black jockey out on the lawn, a couple of Chevelles, and uh I play a lot of golf, sailing, I enjoy my leisure time. And so when me and Marge get just away, we figure, why wait until you're too old to enjoy it? So we dropped everything, said we're finally going to do it and so we went to Yosemite, and boy did we get some shots, you know what I mean?

When I go home, first of all I'm gonna have to throw out all the bums that have been living in my house since I've been gone and then I'll have the place to myself. I usually spend about a week, and I don't go out of the house at all, except to use the bathroom.

**Goldberg:** Do you ever feel like staying in a fancy hotel and putting on an expensive new suit?

**Waits:** What does fancy hotel and putting on a new suit go together? That's like, "Do you ever feel like picking your nose and putting on a pair of socks?"

**Goldberg:** Every story that I've ever read about you talks about the shiny black suit and the tie you can't see through the stains and the pointed ragged shoes that are so—they look like they've been in a garbage can for months.

**Waits:** Hey, I don't look that bad do I?

**Goldberg:** I'm just telling you what they say.

**Waits:** Well look, you read them, and I don't, alright? I'm glad I don't read 'em. My mother read one of those things and just about shit. She thinks I've really, I've gone over the hill. I ain't that bad. I'm not exactly what you'd call a trendsetter in fashion. Actually, I've kinda cleaned up tonight, frankly. You know, I mean I try to be concerned with personal hygiene and all that. But you know, get out here on the road sometimes and sometimes I have to get up so early, so in order to avoid having to get up and do all those things in the morning, get dressed, I just sleep in my clothes. You know. Really.

**Goldberg:** What do you think your audience comes for?

**Waits:** Tonight, they came to hear me. If somebody's never seen me before they come, maybe, out of curiosity. If they have seen me before—I got a lot of diehard fans. They're usually 16-year-old kids with drinking problems. I don't have a young teenage, succulent little pedophile audience. Nor do I have a lot of hardened criminals come either. You're probably better at figuring that out than me 'cause I don't really see the audience except my friends who come backstage. I don't sit in the audience and look around me. You did. So you probably have a better idea. Why don't you tell me.

**Goldberg:** Well, this audience was a lot of college kids . . .

**Waits:** Hippies? Ex-hippies?

**Goldberg:** Well, some employed hippies who could afford the tickets—UC Berkeley students.

**Waits:** There were a lot of students. A lot of English majors?

**Goldberg:** I wouldn't know. How old are you?

**Waits:** I'm 27 years old. Born Pearl Harbor day.

**Goldberg:** How did you avoid the Jimi Hendrix psychedelic scene?

**Waits:** I was in a mental institution. I wasn't allowed to listen to the radio. I was in a straitjacket for 12 years. And they fed me on berries and small rodents. And I wasn't allowed to listen to music. And I had to get my hair cut every day. And though I wanted to wear bell-bottoms and beads and listen to Blue Cheer my doctor said it wasn't a good idea.

**Goldberg:** Do you ever worry about your health?

**Waits:** Sure, I worry about my health. Just as much as anybody else does.

**Goldberg:** You smoke a lot, right?

**Waits:** I try to eat right, and I take Geritol. When you got your health, you got just about everything. *[Spits]* You know what I mean? I'm relatively healthy, on the outside.

**Goldberg:** What is success to you? Do you feel you've achieved it?

**Waits:** Uh, different degrees of it. You can be a big fish in a small pond. I mean I think I—it's expanding a little bit. I'm popular in Belgium and Japan and Philadelphia. [Two decades later Waits would release a song called "Big in Japan."]

**Goldberg:** Is that how you rate success? In terms of how many people see you? Is that how you judge success?

**Waits:** Oh, are you talking about popularity or success?

**Goldberg:** No, I'm talking about to you personally. Are you successful?

**Waits:** I'm successful. I guess I would say I'm successful because I'm—I quit my day job, I'm doing exactly what I set out to do. And it's—so I guess it's something. I'm experiencing a measure of success. Yeah.

**Goldberg:** What do you think about Bruce Springsteen and Patti Smith?

**Waits:** Patty Hearst? Patty Hearst, I like. Patti Smith, I don't like. I'd rather go to a nightclub and see Patty Hearst any day than Patti Smith. And I like Bruce; Bruce is cool.

June 1977

# MICHAEL JACKSON: THE MAKING OF THE "KING OF POP"

**A rare look inside the reclusive superstar's Neverland Ranch and a report on one of the most expensive albums ever.**

*I wrote or cowrote three cover stories about Michael Jackson for* Rolling Stone. *I met the "King of Pop" once. It wasn't much of a meeting. It was at an auditorium in LA where he was rehearsing. At one point he took a break and a number of us, including parents of kids who were rehearsing with Jackson, lined up to meet him. One at a time, one of us would approach him, shake his gloved hand, perhaps say something to him, and move on. What I recall about our "meeting," is that it was as if Jackson had left his body and gone elsewhere. There was no connection. No attempt at connection. He was just going through the motions. Jackson was clearly a troubled individual. At the peak of his success, following the 1982 release of* Thriller, *he was the most popular entertainer in the world. Time's Jay Cocks wrote in 1984, "Jackson is the biggest thing since the Beatles. He is the hottest single phenomenon since Elvis Presley. He just may be the most popular Black singer ever." On June 25, 2009, Jackson died of cardiac arrest; he was 50 years old. In late 1991, when I worked on this story, I was not able to interview Jackson, but I talked to many people who worked with him or for him and spent a night and a day at the compound known as Neverland Ranch in the Santa Barbara hills that was Jackson's home at the time. And it is there, at Neverland Ranch, where this story begins.*

THE SEVEN DWARFS ARE singing. Their voices are floating out of speakers hidden among the trees and lush flora surrounding Michael Jackson's mansion, in Neverland Valley—his 2,700-acre, $22 million oasis in the Santa Ynez Valley, an hour north of Santa Barbara, California. "Michael's very own Xanadu," as his friend director John Landis puts it.

At Neverland Jackson has created a secluded and secure environment far from businessmen, attorneys, managers, music-television-channel VIPs, and even members of his immediate family. Here he can stand in front of his house and the only sounds to hear are the birds in the oak and sycamore trees and, of course, the Seven Dwarfs. And if he chooses to gaze past the expansive lake that stretches out in front of his three-story Tudoresque country home, past the lush green lawns and neatly manicured flower beds, the bronze statues of young boys beating tambourines or playing toy accordions, he sees simply a peaceful hillside dotted with oaks.

In any direction, as far as the eye can see, lies Michael Jackson's Magic Kingdom. "Sure, he's a little afraid of people," says choreographer Vince Paterson. "When you have people that, from the time you're a little kid, want you, they want pieces of you, they want your clothes, they want your—you're going to get nervous around people."

But here at Neverland, protected by armed guards that patrol the grounds around the clock, Jackson doesn't have to be around people. And he never has to grow up.

Michael Jackson and a wax figure of himself at The Guinness Museum of World Records on Fisherman's Wharf, San Francisco, 1984. Photo by © Chester Simpson / Rock-N-RollPhotos.com

Though Jackson is now a 33-year-old man, his associates and friends say he still has the interests and enthusiasms of a child, and at Neverland he has created the ultimate child's playground. "Being with Michael is like being in Santa's workshop," says Paterson.

Santa has been working overtime at Neverland. One can ride a turn-of-the-century C.P. Huntington amusement-park-style train that holds several dozen passengers. Hop on board and it will take you from the main house out past an Indian village (tepees, full-size replicas of American Indians, a totem pole, and campfire), a two-story fort (complete with hefty artillery that shoots water), and an amusement park (including a carousel with custom-made, hand-painted animals, a Ferris wheel, a three-story-high slide, and a heart-stopping ride called the Zipper).

Continue on and you'll see the $2 million-plus Neverland Cinema complex (where *Cape Fear* is playing tonight, according to signs posted at every stop along the train's route). Walk in and feast your eyes on the candy counter, filled with every kind of popcorn and confection imaginable. On either side of the large main projection room you'll find separate glassed-in viewing rooms, complete with beds for children who are ill.

Ride past the zoo, with its horses and zebra, buffalo and chimpanzees, ostriches and swans, deer and llamas. And the zonkey (a cross between a zebra and a donkey). And let's not forget the three giraffes.

Or go boating in the lake. You can choose between a swan boat, a canoe, and a red dinghy. Perhaps you're up for playing some kind of electronic game. The rec building contains two floors of arcade games ranging from Sega's *Time Traveler* hologram unit and *Galaxy Force Version 2* to Teenage *Mutant Ninja Turtles* and something called *Ghosttown*.

At night, Neverland looks like it has been sprinkled with a kind of high-tech fairy dust. Out by the amusement park, for instance, Jackson has had white lights installed up the trunk and on the branches of the oak trees. As these lights flash on and off, glittering trees appear to materialize before one's eyes, only to vanish. A winding yellow-brick road (with recessed gold-colored lights) leads to the amusement park, which is lit against the black sky. Back at the house, the lake, the statues, and the wood and stone buildings themselves look like set pieces from a fairy tale.

Amid this magical environment, Jackson will sometimes get in the outdoor jacuzzi, remove a large piece of stone that conceals a TV and VCR and sitting beneath the stars, watch one of the hundreds of videos that are stored in his tape library upstairs in the main house.

Jackson frequently has children over to play. According to his personal spokesperson, Bob Jones (who first worked with Jackson at Motown when the singer was a member of the Jackson 5), these regularly include "busloads" of underprivileged and terminally ill kids (such as the late Ryan White), as well as young personal friends of the superstar.

"When the children are here, sometimes they get so excited they just can't go to sleep," says Lee Tucker, who helped design Jackson's movie theater and serves as his projectionist. "I'll get a call at 2:00 a.m. sometimes: 'Lee, can you show such-and-such movie?' Neverland isn't about kids going to sleep at a certain time. The kids really run the place when they're here."

Jackson is extremely fond of children. Those who know him believe that one reason he can relax with kids is that he truly believes they like him for himself, not because he's a big star. As one associate observed, "If you're under three feet tall, you can have complete access to Michael Jackson."

Jackson's house is exquisitely furnished. The main floor includes an oak-paneled library stocked with rare editions of classics by Charles Dickens, Mark Twain, and dozens of others. The spacious living room houses a Bösendorfer custom-made rosewood piano and numerous rare art pieces, among them a Raymond Bigot sculpture of a rooster and chickens. There is a roomy den with a Bouquet Canyon stone fireplace, a fully equipped professional kitchen, and a spacious dining room with its own fireplace. Down a hall is Jackson's bedroom, which is off limits to most visitors; it looks out onto a garden enclosed by a six-foot-high stone wall.

While the main floor would make an English lord feel right at home, the upstairs is, like the grounds of the estate, filled with the stuff that children dream about. There is a doll bedroom, a large room with a canopied bed that is crowded with dozens of dolls. Many more dolls, some with sad faces, some smiling, peer at you from every nook and cranny. A three-story, elaborately furnished dollhouse containing miniature figures sits on one side of the room. *Wizard of Oz* plates and jack-in-the-boxes, each featuring Dorothy, the Scarecrow, the Tin Man, or one of the other primary characters, have been placed on shelves. There is an old-fashioned typewriter with a piece of paper in it on which someone has typed: "And all we want for Christmas . . ." Sitting on an end table is Shirley Temple Black's autobiography, *Child Star*.

Another room is jammed with children's games and toys. There are coloring books and crayons, a gun that shoots soap bubbles. A table full of trucks and cars and spaceships. In front of a window stand life-size cutouts of Batman and the Joker. *Simpsons* characters are everywhere.

A narrow staircase leads up to the train room, half of which is filled with an elaborate Lionel set. In addition to the trains on the track, there are more in unopened boxes on the floor. Another part of the room is covered with racecar tracks. Standing against the walls are larger than life Bart Simpson cardboard cutouts and *Roger Rabbit* displays, along with an *E.T.* video display packed with copies of the tape. Peter Pan and Mickey Mouse and Bambi quilts lie on the floor. "The kids have slumber parties up here," says one of Jackson's employees as he takes me through the house.

Ironically, as Neverland becomes even more magical and dreamlike, Jackson himself can't often enjoy it. For most of the three years he's owned it, much of his time has been spent in Los Angeles sequestered in more than a half-dozen darkened recording studios. Now that the album is done, he'll be busy for months, cranking out videos for the various songs on *Dangerous*. He also has plans to star in his first feature film, tentatively titled *Midknight*, for Sony's Columbia Pictures and will hit the road to support *Dangerous* by the middle of 1992. Touring plans have not been formalized, but it's clear that Jackson, in his drive to stay on top of the entertainment world, will want to take his time and make the show as spectacular as possible.

"The plan is for him to start work on his film," says Bob Jones, who for the past three years has been working for the star's own company MJJ Productions. "But with Michael you never know. That could certainly change. Since I've been here, Michael has been in complete control. He knows what works for him and for the public. He's much more fixed in his ideas as to how he wants to do things."

One thing is for sure, Jackson won't be spending much time at Neverland lying by the pool. For as everyone in the world knows by now, the Michael Jackson show is, once again, open for business.

THE "KING OF POP." That's how Fox, Black Entertainment Television (BET), and MTV, the American TV outlets that got the rights to première Jackson's "Black or White" video, now refer to him. That was the deal. You want to get "Black or White" first, you dub Jackson "the King of Pop."

It makes some sense. Bruce is the Boss, Elvis is the King, Prince is, well, Prince. And Michael Jackson? Somehow Wacko Jacko, as the British tabloids have called him, doesn't cut it. So, if the world won't crown him king, why, he'll do it himself.

Which explains the November 11, 1991, memo, typed on MTV Networks letterhead, that was circulated among the MTV staff the week before "Black or White" was first shown. The memo directed all on-air personnel to refer to Jackson as "the King of Pop" at least twice a week over the next two weeks. It also thanked staff members for their cooperation, adding that "Fox and BET are already doing this." "The fact is that a lot of people have changed their names recently," says Tom Freston, chairman and CEO of MTV Networks, in defense of the company's actions. "M.C. Hammer is now Hammer, and Michael Jackson is 'the King of Pop.' Who are we to stand in front of the wheels of progress? Whatever they want to call themselves, we try and oblige."

So MTV and the others dubbed him "the King of Pop" and showed his video, and the world went crazy. It's estimated that half a billion people saw the première of "Black or White," which quickly became MTV's most requested video of the week. As a result of the overwhelming response, the network put the video into what Freston calls "super heavy" rotation. "No artist, including himself," Freston says, "has ever gotten more plays per day."

While "Black or White" has received more concentrated exposure than any other video, it does not have the kind of influential impact that "Thriller" had. "Thriller" clearly broke new ground: Its $1.2 million budget was more than had ever been spent on a video. By combining narrative, dramatic nonmusic sections and ambitious choreography, Jackson and director Landis set new standards for music videos. The "Thriller" video also helped Jackson sell as many as 1 million albums a week for the month following its initial airing.

In the days immediately following the première of "Black or White," in newspapers large and small all over the world, millions more read about it and about the controversy that erupted over the video's last four minutes, in which Jackson simulates masturbation, zips up his zipper, smashes in the windows of a car and throws a garbage can through a storefront window.

*Entertainment Weekly* devoted its cover story to "Michael Jackson's Video Nightmare." Even the *Wall Street Journal* saw fit to tell its readers about the Jackson brouhaha, noting that "the Jackson video wasn't viewed as truly offensive to almost anybody of commercial importance to the singer." Jackson's handlers immediately denied any suggestion that the controversy had been planned.

Certainly, it's not far-fetched to imagine that media-savvy Michael Jackson, a star for more than 20 years, hero to both children and their grandparents, might have had an inkling that if he rubbed himself and smashed up windows, he would get a rise out of his fans. On the other hand, if he didn't plan to create a controversy, it simply means that, yes, Jackson really is quite detached from reality, as many believe.

Yet whatever his intentions, and despite his statement ("It upsets me to think that 'Black or White' could influence any child or adult to destructive behavior, either sexual or violent . . ."), released the day after the video aired, those around Jackson, as well as at least one top Sony executive, seemed overjoyed at all the attention. "No story ever got this much play on the news but a war," said one Jackson associate a few days after the première.

This latest controversy arrived in time to overshadow the attack Jackson had recently suffered from his brother Jermaine. In November, shortly after Jermaine's latest album was released, and just as "Black or White" hit the airwaves, Jermaine's song "Word to the Badd!!," with lyrics different from those that appear on his album, was leaked to radio. This version was directed right at Jermaine's superstar brother: "Reconstructed / Been abducted / Don't know who you are. . . . Once you were made / You changed your shade / Was your color wrong."

Jermaine quickly claimed he didn't know how the song had gotten to radio. And although he said it was written as a way of personally dealing with frustration he felt when his brother didn't return his calls for "eight or nine months," the altered version was formally released on CD to radio and critics by the end of the month.

Jermaine refused to elaborate on the lyrics, saying only that "the overall message is to help mend our relationship." He also said that Michael had "lost touch with reality" but that they had talked recently and that "I love my brother."

But Teddy Riley—who coproduced half the songs on *Dangerous* and is also the leader of the New Jack Swing group Guy—says that, contrary to what Jermaine has said: "Michael does call his family. All this rumor about him not calling anybody, him not answering the calls—come on. I've been there plenty of times when Michael was talking to his mom, and I've spoken to his mom, and I've spoken to Janet. It's a bunch of crap. That record ['Word to the Badd!!'] was a desperate attempt for fame."

"We anticipated a lot of people saying a lot of stuff about Michael," says Riley. "Hammer going after Michael and Jermaine going after Michael. We anticipated that. That's why we wrote songs like 'Trippin' ['Why You Wanna Trip on Me'] and 'Jam.' We know that people are after him, people are talking about him. But we didn't get too direct, we didn't say anybody's name. 'Cause when you're too direct, it gets boring."

Despite Jermaine's denials, it seems clear that the whole thing was calculated to borrow some thunder from Michael.

CERTAINLY, MICHAEL JACKSON COULDN'T have imagined kicking off this round of career activity with a bigger bang. And yet a question remains: No matter how much hype is generated, can Jackson ever surpass his previous sales records? In the headline of a story that ran the week before the "Black or White" video aired, the *New York Times* asked the question on every Jackson watcher's mind: *'Thriller'—Can Michael Jackson Beat It?*

That is the challenge that Jackson is up against. His biggest album, *Thriller*, sold over 40 million copies worldwide and 21 million in the US, while his last album, *Bad*, sold in excess of 20 million, with only 7 million selling in the US. Roughly two-thirds of Jackson's audience is located outside North America. In countries such as England and Japan, Michael Jackson is a hot item. Clearly, he hopes to regain his audience here. And yet Jackson's own expectations seem impossible for any artist to achieve: He is hoping to sell 100 million copies of *Dangerous*. "If it sold 100 million, I don't think he'd be totally satisfied," says Bruce Swedien, one of the coproducers of the album. "But he'd hold still for that."

"With Michael, as with any superstar, reality and fantasy are totally confused," says John Landis. "It's very difficult to remain sane. I think he's doing the right thing by cutting himself off from the press, because the press tends to write what it wants anyway. But I tell you, I really like him a lot. He's very smart; he's a very nice man."

So, in the four years since *Bad* was released, Jackson has, in his own way, attempted to take complete control of his life. He stopped working with Quincy Jones, the man who produced or coproduced *Off the Wall*, *Thriller*, and *Bad*. He fired his manager, Frank Dileo—a former Epic Records promotion man, who deserves much of the credit for keeping singles from *Thriller* and *Bad* at the top of the charts—and hired Sandy Gallin, who has worked with Dolly Parton and Neil Diamond, among others.

He also replaced his business manager and, more significantly, attorney, John Branca, who had not only handled numerous complex legal cases and acted as interim manager at various critical points in Jackson's ascent but had also negotiated Jackson's purchase of the Beatles song catalog, now worth more than $120 million, three times what Jackson paid for it. Finally, Jackson left home, moving into Neverland and, according to several sources, distancing himself from at least some members of his family.

Surprisingly, despite a fresh cabinet of advisers, Jackson's new strategy for topping himself isn't new at all. Instead, he seems to be repeating, with slight variations, what has worked for him in the past.

Yet things have changed since *Thriller* and *Bad*. While rap became a force to be reckoned with, hard rock once again captured the nation's attention. Producers like L.A. Reid and Babyface and Teddy Riley created New Jack Swing, the latest version of soul music. Stars like Madonna and Peter Gabriel, Hammer and R.E.M. have raised the stakes where video is concerned. And the Rolling Stones pulled off the biggest, most flamboyant tour of the decade.

As far as a new album went, Michael Jackson, the biggest star in the world, had to come up with something that looked and sounded new and fresh yet wouldn't alienate his millions of fans, many of whom have decidedly conservative tastes.

Jackson's solution was to create a mass-appeal album in which about half the songs mimic his previous work ("Heal the World" being an obvious rewrite of "We Are the World"; "Who Is It" copping his "Billie Jean" moves; "Black or White" recalling "State of Shock"). He also brought in Teddy Riley to whip up cutting-edge street beats to make the album sound more contemporary.

And then, to announce the new album in a style appropriate for "the King of Pop," Jackson brought back his old friend John Landis for an encore. Landis had last worked with Jackson on the "Thriller" video in 1983. Although Landis says he doesn't have exact figures, he estimates from his experience that "Black or White" may have cost as much as $7 million. (Dave Glew, president of Epic Records, the label Jackson is signed to, denies this figure but would not divulge the actual amount.) It also took about two months to shoot.

The weeks of filming found many celebrities dropping by the set, including Paul McCartney, Nancy Reagan, the O'Jays, Emmanuel Lewis, and, naturally, Jackson's latest friend, *Home Alone* star Macaulay Culkin, who is not only featured in "Black or White" but also appears on the cover of *Dangerous*.

"Michael's really a celebrity magnet," says Landis. Then, chuckling, he adds: "I remember looking over at one of these giant, seven-foot speakers Michael was having the song played through, and Nancy Reagan was standing right in front of it. All I had to yell was, 'Playback,' and that would have been it."

"Black or White" became one of the most expensive one-song videos ever made because of, among other things, the cost of the cast and crew, which Landis says would read like "the credits to *Ben-Hur*," and the extremely expensive "morphing" process used to transform men into women and Jackson into a panther.

And then there were the days when Landis and the crew were all set up on location, ready to begin filming, when Landis would get a call informing him that the star wouldn't be showing up at all. "I was told, on one occasion," says Landis, "that Michael Jackson was doing a commercial for Sony Television, Japan."

Jackson also had his album to finish. "It was a difficult schedule," says Vince Paterson, who will be directing a video for "Jam" should Sony go ahead with the song as a single. "There were days when we were put on hold while he worked on the album. The album had to take precedence. So, the video got scrambled. And if Michael was in the studio for 18 hours, there was no point in then bringing him out to the set and trying to shoot him. He would have been dead, he would have been exhausted, and we would have just had to reshoot it anyway."

"If you've got a sound stage and equipment and people, you have to pay everyone involved whether or not anything gets done," says Paterson. "A lot of the expense was due to that. Bam! A couple hundred thousand dollars—gone!"

Landis says the video's controversial four-minute ending was entirely Jackson's idea. "He wanted it to be even more sexually explicit," says Landis, adding that some of the dancing they shot was even more extreme. As for the negative reaction to that part of the video—which resulted in Jackson's decision to cut out the entire ending—Landis says: "It wasn't so much what Michael was doing but the juxtaposition of simulated masturbation with the violence. And of course, the fact that it was Michael. I don't know that we discussed his intention. It was simply, 'I'd like to do this,' and me giving him what he wanted."

Earlier this year, Michael Jackson's business advisers negotiated a new $65 million contract with Sony Music that gave him not only profit participation in his album's earnings but also his own record company and the opportunity to make films for Sony's Columbia Pictures. It is an unprecedented deal.

"The deal we made—and I don't think it's appropriate to discuss the details—we think is economic for us," says Michael Schulhof, vice-chairman of Sony USA. "If Michael continues to perform the way he has in the past, both he and we will do very well. He's 33 years old. I don't think anybody, including Michael himself, can predict how he is going to exercise that creativity. It may be in music, it may be in film, it may be in totally new areas of entertainment. The fact that the contract with him is unique reflects the fact that he is a unique talent."

Jackson spent an estimated $10 million to record *Dangerous*. (Epic's Glew denies this figure as well.) He used seven recording studios in the process. For over two years he had exclusive 24-hour-a-day access to Record One studios, in Sherman Oaks, California. That studio alone, which contains two complete recording studios, is estimated to have cost $4,000 a day. Then there were the three rooms at Larrabee Sound Studios, in Los Angeles, which Jackson also secured for about nine months. That added another $3,000 to $4,000 a day to the budget.

"Usually, there wasn't a whole lot going on in any of the studios unless Michael was there," says a source who worked on the album. "When they were at Larrabee, they still had Record One booked. It's a little eccentric. Nobody makes records like that. It would be fun to be able to spend that kind of money, I'll tell you.

"It's just 'cause he has so much other stuff going on," the source says. "Trying to help kids. Like if all of a sudden up in Sacramento someone shoots a bunch of kids, he has to go up there and spend time with them. There was a lot of that stuff going on every day. Every day he'd want to go do something else. There were a lot of distractions. Liz is getting married, and he goes and deals with that, but still the studios were booked."

Says one artist manager: "I simply don't understand how it's possible to spend $10 million making an album. People have spent $2 million. But $10 million? That's just beyond comprehension." Jackson worked on the album off and on for nearly four years. "Michael started the day we finished *Bad*," says Swedien. "The next day he was doing demos."

Originally, the plan was for Jackson simply to record four new songs for a multi-CD greatest-hits package called *Decade* that was to have come out before Christmas 1989. Jackson began work on some new songs and came up with about half an album's worth of strong material.

Jackson, in consultation with his associates and Sony Music executives, decided that the new songs he had written were strong enough that he should just make an entire album. The greatest-hits package was thus shelved.

Booked studios accounted for a mere fraction of the high costs. Jackson went on to record about 60 songs for *Dangerous*. In addition to working with Riley and Swedien, he cut tracks with several other producers: Bill Bottrell, Bryan Loren and L.A. Reid, and Babyface. Bottrell describes working with Jackson in near ecstatic terms: "Every time he sings or tells me about a new idea for a song, it's . . . let me just say that there were plenty of extraordinary moments!"

According to Bottrell, "Black or White" developed from something originally recorded for *Bad*. "That piece of music, the beginning part that Slash plays on, was first recorded at Michael's house," Bottrell says. "Michael asked me to dig it out of the vault in August of 1989. He had in mind to use it as the intro to 'Black or White.' It took a long time before we got Slash on it."

Bottrell paved the way for Jackson and Slash to work together. Although Slash is credited with playing on "Black or White," he's actually only on the introductory groove. Jackson wasn't even there for the session when Slash recorded that bit. "He was disappointed," says Bottrell. "He was frustrated that Michael wasn't there."

More than a year later, Slash got a call. It was from Jackson. He had a power ballad, "Give In to Me," that he wanted Slash to solo on. "He sent me a tape of the song that had no guitars other than some slow picking," says Slash. "I called him and sang over the phone what I wanted to do."

Slash, however, didn't have time to record the solo. "I was leaving for Africa," he says. "Our schedules were not in sync. So, they were going to blow me off, but Michael managed to work it out so we could do it when I came back from Africa. I got off the plane and drove to the studio."

"I basically went in and started to play it—that was it," Slash says. "It was really spontaneous in that way. Michael just wanted whatever was in my style. He just wanted me to do that. No pressure. He was really in sync with me. I don't come from this heavy-metal school of guitar playing. All the stuff that I do or dig is from the same place that Michael

Jackson comes from. We may go in separate directions or be on different sides of the fence, but when it comes down to it, it all comes from the same shit."

Working with Jackson in the studio can be tricky. A firm believer in the power of positive thinking (in Jackson's office at Neverland are a batch of books by self-help guru Dr. Wayne Dyer, including *The Sky's the Limit* and *You'll See It When You Believe It*), Jackson almost never comes out and says he doesn't like something. "He doesn't like to be negative," says Bottrell. "He has his own indications, and you just learn what they are. Walking out of the room is one way."

Jackson's approach to coproducing songs is unusual. "He starts with an entire sound and song, musically," says Bottrell. "Usually he doesn't start with lyrics, but he hears the sound and the whole arrangement of the song in his head. I suppose there are exceptions, but this is generally the way it is. He fills in the lyrics later. He hums things. He can convey it with his voice like nobody. Not just singing the song's lyrics, but he can convey a feeling in a drum part or a synthesizer part. He's really good at conveying those things."

While Jackson was happy with a good number of the songs he'd completed, he felt the dance grooves didn't cut it. "Michael's desire was to present something very street that the young people will be able to identify with," says Swedien. "That was a conscious decision on his part."

Enter Teddy Riley. Said to have been the brains behind Bobby Brown's phenomenal "My Prerogative" (although production was credited to Riley's former partner Gene Griffin), Riley was apparently suggested to Jackson by Eddie Murphy as the right producer for delivering the killer grooves.

"He wanted to work on grooves," says Riley. "So I came in with 10 grooves. He liked them all."

"Teddy was very professional," says Swedien. "No problems. He'd come in with a groove, we'd say it wasn't exactly right, and there would be no complaining. He'd just go back and then come back in and blow us away with something like 'Dangerous.'"

Jackson would listen to the music they were working on at window-breaking levels. Riley says they blew a speaker at one studio. "Michael likes to listen even louder than me," says Riley. "His volume is past 19. I'm maybe 9 or 10. His volume is 12-plus. Oh, man, he loves loud music. And he jams! Only way you know your music is right is if he's dancing all over the studio. He starts going, 'Yeah, whoa!'"

Once Jackson and Riley got into it, they just kept coming up with songs. "When the deadline came, he wanted to do more and more songs," says Riley. "And his manager came in there and said, 'Teddy, you and Michael, you're not up to your sneaky stuff. Do not write another song.' And then when Michael saw the commercial for *Dangerous*, the David Lynch thing, we started working hard to get it finished."

For the last two months of work on the album, Jackson and Swedien took rooms at a hotel four minutes from the studio. "We'd drive to the studio and work until we couldn't work anymore," says Swedien. "Then we'd drive back to the hotel, go to sleep and then go back in the morning and hit it again."

One particular day, Swedien found Jackson crying in a room he used as his office at Record One. He was upset because the song he had been trying to sing was in the wrong key. "The day had come for Michael to put the lead on 'Keep the Faith,'" says Swedien. "He sang the first and second verses, and then he disappeared. It was very unlike Michael.

I found him standing in the corner of his office crying his eyes out. He was absolutely heartbroken, cut to the quick.

"I told him, 'Michael, it's not that big a deal,'" Swedien says. "'I'll just record it in the other key.' We'd tried two keys and, unfortunately, picked the wrong one. He was really upset. I told him, 'Michael, we've got to face this right now.' I called the synth player and programmer. I felt we had to get the right key and get Michael to face it before it turned into something ugly.

"I thought we'd have a major, major problem," continues Swedien. "I was visualizing headlines. I told him, 'Pull yourself together, face this now.' And it was late. I said, 'We're not going home until you've sung this all the way through. Then we'll go home and be able to sleep and continue.' That was scary. But he did it. He pulled himself together. We went in the studio, cut a whole new demo and recorded a scratch vocal all way through. A situation like that could have been a real block. We didn't leave the studio till dawn."

The pressure to get the album done in time for a pre-Thanksgiving release was enormous. "He was under extreme pressure to deliver his album," says John Landis. "He had the entire Rising Sun on his ass; they had to drag it out of him."

The album was finally finished early in the morning on October 31. "Michael said, 'We bumped the pumpkin,'" says Swedien. "The last three days of the project, Michael and I got about four hours sleep."

Upon its release on November 26th, *Dangerous* immediately began selling at a healthy clip—more than 70,000 copies a day. The album entered the *Billboard* charts at number one, with sales for the first five days at about 350,000 copies in the US. (Sales figures for a full week were not tallied because of the Thanksgiving holiday.)

Critical response, however, was not as favorable. In the *New York Times*, Jon Pareles called *Dangerous* Jackson's "least confident album since he became a solo star" and criticized the superstar for sounding "so eager to reclaim his popularity that he has ruled out taking chances." The *Los Angeles Times* posed this question: "How dangerous can a man who literally wants to please everyone afford to be again?" and characterized the album as "a messy grab-bag of ideas and high-tech non sequiturs, with something for everyone from the man who has everything. . . . Relatively tame, and wildly unfocused, *Dangerous* is also mostly good, expertly made fun."

Retailers believe the album should do very well. Tower Records president Russ Solomon says it was the number-one seller in most of his stores during the first week of release. "Out of the box, you can't put it in the same league as Guns N' Roses," says Solomon. "But it's selling pretty good. My own opinion is it will build over the next few months. Some records, like the Guns N' Roses album, appeal to an audience that needs to buy it the minute it's available. Others, like this one, appeal to a different crowd who won't line up at midnight. It takes a bit of time. But number one is number one. It outsold the U2 album this week. Sony should have no problem selling the more than 4 million they initially shipped."

Solomon notes that multiplatinum albums do not sell 10 million copies in the first month of release. "It takes time," says Solomon. "If you're lucky, you do that in a year. In the case of *Thriller*, it took two years [to sell close to 20 million copies in the US]."

Critics and retailers alike agree that Jackson has created an album with wide appeal—which is exactly what he intended. "Michael feels a tremendous responsibility to his audience," says Bruce Swedien. "I think this piece of work is a good illustration of the fact that he feels this responsibility to provide the best possible music for the fans. That responsibility is at the foreground all the time with Michael."

JACKSON CLEARLY HAS A lot riding on *Dangerous*. He hopes it will serve as a kind of pop rocket ship that will take him to unimagined levels of stardom and popular acclaim. Already, with the "Black or White" video, Jackson has put himself in the forefront of the public's consciousness. The album's success—and the series of singles that will be on the airwaves over the next year or so—will keep him there, setting the stage for the next aspect of his career: movie stardom. For Jackson wants to be a classic star, like his good friends Elizabeth Taylor and Katharine Hepburn.

Yet times have changed since his cinematic role models achieved fame. Today's stars are public figures whose private lives are open for discussion. And as Landis noted, Jackson, knowingly or unknowingly, has provided the public with a series of personal topics to discuss and debate, ranging from his sexuality to his face.

In trying to create a glamorous image for himself in the years since his first solo album as an adult, *Off the Wall*, was released in 1979, Jackson has literally remade his face before our very eyes. We have all been privy to each new change in the Jackson countenance. He has, of course, been criticized for trying to become white, for turning his back on his roots.

Teddy Riley says that during the *Dangerous* recording sessions, Jackson talked a lot about what he'd done to his face and skin. "I'm quite sure if Michael could have done it all over again, he would not have done that," says Riley. "But there's no turning back. Once you change your description, you can't turn back. You can't get your own face or your own skin back again. But he is still Michael Jackson; he is still the talented man that everybody grew up on."

Indeed, that seems to be exactly what Jackson himself is trying to convey. All of the animals and angels, golden thrones and jeweled crowns, skeletons and funhouse rides that take up much of the cover of *Dangerous* appear to be a gigantic mask behind which the real Michael Jackson hides, through which the real Michael Jackson looks at the world.

There is one thing we know for certain about the real Michael Jackson: He is an extraordinarily talented man with a gift for creating music that people all over the world love. Jackson should put more faith in his talent. That, more than anything, accounts for his more than 20 years of stardom.

*Rolling Stone*, January 1992

# DEVO: SIXTIES IDEALISTS OR NAZIS AND CLOWNS

*The first time I met the members of Devo was in 1978 at their manager's office in LA. Their manager was Elliot Roberts, who also managed Neil Young. I remember Elliot, who I met for the first time that day and who I subsequently spoke to many times over the years, was there for the entire interview, which was not typical. Usually when I interviewed a musician, it was just me and the musician. But Elliot (who died in June 2019) was very protective of his artists, and so there he was. The group had just released their debut album,* Q: Are We Not Men? A: We Are Devo! *It's a groundbreaking album, and it was exciting to interview Devo. The second time I interviewed the band, Elliot wasn't there, and it was nearly four years later. They were in LA, where they now lived (having moved there from Akron, Ohio, where they formed in 1973), and were working on a music video for their fourth album,* New Traditionalists. *They had scored a huge hit in 1980 with "Whip It," so now they were stars, and the pressure was on. Was "Whip It" going to make them one-hit wonders, or was it the start of a long career? I was there to interview them for* Boulevards, *the San Francisco magazine I edited at the time. But I had started freelancing for* Rolling Stone, *and when I got back to San Francisco I pitched my Devo story to* Rolling Stone *music editor Jim Henke. As it turned out, Devo wouldn't talk to* Rolling Stone *because the magazine had panned their second and third albums. Panned isn't strong enough. Critic Dave Marsh wrote at the end of his review of* Duty Now for The Future: *"To say that this critic despises Devo does not go nearly far enough. When I finish typing this, I'm taking a hammer to* Duty Now for the Future, *lest it corrupt anyone dumb or innocent enough to take it seriously. Shards sent on request." So I was in luck. Henke needed a Devo story, and I could deliver. And I did. As members of the group explain in the story that follows, Devo were, to some extent Sixties idealists who were trying to use music to wake listeners up to the insanity of present-day America. Nearly 40 years later, what they say in this story seems prescient. Note that Devo drummer Alan Myers died in 2013; Devo guitarist/keyboardist Bob Casale died in 2014.*

HOLLYWOOD, CALIFORNIA—"SOMEONE WANTED to know where your home is," the waitress said to Mark Mothersbaugh.

"I don't have a home," Mothersbaugh replied softly, peering at the woman through dark glasses, his short brown hair askew so that he looked like a young Dr. Strangelove.

"I told them I thought it was Mars," said the waitress, trying to stifle a less-than-charitable laugh.

"Mars," said Mothersbaugh slowly. "I wish I came from Mars. That's where I'd like to go, anyway."

Mark Mothersbaugh, of course, isn't from Mars. He's from Devo. He writes songs, sings, plays synthesizers, and, together with bassist-songwriter Jerry Casale, is the brains behind the band responsible for adding the phrase "whip it good" to our vocabulary.

Devo at a press conference, San Francisco, 1978.

Mothersbaugh was surprisingly good-natured about the waitress' ribbing. He's apparently used to that kind of thing now. And it was less of a hassle than the fans who come up to him and ask, point-blank, "Why did you sell out?"

"That makes me feel worse than anything, 'cause I don't know what to say," Mothersbaugh said recently while eating dinner at a gourmet health-food restaurant in Beverly Hills. "I try to tell them that it wasn't our fault, that we were just doing what we wanted to do and somehow people ended up buying it."

In fact, Devo have been woefully misunderstood. Until "Whip It" became one of the biggest singles of 1980, Devo had meager record sales; their mix of Fifties sci-fi sound effects, mechanized rock & roll, and offbeat image—five yellow jump-suited industrial ants leaping about the stage in unison—was not well received by the mainstream rock audience. And while the public mostly ignored them, the critics were picking at Devo like vultures going after a dying cow.

"There's nothing older than yesterday's futurism," wrote Lester Bangs in the *Village Voice*. "*Freedom of Choice* [Devo's third album, which contains 'Whip It'] is so pathetic you almost feel sorry for them, but it was their choice to be geeks from the beginning, and there was never any reason to suppose that their routine wasn't a scam." Chris Morris, reviewing a Devo concert for *Rolling Stone*, wrote, "Regrettably missing from the evening's music was the sense that Devo have anything in the least to say." He added, "Devo's show bore all the orgiastic earmarks of a Nuremberg rally for spud boys."

"Well, obviously, we're Nazis and clowns," said Jerry Casale. "They're all right, all those people. They're all right on it. We're assholes. Everything they accuse us of is true. We're subhuman idiots who threaten them." After taking a deep breath, he continued, "You know, really, on the largest level, who cares?"

It seems that Mothersbaugh does, for one. "There are people who buy or don't buy records because of the critics," he said, his resentment obvious. "They call us fascists because we represent something scary to them. It's like all these 'Me Generation' people whose politics are, 'I want to take as many drugs and consume as much energy and own two condos and big recreational vehicles and take up as much space for myself as I can.' They don't want to be concerned about how they relate to other people on the planet and their responsibility to other people on the planet. Those kinds of people are upset by Devo politics. Because if there's a politic behind what we do, it's people being aware of their responsibility to other people."

Despite the group's reputation for theatrics a la silly red plastic hats that look like art-deco flowerpots, Devo has an idealistic bent that is rooted in Sixties activism. Casale and Mothersbaugh met while they were both art students at Kent State University, in Ohio. "I saw Allison Krause from about 30 feet away after the guardsmen blew away about half her torso," Casale has said. "That day was devo. It might have been the most devo day of my life."

The Kent State debacle was just another bit of evidence for Casale and Mothersbaugh. Evidence that mankind was on a steady, downhill plunge. Evidence that they had been gathering since they were kids growing up in Akron, Ohio, a vast wasteland of malls and tire factories, fast-food restaurants and Kmarts. *That* was an inherited reality that nauseated Casale and Mothersbaugh. As they sing on their new album, *New Traditionalists*, "I know a place where dreams get crushed, hopes are smashed but that ain't much."

"They really think the world could be so much better than it is," confided a close friend of the band's. "And they're distraught at all times over the situation that people are ignorant and don't respond to the information that they've been given."

To say that these guys are distraught, troubled by the condition of the world, is to understate the case. They are *freaked out.* They sincerely believe that their songs are imparting important information, and they view the critical attacks that have been aimed at them as a conspiracy of sorts. On Devo's four albums, the group weds minimalist electronics, robot rhythms, and android vocals, satirizing, perhaps, a mechanized, plasticized, programmed, and subdued society. "Things are fucked up," explained Mothersbaugh. As if dissecting an alien species, he continued, "They believe in love, they believe in anger, they believe in jealousy. . . ."

"They believe in God," Casale added solemnly. "We're interested in new traditions." Hence, the title of their new LP. "Well, we were making some kind of play—turnaround—on the word *tradition* and what it's come to mean. The traditions that started a couple of hundred years ago. The industrial traditions. The kind of fundamentalist religious traditions. Traditions based on a certain kind of world. A lot of people are operating under fear of God. All those traditions operating behind every TV station and family in America. The kinds of things that Reagan stirred up with his posters of Reagan country and bygone America, where there're seven icons of the past surrounding his head: Mount Rushmore, a wooden covered bridge and a wheat field and a church steeple. . . . I mean, he should have just had the apple pie and mom and the baby and all the rest of it, and a couple of crucifixes and a Ku Klux Klan outfit as well.

"So we are just using traditions as a springboard and saying what we represent is new traditions. Rethinking the order of things. Which, in my opinion, is what's valid about Devo. We've taken all the same information that everyone has and everyone is affected by and assumes to be true and reshuffled it to make a new picture."

"Use information instead of emotions to make decisions," added Mothersbaugh. "A lot of people make decisions based on paranoia, hatred, selfishness and love.

"If anything, if we were to reduce it to some cliché, we've always represented Spock's attitude toward the world. Not Dr. Spock, Mr. Spock. A kind of world citizen."

Casale and Mothersbaugh claim they have always felt like outsiders. "I never had a good time," said Casale of his childhood. "It was that simple."

"I always knew something was wrong," said Mothersbaugh.

"'Cause of how horrible people were," continued Casale. "The kids in my class. The teachers. The local scene. What you might get beat up for. You'd try to leave school, and the greasers would stand on the corner with a bicycle chain or something and make you pay them a nickel to pass. Playing Mafia. And you would not even believe it. It just seemed too ridiculous. By the time you got to high school, most of the kids you knew were wearing madras shorts and trying to be caddies. And you just always felt uneasy. Like at a party you don't want to be at. You just feel bad."

It was nearly a decade ago—1973—when Devo formed in Akron. Mothersbaugh and Casale enlisted their brothers, guitarists Bob Casale (Bob I) and Bob Mothersbaugh (Bob II), along with drummer Alan Myers. In their hometown, audiences threw things at Devo. "I was always, from the beginning, prepared for a negative response, 'cause we certainly got it," said Casale. "We never did this to be popular. Beer bottles were thrown at us, and people were screaming 'Play Bad Company' as far back as 1974. And to come in the face of a thing [rock & roll] that's based on expendable idols and mythological worship with a group of pretty much provincial middle-class guys who didn't have big drug habits or didn't have long manes of hair and codpieces, you know, and didn't talk about drinkin' and ballin' and losing your girl—I didn't really expect that we'd be popular. I thought, if anything, we'd be popular because there were likeminded people all over the world in little pockets here and there who would respond to it once they were given a chance to find it in front of them."

In 1976, Devo released a single on their own label, Booji Boy Records. The song was "Jocko Homo," and it succinctly summed up the basic Devo creed:

> They tell us that / We lost our tails / Evolving up / From little snails / I say it's all / Just wind in sails / Are we not men? / We Are Devo! / We're pinheads now / We are not whole / We're pinheads all / Jocko Homo / Are we not men? / D-E-V-O.

"Jocko Homo" was an underground hit in America and Europe, and by 1978, they were signed to Warner Bros.

That same year, Devo relocated to LA so that they could "be in touch with our careers." Their careers got a big boost last year with the success of "Whip It." Yet Casale maintains that Devo's one and only hit was misunderstood. "The only reason that they played us on the radio, unfortunately, is there was a song, 'Whip It,' that could be mistaken for sadomasochism and masturbation," he said, adding sarcastically, "two popular themes in America. But we're not proud. We'll take it any way we can get it."

"We thought of 'Whip It' as people pulling together and whipping the problem," explained Mothersbaugh earnestly.

It was getting late, and Casale and Mothersbaugh were tired of trying to explain Devo. "People need an alien shot that would put them one step removed from the world totally but at the same time keep them lucid and pump their adrenaline so that they would just have total observation of the human condition," said Casale, rising from his chair. "It would be fantastic. They wouldn't do 90 percent of all the shit they were doing. They'd never do it again. They'd be too embarrassed and too humiliated."

Then Casale and Mothersbaugh put on their dark glasses and walked off into the muggy LA night.

*Rolling Stone,* December 10, 1981

Neil Young at the Boarding House, San Francisco, 1978.

# THE LONER: A CONVERSATION WITH NEIL YOUNG

*The first time I interviewed Neil Young, it was February 7, 1987, and I was on an airplane flying back to San Francisco from Santa Barbara the day after attending the first Crosby, Stills, Nash and Young reunion concert after David Crosby got released from jail and got his life in order. As I sat waiting for the plane to take off, Neil Young came walking down the aisle and took a seat a few rows in front of me. I waited until the plane took off, and approached him, introduced myself (I had seen him briefly backstage the night before), and asked if I could interview him for a story I was writing for* Rolling Stone. *He said yes. Eight years later he said yes again. Neil Young means so much to me. Here is a brief excerpt from my second novel,* The Flowers Lied; *I think it conveys some of what I feel about Young.*

> I dig Neil the most, beginning in his Buffalo Springfield days. Back then he's the coolest freakster bro in the band with his fringed Buffalo Bill leather jacket. So so serious bummered-out lanky tall plays a big fat Gretsch White Falcon sings us his lonesome. Sure Dylan made up the whole trip, smart young white guy lays the deep poetry over folk-rock, but while Dylan has the East Coast vibe and by the time he plays rock & roll he has that English dandy thing going, Neil's the stoned West Coast free spirit. Neil lays his heart out in those downer chords, not afraid to sing a bad line 'cause he knows the feel is the whole trip, the sound of the words he sings, and the off-kilter rhythm that shows up around *Harvest* but been in the works at least since "Mr. Soul," and the ragged-ass electric guitar. Sometimes it's as if Neil hangs on one note for the whole damn solo. So often growing up I felt lonely as the loneliest Neil Young ballad. "Oh, Lonesome Me" or the other one that's equally downered and out, "The Losing End (When You're On)," where he's all sad-sack singing how he'll never be the same, and yeah it's pathetic, but sometimes it's how I feel. Neil's lonesome sound, sound of my own soul.

WOODSIDE, CALIFORNIA—PINE TREES and redwoods are whipping by as *Addicted To Noise* business manager Steve McConnell and I tool down Skyline Boulevard in Woodside, a rural area of Northern California just south of San Francisco. "Song X," a rousing rock & roll sea chantey off Neil Young's brilliant collaboration with Pearl Jam, *Mirror Ball*, is blasting so loud we can hardly think. I am heading for a Woodside restaurant to interview Neil Young.

In the parking lot, I see Young's 1960 Lincoln Continental parked in the shade of a grove of trees. His dog, Bear, is inside the car, waiting patiently. I enter the rustic restaurant that Young and his entourage have taken over for the day. The restaurant is dark and cool—a safe haven from the heat.

While waiting for Young, I hang with his manager of over 20 years, Elliot Roberts, Warner Bros./Reprise Records chief publicist, Bob Merlis, and MTV's Kurt Loder, an old friend and writing collaborator who had flown in to do the MTV Neil Young interview.

"Anything he seemed touchy about?" I ask Loder, who is brushing some kind of makeup powder off his double-breasted sport coat.

He looked at me like I was crazy: "Of course not," he said. "It's Neil."

I interview Young at the back of the restaurant, light streaming through the window onto him. He is wearing a baseball hat, which conceals his long graying hair.

At 49, Young is indeed the Grand Old Man of raw, primal (OK, I'll say it), grunge rock. He has, simply, lived and experienced a lot. Sitting across the table from him, it is clear that this is someone "connected" to the creative well, one of the rare artists able to be open enough that the universe can, on occasion, speak through him. As the sun slowly sets through the trees, we talk.

**Michael Goldberg:** I've been listening to *Mirror Ball*. I really think it's a powerful album, with a raw, visceral quality to it. I know you recorded it in a relatively short period of time. What made you decide to do an album with Pearl Jam backing you up?

**Neil Young:** I'd gotten to know them through playing a tour together in Europe a couple of years ago with Booker T. and the MGs [Young's backing band for that tour]. Then Eddie inducted me into the Hall of Fame [January 1995], and that night I played a song, "Act of Love," with Crazy Horse, which Pearl Jam recorded with a little DAT recorder, and they learned it. So two nights later I played it with them [at the Voters for Choice benefit in Washington, DC, on January 14]. And it sounded great. So we decided to go into the studio.

**Goldberg:** But it was that spontaneous?

**Young:** It happened eight days after the Choice show [Young and Pearl Jam entered Bad Animals studio in Seattle on January 26, 1995].

**Goldberg:** What was going through your mind once you sat down to write the material?

**Young:** The material became a product of the feeling of not having the time to sit back and analyze. Not enough time for that. So, it was just a matter of opening up and finding what was inside me to write. Once I did that, the songs came really fast, and they were all based on things that were happening right around us at that time. A lot of information from people's lives that were in the room with us. Discussions and talks and things that were happening during the sessions showed up in songs.

**Goldberg:** What's an example of that?

**Young:** "I'm the Ocean." Something in there about baseball players and football players and playing cards came out of a discussion that I had with somebody there. But there's all kinds of things in there, personal things. You can't really tie it to a distinct person. It could be three things that happened to three different people all get put together into the same moment. It's just a matter of stream of consciousness. It's not linear, organized. It just keeps coming out in a rhythm. The thoughts keep coming out. Then when you're done this is as much news to me as it is to you. All I'm doing is writing it down and putting it in a cadence. Once I get into a cadence, then why should I even stop and wonder what it is? You can do that for the rest of your life, but when it's coming out, you don't want to stop it.

**Goldberg:** Obviously it was a very creative period for you.

**Young:** It was a good period. I've made other albums that way, in the past. I've made albums that have taken me years to make. It was just a high energy period. I saw a limited window to do it, because the band was leaving to go [to perform in Europe], and I thought, "God, this feels good right now, if I can stay with this." So I recorded for two days and we got four songs. I was supposed to wait until they came back from a tour, and then we were going to get together and do some more. And that's the way we left it. But after a while, two days at home, I started thinking about other songs. I called up and found out there were two other days they were available, so I said, "I've got a few more songs." Then we recorded until I didn't have any more [songs left]. But there was one day left so I said, "I got some more songs, if we can get one more day, we'll do a couple more songs." Then somewhere in the next couple of days, I wrote the songs.

**Goldberg:** When I first heard "Song X," it sounded like this incredible sort of rock & roll sea chantey *[Young smiles as I tell him this]*. I was imagining you and Pearl Jam, this gang of outlaw rockers, heading out to sea. Tell me your impression of that song.

**Young:** "Song X" was written around the same time as "Act of Love." It's really a story about choice. Both those songs are based around the choice issue: [Whether] to have a baby; the responsibility; why is it always the mother's responsibility? It's so easy for the guy to get out of it. Do people know what they're doing when they're in the act of love? Do they know what's next? Do they know what the fruit of love is? Is anybody thinking about that? Then there's the murder, however you want to look at it, the murder of the fetus, or the murder of the person that did the abortion. The murder aspect brings it into the God-is-on-my-side kind of righteousness of holy war. The whole thing's related [to] the act of love and the willingness or nonwillingness of someone, usually of the guy, to accept responsibility for what's happened. Those first two songs are centered on that 'cause that's what I was focused on, because of the benefit.

**Goldberg:** How did you learn to let yourself be open, to let what's going on around you somehow get through you, into a song?

**Young:** I didn't always know that it was happening. When I started living out here [in Woodside] I started to realize it. I stayed out of the mainstream for a long time and kind of hid down here in my house back in 1970. When I hid out here in the trees, all I wrote about were the trees and what was happening in the country. Then I realized, well, that must be because I'm here. And that's all I write about here. So I should go to New York for a couple of days and come back. So I could see, well, wait a minute, this seems to be directly linked. If I'm going to write, I'm going to be writing about all these things [happening around me at the time]. I just need a jolt of this or that. I'm not looking for anything [in particular], just what you pick up along the way. You don't have to get anything in particular, just be there. Besides being in a relationship, it's also location. It has a lot to do with what you write down. Where you are. I use those things to keep going.

**Goldberg:** So you started to realize this 25 years ago?

**Young:** When I took away the variety and then noticed the music reflected that, I put the variety back in and noticed the music reflected *that*. I concentrate on one thing—you can only see something so many times before you start to count on it in your plan for how you're going to do things.

**Goldberg:** Did you start consciously taking note of being open?

**Young:** You can't improve it by being self-aware of it. It's better to not be aware of it. It's not something you can use as you would a tool. But it's something that you can know. I'm open all the time. There's never a shortage of things to write about, if you pay attention to other people. If there's nothing going on in your own head, that doesn't mean anything. It's like you, him, him, especially him. [He points to *Addicted To Noise* business manager, Steve McConnell, who is videotaping the interview, and then to Elliot Roberts, who has entered the room.] I'll be singing about you, OK? You're next.

**Goldberg:** I was told that in titling *Mirror Ball*, you were thinking of the mirror ball that hung from the ceiling at the Fillmore West in the early '70s. Is that true?

**Young:** I was just thinking of a mirror ball. To me, all the pictures and scenes in the album, if you close your eyes and try to go with where the lyrics are taking you, they're flying. There's movement that keeps going from one place to another all the time. Just like a bunch of little square pieces of mirror all stuck together on a ball that's rolling along. You can only look at one at a time, so you just get to see a little glimmer of this, a little glimmer of that. It's like if they were all little television sets and you were looking in them, up into this ball of televisions rolling along, and they all had different things on them. [That's] sort of what it is. We ought to go build that right away, build a mirror ball television. Four hundred and fifty TVs all on at once rolling down the road.

*Addicted To Noise*, July 1995

# SAN FRANCISCO: THE SOUND OF FREEDOM

*I was asked to write this essay about the Sixties San Francisco Sound for the booklet that the Rock & Roll Hall of Fame passed out at their annual awards dinner, probably because I'd written several stories about the San Francisco music scene of the Sixties and the Eighties for* Rolling Stone *and other publications. I was the right person to ask. I'd been obsessed with the San Francisco scene starting when I was 13 in 1966. I'd seen some of the important San Francisco bands at Bay Area rock festivals, free concerts, and at the ballrooms. A friend and I had attempted to meet Janis Joplin when we drove to her house in Fairfax (and I managed to get her autograph after a Big Brother and the Holding Company show at the Avalon Ballroom). We'd interviewed Jerry Garcia when we were just 17. We knew the great FM DJ, Tom "Big Daddy" Donahue (we were friends with one of his sons). So yeah, I was the guy to write the essay that follows. I wrote it in 1994, a lot of years after the Sixties scene had died. Nonetheless, I can clearly remember some of highlights of those times that I experienced as a kid. I hope this essay will give you a sense of what it was like in the San Francisco Bay Area at that time, if, as is likely, you weren't there.*

## The San Francisco Scene

THE WORD ON THE STREET was that Big Brother and the Holding Company, one of San Francisco's preeminent rock bands, was going to perform in Golden Gate Park. For free. So one morning in 1968, at age 14, I stuck out my thumb and hitched a ride from Mill Valley, where I lived, into San Francisco to see one of my favorite bands.

I was let off near the park, and it took perhaps 15 minutes to reach Speedway Meadow, a long grassy expanse serving as the concert site. Even before my arrival, I knew I was close because of the guitar-driven rock & roll coming through the trees.

A crowd of a few hundred people (which would grow to perhaps 2,000) had gathered. I took in the idyllic scene: Groups of young (though all older than me), long-haired men and women sitting together on colorful blankets digging the sounds, the sweet smell of weed and incense in the air; a frizzy-haired guy blowing bubbles; a woman sunning topless; a few tripped-out souls dancing near the stage; couples making out in the grass.

Eventually Janis, the epitome of the "hippie chick" with her long wild hair, oval granny glasses, numerous bracelets, beaded necklaces, Southern Comfort bottle, and seemingly free spirit, and her Big Brother bandmates—guitarists James Gurley and Sam Andrew, bassist Peter Albin, drummer David Getz—took the stage.

The performance Big Brother gave that day stands as one of my greatest rock & roll experiences.

And not just because I witnessed Janis' bawdy, impassioned, liberating onstage persona and that wiser-than-her-years voice that so deeply conveyed heartache and heartbreak, love and lust, pity and pain.

Big Brother rocked!

Sam Andrew (left) and Janis Joplin of Big Brother and the Holding Company, Mt. Tamalpais, Mill Valley, June 1967. Phil Lesh (right) of the Grateful Dead and Peter Kraemer of the Sopwith Camel (bottom), McNears Beach, San Rafael, October 1967.

They were loud, hard, savage rock & roll rebels tough enough to survive being the house band at Hells Angels' beer busts. Janis' vocals, from a whisper to a hoarse scream, could get you that close to ecstasy.

Big Brother were the Nirvana of their day. Their raw, brutal sound predated both the punk movement of the mid-Seventies and the grunge scene of the Eighties. Their repertoire—"Down on Me," "Piece of My Heart," "All Is Loneliness," "Call on Me," "Ball and Chain," "Light Is Faster Than Sound," "Coo Coo," and others—was exquisite, their delivery visceral and often transcendent.

I like drummer Mickey Hart's off-the-cuff review. Recalling his first Big Brother sighting, at a closet-size club called the Matrix, Hart told me: "Brother were going crazy feeding back and Janis stepped to the mike and it split your head open."

At the end of that magical afternoon, as a cool wind began to blow fog in off the ocean, I walked out of the park, stuck out my thumb and was soon back in Marin. Perhaps there was another place during the late Sixties where you could experience some of the world's greatest rock & roll for free, but I doubt it.

## The Sound of the City

BECAUSE THE "SAN FRANCISCO SOUND" coalesced amid the utopian idealism of the Bay Area's hippie movement, the civil rights effort, leftist politics, environmental concerns, and the psychedelic drug culture, it is impossible (and I believe pointless) to isolate it from its context.

Such trippy, exotic jams as the Grateful Dead's epic "Dark Star," Country Joe and the Fish's "Section 43," or Big Brother's reinvention of "Summertime" are, for me and I think for anyone who had the chance to wander down Haight Street in the mid-Sixties or attend a dance concert at the Family Dog's Avalon Ballroom, the sounds that go with the sights of that strange and wonderful time.

The bands provided the soundtrack for the dance concert "light shows," exotic multimedia wall paintings composed of ever-changing slides, film loops, liquid projections, and other effects staged by such oddly named visual art groups as the North American Ibis Alchemical Co. The soundtrack for a day of dreaming impossible dreams out in the park, of making love for the first time, of LSD- and marijuana-tinged visions, of spiritual possibilities.

Since the mid-Seventies and the arrival of punk and harder drugs, it has been fashionable to dismiss the idealism, optimism, and ecstasy of the San Francisco Scene. One young writer, a Twentysomething born too late to experience the scene firsthand, recently wrote, as if it were something to be proud of, that she has "little empathy for Sixties nostalgia or the remnants of the hippie dream."

Now I'm the last person to pine for what was, but as an adolescent in love with rock & roll, I was there. I walked the Haight, amazed by the freewheeling, bazaar-like atmosphere, "far out" music wafting from open windows, the sidewalks crowded with "groovy" kids. I went to the Avalon Ballroom and the Fillmore Auditorium, the Carousel Ballroom and Winterland. I stayed up listening to DJs at KMPX invent free-form underground rock radio and I dug the psychedelic posters, the handiwork of Wes Wilson and Moscoso and Rick Griffin and Mouse & Kelley, that went up in the windows of bookstores and coffee houses announcing upcoming concerts.

The Twentysomethings have a vested interest in denying a past they missed out on. I can understand that. They want their own culture, and they want it to feel IMPORTANT. But to deny the window into Utopia that existed, at least for a few years, in San Francisco is to deny history.

## Freedom Calling

THE SAN FRANCISCO SOUND WAS THE sound of freedom. Freedom to dress, behave, and live the way one wanted, to escape the confines of a straight, square, normal, inhibited, nose-to-the-grindstone middle-class life. Some of us even believed that a pursuit of one's art took precedence over the pursuit of money.

Today, of course, in the age of AIDs, the homeless, gang violence, a shrinking job market and all the other social ailments plaguing our society, that sounds so naive. Something only a kid (or a spaced-out hippie) could be sucker enough to buy into. Right?

The details of what happened in San Francisco are known. How, to note one example, a bunch of folk and blues musicians plugged in, dropped a lot of acid and, calling themselves the Grateful Dead, created a psychedelic American roots music that has a larger following today than it did in the Sixties.

Most of the important bands have been written up so many times that telling their stories seems redundant. The Jefferson Airplane, the acid-rock combo with the phenomenal singers Grace Slick and Marty Balin, mixing up rock, blues, and folk with lyrics about both love ("Today") and radical politics ("Volunteers"). The Quicksilver Messenger Service, whose mercurial lead guitarist, John Cipollina, took the primal rhythms of Bo Diddley into a mind-boggling realm with his endlessly creative improvisations. Country Joe and the Fish, pioneers of a hallucinogenic brand of spaced-out rock that can be heard on their priceless, appropriately titled debut album, *Electric Music for the Mind and Body*.

So many cool bands: the Charlatans, Moby Grape, the Beau Brummels, the Flamin' Groovies, Sly and the Family Stone, Creedence Clearwater Revival, the Sons of Champlain, Clover, Blue Cheer, Flying Circus, the Mystery Trend, the Great Society, the Sparrow, the Steve Miller Blues Band, the Sopwith Camel.

## The Fans Would Rip You Apart

THE SAN FRANCISCO SOUND WAS SO accessible. At the Avalon and Fillmore, when the musicians weren't onstage, they were often on the dance floor. "As soon as you got through performing you could go down and dance in the audience," Grace Slick once recalled. "I did that. We'd wander in the crowd before and after we played. You can't do that now. The fans would rip you apart."

I remember another day, back in the late Sixties, when I attended an afternoon concert at McNears Beach in Marin and grooved to a wonderful, now forgotten band called the Sopwith Camel (remember "Hello Hello"?). There was no sealed off backstage. Members of the audience could wander behind the stage, talk to the group's charming lead singer, Peter Kraemer, or his bandmates. Phil Lesh of the Grateful Dead was hanging around, digging the vibe, talking to anyone who approached him.

Musicians flocked to the Bay Area during the late Sixties and early Seventies. Most didn't hide behind gated mansions. In those days, you might find Jerry Garcia chillin' out at underground radio pioneer Tom "Big Daddy" Donahue's even bigger house on Mt. Tamalpais, Marty Balin walking the streets of Mill Valley and Jesse Colin Young of the Youngbloods picking up some supplies in the quaint town of Point Reyes Station. No bodyguards.

The late Michael Bloomfield, at the time (the late Sixties) one of America's most popular and influential rock guitarists (ranked up there with Clapton, Beck, and Page) thanks to his work in the Paul Butterfield Blues Band, with Bob Dylan on *Highway 61 Revisited*, and on the *Supersessions* album, had a funky old two-story house not far from the center of Mill Valley. He might have been a big star, but Bloomfield was happy to open his door to a couple of high school kids who wanted to hang out, hear the stories about him recording with Bob Dylan, and learn about the blues.

Now it's all different in San Francisco. Walking down Haight Street, past the crack dealers on the corners, the scraggly-haired and dirty drug casualties sitting on the sidewalk, the blank-faced skinheads and spaced-out Deadheads, it's like seeing what once was refracted in some ugly funhouse mirror that turns dreams into nightmares.

On occasion, I come across new bands that, in their own way, have some of that stubborn, unconventional San Francisco spirit. In years past I've seen it, and heard it, in bands like the Mutants, Romeo Void, and Translator. These days the Red House Painters, the American Music Club, and Counting Crows carry on the legacy of the San Francisco Sound in their own inimitable ways.

No, I'm not nostalgic. Why should I be? I was there. I know what it was like. And it was fine, damn fine.

*Rock & Roll Hall of Fame Ninth Induction Dinner booklet*, 1994

The Flamin' Groovies recording *Rock Juice*, San Francisco, 1992.

# FLAMIN' GROOVIES: LEGENDS OUT OF THEIR OWN TIME

*In 1971 I read a review of the Flamin' Groovies' third album,* Teenage Head. *The writer compared the album by this San Francisco band favorably to recordings by the Rolling Stones, who at the time were still making classic albums such as* Let It Bleed *and* Sticky Fingers. *I bought* Teenage Head; *I immediately became a Flamin' Groovies fan. As time went on, the group released the amazing "Slow Death" and then the brilliant* Shake Some Action *album, whose title track is one of the great rock & roll anthems. Ever. In the late Seventies I interviewed the band's leader, songwriter/guitarist/singer Cyril Jordan on several occasions. The first was for* Trouser Press. *Some years later I hung out with Jordan at his house in San Francisco, in the hills above Highway 280 as it heads toward Daily City, and ended up writing the story you are about to read, for* New West. *I know he didn't like it, but it's an accurate depiction of Jordan and the Flamin' Groovies in 1980. In 1989 Michael Snyder and I put together the Flamin' Groovies compilation,* Groovies' Greatest Grooves *for Sire Records, selecting the songs that appear on it and also writing the liner notes. In the early Nineties I reconnected with Jordan, briefly managed the Flamin' Groovies and executive produced the album,* Rock Juice, *which I released in 1992 on an indie label I had cofounded, National Records. In 2013, Jordan reunited with "Shake Some Action" singer/cowriter Chris Wilson and they reformed the Groovies. They released a new album,* Fantastic Plastic, *their first since* Rock Juice, *in 2017.*

> *It was a Friday night, and I was walking home from Sea Scouts, listening to my transistor radio. "I Want to Hold Your Hand" came on, and I went, "What is this?" All night I stayed up listening to my radio waiting to hear it again. I heard it four more times.*
> —Cyril Jordan

CYRIL JORDAN WAS 16 years old in January 1964, when his parents divorced. As it happened, the divorce came the very week that the Beatles' first American hit was blasting from AM radios—including Cyril's—throughout the country.

Of such coincidences are obsessions born.

For Jordan, now 32, the intersection of his parents' separation and the Beatles hit record threw him in full force into a time warp from which he has never emerged. "I just got immediately far out," he recalls, sitting in the living room of the San Francisco home he grew up in. (Jordan's mother, who gave Cyril the house, lives five minutes away.) "It enabled me to get totally involved in this lifestyle that I've been living for two decades; guitar playin', dope smokin', stayin' up late, comic books, toys...." And the band.

For the last 15 years, Cyril Jordan has led a rock & roll band so peculiar that it could pass for a marijuana-fed fantasy of Jordan's imagination. Only the Flamin' Groovies are for real. These rock purists have single-mindedly dedicated themselves to imitating every aspect of the image and the sound of the mid-'60s "British invasion" rock bands such as the Rolling Stones and the Dave Clark Five and their American contemporaries, the Byrds and the Lovin' Spoonful. And, of course, the Beatles.

It's 1 a.m., and Cyril Jordan (who begins his day at about 5 p.m.) is crouched on the floor sifting through several piles of 45 rpm records. Obscure classics like Duane Eddy's "Because They're Young" and the Troggs' trashy "Wild Thing," along with hits by the Beach Boys, Beatles, Elvis, Stones, Kinks . . . Jordan has them all. "I collect things," he grins.

Indeed. In the living room is a Batman lamp and a Mickey Mouse alarm clock. There's a shelf stacked with *Mad* magazine pocketbooks and a magazine binder whose spine reads *The Complete Tales of the Crypt*. From another shelf, plastic skulls and rubber monster masks stare down ghoulishly. Toy robots and model cars that Jordan recently glued together are set on nearly every surface of the crowded room.

Over the fireplace is a full-color poster of Peter Pan standing at the window, beckoning the kids to join him in Fairyland, where they can stay children forever. Cyril Jordan has, apparently, spent 20 years taking him up on the offer.

"Most people in the world don't have the capacity to get up and groove as much as I do," Jordan says seriously. "Look around here. I have toys everywhere. I get a buzz off the feeling they gave me as a kid. And I still get that feeling."

"Cyril had so much fun as a teenager," explains Carolyn Robinson, his former girlfriend, when I ask her about Cyril. Carolyn is 27 and one of the Flamin Groovies' biggest fans. "What Cyril's sayin' is that the past is great and shouldn't be forgotten," Carolyn says. "The Groovies want to be as heavy as the past. They're following their dreams. How romantic! How idealistic! How far out!"

Jordan looks like he just stepped out of a Carnaby Street boutique, circa 1964. He's wearing a mod black-and-blue striped satin sportscoat with a black velvet collar, a thin black tie, Beatles boots, and the corduroy newsboy's cap that John Lennon once popularized. "You see these pants?" he asks me. "They're made from the *same* material that the Beatles had their pants made from." He rubs a hand almost reverently over his black denim trousers with the gold pinstripes.

"I am telling you," says Jordan, who is losing the hair wars, as he settles into a chair, "we're the biggest fans. Ever!"

He shouts this last word gleefully. "The Flamin' Groovies are living it to the *umpteenth* degree! We played the Cavern Club in Liverpool [where the Beatles got their start]. We're using the same amplifiers as the Byrds and Stones and Beatles. The same Gretsch and Rickenbacker guitars. We're playing the same songs."

Jordan nearly pops out of the chair. "I mean we are so fucking *close*!"

He catches his breath. "I saw the Beatles three times. I still have my ticket stubs." He laughs. "But they never sounded as good as their records. We can do it better than the Beatles live."

Maybe so. The Flamin' Groovies' trip may be weird, but their sound is awesome. They create an unnerving sense of déjà vu. Launching into the Beatles' "Please Please Me" or the Rolling Stones' "Paint It, Black," they perform with a note-for-note, vocal-inflection-for-vocal-inflection accuracy so perfect it's creepy. Even the Groovies' original songs, such as "Shake Some Action" and "Jumping in the Night" could be mid-Sixties pieces, crammed as they are with lush vocal harmonies, jangling twelve-string guitar riffs, short George Harrison– and Chuck Berry–style lead breaks and, of course, the relentless 4/4 beat.

But the Groovies are rarely able to take control of a stage with the authority of the groups they imitate. At a recent gig at San Francisco's Back DOR, the band paused after nearly every number to change guitars, adjust amp settings, and tune. The interruptions sabotaged the spontaneity that marks truly great live rock & roll.

"People don't understand," says Jordan defensively. "They criticize us for doing covers [versions of other people's songs]. But there are orchestras playing Beethoven. Beethoven's dead! He can't do his own gigs. Why can't a rock & roll band go around and do great pieces of music—classics—that sound exactly the same?"

During their 15-year existence, the Flamin' Groovies have recorded six albums and no hits. Continuing obscurity has turned Cyril Jordan into a bitter and, at times, paranoid man. In conversation he bounces between manic energy and bleak cynicism. "When I got into rock & roll in the first place," he says, "I was under some impression that it was the coolest thing in the world. It was like the kids going to the adults, 'You're phony and we ain't. We do what we want.'

"But I guess I was wrong. Rock & roll was a free country at one time, but it isn't anymore."

Jordan can (and does) rant for hours against the music business. San Francisco concert promoters, he claims, shafted the group; the four labels the Groovies have recorded for are "incompetent"; "*Rolling Stone* never wrote about us."

For the last five years the Flamin' Groovies have recorded for the New York–based Sire label (distributed by Warner Bros.). According to Jordan, the label was contractually obliged to release a Groovies album by June 1 of this year. But the group hasn't even been inside a recording studio.

Jordan also claims that it was Sire's lack of promotion that has kept the Groovies' records from topping the charts. "I dare somebody to hype the Flamin' Groovies," he says. "And if we don't sell millions of records, man, I'll jump off the Golden Gate Bridge! That's how sure I am."

"The Flamin' Groovies have been promoted by Sire," counters Sire Records president Seymour Stein. "We've given them tour support. We've supported dates that lost lots of money. We got their records a lot of airplay.

"All through the late Sixties and most of the Seventies the Groovies were like salmon swimming against the musical tide. Perhaps now, with music returning to a more basic form of rock, their time may finally come."

Despite the marginal record sales, the Groovies have accumulated a few supporters over the years. A batch of rock critics praised their 1971 album, *Teenage Head*. Several critics thought the album surpassed the Rolling Stones' *Sticky Fingers*, released at the same time.

And then there are the rock stars. "Rod Stewart likes us. Brian Wilson! Elton John flew from LA to France to see one gig," says Jordan. "And Keith Richards was walking around his house talking about our version of 'Jumpin' Jack Flash.'" Jordan pauses to let this particular fact sink in. "I mean, he said we had a fucking *better* version. That we captured the rawness those guys couldn't capture on that song."

For the last few years, the Groovies' albums have been produced by English rocker Dave Edmunds, who has built a reputation on his ability to recreate, in the studio, the seemingly unreproducible sounds of Phil Spector and Elvis Presley. With Edmunds producing, the Groovies created one album, *Shake Some Action*, that rivals actual mid-Sixties classics such as *Beatles VI*, the Byrds' *Turn Turn Turn*, and the Rolling Stones' *Between the Buttons*. One critic wrote: "I can't recall any album since 1966 that's given me as much pure and simple excitement."

Last fall, Cyril Jordan made a connection he'd been dreaming about for at least a decade. He met one of his idols, Phil Spector. Spector is renowned for the "wall of sound" he created on such records as the Righteous Brothers' "You've Lost That Lovin' Feeling." "Phil told me, 'Really love your fuckin' group. You're the closest thing to the Beatles I've ever heard,'" recalls Jordan with wonder in his voice. Now there's talk of Spector producing the next Groovies album.

In anticipation, the Groovies have worked up a devastating live version of "River Deep Mountain High," a Spector masterpiece that has never (says Jordan) been performed live.

There's another straw in the wind: Former Byrds lead vocalist and guitarist Roger McGuinn wants to cut a mid-sixties-style rock album and wants the Groovies to cowrite some songs and possibly back him in the studio.

The Groovies have headlined in Paris and were recently flown to Germany to participate in a rock festival. On their own, they headlined before 2,000 people at a German club. The poster for that gig read "FLAMIN' GROOVIES—THE SAN FRANCISCO LEGENDS."

Back home, the Flamin' Groovies are lucky to draw a few hundred people to their infrequent gigs. Things got so depressing in the early Seventies that they briefly changed their name to the Dogs "because that's how San Francisco was treating us," Jordan says wryly.

On a drippy weekday night, after the guys had gotten off work (one Groovy fixes jukeboxes; another works for a Bay Area record distributor), the five Groovies gathered for a rehearsal at the Temple, a former Synagogue sandwiched between the former Peoples Temple and the former site of the Fillmore Auditorium. In the semidarkness, they began to run through a new song.

Actually, the song was new only in the sense that it was the first time the Groovies had rehearsed it. Written and recorded by the Rolling Stones, "Out of Time" had been a number-one hit in England for singer Chris Farlowe during the summer of 1966.

"You don't know what's gong on," the Groovies sang. "You've been away for much too long . . . / You're out of touch my baby / My poor old-fashioned baby / Baby, baby, baby / You're out of time."

For the Flamin' Groovies, it made perfect sense.

*New West*, August 1980

# AMERICAN MUSIC CLUB: READY FOR THE AMERICAN MUSIC PUBLIC

## Local underground group on the rise with major labels and new album.

*In early spring of 1996, Mark Eitzel showed up at my house wearing a porkpie hat and a sport coat, carrying his guitar case, a roving troubadour taking a couple of hours to do an interview. Mark Eitzel is a mixed-up genius. Genius? Well his songwriting, as demonstrated on nine American Music Club studio albums and then on a dozen solo studio albums, is the tip off. It's real, real good.*

*Eitzel often writes about the losers, the downtrodden, the freaks, and the throwaways. "The people I was with said you were nothing but a fag hag and a dope fiend," is how he begins "Cleopatra Jones." The song continues: "But the song of your eyes was of the loneliest woman I've ever seen." This is great, great songwriting. This is the stuff of novels but condensed into four- and five-minute songs.*

*I first met Mark in late 1991 and our conversation, which was not an interview, led to a friendship. When I interviewed him for newspaper and magazine stories after that, it seemed like Eitzel trusted me. I was an AMC fan, of course, had been since I first heard their 1987 album* Engine, *with the devastatingly great "Outside This Bar." The group's major label debut,* Mercury, *was released in March 1993, less than a month before I interviewed Eitzel and some of the other members of the band for the story that follows. A year and a half later, a few months after the release of the follow-up,* San Francisco, *I interviewed Eitzel for a Q&A. He came to my Glen Park house in 1996 to talk about his first solo album,* 60 Watt Silver Lining. *During that interview, I asked Eitzel, "Do you think about death?"*

**Mark Eitzel:** Are you kidding? You don't think I do? Don't you? Doesn't everybody? Do you remember in *Don't Look Back*, in the movie when [Bob] Dylan starts to berate the hapless journalist. Do you remember that?

**Michael Goldberg:** Sure.

**Eitzel:** That was beautiful.

**Goldberg:** Telling that journalist that if *Time* magazine was going to show the truth, they'd have a picture of a wealthy businessman next to a bum lying in the gutter.

**Eitzel:** Yeah, and he [Dylan] got serious for a minute and says, "It's all about death. That's the bottom line. That's where all my songs go. That's where they all are." He's right. That resonated so strongly with me. I was like, yeah, baby, that's it. That is finally what art and religion address. Also food. Food and sex and death.

*Those of us in San Francisco who dug AMC were so confident that the group was headed for the big time. How could they miss? Eitzel was a great singer and songwriter, and the band were the best. But it was not to be.* Mercury *was a superb album, as was* San Francisco, *but for whatever reasons, it didn't happen. This story captures a moment when so much seemed possible; the Q&A I did in November 1994 follows.*

"EIGHT MONTHS AGO NOBODY WOULD pee on us," says Mark Eitzel, singer, songwriter and acoustic guitarist for San Francisco's American Music Club. "And now people are walking up to me and saying, 'Hey rock star.'"

He sits in a downstairs dressing room at, appropriately enough, the Great American Music Hall sipping a glass of red wine. With a black porkpie hat set atop his balding head, a mustache, and goatee giving his face a slightly demonic look, a not-particularly fashionable, ill-fitting black suit hung on his skinny frame, Eitzel looks like a down-on-his-luck character out of a Damon Runyon short story.

"I feel it. We're successful," says Eitzel, who in years past called San Francisco's seedy Tenderloin district home. "Even though we haven't toured, we haven't got any more new fans or sold any more records, but still it feels different."

Success? For the American Music Club? Isn't that a contradiction in terms?

For over 10 years this San Francisco band has inhabited the rock underground, recording stubbornly uncommercial albums, performing to hip insiders and bar stool regulars at local nightspots like the Hotel Utah. From a far South of Market vantage point, they've watched as a litany of hip San Francisco rockers—Chris Isaak, Faith No More, the Sextants, Jellyfish, Sister Double Happiness, and on and on—got a grab at stardom's brass ring.

Now, finally, it's the American Music Club's turn.

What Eitzel "feels" is the glow of, finally, being picked for a winner. Last year the group was signed to not one but two major record companies. In the US, they did a deal with Time Warner's Reprise label, once home to Frank Sinatra. For the rest of the world, they now record for Virgin, whose higher profile stars include Janet Jackson and the Rolling Stones.

From the striking black-and-white photo of ancient, decaying ruins they used on the cover of *Mercury*, to the mind-blowing music inside it's clear that the American Music Club is making the most of their opportunity. Almost in disbelief, the group's lead guitarist, who goes by the name Vudi, says, "You have one of the largest media conglomerates in the world [Time Warner] recognizing that maybe they can make a buck off you."

On a weekday afternoon, Eitzel, Vudi and their bandmates—bassist Dan Pearson, drummer Tim Mooney, and pedal steel guitarist Bruce Kaplan—have taken over this San Francisco club to film a $20,000 video for "Over and Done," a song off *Mercury* that they hope will be aired on MTV.

If there is any justice, MTV will rise to the occasion. For the American Music Club are a stunning band, the best thing to rise out of the San Francisco underground in years. They are quirky, eccentric, and resolutely bohemian. At the group's center is Eitzel, 36, a true oddball who has embarrassed himself in years past both onstage doing alcohol-fueled Iggy Pop imitations, and in print. "I don't like having a reputation for being an asshole," he told one reporter, but then added, "I am an asshole."

Asked what Eitzel, who at one point during this interview absently reached into his coat pocket, removed a pair of scissors and began opening and closing them, is really like, Vudi simply says, "The dude's way sensitive."

"Mark sees something horrible and he can't just turn his face away from it," adds Pearson. "That's kind of what this band is about. Looking for a long time at something really bad that's happening on the street."

The American Music Club make a dark, atmospheric music that sounds a million miles away from its rock, folk, and country roots. Electric guitars wheeze and moan through their songs, along with the occasional dreamy piano and gentle strum of an old mandolin. Odd rhythms drive some of their newer material. The songs often have the unpredictable dynamics of a jazz combo jamming, a jazz combo with, say, Tom Waits at its helm.

It's decidedly downbeat music, and it's just the right setting for the hard-luck stories and sad confessions of Eitzel songs with titles like "I've Been a Mess Since You've Been Gone."

Eitzel comes across, both in song and in person, as a kind of beautiful loser. His voice, idiosyncratic, intense, and effectual, is an acquired taste. But one well worth acquiring. He writes with dead-on accuracy about the desperation and loneliness of American life. In other words, he writes sensitively, knowingly of the human condition. "I don't know if I've reached the bottom yet," he confides in "If I Had a Hammer." "Somewhere along the line I passed the point of no return."

So far, the group's fans may be few, but they are fiercely committed. "The music that Mark writes helps them through crisis and trauma," explains Vudi.

"I think everybody is desperate always," says Eitzel. "And I think everybody is reaching. Everybody wants something transcendent. But a lot of what normal behavior is, is people not feeling and not experiencing and not living. And a lot of real joy is stifled because it's too extreme and a lot of real passion is stifled because it's frightening."

Almost from their start, rock critics have loved the American Music Club. For eight years—from the release of American Music Club's first album, 1985's *The Restless Stranger* through their fifth, 1991's *Everclear*—reviewers have raved about the group, while singling out Eitzel for extra praise. England's *Melody Maker* called Eitzel "one of the greatest living songwriters." *The Village Voice* compared him to Steinbeck. The *San Francisco Chronicle* rock critic Joel Selvin has described Eitzel as a "combination of Bruce Springsteen, Van Morrison and Bono."

Over the years the group, whose previous albums have been released on obscure independent labels like Grifter and Frontier, has accumulated a stack of glowing reviews and profiles several inches thick. *Rolling Stone* magazine's critics voted Eitzel 1991's songwriter of the year, and picked *Everclear*, as one of that year's five best albums, alongside the work of such major stars as R.E.M., U2, and Nirvana.

Yet for all the praise, *Everclear* sold a meager 22,000 copies worldwide. Until recently, all the band members held down day jobs. You could find Eitzel working as a page in the main branch of the public library more often than you could see his group perform.

"We've run up against a lot of adversity," says Dan Pearson. "When we've gone on tour before we'll play a place with five people and two of those people have no idea why we're there."

"Or why they're there," grins Vudi.

"I remember we were somewhere in Germany, and we found out about the *Rolling Stone* poll," says Eitzel. "It made me feel really good. But for the next show there were about 20 people in the audience. And they were army guys, and they thought American Music Club were some righteous American freedom-fighting, cool ass Springsteen-influenced Guns N' Roses kind of guys. And we did not rock."

"They didn't know we'd made 'one of the best records of the year' and he was the 'best songwriter,'" adds bassist Tim Mooney.

"They couldn't give a fuck about that shit," says Eitzel. "And they certainly didn't agree."

Group members say Eitzel has quit the band on a number of occasions. A year and a half ago, Eitzel sounded ready to pack it in. He told this writer that his band had just hired new management, but if the guys couldn't get them signed to a major label, the group would break up.

"We decided we wouldn't make another record with an indie," Eitzel now says. "We were sick of not being able to pay rent when we come back from touring. To be broke all the time and know that your albums will never be distributed properly because the majors have a monopoly on distribution."

So what happened? Eitzel looks over at Mooney and Pearson. "We got lucky."

At first, the group's managers, Wally Brill and Ross Schwartz, couldn't get a single American major label interested. "They basically all said, 'This is maybe the most brilliant act we've seen in years, but we don't know what to do with them,'" recalled Schwartz. "We got passes everywhere."

In Europe, where the group has toured repeatedly, Virgin Records began discussing a deal. And then, back in the USA, the group finally got a break. "The crack in the dam came when a guy at Giant Records convinced [company president] Irving Azoff to have a real listen," said Schwartz. "Then all those other companies, knowing somebody else was willing to take a gamble, started coming to the party like dominoes."

In the fall of 1991, in an extremely untypical move, the managers signed the group to both Reprise and Virgin, and for the members of the American Music Club, for the first time in many years life began to take on a rosy patina. "It's a whole different ball game when so much money is involved," admits Eitzel.

Still, as many rockers who have come before him have discovered, the possibility of success can be even more daunting than failure. About a year and a half ago, Eitzel, infamous for heavy drinking, both on and off the stage, went cold turkey. In interviews to promote *Everclear* he declared that sans alcohol, "life is so much better."

So seeing him with a glass of wine came as a bit of a shock. "I stayed on that for eight months and then I started drinking again," he says, shifting uncomfortably in his chair. "It changed my life. It was the best thing I ever did. It was a really good thing. I'll do it again one day. But not right now."

Why'd he start drinking again? "I don't know," he says defensively. "What do you think? I'm an alcoholic. You stop drinking 'cause it stops working for you. It's a drug that stops working for you. Well, I needed some drug. Some legal drug. That's why." The subject, clearly, is closed.

Advances from the record deals have allowed all the band members to quit their day jobs, but no one is living in high style. "People in the band are earning about as much as a clerk makes," says Eitzel.

The band members say they're all ambitious and will not be unhappy if their music brings them financial rewards. But they insist that's beside the point and make sarcastic remarks about the unlikelihood of getting their music on the radio or finding a mass audience.

"I started doing music to change my life, to grow," says Eitzel, who played in a Columbus, Ohio, punk band called Naked Skinnies before putting together an early version of American Music Club at the dawn of the '80s.

"You put yourself on the line and it changes you and you move forward, or at least something happens," Eitzel continues. "That's why I like it. You're always putting it on the line."

As focal point for the group, Eitzel is the one the media always want to interview. "It's becoming really intrusive," Eitzel says. "Finding free time to write and be a normal person. I need three or four months to do nothing and get some good TV going and write songs. It's really hard to get that time now 'cause you're always promoting yourself or talking about what you do to people. Or you're on the phone to the lawyer or one of the two managers or the business manager. And then your friends, who never see you because you're always away, want to hang out and you never have time and it becomes . . ."

He stares down at the floor, sounding temporarily defeated. "I don't know, everything's different. In England we did two weeks solid of nothing but interviews . . ."

He catches himself, perhaps realizing that to many people the idea of an expense paid trip to England where all you have to do is talk about yourself sounds pretty nice. "Yeah, it sounds really great and I do like it," he concedes. "But it's making me really blasé and there's nothing more disgusting than somebody who's blasé. It's like somebody who's overfed."

*San Francisco Chronicle*, May 1993

# AMC'S MARK EITZEL INTERVIEWED: WISHING THE WORLD AWAY

THE FIRST TIME I MET American Music Club singer, songwriter, and leader Mark Eitzel, he arrived at San Francisco's boho South-of-Market Soma Cafe on a bicycle.

At the time, summer 1991, he was at the end of his rope, or so he told me. AMC had received raves in the press for years and had recorded five albums for various indie labels. Yet the band members had to work day jobs to survive, only a few hundred people (sometimes less) showed up to the gigs and when the group toured they often discovered that their albums were not in the record stores.

Our meeting was about the new record company I was starting, National Records, and my desire to have AMC record a country-rock album for me. We drank black coffee and talked for several hours. A few days later Eitzel called to tell me he'd gone home after the meeting and written two songs for the album.

That album was not to be. Instead, AMC signed with Reprise Records in the US and Virgin for the rest of the world; side projects such as mine were put on permanent hold.

In November of this year—two and a half years later—Mark and I once again meet up at the Soma Cafe. He had just returned from a European tour. This time he arrives in a late model car. But other than his mode of transportation, he seems relatively unchanged. In fact, on the eve of another tour, he is once again at the end of his rope. Minutes into the interview he reveals, "This tour is going to be hell."

**Michael Goldberg:** I saw you play for the reopening of the Fillmore Auditorium earlier this year. It sounded like you had been listening to Sonic Youth or Nirvana—very aggressive, charged up, noisy rock & roll, and you were playing electric guitar and just, like, slamming into it. . . .

**Mark Eitzel:** Yeah, well actually, as of today, the band is not allowing me to play electric guitar anymore, and we hired a bass player, and now I just stand there and sing. I wanted it to get more energetic and weird, I wanted it to get kind of psychedelic but the band doesn't, so now I'm not playing guitar at all. That's the news as of today.

**Goldberg:** So you all vote about stuff like that? I mean, how does it . . . ?

**Eitzel:** It's not my band, I can't insist on things. This tour is going to be hell. I hate being the front man, you know. I hate not being able to play guitar so it's going to be really, really bad for me. But whatever, you know. You gotta make them happy. Because the drummer [Tim Mooney] . . . I never play in time. And I play too loud for the other guitar player [Vudi], and the bass player [Danny Pearson] doesn't want to play bass anymore so you know . . .

**Goldberg:** He's going to play guitar?

**Eitzel:** Yes.

**Goldberg:** And then you got another bass player?

**Eitzel:** Yes.

**Goldberg:** Who's the new bass player?

**Eitzel:** This woman named Dana.

**Goldberg:** What's her last name?

**Eitzel:** I don't know. I just met her today for about 15 minutes. [Her name is Dana Schechter; as of 2021 she is founder and main composer for Insect Ark, and a member of the Swans. She only played one show with American Music Club in 1994, but in 2008 she played bass with the group for their entire European tour.]

**Goldberg:** How did you find her?

**Eitzel:** She's been in a band called Torcher [and before that Gifthorse]. She's really cool. Our drummer wanted to play with this one and so fine. I don't get a say in these things you know. It drives me crazy but . . .

**Goldberg:** Why did you call this album *San Francisco*?

**Eitzel:** It just seemed to be logical. There's no concept behind it. It's like . . . it's not about San Francisco. I wanted an album title that would bring it all back to the beginning of something. The next AMC album is going to be really, really different from any of the previous ones and so I wanted an end. I wanted this to be the last album like this and I want the rest of them to be different. For me, it's sort of like the end of the road and the beginning of . . . you know what I mean.

**Goldberg:** When you say it's going to be really different, what are you thinking?

**Eitzel:** Well AMC is more of a vehicle for larger stages and for what we hope to be a more successful career in music, and it never seems appropriate to do my quieter songs with the band anymore, it just doesn't work. So I'm not going to include those on any of the AMC albums. It's going to be the more rock stuff. Because it's just a matter of efficiency and trying to live with it, you know. If you tour doing quiet stuff, it's really hard work and there's no success with it either because people don't want to hear that. Never have, never will. So the next AMC album's going to be really, really different. I hope. This album was supposed to be, but . . .

**Goldberg:** Well, this album has three or four rockers. I mean, obviously "Hello Amsterdam" and "Wish the World Away," "It's Your Birthday," and "I'll Be Gone." So you think the next one is going to be more like those?

**Eitzel:** Yeah.

**Goldberg:** So does this sort of open up the door for you to do your quieter songs on solo Mark Eitzel albums?

**Eitzel:** No, I don't think so. And even if I was, it would be kind of stupid just talking about it before the next AMC tour, right?

**Goldberg:** I mean, it's possible to have . . .

**Eitzel:** Both?

**Goldberg:** Yeah.

**Eitzel:** Sure, it is. And if I can make a solo album, I will. Absolutely. But it's like counting the chickens before they hatch. All I know about right now is I have to get through this American tour and sell this last album and then maybe we'll see what happens.

**Goldberg:** Critics have commented on kind of a hopefulness and belief in the power of love in some of the songs on this album; that's quite a change from your previous material. Obviously today, you're not in the most upbeat, hopeful mood at the moment.

**Eitzel:** I'm tired. I'm just really tired. I'm all jet lagged.

**Goldberg:** Did that have to do with a change in your personal life?

**Eitzel:** I'm writing from a different place. I just don't want to write always from the same place; and in a way you react to the audience and you react to questions just like that. I always get perceived as being this incredibly—as you know, we've had this conversation before—as a really sad, troubled person. All the interviews are about my personal psychology, which is no one's goddamned business. So it's really worth writing some other kinds of songs. I've been saying the wrong things. So I tried and it works.

**Goldberg:** So you can almost be a different character when you're writing a song, it's not like writing a diary.

**Eitzel:** It's not like writing a diary at all. Well, it is in a way because you're writing about some aspect of yourself. You're writing from a different point of view, but it's all me. It's not like I'm changing character dramatically. God, I wish I could, but I'm not doing that so it's just from a different place.

**Goldberg:** Were you feeling more hopeful when you wrote some of the pieces?

**Eitzel:** What's hopeful? Hope is so subjective, you know. It's like the things you say matter. You're not responsible necessarily for how they impinge on people but when you say something, it matters by the way it affects your own life and your own perceptions. I've gotten in arguments with people about hope. Some people say it's the most despairing kind of emotion in the world and I agree. It's sort of something that you only feel out of despair, as a response to despair. I think that maybe indifference enters more into the formula than hope. Just indifference. I don't have any time to care anymore about anything, you know. Just write, you write, you perform, that's it. No time for adolescent angst.

**Goldberg:** What about the line in "In the Shadow of the Valley": "I gave up my cynicism I gave up my hard shell."

**Eitzel:** Well, that's LA though. That's like people in LA. People don't live in LA to respond to others or to live in a society. They live in LA to work and make money and fulfill their dreams. Hopefully, if they're successful at all, they live in a kind of bubble where they really don't have to interact with anybody. You know what I mean? So yeah, you give up your cynicism, you give up your hard shell as soon as you stop interacting with people. *[Quoting from the song]* "If I opened my heart, then you'd be washed away." Yeah, because as soon as you start to live, you know, then, it's destructive in those situations. It's weird, it's all about that city and me being on the freeway in that city. A lot. You know, having to live there. And it's about the [Rodney King] riots in a way because I think the riots are kind of the future, although I don't think it's going to be an uprising, there's just going to be more and more random violence and more and more and more hate. Does that sound hopeful?

**Goldberg:** Sounds real.

**Eitzel:** It's real, yeah. It's real.

**Goldberg:** Things do seem to keep getting worse.

**Eitzel:** But we're also getting older, maybe that's why.

**Goldberg:** Yeah, but I mean, my wife writes about crime and juvenile justice for the *San Francisco Examiner* and what's going on in terms of what 13-year-old, 14-year-old, 15-year-old kids are doing now is just unreal. Just blowing people away. Cold-blooded.

**Eitzel:** Fifteen years ago, Reagan and Bush stopped building schools and started building prisons so in the next 50 years we're going to have a culture—the most, the overriding, strongest, and most dominant characteristic of our culture is going to be prison culture. And if you ever read about any of that stuff, and all I really have read is about prison camps in Europe like during World War II, prison camps in Auschwitz and the kind of societies that are formed—that'll be our culture, that'll be the leading edge.

**Goldberg:** Today, there was an article in the *LA Times* where the police sergeant is saying, "My cops don't have time to check whether someone is a legal or illegal in a school. There's a homicide a day here or more. I don't even have enough guys to deal with all the homicides."

**Eitzel:** Yeah. Tell me about it. It's over, you know. And the way that pornography and the violence is permutated through normal everyday culture is terrifying. It's not just a morality; it's sort of like anti-morality. And it's exactly what people like the born-again Christians and the right-wing—it's sort of the water that they swim in, you know.

**Goldberg:** Are you saying that it feeds their extremism?

**Eitzel:** They're different sides of the same coin, you know, a coin without compassion and a coin without really very much intelligence or thought or passion. It just keeps going. Like most white people do believe that all Black males carry guns and will kill you and do drugs. And so they buy all that shit up. All that hard-core rap is so popular because it totally reflects people's racist ideas of what they are. You know what I'm saying? So they kind of tend to amplify it. It goes into this loop that gets bigger and bigger and, so yes, that culture exists and sooner or later that is going to be America. I don't want to be here for that, I don't like that kind of shit, I don't like people like that. But that's America, you know. Things change.

**Goldberg:** What inspired you to write "It's Your Birthday"?

**Eitzel:** I have a friend who fell in love with a woman who was transsexual, who just had the operation and I told him, go for it, you know, two guys sitting at a bar. He's like, how do I do this, and I said, "Well you love her, right? Do it. It's your birthday, baby. This is what life has dealt you so take it, great."

**Goldberg:** What made you think, "Oh, I'm going to write about this"?

**Eitzel:** Well because I love him. I kept thinking about it. I kept thinking about, well, "You haven't had anyone in your life for several years and you want this person" and it just sort of came out. I don't know.

**Goldberg:** What about "Wish the World Away"?

**Eitzel:** I had a hangover one morning and I remembered a line I wrote in London a couple of years before. "You can wish the world away." I can't really tell you what made me write it.

**Goldberg:** On the one hand, it's an obvious sentiment given just what we were talking about. It reminded me of "Outside This Bar" [off the group's second album, *Engine*].

**Eitzel:** Yeah, it was supposed to be like a companion song to like "Bad Liquor" or something. It's like a double-edged sword. On the one hand wishing the world away is like the highest attainment of human consciousness. On the other hand, it's like yeah, fuck it. You know what I'm saying? I don't think it's my best song ever.

**Goldberg:** The last time I talked to you was just before *Mercury* [AMC's first album for Reprise Records] was coming out. And there seemed to be a lot of expectations that the group was going to break through. Obviously, that didn't happen. Has that been hard for you to deal with, for the band to deal with?

**Eitzel:** It's been expensive. Not that hard. It is hard in a way because I guess we made the wrong album in terms of breaking through. We didn't mean to, we just planned to make the best album we could. Yeah, sure it's hard. For the rest of our lives, we could probably play for the same 300 people. That will probably happen.

**Goldberg:** You play to more people than that.

**Eitzel:** Not really. Not in San Francisco, maybe, not in New York but everywhere else pretty much.

**Goldberg:** But when you were just over in Europe, you were playing to . . .

**Eitzel:** Well, London, we played this 1,500 theater, we filled that out. But mostly, yeah, 300, 400, 500. Those kind of numbers, not very many. It's frustrating but what can we do? We try our hardest.

**Goldberg:** It only takes one song to make the difference between 500 people and Nirvana. . . . Their whole thing hinged on one song.

**Eitzel:** Not really though. Because there was a buzz about them like months before that song. Everybody knew that they were going to be huge. I remember at Reading [one of England's huge rock festivals], like a year before "Smells Like Teen Spirit," not a year, more like seven months before. I remember everyone was like, "Nirvana, they're going to be fucking huge." And I went and saw them, and I wasn't too blown away. I don't remember much about it. I thought they were cool but, yeah, they were great. They were great.

**Goldberg:** There's been a buzz about AMC.

**Eitzel:** Not like this. Not like this though. Not like ours. This band is not a teen band. Never has been. Probably never will be. And Nirvana always was, which has a whole different kind of buzz. There's a different kind of excitement.

**Goldberg:** There's sort of a cliché idea that a band gets to a major and now they have to conform to this and that and the other thing. But it hasn't been like that for you guys.

**Eitzel:** Not really. We're on Warner Brothers [Reprise] and Virgin and they're not like that as labels. I mean, they'll probably drop us. This is probably our last album with either of them, but you know, they're not like that. They're pretty cool.

**Goldberg:** What do you listen to these days?

**Eitzel:** Umm, geez, not much because I'm always on the road.

**Goldberg:** Don't you take tapes along on the road or . . . ?

**Eitzel:** No.

**Goldberg:** What was the last thing that you actually dug a lot?

**Eitzel:** The Afghan Whigs record, *Gentlemen*. No, not *Gentlemen*. *Congregation*. I never heard *Gentlemen*. *Congregation* was really good. Also the new Palace Brothers album. I liked that for the two weeks that I had to listen to it. There's good stuff coming out all the time. I never get it. Because I never seem to be home.

**Goldberg:** Do you think the success of this whole wave that's continued—now with Green Day—the whole left of center becoming the center, has been good for you guys?

**Eitzel:** I don't know. I don't know because I never really thought that late '70s punk rock was ever left of center. I always thought that it was pretty center. Nirvana helped because they actually had words, and lyrics, and they were intelligent, and they weren't assholes. I'm so glad that they bumped Guns 'N Roses, although Guns 'N Roses, as soon as MTV starts to lose a few ratings, will start pumping those Guns 'N Roses videos right back on. You bet they will. Yeah, it did help us, I think. It opened everyone's eyes up and it gave a whole generation of kids a fashion to latch onto that they hadn't had. During the '70s and '80s kids didn't really have a fashion at all. They didn't have, like, the big baggy shorts and that's good; it's good for kids to have a fucking rebel stamp. Especially kids in the suburb, white kids. And it's a good thing because they don't care if they listen to Black music or white music, which is really cool. It's good. I don't necessarily like gangster rap very much. I do like a lot of it and that's changed things too. That's changed everything as well. As much as Nirvana, I think. Because again, it's people telling stories, and it's people talking about their real lives. It's not like some fake heavy metal rocker guy fresh from the gym singing about being a pig. It's about people talking about their lives. Of course they may be pigs. But it's better.

**Goldberg:** This generation of kids has their own culture. They have all their own bands. It's just a whole thing that really wasn't there throughout the '70s. There was the punk movement in the mid-'70s, but it really wasn't there in the mainstream.

**Eitzel:** Yeah. I was there in the mid-'70s, in the punk movement and boy, did the radio and the TV and all the major media close that down as quickly as they could. Because they had invested so much in the Eagles and—So they closed that shit down. They would not play it; they would not respond to it. So no, it really never got a toehold at all and that's why it continued to be so influential. It's because it never got a chance to live itself out. And in America, when I lived in Ohio, for instance, there were about 50 people that I knew when I was 19 who were into that music. Everybody else was into, you know, Springsteen and the usual crap, the crap they still play in Ohio. I mean, it's really changed everything. And in the '80s there was nothing either. It was like that weird time. Do you remember somewhere in the middle '80s when thousands of people were going to see the Cure and thousands of people were going to see Depeche Mode and everybody was saying, why? Suddenly they were huge. It's so cool when that happens. And then you had all those other bands like the Pixies or the Replacements or Nick Cave and all those bands that people would go see. But it was never anything like a youth movement. It was mostly rockers, people who were a little older than the usual punk rockers. It was never 17-year-olds who saw those people. It was always a little older. Hüsker Dü. Great, great music but it's nothing like it is now. This is a really good time. Counting Crows. I'm amazed that they're huge. Everybody accuses the singer of being a Van Morrison rip-off, and why not? OK, rip him off? Go ahead, rip Van Morrison off, why not? Van Morrison sure can't do it anymore. Oh, he can, maybe.

**Goldberg:** Adam [Duritz, of Counting Crows] is a good writer though. When you look at some of those songs—

**Eitzel:** They're interesting.

**Goldberg:** They're good songs. "Mr. Jones" is a great story, and it operates on several levels.

**Eitzel:** It's fine. I think it's fine. I'm in support of it. I love it.

**Goldberg:** I'll tell you, if you're 17 right now, you don't go, "God, that's a Van Morrison rip-off."

**Eitzel:** I know, you go, "Wow, fucking cool."

**Goldberg:** It almost seems a cliché that people who are older and who have listened to rock & roll in the '50s or '60s or '70s, those people go, "Oh, look at that, the Beatles, they're just playing Chuck Berry or the Stones, they're just doing Muddy Waters." You know what I mean?

**Eitzel:** It's stupid. It's just crazy. I don't do that.

**Goldberg:** Are you angry these days?

**Eitzel:** Of course.

**Goldberg:** Is that a reaction to the Republicans taking over the Senate and House yesterday?

**Eitzel:** I didn't vote so I can't really comment. I'm not allowed. America wants to slash its own throat so it's doing it.

**Goldberg:** You feel anger is the only reaction to have because we're really impotent to actually change things?

**Eitzel:** I don't know. I don't understand those people. I'm not one of those people. I'm the kind of person that most people consider as weird or outside it. I've never seen it as my job to make too much sense, so I don't bother. I can't comment. I don't know why. All I know is that it's just against the future, it's just completely against the future. I'm certainly not a liberal. I'm not at all a liberal. I'm actually pretty much a reactionary. I just think that if you advocate building more jails, if you advocate mandatory sentencing, if you advocate slogans that at their root are evil and divisive and vindictive and if you're on your way to building prison camps, which is what seems to be happening, then I can't help but say it's wrong. But on the other hand, I don't know what America thinks. I live in San Francisco. We're like one of the most hated cities in the country, you know? Because we're so liberal, supposedly. And we are, though.

**Goldberg:** Is "Hello, Amsterdam" based on what you've seen over there?

**Eitzel:** It's just us playing bad shows. We used to play there at a place called Milky Way. We used to play this club all the time and we played there like three times and every time we played there, we just sucked. We'd been terrible and just trying to find out why. I just want to be an ABBA. *[laughs]*

**Goldberg:** Is that about what the audience would have preferred?

**Eitzel:** I don't know. We had a great show there when we played last time. We played a different club. This time it was great, so I think that sort of blanks out the other three times. I love Amsterdam. It's a wonderful place. It's funny that people there, especially when people judge America or anything, they don't realize how fucked-up it is here, how violent people are here. How much fear is a factor. In Europe, nobody understands fear. We do. A nation of cowards. No we're not. I mean, you know what I'm saying? I was trying to explain this to a Dutch journalist. He was like, "Oh, what do you mean?" *[He quotes from the song]* "We came from America so you could share in our pride, guilt, greed and genocide." I was like, "Well do people shout at you threateningly from cars ever?" He was like, "Never in my life." I'm like, "Oh, OK. Do people look at you with hate?" "No." You know what I'm saying? How many times do you see an ambulance? How many times do you see a cop car wailing down the street? I mean, just basic things. They don't have them there. It doesn't happen. So maybe our music gets lost a little bit in the translation. Not that we play violent or mean music, but we play it with that being part of our background and I think that gets lost in the translation from English to Dutch.

**Goldberg:** Where do you look for inspiration?

**Eitzel:** I don't. I just always keep it in mind that I'm going to write another song. I never look for inspiration anywhere.

**Goldberg:** Where is the creative wellspring that you're drawing on?

**Eitzel:** I don't know. If I knew that, I wouldn't write songs. I mean, I'm not my own psychiatrist. I just write songs. I don't know why. I don't know where it comes from. I could waffle on and on and on about it, but you know what, I don't think it matters. I mean, you listen to the songs, and you know where they're coming from, that's where they're coming from, you know? It's pretty much that easy. I mean, having me talk and talk and talk about what my inspiration is—so what?

**Goldberg:** There is this mystery, I mean, not just with you, but whether it's a painter, whether it's . . .

**Eitzel:** I don't know, man. I just try to find the things that I want to say and I say them. You write and you write and you write and you cross shit out and you go, "oh, that doesn't work, that doesn't work, that works, that works, that doesn't work," and you just end up with something that works. And that's what you've been trying to say, whatever that thing is. Usually, it's a lot less intelligent than I thought it was going to be. But you just have to go with it. I don't think I ever really want to know what inspires me. Everything does. Nothing does.

**Goldberg:** There's a quote on a sticker on the cover of this new album, from a *Melody Maker* review: "One of the greatest living songwriters."

**Eitzel:** Oh yeah. That was from 1989 or something? '88 maybe? Old news.

**Goldberg:** Do you feel a weight on your shoulders? Is it hard to write? Do you say, "Oh my God, people are going to look at this song . . . ?"

**Eitzel:** Well, you know what. What it is, deep in my heart, I believe it. You have to. But it's like having people say that or having that person say that several years ago, it's like, what? How can it be true? There's no way it can be true. All it means is that I can walk into a party of people, and I can just sort of stop somebody and say, you know who I am? I'm the greatest living songwriter, how're you doing? And I can have them look at me and go, "Fuck off." That's what it means. I'm a small headline in a newspaper from six years ago. I had someone come up to me and say, "Weren't you the hot band in 1991?" I said yeah, we were. *Rolling Stone*. It's embarrassing, it's worthless. But I think I'm great. *[laughs]* I always will.

**Goldberg:** But I mean it's not as if this current album hasn't gotten any, from the reviews I've seen, it's been well received.

**Eitzel:** I'd much rather have like a million dollars and live in a giant mansion with several Rolls-Royces, and I would put on the gate of my mansion, "World's Greatest Living Songwriter." When I have the security gates with a few television cameras constantly swiveling and the proximity monitors keeping people away and then an inner area with dogs—submachine gun posts—and then outside I'll have this incredibly incongruous ornate gate with wrought iron. Well, I'll probably buy the gate from Buckingham Palace but at the top I'll tear out the Queen's sign and I'll put, "World's Greatest Living Songwriter." That would be great. That would make sense. Doesn't make sense at this point at all. Either I'm a contender or I'm not. Either I'm selling or I'm buying. And if I'm the world's greatest living songwriter, I'm doing nothing but buying. I'm buying shit. I'm buying other people's shit. So really, I kind of don't care. I have to sit at my desk, and I have to go, "Well, this week, you really sucked." And every once in a while, I'll have a breakthrough. You know, and I really will think I'm the best songwriter. Otherwise, you know, you just write.

**Goldberg:** There is a tradition of good songwriters like a Leonard Cohen for example who don't get the Smashing Pumpkins kind of success but yet here he is, 30 plus years later—

**Eitzel:** His first record probably sold more than all of my records combined. So he can afford to live that way 'cause his albums are still selling and always should 'cause he's brilliant. He's brilliant and he still writes great songs, still writes brilliant songs. I just wished he'd find a new producer.

**Goldberg:** In other words, you feel that you need to get a validation from the public for it to really matter?

**Eitzel:** Yeah, that's all that matters. What critics say, pardon me, but what critics say doesn't mean shit. I mean critics cannot keep you from starving to death, critics don't buy records, they get them for free. Critical acclaim is something that I have to deal with. It's like doing interviews. If I had my druthers at this point, I would not do them at all. They don't sell records. Journalists read about American Music Club and nobody else cares. So it's almost like something's wrong with this band. I don't know what it is, but it drives me insane. I love journalists. They're writers. I love writers. Usually they're very cool people but it's like, hey, you buy it. OK, I'll give you an interview if you buy it. Thirty of my records. Thirty records. Help me out. Come on.

**Goldberg:** Has it become more difficult to write, or is it always hard to write?

**Eitzel:** It's always hard. It's always, like, really hard to write a good song. Takes forever for me. I'm more like Leonard Cohen than anyone. There's this great short interview I read with him in *SongTalk*. God, I'm the greatest songwriter? OK. I met the editor of *SongTalk* at a party, and he said, "Are you a musician?" I said, yeah, yeah. I'm in American Music Club. That was like three months after *Rolling Stone* named me as "Songwriter of the Year." He said, "Yeah, you're in a band?" Yeah, American Music Club. "Oh. Well, um, do you ever play out, do you have any records out?" It was like, yeah, a couple. "Cool. If you send me some demos, I'll tell you what, I'll send you a free copy of the paper." All right, I'll buy it. Cool, cool. I like your paper a lot. I'll buy it. It's weird. There you go. Success, right? I read this interview with Leonard Cohen in this magazine, and he was great, great. He talked about how he sits at his computer and just works and works and works. I love it, you know. I love reading how he works.

**Goldberg:** I know a few years ago you told me you had rented an office. You went there during the day and wrote. Is that how you still work?

**Eitzel:** I've got a house, so I have a basement room set up.

**Goldberg:** Do you write from nine to four?

**Eitzel:** No, I don't have time for that. The fucking phone constantly rings. Doesn't do anything but ring. Then I have a message machine with like an hour of messages and then I have people complaining that my beep's too long. I mean, it's insane at home. I have an unlisted number and I still get like, between my managers and my business manager and my lawyer and my two agents and you know, all the five members of the band and between everybody, I can't get any fucking work done.

**Goldberg:** So when do you write?

**Eitzel:** Every chance I get until the phone rings. Everyone thinks I'm so rude on the phone. I pick it up, I have headphones on, I've got my computer on, I've got my keyboard going, I've got like all this stuff going, I've got my four-track on, I'm trying to do some work, I'm recording something, the phone rings, I go, "What?" "Oh, we've got five interviews to do tomorrow. Please, Mark, give them 45 minutes each." I'm like, "No, no, no." It's crazy. So I don't. This poor guy wanted five minutes with me today and I told him, no. I couldn't believe how snotty I was but—but this album, I can't wait 'til this album is sold or done so I don't have to work on it anymore.

**Goldberg:** You're already sick of dealing with it? It's only been out like—

**Eitzel:** A month. Well, we started recording it in August of last year and then we had like five months of recording it. Then I finally kicked the producer out and I kicked the whole band out of the studio to mix it with the engineer. It was like thousands of dollars over budget. The producer didn't care. It was awful. Awful. And then I tried to do a promotional tour of America so I could do promotion outside of the tour, so I didn't have to like, sing and do two hours worth of interviews. And they couldn't get anybody interested in the album, so it was like, "OK, then I won't do any interviews during the tour, right?" They're like, "Fine, no one's interested." So, I'm like, great.

We did a video, a really fun video with Adam Bernstein. We tried to make a copy of *Baywatch*, the most popular show in the world. So we got hard-bodied people and they're advertising an AMC soft drink and MTV banned it because we showed torso shots of women and men.

**Goldberg:** I guess if it had just been women it would have been OK?

**Eitzel:** No, if we had been David Lee Roth or if we had been like Ice Easy, what's his name, Ice Cube? Coolio? Or somebody like that. If we had like wanted to show naked people, we should have been a lot more famous, goddamnit. So they banned it. The record companies spent an insane amount of money on this video. So yeah, I've really worked my fucking ass off already for a year and a half almost and I'm sick of it. And I want to move on to another album as soon as I can. And they're already talking about another more extensive European tour in January and another American tour in February and March. So, I'll just fulfill my contracts to try to help sell the record and I'm over it.

**Goldberg:** It sounds like you're cornered in a way, right now.

**Eitzel:** That's how I feel.

**Goldberg:** You've got all this ahead of you that you don't want to do. It's almost like you're part of the chain gang for the next six months.

**Eitzel:** Yeah. Because it doesn't seem to make us more successful. It doesn't seem that way at all. It just seems like the same 300 people come to see us and nothing changes. If we had any chance—and it doesn't look as if we're getting any major interest in the album and we're certainly not getting any help from MTV—if there was some sort of success, sure, I'd be totally into it. But nothing seems to be happening. So, it's like, OK, let's go through the motions again. After 12 years you get bitter, you know?

**Goldberg:** So if when you toured you kept seeing bigger and bigger crowds?

**Eitzel:** It would be great. I'd love it. It would be what we need to do. But at this point I'm looking towards the band being completely broke. This album took so long that the band went broke. So until we get some advance money from Virgin for the next album— Basically it just seems as if in January the band is going to be completely broke again and I ain't paying anybody's rent so I don't know where the money is going to come from. So we'll see. And nothing is going to happen until we start playing to larger audiences, and we probably won't be doing that, so I don't know what the answer is.

**Goldberg:** What did recording *San Francisco* take so long?

**Eitzel:** Because the producer just wanted to do more and more overdubs. We were coproducing with him but—He would say, "I think you should look at that middle section again. You know. It's really no good. Something doesn't happen." And you go, "Really?" "No, it's not happening. It's really sort of bogus. It kinda sucks." "Oh. OK. OK, great! Well then, we'll do a distorted guitar and some congas and then we'll do some accordion" and three weeks later you're like, "Oh, this song's done. Is it done?" That's why. I'm such a nice guy. It didn't occur to me until we were $50,000 over budget. That's when I thought, wait a minute, something's not working here. I told the coproducer I wanted this album done it two months. And it had to be done in two months and now it's like, whatever. I don't want any bitterness or bad blood.

**Goldberg:** So you feel the band could go into the studio and cut an album fast?

**Eitzel:** If we didn't have to use any goddamn motherfucking producer, absolutely.

**Goldberg:** If you guys were self-producing?

**Eitzel:** Well, I would insist on producing it myself. Fuck the band. If they don't want it, quit. I don't care anymore. I know exactly how my songs sound. Nobody else does.

**Goldberg:** Just get a good engineer.

**Eitzel:** Yeah. Jim Scott who engineered the last album is awesome. Chad Blake, good people. It's not that I hate Joe Chiccarelli at all, he's wonderful, he's a great guy. It's just that he went a little crazy. He thought he was making the album of his life. He wasn't. He was making another album, just like we were.

**Goldberg:** Do you like the album as it stands?

**Eitzel:** Look, I had to live with it, and I know it inside and out and it's really hard to listen to because of a lot of the compromises. A lot of endless discussions about it that I had to have. I like a lot of it.

**Goldberg:** You could imagine it—

**Eitzel:** We're rehearsing that song that's called "In the Shadow of the Valley." Nobody was sure if that was going to be the song or not. Nobody was sure if it was good or not and it ends up being the best thing on the album. "How Many Six Packs Does It Take to Screw in a Light." That was going to be a B-side. The drummer hated it; the guitar player hated it. No one liked it. Producer? "No. It's kind of stupid, blah, blah, blah." I said, "We have to record it. We have to do it." We recorded it the very last week, it was rough, it was sort of a throwaway. It ends up being a great song, you know? On and on and on. Every time. I'm sick of it, really. Or like "Cape Canaveral." No one was sure. Some people at the record company kind of thought it was the weakest one, maybe drop that one, maybe we need more rockers, maybe this, maybe that.

**Goldberg:** On and on and on.

**Eitzel:** It's on and on. You're like, "No, just do it."

**Goldberg:** It sounds like you had to convince someone all down the line.

**Eitzel:** Everyone. And it shouldn't be that way. I have to convince everyone. It's awful. Yeah, it's hard. This album was so hard for me. I want to do vocals. It takes two hours to get a mix up so I can sing to it. Two hours. When you want to work, you want to work now. You don't want to wait in another room staring at the wall, watching some stupid TV show. It's ridiculous. This album was so hard for me to do. And I didn't have the guts or the balls or the gumption to stop it and say, "I'm out of here." I didn't. So it's my fault. But it'll never happen again. I learned so much. It made me so bitter.

*Addicted To Noise*, December 1994

Laurie Anderson, San Francisco, 1982: "Obscure art basically leaves me cold. One of my goals is to communicate." Photo by © Chester Simpson / Rock-N-RollPhotos.com

# LAURIE ANDERSON

*Fifteen years before I interviewed Lou Reed, I met his future soul mate, the performance artist Laurie Anderson. In early 1981, Anderson had a remarkably unexpected international hit with her mesmerizing "O Superman (For Massenet)." She had made the recording in the hallway of her home with an NEA grant of $500. "It was the quietest place she could find," said Bob George, who pressed up 1,000 copies initially for his small indie label, One Ten Records. "I suggested she slow it down slightly to make it longer—it ended up eight minutes long—so I'd get paid more royalties if it was played on the radio." The international success of "O Superman (For Massenet)" led to an eight-album deal with Warner Bros. I hung out with Anderson when she came to San Francisco in the spring of 1981 to perform at the Market Street Cinema with William Burroughs. At the time I was the managing editor of* Boulevards, *a monthly San Francisco–focused magazine. By the time this piece was published, the magazine had been bought at a bargain price by a collective of San Francisco journalists led by the once-great editor (*Ramparts*), Warren Hinckle, who renamed it* Frisco. *Decades later, when I contacted Anderson by email after Lou Reed's death, she got right back to me and wrote that she remembered me. I think she was just being nice.*

SAN FRANCISCO, CALIFORNIA—LAURIE ANDERSON, the performance artist, had been up all night. She was leaning, exhausted, against a crate full of the electronic equipment she uses to make strange noises and weird music. We were in the alley outside the Market Street Cinema (a porno movie theater that occasionally doubles as a concert hall) where she had performed the night before. "I was afraid to go to sleep," she said, with a voice as faint and muted as an oriental watercolor. "Once I fall asleep, nothing will wake me."

Her soft brown hair was cut short and spikey. In the stark, bright morning light, she looked a lot like former Sex Pistol Johnny (Lydon) Rotten. Like Rotten, she seemed fragile, vulnerable, a rag doll about to fall apart. Yet she lacked his pugnaciousness. And unlike England's arch rebels, Anderson is gracious and accommodating, if a bit reserved.

The night before, dressed all in black, Anderson looked like a punk mystic as she stood on the stage before the huge, white movie screen, surrounded by the kind of machines that modern composers use to make music that sounds like a typing pool, or the inside of a factory. When she finally began to speak before the hushed crowd that filled the theater, the voice did not sound like her own. One heard a mechanized, technologically altered man's voice: Jack Benny as a robot. The audience laughed. "Good evening. Welcome to difficult listening hour . . . that impenetrable sound of unlistenable music. Get set for some diff-i-cult music. Ooh la, ooh la."

The performance, a kind of 21st-century vaudeville, combined singing, the spoken word, music, and electronic effects, shot through with healthy doses of sarcasm, humor, and some cultural and political commentary all performed by Anderson using a violin, vocoder, synthesizer, tape recorder, and a few mysterious boxes that she says are harmonizers and filters. Everything was manipulated by electronics. Nothing was what it seemed. She played her violin, and it sounded like a banjo. She sang, and it sounded like a violin. At one point, she put on sunglasses that contained a pickup and played her own head like a drum. By using prerecorded material and devices that repeat, multiply, and/or alter the pitch and tone of her voice, Anderson, alone onstage, becomes a futuristic orchestra and chorus, creating a modern, appropriately gloomy soundscape. One got the impression that she was having a hell of a good time doing these things.

But she was also making a number of potent, if somewhat abstract, statements about the times in which we now find ourselves. "O Superman (For Massenet)," a song originally released on a small New York record label early last year, that has gone on to become a major pop hit in Europe, selling more than 300,000 copies to date (Anderson is now signed to a contract with Warner Bros.), touches on numerous indelicate areas of contemporary American life. Anderson deals with alienation ("Hi! I'm not home right now. But if you want to leave a message, just start talking at the sound of the tone . . ." states an overly cheerful mechanical voice); with the proliferation of arms and the current pro-war mood of the Reagan gang ("I've got a message to give you. Here come the planes . . . they're American planes . . . and the voice said: Neither snow nor rain nor gloom of night shall stay these couriers from the swift completion of their appointed rounds"); with the detachment many of us feel due to the increasing number of machines (phone answering devices, taped messages, computers, video games, etc.) impinging on our lives and pushing people apart; and with a profound sense that America itself (and all that it once stood for—liberty, freedom, the pursuit of happiness, etc.) has betrayed us, and left us, as they say, up shit creek without a paddle. "So hold me Mom, in your long arms," sings Anderson at the end of "O Superman (For Massenet)." "In your automatic arms. Your electronic arms. In your arms. So hold me Mom. In your long arms. Your petrochemical arms. Your military arms. In your electronic arms."

In the morning, out in the alley, Laurie Anderson wore a long dark brown wool overcoat that looked pinched from one of the grizzled winos that stumbled past the entrance to the alley as we fumbled with the boxes. Under the overcoat, she wore a wrinkled black pinstripe suit, a black dress shirt, a black silk tie and black shoes. She lit a Camel. Her green eyes were clear, alert, despite the lack of sleep. Her lips were a pale pink—no lipstick.

"I've never liked dresses," said the first performance artist to become an international pop star, when I asked her about her outfit. "I'm not interested in being a cliché of a woman or some kind of imitation of a man." She lit another Camel, and I glanced at her. She looked young and pretty, despite the fact that her black eye shadow was smeared. "In terms of the way I work," she continued, "I like to be as simple as possible. And that carries over to what I wear. It refers to a way of being the interlocutor and it also refers to being able to use the dress system—system of address—and not be immediately pegged as a man or a woman. It's freeing. That, I guess, is what I'm trying to say."

Laurie Anderson is a woman of many talents. She is a sculptor and a poet, a singer and a musician, an actress and a filmmaker, a photographer, and a pop star. Part Brian Eno, part Patti Smith, part William Burroughs.

"I like combining as many things as possible," she said of the performances that have made her famous within the art world. "And with most of those things, you're not seeing what you're hearing. Just the way we receive information through TV, telephone, radio, conversation, advertising, pictures—all of this barrage coming in. What you may be seeing is a picture of an incredibly contented couple and they may be trying to sell you some really horrible insurance."

"And it's a way of trying to use that technique, that mode of perception to say a couple of different things at once that appeals to me. Have them resonate against each other. Or with each other. So it becomes a much more complete situation."

Laurie Anderson tells stories: off-kilter, surrealistic tales set in a landscape of Americana. Dolly Parton and Superman, Mom and Dad, telephone answering machines and airline pilots instructing their passengers on proper seating methods, snake charmers, and fed-up lovers. They all populate her work. She pits the clichés of America against cool technology. "People are going to have to come to terms with the creation of totally electronic cities," she said seriously, "because that's absolutely what's going to happen. And to live with these sort of romantic ideas about, as Reagan says, Main Street—it's going to make life very, very difficult to live with such totally outmoded ideas and get along in the world."

In San Francisco, Anderson, who works with the tools of a small rock band, set up and tested her equipment by herself, with only minimal assistance from a man at the soundboard. Though this is partially out of financial necessity, it appeared that Anderson took pride in handling everything by herself. As an independent woman who has struggled on her own for 10 years, gradually gaining recognition, I wondered: 1) If Anderson considers herself a feminist; and 2) If so, why feminism as a theme doesn't figure in her art?

"I used to be politically active," she said. "And the last time I was in a demonstration was in the early '70s. I was marching in a demonstration in front of the Playboy Club in New York. A woman showed up for work at the club and she was surprised to see us there and said, basically, 'Listen, I make $800 a week at this job. It's the best job I've ever had. I support two kids. I have no husband. And if you want to talk about women and money, why don't you go down to the garment district where women make 23 cents an hour and why don't you just march around down there?'

"And I didn't have an answer for her for I thought that was an excellent point. And that was the last demonstration I went to in terms of politically oriented things. I consider myself and my work to be—Well I consider my work to be political activity in a certain way and probably in a very broad sense, because I'm not offering solutions. I mean I'm not running for office and so I don't present solutions.

"I mean I try not to run into the situation where I do something that doesn't fit the bill politically and yet is very beautiful. I always feel that somehow I can work so that I feel comfortable with it and can also use it in terms of the work. I think that one's political ideas—I mean, at least I know that mine are already so built in that my work expresses them whether I make it explicit or not."

For Laurie Anderson, this all started back in the late '60s when she was teaching art history at City College of New York. The classroom was dark; Anderson would show slides and lecture about them. Only there was a problem; she kept forgetting the facts. So she just began making up some of her own. "And people were writing the stuff down as facts," she said, still a little surprised by the students' gullibility. "From that it was pretty easy to move to what was being called, at least in Europe, action art."

Anderson's inspiration was Vito Acconci, a poet who got fed up with the written word and started using his own body to express himself. She was impressed by a performance where Acconci sat blindfolded at the bottom of a staircase holding a stick and threatening to kill anybody who came down the stairs. "He called himself a poet, but he was really interested in kinds of space—public and private space," said Anderson, becoming more animated. "Everyone else was doing real precise, efficient things, hard-edged things and he was just doing very personal, emotional things. Using 'I' in this really interesting way."

Born and reared (along with three sisters and four brothers) in Wayne, Illinois, Anderson earned a BA at Barnard and then an MFA in sculpture at Columbia while teaching art history and Egyptian architecture at City College in New York. At the same time that her lectures were becoming performances, her sculpture was becoming preoccupied with the written word. In one instance she cut up the *New York Times* and the *Chinese Times* and wove the strips together.

"Then I realized that it was just kind of silly to do it that way because I really like words when they're spoken. It's like when you get a letter from somebody, and it can get kind of abstract and it's not always easy to tell exactly what they're saying because the whole element of tone is missing. The same person calls you up and you can tell in 10 words really a lot more about them. So I decided that since I was interested in spoken words, I would just speak the words."

Soon she was combining words and music. And beginning with a piece in 1974, "Duets on Ice," Anderson started using transposed objects in her performances. "Duets on Ice," performed on the streets of New York and Genoa, Italy, found Anderson playing a violin that had a small tape recorder concealed inside it. She played duets (she is an accomplished violinist, having studied the instrument until she was 15) with the prerecorded music ("spaghetti western cowboy songs," she says) while wearing a pair of ice skates frozen in blocks of ice. "When the ice melted, I would lose my balance and the piece was over," explained Anderson. On another occasion, she affixed a tape playback head to her violin and strung the bow with a piece of recording tape. As she "played" the violin, prerecorded sounds unrelated to the violin were heard.

As Anderson's work has gotten more and more dependent on electronics, she has moved off the street and into auditoriums, concert halls, and even rock clubs. "Basically, I wanted to refer to things that were already done," said Anderson, explaining her use of audio and visual technology. "At first, when I was just recording talking, it became a way of having another voice that was definitely in the past tense. And so there could be some dialogue between the past and the present. And I like electronics because it's fast. It's the closest thing to the mind."

At the airport, we unloaded Anderson's boxes, hassled with an airline clerk about whether the boxes would fit on the plane, and, after that conflict was resolved in Anderson's favor ("I always take them on the plane," she calmly told the clerk), we sat in the waiting area.

She told me that when she first turned to performance art, she had "gotten very tired of making objects because they took up so much room and there were way too many of them already." And until this year, recorded examples of Anderson's art have only been available on fairly obscure anthologies of poets, performance artists, and creators of New Music.

But now, Anderson has made an about-face; she is back in the business of making art objects for public consumption. Her 33 and 1/3 RPM EP was her first stab at the pop market. Its success has been very surprising to Anderson. "I'm real happy about it," she said.

"I got tired of people asking me what I did, and I'd have to say, well I do performances but I can't really explain them because, well, they're pictures, lots of movies and slides and there's talking and it's music—You can't say, 'Here's my painting,'" said Anderson, explaining why she put out "O Superman (For Massenet)."

Warner Bros. is set to release Anderson's first album, *Big Science*, which will contain a remixed version of "O Superman (For Massenet)" and other original compositions including "Let X=X" and "Greener Pastures" in early 1982.

I wondered about Anderson's intentions of finding a mass audience for her work (in Europe, of course, she already has one; and in the US she has performed for audiences containing as many as 4,000 people). And I also wondered if, in the process, she is leaving art behind, replacing it with entertainment.

"Obscure art basically leaves me cold. One of my goals is to communicate," said Anderson, fishing in her overcoat pocket for the Camel pack. "So it affects me a lot whether people seem to get it. One of my hopes for what would happen in the United States is that American artists could finally decide to actually participate in their own culture. The United States is totally AM pop culture. Totally uninteresting on a mass media level."

"Of course, the first thing an artist does is go—" Anderson adopted a shocked tone, "'I'm going to dilute this so that more people—' I think it's obvious that a great work of art can be a great work of art even if only two people understand it. Or maybe one. And it in no way means that if more people vote it's a good work of art, the better. Obviously. But if the work is appropriate to media like that, and if its integrity can be sustained, I would love to see that kind of work moving in different directions than circling around in this whirlwind of our own little world of the elite. And there is the possibility of people taking part in an artist's work in some way or being interested in it or letting it contribute to their society. It would be thrilling. It would be thrilling!"

And with that, Laurie Anderson got up and walked onto her plane, headed back to New York.

*Frisco*, March 1982

Lou Reed, Old Waldorf, 1978: "I have no idea what prompts me to write any song ever other than things going on around me and I react to it."

# LOU REED'S ROCK & ROLL HEART

**At 54, Lou Reed has mellowed out a bit—but not too much. A conversation with rock's avant-garde avatar about censorship (on the internet and elsewhere), art, recognition, and heroin.**

*I was scared to interview Lou Reed. After all, he once released a live album in which he trashed Village Voice critic Robert Christgau. Reed was notorious for his treatment of rock critics, including Lester Bangs. My interview with him had been arranged by then-Sire Records president Howie Klein, who had assured me Reed was a different person since falling in love with Laurie Anderson. In anticipation of our interview, I feared that the wrong question might set Reed off. Still, this was the onetime leader of the Velvet Underground, one of the great rock bands, taking rock far into the avant-garde so there was no way I wasn't going to meet with him. I first heard the Velvet Underground in '70 or '71. I remember standing next to my dad's stereo in the living room listening to "Heroin" and being surprised more by how beautiful the song was, than its subject matter, which I knew about before hearing the song 'cause so much had been written about that song. For a while back then, when I was 17 and 18, I was obsessed with the Velvets. I dug the darkness of the Lou Reed written, John Cale recited "The Gift" on* White Light/White Heat, *and many tracks on* The Velvet Underground & Nico, *but it was the third and fourth album,* The Velvet Underground *and* Loaded, *that I listened to over and over. I lost my bearings in '71 and '72, my first two years in college and away from home. Somehow those two albums, for better or worse, were a serious part of the soundtrack that kept me going in those difficult times. So Lou Reed is important to me on a personal basis. Yeah, I had to interview him. As for my fears of the interview going off the tracks, they were unwarranted.*

NEW YORK, NEW YORK—LOU REED IS dressed in black. Black leather pants. Black T-shirt. Black shoes. Electricity is, literally, crackling off him, as he stands in his elegantly cool, private sixth-floor office at the back of Sister Ray Enterprises, overlooking Broadway in the Village.

"Did you hear that?" he asks, walking over to an open window and closing it. I think he's referring to the street sounds, but I'm wrong.

At Sister Ray, there are Lou Reed and Velvet Underground posters on the walls, as well as framed gold and platinum albums for *New York*. A rack holds copies of many of Reed's older albums; boxes of the recent Velvet Underground boxed set sit on a bookcase. A photographer is setting up to shoot Reed up front. Reed's publicist is on the phone, dealing from a couch at the back, just outside the room where Reed and I are talking. Nearby is Reed's internet expert, Struan Oglanby.

"I'm getting a shock every time I get up," Reed says with a grimace, taking a seat back at his desk. "That was that snapping sound." Then, in that classic Lou Reed monotone, "I conduct a lot of electricity. It's really strange."

Maybe not so strange. We are, after all, talking about Lou Reed, founder of the Velvet Underground. Writer of such highly charged songs as "Heroin," "I'm Waiting for the

Man," "Sweet Jane," and, of course, "Rock & Roll." And "Lisa Says." And "Walk on the Wild Side." And "Satellite of Love." And "The Blue Mask." And "Romeo Had Juliette." And "Dirty Blvd." And . . .

For over 30 years, he has recorded albums that have ranged from truly brilliant (*Street Hassle*) to downright annoying, yet revolutionary (*Metal Machine Music*), from insightful (*New York*, *Magic & Loss*) to, well, not so hot (*Mistrial*). Mostly though, Reed has managed that difficult feat of simultaneously making rock & roll and art.

"I don't want to be pretentious to call it art," he says quickly, when I bring up the A-word. "But I hope that it's pure and good enough and honest enough of thought and expression to be—" His voice trails off. He lays his hands flat on the desk that separates us. Then, as if to say to hell with this humility bullshit, he says, "I'm trying to make art out of it."

Lou Reed at 54. 54? He sure doesn't look it. Thin, wiry, intense, Reed has the energy of a man half his age. But with the wisdom and the authority of one who has lived a lot of life, which he certainly has.

This may be an office, but that doesn't mean Reed can't make music here. I notice several amplifiers including an old tweed Fender champ. There is a photo of Reed and the great songwriter, Doc Pomus, on a shelf, along with some books on the Velvet Underground.

He was a troubled kid who was subjected to shock treatment therapy when he was 17. *I conduct a lot of electricity.* No lie. Reed's story is a long one, and if you want one version of it, check out Victor Bockris' bio, *Transformer: The Lou Reed Story*.

From early on, Reed (certainly inspired by Bob Dylan) was doing something that few rock & roll songwriters had done before him. He was attempting to write more than just silly love songs. "I wanted to write a novel; I took creative writing," Reed once said. "At the same time, I was in rock & roll bands. It doesn't take a great leap to say, 'Gee, why don't I put the two together.' I wanted to write simple words to cause an emotion, and put them with my three chords."

Reed hooked up with guitarist Sterling Morrison while in college. A few years later he met John Cale (bass, viola, etc.) when the two were attempting to crank out hits at Pickwick Records, a New York-based budget label. Eventually Moe Tucker came in on drums. They named their group after a 1963 paperback book by journalist Michael Leigh about "aberrant" sex between willing adults.

With Andy Warhol as their manager, and the model Nico on occasional vocals, the group made waves in New York (their fans included no less than Beatles' manager Brian Epstein), before recording the first of four albums that contain some of the greatest rock & roll ever made: *The Velvet Underground and Nico*, *White Light/White Heat*, *The Velvet Underground*, and *Loaded*.

At a time (1967) when American youth were caught up in the peace and love hippie vibe emanating from San Francisco, the Velvets offered dark songs about hard drugs, kinky sex, and emotional dead ends. But they also delivered songs about transcendence ("Beginning to See the Light"). Despite the raves of a few rock critics who loved them from the start (Ellen Willis for one), the Velvets were, for the most part, hated. After an appearance at the Fillmore Auditorium in San Francisco, the nationally respected critic Ralph J. Gleason (who advised *Rolling Stone* founder Jann Wenner and wrote a column for the *San Francisco Chronicle*), described the performance as "nothing more than a bad condensation of all the bum trips of the Trips Festival." Gleason was referring to a pivotal San Francisco "happening" that had taken place a year or so earlier.

Hated by some critics, ignored by the public. As Reed now notes: "When the Velvet Underground was around, we sold almost no records. Literally."

Though to this day when one thinks of Lou Reed, it is impossible not to also think of the Velvet Underground, the fact is that Reed has recorded several dozen solo albums.

Brilliant songs can be found on just about every one, from his very first solo release, *Lou Reed*, which, for example, includes "Lisa Says," through the brand new *Set the Twilight Reeling*, which has at least four songs ("NYC Man," "Trade In," "Riptide" and the title track) that after many, many listens, sound like classics.

The new album was recorded at Reed's "home" studio, The Roof. He is especially proud of the true-to-life sound quality of the album. What you hear is exactly what it sounded like at The Roof when Reed and his musicians—Fernando Saunders on bass, Tony "Thunder" Smith on drums—played the music, live.

I had spoken to Reed on the phone a few months earlier about the album, and at that time he had told me about one of the songs, "Sex with Your Parents," a stinging indictment of right-wing politicians.

**Michael Goldberg:** I spoke at a rally about internet censorship back in December and at the end of a brief statement, I told people about your song "Sex with Your Parents" and said it was the kind of thing that if some congressmen just heard the title, they would think it was something that should not be on the internet. But in fact, this song is a statement about those very congressmen. It got great applause when they heard about this song on the album. Afterwards, people came up to me and would say, wow, that was so perfect, that thing about that Lou Reed song. I wonder if you had any feelings about the fact that Congress just passed, and the President just signed in, a bill that puts more restrictions on internet content than constrain the content of any other medium right now.

**Lou Reed:** In one sense, it's completely incomprehensible to me. I would have thought those days were over, but when you see what's going on with the NEA, you realize this is not as surprising as you might have thought. And you correct me if I have it wrong, but it seems that electronic mail doesn't receive the same constitutional guarantees as written mail. Or as someone else said to me, "I have it here, I write it, it's OK. You have it over there, you read it, it's OK." It's the in-between, when it's going in-between. And that's because, as I understand it, again correct me if I'm wrong, they're—the bad guys—saying that it's broadcast, that it's being broadcast, and therefore it's subject to the same things as TV.

What can you say to anyone who says that? It's so either maliciously off base and a convenient thing just to—to what, what are they talking about? What are they talking about?

**Goldberg:** What in particular prompted you to write "Sex with Your Parents"?

**Reed:** I have no idea what prompts me to write any song ever other than things going on around me and I react to it. And certainly, this stuff has been going on around for awhile so I guess, for whatever reason, it set me off in a writing mode about this. I know it's not going to affect anything. I know it's not going to change anybody's mind. I know I'm talking to the converted. I know all that. I know that. It's just an expression of something. It'd be nice if it could become a theme song for something, as far as I'm concerned. Although I'm not into being part of a group even though right now I'm advocating the only way to stop these people is to get organized yourselves and do something. I would love to have that song as a reference point. I would love it, if you called up the national anti-censorship line for the internet, when they put you on hold, you heard "Sex with Your Parents" or something like that.

It's a nice expression of something. I'd like people out there to see that. But I'm talking to the converted. I'm not going to convince anybody from the Right by that song. But it would be nice to get a chuckle out of people who do agree with you and give them a little spirit from it. This misery we had hoped vanished years ago. They couldn't do it in books, they couldn't do it in movies, they're trying it on TV and now here they are, here's a fresh thing. We couldn't do it over here, they couldn't do it in a book. Not for lack of trying.

This is a country that banned *Ulysses*. James Joyce. Are we proud of this, this Puritan country? Is this something to be proud of? Henry Miller having to go to France to be published. William Burroughs to France to be published. And then the books are stopped over here. Then it's no big surprise that they want to leap all over the internet and make it like that. It always surprises me, you go to a beach in countries like France or wherever, the women are topless. No one thinks about it. You go in a sauna. Everybody's in the sauna. If you did it in New York, there'd be pillage. God only knows what would happen. It's such a big forbidden thing. It's such a big deal. Blown out of proportion. Where's the undefended soft little thing to go after right now with all that vehemence that's been geared up to go after books and movies and really try to censor things. The internet. There it sits. This glorious thing with access to this and that. And guess what? Who leaps in? *Them*.

**Goldberg:** Is there a typical Lou Reed writing thing? Or does it happen a lot of different ways? And let's look at this particular album and talk about that.

**Reed:** It pretty much happens the same way all the time. I don't write stuff in advance. Anything you hear is written for this album. And it's been written within the time period of the album. It's not from before. Generally speaking, I hear music and songs in my head all the time. Like there's a permanent radio. Solely for my own amusement. And when I decide to do an album, I start taking down things that I'm listening to. That's it. And I do it because there's an album to make and it's fun to play and all that. Otherwise, I don't bother. It's just going on and on and on. Sometimes it gets intense enough that I have to put it down. It just won't leave me alone. It's kind of an interesting thing. But on the other hand, if I don't put it down pretty quickly, it'll go away, and I'll never see it again.

**Goldberg:** Was that the case with any of the songs on this album where you just had to put it down?

**Reed:** They're all like that. I was in writing mode. All the lyrics except one were done that way.

**Goldberg:** You said in the past about writing that sometimes it was putting it down and kind of removing words to get it as concise a statement as you could make.

**Reed:** Yeah, but I self-edit in my head.

**Goldberg:** So there's been an evolution. So now it comes more from your head to the page.

**Reed:** There's a more effective editor operating because I have more experience. Experience leads to improvement in my particular case. It's practice. It's like you practice guitar, you practice writing. After a while, certain things get a little easier, you're faster, better at it. I edit in my head better. And then I do a little bit of rewriting but it's real small. And it's all on computer because I can't even imagine anymore not doing it with computer. It saves me so much time. It's frightening to think the way I used to have to go through doing it.

**Goldberg:** It used to be notebooks and stuff?

**Reed:** Yeah. Matchbook covers. Pieces of paper. Arrows with rewrites pointing to another piece of paper and it's written upside down. Now there's version one, version two, three, four, *ad infinitum*. But, of course, I would do that. I'm not even talking about cut and paste, by the way. I don't even have to go that far with it. These are little bitty changes. It's nothing heavy like that. I wrote the whole album on a Mac. All my latest albums, I've written them all on the Mac. It saves me so much time. I can write in a week what would take me a month.

**Goldberg:** Why is that?

**Reed:** I can read the writing. I can read my writing. I can do nine different versions and see them all. I think a lot of the secret of things is to rewrite. The rewriting. A computer is made for rewriting. The speed and the accuracy that you can rewrite, that's a real telling thing, for me anyway. I'm one of these people, if I write something and go back an hour later, I can't read it. So this is made for me. My mother made me take typing in high school 'cause she never thought I'd have a job. That's the only reason I know how to pick and peck my way through the computer.

**Goldberg:** This album—one of the things it's about, it seems to me, is sort of rebirth and transformation. I could quote you some phrases. There's lines in here about "new self is born / the other self dead," "talk about a new me" and "talk about accepting the new found man." Are you feeling kind of revitalized or reborn these days?

**Reed:** Well, look at me. *[beats on the desk with his hands]* Yeah, I feel pretty good. I feel really great. I'm just feeling really good these days. You never know. Talk to me in a week. Maybe it's the opposite.

**Goldberg:** I only ask you this because you've already been public about it. But do you feel having a new relationship [with singer Laurie Anderson] has helped or sparked feeling revived?

**Reed:** I feel like I walked into one of those 40 billion new galaxies that Hubble found. That's what I think. Lucky me, *major domo* lucky, that's what I would say. I mean I write about everything, to my own detriment in some ways; how many secrets can you keep? But on the other hand, I am a writer, I do move things around. People forget about that. Things do get—well, *you* write, you must know what I'm talking about. It's real up to a point. It's true up to a point. I mean, it's all true in its entirety. It's just not exactly that way maybe or it's an amalgam of different things. I don't completely really understand the whole process myself.

I just think that I'm lucky that it chooses—and I don't want to sound New Age-y but I can't help it, this is the way it is—it's just this talent and ability and it goes through me like water. And I've learned how to treat it respectfully, to try and get the most out of it. I take it for granted in the sense that I'm listening to it most of the time anyway. So I never thought of it as like having brown eyes. This thing is always there, I'm always listening most of the time, it's going on and on and on.

Sometimes it's not my stuff either; some of these lyrics that I wrote, they were so good, I was concerned I was quoting Yeats or something or there was something biblical. I had people check. I said, "Listen, 'set the twilight reeling.' Has someone used that?" And somebody said to me, "It's from the 'Star Spangled Banner.' Starlight's last gleaming. Twilight's last gleaming.'" Close, but that's not what I said.

**Goldberg:** A line like "I was thinking of Van Gogh's last painting / was that perhaps what you've been feeling?"; a line like that is so beautiful and moving. You think of saying that to somebody. That just pops into your head, those lines?

**Reed:** Oh yeah. My favorite line in the whole album is "first came fire / then came light / then came feeling / then came sight." Oh my. Oh my! Who am I quoting? Where is that coming from? I had an interview with a younger guy, and he explained back to me what it meant. And it was so stunning because I hadn't really gotten that far into thinking what it meant. He said this means—Wow. I said I'm going to use that from now on. I don't get into what it means very much, because it's like the centipede that starts thinking about which leg comes first. It would grind to a—unless in the process I say something awful, then I say, "Please, no one must ever see this, *I* don't even want to see this." And I'm the one who wrote it.

That's part of the thing about writing. Some of what you write, you say, "Let's get that out of here and burn it." So these are only the things I want you to see. They've been polished and buffed and set in a little crown and off they go. But as far as the actual meaning of some of it, if it's not a hurtful, ugly destructive thing, if there's a purity of heart there, then out it goes whether or not it points at me in a way that may or may not be flattering. I don't get into a deep thing of what it means. But it is amazing to me to find out from other people what I thought it meant and these other layers of meaning. And these other layers are really there and there's a very good argument that can be made for them.

And people get into psychological—well there's this, *this* is what that meant. And it's all true. It's just that I don't sit down to officially write a song. I don't do that. So I also don't make these—there [are] some serious link ups on this album, but that's just because it's written by the same person who's interested in the same subject so it's running through all of it. It's not this calculated—well now we'll reiterate. It's not that.

**Goldberg:** It's sort of what was going on in your life turned into art.

**Reed:** Whatever I'm around, oh yeah. Sure. I don't want to be pretentious to call it art, but I hope that it's pure and good enough and honest enough of thought and expression to be—I'm trying to make art out of it.

**Goldberg:** Very early on, there's that idea of taking poetry and wedding it to rock & roll and writing about things that hadn't traditionally been written about in rock & roll. Keeping it very simple but powerful. That's something that you've done consistently.

**Reed:** That was the idea from the beginning.

**Goldberg:** Yeah, it's amazing. And listening to this album, listening to the blues guitar playing on "Sex with Your Parents"; to my ears, it could be a Howlin' Wolf session or something. And the rawness of the guitar on some of the other things—sometimes I think people don't realize how hard it is to get that right.

**Reed:** Let me tell you, I know how hard it is to get that right. Because someone who has been trying to get it right for lo, these many centuries . . . all the way back to the very beginning, I had my dream about what you could do with this music, with lyrics and the sound of the guitar. Keeping in mind that you're talking to a person who has been in bar bands since he's 14, but graduated honors in English.

Now you cross that with someone who's reading Hubert Selby Jr. and William Burroughs and really likes it. And some of the stuff that Delmore Schwartz did, and I was a student and friend of Delmore Schwartz. You mix that all up together and on top of that, there I land in with Andy Warhol. What an amazing bouillabaisse of influences is going on there! And it stays that way from my very first record on up. Now I may have fucked up here or there, I may have fallen down or stood up or flied or this or that but it's always there for better or worse.

That's why I said, if you plan them in a row, it's kind of interesting. I was astonished when I saw a magazine the other day in Spain: they had all the albums in a row . . . holy shit. Now I know someone would say, "well they ain't all good." I say, well, that ain't even the point either. There's a thread that goes through there that I think is really fascinating including the focus. It's someone trying to focus this thing starting from the very bare bone beginning to where you get up to now where this is high intensity focus.

The recording techniques I used, what I did on [*Set the Twilight Reeling*], heavy duty focus. If you want to hear it, it's there, you know. And the more you want to hear, the more that is there. It seems like a simple record; there are many, many, many things going on and I don't like to tell people about it.

I like them to . . . it's like I usually say, well, you know, it's a rock thing and if you get into the lyrics you could and if you don't want to, it's just some caterwauling going on over there. But there's all these other things going on there but it's interesting to me.

Have you heard it on a good system?

**Goldberg:** I actually listened to it on a portable CD player with headphones.

**Reed:** That's all?

**Goldberg:** Yeah, that's the way I've been listening to it.

**Reed:** It's the only way you've been listening to it?

**Goldberg:** Yeah. Because I'm traveling around a lot.

**Reed:** Well, you're in for a real treat. I'll play it for you outside for a minute on one of my systems. We mixed over six different systems, *six*, to make sure it sounded great no matter what the hell you listened over. This is not an elitist CD by any stretch.

**Goldberg:** Oh yeah. Like I say, it sounds great on a portable CD player with headphones.

**Reed:** Oh yeah. It's supposed to and it really ought to because we had a little mono rat speaker to check that out, you know, all the way up to big guys out there. It can sound monumental. There are things going on in there that are truly . . . keep in mind everything except one, the vocal is being done at the same time the guitar is being played. It's all being done live in The Roof, my home studio, available to only me. There was a problem in the studio. I just didn't want to go back in the studio until I could cure this problem.

It has to do with recording in a professional studio, the disconnection that you can feel. I knew I'd gone as far as I could go with *New York* and *Magic and Loss*, as far as using those techniques to record. That it had to be something that went past there. There was no way I could do better than that. I would do just another one of those, but I couldn't do better than that sonically and performance-wise. I think this is a new level of sound, and that I guarantee you, which you may or may not pick up over headphones. But the guiding principle here was really simple, and it's very hard to do.

You can go ask other musicians when you talk to them. This is the question. Say to them, "Are you happy with the sound you got on your album? Is that the sound that you had? Are you happy with the mix on your album?" Just hear what they say. And say, "Are you happy with the sound of your instrument? Is that what it really sounds like?"

OK? The guiding principle on the recording of this album was really simple, and that was: whatever you hear, that's what I heard. Not almost. Not sort of. Not constructed at the console. If you hear a sound, that's what it sounded like for real, starting with my voice which you can hear right here. I'll guarantee you that. One hundred percent successful transfer from point A to point wherever it is. Total. That's very, very . . .

**Goldberg:** That live-in-the-studio thing: there is a looseness or spontaneity and it certainly comes across listening to it.

**Reed:** Well, yeah. But I mean it's also a very sophisticated recording of raw. It's not so easy because, think about it: if you want to get that raw thing, you've got to get it while people are playing it, while it's there.

I was listening to a record today that just showed how sad it is what's going on as far as music that you don't get to hear. But I don't want to sound like one of those old people saying "oh, the music was better than it is now." I was listening to this CD that you must, you *owe* it to yourself to get: *The Loma Records Story*, which contains the soul records of Loma Records. In that collection is one of my favorite records of all time ever. If I had the top three records, this is in there, of anything available on the planet Earth as we know it, and it's called "Stay with Me" by Lorraine Ellison . . . came out in the late '60s.

They did a magnificent job in the transference from analog to digital. They really worked on it. Whoever did it, Lee Hirshberg . . . this guy must be real serious. What a transference. And then, if you've heard "Stay with Me, Baby," go to "Heart Be Still" and there you will get an example of what it was all about.

And to me, that's the inspiration: to try to get that on a record. It's the most amazing thing I've ever heard. I was thinking of carrying it with me so when people say, *what do you like, what do you listen to, what turns you on*, I just play this and say *this* turns me on. Amazing.

**Goldberg:** How did you feel about the Velvets finally getting into the Hall of Fame?

**Reed:** Better late than never. I was very honored by it. Nice to be included among some of the people who are my idols, also my peers. I just wish Sterling Morrison had been alive to experience it.

**Goldberg:** I was a kid when the first Velvet Underground album came out . . .

**Reed:** Let's talk about my new record . . .

**Goldberg:** I was just going to point out the irony of it taking so long for the establishment to accept the group . . .

**Reed:** Well, I hope it doesn't take them that long to accept *me*.

**Goldberg:** Why did you call the album *Set the Twilight Reeling*?

**Reed:** Oh, I have no idea. Well, actually I do. Because it's about transformation and rebirth. That's why.

**Goldberg:** That runs through the entire album.

**Reed:** It's a rock & roll album. That's the theme.

**Goldberg:** This is the first album you've recorded at your studio.

**Reed:** High above the city.

**Goldberg:** Can you look out on the city from the studio?

**Reed:** We were looking out all the time. It was particularly amazing when it was storming out. All of this was cut live, all live vocals, all live tracks. Cut live in the studio.

**Goldberg:** There's a lot of guitar on this album.

**Reed:** A lot of loud guitar.

**Goldberg:** What motivated you to make this kind of record?

**Reed:** I just wanted to make a rock & roll record. That is what I do, after all.

**Goldberg:** You were recently in Europe working on a play with Robert Wilson?

**Reed:** I did the music for a play with Robert Wilson called *Time Rocker* in Hamburg. He did the sets and designs, and I did the music and the lyrics, and we worked with a guy named Darryl Pinckney. He did the book.

**Goldberg:** What's that about?

**Reed:** Well, it's taken from H.G. Wells' *The Time Machine*. It's about traveling around in time.

**Goldberg:** Well, of course that book was about an underground civilization that was struggling against this society above.

**Reed:** It was a tract for socialism. The play we're going to do isn't.

**Goldberg:** It seems like you're one of a few artists that have had really long careers. You have this huge body of work, like you were talking about earlier—

**Reed:** *[Laughs]* Gargantuan!!

**Goldberg:** . . . but who are still able to make vital and contemporary records. Neil Young's another one that comes to mind, for me anyway. But there's not a huge list.

**Reed:** No, but like the generation before us, I would have hoped you could look to them that they would be doing new things. Why not? Jazz guys do. The blues guys do. I mean, I went to see B.B. King at the Blue Note three weeks ago. He was at a club, no less; people were killing to get in there. He was amazing. A true master. He'd attained the level of a true master. And it was astonishing to watch him going through an amp anyone can buy and do that. Just sit in awe. Seventy. And he sang some stuff I never heard before, and he sang stuff he's done two million times before and it sounded like he loved it. It was great.

So, what do I have to fear? What I'm told is rock is a young guy's thing. That's what rock was made about. I say, OK, call it Lou Reed music. Then am I allowed to play, or do I have to be led out to pasture? I would have hoped the generation before, instead of running around doing oldies—but that's what they did. Oldies. So now you got this other generation, and you got some people who are not and don't want to be nostalgia acts who have a serious agenda. They want to play rock, whatever version you like and that's what it comes down to. Now it may not be something necessarily appealing to a nine-year-old, but I was never aiming at a nine-year-old anyway without offending any nine-year-olds out there.

My stuff can be checked out. I'm not just talking. I have records. You could check the records out. Is it true or isn't it true? Look at what I started with. I've been going all this time from the very first record being told, "That's the best song you ever wrote, you're downhill from now on." Meaning "Heroin."

"Thanks. How would you know? Why? Do *you* write? How would you know?"

**Goldberg:** You were saying, right from the beginning, people were telling you you'd written your best song. Back in 1965 they were telling you that?

**Reed:** Oh yeah. If they thought anything, other than that the Velvet Underground was a horrible thing.

**Goldberg:** How do you feel about the fact that you had a tremendous influence from it seems, almost from day one to right now. Generation after generation of musicians that have come along—I don't have to name them, but Sonic Youth, Yo La Tengo, we can go on and on, Jesus and Mary Chain—

**Reed:** Usually I don't catch the influence, to tell you the truth. People say that to me and I'm like, "If you say so." *[laughs]*

I don't get it. I don't get it myself. And certainly, when the Velvet Underground was around, we sold almost no records. Literally. Minuscule. All of this happens way later, and then it kind of builds up until all of a sudden, it's a staple. But it was not like that at the beginning. It wasn't like that after the beginning. It wasn't even like that in the middle as far as I could tell.

**Goldberg:** But you know, the New York Dolls, Patti Smith—really quick it seemed to me, your influence was seeping into other things. Fast.

**Reed:** Maybe it was just an idea that was commonly floating around in the ether, I don't know. I wasn't keeping track of that. That's not for me to say. It's not for me to say, "Oh, this that and the other thing." Other people can say that.

**Goldberg:** Do you like it that it happened? Because it has happened, it's not—

**Reed:** If there's any truth to it, I find it very, very—it makes me feel very nice. And it's flattering if it's true. For me to know that it's true, I would probably have to have the artist himself say to me, hey . . .

**Goldberg:** Do you pay any attention to what else is going on? Do you listen to other stuff?

**Reed:** I listen to other stuff. I'm always asking people to keep me up to date, what's going on out there, what's something to listen to that's really great fun. I was listening to a ['90s group led by British electronic musician Mike Paradinas] called u-Ziq: it's the symbol for "Mu"—amazing drums. Amazing. Really interesting. I just was listening today—the Lorraine Ellison thing on this collection, it's the pinnacle. It's illuminating and revelatory, it's unbelievable, you have no idea. I'd give anything if I had a copy here. I'd tie you up and make you listen to this thing—well, I'd let you do it voluntarily. It's just unbelievable. Maybe I've got a copy over here. Some of the problem here is before we started taping, we've been talking, I've been flying in and out. But even before then, we were talking about different things, we've been officially doing that, there was some peripheral yammering going on—so, what's another question?

**Goldberg:** Well, the last question was: starting in the late '80s, unfortunately, the drug heroin has, as you know, become sort of trendy or something. And Alice in Chains, all these bands—I just wonder how you felt about that, given that long ago you wrote a song that, at least in my interpretation, was a warning. At least, that's one way it can be interpreted.

**Reed:** You know, I don't think people take things or don't take things because they heard somebody say something on a record.

**Goldberg:** No.

**Reed:** I haven't noticed that. I stopped smoking and I haven't noticed people stopping smoking because I did it. Quite the opposite. People do what people do. I personally think, generally speaking, you can't tell anybody anything. That's a line, by the way, that pops up in *Songs for Drella*. Some of the lines are really the way I talk, but it was Andy who in fact said that, but I believe that about certain things, I just think people do what they do.

And banning things and outlawing things and the rest is not going to change it. It doesn't seem to change it. I personally would legalize it: I'd take the profit out of it, that's what I would do. I would have treatment centers funded by taxes, make sure it's pure—no marijuana smoker ever died of cirrhosis of the liver, the last time I looked. It's so helpful for people who are ill. It's a very repressive society.

*Addicted To Noise*, February 1996

# SLY STONED NO MORE

*In March of 1982, I spoke to Sly Stone on the phone. He was coming to the San Francisco Bay Area and doing interviews to promote his appearances. I was a huge Sly fan. I thought his 1971 album,* There's a Riot Goin' On, *was a masterpiece. And I love Sly and the Family Stone's hits. He was a creative genius, and I was excited at the chance to talk to him. But I also knew that Sly had destroyed his career, and drugs, cocaine in particular, were a big part of it. I was told that Sly had cleaned up but as it turned out, that wasn't the case. When Sly did perform at a club in the South Bay, it was obvious he was high; his performance was a disaster. A month or so later, when I was waiting to talk to Rick James at the Record Plant recording studio in Sausalito, James and Sly were in James' bedroom at the studio freebasing cocaine. By 2011, it seemed that little had changed. Sly was living in a van in a rough part of LA; in the years since he's been trying to recover monies he says he was cheated out of. In February 2021 it was announced that Questlove was going to make a documentary film about Sly.*

IT WAS, SLY STONE DECIDED, time to put up or shut up. Sly had been basically inactive for years, and his manager and close friend Ken Roberts couldn't go on any longer. Two months ago, he gave the onetime Sly and the Family Stone superstar the boot.

Roberts had been there in some capacity during the good times—from the late '60s through the early '70s, when Sly's hits were blasting out of every Top 40 radio station, and his albums were million sellers and the bad—when Sly had been busted for possession of cocaine, failed to show up for numerous sold out concerts, and, later, by the mid-'70s, stopped having hits, and then stopped making records altogether.

Sly's marriage, which took place before a crowd of 23,000 people at Madison Square Garden, had ended in divorce. The bad times had been going on for too long. His fortune had dwindled to nothing, and Roberts had, he says, helped Sly out financially many times. "For so many years, I was basically the one who kept him alive," says Roberts. "But about a month or so ago I told him that I wasn't going to continue to do this for the next 20 years."

Roberts' decision to cut off his relationship with Sly may have been just what the man who wrote and sang hits like "Dance to the Music" and "I Want to Take You Higher" needed. "He told me that he was going to show me that he was serious about going back to work," says Roberts.

Which is just what Sly seems to be doing. First, he put a new version of Sly and the Family Stone together. Then he hit the road. So far, Sly has performed at every club he's been booked into—some 18 concerts. "I feel valid again," says Sly, now 37. "The magic is here to stay for a while. I mean I know. I feel cocky about it. I feel exactly like I felt when I made all the hits."

Sly was calling from a rehearsal hall in South Carolina. "If I wasn't talking to you right now, I'd be working on some music. I'm sitting in a room surrounded by guitars and talented people. And that's what I do now. All day. I want a hit record."

If anyone deserves another chance, it's Sly. He is one of most influential musicians of the past decade and a half. "There should be a Sly Stone Day," says superstar Rick James,

Sly Stone, Record Plant, Sausalito, 1982. "It was the drugs, man," said Rick James. "It was the drugs that did it. Too much cocaine." Photo by © Chester Simpson / Rock-N-RollPhotos.com

whose hit "Super Freak" and tremendous live show has made him (currently) the most popular Black singer/musician in America. "And the Commodores should be there and Stevie Wonder and Rick James and the Ohio Players and everybody else who made a million dollars by letting this man open the door."

For Sly, it all began in San Francisco. Born Sylvester Stewart, he first entered the music business as a record producer, working at the late music mogul Tom "Big Daddy" Donahue's San Francisco–based Autumn record label. Sly produced hits for the Beau Brummels, Vejtables, Mojo Men, and others. And when he wasn't producing, he taught himself how to play all the rock instruments—drums, bass, guitar, keyboards, horns.

Sly's ascension to stardom began in 1968 with "Dance to the Music," a Top 10 hit. Sly's music wasn't conventional soul stuff. It contained rock & roll and gospel and jazz, as well as doo-wop and soul influences. "My ears are always open," Sly says today. "And I like input from across the street. If I hear a Black cat say, 'What's that white boy doing?' and I hear the white boy say, 'What's that [N-word] doing?' that gives me material. (In fact, Sly wrote a song in his heyday called, "Don't Call Me [N-word], Whitey.")

Sly had 15 hit singles on the soul charts (10 pop hits), and nine hit albums (five on the pop charts). At the height of his popularity, only Jimi Hendrix could compete with Sly's universal acceptance by both Black and white audiences. "Well, it seems to me, if you mean what you say, you don't only mean it among the people you associate with," Sly says. "If you mean what you say, it's a universal feeling.

"And if it's a universal feeling, then the colors of the human beings involved are only a misdemeanor. Music can't be isolated. If my music had been isolated or categorized, you right now would be saying to me, 'Man, how come your music only related to Black people?'"

Sly's message was peace and harmony. He wrote beautiful songs that expressed simple truths: "Everyday People" preached, "We got to live together!" In "Everybody Is a Star," Sly sang, "I love you for who you are / Not the one you feel you need to be." "You Can Make It If You Try," "Stand!," "I Want to Take You Higher," and many others were all positive, affirmations of life. In the context of the times, the late '60s and early '70s, before the idealism of the '60s had dissipated, Sly's music and message made perfect sense to millions of people.

Sly was a star and he acted like one. He wore flashy custom-made clothes, was chauffeured in long black limousines, and was constantly surrounded by an entourage of at least 10 people. He had homes and recording studios in San Francisco, LA, and New York. He loved to be the center of attention. "He'd do funny things," recalled Tom Flye, who was Sly's engineer for three years (including for the hit album *Fresh*), working with him constantly from 1973 to 1976. "Like he went into this music store in New York wearing a Nudie-designed cowboy outfit. He had two guns in the holsters—fake guns. And he pulled them out and said, 'Hey, give me all your guitars.' And they all freaked and called the police and all of a sudden it was a big deal."

But if Sly liked to show off, he also liked to work—and work hard. He spent two years in the studio working on *Fresh*, his last quality album (released in 1973), then rerecorded the entire album in a week. "He'd have a song that was all finished, then he'd decide that the guitar part could be better," Flye said. "So he'd put a new guitar part over the old guitar part and sit and listen to that and say, 'Wow, that's a lot better!'" And on and on it went like that.

His former manager, Ken Roberts, believes that it was after Clive Davis, onetime president of Columbia Records, was fired in the early '70s, that Sly started going downhill. But there were other problems.

"It was the drugs, man," Rick James told me. "It was the drugs that did it. Too much cocaine."

Sly Stone avoids a direct answer when I ask whether he still uses drugs today. "I'm not going to say no, 'cause if I say no the majority of anybody in the world is going to say, 'Well he's lying.' And if I say yea, I'm incriminating myself."

Asked what led to his fall, Sly himself says, "I got tired. You know how you get tired of drinking water when you're thirsty? You know how you get tired of making love, and it crosses your mind that you may be merely fucking?

"All I did was make money. I didn't need money. I like to need money. I like to hear people like you calling me and asking what the hell have I been doing."

"From '68 to '75 there was nothing but hits. And after a while it gets boring that there could be an animal that could be called a genius. I am not a genius. Or if I am, I'm going to lie and say that I'm not. Between those years, everything was so perfect.

"There was nothing wrong I could do. There was an entourage around me and every time I opened my mouth, it would be, 'Right on Sly, right on Sly.' And you know nobody is gong to be right on all the time.

"And if you think about it, what could I do after 'Higher' or 'If You Want Me to Stay' [his last hit]? I wanted to go fishing man. Or drive my own car. For a long time, I didn't understand anywhere but hotel rooms, the inside of airplanes, and trying to figure out a way that didn't come off wrong to human beings."

During the second half of the '70s, Sly recorded a few poor selling albums. In 1979, he half-heartedly attempted a comeback, recording a decent album with an outside producer (Sly had produced all his own hits) for Warner Bros. that was a commercial flop. His most recent record was a George Clinton/Sly Stone collaboration called *Hydraulic Pump*. But Sly now disassociates himself from everything he's recorded since *Fresh*. "I was doing some music, but it wasn't my own music."

And, as for the future, Sly says, "I've got to play. I'm concerned only with reestablishing the fact. Reestablishing the fact! And music is my best buddy."

*San Francisco Chronicle*, April 11, 1982

# GEORGE CLINTON: THE RETURN OF DR. FUNKENSTEIN

*George Clinton emerged from a long black limousine. Wearing military fatigues and a red beret with several military pins dangling from it, Clinton looked ready to lead the revolution. Certainly, he was a participant in a music revolution, taking the funk of James Brown, Sly Stone, and others and mixing it with the dark weirdness of Frank Zappa's Mothers of Invention and creating a new psychedelic funk vision on such albums as* Free Your Ass . . . And Your Mind Will Follow *(1970) and* Maggot Brain *(1971). It was November 1979; his T-shirt, peaking through his unbuttoned army shirt, had a cartoon-style drawing of the American flag on it. And written where the stars should be was Clinton's motto. The motto, around which he hoped to rally the millions of disaffected youth, was not "Black Power" or "Kill the Pigs." Clinton's motto was "One Nation under a Groove" (the title of a 1978 Funkadelic album). I met Clinton for the first time that day, and we sat in the living room of a borrowed house in San Francisco, and he answered my questions. At one point he was talking about free will versus mind control, a theme present in many of the songs he'd written during the previous 10 years. "Who's gonna have the rights to the airways of your mind?" he said. "The FCC don't have no ruling on that yet. But they gonna want to in a minute. 'Cause mind control conditioning is going on right now through TV, most of the media. They're all focused on the one basic concept of putting us to sleep. They're tampering with our responses. You know, like equating toothpaste with sex on TV commercials. There's some serious behavior modification going on and people can't take it. Every once in a while it explodes and you've got Son of Sam. At our concerts there's a chant we do which goes, 'Think, it ain't illegal yet!' We say we can be revolutionary in our minds 'cause you can burn down the ghettos in your mind, you can rob and loot and whatever it takes to wake you up." Many years later, in 1994 or early 1995, I spent a few days at George Clinton's farm, which was located about 50 miles outside of Detroit, where he was living with his wife, Stephanie (who he divorced in February 2013 after 22 years of marriage). I was there looking at his stage clothes, stage props, and other items that, as a curator at the time for the Rock & Roll Hall of Fame, I was considering for inclusion at the museum that was scheduled to open in December 1995. It was extraordinary hanging with Clinton, but what I remember most about that visit was the dining room in his house where the heads of a half dozen, maybe more, deer hung from the walls. Under each head was the name of a different record company president. Clinton married Carlon Thompson later in 2013; she became his manager. I wrote the story that follows in 1983, half a year before I joined the staff of* Rolling Stone *as a Senior Writer. It was a good time for Clinton, as he was experiencing a hit single and album.*

HEADS TURN WHEN GEORGE CLINTON enters a room. Any room. At the moment, the people in the lobby of the Beverly Hills Hotel are staring at him.

A wedding reception is taking place at this plush hotel, and handsome men in tuxedos are escorting gorgeous young ladies in taffeta through the enormous lobby, with

George Clinton, San Francisco, 1979: "At our concerts there's a chant we do which goes, 'Think, it ain't illegal yet!'"

the curved pink walls, the art-deco couches, and the marble-topped tables. It is a lobby designed for legendary movie stars; there is nothing funky about this hotel. Except for George Clinton.

The 41-year-old mastermind behind Funkadelic, Parliament, Bootsy's Rubber Band, Zapp, the P-Funk All Stars, and so many other acts is wearing blue jeans, Nike running shoes, a black leather jacket, and a gray sweatshirt. He is taking gulps from a bottle of Beck's and giggling. It is the giggle of a man who is stoned: stoned on life, stoned on drugs. A religious man, if you will. And right there, on the front of the sweatshirt, printed in black, six-inch-high letters, is the gospel of George Clinton: FUNK!

A member of the hotel staff walks over and informs the man known to millions as Dr. Funkenstein that he'll have to do something with the bottle. Clinton laughs, tells the guy he doesn't even really like beer, and hides the bottle under his jacket. Of course, it could have been worse. When Clinton left his hotel room a few minutes earlier, an aide had to remind him to get rid of the joint hanging from his lips.

Here in the lobby, most people haven't noticed the bottle of beer. They are too busy eyeing the hair. The two-inch-wide mohawk. The luminous purple mohawk. And the rows of luminous purple cornrow braids a la Bo Derek. But George Clinton doesn't worry about what these people think of him. "Too many beautiful people in Los Angeles," he says. "That's why I couldn't stay in LA. 'Cause every time I see something I like, it snatches my head around." He laughs again. "I can't control it. Ain't no time for going to bed or getting up, walking down the street and just being a person. 'Cause everybody come here to be a star, and so everybody look especially good. Too much of a good thing in LA. So I had to move."

That may be why, when he is not on the road or in the recording studio or taking care of business, Clinton leads a reclusive life with his wife, Stephanie, on a farm outside Detroit that has no phone. There he hunts and fishes and plays video games and reads science-fiction novels and meditates and practices yoga and dreams up the strange concepts for his albums.

Clinton leaves the lobby and walks to his limo. A movie producer is getting out of a car parked directly in front of the limo. He stares at Clinton, shakes his head, smiles.

"You laugh," someone says to the movie producer, "but at the moment, he's got a number-one record."

Inside the limo, Clinton is laughing, too. He takes a sip of the Beck's and stretches out his legs. How does it feel to be back, he is asked. "I don't even know yet," he says with a grin.

AH, BUT HE KNOWS. And it feels good, mighty good to be back, to be out on the road again, playing to crowds of up to 20,000 fans, six nights a week. Feels oh so fine to be back on the charts with a hit single, "Atomic Dog," and a hit album, *Computer Games*. It feels very good indeed.

Clinton's comeback was quite unexpected. Even the fact that he got to make another record for a major label came as a surprise. For George Clinton had been in a bad way for the past two and a half years.

To appreciate just how bad things had become, however, one must first consider what the man had accomplished. At age 39, Clinton was the producer, writer, and brains behind a stable of bands that each went under a different name but actually included many of the same musicians and singers. At United Sound Studios in Detroit, Dr. Funkenstein would work around the clock with his crew of 30 or so musicians and singers, laying down tracks that would later surface on albums by Funkadelic and Parliament, the Horny Horns and Bootsy's Rubber Band, Zapp and Parlet and the Brides of Funkenstein.

Every record he produced has a distinctive George Clinton sound, yet none of them sounds the same. Some are indulgent psychedelic jams. Some feature raps recorded 10 years before rapping was in vogue. Some are hard-core James Brown funk chants. Some are Sly Stone-meets-the-Temptations vocal extravaganzas. Some sound like the Supremes spent a few nights with Frank Zappa's Mothers of Invention, and some sound like Stevie Wonder on acid.

By the end of 1980, Parliament, Funkadelic, and Bootsy's Rubber Band were all platinum acts, and the first Zapp album had gone gold. Clinton was on a roll. Having sold more than 10 million albums within five years, he truly was the king of a funk empire. He figured the party had only just begun. He had negotiated label deals with three major record companies: CBS would distribute Uncle Jam, Warner Bros. would handle Park Place, and Casablanca would take care of Choza Negra.

And then, like a house of cards, George Clinton's empire collapsed.

His road to ruin began when he filed three separate lawsuits for breach of contract (claiming a total of $100 million in damages) against Warner Bros., the label to which Funkadelic, Bootsy's Rubber Band, and Zapp were signed. One consequence of the lawsuits was Warner Bros.' decision not to distribute Clinton's Park Place label. Another was that Funkadelic became tied up in the courts. More trouble was brewing over at Casablanca. That company was sold to PolyGram, Clinton's Choza Negra label never materialized, and soon Parliament, like Funkadelic, was on ice. The final blow came when, according to Clinton, Zapp singer/songwriter Roger Troutman took his completed album to Warner Bros. CBS had advanced Clinton's company, Uncle Jam, $200,000 to produce Troutman's LP and when they didn't get the record, Uncle Jam joined Park Place and Choza Negra on the shelf.

As all these business headaches developed, Clinton was going broke. It was costing him more than $150,000 a week to keep his 88-man entourage of musicians, singers, and crew on the road. Without new hits to keep the fans coming and with royalties tied up in the courts, there was no money; personnel couldn't be paid; and debts accumulated. He was locked out of recording studios because of unpaid studio bills. No major label would deal with him.

It appeared that it was all over for Clinton. "He hit rock bottom," says Armen Boladian, an independent record-company president who has been a friend of Clinton's since the late Sixties, when he signed Funkadelic to his label, Westbound Records. "It was like a bad dream."

That's when drugs entered the picture. Not that drugs were foreign to George Clinton. He had smoked marijuana, dropped acid, popped Quaaludes, and snorted coke for years. But now he established a rather intense relationship with a more lethal chemical: freebase cocaine.

You may remember the newspaper reports: George Clinton and Sly Stone busted in LA for possession of narcotics. (The charges were eventually dropped.) Clinton vacillates when talking about his "lost weekend" of drug use. He denies that things got out of hand, but then he agrees that perhaps he was in over his head. "I got frustrated," he says. "I came to LA and spent three or four months in the Beverly Comstock Hotel and didn't have nothing to do but get high."

"I didn't look at it as no frustration; it was just something to do while I couldn't get any records out. But I wasn't going to feel frustrated 'cause that wouldn't have helped me get back at all. 'Cause then you would do drugs with another attitude. Then you do drugs to totally escape, and with freebasing, it makes it easy 'cause it takes all your time. I wasn't into it like that. I was into it just like I'm into any other drug—I liked it. I tell you, it could have worked out the other way, 'cause I think I took a chance. I was being rather cocky. I really was having a ball. I don't want anybody thinking I'm bragging that I had fun, but I did. I mean it got scary, but drugs are like that."

While Clinton was busy "having a ball," his business advisers and lawyers were trying to arrange a new record deal. It was not easy, but eventually Capitol Records signed him to a deal and, according to Clinton, advanced him around $300,000. Then the Warner Bros.' legal department called, claiming Clinton was signed to them. Clinton contended, however, that he wasn't signed to the label, even though Funkadelic was. (David Berman, vice-president of business affairs at Warner Bros, refused to comment when approached for his side of the story.)

In any case, Capitol was getting cold feet. "There were all sorts of problems dealing with claims from Warner Bros., claims from CBS, and an attachment from a former manager," says Mark Levinson, vice-president of business affairs for EMI America/Liberty Records. "At one point, we said, 'This has got to stop. What are we getting ourselves into?'"

According to Clinton and his business advisers, Nene Montes and Archie Ivy, Capitol wanted to cancel the deal. "Levinson actually said, 'Give me back my $300,000, and you can have your album,'" says Ivy. "And we said, 'We don't want the album back; we want it out.' We forced them to release it. He saw that if they didn't release it, they were going to eat $300,000."

"They were scared to death," says Clinton.

"We forced Capitol to make a funky million dollars," says Nene Montes.

SUCH "HUMPS," AS CLINTON calls them, have always been a part of a life that began on July 22, 1941, in Kannapolis, North Carolina (about 50 miles south of Winston-Salem). He was the first of nine children born to Julia Keaton, a poor woman who cleaned house and babysat to support her family. "It was very hard. Had to do a little bit of everything to make ends meet," she says, calling from a pay phone in Greensboro, North Carolina, where she now lives. "It really put a strain on mom."

In 1956, after his family had moved to Newark, New Jersey, 14-year-old George Clinton heard a group on the radio that changed his life. "When he heard Frankie Lymon [and the Teenagers], he knew that's what he wanted to do," says his mother.

Young George Clinton got a job running a barber shop by day and sang doo-wop with his buddies at night. "We processed hair," says Clinton. "I majored in making other [N-words] look cool. Doin' the superflys." He also sold drugs. "Yeah, that was part of survival. Weed. But everything was survival there. And after dealin' with all the jive on the street, I thought the record business was just an ill-equipped, simulated version of the same thing. So I said, 'why the fuck should I settle for a Cadillac and three or four bitches when that same concept works better with them big bitches, the corporations.'"

It was easier for Clinton and his buddies, who were calling themselves the Parliaments, to process hair and talk big than to make it big. But after recording some flops for ABC and cooling their heels at Motown, in 1967 they finally scored a hit, "(I Just Want to) Testify," for the small independent label Revilot.

Legal problems developed with Revilot, and the name Parliaments was tied up. So Clinton renamed his group Funkadelic and signed with another independent label, Westbound Records. But Funkadelic was something else. Clinton and his band had discovered LSD, and their music took on a very psychedelic glow. "Psychedelic music was kind of starting at that time," recalls Armen Boladian, then president of Westbound. "George loved that music, but thought there should be some good old funk connected to it. That's where the Funkadelic came in."

Early Funkadelic albums had ghoulish graphics and titles like *Maggot Brain* and *America Eats Its Young*. "It was wild onstage," says Boladian. "One would be dressed in an Arab costume, another would come out wearing a garment bag with the hangers sticking out of it, and another would have diapers on. If George didn't have his costume, he would take a sheet off the bed of the hotel, cut a hole in it, and pull it over his head, and put some paint on his face and go out there. Of course, he had nothing on under the sheet. It would just freak everybody out."

Funkadelic was a cult item, but in the early Seventies, Clinton reactivated the Parliaments as Parliament. The sound of that group, which played up horns and vocals and played down the guitars and the weirdness, clicked. Clinton soon had a platinum act on his hands.

From 1975 until 1980, Clinton proceeded to become one of the most powerful forces in contemporary Black music, influencing everyone from Earth, Wind and Fire to Rick James. Along the way, he attempted to revive the career of Sly Stone (who appeared on several records) and held a joint congress of funk when he brought James Brown, Sly Stone, Bootsy Collins, and himself together. Tracks were cut, including a song called "Go for Your Funk," but nothing has been released from those sessions. There were tense moments when the foursome got together. "George started cussing in front of his old lady, and James didn't like that," recalls Bootsy Collins. "But we laughed that off."

Now, with a hit record on the charts, George Clinton is ready to rebuild his empire. CBS is once again talking about distributing Uncle Jam, and a single, "Generator Pop," by the P-Funk All Stars on Hump/CBS is due soon. Clinton won the rights to the Funkadelic name and is talking about new Funkadelic and Parliament albums. He will probably coproduce Bootsy Collins' next album. Then there's the next George Clinton album to think about.

As Clinton said two years ago, when dark clouds were overhead: "They said the empire was falling; I say the empire strikes back."

*Rolling Stone*, June 23, 1983

# RICK JAMES: SEX, STREET SMARTS, & SUCCESS

**Street songs from the ghetto to sweet songs in the limo—Rick James is livin' the life he's always dreamed of.**

*The second time I did coke, Rick James was freebasing with Sly Stone. The first time was in college, sophomore year, when I bought what may or may not have been coke from The Dealer, this tall, lean cat out of a Steely Dan song, maybe "Kid Charlemagne," who knew I knew nothing about coke and could have sold me any white powder and what did I know. When I snorted it nothing happened. That second time, I was a Contributing Editor (aka a freelance writer who frequently contributes stories to a publication) at* Rolling Stone. *It was in 1982, early evening, when I arrived at the Record Plant, a recording studio in Sausalito where James was living while he recorded the follow-up to his smash hit album,* Street Songs *(which included "Super Freak"). I was there to profile James for a story that would run right as that follow-up,* Thrownin' Down, *was released. I was supposed to hang out with him and interview him at length for the first major story on Rick for* Rolling Stone. *Only when I got there I was told, nicely, that he was indisposed with Sly Stone. Rick knew me. I had interviewed him at least twice, maybe three times already for other stories, stories that he liked enough that he kept letting me come back. I'd watched him work in the studio on two occasions, even bringing my five-year-old son along once. One of his aides told me he knew I was waiting, and he'd be able to talk to me pretty soon. Only pretty soon dragged to an hour, and then two and then the aide appeared with a baggie of white power for me, courtesy of Rick, who was really sorry, but he was still busy with Sly. Eventually Sly split (I didn't meet him) and at some time after 2 a.m. I was ushered into the room Rick was living out of while recording and our interview began. The first story here is the one I wrote for* Rolling Stone *after spending a couple days with Rick; it is Rick James at the peak of his success. A lot of what he tells me is true, but he concealed his freebase coke habit from me and other darker aspects of his life. The second is an interview I did for* Vibe *magazine with Rick; it took place in early 1994 over the course of multiple visits to LA County Jail, where he was incarcerated at the time for numerous crimes, including allegedly torturing a woman with a hot knife and forcing her to have sex with him and his fiancée. You could say this was a low point for Rick. Because of the first story, and others I had written about Rick, he trusted me, which is how I came to talk to him in jail. He served two years in prison and was released in August 1996. Eight years later, August 6, 2004, Rick James died of a heart attack; he was 56. He had nine drugs in his body at the time of death according to a coroner's report, including coke, Xanax, Valium, and speed.*

SAUSALITO, CALIFORNIA—RICK JAMES LIES sleeping on the plush burgundy velvet seat in the back of the long black limousine. It has been 48 hours since he last slept. Nonstop work on his new album, *Thrown' Down*, and a night spent partying and scheming with Sly Stone have finally taken their toll.

Rick James, 1982: "You see, I have to buy marijuana. I don't buy ounces, I buy pounds." Photo by © Chester Simpson / Rock-N-RollPhotos.com

A cassette of Brahms' Concerto no. 1 in D Minor, one of James' favorite pieces of music, fills the rear of the limo—a lullaby for a superstar. Rick James can afford to sleep easy. He is now the most popular Black rock & roll star in the world. His last album has sold more than 4 million copies. He is a millionaire many times over. Yes, life has been good to Rick James recently. Let him sleep.

THERE WAS SOMETHING WRONG with the little Black boy. James Ambrose Johnson Jr. was nervous, hyper, irritable. He couldn't seem to settle down. It was as if something were constantly bothering him. *Disruptive* was one of the words his mom used to describe him. *Mischievous* was another, and it was an accurate description of a boy who was always playing tricks on his three brothers and four sisters. Like the time he poured itching powder down his baby sister's back. Or the time he slipped a pearl from his mother's necklace into his brother Roy's ear and his mom had to rush Roy to the hospital to have it removed. Then there were those damned animals. One time he put a hamster in his brother's bed; on another occasion, his mom found the bathtub in their Buffalo, New York, home full of stray dogs.

Mom thought he was crazy. How else to account for this precocious kid who would strut around the house like Superfly Jr., yapping about how he was going to be a star? "I'm going to be rich and famous and real big one of these days," James would say. "I'm going to have a big house and set you out in fur coats."

"What you talkin' about?" his mom would reply. "Get away!"

When James didn't seem to be coming to his senses, she sent him to several psychiatrists. But they all told her the same thing: Betty Gladden's wild son was "bright and brilliant." There was something inside of him that he had to do; he just didn't know what it was yet.

This internal turmoil began to surface in more serious, disturbing ways. At age 13, James Johnson started making a habit of stealing Chevies. "Guy's got to have some fun," he would say. "I need a car. I have women on the other side of town. I *have* to see them. I need to have a car. Just for four hours."

The police in Buffalo didn't see it that way. First, they threw him in juvenile hall, and then they put him in jail for seven months. "I was a serious juvenile delinquent," he says today. "I perfected juvenile delinquency. I'm not ashamed of it."

When he wasn't in jail, stealing cars or hustling "hot chicks," James Johnson used to hang out with his gang on the corner of Jefferson and East Ferry streets. They would sing Temptations songs in five- and six-part harmony, and between songs they would try to convince one another that the future held more for them than a life in the ghetto.

"We used to do some serious fantasizing," says Johnson. "It was always the same things. Lots of cars, lots of clothes, lots of women. Being recognized all over the place. Private planes, Learjets. *Tons of women*. All that bullshit that never comes true. *But this time it did.*"

"YOU GOT TO HAVE THE MONEY," says James Johnson, who is known today as Rick James. "*I* got to have it. You see, I *have* to buy marijuana. I don't buy ounces, I buy pounds. I buy clothes. I don't buy one pair of shoes; I buy 30 or 40 pairs. I don't buy one shirt; I buy 15 or 20. That's just the way I am. I'm very extravagant." He's talking seriously now; Rick James is serious about his lifestyle. "I ain't playin'" is how he puts it.

James is stretched out across his double bed in a small room within the Record Plant, a Sausalito recording studio that has been his home for the past four months. A little over a year ago, James wrapped up an album called *Street Songs* at this same studio. The LP hit the number-three position on the pop charts, contained the two hit singles "Give It to Me Baby" and "Super Freak" and held the number-one position on the soul charts for some 20 weeks. ("Super Freak" reached number 16 on *Billboard*'s Hot 100 and was certified Gold.)

James scratches his crotch, then takes a hit from a joint of sinsemilla. He's wearing a pair of baggy green-and-brown camouflage pants and no shirt. His black cornrow braids hang down past his shoulders, a trademark as instantly recognizable as Kiss' makeup or Alice Cooper's ghoulish mug once were. James takes a sip from a bottle of Beck's, then licks his full lips.

Now he's talking about why the cars and the houses and the clothes and all the things that he spends his millions on matter. "What does it matter?" James asks, screwing up his face for a second. "I don't know. I don't have one car! I have five cars. I can't drive five cars, but I like every one of them. And I wanted every one of them. I wanted a house with a swimming pool. I mean, these things I *wanted*. Always wanted! I wanted a whole fucking closet of fucking clothes. I got to be sharp. *Got to be sharp*."

*Sharp* is not the word. Try *bad*. Rick James is the baddest-looking dude in rock & roll, and don't try to tell him otherwise. Onstage, he shows up in a flash of lights and explosions and dry ice. That larger-than-life head of cornrow braids, dusted with sparkling silver and gold glitter, seems to have a luminosity all its own. His body is sheathed in skintight spandex covered with sequins. A giant serpent wraps itself around his thigh and snakes between his legs, past the bulge at his crotch, like a deadly phallus. And don't forget the knee-high space boots. James is in constant motion, rapping to his fans about love and sex between every song. For "Mary Jane," his tribute to the joys of smoking weed, two towering, fabricated joints are brought onto the stage as Rick lights up a real one and takes a few exaggerated hits.

Offstage, he will tell you that "Rick James" is just an act, a character he invented one night in Buffalo when he was living in his mom's house on Rich Street (which the city of Buffalo has renamed Rick James Street). He'll tell you there's a James Johnson and a Rick James, and that the two are completely separate; that James Johnson is really a quiet guy who likes to ride horses at his ranch near Buffalo and write songs and listen to classical music. All of which is true, of course, and all of which is also beside the point. For what's also true is that Rick James and James Johnson have merged, or maybe they were always two sides of a man who can't be contained by a one-dimensional image.

Tonight, as he lies on the bed smoking his joint, munching on popcorn prepared by one of his bodyguards, sipping beer, rapping nonstop about everything from drugs to sex to his troubled childhood, Rick James *and* James Johnson are both talking to me.

"What about drugs?" I ask.

He laughs. "What about them?"

There was a time, after his first wave of success, when Rick James had gone clean over the edge, ending up in a hospital nearly dying of hepatitis. "How do you keep it in control now?" I ask.

"There's something I want greater than drugs," says James. "Usually, when people lose control to drugs, it's because that is the greater thing to them. And they can't deal with it. Entertainers are sensitive people, overly sensitive. And when you become sensitive and susceptible to a lot of the shit around you, it becomes easy to want to take yourself out of it.

"You find that all the abundance of material wealth you've acquired really doesn't mean much. In your heart you really know that so much is superficial and so much is bullshit, and it's a heavy reality to deal with. There are only two things you can do: rise above it and treat the business you're in like a business, or fall below it and take your life with drugs or a gun to your head, which is a very easy, simple way to do it. But drugs are very easy for me to deal with. I went through my little drug flip-out trip and decided that my life and this career the creator has given me are more important. I enjoy a snort or two with friends. A nice joint. But I don't overindulge in anything anymore."

SOME PEOPLE THINK RICK JAMES is only in it for the money. It's an idea that he generally doesn't do much to contradict. On several occasions he's told me that Rick James is "strictly business."

But Rick James isn't strictly business at all, which is something that he'll rarely admit, but that his friends and business associates will tell you.

"Well, I think he might *think* that's true, but I don't think it is. No one can do what he does as well as he does it strictly for money," says Berry Gordy Jr., the founder of Motown Records. "If he were strictly in it for the money, he would not be as good as he is. Sure, he wants to make a lot of money, like all of us do. Money is a measure of success in our society. But underneath it all, Rick is a real pussycat. He's one of the most wonderful, soulful people you would ever want to meet."

James' last album, *Street Songs*, was the most powerful record by a Black artist since Stevie Wonder's *Songs in the Key of Life*. It's a soul opera of sorts about life in the ghetto. The LP begins late one night when a drunken Romeo rolls into bed and tries to get his woman to put out ("Give It to Me Baby"), then moves to a flashback of this Romeo's youth on the street ("Ghetto Life"), cuts to a tender ballad that conveys the intimacy and intensity of making love ("Make Love to Me"), and finally hits the street again just as a cop has killed an innocent man ("Mr. Policeman"). That's just side one, but you get the idea.

Rick James' great contribution to our culture is to have painted this big, dramatic, vivid picture of a world that few whites know anything about. And for Blacks, James' songs must surely be powerful and cathartic.

"What makes him so popular is that he's from the street," says Gordy. "It's about the street, it's about life, it's about what people are feeling. There is only one Rick James. He's an original."

His mother agrees: "His songs are him. I mean 'Ghetto Life' is his life. That's the soul life, 'cause we lived in the ghetto. And he did hang out around the corner with the boys. That's his life."

At about 5 a.m., after a day and a night in the studio without sleep, followed by hours and hours of conversation, Rick James finally admits just how personal his music is: "I am the music I make."

For James Johnson, it all started in Buffalo, New York, on February 1, 1952. Right from the start, he wanted to get out of the ghetto—"probably from the time I came out of the womb," he says, his eyes flashing. "My mother said I was the hardest birth she had. I did not want to come out. It was like I didn't want to come here. But now that I'm here, look out!"

Betty Gladden worked several jobs, the most profitable of which was running numbers. She was able to provide a lower-middle-class childhood for James and his brothers and sisters. "We were never really poor, but we grew up in poor surroundings," recalls James. "The ghetto is a poor state of mind, no matter how much money you have or what you're doing. You're still not living in a house with grass, the way you want to live, where your mind is going to be relaxed. The crazy thing about the ghetto is that there's something that really seems to hold you there. Makes you kind of lazy and dumb and lackadaisical. Your motivation plug is kind of out."

But James Johnson was always motivated. He says it was the image of his dad—who was separated from his mother when the boy was only three—that pushed him toward a career in entertainment. "I was too lazy to work," James says. "Music was always going on around me. I've always been kind of a ham, kind of an entertainer. It was easier than working. I used to watch my father come home real tired from the Chevy plant with these big boots on, and he was real dirty. Every day he did this, and it looked really boring and like a real drag. So I said, 'What else is happening?' And I decided music was what was happening."

When he was 15, James ran away from home to join the US Naval Reserve. He says he had to escape the dominance of his mother, who used to whip the kids for the slightest infraction. He lied about his age and got a friend to forge his mom's signature so he could enter the navy.

But James Johnson didn't take to the navy, and when they started talking about shipping him off to Vietnam, he went AWOL. James spent some time in Greenwich Village, where he sussed out the folk rock of the Lovin' Spoonful, then headed for Canada, where he discovered he could make a living playing music in the Toronto clubs. It was there in the late Sixties that James put together a rock & roll band that included future members of Steppenwolf and the Buffalo Springfield. Bruce Palmer, who played bass, and a longhaired singer-songwriter-guitarist named Neil Young were both in Rick's band, the Mynah Birds. "Neil and I got this little apartment and stayed together and wrote a lot of great songs together," says James. "We were happy. Only thing I worried about was stopping Neil from having an epileptic fit. And us catching VD from all the chicks we were messing around with. We didn't worry about being rich. We thought we were going to make it."

JAMES TOOK THE MYNAH BIRDS to Detroit, where they signed with Motown Records and recorded an album that was never released (in 2012 a single with two songs, "It's My Time" and "Go on and Cry," was released). The problem was that James was still on the lam from the US Navy. Motown executives convinced him to turn himself in, and he spent nearly a year in a government detention center in Connecticut. "That's when I think he got deeply into his music," says Betty Gladden. "The severity of the punishment really did him in. After that, I didn't have any more problems with him."

When he got out, James went to work for Motown as a staff writer and producer. Though he didn't write or produce any hits, he took advantage of the opportunity to learn from some of the great hit-makers of the day, Norman Whitfield and Holland-Dozier-Holland. But he felt his talents weren't appreciated, and eventually he left Motown.

James spent several years traveling in Europe and South America before returning to Buffalo, and in 1976, he began working on the material that would appear on his debut album. "I had a baby grand piano, and he'd get up in the middle of the night," says his mom. "I remember it well, because I would come home and want to get some rest, and he would be down at the piano, three or four o'clock in the morning, getting this album together."

Motown signed Rick, and his first single, "You and I," and the LP, *Come Get It,* both sold over a million copies. James' next two albums, *Bustin' Out of L Seven* and *Fire It Up,* were both successful, selling, respectively, a million copies and more than a million. But his fourth album, *Garden of Love,* a collection of mellow ballads, sold poorly.

"After *Garden of Love,* I thought I was through," says James. "Really. I didn't get in this business to be number two. Number one is what's happening. Always!"

So Rick James took a short vacation. When he returned to the studio, he was ready to try it again. "Everybody kept telling me I should go back to my roots. So I said fuck it, wrote about ghetto life and growing up and decided to call the album *Street Songs.*

"My attitude was that it was going to be the biggest album I ever had or it was going to be the worst album I ever had. Fortunately, it was the biggest."

THE SUNLIGHT THAT FALLS across Rick James' body is muted by the tinted glass of the limousine we're riding in. Rick is asleep as the vehicle heads toward the San Francisco airport. His next album, *Throwin' Down,* is finished, and he's heading out to LA to play it for Berry Gordy. Already, the single, "Dance wit' Me," is a hit in New York.

But now, as Brahms fills the limo, Rick is sleeping. His eyes are covered by powder-blue sleep shades, and he looks like a star, royalty. He is wearing a white-and-red velour shirt, white cotton slacks, red plastic Fiorucci shoes, and a mess of gold rings and bracelets studded with diamonds. One of the rings is in the shape of a heart with wings; Rick's name is etched across the center of that gold heart.

Rick James has come about as far from the ghetto as is possible. And now he is sleeping. And there is a smile on his face.

*Rolling Stone,* June 1982

# RICK JAMES: THE UNTOLD STORY

**While Rick James was ruling the charts with hits like "Super Freak" and "Give It to Me Baby," he was descending into the drug addiction that led to his arrest last year. From behind bars, James tells Michael Goldberg how he fell so far so fast, why he hates Prince, and how being arrested may have saved his life.**

LOS ANGELES, CALIFORNIA—THE FIRST TIME I went to LA County Jail to visit Rick James, I didn't recognize him. I walked along a corridor past prisoner after prisoner, each locked into a narrow booth with a Plexiglas window and a phone, each looking very much like the others in their drab prison garb. I had just passed booth number six when I noticed a prisoner frantically waving to me through the glass.

It was Rick James, all right. He had shaved off his signature braids and put on a few pounds since I'd seen him last, in the mid-'80s. This past September, James was convicted on three counts: assaulting and imprisoning a woman in November 1992 at an expensive West Hollywood hotel and furnishing cocaine to a second woman in July 1991. The jury deadlocked or acquitted James on nine other charges, including his alleged torture of the second woman with a hot knife and forcing her to have sex with both his fiancée, Tanya Anne Hijazi, and him.

At his peak in the late '70s and early '80s, James built on such influences as James Brown, Sly Stone, and, naturally, Motown (where, as a teenager, he had worked as a staff writer), and concocted a sound of his own, a killer punk funk blend. His image—long, jet-black braids, skintight spandex, and knee-high boots, a joint in hand, scantily dressed women at his side—remains unforgettable.

But as the 42-year-old James now freely admits, throughout the '70s, '80s, and early '90s, he was a drug addict. By the mid-1980s his star was rapidly fading. In the months leading up to his first arrest in August 1991, he became a recluse, seldom emerging from a trash-strewn bedroom filled with smoke from around-the-clock freebasing.

After his arrest, I met with James on four separate occasions. Each visit involved a three- to four-hour wait in a large, crowded visitors' area. Eventually, James' name would be called over a loudspeaker, and we would talk for about 30 minutes. He'd speak excitedly about a multi-CD career retrospective due from Motown this spring, and he remained hopeful that his jail time would be short. Then the phone would go dead, and the guards would handcuff and shackle him before leading him back to his cell.

In January, his attorney worked out a deal with the LA County district attorney's office that placed James in rehab, not prison, after allegations of misconduct during the trial surfaced. The *LA Times* reported that an investigator for the DA's office had allegedly provided heroin to a key witness and that an internal investigation had begun. On January 21 the court sent James to the California Rehabilitation Center in Norco. If James successfully completes the rehab program, he could be out by September.

During the trial, and throughout our interviews, James admitted to having shared drugs with the two women but vehemently denied all other charges. "A lot of lies went on in this case," he said during one of our jailhouse conversations. "A lot of girls told a lot of lies."

**Michael Goldberg:** Following your arrest, you wrote and recorded a song called "Down by Law," which begins: "I've got no reason in this cloudy room / I've got no reason to live." As you sit here today in jail, do you still feel the way you did when you wrote that?

**Rick James:** No. But at the time that I wrote it, that's the way I was feeling. When you're sitting there and you got a pipe in your hand—you're smoking drugs, you're doing dope—there isn't much reason to be in that room other than the fact that you're getting high. Those were my thoughts, looking around at myself. Not caring about living, spending $6,000 to $7,000 a week on cocaine. The loneliness setting in and the viciousness.

**Goldberg:** In revoking your bail after you were convicted, the judge said, "I'm concerned about the community's safety. I think he's a danger." Is Rick James a danger to the community?

**James:** If Rick James was getting high as he was getting before, that might be true. Other than that, I don't think I'm any danger to the community. But I love the fact that my addiction is now restricted. I would like to be out. But I have to be out with this addiction under control. 'Cause, man, I feel whole now. I'm back to Rick now. The shit is all out of me. The last thing I want to do is get high again, but the first thing I want to do is get high again. *[Laughs]* It's like that song I sang on by the Lemonheads ("Rick James Style"). It goes, "I don't wanna get high, but I don't wanna not get high." When I heard that, I was so excited about singing on it because the hypocrisy and denial is so wonderful.

**Goldberg:** The district attorney who prosecuted you described you as a "sadistic animal." Is Rick James a sadistic animal?

**James:** I think of myself as a sadistic animal as much as I think of Peter Pan as a serial killer or Rev. Martin Luther King as a Ku Klux Klansman. But he's doing his job. His job is to make me look as bad as he can, and he's done a good job of that.

**Goldberg:** What's jail been like?

**James:** I'm in a six-foot-by-eight-foot cell with mice and rats and roaches and criminals 23 hours a day. See, the section where I am is the protective custody section. A lot of the people in there are in for 187s, murders. A lot of child molesters who have killed children. Rapists and bank robbers. I was next to Lyle and Erik Menendez for a while. Found them to be nice guys—above and beyond what they're charged with.

I relate to my fellow inmates as brothers. We talk about what brought us here, the things we've left behind and want to leave behind and change. Sometimes it's a lot of fun. The guys I'm around seem like nice guys who got caught in weird circumstances. I believe in Innocent until Proven Guilty. But that's not the way it is. I was a guilty man as soon as I walked into the courtroom. My thing was that I had to prove I was not as guilty as they said I was.

**Goldberg:** Back in 1982, while you were enjoying the success of *Street Songs* and "Super Freak," we spent some time together. On one occasion, I remember you were up all night in a room at the Record Plant arguing with Sly Stone. All night you were trying to convince him . . .

**James:** To stop getting high. Yeah, I remember that. I was telling Sly that getting into the pipe was the reason for his demise. I tried to tell him, "That fucking cocaine, man, has darkened your senses. You're not making the music that you used to make. And it's all because smoking that pipe has become your main thing."

**Goldberg:** He wasn't buying what you were saying.

**James:** No. How am I going to talk somebody into it? I'm sitting there smoking! I'm giving it to him; he's smoking. And I'm saying, "Yo, Sly! I think you're a genius, and I think you're incredible and an innovator, and here you are freebasing your whole life away." I was a big hypocrite, and I didn't even know it. If I could apologize to Sly, I would. Same things I said to him, I heard from so many people who loved and cared for me. And it went in one ear and came out the other.

**Goldberg:** When I heard you were doing base, I couldn't understand it. You used to be really down on freebase and people who did that.

**James:** Yeah. I used to throw people out of my house, man. I never permitted that shit around me.

**Goldberg:** So how'd you get started?

**James:** It was a freak accident. It happened in 1981. All I was doing then was snorting. But no matter whether you shoot it up your ass, whether you inject it, or you snort it, a drug's a drug. I was in a hotel room in Chicago. I had these two chicks with me. I was almost in the middle of doing some sex and shit when I decided I wanted to find my friend.

So I went looking for my friend, and he was in a room with some members of the Blackstone Rangers. And they had this big suitcase full of paraphernalia and rocks and all kinds of pipes. They asked me if I'd done it before. I told them the truth, that I hadn't. They immediately started closing the case back up. So I lied. I told them I was kidding, that I had done it. So they said, "Good, 'cause if you hadn't, we weren't going to be the ones to turn you on for the first time."

In 1981 I took the first hit. And then, next thing I know, during the *Street Songs* tour, I had a guy traveling with me who I hired just to cook it up for me. And I was gone then.

I went from spending $1,000 a week on coke for snorting, to $300,000 to $400,000 a year. That quick, that fast.

**Goldberg:** Did you feel that you were immune, even though you'd seen what freebasing did to someone like Sly?

**James:** In my insane way of thinking, I thought that Rick James could never get hooked. I didn't realize I was an addict, and if I had, I wouldn't have given a fuck anyway. All I knew was I had to have it. I had to wake up in the morning and stick cocaine in my nose to function. I had to go to a restaurant and be the big shot and pull this Rick James thing off, pull this image off. And this image was a coke-snorting, reefer-smoking sex maniac.

**Goldberg:** How did things go so wrong?

**James:** In the late '80s, my mother started to die from cancer. She passed in '91, but those two years before '91 were when things started to really get dark. When she starred to die, I was living in the house I bought from Mickey Rooney. It was a fabulous home. Had a rose garden, gazebo, Olympic-size pool outside, big brick fireplaces, sunken living room, wood-beam ceilings. It was a beautiful place. And I never appreciated it. It took me four months before I even realized I had a rose garden outside the house, that's how out I was.

I spent most of my time in the bedroom with the door closed. Those were the dark days. Once I moved up to that house, I started associating myself with street people, people who were out to get me, people who I *knew* were out to get me. It wasn't paranoia; it was a fact. And I didn't give a fuck.

My friend Eddie Murphy and actor friends and musician friends of mine would come up to that house, and then they would never come back. Because they saw the kind of people I was associating with: hustlers, dope dealers, crack dealers, thieves, pimps, prostitutes, killers, gangbangers. It was like a den of thieves was around me. I kept myself involved with the lowest. Because I felt low and I felt I was in a depraved state, so I might as well keep depraved people around. The darkness started to get sadistic, depraved, ugly.

**Goldberg:** Did the drugs make you crazy?

**James:** Yeah. It's like looking Satan in the face. For me to be up 10 days or 12 days getting high was nothing unusual. You start losing your senses. You start losing your balance. You start losing your insight. I mean seven, eight days smoking dope on a continuous basis! Satan was really pulling on me; the darkness was pulling on me, man. I consider freebasing to be sucking on the devil's dick.

**Goldberg:** It became this downward spiral . . .

**James:** Yes. The last time I saw my mother before she went into a coma, she came up to that house. She was a very magical, very spiritual woman. And she knew. She told me I was going to either go to jail or die in that house.

**Goldberg:** When you look at Black music today, what influence do you see that you've had?

**James:** I see a lot. A lot of stuff that me and George Clinton are responsible for, in terms of song structure, bass lines, how they texture things. Their harmonies. And the production. Writing *Street Songs*, I think I was the first one to really talk about life on the street. There was nobody else talking about pimps and hoes, cops shooting people and shit.

**Goldberg:** What do you think of gangsta rap?

**James:** I don't like it. Ice Cube's a millionaire, and he's talking about gangbanging and bullshit. To me, it doesn't make sense. It's silly and it's stupid. And I think eventually that shit is going to change. There are going to be some rappers who are going to write about real relevant shit and positive shit other than going out and shooting cops or going out and getting pussy and drinking a 40-ounce and gangbanging.

**Goldberg:** Are you disappointed that some of your celebrity friends like Eddie Murphy and Arsenio haven't spoken out on your behalf?

**James:** I'm very disappointed. They're protecting their own rich asses. I'm mad more at the Black stars than the white ones. I've had more white people come on my behalf. In times of trouble, man, that's when Black people need Black people to stand up for them. Some of my rich, so-called good friends could have come and offered some assistance, but they didn't. All they did was run. 'Cause they didn't want to have their little careers tainted with the fact that they knew me, when everyone in the world knows they know me anyway. So they can all kiss my ass.

**Goldberg:** Teena Marie came to visit you.

**James:** Yes, she did. And Teena Marie was in court too. That's what I'm saying. I had more white people defend me than Blacks. Eddie didn't come up there. Arsenio didn't come up there. M.C. Hammer didn't come up. None of the people that used my music . . .

**Goldberg:** Speaking of people who used your music, how did you feel about Hammer using "Super Freak" for "U Can't Touch This"?

**James:** I felt okay about it because I got paid. But I don't consider M.C. Hammer to have a lot of integrity. Did you see him in court? Did you see him say anything to try and help me? It was my song. He won a Grammy award for it. He still hasn't sent me one. But I never looked at M.C. Hammer like any top-flight artist. M.C. Hammer is a passing nothing. He's not even worth my talking about.

**Goldberg:** What about Prince? Haven't you had some trouble with him?

**James:** He was very disrespectful to my mother at a party after the American Music Awards. She asked for his autograph, and he kind of looked at her and ran away and stuff like that. But he was also disrespectful to the Mary Jane Girls when we did the Universal Amphitheatre. He had his bodyguard carry him around while the girls were onstage, trying to get attention. He's a little, arrogant, snooty-nosed motherfucker. I think he's a brilliant musician and a great composer, but as a person he needs a good ass kickin'. I mean, he could do with a can of "Get Right." He could use a can of "Act Right." I don't have any love for Prince. Prince is one of those kinds of Blacks who don't really want to be Black and don't want to be a man. He's one of those confused little motherfuckers, and I really don't have any time for that in my life.

**Goldberg:** Your mother-in-law-to-be told me she thinks that you're very insecure and that you feel you don't really deserve all the fame and money.

**James:** I think that has a lot of validity. When I was growing up, I never felt like a whole person. I always thought there was something mentally wrong with me. I ran away from home a lot as a kid, looking for something. But I didn't know what it was. There was something missing inside of me, I felt. I didn't feel I was 100 percent human.

**Goldberg:** Was that partially due to your not having a father around?

**James:** Of course, not having a father had a lot to do with it. Being raised by a mother who had to work two jobs all her life had a lot to do with it. Being Black and born in the ghetto and not thinking that you can get out. That's what most of us go through. Most Black people born in the United States today have a psychological defect. We're born into something that's not what we perceive life to be.

We're born in fucking ghettos of poverty, drugs, pimps, gangsters, prostitutes, guns. That is what you call mental illness. So from jump street, Black people are mental patients in the hospital of fucking life. A lot of Blacks don't understand this. So I'm here to tell them: Look at it like it's a mental hospital. And like in any hospital, the first thing you have to do is get well. And to get well, we have to say we are somebody, we are relevant to life, we can get out of here, and we don't have to pick up guns and kill people and pimp our sisters. We don't have to gangbang. And we can get out.

**Goldberg:** During the trial you repeatedly and adamantly stated that, with the exception of sharing your drugs with people who were already drug users, you did none of the things you were accused of.

**James:** I stand by what I said at the trial. I have been railroaded and subjected to some shit that I brought on myself by just having the wrong people around me. But it's deeper still, and this gets really political within the office of the district attorney. Pretty soon, all that's going to come out. There's a lot of lies and fabrication going on.

People have been after me to put me behind bars for a long time. Because I'm Black, because I'm who I am, I say what I say. Whites don't like that, and they never have. They never wanted to accept an intelligent Black man with any kind of power whatsoever. Never. They never have and they never will. Especially when the Black man can have it on his terms, not their terms. And he's not an ass-kissin' boy.

And I did a lot of having a good time. Green women, white women, Brown women, Black women. It didn't make any difference. I love women. I got high. I rode in Learjets. I associated with presidents and queens, pimps and hoes. I spoke what was on my mind and had a great time. There's a lot of people in the bureaucracy who didn't like that. And they followed my behavior patterns for a long time. Finally, they got a chance to use it all against me, and they did it very well. But it's all backfiring in their face, pray to God. And I'm excited about that. It will all come out in the wash.

**Goldberg:** You told me the other day that ending up in jail may just be one of the best things that's happened to you.

**James:** It stopped me from doing drugs. It gave me a good chance to see who my friends are. It gave me a chance to get clear—my consciousness. It gave me a chance for my eyes to finally see. It gave me a chance to rest, to get my thoughts together. It gave me a chance to eat three meals a day, get healthy again. It gave me a chance to get closer to God. It gave me a chance to thank the Lord for each and every precious day that I live, incarcerated or free. That if I have another day on this planet, that I owe it to God and not to man.

It gave me a chance to see all the beauty that I've missed. It gave me a chance to finally look at my life for what it can be and not what it was. It gave me a chance to see that I could love again, that I could love me again. That I wasn't a hopeless case, and I wasn't a has-been and I'm not just a nobody. I'm a child of God and I'm a child of this universe and there's still a lot of love in me and I'm not cold-blooded and I'm not a maniacal killer and I'm not a Black Marquis de Sade. I'm James Johnson, also known as Rick James, who happened to let his life run amok because of a fucking pipe and a rock of cocaine.

Every day that I'm here, man, I get stronger and I get stronger and I get stronger. I think God has something planned for me. This isn't something I have to worry about for today or tomorrow. I think it's down the road. Right now, he just wants to keep me living, and keep me getting back to me.

*Vibe*, April 1994

# THE LAST DAYS OF DENNIS WILSON

**He was the wild one. He could never get enough of anything: drugs, women, or booze. But in the end, he had nothing.**

*The Beach Boys did not want me writing a story about them. They made that clear when I attempted to set up interviews with the band members, and when I drove up to Lake Tahoe, California, in January 1983, to watch one of their shows. They didn't want a story and they weren't cooperating. No access, no story. The Beach Boys were a major band for me. As a kid I remember lying in bed at night, my small transistor radio on, listening to "Fun, Fun, Fun." And when I was 18, after I broke up with my first serious girlfriend, I listened over and over to "Caroline, No." It perfectly captured the heartbreak I felt. When Dennis Wilson drowned in December 1983, Beach Boys management still wouldn't cooperate. Whatever. I interviewed dozens of the Beach Boys' friends, associates, current and former business partners to report my Dennis Wilson story. Six years later, shortly before the release of Brian Wilson's first solo album, I got full cooperation from Wilson's people, as well as Warner Bros. Records, when I reported on the precarious state of Brian Wilson in 1988. I'm proud of both of these stories, which were unique at the time they were first published and continue to provide insight into the lives of two key members of an important rock band that in addition to recording dozens of amazing hits, under the guidance of Brian Wilson recorded one of the greatest albums ever,* Pet Sounds.

SANTA MONICA, CALIFORNIA—IT WAS ALMOST midnight on Christmas 1983, and Dennis Wilson's head was a bloody mess. The 39-year-old Beach Boy had been beaten up by a male friend of his estranged wife—19-year-old Shawn Love Wilson—at the Santa Monica Bay Inn. Wilson had checked himself out of the detoxification unit at a local hospital and had been drinking in the area when he ran into Shawn's friend, with whom he picked a fight. He lost that fight.

Several hours later, drunk and puffing on a cigarette, his face a ghastly gray, Wilson was vowing revenge outside St. John's Hospital and Health Center in Santa Monica. "I just want to go down there and kick his ass," said Wilson in a gruff croak. "Call the cops. Close the place [the Santa Monica Bay Inn] down. Bust everyone." Steve Goldberg, a close friend who had brought Dennis to the hospital, did his best to calm him down.

Inside the hospital, Chris Clark, another buddy of Wilson's, was on the phone, trying to convince Dr. Michael Gales to readmit Wilson, an alcoholic and drug abuser, to the hospital's detox unit, from which the Beach Boy had checked out earlier. But Gales didn't want to have anything to do with Dennis Wilson.

"He's just too much trouble," Gales allegedly told Chris Clark.

"He may die, you know," Chris Clark told Gales.

"He might have to," the doctor allegedly replied.

Three days later, on December 28, Dennis Carl Wilson was dead, his body pulled out of the cold, murky water of nearby Marina del Rey. Toxicological tests showed Wilson's blood alcohol level to be 0.26 at the time of death—more than twice the legal limit for driving. A week after his death, Dennis Wilson's ashes were sprinkled into the Pacific.

"DENNIS WILSON WAS THE ESSENCE, the spirit of the Beach Boys," recalled Fred Vail, a longtime business associate of the band. "We used to think of him as the Steve McQueen or James Dean of the group."

For one thing, Dennis was the only Beach Boy who knew how to surf. He was also the band's sex symbol. But while he was breaking hearts at their live performances, he wasn't always playing on the records.

By the time the Beach Boys' fifth hit single, "Little Deuce Coupe," was released in 1963, Dennis was frequently being replaced in the studio by session drummer Hal Blaine.

It apparently didn't bother Dennis that Blaine was drumming on the Beach Boys' records. "I think as soon as the checks started rolling in, Dennis had other things," says Blaine. "He was buying things; he was appreciating his motorcycling and hobbies and so forth. When you're 16 years old and you're literally handed millions of dollars, you get crazy."

And Dennis Wilson loved to spend money. "He was a Sixties type of person," said Robert Levine, his personal manager. He wasn't concerned about materialistic things. He would give away clothing, money...."

Wilson was famous for letting people crash at his house—when he had one. In 1968, Charles Manson and his "family" moved into Dennis' Sunset Boulevard home. By then, Dennis had divorced his first wife, Carole Freedman, and was participating in orgies and other debauchery under Manson's direction. During this period, he also tried heroin for the first time. The Manson Family spent $100,000 of his money and wrecked an uninsured $21,000 Mercedes. But rather than kick them out when things got too heavy, Wilson himself split, moving in with Gregg Jakobson, a friend and musical collaborator.

Wilson's involvement with Manson was not atypical in at least one respect: The drummer loved to flirt with danger. In the early Seventies, he would drink a six-pack or two, smoke some grass, and then get in his jeep and drive through the desert at top speed with the headlights off.

"Whatever he did," said Chris Clark, "he did in excess." Including sex. Dennis was a notorious womanizer; he was never able to remain faithful to one woman. "He called himself 'the wood,'" says one friend. The wood? "Yeah," the friend said, gesturing to his crotch.

Even his manager acknowledges Dennis' satyriasis. "Dennis was a sex fiend, plain and simple," said Levine. "The man used to think more with his sex organs than with his brain."

Wilson was married five times, and had filed to divorce Shawn—the illegitimate daughter of his cousin and fellow band member, Mike Love—a month prior to his death. He is survived by four children: Jennifer Beth, by his first wife, Carole Freedman; Carl Benton and Michael Dennis, by his second wife, Barbara Carol Charren; and Gage Dennis, by his last wife, Shawn.

Wilson's relationship with actress-model Karen Lamm was by far his craziest. Their first date was in 1974 at Mr. Chow's, a Beverly Hills restaurant. "He reached over and grabbed my right breast and said, 'Great tits!'" Lamm remembers. "I ran to the bathroom; I was so humiliated. I thought, 'I never want to see this guy again.'" But Lamm and Wilson saw each other for the next six years, a period during which they were married and divorced twice. "We were so out of control," said Lamm. "It led to a very wild existence with each other."

Indeed. Like the day in 1975 when Wilson hit Lamm, prompting her to fetch a .38-caliber revolver from her house. She had decided to put on an act to keep Dennis in line. "You get your ass off my property and don't come back," said Lamm, waving the gun. Then she shot a hole through the side of their Mercedes, just missing the gas tank. Lamm says they both broke up laughing. In 1978, Dennis drove Lamm's Ferrari down to Venice Beach and, in another fit of rage, doused the interior of the car with lighter fluid and torched it. "Then he went up to a house on Venice Boulevard and played the piano while it burned, like Nero," recalled Steve Goldberg.

All was not wanton destruction while Dennis and Karen Lamm were together. Dennis' most creative period came in the mid-Seventies, when he wrote and produced a marvelous solo album titled *Pacific Ocean Blue*. Released in 1977, it sold a respectable 200,000 copies.

Wilson recorded about half of a follow-up album, though most of the songs were never finished. "Dennis was not what you would call a completer," said Levine. Part of the reason may have been his use of heroin. According to sources close to the band, Dennis had started to use the drug in 1978, and during a tour of Australia that year, he was allegedly sharing his supply with Brian. At one point, the drummer checked himself into a hospital under an assumed name and cleaned up, but his overindulgences were creating problems within the Beach Boys.

Toward the end of 1978, Wilson took up with Fleetwood Mac's Christine McVie. The romance began while Fleetwood Mac was recording *Tusk*. "Dennis walked into the studio one night and whisked me off my feet," McVie recalled. The two went out for nearly three years, and Wilson even moved into Christine's house in Coldwater Canyon. "It was probably the experience of a lifetime. Dennis was such a character. Half of him was like a little boy, and the other half was insane. A really split personality."

With McVie, Dennis was both a great romantic and a drug abuser and alcoholic. He had a heart-shaped garden planted at her home in 1979, and at a surprise birthday party the following year, Dennis hired a symphony orchestra to serenade her as he sang "You Are So Beautiful." McVie and Wilson sang and wrote songs together at the piano. They considered recording an album together, and she dedicated a song on the last Fleetwood Mac LP, *Mirage*, to him.

Still, along with the romance and good times came bouts of drunken destruction, when Wilson would storm through the house breaking anything within reach. "He used her place like a hospital," said Steve Goldberg. "Then he'd call me, I'd go and pick him up, and she wouldn't see him for a week. When he was totaled out—he wouldn't sleep for a week—he'd go back. Over and over again. He cared about her, but his priority was having a good time."

In 1979, the Beach Boys had had enough. Dennis was frequently missing tours, and when he did show up, he was often too messed up to play. Finally, he was kicked out of the group.

With his business affairs in disarray, the drummer hired Levine as his business manager. Within a year, Levine also became Wilson's personal manager. "It wasn't the easiest situation," said Levine. "He was heavily in debt when he came to me. The whole gamut. Two years of back taxes. He owed everybody in every store money. We set up a program where it took us about two and one half years to work down the most pressing debts." In 1980, Dennis rejoined the Beach Boys and began to tour again.

By the beginning of 1981, Wilson and McVie had split up. Dennis moved into a house in Venice Beach with his 17-year-old daughter Jennifer and some other friends. "Things got real bad," said Steve Goldberg, who was also living at the house. "When he was living at Christine's, he was doing a lot of coke. [The drinking] kind of started to ease the shakes from the coke. By the time he moved to Venice, he was carrying around a ready-mixed jug. It just progressed to a continual drink."

Up until his death, Dennis Wilson would show up at the Venice Beach home of Garby Leon, a friend with a doctorate in music composition from Harvard. There, Dennis, Garby and sometimes Brian would hang out and make music late into the night, with Brian on Hammond organ and Dennis on grand piano or harp. During that time, Brian wrote nearly an album's worth of material.

But, Garby Leon says, the other Beach Boys didn't like Dennis and Brian's new songs. In late 1981, the Wilson brothers spent a few days making demos of several songs in the studio, but money to pay for the sessions was cut off.

It was while Dennis was living in Venice that the affair with his illegitimate second cousin, Shawn Love, began. Shawn, then 16, recalls showing up at Dennis' house in Venice with a mutual friend.

"What's your name?" asked Dennis.

"Shawn," she replied.

"What's your dad's name?" asked Dennis.

"Mike."

"Mike what?" he asked.

"Why?"

"Just tell me who your dad is," insisted Dennis.

"His name is Mike Love."

Then, she recalled, "he started talking to me like a big brother. He said, 'It's not safe for you to tell everybody who your dad is.' All of a sudden, he changed the conversation. At first, some people thought he was coming on to me to get at Mike." Soon they were living together.

Dennis did go back on the road with the Beach Boys, but it was rough for everyone. Bodyguards were needed to keep Dennis off the bottle prior to performances. When he drank, he could be boorish onstage, as well as an erratic drummer. There were raging battles between Dennis and Mike Love. Finally, restraining orders were issued to keep them apart.

Wilson used to get a kick out of hassling Love. Once, on the way to a concert date, Wilson walked up to the area on their private jet where Love was meditating, pulled open the door, and threw up.

By the end of 1981, Dennis and Shawn's relationship showed signs of strain. "He was acting like a real punk," said Shawn. "He was drunk and high. It was embarrassing to me. One of my girlfriends told me he was trying to take another girlfriend to bed."

Shawn was furious. "I ran up to him in the alley, and I just slugged him in the face," she said. "I came up to him like, 'I am going to kill you.' We got into a full-on fight. He didn't actually punch me, but he had me down. He dragged me by my hair."

Despite the ongoing friction, Dennis and Shawn were married in July 1983, nearly a year after their son, Gage Dennis, was born. By the fall of 1983, there wasn't much of a relationship left. Scrawled in crayon on the walls of their house at 6120 Trancas Canyon Road in Malibu were the phrases "No love" and "No respect." The house was a shambles. Doors were broken. On one occasion, Shawn nearly drove her silver BMW into the front door. Less than a month before he died, Dennis smashed the windows of the same car with a baseball bat.

Dennis and Shawn separated. "I left partially because of me and Dennis not getting along because of personal things—jealousies and stuff," said Shawn. She moved into a $150-a-week room at the Santa Monica Bay Inn, a stone's throw from the drug connection Dennis Wilson turned to when he needed cocaine. A divorce was in the works at the time of his death. Shawn claims that they were working things out, but adds, "We probably would have been together, then apart again."

IN 1982, THE MORE BUSINESS-MINDED BEACH BOYS—Carl Wilson, Al Jardine, and Mike Love—and their manager, Tom Hulett, felt there were two big problems that had to be solved: Brian Wilson and Dennis Wilson.

Brian had ballooned to over 300 pounds. He wouldn't bathe, he would eat and then throw up his food, and if drugs were around, he would use them. He was, as one associate put it, "extremely nonproductive as a human being."

The task of curing Brian eventually fell, as it had once before, to psychologist Eugene Landy. Landy had once worked for a fan magazine, *Teen Screen*, and was later a record company A&R man before becoming therapist to the stars. In 1976, he became a celebrity for his role in getting Wilson out of the bedroom and into the recording studio. Eventually, Landy was fired when he allegedly began asking for a percentage of the Beach Boys' income and wanted to become active in the management of the group.

Nevertheless, it was Eugene Landy whom Tom Hulett turned to. Though Hulett refused to be interviewed for this article, he told the *Los Angeles Times* last summer that he had Brian Wilson's interest at heart when he enlisted Landy. "I told the other guys in the band that if we didn't do something, Brian was going to be the next headline (death) in *Billboard*."

In late October 1982, Brian Wilson was told by his accountants that he was broke and that he owed the government tens of thousands of dollars in back taxes. A week or so later, at a meeting attended by Mike, Al, and Carl, plus various managers and accountants, Brian was fired. He was handed a letter dated November 5, 1982, that read, in part: "This is to advise you that your services as an employee of Brother Records, Inc., and otherwise are hereby terminated, effective immediately." Though it was signed by the four other Beach Boys, Shawn Wilson claims that Dennis didn't know what he was signing, if indeed he signed it at all.

"They told him that the only way that he could be a Beach Boy again, and the only way they would release his 1982 tour disbursement money, was if he would agree to see Dr. Landy," says Brian's girlfriend, Carolyn Williams, who was present at the meeting. "Brian started yelling that he didn't like Dr. Landy and that [Landy] was charging him $20,000 a month the last time. He was willing to see anybody to get the weight off, but he didn't want to see Landy. And they said, 'Well, no, you have to see Dr. Landy. That's the only way.'"

A while later, Brian was taken to Hawaii to begin a program with Eugene Landy. Brian remains under Landy's care to this date; his fee is rumored to exceed $50,000 a month.

Landy has recently become the Beach Boys' "recording manager" and may share song writing credits (and, thus, royalties) with Brian Wilson on the next Beach Boys' album. Because of his relationship with Brian, Landy actually told a reporter from *California Magazine*, "I'm the one who's making the album."

The three Beach Boys and their manager then apparently turned to the other problem: Dennis Wilson. "When they put Brian in the Landy program," said Shawn, "A couple of our friends said, 'Dennis, as soon as they have Brian done, they're going to try to do the same thing with you.' He said, 'No, they're not going to do anything.'"

Dennis was wrong.

Mike, Carl, Al, and manager Hulett had already banned Dennis from some concerts during 1983. Finally, Dennis was told he would not be allowed to tour with the band unless he went through a detox program. "Which was okay," says Levine. "They were all interested in helping him. I was in full agreement with that."

To hear Dennis' Venice Beach friends tell it, the rock star was literally put out on the streets. For a month prior to his death, Dennis was without a home. He had no car and little money. He lived a nomadic life, crashing with various friends. "If Dennis had had a place to live, he might not have died," said Garby Leon.

At least one member of Dennis Wilson's immediate family agrees. "I feel if Dennis had had a place to stay, he might not have been down in the marina that day," said his daughter Jennifer.

Though Bob Levine feels Wilson was fairly serious about straightening out his life, Steve Goldberg maintains he was just telling people what they wanted to hear. In late November, Dennis checked into a country club–style therapy center in Arizona. He left after two days.

Over the next month, he bounced from friend to friend. There was a scene outside an Alcoholics Anonymous meeting, where Wilson and Beach Boys manager Tom Hulett argued about money. Hulett reportedly pulled out a wad of bills, peeled off 15 dollars and offered it to Wilson, who wouldn't take it. Hulett threw it on the ground. The next day. Hulett apparently gave Wilson $100.

On Friday, December 23, Dennis Wilson checked into St. John's Hospital and Health Center in Santa Monica. Dr. Jokichi Takamine, the doctor caring for Wilson at St. John's, says that "he was very serious" about the program.

Wilson and Takamine spoke at length on Saturday; the doctor says he told Wilson he would be away on Sunday, Christmas Day, but would see him on Monday.

But Dennis checked himself out of St. John's Hospital early in the evening on Christmas Day. Although Shawn had apparently agreed to come to the hospital with Gage to visit, she never made it. "He just showed up at my mom's," said Shawn. "He said he was really lonely and that he wanted to be with us on Christmas."

He spent about an hour with Shawn and Gage, then left. A friend bumped into Dennis walking along the road near the Santa Monica Bay Inn. They went for a drink at a club. It was later that night that Dennis stopped by the Santa Monica Bay Inn and was beaten up by Shawn's male friend. After being denied medical attention at St. John's hospital, Dennis was admitted to Daniel Freeman Marina Hospital at around 2 a.m. He spent the night.

Wilson checked himself out at 11:30 a.m. the next day and called Steve Goldberg an hour and a half later. "He was at a beer bar two blocks down the street He wanted me to drive down and pick him up," said Steve Goldberg. "I told him I was working on my van and said, 'Why don't you just walk over here?' "He kept calling me back. He wanted money and a ride. He ended that conversation [with the word] termination. Click. I don't know if he was referring to the conversation, our friendship or his life."

ON TUESDAY, DECEMBER 27, AT ABOUT 8 p.m., the phone rang on Bill Oster's boat, the *Emerald*. Dennis wanted to visit. The old friends had been out of touch for nearly a year, but Oster was happy to hear from him and agreed to pick up the Beach Boy and the girl he was with, Colleen "Crystal" McGovern.

Wilson had met Oster, a mechanical engineer, a few years earlier when his boat, the *Harmony*, had been docked next to the *Emerald* at a Marina del Rey slip. After Wilson lost his boat, Oster hid a key on the *Emerald* so Dennis could have use of the boat. Dennis had called Oster from Colleen McGovern's house in Culver City. McGovern was a casual friend; she and Dennis had been seeing each other only for a few weeks. After talking with Oster, Dennis was excited. "He said, 'We're going to the boat; we're going to have a good time. And tomorrow I'm going to go to detox,'" recalled McGovern.

When Oster picked the couple up, Dennis said, "Gotta get a bottle." They stopped at a liquor store, Wilson bought a fifth of vodka and some orange juice, and they drove to the boat.

Oster, his fiancée, Brenda, McGovern, and Wilson sat around in the boat's small cabin that night, reminiscing and drinking. At one point, the conversation turned to Dennis. Oster told the Beach Boy, "It wasn't six months ago that I said to Brenda, 'I hope the next tune we see Dennis, it's not at his funeral." Wilson looked right at Oster and said, "Don't you worry about that."

"We talked about his alcohol rehabilitation, detox and why he didn't want to go in," recalled Oster. "He said, 'They won't let me back in the band until I do it.'" He didn't like the atmosphere [at St. John's]. There was a place in New Mexico he was willing to try."

Wilson was drinking heavily. "If anybody else had been drinking the way Dennis was drinking, they would have been smashed," said Oster. "But Dennis drank like that normally. I don't think I ever knew him sober."

At about midnight, Dennis passed out. He slept fitfully. "Dennis was just sweating like I'd never seen him sweat," said McGovern. "It was just dripping down his face. I was mopping his forehead constantly."

McGovern eventually fell asleep, but was awakened an hour later by Wilson. "I could see right away he was wound up again." Wilson made several phone calls, apparently including one to Shawn. "Dennis and I ended up staying up all night," said McGovern. "We would sleep a few minutes, then he would wake me up again. Every once in a while, he'd say, 'Honey, what are we going to do?' And I'd say, 'We're going to get some sleep.' And he would say, 'I can't sleep, I can't sleep.'"

The next morning, the foursome sat around talking. At about 10, Oster suggested that he and Wilson go rowing. "We set it up, put the oars in it," said Oster, "and he's wandering around. 'I want a drink. I want a drink!' The girls had hid the stuff. He finally found it and mixed himself another drink."

They returned an hour later; at noon, they had turkey sandwiches. Wilson had consumed three-quarters of the bottle of vodka by this point. When he spilled a drink on his pants, Oster loaned him a pair of cutoff jeans. That's when Dennis began diving into the slip next to the *Emerald*. He surfaced and handed Oster an old piece of rope.

"That was the first thing he brought up," recalled Oster. "He kept diving down, scrounging around, bringing up junk. Why he was doing it, I don't know."

Wilson came out of the 58-degree water after 20 minutes; back on the dock, he was shivering, and his teeth were chattering. He sat in front of a heater inside the cabin. His friends brought him towels, and after about 15 minutes, he stopped shaking. He ate another sandwich and had another drink.

Then he made a few more dives. He found a silver frame that had held his and Karen Lamm's wedding picture. He had thrown it off the *Harmony* in 1980, when they were divorced.

"He was really excited," said McGovern. "He said, 'Guess what I found! A chest of gold!'"

Back on board, the Beach Boy sat around for about two and a half hours, relaxing and drinking. He finished off the fifth of vodka. He was talking about what he thought was at the bottom of the slip: a tool box, the "chest of gold," a sack of silver dollars. "He was psyching himself up to go back in after his treasures," said Oster. "I told him there was nothing down there. We tried halfheartedly to talk him out of going back in. There was no talking him out of it."

At some point, he found a bottle of wine on the boat and drank from it. Around 4 p.m., Dennis was ready to go back in the water. But first he walked to another houseboat on the other side of the dock in search of booze. He managed to talk a friend into giving him a partially filled fifth of vodka and had another drink.

Then he made his last dive. Oster was standing on one of the slender piers that extend between the docked boats, across the slip from the *Emerald*. From there, he saw air bubbles. "I saw him come up to within two feet of the surface," said Oster. "Then I saw him swim behind my rowboat, where I couldn't see his face or what he was doing. I think I heard him take a breath of air."

Oster called out, "Dennis, what did you find?" There was no response.

"At that point, I saw him go straight down and back out of sight. I said to myself, 'That sucker's playing a game on me, he's trying to hide.' That was my fatal error. Because that was the last time he went down. I took a few puffs on a cigarette, waiting for him to come up. Didn't hear or see anything. So, I quietly walked around to my side of the empty slip. I didn't see him, so I stomped on the dock and made a whole bunch of noise and said, 'Hey, Dennis, where are you? Ha ha. I can't find you.' Still no response. Then I started looking. It was just clear enough that you could look under all the docks and see if there was an object under there. There were a lot of places where he could have come up and hid."

But when Dennis didn't surface, his friends became worried. Oster was going to dive in himself when he spotted the harbor patrol. According to the autopsy report, "The harbor patrol searched the waters for approximately 30 minutes before finding the body. The time that the body was pulled from the water was approximately 1745 hours [5:45 p.m.]. Dennis Wilson was pronounced dead three minutes later.

"WE ARE NOT DISBANDING," ANNOUNCED Carl Wilson at an LA press conference on Monday, January 9, some 12 days after Dennis Wilson's death. "We are postponing currently scheduled dates during this period of mourning."

Regardless of their personal feelings about Dennis, the Beach boys will continue—and at least one member thinks the band will be stronger. "A chain is only as strong as its weakest link" is how Mike Love characterized Dennis' effect on the band during his decline. "Dennis had his problems: drugs, alcohol."

Now middle-aged men—Love is 43; Brian Wilson, 41; Al Jardine, 39; Carl Wilson, 37; and Bruce Johnston, 40—the remaining Beach Boys are caught in a bind. Their last studio LP, *Keepin' the Summer Alive*, sold fewer than 200,000 copies, and the band members have reportedly been unable to hang onto their money. (Mike Love filed for bankruptcy last year.)

As a result, they must tour constantly to afford their extravagant lifestyles. So, to no one's great surprise, the Beach Boys were performing at Harrah's, a casino in Lake Tahoe, a little over a month after Carl's announcement.

Renewed concert activity is not the only front the Beach Boys are now active on. A million-dollar deal with Vestron Video to make a home video, *The Complete Beach Boys*, has been made. Culture Club producer Steve Levine, who has recently spent time working on music with Brian in Jamaica, will produce a new Beach Boys album in London. Recently, the Beach Boys contributed a song to the soundtrack of *Up the Creek*. A collaborative Beach Boys-Four Seasons single titled "East Meets West" has been cut, and the band is pairing up with international pop star Julio Iglesias on a remake of the Hollies' "The Air That I Breathe."

At the late show at Tahoe, Brian Wilson did not perform. The others, backed by an 11 piece-band, including a horn section and two drummers, offered an unexceptional rerun of the Beach Boys' oldies. With the exception of "Rock and Roll Music," which reached number five on the pop charts in 1976, and a couple of tunes off Carl Wilson's solo albums, the Beach Boys performed music that was nearly two decades old.

Toward the conclusion, the band sang a weary version of "Fun, Fun, Fun." Conspicuously absent was any mention of Dennis Wilson. The period of mourning was apparently over.

*Rolling Stone*, June 1984

# BRIAN WILSON: GOD ONLY KNOWS

## The troubled pop genius who made the Beach Boys great has finally released his first solo album. Is Wilson really back?

SANTA MONICA, CALIFORNIA—BRIAN WILSON HEARS voices. They talk to him. They distract him, frighten him, confuse him. Right now, as the creative genius behind the Beach Boys' classic surf-rock sound sits for an interview in his darkened living room, the Pacific crashing loudly outside his million-dollar Malibu home, the voices are calling.

The 46-year-old screws up his face. His eyes roll toward the ceiling; they've gone blank. His brow is furrowed with thick worry lines. He is silent. Gone.

"Brian," says Kevin Leslie, a 24-year-old who is with Brian around the clock, looking after him and acting as the "eyes and ears" for Wilson's therapist-manager, Dr. Eugene E. Landy. "Uh, Brian, come on."

This tortured rock & roll legend—who changed pop music irrevocably with the string of masterpieces he created for the Beach Boys—snaps out of it. He looks up, jerks his head back and forth for a few seconds, as if physically shaking away the voices.

"I get calls, in my head, from people in the vicinity or maybe 10, 20 miles out," he says. "They get to me. They say things like '*You're going to get it, you* motherfucker!' Cruel talk." He frowns, and then, as if he were a 12-year-old resigned to the teasing of schoolyard buddies, says, "That's a drag."

Wilson is silent again. But this time he's just thinking. The voices have stopped—for now. He flashes a nervous, boyish smile, summons up some inner resolve and says firmly, "I'll get through it." Brian Douglas Wilson has been diagnosed as having a schizoid personality (extremely introverted, unable to express or show emotion, pathologically shy) with manic-depressive features. Untreated, he could shift from delusional highs to possibly suicidal depths of depression and despair. But according to his psychiatrist, Dr. Solon Samuels, 81, controlled use of certain medications—including lithium (Eskalith), sedatives (Xanax and Halcion), and antidepressants (Elavil)—allow Brian to remain somewhat emotionally balanced. Still, Brian remains, in the words of Warner Bros. Records president Lenny Waronker, "a troubled soul."

YET DESPITE HIS PROBLEMS, for the first time in over 20 years, Wilson has completed a brilliant album. This month he's releasing his first solo record, *Brian Wilson*, a delightful, engaging pop masterpiece. His chief coproducer, Russ Titelman, proudly calls it *Pet Sounds '88,* referring of course to the legendary 1966 Beach Boys album that helped inspire the Beatles to make *Sgt. Pepper's Lonely Hearts Club Band.*

If there is one man responsible for Brian's return to the recording studio, it is Landy, who, in addition to being Brian's psychotherapist and personal manager, is also his executive producer, business partner (they recently formed a company called Brains and Genius), and songwriting collaborator (Landy receives cowriting credit on five of the 11 songs on the new album; Landy's girlfriend, Alexandra Morgan, receives cowriting credit on three of those five songs). Beginning five and a half years ago, using a controversial 24-hour-a-day "milieu therapy" program in which Wilson's entire environment was under Landy's control, the doctor miraculously brought Brian back from a state of near death.

But Landy's involvement in every aspect of Wilson's personal and professional life has caught the attention of the California attorney general's office. This past February, following what Landy describes as a four-year investigation, the attorney general filed formal charges against him for gross negligence in his treatment of Wilson. He is accused of acting as "the business manager, business adviser, executive producer, and co-song writer with his patient while also serving as his therapist." Landy is also accused of prescribing drugs to Wilson—something he is not licensed to do, because he is not an MD—and of directing his assistants to dole out the drugs. (He is additionally charged with gross negligence in his treatment of a female patient identified only as R.G. He allegedly gave her illicit drugs and forced her to have sex with him.) At the earliest, the Landy case will be heard this fall.

*Brian Wilson* cost a million dollars to make. The project is considered so important at Warner Bros. Records that although Wilson is signed to Sire Records (a Warner subsidiary) and would normally deal exclusively with Sire president Seymour Stein, Waronker—a longtime Beach Boys fan—has also been heavily involved. In fact, he went so far as to enter the recording studio and coproduce one of the tracks, "Rio Grande," something Waronker (known for producing Randy Newman and Rickie Lee Jones) hadn't done in five years. "For the past six months," says one Warner executive, "we've practically been a record company without a president, Lenny has been so preoccupied with the Brian Wilson album."

For any major recording artist, the release of a new album is a high-pressure experience. There are interviews, photo sessions, video shoots, industry functions, TV appearances. But the resurrection of Brian Wilson has put even more than the usual amount of stress on Wilson and the others involved with the record.

They want the world to perceive Brian Wilson as being back in the saddle in all the important ways: as a recording artist and as a healthy, mentally alert adult.

It's an uphill battle. In 1962, Brian Wilson and the Beach Boys emerged from the nondescript suburban community of Hawthorne, California, with a Top 20 hit, "Surfin' Safari." With Wilson writing the songs, composing the music, and producing the records, the Beach Boys quickly became America's most popular rock band. Until mental illness and drugs sabotaged his life in the mid-Sixties, Wilson was considered a genius as a songwriter and record producer.

But that was 20 years ago. Since then the image of the youthful genius has been replaced by the image of Brian Wilson as a crazy man, the eccentric with the piano in the sandbox and the tent in the living room, the 303-pound "lumbering hulk" wacked out on both legal and illegal drugs—acid, cocaine, marijuana, hash, and, in the mid-Seventies, black heroin—living in a stupor induced by drinking and overeating, stumbling down to Venice to get drugs from his brother Dennis as recently as 1982.

"I lost interest in writing songs," says Wilson. "I lost the inspiration. I was too concerned with getting drugs to write songs."

If Brian were completely recovered, his publicists would simply have to expose him to the world, and the new, improved Brian would replace the old preconceptions. But for

Brian, the recovery process isn't over—and may never be. "There is a kind of boyishness about him," says Samuels, who tends to downplay Brian's continuing emotional and mental problems. "He still has growth to go to become, as it were, a mature man. He's become, shall we say, a well-adjusted adolescent."

Except for those moments when the voices beckon and he spaces out, Brian Wilson looks great. Standing at about six feet two, wearing jeans, running shoes, and a colorful Hawaiian shirt, he is 180 pounds of sinew and muscle. Thanks to Landy, he's become a fitness junkie—the flip side of his new single, "Love and Mercy," is a pro-fitness anthem called "He Couldn't Get His Poor Old Body to Move." His mornings are spent jogging, working out with a trainer, or lap swimming. He avoids junk food, doesn't smoke, and says he steers clear of street drugs save for the rare toke from a joint.

But inside Brian's head, things aren't so sunny. Actually, within the Beach Boy's brain, there seem to be many Brians. "There are a lot of different people there," says Waronker. "I've met five different people."

One Brian is like a 10-year-old; after tripping and mildly scraping his leg during a run, he told Landy he thought he was going to die. Naive and uninformed in many areas, he knows nothing of Woodstock, hasn't heard of R.E.M., and apparently doesn't read books. Another Brian is a teenager—sometimes stubborn and moody, other times lazy or bored—who talks in a kind of boyishly appealing Sixties teenage slang: "I had to, man," he'll say about an accomplishment. "I didn't want to goof up." Or "That would be a real groovy kind of a thing."

There's the musical genius who, when placed in a recording studio with the right support team of producers, engineers, and studio musicians, instinctively comes up with brilliant, original ideas. There's a guy whose fantasy life is so real he can state with all seriousness that he expects his album to generate six hit singles. Then there's the Brian who's fully aware of his fantasy world. "Reality checks," he'll say about how he differentiates between reality and fantasy. "I have a series of reality checks. Am I still in reality, or am I going off into fantasy?"

There's the Brian who literally can't make a move without directions from Landy (he was recently observed calling Landy to ask if he could remove a framed poster of the Beach Boys from his wall because, he said, "it's bumming me out"), who spouts out lines Landy has fed him like a robot. But there's also a sharp, intelligent guy in there somewhere, a man who understands that he's working his way through a mass of problems, who'd like to reestablish his relationship with his daughters, Carnie, 20, and Wendy, 18 (he says he can't handle seeing them at this time), and the Beach Boys (he believes that if his solo album is successful, it will destroy the group), who'd like to someday live some kind of normal life, perhaps even get married again (although at the moment he finds the mere idea of a steady girlfriend intimidating).

"Being called a musical genius," he says, quite rationally, "was a cross to bear. Genius is a big word. But if you have to live up to something, you might as well live up to that. God damn!"

THE PHONE IN WILSON'S DINING ROOM rings. Brian involuntarily stiffens. It's the "E.E. Landy line," a kind of Batphone, but instead of finding Commissioner Gordon at the other end, one always gets Landy.

Landy, 53, may be the most unorthodox therapist in the world. Beach Boys manager Tom Hulett calls him "this outrageous-looking doctor." Even Samuels, Landy's longtime mentor and associate, volunteers that Landy has a "personality problem" and is "emotionally explosive."

Landy likes to say that he's "Eugene Wilson Landy" and that Brian has become "Brian Landy Wilson." "We've exchanged names," says Landy. "We've kind of merged. I've taken from him, and he's taken from me. Brian and I are partners in life—we're sharing a life experience."

Landy drives a $34,000 black Biturbo 425 Maserati with a license plate that reads, HEADOC. At times, he acts like *he's* the pampered star. He showed up for one interview wearing black nylon running pants stuffed into cowboy boots, an orange silk yoked cowboy shirt and a small earring in his left ear; his hair was cut in a modified Rod Stewart shag. "Gene is sort of like a rock star," says Hulett. "He's caught up in showbiz."

Landy has always been attracted by the glitter and the glitz. He says that as a teenager working at the 500 Club, in Atlantic City, he was a flack for Frank Sinatra. Later he was a producer for a syndicated radio show for teens and then worked as an A&R man for a small record label. He also discovered George Benson. Landy got his BS in psychology from Cal State at Los Angeles in 1964 and his doctorate in psychology from the University of Oklahoma in 1968. In the late Sixties, he was involved in drug counseling and served briefly as director of the adolescent program at an LA hospital. In 1971, his book *The Underground Dictionary* was published by Simon and Schuster. Soon after, he was earning $200 an hour as a therapist to the stars; in addition, he was a consultant on *The Bob Newhart Show.*

Landy has a charismatic, manipulative personality. But associates say that he drops the charm once he's gotten what he wants. He is prone to loud arguments and hysterical shouting matches. Recently, when he arrived at the Los Angeles airport and found that Warner Bros. had sent a town car instead of a stretch limo, he exploded, fuming for 20 minutes. He later put in calls to both Waronker and Stein to straighten out the limo problem. "This is one of Warners' cheap little numbers again," he muttered to his girlfriend. "I'm sure this is the bright idea of some junior-accountant type at Warners who wants to save a few bucks."

Of course, Landy has more than limos on his mind. If found guilty of the attorney general's gross-negligence charges, Landy could have his license as a clinical psychologist revoked. Ask Landy about the charges involving Brian, and he is expansive, going on for nearly an hour as he tries to explain why rules that other psychotherapists are bound by shouldn't apply to him in this case. "*This is not a normal situation,*" Landy says, rising and pacing around his office. "Brian had been with 38 other therapists, and they had failed to somehow motivate him under the conditions that existed in normal-process therapy. He had been hospitalized many times in mental hospital. . . . I didn't have a dual capacity with Brian; I had a multicapacity with Brian. I'm insulted they only have it listed as dual capacity. If I hadn't, this man would be dead." (In fact, the attorney general's complaint against Landy charges him with "various dual, triple and quadruple relationships with his patient.")

As for the charges involving the female patient identified as R.G.—Landy is accused of furnishing her with cocaine and amyl nitrate from the fall of 1982 through the spring of 1983, of having sex with her on several occasions, of forcing her to perform fellatio on him, and of engaging in sex with her at an "orgy"—he says only, "It's untrue. It's all *untrue*. This is all fantasy."

The press has painted Landy as a Svengali who plucked Brian from the jaws of death only to transform him into a kind of malleable rock & roll zombie. But even Landy's enemies use words like "miracle worker" when describing what Landy has accomplished with Wilson.

Landy first began treating Wilson in 1975, after being approached by Wilson's then wife, Marilyn (they divorced in 1980). Although his program seemed to be working, by the end of 1976, Landy and the Beach Boys' management had had a falling out; Landy was fired. Over the next six years Brian regressed, so Landy was called in again at the end of 1982. "I was a vegetable," says Brian. "I didn't do shit."

"The program" began in January of 1983. With the consent of Brian's family, the Beach Boys, and their management, he was whisked off to Kailua-Kona, a secluded area in Hawaii. There, according to Landy and his associates—Samuels, Dr. Bill Flaxman, and Dr. Murray Susser—Wilson was put on an extreme diet and vitamin regimen (Susser says this included daily intravenous injections of "ridiculous amounts of vitamin C"), an exercise program, and a resocialization program.

Wilson was so far gone that he'd actually forgotten his own songs and had to attend daily music lessons in which, using a Beach Boys song book, he relearned "Surfer Girl," "I Get Around," and many of the others.

"I've taught him a new way to react to situations and circumstances," says Landy, who until recently reportedly earned $50,000 a month treating Wilson. "A way to do it with logic, with sanity, with consideration for the consequences and the responsibilities. What a *yes* means, what a *no* means."

According to Brian's lawyer, John Mason, whose clients include Elton John and Kenny Rogers, Brian is now in control of his business affairs. "During the last year," Mason says, "Brian has made all of his own decisions about business."

If Mason really believes that, then he's not as sharp a lawyer as many in the music industry believe him to be. Brian himself says it's Landy who calls the shots. "He's my boss, and I like him as my boss," Brian says. "I'm in step with Gene. He gets what he wants. I just toe the line."

The problem, says one associate, is that although serious attempts are made to keep Brian informed of his business, Brian's extremely erratic memory (he frequently forgets things that happened just hours earlier) and his apathy about business keep him in a state of semiconfusion about many of his affairs.

AT LANDY'S OFFICE RECENTLY, Brian sat signing a sheaf of papers provided by one of Landy's assistants. A little later, upstairs in Landy's private office, Landy asked Brian about the papers he'd just signed. "I signed everything that was before me," Brian said, sounding like the dutiful son. "It all has to do with . . . I signed . . . I think . . . God damn. I was so shook up being here. . . ."

"Well, check it before you go," said Landy. "Don't sign shit you don't know." Then he added, "Rule that I put into effect at the very beginning: that you don't sign shit unless you know what it is."

Landy's control of Brian's affairs extends to the Beach Boy's personal life. Whenever Brian leaves his house, he wears a beeper to stay in touch with Landy. It is Samuels, a longtime associate of Landy's, who prescribes the potent drugs that hold Brian together. But it is Landy who monitors Brian's drug intake, and it is one of Landy's assistants, Kevin Leslie, who stays with Brian 24 hours a day and doles out Brian's "meds" at Landy's direction. Leslie used to be paid by Landy; now Brian pays his salary, although Leslie still reports to Landy dozens of times a day by phone.

During the course of eight days spent with Landy and Wilson, it became clear just how much control Landy exerts over Brian's life. With the exception of taking a brief drive by himself to the market to pick up groceries, Brian appeared to be incapable of making a move without Landy's okay. During one interview session, the Landy line seemed to ring every 30 minutes.

Yet Brian appears to be a willing participant in the program. "Gene told me that the program was legally over about two months ago," he says. "But I don't believe it. I just don't believe that I could walk away. First of all, I'd be afraid. I'd be scared. I wouldn't know where to live; I wouldn't know how to live."

Landy says simply that the program ended last year. "Nobody," he says, "tells Brian what to do."

Sitting in his living room, as Leslie disappears into another room, Brian vents his frustration. Pointing in the direction of Leslie, he says he doesn't like living with him: "It's like the first two months of the army." When the Landy line rings again, Brian says softly, "He calls all the time." Then, to distinguish those calls from the ones that come only in his head, he adds, "On the phone. The sound of that bell is kind of frightening. It's like a nightmare. A recurring nightmare. The phone keeps ringing. I'm scared of Gene. Obviously. What's there to be scared of? Nothing really. Kind of a nightmare that's gonna get easier." He pauses uncomfortably. "I hope."

Brian is also uncomfortable when he discusses the Beach Boys. He says that Mike Love's rambling putdown of Paul McCartney, Bruce Springsteen, Billy Joel, and Mick Jagger at the Rock & Roll Hall of Fame dinner this year was "an embarrassment." He's extremely worried about the negative effect he believes the success of his album will have on the other guys. "Our personal relationships aren't working," he says. "Do you know they had, or tried to have, a meeting without me? It's been four months since I've seen the other guys." He also says that he and Landy suspect that Wilson's family filed the complaints against Landy with the attorney general's office. "Carl and my mother and Mike Love. I think they're trying to get Gene out of there. My brother Carl never liked Gene anyway. He and Gene never got along. If I could, I'd wring Carl's neck. He makes me mad."

According to manager Tom Hulett, the Beach Boys "want Brian to have success. I gave the album to each of them, and they were tickled to hear it. They were all positive about it." Still, although Hulett said he'd get Mike Love on the phone to talk about Brian, Love did not return repeated calls. As for Landy, Hulett said "I'm proud to be associated with him. Brian's not ready to be on his own. I could see the world hurting Brian. Now Brian's in a place where things are good."

"GIMME 10 TRACKS FOR VOCALS," says Brian Wilson. "I'm going to do it *now*." Seconds later the Beach Boy is out in the studio, adjusting his headphones. And then seasoned studio veterans like Russ Titelman and Lenny Waronker watch in awe as Brian Wilson, on his own, creates the melodious, breathtaking wall of voices that is the Beach Boys' trademark.

Titelman, who coproduced all but three of the album's songs, still can't get over the sessions for "There's So Many," the achingly beautiful romantic ballad that ends side one of *Brian Wilson*. "I said to Brian, 'Go out and do the background vocals—kill it!'" he says. "It took 15 minutes. He sang a part, then he'd double it, sang another part, doubled that. When he was finished, it sounded like an old Beatles record, like John Lennon. I said, 'Brian, I'm so proud of you.' He leaned over to me and said, 'Yeah, who needs the fuckin' Beach Boys!'"

"When it comes to music, he *is* a genius," says Waronker.

The album took over a year to record. As the budget doubled, then quadrupled, Warner Bros. Records chairman of the board Mo Ostin, who could have pulled the plug at any moment, didn't say a word. Sessions were held at eleven recording studios, in Los Angeles, New York, Boston, and Honolulu. Six producers—Titelman, Waronker, Andy Paley, Jeff Lynne, Hugh Padgham, and Lindsey Buckingham (whose contribution, "He Couldn't Get His Poor Old Body to Move," didn't make it onto the album)—were involved. Numerous songwriters—including Bob Dylan, John Sebastian, Van Dyke Parks, Carole Bayer Sager, Harry Nilsson, Jeff Lynne, and the Dream Academy's Nick Laird-Clowes—had meetings with Brian. A room in Landy's office contains over 100 reels of recording tape used for the album. "You can't put a price on art," says Brian matter of factly. "Do you realize that a person can walk in a record store and can buy art that's worth millions of dollars? If you could put a value on art—I don't think you can, but if you could—it would be much more than $2 or $1.50 or whatever they charge for records. It kills me. It blows me right out."

The album began in the small music room downstairs at Brian's house. That room, which contains only an upright Schafer & Sons piano, two synthesizer keyboards, a Fender precision bass, and a boom box, was where Brian, encouraged by songwriter-producer-multi-instrumentalist Andy Paley, worked on many of the songs. Three briefcases sit next to the piano: They contain rough piano-vocal demos of close to 170 mostly unrecorded songs that Wilson has written over the years. "There's great stuff," says Paley, who considers himself a student of the Brian Wilson-Beach Boys sound. "But there are also what I call the 'hamburger songs.'" Reportedly, in the early Eighties, Dennis Wilson would go to McDonald's and buy a bag of hamburgers; he'd then give Brian a hamburger for each song he completed. "A lot of those are real junk," says Paley.

Sire Records head Seymour Stein impulsively decided to sign Wilson after meeting him backstage at the Rock & Roll Hall of Fame dinner in January of 1987. But before the deal was concluded, Stein made two trips out to the West Coast to hear Brian's recent material. As Stein listened patiently, Brian sat at the piano banging out song after song after song. "When he played 'Love and Mercy,' I got chills," says Stein. "I said, 'For this song alone it's worth doing the album.'"

Now Stein feels differently. "The recording of the album was like hell on Earth," he says. "Because Dr. Landy seems to thrive only on turmoil, tumult, and confusion. He would completely destroy the harmony that was going on in the studio. For example, Russ would be ready to work on one track and Landy would send the wrong tape, just to drive Russ crazy."

"It was absolutely frustrating," says Titelman. "I don't know how to stress it enough. Landy has no qualifications to make creative decisions. In your wildest imagination you couldn't find a qualification, from songwriting to sound to anything to do with the record-making process. To deal with him and try to convince him—these lyrics are good, these are bad, 'Melt Away' should not have a gypsy violin. All of a sudden, I'm in a Marx Brothers movie instead of making a record."

Landy agrees things were strained. "Titelman and I were always nose to nose, pushing, pushing, pushing," he says. "Russ Titelman is not my favorite person. But I must give him his honest due. He came in, rescued an out-of-proportion situation and brought it together. Russ has to be congratulated for having the balls to stand up to Brian and Dr. Landy."

When Titelman entered the picture, Brian had already been working with Paley in California for several months. But after Waronker came down to the studio and heard what he felt were six promising but seriously incomplete tracks (Titelman describes them as "sloppy sketches—and that's being kind"), he realized that another producer was needed. "Each song had moments, but they needed help," says Waronker. "But Brian had all the inspiration. All Russ did was make it stand up, make it be a record."

Wilson's studio collaborators were able to coax brilliant ideas out of him. Brian was inspired to try to work the sampled sounds of crickets, frogs, wolves, water, and a saw into the texture of his songs. At one point he asked for a nuclear explosion, although that didn't make it onto the record. "This is how he works," Waronker says. "You get him the sound, he fiddles around for a minute, and then he's done. And it's great."

Around Brian there was constant chaos. Wherever he went, Kevin Leslie accompanied him. As work in the studio inched along, Leslie—whose long blond hair but often stern demeanor earned him the nickname Surf Nazi among many of those who worked with Brian on the album—took notes, made tape recordings of everything Brian said and reported by phone to Landy. In one studio, Leslie rigged up an intercom system so he could listen in on conversations between Brian and Titelman. And of course there were constant calls from Landy. Titelman says that during the mixing sessions things got so out of hand that Hugh Padgham said that he would head back to England if Leslie wasn't removed from the studio. "I told Leslie, 'You can't be in here,'" says Titelman. "He said, 'My instructions are I must be here.' Finally I said to him, 'You come in, the record's over.' Next day—after he talked to Landy—he was gone."

The record was finally completed earlier this year. "I don't care if Warner Bros. makes one dollar," says Waronker. "I'd like us to break even, that's all. But I'd really like to see Brian Wilson come back and make more music. That's what it was all about for me. It was never about hits. The fact of the matter is, if you're a Brian Wilson fan and you get to hear new Brian Wilson stuff, it's great. I think he deserves this shot, and if he doesn't mess up and if he does take advantage of it, then he deserves to have a career. All this work has been done. Unbelievable amounts of energy have been expended, incredible pain inflicted on everybody. One of the most difficult situations I've ever been through has occurred, and we still have this thing that I think is good. And now he's got a shot."

"It was a labor of love," says Brian.

"HEY," SAYS BRIAN, "LET'S GO in the hot tub." He heads up to his room to undress. A few minutes later, he leads the way through the living room, out onto his deck and down a short flight of stairs to a steaming redwood hot tub that looks out on the ocean. Dropping his robe, he eases his body into the warm water.

Out here in the tub, with Kevin Leslie inside the house, Brian suddenly seems to feel less inhibited. "Don't tell Dr. Landy about this," he says conspiratorially, then pauses for a moment. "I hate the feeling of looking up in the morning when I wake up in bed. It is like a mountain ahead of me. Nothing seems right. About two or three o'clock in the afternoon, 'Hey, what was I worried about?' But you can't tell yourself that when you're worried. You say, 'I'm worried.' That's one of my big problems in life, dealing with morning. So now you know!

"I want to be able to pop out of bed at six or seven in the morning and meet the day," Brian says. "But I can't. I'm negatively programmed to think that each day is a bummer."

Above the huge expanse of ocean, clouds are blowing in against the black sky. "I'm going to get out," Brian says abruptly. And with that he's out of the tub, draped in his robe, hurrying back into the house.

In the living room, Brian's mood has changed. He seems giddy. It's nearly 11:00 p.m., his bedtime, but first he wants to listen to music. He gets up to walk over to the stereo but stops himself.

He stands there, a towering figure wearing only a long, white terry-cloth bathrobe. "I prove to myself over and over again that I can do things," he says. "I can do music. I go in the studio, and I don't fuckin' crack up.

"Everyone in the world has the same hang-ups, only in different ways," he says. "Same hang-ups. It's quite an ordeal. Getting things together can be quite an ordeal, I'll tell you that right now. But once they're together, you go, 'Hey, yeah!' You feel good. Getting used to yourself is hard. I find it hard to get used to myself. But you can get used to yourself. Anybody could. Jesus! *Anybody could.*

"To be, or not to be," he suddenly exclaims. "That is the question." He means, of course, that after 15-plus years of trying not to be, Wilson has decided that it's time to be. A few days later, while looking at some old photos of himself in his days as a 300-pound blob, he will say, "I was ready for death. I had a dying thing."

But that's all behind him now. And despite the voices, despite his bad mornings, the sometimes nerve-racking anxiety, the memory lapses and, yes, the omnipresent Landy, Brian Wilson appears to be back in action. He's already got half of a second album written, talks of producing both the Beach Boys and the Ramones and is contemplating a solo tour. "We're not going to die," he says. "We're going to live!"

*Rolling Stone*, August 11, 1988

## Postscript

IN THE *NEW YORK TIMES* OBIT for Dr. Eugene Landy, who died on March 22, 2006, the paper reported that in "1989, after the California Board of Medical Quality Assurance accused Mr. Landy of 'grossly negligent conduct' in the Wilson case and others, he voluntarily surrendered his license for at least two years. . . . At the start of 1992, as a result of the settlement of a suit by Mr. Wilson's family, Mr. Landy was barred by court order from contacting Mr. Wilson." Since 1988's *Brian Wilson*, Wilson has had 13 additional solo albums released. The most recent, *Brian Wilson: The Long Promised Road*, was released in 2021.

Captain Beefheart, San Francisco, 1977: "DDT is immortal. They've made DDT immortal. Boy, what's the matter? What's the matter with people?"

# CAPTAIN BEEFHEART

I AM NOTHING LIKE WHAT PEOPLE have heard about me. I've never killed an animal in my life. I've never stepped on another human being. I'm not speedy. I don't drink coffee. I don't drink. I don't use drugs and I'm a vegetarian. All I do is smoke. That's bad. It's a habit. Boy, that's a habit. My dad gave me my first cigarette. He said, "Here," and handed me one. He couldn't relate to me.

I try to raise art culture. And it's very difficult. They've made me a weightlifter. I was trying to be an artist. But now I'm a weightlifter, a babysitter. I'm babysitting all the parent neglect. I'm saying, "Why don't you cultivate the grounds / They're the only ones around." I mean gravity isn't going to let us go. We're here. What we do here is here. DDT is immortal. They've made DDT immortal. Boy, what's the matter? What's the matter with people? Bad nutrition. Lack of vitamin B creates paranoia, although a little paranoia is a good propeller. I'm just kidding. But it does create, well, what they say is insanity, which is varying degrees of disconnection. If somebody's body doesn't feel good, that's the whole of the body. If the ocean is wounded, it takes the whole world to heal it. And nobody seems to care.

The ocean gave me oysters, the people watching gave me ulcers. I can't believe it. The blue million miles. You've heard that song ["Her Eyes Are a Blue Million Miles"]. I did it on *Clear Spot*. That was about the ocean. "She looks at me / Her eyes are a blue million miles." What do they want to put her eyes out for? Why don't they put their eyes past their nose and shake a wet hand.

I've heard cynic people say that love is a delusion. It isn't. It's love. Man and woman, very good. I mean *very* good. Very good energy. Perfect. Perfect, that is to say: imperfect, perfect; imperfect, perfect. Very good. I've been very happy. I don't have any money but I'm happy.

Art culture must raise the drawbridge. Boy, they better raise the drawbridge or else it'll be a drawstring around everybody's neck. I can't help but think they treat love like a joke. Time's running out and all they ever do is blabber and smoke. Clean up the air and treat the animals fair. Boy, that's all I'm about. You know that. That's all I'm about. I say that. I'm truthful or at least that's my truth. Full. Really!

April 1977

Frank Zappa at the Miyako Hotel, San Francisco, 1975.

# ZAPPA AS REPORTER, HISTORIAN, & CYNIC

*In the fall of 1975, my then-girlfriend Leslie Robinson (now Leslie Goldberg) and I were fairly new to both journalism and the art of interviewing rock stars. This interview with Frank Zappa was one of the first pieces of journalism either of us was paid for; I believe we got $25. Prior to this one, I hadn't conducted many interviews. All of those, which included a conversation with Jerry Garcia, another with Mose Allison, and one with Paul Krassner, had gone smoothly. So this conversation with Frank Zappa was our first introduction to the uncooperative rock star. Zappa was a dark, bitter presence all wound up tight at the corner of the couch in his room on an upper floor of the Miyako Hotel in San Francisco, smoking cigarettes and drinking black coffee. He wouldn't let us record the conversation, so we had to take really perfect notes since the interview was to run as a Q&A. At one point I said something that angered him. To try to cool things out I told him I was one of his biggest fans. He responded that if that were true, he was in big trouble. The interview ran in the* Berkeley Barb *with a double byline. Five years later, in 1980, I went to Zappa's house in the Hollywood hills and spent several hours with him. That story follows the Q&A interview.* Frank Zappa died of prostate cancer in 1993; he was 52 years old.

### By Michael Goldberg and Leslie Robinson

SAN FRANCISCO, CALIFORNIA—WHEN FRANK ZAPPA was a kid he wanted to be a chemist. Although he couldn't afford a chemistry set, he said with a gleam in his eye, "I could always get the materials I needed." One wonders if Frank Zappa may have, in a sense, realized his childhood dream. Not only does he manage to produce lyrical bombs by mixing diverse elements from unlikely sources, but he also reaches beyond the sterile white laboratory of a technician to the purple velvet underworld of an alchemical magician, where black primal matter is turned into pure gold.

Along with Captain Beefheart, Zappa and the Mothers of Invention will be playing the Paramount Theatre in Oakland, Friday, December 26, and Winterland the following night. The *Barb* interviewed Frank Zappa at the Miyako Hotel in San Francisco last week. Zappa thoroughly dislikes interviews but submits to them, he says, because he has to remind people he "is still around." He was defensive, sardonic, and at times condescending. He smoked cigarettes and drank black coffee throughout the interview. After parleying back and forth for over an hour, we confronted Zappa with our impression of him as an extraordinarily uptight person. Whereupon he replied, "Hasn't anyone ever told you the truth?"

**Barb:** Ten years ago, your debut album could be defined as freaky by most standards. It seems that the times have caught up to you.

**Zappa:** What do you mean "freaky"? Define your terms.

***Barb***: Well, the lyrical content of *Freak Out!*, which came out in 1966, was outrageous. No other musicians had presented those themes in a rock & roll context. Now other artists like the Tubes and Alice Cooper are imitating you and it seems like you may no longer be at the forefront of the outrageous.

***Zappa***: I don't see what's so outrageous about a plastic dick in "Mondo Bondage" or choreographed dancers. *[pause]* Have any of my songs offended you?

***Barb***: Well yes, several years ago "Dinah Moe Humm" was offensive to me.

***Zappa***: You know "Dinah Moe Humm" is our most requested song.

***Barb***: I thought it was anti-feminist . . .

***Zappa***: But it isn't.

***Barb***: . . . but I re-read the lyrics this morning and realized it wasn't.

***Zappa***: And you just figured it out this morning. It took you three years to understand what that song meant. How do you expect to understand my show next week, if it took you 'til today to understand something I wrote three years ago? How can you say the times have caught up to me?

***Barb***: Bob Dylan and Frank Zappa write songs to listen to rather than to dance to. What would you say is the major difference between the two of you?

***Zappa***: He doesn't have a sense of humor. I do not choose to write songs that leave people feeling morbid, where you have an audience contemplating the sensitivity of the great inner hurt of the artist. When a songwriter does that it's just a classic example of neurotic behavior.

***Barb***: Your lyrical attitudes are very cynical. Do you like people?

***Zappa***: Yeah, I am cynical! People always ask me that. They don't understand that cynicism is a positive value. It's the only rational value. People should strive for cynicism. In fact it's dangerous not to. The US would be much better off with a wave of cynicism instead of Transcendental Meditation.

***Barb***: Back to my original question, do you like people?

***Zappa***: If I have to choose, do I like people or do I dislike people, I say I love 'em. I love 'em enough to tell 'em the truth about stuff they don't want to hear.

***Barb***: Have you ever written a serious song?

**Zappa:** They're all serious.

**Barb:** Wait a minute. Comedy plays the preeminent role in your work. Have you written a song without satirical lyrics?

**Zappa:** Sure.

**Barb:** Which one?

**Zappa:** All the instrumentals.

**Barb:** Alright. Have you ever written a serious song with lyrics that aren't satirical?

**Zappa:** You mean without funny lines?

**Barb:** Yeah.

**Zappa:** No.

**Barb:** Will you ever write a serious song without funny lines?

**Zappa:** Look, I can do anything I want. I do not choose to write serious songs without funny lines. If I didn't write funny lines I'd be finished.

**Barb:** What gives your life meaning?

**Zappa:** Music gives my life meaning. Music and fucking, in that order.

**Barb:** What do you want most?

**Zappa:** A larger audience.

**Barb:** Do you think the audience you have understands you?

**Zappa:** Who I am—no. What I'm trying to do—no. The lyrics—yes. The music—maybe.
 (So what is Zappa doing? "How long have you got?" he asks. Not that long. In essence, Zappa sees his work developing into one Hieronymus Bosch type of painting. "One album is equivalent to a corner of a large picture, to the overall work." Zappa is truly ambitious. "I tend to resemble *Encyclopedia Britannica* in cartoon form. In terms of the various subjects covered, it's an historical work, but coming from more angles than the traditional historian who merely reinforces the socioeconomic theories of the day. My work also fills in all the blanks in the entire body of pop music in this century.")

**Barb:** What do you think of San Francisco?

**Zappa:** I'd rather not discuss San Francisco.

**Barb:** Does performing live still give you the rush it initially did?

**Zappa:** It gives me more of a rush now because I don't have to argue with the audience. The basic understanding is there. They already know what they're getting into. I can get down to business and play. The audiences come and listen.

**Barb:** Why has there been such a turnover in the personnel of the Mothers?

**Zappa:** The main reason is because they leave. There are no contracts. People just come and go as they please. George Duke left several months ago to work with Billy Cobham. If I fire them, it's because they're not doing their job right. Recently I fired three people who had been rehearsing material for a month because they couldn't retain information; they wouldn't have survived the tour. Ray Collins holds the record for quitting and rejoining the Mothers. He's left five times. Roy Estrada left three times.

**Barb:** What brought you and Beefheart back together?

**Zappa:** Beefheart called me up last year and apologized.

**Barb:** Is Beefheart in your band right now?

**Zappa:** No. He'll be opening the Paramount and Winterland shows with his own band.

**Barb:** We've heard that you don't allow the musicians in your band much of a chance to improvise.

**Zappa:** What do you mean "allow." Are you going to allow the violinist to play what they want for an orchestra performance of Stravinsky? I compose songs. The song goes like this. It's not open for interpretation.

**Barb:** How is a song successful?

**Zappa:** A song is alive in my head. I translate it onto the two-dimensional surface of a piece of paper. Then I have to get it from the paper into the hands and minds of the people who will perform it. I am successful when the performance is close to the way I heard the song in my head. Different people give it new life. When it comes closest to my imagination, its successful but it's never 100 percent.

**Barb:** What songs do you feel are 99 percent successful in realizing on record or in concert what you heard in your head?

**Zappa:** "Zombie Woof," "Montana," "Muffin Man," "Andy," "Later That Night," and "Fountain of Love."

**Barb:** Do you think there's a different mood in the Seventies then there was in the Sixties?

**Zappa:** Yes. All the older brothers and sisters of the Sixties got into acid and Timothy Leary which was CIA and government sponsored. Their younger brothers and sisters of the Seventies viewed them and rejected the older brothers' and sisters' values. They have ended up somewhere between their parents' values and the values of their older brothers and sisters, which is all right. We have seen a reaction of the Sixties against the Seventies and the Seventies against the Sixties. The Fifties were a very conservative time. The teenagers of the Sixties compensated for what was missed in the Fifties. You know, teenage history started in the Fifties. There is no record of teenagers in the Forties or before. It used to be you were a child and then an adult. Nothing in between. The concept of teenage exists today only because someone found you could sell them things. They found that a teenage market exists.

**Barb:** What significant changes have you gone through in the last 10 years?

**Zappa:** I lead a different life. I have to accommodate more people who want to impinge on my lifestyle. I mean how do you rationalize someone coming up to you on the street and asking for an autograph, and if you don't have paper, they want you to bite their pencil. I lead a different life because I have a wife and three children.

**Barb:** Are your children in school?

**Zappa:** Yes.

**Barb:** How does that fit in with your drop out of school and educate yourself philosophy as articulated on *Freak Out!*?

**Zappa:** Every school needs a good student. And I'm proud to say my kids don't take shit from nobody. And I didn't even have to teach them that. Those schools will benefit from Dweezil and Moon Unit.

**Barb:** You don't think the schools will corrupt them? *[Zappa smirks and shakes his head.]* What pisses you off the most?

**Zappa:** Incompetence—I can't stand it. Injustice. Outright malice and stupidity. Stupidity is different than the other two. I can almost tolerate it.

**Barb:** Do you consider yourself a moralist?

**Zappa:** What do you mean moralist? When I talk about incompetence, I mean someone who says they can do something and then either they can't or they're incompetent. There's no morality involved.

**Barb:** You've written songs against social institutions, riots, etc., aren't you trying to change the world?

**Zappa:** No, I'm a reporter. If people hear my songs and try to do something because of them, that's okay. I see things and I write songs about them.

**Barb:** Don't you feel you miss things?

**Zappa:** Oh sure, I miss 99 percent of things but that's better than most people who miss 100 percent.

**Barb:** Do you read?

**Zappa:** I read news magazines, *Scientific American* occasionally, technical books on music, and an occasional science fiction novel. Other than that, I hate all printed material. I hate incompetent writers. Few people have learned to write anything and extract the bad part of themselves to give truth to the matter at hand. It's that extra piece of shit in the work that spoils the work. The guy wants someone to like him, to listen to him, pay attention or whatever. He should keep his crap out of it. Objectivity, that's what it is. I don't want to know about the author's deep emotional hurt or self-analysis. I don't like fiction except some science fiction. I like monster movies, childish entertainment. When I turn on the TV, I keep changing the channel 'til I see a giant spider or something. The challenge of fiction is the invention.

**Barb:** What do you think you'll be doing when you're 50?

**Zappa:** What month?

**Barb:** December 21, when you turn 50.

**Zappa:** I'll be finishing a fall tour.

**Barb:** What will your performance at the Paramount and Winterland be like?

**Zappa:** Wonderful, and if the acoustics are good, exquisite.

*Berkeley Barb*, December 1975

# ZAPPA COMES CLEAN

## An interview with rock's favorite anti-hero.

HOLLYWOOD—EVERYTHING LOOKED *so* normal. The large, ranch-style house glistened. Here, up the winding road that leads from Hollywood to Laurel Canyon, only the sounds of kids playing interrupted the calm.

"How are you doing, Dweezil?" the man asked a young boy playing in the driveway. The kid said nothing for a moment. Then, looking down at the pavement, he whined, "Fine."

A teenage girl came skipping down the stairs from the house. "Where's your dad?" asked the man, Marv Greifinger, Zappa's longtime publicist.

"He's in there," she said, pointing to a door slightly ajar.

As I said, it looked normal. But looks can be deceptive.

Greifinger pushed open the door. "Frank," he called out. The metallic sting of an electric guitar was the only answer that came from the dark room.

"Frank, it's Marv," repeated the man.

Here, amid the wealth of film, TV, and music biz stars, lives that saboteur of American culture, Frank Zappa. After my eyes adjusted to the light, I focused on the silhouette of a tall, skinny man with short, black, curly hair, bending over an electric guitar.

It was my second confrontation with Frank Zappa. The first had occurred over five years ago when he had flown up to San Francisco for a day of quickie interviews. *San Francisco Chronicle* in, *Chronicle* out. *San Francisco Examiner* in, *Examiner* out. *Berkeley Barb* in . . . You get the picture.

On that occasion, Zappa had slouched into the couch at the farthest corner of his hotel room, smoking cigarettes, drinking coffee, and looking the epitome of the jaded cynic. His hair hung down past his shoulders then, and an expression of constant irritation crossed his face.

"If people like you are my fans, I'm in big trouble," he said at one point.

"Frank has mellowed in recent years," Marv had explained on the drive up to Zappa's house.

Oh yeah? Wearing a black silk shirt, collar up, high-waisted slacks, and brown and tan saddle shoes, Zappa looked well off, but not the least bit decadent. And in contrast to the persona of his records, not the least bit weird. As he said during the interview, "I'm a no-nonsense person with a sense of humor who is very creative."

But if Frank Zappa, age 39, is less apt to insult journalists these days, and if having a wife and four kids (along with 22 employees for whom he feels responsible) has made him a more "mature" person, one thing is certain from listening to his recent recorded output: Zappa's art is as tough and scathing as ever. Frank Zappa is still OUT THERE.

"I think that you have to have the desire to be out there and the strength to deal with the consequences of confronting what's out there," says Zappa. "Most people have the horrible suspicion—which I will tell you is grounded in fact that if you knew what was out there, you wouldn't like it. Once you step beyond your everyday existence and start realizing facts that you haven't dealt with before, then that changes your relationship to your prior existence."

Zappa is sitting on a purple, velvet hardback couch. During our three-hour conversation, he talks in a low monotone. His deadpan humor alternates with cynicism and occasional flashes of humanitarianism throughout the interview.

"If I presented to you absolute proof that there were three people in the world who were running everything and planning to have you gassed tomorrow, do you think you could relate to your everyday life?" asks Zappa matter of factly. "To be able to contemplate seriously that such acts are right around the corner, that changes your relationship to the everyday environment."

"Most people would rather have a beer, go to a football game and forget it because that's more fun," Zappa claims. "Where's the get-off in thinking about the three guys with the gas? Anything that becomes a subdivision of the three-guys with-the-gas syndrome is threatening in various degrees.

"Just pick any phenomenon that would be the ultimate revelation of how shitty the world is, that's what you fear. To know, deep in your heart, how shitty everything really is and how you have no chance, you have no future. It's all gone. YOU HAVE BEEN BOUGHT AND SOLD. YOU'RE DEAD. OK? That would be the thing nobody would want to know. It's one thing to suspect it. But to know it! That ruins you. Anything that hints toward that is stuff that people get afraid of. They don't want to deal with it."

"But in a lot of ways, that is the reality," I say, thinking of Three Mile Island and the recent nationalist "get the Russians" fervor that stuck its ugly mug into the collective consciousness.

"Hey," pops Zappa, "remember the old saying? 'Know the truth and the truth shall set you free'? Some people don't believe that knowing the truth will set you free. They would rather know the fear and pitfalls. These are things that scare Americans. These are the taboos of this culture."

"But how does it set you free?"

"Once you realize . . . now I'm not saying I know everything about everything. Don't get me wrong on that account. I'm sure there's lots of stuff I don't know and plenty of stuff I don't want to know, 'cause I'm too busy to know it. But I think people have such an infinite potential for evil. I think that at a moment's notice your best friend can be so fucking shitty that it's not worth having a best friend. Once you get to the point where you can understand that, and live with that, and get past the point of feeling sorry for yourself, feeling sorry for your condition or hating things, then you can get to work. Just go to work and have a good time.

"I take this approach," he philosophizes. "Music is my religion. Music is the only religion that really delivers the goods. I've found something that I really like. And until such a time where I'm so polluted with radiation, and all the rest of the things that are negative in this society finally put me in a condition where I can't work, I'll devote everything I've got to something that I feel is positive. That's what it's all about."

IT HAS BEEN NEARLY 15 years since Zappa himself picked something he liked and "hit it." It was in 1965 that he led a band of cranky musicians he called the Mothers of

Invention out of some low rent LA garage and into the hearts and minds of a countercultural that took the title of the Mothers' debut album, *Freak Out!*, very seriously.

Since that time, Zappa and the Mothers have parted ways, but the skewed humor, schizophrenic music, and daring concepts have continued unabated. Just last year, Zappa released three albums, two of which were two-record sets. His most recent concept, *Joe's Garage Act I* and *Joe's Garage Acts II and III*, managed to be as outrageous, dirty, funny, and musically inventive as most of his previous efforts.

Zappa's live performances are typically amazing tours de force that include healthy chunks of his inspired guitar gymnastics. And *Baby Snakes*, Zappa's second film project to see the light of the projection booth (the first was the cult classic, *200 Motels*), is even now making the rounds in the US and Europe.

Frank Zappa is beyond trends, beyond contemporary fashion. If the Mothers' debut in 1966 seemed a part of the swirling psychedelia of the counterculture that was developing in LA, San Francisco, and England, well, as I said earlier, looks can be misleading. For if Zappa was as anti-establishment in his message, music, and image as any Haight Street hippie, circa 1966, he was also firmly anti-drugs and *just* as down on the hippie culture.

In "Are You Hung Up?," which appeared on the Mothers' 1968 album, *We're Only in It for the Money,* Zappa mocked the Summer of Love. "Think I'll just drop out / I'll go to Frisco / Buy a wig & sleep / On Owsley's floor / . . . I'm just a phony / But forgive me / 'Cause I'm stoned." Not exactly in sync with the love/peace/wear-a-flower-in-your-hair crowd.

Still, Zappa's freaky image—his band was pictured on the cover of *We're Only in It for the Money* wearing dresses—has given him the appearance of being part of the late '60s' psychedelic army. However, when the '60s came to a close, Zappa stood out for the idiosyncratic anarchist that he is. And he has continued to create music on his own terms that steadfastly avoids any pop music trend, fad, or cliché.

Although he has commented on successive changes in pop fashion, his body of work (29 albums [as of 1980], 8 of which are two-record sets) ultimately refers only to itself. I would expect that 15 years hence, Zappa will still be single-mindedly pursuing his own phantasmagorical visions, whether the latest trend is zydeco-disco or surf funk.

Frank Zappa has paid a certain price for his uncompromised individuality. Though the critics seemed to be siding in his favor in the late '60s and early '70s, the last five years have found them blasting Zappa's records as "dated, adolescent, redundant and repetitive." Critics have been particularly offended by Zappa's preoccupation with sex, his humorous look at groupies, and crew sluts. Some see Zappa mining the same vein over and over.

"Well, have I written about a crew slut before?" he asks, when I mention the criticism.

"Not specifically."

"These songs are based on facts," says Zappa adamantly. "Same thing with my song, 'Jewish Princess.'"

The Anti-Defamation League of the B'nai B'rith took particular offense, for some reason. Zappa's follow-up was an equally tender number, "Catholic Girls," about fellatio training in the rectory basement.

"Nobody is going to prove to me that Jewish princesses don't exist, not when they call me up and thank me for writing a song about them. I don't make these things up. I'm only the Roman messenger, so to speak. I'm just telling you these things exist. If you want to stick your head in the sand and forget it, that's your business. But this stuff is real. It's journalism."

Asked about the criticism of such songs by rock critics, Zappa says, "What sort of a person would criticize that process? Should we analyze that person's social problems? It's a very simple process. A person who writes for a rock & roll newspaper. . . . I'll requote myself. Basically, it's people who can't write talking to people who can't talk in order to prepare articles for people who can't read. And all this is done under the auspices of a publisher who is only interested in raising the ad revenue of his publication.

"My function over the last 15 years in rock & roll has turned out to be that of the object that is held up as the opposite end of the spectrum of everything that is good and holy in rock & roll. They always compare all this good stuff over here to this stinker—me. It's totally unwarranted, 'cause basically what I do is quality work. In many instances it's superior musically, and on a number of other levels, to the things that are raved about two pages over in the same publication.

"But I'm a convenient kind of a personality to use for that function. It's getting to be a very old joke. They ought to find somebody else for the '80s to use as the doormat for rock & roll."

OF COURSE, IT'S MORE THAN Zappa's musical genius that has allowed him to remain on top. He has been with three different record labels and has sued two of them. After making three albums with Phonogram Mercury, he has just severed his relationship with the company because it refused to release a timely, topical single, "I Don't Want to Be Drafted," that Zappa recently recorded.

Zappa is one of the most business-minded of rock musicians. His knowledge of the music business has allowed him to use it to further his ends, while most groups find themselves kicked about like empty beer cans on the street.

"Well, I do business in a way that will make it possible for the music to get to the people who want to hear it," he says, "whether it's in concerts or through records or video tape or whatever. I have to engage in certain processes that I don't really enjoy, such as talking to some of the people in the business who actually do the nuts-and-bolts work. If you don't do that, then bad things can happen to you.

"To give you an exaggerated example, there have been people who have had problems with record companies and given the choice between fighting it with a long lawsuit or giving up and starting some place else, they gave up.

"Well, I'm not that kind of guy. One of the reasons I've lasted so long is 'cause I'm too mean to quit. I never felt like there was anybody at any company who was going to keep me from doing what I wanted to do. A lot of the process of staying in the business is really unpleasant. It's not musical. It's not fun. But if you don't do it, you won't survive."

Frank Zappa has been an individual who has stood up to abuse from his contemporaries since childhood. "I got a lot of training being ridiculed," he recalls. "I lived on the East Coast during the tail end of WWII. Because my family was Italian, and we were living in a hillbilly area, there was a lot of ridicule. You get used to it and it doesn't affect you. What's the difference if people talk about your nationality or your clothes or your behavior? Once you're into it, it's all the same."

When he was 12 years old, Zappa turned his attention to pop music. It was drums, not guitar, that first obsessed him.

"My dad had a guitar he used to play in college. I couldn't figure out how it worked. I thought drums were more fun, got a pair of drumsticks, and began beating up furniture. My parents were horrified that I was interested in music as a career, because they couldn't see—and rightly so—how anyone could earn a living playing music in the US. It was just not a thing to do."

Zappa became a commercial artist after high school and played in bar bands on the side. It was in the early '60s that he worked with his high school buddy, Dan Van Vliet, better known as Captain Beefheart, and gradually assembled a band that became the Mothers of Invention.

"What I had in mind when I formed the Mothers," says Zappa, "was that I liked blues music. By experimenting around, I noticed that blues scales took on an entirely different character if they were placed in another harmonic climate. I had been writing a lot of orchestra music and chamber music, but couldn't get that played. I was interested in certain rhythmic things that weren't common to either popular or orchestral music, and I wanted to mess around with those. The band was the only thing that would allow me to do that."

The early Mothers were, for the most part, former R&B and rock & roll musicians who wore their hair straight and greasy. According to some accounts, Zappa had to insist that they dress "freaky" to fit the times. "As far as what the band would look like," says Zappa, "that was pretty much governed by where we could play. The clubs in Hollywood that hired rock bands wouldn't hire you unless you had long hair, so that was one thing I specified to the guys in the band. They'd better start growing their hair out.

If Zappa and his Mothers purposefully presented, both in concert and on album covers, a persona of the bizarre, it was only to prepare the potential record buyer for what was in store musically. "If you thought the record cover looked nontypical," he explains, "wait until you heard what was on the record. It's a public service, doing it that way."

Zappa's nonconformity has never fit with the ever-trendy music biz. He had to constantly watch for potential sabotage while recording for Verve Records, his first label. "We had problems at Verve because it was a subsidiary of MGM and some lawyer or top exec at MGM in New York was a personal friend of Lyndon Johnson. When we did 'Brown Shoes' with the line, 'I want to make her do a nasty on the White House lawn,' he went ape shit. They were afraid, given the climate of the times—the whole war syndrome—that whatever leverage a company of that size might have with certain friends in Washington might be compromised by having artists on their record label that those friends wouldn't agree with."

If the critics have mostly disowned Zappa, his fans have continued to multiply. "They get younger and younger," said one of Zappa's roadcrew, who I talked to briefly after speaking with Zappa. It also seems that Zappa has managed to keep many of his original fans, while appealing to each new generation of rock fans. His albums sell close to a million copies worldwide, which isn't bad for a guy who Clive Davis (former president of Columbia Records, now president of Arista Records) once said had "no commercial potential."

In fact, it's quite amazing that Frank Zappa has managed to not only maintain but expand his popularity in a business known for its here-today, gone-tomorrow stars.

"It's 'cause the music is nontypical. And we deliver something that has some lasting musical value, as opposed to manufacturing a product for instant consumption," says Zappa.

*Berkeley Barb*, March 27–April 2, 1980

# STEVIE WONDER: THE TIMELESS WORLD OF WONDER

**When you've sold 70 million records and persuaded Congress to make your hero's birthday a national holiday, you can afford to keep people waiting, and waiting, and waiting.**

*I hung out in a hotel room for at least two days waiting to interview Stevie Wonder. Really! It wasn't until the 1990s that cell phones became common, so it wasn't like I could do other things in LA while waiting. No, I had to be there so when Wonder was ready, and his guy called, I'd be there, ready to go. So in 1986, I was pretty much stuck in my room—waiting. Every few hours I'd hear from his guy, who would let me know that Wonder still wasn't available. One night, two nights, I can't remember. What I do know is that it was in the evening when I finally got to Wonder's recording studio. These days, if you are under 40 and aren't into the history of pop music, you might wonder why anyone would care about Stevie Wonder. I would say his last solid album was 1980's* Hotter Than July, *but that you have to go back to the first half of the '70s and such albums as* Talking Book, Innervisions, *and* Songs in the Key of Life *to understand why Wonder is considered an important artist. But he is an important artist, and this story will help you understand why; it ran in* Rolling Stone *and captures what it was like to spend three days around Steve Wonder.*

LOS ANGELES, CALIFORNIA—STEVIE NEVER MADE it down to the studio that day. Or the next. He was, "uh, still preparing," as one of his aides put it. He was "sleeping." He was "meeting with Motown." But as Wonder associate Birdis Coleman says, "What's an hour to Stevie?" Or a day? Or a year?

Or five years? That's how long Motown had to wait for Wonder's latest album, *In Square Circle*. "Five years is much too long to spend making an album," says Berry Gordy Jr., chairman of the board of Motown Records. "We disagree tremendously on that. He could have had two or three albums out in that time."

But Gordy, like nearly everyone else who finds himself waiting for Stevie Wonder (and everyone does), puts up with it, expects it. After more than 20 years of hits—and with about 70 million records sold—Stevie Wonder is a living, breathing, still bankable legend. Just over a year ago, he wrapped up a little ditty, "I Just Called to Say I Love You," that is one of the biggest-selling singles, worldwide, in the nearly 30-year history of Motown Records. So, Berry Gordy waits.

The "Brothers" are slumped, exhausted, around the lounge in Wonderland, Stevie's LA recording studio. Brian LaRoda, a dapper personal assistant with a pencil-line mustache, is snoring loudly, stretched across a black Naugahyde couch beneath an immense concert photograph of his boss. James Kennar, a hair stylist, is dozing off on the other couch. Barely holding on to consciousness are Birdis Coleman and publicist Ira Tucker Jr., who's so tired he's wearing shades to keep the fluorescent lights from hurting his bloodshot eyes.

Stevie Wonder at the Berkeley Community Theater, Berkeley, 1972.

It's 2 a.m. on a Friday morning. Gesturing toward the slumbering bodies, Tucker, who likes to keep things light, smiles weakly. "Perfect pitch," he says. "Only by being around Stevie Wonder does one learn to snore like that. Listen to those tones!"

This is the usual state of affairs at Wonderland. Stevie often gets by on three or four hours of sleep. He has been known to work in the studio, around the clock, for two and a half days. His staff, mere mortals, struggles to keep up. "When it comes to music, if he decides he wants to do something, he wants to do it instantaneously," says Mick Parish, one of the technicians who keep Stevie's collection of state-of-the-art synthesizers and computers, valued at more than $3 million, in running order. "He called me from Africa one time. He wanted all his synthesizers and recording equipment flown to Africa—immediately. Thirty-five of us flew to Africa that day."

Drifting in from the studio itself comes the muted sound of Stevie playing "Stormy Weather" on a Yamaha grand. He is smiling happily, lost in a melody, oblivious of the fact that people are waiting for him to get back to the task at hand: writing a jingle for Hansen's natural soda pop. Stevie's smile is euphoric, childlike. His beaded cornrow braids bounce against his shoulders as he bobs his head—to the right, to the left, to the right, to the left.... He calls that a "blindism." As he once explained: "When you're blind, you build up a lot of excess energy that other people get rid of through their eyes. You got to work it off some way, you know, and it's just an unconscious thing." Light glints off a large gold musical note that hangs from one braid. He shifts into a jazzy, Keith Jarrett–style improvisation. His whole body sways to the rhythm. Time seems to stand still for a few dreamy minutes. Birdis Coleman calls this "the timeless world of Wonder."

Then it's over, and Stevie snaps back to real time. He asks Richard Runyon, president of the marketing company that has put the Hansen's commercial together, to press a button on his Linn drum machine. As the synthesized beat begins, Stevie's large hands start working up a melody, and he improvises a lyric: "I like the taste of natural, natural. Give me the taste of natural. Give me the taste of life."

Stevie Wonder is endorsing Hansen's soda pop for what is, in the entertainment world, the oddest of reasons: He likes the product. He drinks the stuff all the time. So one day his cousin Damien Smith suggested that Stevie hook up with Hansen's. Though no one will say how much Wonder is being paid, it is, according to Runyon, "a fraction" of the $5 million Michael Jackson and his brothers got from Pepsi.

Another 20 minutes and Stevie is finished writing the jingle. Giving the advertising people a warm send-off, he enters the lounge. His presence is overwhelming. He is a big man, standing at just over six feet. And hefty. He probably weighs more than 200 pounds. (He's touchy about his weight; he got a talking scale for Christmas, though according to his secretary, "he turned the volume down.") He's also got a scar across his forehead, a reminder of a near-fatal car crash that occurred in North Carolina in 1973, when the car he was traveling in ran into a lumber truck. A log from the truck came right through the front windshield and hit Stevie in the forehead. He was unconscious for more than a week. As the story goes, Tucker sang "Higher Ground" into Stevie's ear, and he came to. Now Tucker is instantly at Stevie's side, rubbing his neck. "That hurts," says Stevie.

"It's supposed to," says Tucker.

"Well, dig in, brother," says Stevie, now welcoming the massage. Hearing the snores of his two employees, he laughs. "Welcome to my studio and dormitory."

Tucker leads the blind superstar over to a desk that sits beneath a framed poster for one of the marches Stevie led in Washington, DC. a few years back while working to make Martin Luther King Jr.'s birthday a national holiday. Judging from the many posters of King around the studio—and the two-hour NBC special that Stevie organized this year to commemorate King's birthday—it is a victory he still relishes. "I had a vision of the Martin Luther King birthday as a national holiday," Stevie will say a few days later. "I mean I saw that. I imagined it. I wrote about it because I imagined it and I saw it and I believed it. So I just kept that in my mind till it happened."

That is Stevie Wonder, cosmic visionary. The soulful seer who is wont to say things like: "Three will make the difference. *Three*. That other, you know, extraterrestrial kind of whatever that comes along. Or any three. That'll be the thing."

But at the moment, another side of Stevie Wonder is presenting itself. Removing his shades, Stevie rubs his pale, sightless gray eyes. He reaches in the direction of the phone, gropes for a half second before locating it, places a call. It is 3:30 a.m. "Bill it," he shouts at the top of his voice. "If you can't charge it, *bill it*. Billy, listen. . . ."

That is Stevie Wonder, practical joker. The lovable boss who calls at any hour of the night or day. "He'll call me, but he'll disguise his voice," says Chrysanthemum James, Stevie's secretary. "He'll say, 'I got your number, and I think you're swell.' Obscene calls. Crazy stuff. He's a clown. He loves to joke and tease. He does something every day, unless he's having a bad day."

Stevie has been known to impersonate Berry Gordy Jr.—for a laugh. "He's called my secretary," says Gordy, "and said, 'Send Stevie Wonder a check for half a million dollars right away. He needs the money right away.' So my secretary says, 'Wait a minute, boss. Just like that?' 'Yes, just like that, and do it right away.' She says, 'Have you lost your mind?' He says, 'No, Stevie's my friend, Stevie's a fine young man, just give him a check. He'll be in there shortly.'" Gordy chuckles. "I don't think he got any checks, but who knows?"

In the studio lounge, another line rings. For five minutes, Stevie bounces back and forth between calls, carrying on two conversations, occasionally firing a question at Tucker. Stevie Wonder *loves* the telephone. And it's not hard to understand why. On the phone, Stevie's blindness becomes irrelevant. Wonder is constantly struggling to overcome his handicap. He uses a Versa braille address book that allows him to note phone numbers in braille and find them when he wants to make a call. At his home he uses a Kurzweil reading machine; he can place a book or magazine in it and a synthesized voice will read to him. "He is determined to keep it from being a handicap, to overcome the obvious restrictions it might place on him," says Ewart Abner, a former president of Motown Records who has been Wonder's business manager since 1978. "He has devised means to make himself totally independent. He's been involved with manufacturers in designing things so that the sightless can be independent and free and capable of doing the things that the sighted can do."

Tucker brings over a Manila folder full of correspondence requiring Stevie's attention. Some of the letters have been transcribed in braille. Stevie's hands touch the dots. "Ah," he says, laughing. "Trying to butter up the Wonder."

The phone rings again, and Stevie answers in a weird, high-pitched voice. "Is he up? Stevie? He's on the phone. He's busy. Call him back in 10 minutes." He hangs up; those in the room laugh with him.

Tucker starts pitching an upcoming performance at the Statue of Liberty that he claims Stevie agreed to. Stevie doesn't remember the conversation. "I must be getting senile in my old age," he says. Though he has been a star for more than 20 years, ever since "Fingertips (Part II)" reached number one in 1963, Wonder is all of 35 years old.

"Man, a billion people will see you," pleads Tucker, making the case for the concert.

Stevie leaves the subject hanging. He nibbles on a cookie, then addresses the room. "You know I heard this song by Doug E. Fresh: 'The bitch was strong!'" Pause. "'Six minutes! Six minutes!'"

Kennar, the hair stylist, sits up. "Stevie, you heard that other line, 'I don't want no wrinkled pussy'?"

Stevie is incredulous. "Does it really say 'wrinkled pussy'? You know, I might be for labeling some records." Wonder isn't for censorship, but he thinks some acts have gone too far. "You want your five-year-old kid hearing 'motherfucker' on a record?"

Four-thirty a.m. Stevie's on the phone again, fingering one of his braids. "Get down here. I got to cut this Hansen's thing. Yeah. Not only that, I got to cut a demo for Dionne [Warwick]. . . ."

"And," says Tucker, grimacing, "be on the set for the Hansen's commercial by 11 a.m. With his hair braided."

"You know what I said to Stevie?" says Jay Lasker, president of Motown Records. "I told him: 'Stevie, you were working on two cylinders instead of eight on *The Woman in Red*. Let's hear the eight-cylinder job.'"

That was before Stevie delivered *In Square Circle*. Now one can practically see dollar signs lighting up in Lasker's eyes. "This will be the biggest album of Stevie's career," he says. "Part-Time Lover," the first single from the LP, reached the top of the pop charts a few weeks after its release. The second single, "Go Home," made it into the Top 10, and a third single, "Overjoyed," is currently bulleting up the charts. The album itself is selling by the truckload; it entered *Billboard*'s pop charts at number 12, which, as Berry Gordy Jr. notes, "made it the fastest-moving album in the country" upon its release last October. It has, to date, sold more than 2 million copies.

Ask Stevie why it took him five years to make *In Square Circle*, and he becomes vague: "I was involved with the King-holiday bill and performing, touring, and I was enjoying my family, and I was just *living* the experiences that would help me write."

But five years? After all, Stevie cut four of his best albums—*Music of My Mind, Talking Book, Innervisions,* and *Fulfillingness' First Finale*—between 1971 and 1974. Just two years later he delivered the masterpiece of his career, a two-record set (with a four-song EP) called *Songs in the Key of Life*.

Stevie's problem wasn't writer's block. According to his secretary, he writes a song nearly every day. When he travels, he carries a Yamaha DX7 synthesizer and a Linn drum machine, so that when the mood hits, he's ready. "He has 500 songs," claims Chrysanthemum James. "He could release an album a month for the next five years."

And despite what he says about "living," it wasn't like Stevie was on some extended vacation. He was in the studio "practically every day," according to Lasker. During the three years preceding the release of the LP, Wonder would periodically show up at Lasker's office, accompanied by a sound crew that would set up a digital sound system. Then Stevie would play bits of songs—just a few bars or a chorus—for the Motown president.

"He loves to play little pieces and get reactions," says Lasker. "He'll never play the whole thing. He loves to come up and tease you. He'll get everybody here to say, 'Jesus, give us that record, Stevie. That's a smash.' Then he'll smile and just walk out. He's very mischievous."

But something prevented him from finishing the album. "There must have been things going on in his personal life," figures Gordy. "It could hardly have been a problem with his creativity. I know it wasn't. He's written songs while we've talked on the phone. It was something else."

Whatever demons were preventing Wonder from completing his album were chased away by Dionne Warwick. Warwick persuaded Stevie to contribute a song to the soundtrack of *The Woman in Red*. Before long, he had completed a batch of songs, including "I Just Called to Say I Love You." Stevie claims he wrote the music in 1978, then "modernized" the sound and wrote the lyrics while working on the soundtrack. He won an Oscar for that one.

Working on *The Woman in Red* got Stevie back on track. "Artists get lost in the studio," says Lasker. "Sometimes it takes something to get them back in the world. Dionne was a catalyst. She got him out and moving. He got new energy. She got him into the race again. Got his juices going. Got him rolling. Enough is enough."

WHEN STEVIE LEFT HIS STUDIO and headed for home at about 5 a.m. Friday morning, this was his plan:
1. Have his hair washed and braided.
2. Return to studio and record the Hansen's soda jingle.
3. Record a demo for Dionne Warwick's next album.
4. Show up at the Culver City sound stage by 11 a.m. to film the Hansen's commercial.

Of course, none of that happened as planned. Instead, Stevie went to bed. When he got up, he decided that rather than cut the jingle at his studio, he'd cut it live, right at the sound stage. And while he was at it, maybe he'd buy himself a mobile recording studio. What the hell?

"At about 10:30 he called me up and wanted to know if he could bring down a sound truck," says Richard Runyon, who is directing the commercial, as he stands in the doorway to the sound stage. "That was fine with me. Right this very minute, he's negotiating to buy a mobile studio. I said, 'Stevie, we'll see you at 12:30 or 1?' He said, 'Something like that.'"

Twenty-odd people—cameramen, gaffers, lighting people, technicians, soundmen, and others—stand around the sound stage, waiting. And waiting.

And waiting. Hours pass. "This thing has been a nightmare," says one woman. "This has been the third time it's been rescheduled. I can't understand how he can have no consciousness of the value of other people's time. This is typical. Sure he's Stevie Wonder and everyone wants him, but . . ."

At 3 p.m., a procession of Stevie's people arrives. Gary Olazabal, his coproducer. Mick Parish, the sound technician. Aquil Fudge, a producer who uses Wonderland, and Abdoulaye Soumare, one of Stevie's synthesizer experts. And members of Stevie's family—his brother Calvin, his cousin Damien—who work for him. "Stevie's a great procrastinator," says Olazabal. "He's the best."

Sometime after 4 p.m., Stevie's chocolate-brown '79 Rolls-Royce Silver Shadow pulls up. Stevie is on the car phone, rapping. "It's amazing," says one onlooker. "Just watch. People can be bitching about him all day, but as soon as he shows up, none of it matters. Everyone is totally charmed by the guy."

Stevie is led to a dressing room where three makeup girls have been waiting since 8 a.m. They apply some makeup to Stevie's face, do some work on his fingernails, then leave. Stevie's brother Calvin then helps him dress. Beige slacks. Beige coat. Beige boots. "Shirt inside or outside?" asks Stevie.

"Inside," says Calvin. Stevie tucks in the shirt, then Calvin assists him in slipping on the coat.

"You gonna wear a second bracelet?" asks Calvin.

"It's too much," says Stevie, who's already wearing a gold bracelet with his name written in diamonds on it.

"No, man, you should see Sammy Davis Jr.," says Calvin.

"*You* should see Mr. T," retorts Stevie.

The filming of the commercial will take all night. First, Stevie begins laying down the track with his synthesizer and drum machine. As Stevie works, Runyon motions his photographer to take pictures, then gets Tim Hansen, the owner of the soda company, and finally himself photographed with Wonder.

At about 5:30 p.m., Dick Clark and film crew show up. Clark is putting together an *American Bandstand* special and needs to interview Stevie for a 30-second spot. On an adjacent sound stage Clark's crew arranges some potted plants with blue Christmas-tree lights twinkling among the leaves, a round table covered with a red tablecloth and a couple of wineglasses, and a backdrop that says, AMERICAN BANDSTAND'S 33 1/3 CELEBRATION.

Meanwhile, Stevie is still working on the music. The computer memory screws up twice, forcing him to painstakingly create the track from scratch a total of three times. Hours pass. Dick Clark periodically pokes his head through the doorway. "I've had 20 years of this," says Clark, gritting his teeth.

"I heard he kept Barbara Walters waiting 13 hours once," someone says. A thin smile appears on Clark's face. "Good."

Five hours after his arrival—and with no interview in sight—Dick Clark calls it a night, has his crew pack up the trees, the table, and the colored lights and goes home.

At about midnight, a pizza break is called. Stevie retires to his dressing room. Without being prompted, he starts to talk about his tardiness. "People seldom have a real perspective on what it takes," he says. "They just go, 'Damn, he took so long.' They don't realize all the many experiences you have to go through."

He sips from a can of Hansen's. "People do not understand lots of times. Which is okay. I mean, I'm not saying people have to change their lives for me. But if I'm what they want to be involved with, if this situation means that, as opposed to being 3 o'clock, it's gonna be 9 o'clock or 10 o'clock, and if during all of that time between when it was supposed to be and the time it's gonna be, I am honestly dealing with something else, then that's just what that is. I can't say that a computer's going to break down. Basically all you can do is the best you can do."

He leans forward in his chair. "It isn't like I'm not sorry, because I am. But then again, if everyone understands the situation, I can be sorry, but that's the way it is."

It's time to return to the set.

Nearly five hours later, at about 5 a.m., the shoot is completed. Stevie is led back to the dressing room. In the sound stage, at least five members of Stevie's staff can be seen sleeping. Some of them are awakened; they hurry to take care of the boss. In the dressing room, Stevie collapses in a chair. Calvin pulls off his boots; one of the makeup girls wipes his forehead; a box of fried chicken is produced.

Stevie reaches for a piece, finds it, takes a bite. "Never again," he says of this night spent making a 30-second commercial. But that's just exhaustion talking. He's already agreed to make a second Hansen's commercial in just a few days.

Inside his head, Stevie Wonder "sees" things. "Yeah, I think I see . . . I'm almost sure that the forms I see look exactly like yours," he says sometime after two one morning, as he sits and eats chicken in a lavish LA hotel suite. "I mean even with textures of skin, or the different colors of skin, you can touch someone, and you can get a pretty good picture in your mind. I assume that when you see something, you see it right in front of you, but you also take that image and it's in your mind, your mind's eye. It's no longer coming from your eyes, it's coming from inside you."

He takes another bite of fried chicken. "Well, the same thing happens to me. It's kind of like I touch certain things, so that in my mind that visual thing . . . It's closer to being tangible than intangible. Sort of like . . ."

He interrupts himself. "Which brings me to an interesting thought I was just thinking of while I was saying that. I bet you there is a way where the hands can actually see as eyes, connect to the optic nerves. I really believe that is possible, in a kind of way. Because basically it all gets back to being the same. If you think of a cake and you feel a cake, after a while in your mind you're thinking about how it looks."

He wipes his hands with a napkin. "I see it from how I perceived it, from touching it. But I don't touch it in my mind. I think about how I see it. I see the full shape of the cake in my mind. I imagine the cake. I'm seeing it in my mind now, a round cake . . ."

Stevie leans forward, his hands outlining an invisible cake on the tabletop. "I see it being round here and layered, and then it curves over to that side, and it has icing, and there's maybe cream over in the middle. And the candles. And I'm imagining I can see the plate and the little napkin that goes under the cake. Right? Can you see that when I'm talking?"

THE FIRST TIME BERRY GORDY JR. met Steven Judkins (he later had his name changed to Stevland Morris) was at Motown Records in 1961. The 11-year-old kid sang the Miracles' "Lonely Guy" for the Motown kingpin. "He was playing bongos, sitting on the ground in the studio," says Gordy. "He was mainly a little bongo player, and he had a little voice that wasn't that great. My first thought was 'Very nice—a blind kid playing bongos and sort of making some sounds.' I thought he was cute. I had no idea that he was a genius. We didn't sign him right away."

Stevie Wonder was born four weeks premature on May 13, 1950. According to Nelson George's recent book about Motown, *Where Did Our Love Go?*, he was kept alive for the first month of his life in an incubator. "Too much oxygen was pumped into the incubator," writes George, "and as a result Stevie developed retrolental fibroplasia, which creates a fibrous membrane behind each eyeball, and would render him permanently blind."

His parents separated early on, so he was raised by his mother, Lula Mae Hardaway. While Steven was still a baby, she moved the family from Saginaw, Michigan, to Detroit. For the soon-to-be Little Stevie Wonder, it was a fortunate move, bringing him to the future home of Motown.

By age eight, Stevie could play harmonica, bongos, drums, and piano. When he was nine, as Motown was just getting started, Ronnie White, one of the Miracles, brought Stevie down to the label's offices. It was the first of many visits. "He had something about him that was very nice in terms of his so-called handicap, his blindness," says Gordy. "He wasn't really sensitive about it. So we basically would forget that he was blind. He started hanging around the studio. *A lot.*

"We allowed him to come in and play on the drums," continues Gordy. "It was always very irritating to me, 'cause he would play very loud. I remember coming into the studio and hearing this noise and always getting quickly to my office, which was upstairs, so I would avoid the pain of hearing it."

By the time Stevie was 13, he had been dubbed Little Stevie Wonder by Gordy, was touring as part of the legendary Motortown Revue and had scored his first number-one hit. Eight years later, with 21 Top 40 hits under his belt, Stevie Wonder rebelled against the constraints of Motown. "He sent us a wire telling us he was 21, and because he was 21, his contract was voidable and he exercised that option to void it," recalled Ewart Abner, who was president of Motown at the time. "We had expected it because he had been chafing at the bit, he had been saying to us that he didn't think we understood where he wanted to go and what he wanted to do. We knew that when he got to be 21, he was going to demand absolute total creative control over his own product, which is what he did."

He received nearly $1 million, which had been held in trust for him, and he negotiated a new contract with Motown, getting Berry Gordy to acquiesce to a list of demands the record mogul had never before agreed to: Stevie got his own publishing company, complete artistic freedom, and an exceptionally high royalty rate.

Stevie took total control of his music, and he considers the results the "body of my work." The records—*Music of My Mind*, *Talking Book*, *Innervisions*, *Fulfillingness' First Finale*, *Songs in the Key of Life*, and *Hotter Than July*—are classics, on a par with just about anything else produced during the Seventies.

"The key to your success—not success but being always innovative—is how open you are to change," says Stevie. He listens to music constantly and, at the moment, is taken with rap, particularly Run-D.M.C. and Doug E. Fresh. When asked to come up with a group he's been impressed with, he mentions Culture Club. "I think Prince is incredibly talented," he adds. "He's definitely created a style. A very exciting, unique style of chord progressions, as well as kind of innovating some of the older music. Like, if he produced James Brown, it would be incredible.

"Then again," he continues, "I think that Michael [Jackson] is also very talented. And I say that also because there's so much of what he does along with Quincy [Jones]. . . . People don't realize how involved he is in the actual production."

Creatively, Stevie himself seems to have reached a plateau. *The Woman in Red* was a gooey MOR confection; the hit "I Just Called to Say I Love You" a Hallmark card set to an advertising jingle. *In Square Circle*, though obviously a more substantial record, is a consolidation of what Stevie has done before, rather than a creative leap forward.

Stevie disagrees with that assessment. Asked if he feels the material on his most recent albums is as adventurous as his work in the Seventies, he says: "Technically, yes, I think it is. 'It's Wrong (Apartheid)' is adventurous. See, my thing is, I don't really think in that sense of asking myself, 'Well, how adventurous can you get?' I know how adventurous I can get, and I know what I can do and what I'm going to do. 'It's Wrong (Apartheid)' is really the beginning of the next album. That's like an indication of the kind of stuff that's going to be on the next album."

His mouth forms into a big smile. "I haven't gone to sleep yet."

"I DON'T WANT TO talk about Stevie's personal life," says Ewart Abner. "It's nobody's business."

Stevie Wonder is a very private man. He won't allow reporters in his homes. He doesn't talk about his girlfriends. Having been a pop star for most of his life, he is skilled at deflecting inquiries into his personal life.

Ask him about women, and he is typically vague. "You meet girls," he says. "Guys like girls, girls like guys. You know that happens. And for me, it's not been an exception. But when it gets into what you want in your life and how much of a certain thing you want . . . letting someone in your life is a personal thing. That doesn't say that in my life I haven't hung out. I'd be lying to say that I didn't. But you can only really live a life with real relationships. Most of my friends are still my friends."

He's been married only once, in 1971, to Syreeta Wright, a Motown secretary turned singer. They were married for only a year and a half. "He wakes up with the tape recorder, and he goes to bed with the tape recorder," Wright said a few years ago. "If you were able to get in between, that was great."

After his marriage to Wright ended, Stevie had a daughter, Aisha (now 10), and a son, Keita (now 9), with a girlfriend, Yolanda Simmons, who currently lives in a house Wonder owns in Alpine, New Jersey. Two years ago, he had a second son, Mumtaz, with another girlfriend, Melody McCully.

In addition to his New Jersey house, Stevie owns a brownstone in New York, two houses in LA, and one in Detroit, He also owns an LA radio station, KJLH; his studio; a publishing company, Black Bull Music Incorporated; and a record label, Wondirection. He employs more than 80 people, including his sister, Renee, and his four brothers, Milton, Calvin, Larry, and Timothy.

One recent morning, he sat in the studio lounge and had a long phone conversation with Wright. "I'm friends with them," Wonder says of Wright and Simmons. "Everybody's fine with me. It gets into, like, do you love someone, or do you love them because of what they do for you, with you, to you? . . . And I mean that isn't to say that situations can't be bitter, but I think that whole energy of bitterness is something I don't ever like to have in my life. And I would sacrifice a lot just so that bitterness is not part of my life."

"Wonderboy, he can eat and talk at the same time." Stevie Wonder grins, picks up another piece of fried chicken, and takes a bite. Then he gets serious.

"I knew John Lennon would be the Beatle that would die first," he says, this particular thought triggered by a question about Marvin Gaye. "I knew that. I feared it for a long time. Because, in my mind, I felt, when I heard the song in which he sings, 'God is a concept by which we measure our pain,' I knew that somebody somewhere had a problem with that. Didn't understand it. . . . You know, when John Lennon died, for a long time I cried every time I heard 'Imagine,' because I could feel his soul in that song.

"I still can. If I'm in a certain mood, I will still cry, because, you know, I just don't understand how someone can just take someone's life like that. Which brings me to a whole other thing. I have this thing about this society, this culture, this civilization. And that is, I don't believe that whole thing about 'It's God's will.' I don't believe in that. I believe that certain things, yes, are definitely God's will. The power of the Creator. But I believe that a lot of things are man's fuckup."

He hesitates. "Excuse my language. Certain things are meant to be, but those are natural things, things that happen naturally. But any participation that man has, because of man having the ability to think and to reason, makes us responsible. We are *responsible*. But people become very irresponsible and negligent because they say, well, 'That was meant to be. It happened because it was meant to happen.' If someone in this hotel decides that they're angry with somebody else and says, 'Look, I'm going to blow this hotel up in two minutes,' and we are here doing this interview and all of a sudden this place is engulfed in flames and there's no way we can get out and we all blow up and die, I would not believe that that was meant to be. I refuse to believe that. But a lot of people, 'cause they don't understand it, say, 'Well, it's meant to be.' People that abuse children or beat their wives or stuff like that. You know, that's not meant to be. That's stupid ignorance. People who use guns. People who drink and then drive and kill families or themselves. I don't believe it. I believe that we are given this life and it really depends on how special and precious it is to us.

"That's the major thing that concerns me with crime. I understand that a lot of frustration exists. I believe there's a lot of idle time. They say that idle time is the devil's workshop. I really believe that. It really gets down to caring, and people beginning to care about themselves as well as other people."

HE IS SIX HOURS LATE. Tonight, Stevie Wonder is to be the guest of honor at a $250-a-person benefit for the American Cancer Society being held in the Los Angeles Ballroom of the Century Plaza Hotel. Smokey Robinson is the master of ceremonies. Dionne Warwick is to sing with Stevie. Berry Gordy will be in the audience, as will other top Motown executives.

As usual, Stevie is way behind schedule. He was supposed to have rehearsed yesterday evening at a Burbank sound stage. He blew that off totally. Today, the calls from the Century Plaza have been coming since noon. "By about 3:45 this afternoon you'll begin to see people tense up," says Stevie, laughing, in the early afternoon. "Panic time," he adds, obviously amused by the way people react to his tardiness. "People will start to panic."

He is sitting in the studio lounge, facing two 3/4-inch digital video-playback units. Because of its excellent sound quality, Stevie records his music on videotape. He is putting together a tape of the instrumental tracks to the songs he will sing tonight. But, as usual, there have been technical difficulties. It took hours to locate the master tape to "Part-Time Lover." A note or two of "Signed, Sealed, Delivered I'm Yours" "dropped out" of the tape, and so a new mix had to be made. Then there were the three hours spent recording an updated version of his 1969 hit "My Cherie Amour." "I'm a marathon man," says Wonder.

Stevie's assistant Brian LaRoda is nearby, staring at the TV. On the screen, the Three Stooges fumble through some harebrained shenanigans. "Reminds me of this place," he says.

Stevie has to go to the bathroom. "Can I have my shoes," he says. "I don't want to get done in by our little friends."

His voice becomes high, squeaky. "Stevie Wonder has rats in his place from the restaurant next door."

"You got roaches, too," says one of his aides.

"Rasta roaches, mon," says Stevie in Jamaican patois.

In a normal voice he says: "Not Stevie, man. He's too square, man."

Finally, at about 4:30 p.m., the tape is ready. Stevie wants to be driven to the cancer society event. One problem. His personal assistant has disappeared, along with the Rolls. So Stevie stretches out on a couch to wait. After 30 minutes, he gets impatient and asks his brother Milton to give him a ride. They load into a shiny white Mercedes convertible and take off.

At the hotel ballroom, while waiters rush about carrying platters of food to the tables, Stevie runs through a few tunes. Then he goes upstairs to his penthouse suite. As the dinner begins 19 floors below, he lies down on the bed and falls asleep. While Smokey Robinson and others make speeches honoring Stevie Wonder, Stevie is dreaming.

While he dreams, his brothers Calvin and Milton and other members of his staff change into tuxedos. Shortly after nine, Stevie emerges from the bedroom, and Val and April, his makeup girls, start to work on him. Val smooths makeup onto his face; April rubs something into his hair. The phone rings; Stevie is needed backstage. He is led down the hall, into an elevator, through the lobby and the kitchen and up some stairs into a dressing room.

Dionne Warwick arrives and plants a big kiss on Stevie's face. "How are you!" she gushes.

"Sleepy." They embrace for a good minute.

"Well," she says. "I'll go down and enjoy myself."

After she leaves, Stevie says, "I need my headphones." To monitor his performance, he uses headphones plugged into a pocket-size radio transmitter. One of his brothers hands him a pair. Stevie is irritated. These are not the right headphones.

"Where are they, Stevie?" asks his assistant.

"Things get moved around. You don't put them in the same place, and they're lost." He seems close to exploding. "They were in my bag." The assistant and a brother run over to a black leather bag and begin searching through zippered pockets. Another pair of headphones is produced. Still not right. And another. "No," says Stevie. "Where's that first pair?"

"Stevie," someone says, "they're waiting for you." He slips on a striped formal jacket as he is led into the hall. People crowd around. The hallway feels chaotic, claustrophobic.

"Where's the transmitter?" snaps Stevie, slowly descending the stairs. It is produced, and he plugs in the headphones as he reaches the stage entrance. "It's not working." He's frantic. "I don't hear anything. The battery is dead."

There is much fumbling by his aides as they locate another transmitter. Then Smokey Robinson appears. He throws an arm around Stevie. "We took down the microphones and the equipment," says Smokey. "No piano, either, Stevie." Stevie Wonder practically jumps, then realizes it's a tease. "If anyone can go out there and do it alone," Smokey says, "it's you, Stevie."

Stevie Wonder walks calmly out onto the stage to a deafening round of applause. "I heard all that stuff about Stevie Wonder," he says. "Stevie who?"

There is laughter.

He gets serious. "I was listening to all the things you were saying about me. . . . I'm appreciative of what you've said about me and what I've done."

Minutes before he had been exhausted. Irritable. Now, before the public, all that is visible is a smiling, charming Stevie Wonder. A gracious superstar. No one in the audience could possibly suspect that he slept through the speeches. "When we see people far less fortunate than we are, then we will do all that we can so they can enjoy that which God wants us to have. . . ."

When the speech is over, he is led to a bank of synthesizers. Taking a seat, he begins to sing and play "Did I Hear You Say You Love Me" to a taped backing track. "Master Blaster (Jammin')" follows. At one point the tapes are stopped, and he performs the modernized version of "My Cherie Amour," using the musical tracks that he had played and stored in the synthesizer memory that very morning. It is a phenomenal one-man show.

A FEW HOURS LATER, BACK in his hotel suite, Stevie speaks to a small group of friends and associates, including Adrienne and Elliott Horwitch, the couple who organized the benefit, about a vision he had after visiting a close friend who has cancer.

Stevie dreamed there was a lake. And near the lake were cedar trees. And in the dream, the sap from the cedar trees was a cure for cancer. "I called up my friend," says Stevie. "I asked him if there was a lake near where he lives. He said there was. I asked if there were any trees. He said. 'Yes, cedar trees.' That really struck me. So I've been talking to some doctors. I think there may be a cure there. It's something I really believe. It's something I intend to pursue."

*Rolling Stone*, April 1986

# RICHARD THOMPSON SHOOTS OUT THE LIGHTS

*There are a lot of great guitar players, and then there is Richard Thompson. He cofounded Fairport Convention when he was 18 and recorded five studio albums and two live albums with them before he left to pursue a solo career. He recorded six studio albums with Linda Thompson, who he was in the process of splitting up with at the time I wrote this story. As a session musician, he played on such incredible albums as Nick Drake's* Five Leaves Left *and* Bryter Layer *and John Martyn's* Bless the Weather *and* Solid Air. *He also played on albums by The Incredible String Band, John Cale, Sandy Denny, David Thomas, and many, many more. And he has had 19 solo studio albums released, plus a bunch of live albums. No one sounds like Thompson. While he is known for his glistening guitar work, he is also a distinctive singer and a brilliant songwriter.* Shoot Out the Lights *(1981), which he made with Linda Thompson, is one of the greatest rock albums every recorded. Thompson became a Sufi in early 1974, and I've always felt that there is both a spiritual quality to Thompson's playing and a Middle Eastern feel to it. It was an honor to get to hang out with and interview Richard Thompson.*

THERE IS A STORY CIRCULATING about Richard Thompson. The way I heard it, the Eagles approached him, prior to hiring Joe Walsh: They wanted Thompson in the band as lead guitarist. Living in obscurity in England, Thompson allegedly replied: "What? And spend the rest of my life working with a bunch of Southern Californians?"

The world's greatest living rock & roll guitarist was sitting in a rundown hotel room in San Francisco, looking more like a rumpled character out of a song by The Band, or from a John Steinbeck novel, than a rocker.

Richard Thompson is 33 years old and speaks with an English accent as thick as the head on a mug of English ale. He might have been a farmer from the turn of the century with his receding hairline, trimmed beard and mustache, green army pants, and pale blue cotton shirt. He screwed up his gaunt face into an exaggerated grin and stared down at the fake wood table between us. I had just mentioned that in many reviews, Thompson is favorably compared to Robbie Robertson.

"Really?" he said, his voice almost a mumble. "Very flattering." He looked over at me. "I love Robbie Robertson's guitar playing. I wouldn't mention myself in the same breath as him. I think he's great."

The word "modest" might be appropriate at this point. Didn't he think he was a good guitarist?

"Sometimes. I think it varies from night to night, actually. After the last two gigs, which were in Santa Cruz, I don't think I'm a good guitar player." He laughed nervously. "'Cause I didn't play very well." What Richard Thompson didn't say, but which I will, is that on a bad night, Richard Thompson can walk all over everyone from Eric Clapton to Eddie Van Halen. He is a purely intuitive player who sounds like he's letting a drop of his soul out with every note he fires from his Fender Strat. As often as not it's a mess of notes. He'll somehow stretch a string with one finger while other fingers are picking out a fluid solo—he sometimes sounds like two guitarists playing together (cf. the solo at the end of the title track of Richard and Linda Thompson's recent LP, *Shoot Out the Lights*, for evidence).

Unlike so many of the younger guitar slingers, Thompson is a man who takes note of tradition. His is a tradition of rock guitar defined by people like James Burton (Elvis Presley's hired gun), the late Clarence White (who helped Gram Parsons and the Byrds invent country rock), Muddy Waters and, of course, Robbie Robertson.

It's a tradition of guitarists who play with emotion and technique. But it's a tradition that never sacrifices emotion for technique. In other words, sometimes a wrong note has more emotional TRUTH than a perfectly played noted. Dig?

"I think if you play an instrument, you're expressing something. I think instruments are a substitute for the voice," explained Thompson, as he rubbed a bare foot against the worn beige carpet. "You are trying to speak, you're trying to be eloquent in a way. It's a kind of a language. You are trying to communicate something. But it comes, really, without thinking. You don't sit down and go, 'Well, right now I'm going to play a solo, it's going to be very eloquent and it's going to convey the pathos of an Armenian peasant toiling in the fields for hours. I want to convey that in a solo.'" He chuckled.

Did he think of that right before he played, I kidded?

He grins. "Uh, no. Not usually. I think it's really just unconscious. Thinking as little as possible. The less you think the more it plays itself. And the more it plays itself, the better it gets. The less you interfere with it. The more it's music and the more you get those real notes, the good ones. And there's not many of those. So you're playing for those real notes."

If Richard Thompson was merely an amazing guitarist, that would be enough. But he's not. He's one of these multitalented characters; a band leader, currently leading the Richard and Linda Thompson Band, one of the greatest songwriters of his generation, and the man can sing with the kind of voice the Levon Helm might have had if he had grown up in England rather than the South.

Because he was a founding member of Fairport Convention, Britain's answer to the Byrds, back in 1967, and because he continues to work in a corner of the musical universe where rock and folk, country and blues, acoustic and electric all fit together in a magical, mystical way, he has been dubbed a "British folkie." But in fact, Thompson's music has about as direct a relationship to folk as Fleetwood Mac's. "The music we play, it tries to be contemporary," said Richard flatly. "It's not trying to be old worldy. Sometimes people think that if you have anything to do with traditional music, then you're being old worldly or something. A lot of the reviews of Fairport used to take that stance. That we were reviving this rich English history of music. Which wasn't true. English traditional music is still sung and goes on. It's not this old thing. It's this contemporary thing. So what we try to do is contemporary. I think if you listen to a lot of traditional music and it influences you, then inevitably, what you do will have a timelessness, because you absorb something that was written over a long period. In the case of British music, 700 or 800 years. And you could say that that's the only way to be contemporary in England, to understand traditional music. Because then you understand what's possible. And what's been done. And you can be truly contemporary.

"In another sense it's just rock & roll. I hate definitions. I really do. I shouldn't have gotten into this. I just cut my own throat."

As you are probably beginning to gather, Richard Thompson is not your typical sex, drugs, and rock & roll type guy. He's very . . . *serious*. Consider that he doesn't drink or smoke, and that he became a Muslim six years ago.

"If you're a Muslim, then you believe there's more to the world than what is apparent. And after you die, that isn't the end of things. You carry on. And if you believe that, then obviously you live life differently than somebody who thinks that's nonsense. It gives you a totally different attitude to living."

Thompson was 18 years old when, together with a bass player named Ashley Hutchings and guitarist Simon Nicol, Fairport Convention was formed. It seems natural enough that this kid who was born in London and grew up there, listening to his father's Fats Waller and Duke Ellington and Django Reinhardt and Les Paul records, not to mention the Scottish country dance records, would end up in a band that mixed jazz and folk with rock & roll.

As Thompson tells it, the arrival of American rock & roll records in England had a major effect on him. "Oh, it was wonderful. It was kind of naughty music," he laughed. "You had to hear it wherever you could. I was fairly young at the time. I had a big sister who started to collect rock & roll records. She had a good collection of Buddy Holly, Presley, Jerry Lee Lewis. That was the first stuff I heard, yeah. That was the only stuff that came to England. Stuff like rockabilly never appeared in England until 1975." He laughed again. "Earlier than that, but there wasn't a lot of that around. A bit of Carl Perkins."

When Fairport formed in 1967, Dylan had already shifted from folk to rock, had toured England with The Band (then known as the Hawks), and had demonstrated that rock & roll and brains *were* compatible. Thompson and his friends were bowled over by Dylan and the Byrds. "We were very impressed by the lyrical content, more than anything else," he recalled. "The fact that you could have rock & roll with very strong lyrics was very appealing. We always wanted to do the equivalent. And our interest in it started by imitation. We used to do Byrds numbers, Dylan numbers, and Joni Mitchell numbers until we had a style of our own."

Fairport Convention were never particularly popular, in England or the US. Yet they managed to record a batch of wonderful records with titles like *What We Did on Our Holiday, Unhalfbricking, Liege and Lief,* and *Full House*. Richard left the band in 1971 and released his first solo album, *Henry the Human Fly*, a year later. By that time, he had become romantically involved with Linda Peters, a friend of the late Sandy Denny, Fairport's striking lead singer. Peters was also a singer, and after Richard married her in 1972, they began working together as Richard and Linda Thompson, recording a series of albums, most of which the critics loved and the public ignored: *I Want to See the Bright Lights Tonight, Hokey Pokey, Pour Down Like Silver, First Light, Sunnyvista*, and, most recently, *Shoot Out the Lights*.

Over the course of those six albums, the duo has taken the tentative folk and rock fusion of Fairport Convention and developed it into a rich music that is quite unique. Linda's voice has that proper English quality about it that reminds one of afternoon teatime; it is a gorgeous instrument, far more emotive and beautiful than more popular singers like Linda Ronstadt and Emmylou Harris. Contrasted to the rough grain of her husband's vocals, the two come off like a hip, very English George Jones/Tammy Wynette.

The songs that Richard writes are not slight. In fact, some people wonder about them. About the, shall we say, morbid and depressing nature of many of the lyrics. On the new album, for instance, there is a song called "Did She Jump or Was She Pushed?" Sings Linda in an almost hushed tone: "She was there one minute / And then she was gone the next / Lying in a pool of herself / With a twisted neck . . . / She thought she'd live forever / But forever always ends."

Another of Richard's songs is called "The Wall of Death." And when he writes about love, "Don't Renege on Our Love," it's in this manner: "Remember when we were hand in hand / Remember when we sealed it with a golden band / Now your eyes don't meet mine. . . ."

When asked about the dark nature of his songs, Thompson was surprised. "Well, if you switch on the television," he says, pointing over at the hotel room set, which is turned off, "at least half the channels are showing something comparable. Is that dark? If you go to the cinema, at least half the films are a lot heavier than that. I don't see that it's dark or heavy."

"I try not to locate them too precisely myself," he said. "I prefer the ambiguity of them. I hate to pin stuff down and say this means this. It's not the way it's intended. It's intended to be how you like it. It's one of the great things about music. It's different to each person. And I think within the confines of a song . . . a song isn't any big deal. It lasts three minutes. It's not Shakespeare and it's not Mozart. It's neither of those. It takes elements of music and elements of words and puts them together. And you can do something with that. In three minutes you can put something across. But it's not a really big deal."

But it's important to you, you've spent your life doing it.

"Oh, I love it. I really enjoy it. But I know its limitations."

At this point, it must be rather sadly noted that when I interviewed Richard, on the final afternoon of the Richard and Linda Thompson Band's first American tour, things were not looking too good for the future of the Richard and Linda Thompson Band— or, for that matter, the future of Richard and Linda Thompson's marriage. Richard was staying in his own hotel room—and there was no sign of Linda in the room. Rumors were flying fast and furious that this would be their last performance together, that their marriage was on the rocks, that kind of thing. Linda was not available for interviews. And all Richard would say about it was: "It's always been hard to balance domestic and career. It's an endless problem. That's all I can say. Really difficult."

Richard Thompson likes punk rock. "I thought the Sex Pistols were the outstanding band of the '70s, actually," he said with utter seriousness. "They just sounded great to me. Phenomenal energy. I think Johnny Rotten was a great singer. His new band, Public Image, is just excellent. Possibly by accident, one of the most interesting bands around."

The fact is that Richard Thompson is a fan of good music, music that conveys emotion and life. "Heart" is his word for it. Which is why he can dig the Pistols, but has contempt for, say, Journey.

Asked for his take on the Styx/Journey contingent currently dominating American FM rock radio, he said: "Oh, that stuff. In England you don't hear too much of that stuff. Before I left England, I was despairing because English radio is so awful. It's just the same old stuff all the time. The same old hits, real narrow programming policy. I thought, this is terrible here. I thought there must be something better in America. And I got to America, and I couldn't believe it. It's so abysmal. It's really conservative. It's like frightened music. Frightened to make anything that someone might object to or might stick out too much. It's just elevator music as far as I'm concerned. I'd rather listen to elevator music, really. I think it serves a better environmental purpose than Journey, Styx, Foreigner, etc."

Those bands just seem to be in it to make money.

"And having made it, they're desperate to keep making it. And so they make more and more conservative records. Take less and less chances. They probably take a million hours recording every album making sure they get everything absolutely right. Get the tempo unspeakably steady. Get the notes excruciatingly correct. It's extremely distressing. And I hope there are enough people in America with decent taste that it would eventually overthrow this tyranny of blandness."

And with that, Richard Thompson, the man who wouldn't join the Eagles, got up to go watch a bootlegged videotape of Bob Dylan's 1967 documentary *Eat This Document*.

*Creem*, September 1982

# THE SECOND COMING OF ROBBIE ROBERTSON

**The enigmatic leader of The Band returns to the rock world with his brilliant solo debut.**

*I spent a year reporting and writing this profile of Robbie Robertson. It wasn't supposed to take so long. But then recording his first solo album,* Robbie Robertson, *wasn't supposed to take Robertson so long, nor cost so much—an estimated million dollars. I'm glad it all took so long. I wasn't working on the story full-time for a year (I wrote many other stories too during that time), but it gave me a chance to see Robertson over time, to be with him in a number of different places including three recording studios. I was also able to see him in Woodstock, where of course The Band came together at Big Pink, and where the famous* Basement Tapes *were recorded, before The Band cut* Music from Big Pink. *The Band is one of my favorite groups and Robertson is one of my favorite songwriters and guitarists. His playing with Bob Dylan during the touring they did in 1965 and 1966 is exceptional. And that first solo album Robertson made during the year—1986–1987—I spent reporting on him, remains a favorite. So I was a driven man as I worked on this story. I wanted it to be a classic of music journalism. I don't know if it is, but what I do know is that when I finished this story, I felt it was a breakthrough for me. I felt that because I'd been reporting it for a year, I was able to put the passage of time into the story, something that you don't often experience in a piece journalism. To this day I think this is one of the best stories I've written.*

SANTA MONICA, CALIFORNIA—A FEW YEARS ago Robbie Robertson decided that he wanted to make a film called *American Roulette*. The script tells the story of a Sixties rock & roll legend who has disappeared for some 15 years. A notorious abuser of drugs and alcohol during his heyday, this onetime guitar hero is believed by many to be dead, perhaps of an overdose. But no one really knows what has happened to him. And by the Eighties, no one cares.

The film would focus on this rocker's teenage son, who is searching for his father. The journey is a coming of age for the boy, who dreams of someday becoming a big-time rock guitarist himself. Along the way, he plays in a roadhouse band, gets beaten up in a parking lot for flirting with the wrong girl, smokes dope for the first time, loses his virginity, and comes face to face with his dad's old manager, an eccentric character now living on a grand estate in Woodstock, New York.

Eventually, the boy finds his father, who is alive and well, living a quiet, anonymous, and drug-free life since he dropped out of the rock & roll world.

Robbie Robertson still hopes to turn this script into a movie. It's easy to understand why: if you could combine the father and the son into a single character, you'd almost have *The Robbie Robertson Story*.

Eleven years ago, Robbie Robertson shut down The Band and walked away. At the time, The Band was a living legend. One of the first rock groups to appear on the cover of *Time*. Headliners at Woodstock. Like their friend and former boss Bob Dylan, the

Robbie Robertson playing in The Band at the San Francisco Civic Auditorium, 1970.

members of The Band cloaked themselves in myth and mystery. And just before they called it quits, Robertson assembled a cast of some of the most prestigious names in Seventies rock—Neil Young, Bob Dylan, Van Morrison, Eric Clapton, Joni Mitchell—to perform at their final concert, an elaborate affair called the Last Waltz.

After 16 years—Robertson had hit the road in 1960, at age 16—the rock & roll life had lost its allure for Robertson. What had begun as a fantastic adventure had become a job—"like selling shoes," he says. He had other plans—perhaps a career in films. "The Band was just fine until we became successful," says Robertson, who is now 44.

"And then here came this strange phenomenon. It's like a disease. . . . It just wasn't a creative process for me anymore. And I felt guilty of being one dimensional in my life. I wanted to just be able to sit down or play with the dog or *something*. I was dying to be able, when someone asks, 'What are you doing?' to say, 'Nothing.'"

The author of such classics as "The Night They Drove Old Dixie Down" and "The Weight" had run dry. "I just had nothing left to say," Robertson says. "I would look around, and I would see all these other people who had nothing to say either, but they insisted on making records. I thought, 'I don't want to do that.' I felt like I'd made a hundred records. I thought, 'I just want to clear the air, do something else for a while, and maybe, at some point, I'll feel inspired, and I'll do it again. Or maybe I'll never do it.'" He pauses for a moment, and a sly smile creeps across his face. "Either way, it intrigued me."

"I CAN'T JUST MAKE A record," says Robbie Robertson one night as he cruises through Santa Monica, California, in his jet-black BMW 733i sedan. "I have to make a *move*."

After a decade in the shadows—which included a separation and reconciliation with his wife of 19 years, a flirtation with the movie business, a period of wild living, fueled by drugs and alcohol, and the tragic suicide of Band singer-pianist Richard Manuel, who hanged himself in a Florida hotel room last year—Robertson is, finally, making his "move." "All of a sudden, I had this yearning, I had this need," he says. "I felt angry. I felt possessed. It was all very instinctual, like breeding time."

His first solo album, *Robbie Robertson*, a brilliant, autobiographical work, should reestablish him as one of the preeminent rock & roll artists of his generation. The album, produced by Daniel Lanois (U2, Peter Gabriel) and Robertson, with contributions from Gabriel, U2, the BoDeans, former Band members Rick Danko and Garth Hudson, and jazz arranger Gil Evans, is a lyrical and musical masterpiece.

"It's really Robbie's story," says Daniel Lanois. "I was talking to Bono about this. 'Testimony' and 'Fallen Angel' and 'Broken Arrow'—they're all about *him*. Not that many writers of songs have seen enough of the world to make a record like that sound interesting. But Robbie has. It's fiction based on truth, based on his life."

One of rock's great enigmas wants another shot at stardom. The star-making machinery is already in high gear. Geffen Records has committed over a half million dollars for the initial marketing and promotion blitz. MTV will air a half-hour special on Robertson. He may host *Saturday Night Live* in December. "I think he's hungry for success," says Peter Gabriel, a good friend of Robertson's for the past five years. "But there are two ways of going after it. The work can ride on the ego, or ego can ride on the back of the work. With Robbie, the latter is true. The music wouldn't sound like that if it were the other way around."

If all goes as planned, this will be the year of Robbie Robertson's second coming.

THE DOOR TO ROBBIE ROBERTSON'S "workshop," a recording studio in West LA, opens, and there he is, looking tired, a cigarette between his fingers, a half-empty bottle of Corona in his other hand. "Come on in," he says in a low, cigarette-worn voice. "Have a seat. Want a beer?"

It's early November of 1986, and Robertson is hard at work on his album. For the past few years this $12,000-a-month studio has been his base of operations. He's done much of his recent recording here. Wearing a dark, oversize shirt that hangs over black jeans, Robertson leads the way into a room that he has converted into a kind of serene den, complete with two couches, a coffee table, a mess of guitar cases and walls hung with paintings and drawings by an American Indian artist, Darren Vigil.

He collapses onto one of the couches. As the smoke curls up from his Marlboro, he peers through the dark lenses of his oval sunglasses and launches into a few of the stories he's collected during the making of his album. But as he tells these stories, one begins to realize how little they actually reveal about Robbie Robertson. Perhaps this is something he learned from being around Dylan; his essence remains frustratingly out of reach.

Robertson's friends describe him as a very private person. Although Gabriel has known him for five years, he's been out to Robertson's house only once; all their other LA socializing has taken place at restaurants and clubs. Gabriel says that he was surprised at how "nervous" Robertson was when he came to Bath, England, to work on songs with him. "He's a very kind person with a wild imagination," says Lanois. "He's got a heart of gold. But he's got some mischief in him as well. He's a street kid from way back. He learned the ins and outs playing in scuzzy bars, and he's always got the point of view of that same young man."

"I've always had the sense," says Gabriel, "that there is some strong spirit of brooding within Robbie that needs its expression."

At the studio, most of the recording takes place in a cramped control room filled with synthesizers, speakers, guitars, and multitrack recorders. Asked to play some of the songs he's been working on, Robertson hedges. He offers some excuses—the vocals aren't done; the tracks aren't finished; everything is incomplete—before stating flatly, "I'm not into playing tracks." Instead, entering the control room, he removes his shades and puts on a finished piece he recorded last year with Gil Evans when the two of them worked on *The Color of Money*.

Up close, Robertson's face looks weathered from the years of fast living and the recent nights of little sleep. Yet he's still remarkably good-looking and undeniably charismatic. And as Gabriel puts it, "Both his lyrics and his voice sound like they've been lived in."

An hour later, seated at a table at Chinois on Main, a pricey Santa Monica restaurant he frequents, Robertson orders a glass of champagne. The conversation has turned to his foray into film, a strange adventure that began at the end of 1976, as Robertson and Martin Scorsese started editing the raw footage of *The Last Waltz* into the best rock concert film ever made. By the time the film was released, in 1978, Robertson had the film bug—bad. And when film critics started predicting that the handsome guitarist would become another Robert Redford, Robertson ate it up. Now *this* was a move he was ready for: Robbie Robertson, *movie star*. He liked the sound of that.

He was given an office—Carole Lombard's old dressing room—at MGM. And off and on for a few years, he would drive out to the MGM lot and read scripts. Many, many scripts. But nothing grabbed him. Nothing swept him away. Nothing made his "blood boil." Until he came across *Carny*, a 1980 film about a traveling carnival, which he not only starred in, along with Gary Busey and Jodie Foster, but also coproduced. A provocative but flawed film, *Carny* bombed, and none of the acting roles that came Robertson's way after that were quite right. "Several things came up that I almost did," he says. "But something would stop me at the last minute. I would go for meetings with directors, and as I talked with them, I'd end up saying, 'You know who you should get for this part? Get somebody who's dying to do this. People would cut off their little finger to play this part. For me, it's medium.'"

In the meantime, he was "musical producer" for two Scorsese films, *Raging Bull* (1980) and *The King of Comedy* (1983). By 1983 he had pretty much given up on an acting career. "I was working with this agent, and he kept sending me stuff. This is what I did every day for a couple of years: reading scripts, meeting with people, flying to see some director somewhere. Finally, my agent said to me, 'You know, I don't know what I can do here, because you say no every time. Maybe you're just not interested in doing this.'"

DURING THE PAST YEAR, gossip around the music industry had it that Robbie Robertson's album was a runaway project.

"There's this vibe going around," Geffen Records A&R executive Gary Gersh said in June. "People start to think that you're dealing with *Heaven's Gate*."

Robertson labored for three long years. Most of the songs were written in the studio. There were months upon months of musical experimentation, countless rewrites and rerecordings of the songs, and even an 11th-hour decision to bring in Bob Clearmountain (Bruce Springsteen, the Rolling Stones) for a remix.

Robertson began preliminary work on the album in the fall of 1984, prior to signing with Geffen. He spent "at least $50,000" on preproduction, including trips to the East Coast and Europe to meet with a half-dozen record producers. Formal recording with Lanois began in June of 1986. Session musicians were flown in from Canada, New Orleans, and even France. Sessions eventually took place in Dublin (with U2), Bath (with Peter Gabriel), LA, and Woodstock.

Gabriel believes the album took so long because in Robertson's mind it became "some kind of monster he had to live up to." Robertson admits that he procrastinated. "People would mention it," he says, "and I would say, 'Yes, yes, yes, I'm working on the album.' But I didn't have *any* songs written."

Robertson was also nervous about his singing voice; it was Levon Helm, Danko, and Manuel who provided most of the vocals in The Band. "Robbie was always one of my favorite singers," says Danko. "But he was always shy of the microphone. Might have been an element of stage fright there. He would sing the parts for us, and we would reproduce them."

The project dragged on for so long that Lanois had to take a leave of absence midway through it to produce U2's album *The Joshua Tree*. At one point Geffen Records refused to advance additional money for the mounting recording costs, so Robertson's manager had to raise funds for its completion. "I was uncomfortable about what it was costing," says

David Geffen. "Frankly, I think Robbie is a musical genius. I have complete faith in him as a musician and a songwriter. The only question that ever came up was how much this was going to cost, and ultimately that was okay, too."

In the end, the cost of making the record, including a several-hundred-thousand-dollar advance Robertson got for signing with Geffen, came to nearly a million dollars. "It wasn't a cheap record," says Robertson. "But I wasn't trying to be extravagant. But it's so hard not to be, because every step you take is like 'Whoops, there goes another $20,000.'"

JAIME ROBBIE ROBERTSON WAS BORN in Toronto on July 5, 1943. His mother was "this little Hiawatha girl," an American Indian who had grown up on the Six Nations Indian Reservation, located above Lake Erie. His father was a "sharpie guy who gambled for a living," says Robertson. "So it was kind of a strange combination."

Robertson spent his summers on the Indian reservation, visiting his relatives. He says hearing his uncles playing "fiddles and mandolins and guitars, and singing" was "just like a burning spear through my heart."

And then, when he was about 11, he heard some rock & roll. "The next thing you know," he says, "there's this music seeping out of the cracks in the walls. It was all over for me. Elvis was part of it, but so was Chuck Berry and Fats Domino and Bo Diddley. You put all these things together, and what are you going to do? After that, I couldn't concentrate on anything else. It was the *only* thing."

In 1960, after leading some bands of his own, with names like Thumper and the Trombones, the Robots and the Consuls, Robertson got a phone call from the Arkansas rockabilly singer Ronnie Hawkins, who offered him a job in his backup band. "You'll get more pussy than Frank Sinatra," Hawkins told the young guitarist, and that was all he needed to hear. "He was right about it to a certain degree," Robertson says with a laugh. "What we never got to discuss, on a grand scale, was quality."

Hawkins' backup band also came to include Richard Manuel, Rick Danko, Garth Hudson, and Levon Helm. The next five years on the road—first with Hawkins, then on their own as, at various times, Levon and the Hawks, the Crackers and the Canadian Squires—transformed them into the toughest rock & roll outfit around.

In 1965, word reached Bob Dylan, the folk singer who had decided to "go electric," and soon they were touring the world, minus Helm, as Dylan's backup band. The tour was a real trial by fire—audiences weren't yet ready for Bob Dylan, rock star. "They'd throw bottles at you and boo," says Robertson. "Sometimes it was very funny, and sometimes it was heartbreaking."

When Dylan and the Hawks played London's Royal Albert Hall in 1966, the Beatles were in the audience. "After the show they came back to say hello to Bob," says Robertson. "We were still basically scroungy street kids, you know, and we were astonished at how naive they were. How very sweet and nice and everything. They all had on, like, matching boots and matching clothes. And they talked about mystical things that were very corny. From the American side of it, it wasn't so sweet. It was tougher. Different rules to the game, I guess, is what it was."

Soon after they returned to America, Dylan had his infamous motorcycle accident. As he recuperated, the Hawks were encouraged to join him in Woodstock. "It was summertime in New York City," says Robertson. "It was expensive, and we were just these road musicians that had no road to go on. We were scrounging around trying to figure out a place to work on some music. And Albert Grossman [Dylan's manager] said, 'This is silly. Why don't you guys move up to the country up here?' And it just simplified everything. So that's what we did. We got this pink house."

The scene at Big Pink was casual, like "a clubhouse." People would toss a football around in the backyard or play checkers; they were having a good time. Things were just as relaxed in the basement. There, with Garth Hudson manning a reel-to-reel tape recorder, Dylan and the Hawks (who decided to change their name to The Band; that's how people in Woodstock were referring to them anyway) created some of the greatest rock & roll ever made. "You would experiment," says Robertson. "And it wasn't all these long intellectual songs and big statements and poetry. I didn't want to write Bob Dylan poems. Not because I didn't like them, just because it wasn't my job. I always felt I had to connect it with this world that was true to The Band's music. We came in on a different train. It wasn't folk music, and it wasn't poetry. It was rock & roll."

At some point Grossman—a colorful character who was at the time perhaps America's most powerful rock & roll manager—suggested that if they wanted to make an album, he would get them a deal. *Music from Big Pink*—composed and arranged at the pink house but actually recorded over a few weeks at A&R Recording Studios, in Manhattan—was a big hit with the critics but not a commercial success. Nonetheless, The Band was planning to go out on tour; then Rick Danko broke his neck in a car accident.

So instead of touring, Robertson wrote another batch of songs; he and The Band rented Sammy Davis Jr.'s old house out in LA, installed some multitrack recorders in the pool house, and spent two and a half months recording the group's masterpiece, *The Band*. It was a critical and commercial success, selling a million copies and yielding a Top 30 hit, "Up on Cripple Creek."

They subsequently did their first American tour as The Band, then returned to Woodstock to begin work on *Stage Fright*. That was when a cloud of sorts—what Robertson calls "the darkness"—settled on The Band. "Ever make a million dollars fast?" says Rick Danko. "Well, I have. I've seen it ruin people. I've seen it kill people. It's a goddamn crying shame what success can do to some people. Try having the money and having all the drugs you want."

"It was the drug age," says Robertson. "In the late Sixties and early Seventies, it was just wall-to-wall. Everybody wanted to turn me on to something new. There were a lot of people around. Crazy people. Wonderful people, too. But a lot of them were crazy. And a lot of them were druggies. And some of them were heroin addicts. Everybody's trying to do you a favor. Some people are trying to do you the wrong favor. And for the guys in The Band, it wasn't like all of a sudden they got successful and immediately people were running into the bathroom with needles. It wasn't dramatic at all."

Robertson is understandably vague when asked specifically about the extent of The Band's drug use. "Heroin was a problem," he says cautiously. "I never liked heroin. I never understood the drug. And I was scared to death of it, too. But it was a problem. It was just not something that I ever got into. But it came through, you know, like everything else came through. Just flavor of the month."

In 1973, at the suggestion of David Geffen, Robertson moved out to Malibu to escape all of that. Soon he encouraged the other guys to try the California sun. And in that year

The Band reunited with Bob Dylan to cut *Planet Waves*. "We went in and made that album in three or four days, just hammered it out," Robertson says. "It was like making a blues record for us." That was followed by a major 1974 tour of sold-out arenas across the country. "That's when the wretched excess began," says a former Band employee. "Just 'cause there was too much money floating around. It was private jets, best hotel room, limousines everywhere and, of course, white powder."

In talking to Robertson, though he never comes right out and says it, one senses that these problems contributed to the end of The Band. "That was the first sense I had of Robbie's slight alienation from the whole thing," says Jonathan Taplan, a former tour manager for The Band who went on to coproduce *Carny* with Robertson. "He'd made a good bit of money. He had a beautiful house on the beach. He didn't really want to be the babysitter."

It was soon after The Band split up that Robertson had what Taplan calls his "midlife crisis." "Once he got out of being responsible for a whole band and all of a sudden he was just responsible for himself," says Taplan, "he just kind of threw caution to the wind."

"MARTY, CAN YOU TURN THAT stuff down?"

It was 1977, and the Sex Pistols' "Anarchy in the U.K." was blasting through the house on Mulholland Drive, in Hollywood.

But the music was so loud that Martin Scorsese, the famous film director, couldn't hear Robertson's plea. And anyway, it was Scorsese's house, though Robertson had been sharing it with the director since their marriages had self-destructed following the filming of *The Last Waltz*.

Robertson was beginning four years of what Peter Gabriel describes as "wild living." Cocaine, champagne, and beautiful women—including some well-known actresses—were always around.

Robertson and Scorsese would work on *The Last Waltz* all day, then unwind all night. "We had a kind of daily ritual," Robertson says one afternoon at his studio. "Marty had things to do on the film, I had things to do on the soundtrack album. So, we'd get back to the house around midnight and have dinner. Then in the middle of the night we would screen a movie or two. I'd want Buñuel and Jean Renoir, and he'd want these sleazy B-movies: Sam Fuller films and these weird vampire movies. We would usually watch them until it seemed like the sun was going to start coming up. It was like 'Uh-oh, uh-oh,' and we'd have to scatter."

Robertson was separated from his wife, Dominique, a beautiful freelance journalist whom he had met in Paris while he was touring with Dylan in the spring of 1966. (They have three children: Alexandra, now 18, Delphine, 17, and Sebastian, 13.) Freed from his responsibilities as a husband and a bandleader, Robertson experienced something of a second adolescence. "It was a crazy period," he says. "Marty and I were the 'misunderstood artists,' and our wives threw us out. We were just kind of lost in the storm. You are a tame house pet and you get thrown out in the woods for a while and pretty soon you're not tame anymore. All of a sudden you are like a wild dog. We just ran amok."

He stares down at the floor for a moment. "It was probably to cover up the hurt," he says. "The pain and the loss in our lives. . . . And drugs were everywhere. It wasn't that much a part of my life. I didn't drink my blues away. It wasn't my problem, but everywhere I looked, there were people doing drugs and alcohol."

"You go through periods like that time," says Scorsese. "People just searching for things, looking for things. Sometimes it takes one form, sometimes it takes another. That's the form it took at the time."

The wild times with Scorsese also included many highflying jaunts to Europe to promote *The Last Waltz*, attend film festivals, and pick up awards—trophies and gold records—garnered over the years but never collected. "Seems like there was always a commotion wherever we went," says Robertson. "Marty has big extremes in his personality. One minute he would be laughing, and the next minute there would be telephones flying out the windows."

As the months of extreme living drifted by, word inevitably leaked out. "There was a magazine article," Robertson says, "and it was called 'Bel Air, Bel Air.' It said something like 'I went to Martin Scorsese's house. He and Robbie Robertson are having these wild parties, and there are women everywhere, and there are drugs, and it makes Hugh Hefner's place look like a kindergarten.' So we get a copy of this article and Marty goes crazy." Robertson laughs. "He starts breaking glasses immediately. Smashing things. Talking with lawyers, ripping phones out. He says, 'Look at this! Look at this article! Read it! I'm suing these people. I'm taking them to court.' And I looked at it, and I said, 'Marty, the only thing inaccurate here is that we don't live in Bel Air.'"

That chapter came to an end when Scorsese, an asthmatic, suffered health problems brought on by the fast living. "He got real sick and ended up in the hospital," says Robertson. "It was either change your lifestyle or die. I remember seeing him in the hospital and thinking, 'Boy, this is definitely the end of an era right here.'"

But not for Robertson. It wasn't until after another "crazy" period—with Gary Busey during the making of *Carny*—that he finally decided it was time to slow his pace and patch up his marriage. "These rock & roll ways were getting old," he says. "I smartened up a little bit, maybe. I just felt like I just wasn't satisfied living that way anymore. I just wanted to be with my family, so I did everything I could to work it out."

Though he reestablished his relationship with his family, Robertson had no desire to join his old bandmates in a reunion they were putting together. Asked what he thought of the group's touring as The Band without him, Robertson picks his words with care. "It's hard to say anything against anybody who's just trying to do what they do and make a living. You can't say, 'How dare you do this?' So I said, 'I have no problem with any of it.' My attitude was 'Do it with my blessing.' I didn't know what else to do."

He admits that the film work he did for Scorsese didn't bring in a lot of money. So how did he support himself through the "lost years"? "I don't know," he says. "I guess just the money I had made before and the money that I make from publishing or whatever. I just never got to the point where I was on the street, fortunately."

Money was a factor, though not *the* factor, in Robertson's decision to get to work again. "It was a good time to do something: produce a movie, act in a movie, make a record, *something*. I didn't want to one day just find that I was in a desperate situation. I mean, I didn't decide to make a record because I needed money. It was *time* to make a record, but it was time to make some money as well."

In 1983—while cooling out in Rome with movie producer Art Linson (*The Untouchables*)—Robertson made his decision. "We were drunk," says Linson. "I'm sitting there having wine with one of the great rock composer-guitarists in the history of rock & roll. I said, 'Hey, you're not serious about retiring. Why start at the beginning as an actor? You're out of your mind. Go back and get to work! Make a record!' He looked at me like 'Oh, I guess I have to.'"

THERE IS A BOOMING CRACK of thunder, the sky opens up, and the rain comes pouring down on Woodstock. It's early July. Robbie Robertson closes the door to an upstairs apartment at Bearsville Studios, where he's staying for a few weeks while completing the album. Being back in Woodstock is bringing up some old memories, and Robertson begins to talk about his lost friend Richard Manuel. "It makes me uncomfortable to talk about Richard," he says, lighting a cigarette and taking a seat at a large wooden table. "He's not here to talk for himself. When I first met Richard, when he was 17, he was a drunk. He said that he had been drinking since he was very young. He was always an alcoholic. And he decided to pursue it, you know, to the darkest degree that he could at some points in his life."

Robertson glances out the window; maple and pine trees are swaying in the wind as the sky darkens. "I can't tell other people's stories," he says. "It's not right. You know, they wouldn't say, 'Well, you know Robbie did this and Robbie did that.' It's like you were in this club. All I can tell you is you know it existed. And it went from bad to worse to the ultimate nightmare imaginable. And people survived it. Got smarter. Changed. Some people were able to help themselves. And some people weren't. And you see in a case like Richard, where you can't help yourself—there's the poor guy left at the end of the pack who's saying, 'Wait for me. I can't help myself.' But you don't know that. You just think, 'This guy's just got to get a grip.' Well, it's not like that. But how do you expect everybody to be so knowledgeable and so smart? Saying, 'Oh, I know what this fellow needs. This fellow needs to go into a certain clinic. Get into a program. And that's his one chance of getting through this alive.' We don't know those things. You know those things when it's too late."

Robertson is silent for a while. "When he died, I wasn't expecting it. I guess you should say, 'Well, maybe I shouldn't be too surprised, because of Richard's past and everything,' but I was. I was devastated. I couldn't get used to the idea at all. You know, you are just never ready for those things until they happen, and then you're really not ready for them."

"I FEEL LIKE A BIG WEIGHT has been lifted," says Robertson. It's late July, two days after he has completed his album, and Robertson does seem like a different person. At his West LA studio, he sits and talks freely about some of his new songs. He's asked about the album's most autobiographical song, "Testimony," on which he sings, "Bear witness, I'm wailing like the wind / Come bear witness, the half-breed rides again / In these hands, I've held the broken dream / In my soul, I'm howling at the moon."

"I'm not gazing at the moon," he says. "I'm not strolling beneath the moon. I'm *howling* at the moon. It's just part of the picture of someone standing on the mountain with their arms stretched up to the sky, screaming in the ceremony of life.

"That's the business, that's the real item," he says. "It's like some kind of sin when you see somebody great in a movie and you say they walked through the movie. And that's only a movie. This is life. Who wants to grow old and think, 'God, I walked through it'?"

*Rolling Stone*, November 1987

# INVENTING (PUNK) ROCK AT THE MABUHAY

*In early 2018 I got an email from the editor/writer/photographer James Stark, who I had vaguely known in the late '70s, in the early days of San Francisco's punk scene. He was working on a book about the late Dirk Dirksen, who had promoted punk shows at San Francisco's first punk club, the Mabuhay Gardens. He wanted to reprint an old article of mine in his book. I started thinking about the Mabuhay, and the many unique bands that played there. Crime. The Avengers. The Mutants. Devo. The Sleepers. Flipper. Dead Kennedys. Silverstone. Romeo Void. Tuxedomoon. And so many others. The Fab Mab was an important club. An influential club. The scene at the Mabuhay came back to me, and soon I was contacting Stark, wondering if in addition to reprinting that old article, there was interest in an essay about the import of the Mabuhay. So that's how I came to write this essay, which I finished in June 2018 and which was published in* Shut Up You Animals!!! The Pope Is Dead: A Remembrance of Dirk Dirksen *(Last Gasp) in January 2021.*

> *Better watch out for the new world.*
> —"Sister Little," performed live at the Mabuhay Gardens by the Sleepers, 1978

AS IF ROCK NEVER HAPPENED. No Chuck Berry, no Elvis, no Beatles, no Stones.

Sometimes it was like that. Other times it was a raised middle finger to all that preceded them, *the punks*—a fuck you to the past from the present, from the future.

When you least expect it, the world reinvented in some small out-of-the-way place that no one is paying attention to, and in 1976, in San Francisco, because Dirk Dirksen, a former TV show producer who had since run a surfing business in Santa Cruz, convinced Ness Aquino, owner of a tired Filipino nightclub at 433 Broadway, to let him promote occasional shows there in the evenings, that place, located among topless bars and strip clubs, was the Mabuhay Gardens.

What took place at the Mabuhay felt brand new, it was a new society with new values, coming together night after night, participating in a kind of ritual: a series of bands, alienated from the mainstream, on the small stage expressing their emotions in a raw, visceral manner, and an audience of equally alienated music fans there to hear the emotional (and political) news those bands were delivering.

"It was so thrilling and bracing to see these people whose every aesthetic choice was about repudiating everything that the ['60s] counterculture had stood for," novelist Jennifer Egan told me. Egan, who says that as a teenager she went to the Mabuhay weekly during the late '70s, set part of a chapter of her 2011 Pulitzer-winning book, *A Visit from the Goon Squad*, at the Mabuhay.

Of course in the mid-'70s this *new world* I am talking about, this world that acted like nothing that came before it mattered, was seemingly being invented *everywhere*. There were numerous ports of entry—in New York, in Cleveland, in Seattle, in LA, in London—but if you lived in San Francisco, yours was the Mabuhay aka the Fab Mab, or simply, *the Mab*.

The Avengers at the Mabuhay Gardens, 1978.

"In terms of San Francisco punk rock, it was a community epicenter," Egan said. "It was so original.... The anger, the pace, the energy and the rage were all incredibly compelling to me. As a sort of troubled teen I could not get enough of it."

Low-ceilinged and brick-walled, the first maybe three-quarters of the club was a terraced hillside of tables descending to a crowded dance floor. Except that amid the people on the dance floor were small round tables and rattan chairs and sometimes Penelope Houston of the Avengers might be sitting in one of those rattan chairs and some nights, such as on January 3, 1978, Negative Trend singer Rozz Rezabek would climb on top of the huge loudspeakers and leap off what artist Bruce Conner called the "shin high" stage, knocking over people and chairs. The stage was small, but there was room for a drum kit up against the brick wall, two or three musicians in front of it, a singer up close to the edge and plenty of drama.

When the Mab was empty in the afternoon or after everyone finally went home, and you could actually see the place, it was worn out, more than worn out. It had been kicked in the stomach and never recovered. But at night, alive with punks and high school kids like Egan, that didn't matter; in fact, anything less fucked up would have been so *wrong*. The Mab was where survivors of WWIII converged, a kind of postapocalyptic hideout for conspiring the new.

Howie Klein, at the time a DJ/writer who started 415 Records during the Mabuhay's heyday and released records by The Nuns and Romeo Void, says he hung out at the club "every night for years. *Every single night*. Seven nights a week. *Literally* for years.

"Especially in the beginning it [the Mabuhay] was very much dedicated to punk rock and a punk ethos," he recalled. "The idea of rejecting that which was the establishment at the time and starting something completely new on every level, whether it was the way you dress or the way you think or look at politics. And the Mabuhay was the central place for it to be happening."

At first "punk rock" didn't mean bands conforming to a dress code of Mohawks, black leather jackets, and dog collars playing loud, fast, short songs. The punk movement of the mid- to late '70s began in New York in '74 and '75, then spread to London in '75 and '76. In San Francisco in '76 and '77, the city's version of punk ranged from Sex Pistols-influenced bands like the Avengers to indefinable bands like the Mutants. There was little in common musically or visually between the Avengers, Flipper, the Mutants, Crime, The Nuns, the Sleepers, and U.X.A. While Crime sometimes appeared wearing police uniforms, the Mutants might show up all wearing white, or as characters out of *Alice in Wonderland* complete with huge playing cards attached to their chests. Two few months after her boyfriend Michael Kowalsky died of an overdose, De De Troit, singer for U.X.A., appeared onstage wrapped in white gauze like some femme fatale version of the Mummy, at one point lying on the stage, eyes closed.

In the early years at the Mabuhay, Dirk Dirksen always said he was presenting "avant-garde theatre." After the police raided the club and shut it down one night, Dirksen told me: "They [the police] see it as a punk scene. But punk is just a part of what we do here. . . . We've had great jazz performers like Sun Ra and George Shearing. And people do not understand the satire of punk. Our people are in costume, they are not thugs."

Still, despite what Dirksen said, various versions of "punk rock" were what mostly happened on the Mab stage.

If you wonder what was so different about the club, maybe this will help: "One time The Nuns' bass player got stage fright and vomited and couldn't go onstage," Klein said. "So, The Nuns threw his bass at *me* and said, 'You play, just do this and this.' I had never held a bass before. But I went onstage and played, and no one knew the difference."

The scene at the Mab was like a secret society, only it was right out in the open, and anyone could join. The price of admission? Simply wanting to be there.

Egan said, "The fact that a Lowell high school student like me and her friends, who, I mean we took drugs, but we were basically pretty straight arrows, could go there and enjoy it was part of the magic . . . it really did help for that moment to penetrate the larger culture, which would be me, a pretty ordinary high school student who was looking for action with her friends."

Another San Franciscan who visited the club, dug the scene and never left (well, at least for a year), was the famed Bohemian artist Bruce Conner, who had moved to the city in 1957 and become part of the Beat scene, and then in the '60s participated in another countercultural shift as a member of the rock & roll light show troupe, the North American Ibis Alchemical Company, projecting psychedelic collages of film loops, photographs and colored liquid light paintings onto the walls of the Avalon Ballroom as Big Brother and the Holding Company or Country Joe and the Fish rocked the place.

Beginning in January 1978, Conner found needed inspiration in his frequent nights at the Mab, and proceeded to photograph the bands and the scene there for *Search & Destroy*, the San Francisco–based punk magazine.

"In its own way, it [the Mabuhay scene] reminded me of the energy of the poets, artists, filmmakers, and dancers who had been characterized as the Beat generation in the 1950s," Conner said during a 2005 interview with journalist/publisher Mike Plante for his *Cinemad* magazine. "Then in the '60s some of the same people were called the Hippie generation. This creative phenomenon appeared to become publicly conspicuous in San Francisco every 10 years.

"I wish we could find more people with that kind of intensity today," Conner continued. "It's worth gravitating towards that type of environment. A kind of activity that compels people, despite the limits of their technological or professional abilities, to produce, perform, and have their say."

I went to the Mab in 1977 to see the band Crime, who at times appeared onstage wearing police uniforms. Writing for *New York Rocker* in 1978, I described what I experienced that night at the Mab:

> Crime play loud. So loud that the plate glass window at the opposite end of the club shakes, tables tremble and people hang onto their drinks. Loudness may be Crime's only musical raison d'être. This band is a literal translation of the concept "minimal." Drummer Hank Rank thumps out a simple Bo Diddley beat that is only adequate in the context of the rest of the band. Bassist Ron the Ripper coaxes a thick rumble from his amp that reminds one of the thunder of a bulldozer rolling over rugged terrain. And the guitar playing of [Johnny] Strike and Frankie Fix make you feel like you've been forcefully held underwater for the full 25 minutes of the set.

If you saw Crime or the Avengers or Negative Trend at the Mab, you never forgot it. For many who attended in the early years, these weren't "shows" or "concerts," these were life and death important experiences.

"One of the key things about the punk scene, it was a do-it-yourself scene, there was a oneness between the audience and the artists," Howie Klein said. "There was no, 'we're the artist and you're the audience and there's this impenetrable wall.' That was what we were against. With Journey and Led Zeppelin there was this wall that you couldn't cross over to. But it was the opposite in the punk scene. Anyone could start a band."

It was common for audience members to turn up onstage. Debora Iyall attended many Mab shows before founding Romeo Void, who eventually scored two hits, including the sneering "Never Say Never," and the same was true of Eric Boucher who was a fan in the audience before he appeared on the Mab stage fronting the Dead Kennedys as Jello Biafra. Klaus Flouride, East Bay Ray and Biafra formed the DKs in June of 1978; a month later they played their first show at the Mab opening for The Offs and Negative Trend.

Biafra said in one interview that Dirksen "stuck his neck out and had the sense to make the shows all ages, which allowed me to get the Dead Kennedys off the ground, since I wasn't 21 when we started."

In another interview: "It [the Mabuhay] meant the world," Biafra told Michael Stewart Foley, professor of American Political Culture and Political Theory at the University of Groningen in the Netherlands and author of the book "Dead Kennedys' Fresh Fruit for Rotting Vegetables." "It meant seeing some of the greatest music you'll ever see in your life, blisteringly loud, three feet away from you, and you can watch the sweat drip off the guitar strings while you bounce off people . . . that was a big adrenaline rush, just all the people bouncing off each other."

The Mabuhay was where "we were all joined together as punks," Penelope Houston, 18 at the time and lead singer/lyricist for the Avengers, told Foley. "I just registered that I was a punk in a world that wasn't punk. . . . Whether we were male or female, Black or white or Mexican of queer or Asian or whatever, we were all just punks, and we were all joined together in that way. There was this great feeling musically, as well as how you looked, you could do whatever you wanted. You just made it up."

Other notable bands that played the Mab: Black Flag, the Dils, Rank & File, Silvertone, Screamers, the Damned, the Descendents, Blondie, Devo, Jim Carroll, the Ramones, Situations and Tuxedomoon. And there were many more.

When the Sex Pistols came to San Francisco in January 1978 and played for the last time (until they reformed to cash in decades later), the three opening acts were all Mabuhay regulars: The Nuns, the Avengers, and Negative Trend (who never made it to the stage).

The punk scene, including the Mabuhay, spread a DIY message throughout the world. It led to the proliferation of independent record companies like Klein's 415, Biafra's Alternative Tentacles, and Bob Biggs' Slash, Xeroxed fanzines and punk magazines like Jean Caffeine's *New Dezezes* (San Francisco's first punk zine), V. Vale's *Search & Destroy*, Brad Lapin's *Damage*, and Ginger Coyote's *Punk Globe*, and the alternative network of performance spaces and clubs. I believe that DIY idea carried over years later to the internet (it certainly inspired me to start an internet magazine, *Addicted To Noise*, in 1994), to the widespread self-publishing of books and, most recently, Facebook live streaming, which lets anyone have the power to broadcast video worldwide.

Today, there are videos and audio recordings of early Mabuhay performances on YouTube by bands including U.X.A., the Dils, the Avengers, the Sleepers, the Mutants, Negative Trend, Flipper, and the Dead Kennedys (in particular, seek out Mindaugis Bagdon's 17-minute film, *Louder, Faster, Shorter*, and an audio recording, "Miner's Benefit Compilation," also on YouTube). Additionally, studio recordings by Crime, the Avengers, the Sleepers, U.X.A., Flipper, and others can currently be heard on YouTube.

Since the club shut its doors in 1986 (and by then the San Francisco punk scene was dead) its reputation has only grown, and more than 40 years after the first shows there, the Mabuhay lives on in ways that are obvious and sometimes not so obvious.

In 1987, Sonic Youth included a cover of Crime's 1976 recording, "Hot Wire My Heart," on their album *Sister*.

In 1990, the year Bikini Kill formed, the band covered the Avengers' 1977 song, "The American in Me," which the Avengers frequently played at the Mabuhay. Bikini Kill not only became *the* major Riot Grrrl band, inspiring thousands of young women to form bands or assert themselves in some way, but had a major influence on Sleater-Kinney, who remain popular to this day.

In 1991, Chris Isaak, who initially led a trio called Silvertone that played the Mabuhay, scored a Top 10 US hit with "Wicked Game." The guitarist who wrote the spooky guitar hook that opens the song is former Avengers' bassist James Calvin Wilsey; after the Avengers split up in 1979, Wilsey did sound for Silvertone at the Mab in mid-1980 and taught Isaak guitar parts leading to Isaak asking Wilsey to work on music with him; when Isaak broke up his trio, he and Wilsey cofounded a new version of Silvertone in late 1980.

When Nirvana played "Smells Like Teen Spirit" on *Saturday Night Live*, January 11, 1992, Kurt Cobain wore a hand drawn Flipper T-shirt. Both Cobain and Nirvana bassist Krist Novoselic named Flipper as an influence, as did Jane's Addiction's original bassist Eric Avery. Flipper's classic debut album, *Album—Generic Flipper*, was first released in 1982; it's currently available in MP3 and streaming formats, as are Flipper's other studio albums and live recordings. There is also a DVD, *Flipper: Live—Target Video 1980–1981*, currently available.

In 1994 a Swedish band, Sator, covered The Nuns' song "No Solution," which reached number two on the Swedish charts. In 2006 The Nuns' debut album, *Nuns*, recorded in 1980 without guitarist Alejandro Escovedo, was reissued. It is currently out of print and used copies are selling for $65. The Nuns' first record was a three song EP released in 1979 on 415 Records; two of the songs, "Decadent Jew" and "Suicide Child," were recorded live at the Keystone Palo Alto in March 1977; it is currently out of print.

In 1995, punk artist Winston Smith, whose collages appeared inside or on the cover of such Dead Kennedys' albums as *Fresh Fruit for Rotting Vegetables* and *Let Them Eat Jellybeans*, had one of his collages, "God Told Me to Skin You Alive," used for the cover of Green Day's hit album, *Insomniac*.

In 1996, a compilation album, *the less an object*, with all the Sleepers' recordings including all the songs on the group's amazing 1978 "Seventh World" EP, was released. The Sleeper's gifted singer, Ricky Williams (who was also Flipper's first singer and is credited with coming up with that band's name), died of a heroin overdose on November 21, 1992.

In 1997, the Avengers' singer/lyricist Penelope Houston and Green Day's Billie Joe Armstrong wrote and recorded a song, "The Angel and the Jerk," which was used in an episode of *Friends* and appeared on the 1999 *Friends Again* soundtrack. Houston and Armstrong also recorded the Avengers' song, "Corpus Christi," with lyrics by Houston, which appeared on Houston's 2003 album, *Eighteen Stories Down*. The compilation album, *Avengers*, made up of singles recorded in 1977 and demos produced by former Sex Pistol Steve Jones in 1978, was first released in 1983 and was rereleased in 2010; another compilation album, *Died for Your Sins*, including studio and live recordings, was released in 1999. The Avengers' live set at Winterland opening for the Sex Pistols in January 1978 can currently be watched at YouTube or purchased as an album.

In 2001 *Dils Dils Dils*, which compiles the group's singles and live tracks, was reissued on CD; it was first released on vinyl in 1991.

In 2004, U.X.A.'s first album, *Illusions of Grandeur*, was reissued. It is currently out of print.

In 2005, a reformed version of Crime headlined the Road to Ruins festival in Rome. A compilation album, *Murder by Guitar*, was issued in 2013 and is currently available in vinyl, MP3, and streaming formats.

In 2006, a book of Bruce Conner's 1978 Mab photographs, *Mabuhay Gardens*, was published in Germany in tandem with a show in Dusseldorf of those 53 photos. In 2007, the Berkeley Art Museum acquired a set of the photos and in 2008 exhibited them in conjunction with a film/video series at the Pacific Film Archive: *Louder, Faster: Punk in Performance*.

In 2007, the Dirk Dirksen/Damon Malloy–produced documentary on the Mutants, titled *Mutants: Forensic Report*, was released on DVD. The Mutants one and only album, *Fun Terminal*, was reissued in 2004. While the CD version is out of print, an MP3 version is currently available, and it can be streamed at Spotify.

In the March 8, 2010 *New Yorker*, a short story, "Ask Me If I Care," by novelist Jennifer Egan was published. A portion of the story takes place at the Mabuhay, Egan's characters listen to the Mutants, Negative Trend, the Dead Kennedys, and The Nuns, and Dirk Dirksen gets a mention. That story is also a chapter in her 2011 book, *A Visit from the Goon Squad*, which won a 2011 Pulitzer. The book also won a 2011 National Book Critics Circle Award.

The Bruce Conner retrospective, *It's All True*, included a room devoted to his 1978 Mabuhay photos. That exhibit was shown during 2016 at the Museum of Modern Art in New York and at the San Francisco Museum of Modern Art. In 2017, the exhibit traveled to the Museo Nacional Centro de Arte Reina Sofia in Madrid. Conner's Mabuhay photos were seen by thousands of people who had previously never heard of the club.

The first major showing of Conner's work in Southeast Asia took place in 2018 at multiple venues. One of the events, held halfway around the world from 433 Broadway on March 3, 2018, in Bataan, Philippines, was a "Mabuhay Gardens Punk Party."

*Shut Up You Animals!!! The Pope Is Dead: A Remembrance of Dirk Dirksen* (Last Gasp), January 2021

Eyes' frontwoman Alicia Pojanowski at Mona's Gorilla Lounge, 1973. Photo by Michael Goldberg; Copyright Michael Goldberg

# EYES: THE FIRST FEMINIST ROCK & ROLL BAND

*The all-woman feminist rock band Eyes never recorded an album. There are no bootlegs of their live gigs, no collections of their demo tapes, no YouTube videos, and no Facebook groups celebrating them. Unless you were one of the few who saw their amazing live gigs, mostly at crummy bars in the early to mid-Seventies, you have likely never heard of them or heard them, and certainly never seen them. Until now, they would be nothing more than a memory shared by fans like me if not for* New Yorker *rock columnist Ellen Willis, who wrote about them briefly in the second half of a piece called "San Francisco Habitat" published in the magazine in 1973 (and in her 1982 book,* Beginning to See the Light: Pieces of a Decade *and later included in the 2011 collection* Out of the Vinyl Deeps: Ellen Willis on Rock Music*). Well, "it's not enough" as onetime Eyes frontwoman Alicia Pojanowski sang. I wrote about Eyes when I was 20 for an underground paper. What I wrote isn't good, and so I hope to rectify both problems with this new essay.*

> SOMEWHERE IN THE SHADOWLAND of Santa Cruz County, the beginnings of a rock & roll transition are in process. Within a small, two room bar off Highway 1, Eyes pulsates with 1984 energy and excitement.
>
> Eyes, when they choose to play in Santa Cruz, perform exclusively at Mona's Gorilla Lounge. Mona's is a unique bar. . . . A bar that caters to people of all sexual preferences. The atmosphere is one of intense sensual vibrations when Eyes perform. This may be caused by their tight, raunchy, hard-rock, and bluesy sonic moonbeams.

So begins a story I wrote in October 1973, three months after I turned 20, for the long-gone underground Santa Cruz weekly *Sundaz!* During the spring of that year, a woman friend of mine, a self-identified feminist who was friends with Kate Millett, author of *Sexual Politics*, took me to Mona's to see the all-woman rock band Eyes for the first time. We entered the dark, smoky club, walked through the front room where people were drinking, smoking, and talking, past the bar and into another room crowded with mostly lesbian couples dancing. The band across the room on a low stage was playing the Marvelettes' "Danger! Heartbreak Dead Ahead." I had liked the Motown hit, but this version was better, there was a desperation in the vocal, this was life and death rock & roll, intense and vital, and in that moment, Eyes was the best band I'd ever heard.

Eyes were an incredible *rock band*. Not just a *feminist* rock band. Not just an *all-woman* rock band. No. They were an incredible flat-out *rock band*. They were the Velvet Underground. They were the Clash. They were the Patti Smith Group and the Rolling Stones. *That* kind of flat-out incredible rock band.

Even before we got to Mona's I was intrigued. My friend, who taught a class called "Women in Film" at the University of California, Santa Cruz, had made a short film of Eyes performing, which I'd seen, and in talking about the band she favorably compared singer Alicia Pojanowski to Mick Jagger.

Pojanowski was a captivating and at times forbidding figure, both in the film and live. Thin and tall, her hair curling down to her shoulders, dancing on the low stage as she sang, raising her arms so they stretched out from her sides like wings, she was, at times, androgynous as Dionysus, deadly as Medusa, wise and beautiful as Aphrodite. She balanced the seriousness of the songs with a casual insider's sense of humor, joking to the mostly female crowd after the band finished one song, "It appears to be feminist bandstand. All you young couples, we're *watching you*."

From the audience: "We're watching *you!*"

Eyes were a groundbreaking band: the first all-woman *feminist* rock & roll band. There had been a handful of all-woman rock bands before Eyes (Ace of Cups, Fanny, Joy of Cooking) and others also formed in the early *Seventies* (Sweet Chariot), but Eyes were the first to combine feminism and an original rock sound. In addition to Pojanowski, who wrote lyrics, fronted the band, and sang in a voice that could be strong and hard (but, when appropriate, could be softer too), there was ace guitarist Peggy White, sophisticated Fender Rhodes keyboardist Janet Small, melodic bassist Nikki Nutting, and a powerhouse drummer named Vicky Gilliam.

Eyes, originally named Isis after the Egyptian goddess of fertility, was birthed by Peggy White (who described herself as "the founding mother" in a press flyer about the group) in January 1972. None of the other women had played in bands before and didn't have the opportunities in the late *Sixties* that preteen and teen guys had to be in bands. Girls just didn't play electric guitars, electric basses, electric keyboards or drums in the Sixties. Janet Small studied classical piano for years, but that might have been detrimental to playing the simple chords and melodies of rock music.

Peggy White made use of feedback, distortion and a wah-wah pedal. At the beginning of "Siren Sniper" she added surging feedback to lift the song. Many of her solos used distortion reminiscent of Quicksilver Messenger Service guitarist John Cipollina or even Hendrix. She played the song's melody when appropriate but often took off into psychedelic flights. The music she wrote for Eyes could be ominous, and there was an anger and power in her solos.

There were plenty of female rock & roll singers in the Sixties, but Pojanowski, who grew up in New Jersey, wasn't focused on rock music then; she wanted to be an opera singer, but her family was not keen on her going to New York to pursue opera. Her focus on opera—she's a dramatic soprano and told me she sang using chest tone in Eyes—likely contributed to her distinctive rock singing voice.

The group called themselves Eyes for a reason—they were turning the idea of "the male gaze" on its head. "We played the Overcast, a club on Haight Street, every week," Pojanowski said during an interview in late January 2022. "And the guy who owned the club claimed he had 'made Carol Doda.' There was always that element in what it meant to be a girl rocker. You were just—there was always this legacy of women as sex objects. We tried to own it in a positive way. We saw ourselves as sexual subjects, but not as objects. We were the *eye*. Not the one who is seen but the one who is seeing. [We were Eyes] because we were the ones doing the looking."

Eyes—the five women were all in their 20s back then—formed just as the second wave of feminism was hitting its stride, and feminism had everything to do with what the band was about. This was a time in American history when young women stopped putting up with shit from their boyfriends or husbands. They were willing to kick the guy out ("I asked you over a month ago / Please move out your things," goes one lyric), or walk away ("You got to break your bonds"), if they weren't treated with respect, as equals.

Pojanowski told me that the Eyes women considered themselves part of the women's movement. "Eyes really was a cultural project," Pojanowski said. "For me it wasn't a musical project as a much as a cultural project. It was about feminism; it was about being involved in a movement that was about my own particular place in history."

Guitarist White described Eyes as "the musical arm of the women's movement."

Pojanowski wanted it to be clear that "the Gloria Steinem brand of feminism didn't really speak to us. Because we weren't middle-class professionals trying to make it. That brand of feminism didn't speak to women who wanted to stay home with their children and certainly not to—and I hesitate to say this because I'm a white person—but it didn't speak to Black or Brown people either, as a group, in my opinion. We were looking for something else in feminism than just to become just like our male counterparts who would be cogs in the big economic . . . We saw ourselves as artists, perhaps misfits in the sense that homosexuality, for those of us who were homosexual, was not . . . accepted by the general public. Our goal was to feel powerful in who we actually were. Be comfortable, be happy about it."

They all lived in Berkeley or Oakland where protests, activism, and the counterculture were still the currency of the day. Eyes was a collective, with each member contributing to the good of the whole in their own way: Peggy White with her lightning strikes guitar, Vicky Gilliam with her rock-solid drumming, and so on. Everyone made an important contribution, and they relied on each other to fulfill their roles; there was a strong sense of comradeship.

Small, White, Nutting, and Pojanowski wrote or cowrote some of the original songs Eyes performed, sometimes contributing lyrics, sometimes music, sometimes both. The group's manager, Ella Hirst, also wrote lyrics and sometimes music too.

Eyes helped set the stage for all-women bands or bands fronted by women, that came along later like Joan Jett and the Blackhearts, the Patti Smith Group, the Avengers, the Pretenders, and later still, feminist bands like Bikini Kill and Sleater-Kinney. Eyes saw themselves as something new. And they were.

Pojanowski, who like Patti Smith grew up in New Jersey, was (and probably still is) an excellent singer. She could handle everything from the Staple Singers' "Respect Yourself" and the Supremes' "You Keep Me Hangin' On," to Neil Young's "Mr. Soul" and David Bowie's "John, I'm Only Dancing." Other covers included the Stone Poneys' "Different Drum," Spirit's "I Got a Line On You," the Marvelettes' "Shop Around," Neil Young's "Mr. Soul," and Bowie's "Suffragette City." Eyes were adept at picking covers that kept the dance floor full while often conveying empowering messages or providing the context for their original songs.

The four musicians together created a sound at times vaguely reminiscent of the Doors due to the dominance of Small's electric keyboards, but it was the original songs, along with Pojanowski's deep, expressive voice, that made Eyes unique—and made audience members and rock critics like the *New Yorker*'s Ellen Willis pay attention to this band that didn't have a record contract.

Those original songs that Pojanowski sang could be very dark. "Siren Sniper," "Happy in the Attic," "Night Blindness," and others confront sexism, physical and emotional abuse, and female empowerment. The songs have a real depth to them, and there's a Dylanesque sarcasm but also a real sincerity. In one song, Pojanowski sings, "You got to know what you want / You got to break your bonds / You got to look for something new."

Pojanowski was a fan of folk music when she was younger, particularly Joan Baez, Bob Dylan, and the blues duo of Dave Ray and Tony Glover. "I learned every single song on Joan Baez's albums," Pojanowski said. She also told me she spent four years trying to sing like Dave Ray. She also dug female singers and "girl groups" as a kid including Martha and the Vandellas ("Nowhere to Run," "Heat Wave"), the Marvelettes ("Danger! Heartbreak Dead Ahead"), and Lesley Gore ("You Don't Own Me").

She was "steeped in Surrealism" at the time, she said. "I was absolutely fascinated by Surrealism and Dada and Marcel Duchamp. I wore a cartridge belt onstage with Tampax where the cartridges go. Juxtaposing things that don't go together that I thought represented personal female power. I thought it was art."

In Pojanowski's (lyrics) and White's (music) "Happy in the Attic," Pojanowski sang, "You were so afraid / To show me to your friends / I was out of step and you were not impressed . . . / Listen to you never were the monster you pretend / . . . If you think I'm leaving now / You better think again."

In the chorus, Pojanowski sang in her defiant voice, "I was happy in the attic / I could be alone all day / I drank my Coca Cola / And threw the cans away / Once you put me up there / I knew I had to stay / 'Cause I was happy in the attic," while other band members echoed her in a singsongy falsetto.

"I think I must have been thinking of *Jane Eyre*," Pojanowski said. "I guess the message is, 'I know you were ashamed of me, basically, and kept me in the background but you were never the monster that you pretended. I actually was having a good time in the attic. I was happy in the attic. You don't have the power over me that you think you do. And now—and I really don't know if it's because now I have some notoriety [as a singer?]—I'm looking better to you, you're willing to bring me out in the open more, and not act like I'm out of step. But frankly, I just want the relationship we had in which I could spend lots of time by myself.'"

In another song Pojanowski wrote the lyrics for and White the music, "Siren Sniper," the protagonist is a powerful, independent woman. "I'm the siren sniper / I bide my time / I'm the ruler of the earth / I bide my time / I'm the rock and basalt soul stopper / The foam and cool fire death dropper / You'll know me when I come / I'm the kind of woman you warn yourself about / And I won't let you down."

"I don't see us as being anti-male," Pojanowski said. "We just wanted the power we had. That's how I saw what we were doing. We were just stepping into our rightful sense of power, which is what all the women in the women's movement, let's say the whole Bay Area scene, were trying to do. I know there was a lot of anti-male feeling [in the women's movement] but I don't think that's what we were doing."

It was male musicians that the group members had a problem with. "Rock was such a male domain," Pojanowski said. "I thought that most of the rock guys, as opposed to men in general, were really dinosaurs in terms of their consciousness. They seemed to be really retrograde. They inhabited a cultural world that didn't have to accommodate women much at all other than as groupies or whatever. I don't think the real world was that bad, as bad as it was in the rock world."

Pojanowski worked in a law office and before that she'd been a draft counselor. At least one of her songs dealt with the politics of the day. In "Closet Queen" (lyrics Pojanowski, music White—also referred to as "Queen of Tangerine" because of the chorus, which begins "I'm the Queen of Tangerine"), Pojanowski sang, "My brother he's a frager / My sister's underground / There are post office pictures / Of my friends all over town / The judge who gives the sentence / Says it hurts him more than them / But I'm not taking any chances / 'Cause you know my crimes much worse."

"I thought that speaks to all the political ferment that was happening," Pojanowski said, then added when I asked her about the phrase "Queen of Tangerine," "You've got the House of Orange in European royalty. Queen of Tangerine is not only a lovely rhyme (to me) but also a spoof."

Pojanowski also mentioned that one of the women who died in the Symbionese Liberation Army (SLA) shootout in LA "had come to our gigs. I didn't realize it until I saw her picture in the paper."

Guitarist White, originally from New York, studied violin for five years as a kid, then folk guitar as a teenager in the Sixties. She was the only member of Eyes who had previously been in other rock bands. She was in three groups: The Lunatic Fringe (1970), Flash Mama and the Little Honeys (1971), and Wizca (1971). Keyboardist Small was born in New Jersey and grew up in Las Cruces, New Mexico. When she was eight years old she had her first song published in the Unitarian Universalist magazine. Now deceased, she also played violin, viola, recorder, guitar, harpsichord, and organ; she was in the El Paso symphony. She said her greatest honor was picking sugar cane with Fidel Castro and her greatest dishonor was shaking hands with President Lyndon Johnson.

Bassist Nicole (Nikki) Nutting, born in Oakland, started playing acoustic guitar by ear when she was 10. She'd never played bass before she auditioned for Eyes in January 1972. Drummer Victoria Gulliam got her first drum kit in December 1971 and started playing in Eyes a month or so later. The last to join was Pojanowski, who answered an ad in a local paper (either the *Oakland Tribune* or the *Berkeley Barb*) and auditioned at an Oakland rehearsal studio the group rented.

While together, in addition to playing regularly at Mona's in Santa Cruz, Eyes played many women's movement events as well as Berkeley clubs like the Long Branch and Keystone Berkeley and at the Overcast Club in San Francisco. They also made the occasional trip up to Portland.

Ellen Willis saw Eyes at the Long Branch and wrote in an August 1973 issue of the *New Yorker* that Eyes were doing what "no other female band has managed: integrating a feminist consciousness with a love for rock and roll and an acute fan's sense of their own place in its tradition."

Perhaps because of what Willis wrote, Eyes was pursued by major labels, but the women were not receptive to the companies' overtures; collectively Eyes chose not to sign with any of them. "We were Berkeley people," Pojanowski said. "They were big LA record companies. Not really our cup of tea. We would have been chewed up and spit out. We would have been destroyed—personally and artistically. Some of us pretty much knew that was a situation where we would have zero power and we would not get to represent ourselves the way we wanted to be represented. We would have been victimized."

So what happened? Toward the end of 1974, less than three years after forming, there was a parting of the ways. If Pojanowski remembers why they broke up, she's not telling. "I would imagine it was because it could no longer go on," Pojanowski said. "That's usually the way of things. If the things don't go on it's because they couldn't."

Pojanowski, Small, and White immediately formed Lip Service with a different drummer and bass player; Gilliam and Nutting went off to pursue their own musical projects.

Though Eyes were together less than a year and a half when I first saw them at Mona's, they were really good that first night, and each time I saw them after that they just kept getting better. I made a crude cassette recording of one of their shows in the fall of 1973 and 47 years later, in late 2020, while looking through a box of old cassettes, I came across the Eyes' tape and it was a revelation. For more than a year I've listened to it again and again and it confirms my memories. There was no band like them. They deserve to be remembered, to have their place in written history, and now they will.

January 25, 2022

# DISCOGRAPHY

For those unfamiliar with some of the artists or bands written about in this book, I have provided one album (in most cases), that will provide a great introduction to each artist or band.

John Lee Hooker, *The Ultimate Collection* (Rhino)
Ramblin' Jack Elliott, *Hard Travelin'* (Fantasy)
Bob Dylan, *Highway 61 Revisited* (Columbia) and *Blonde on Blonde* (Columbia)
Black Flag, *Damaged* (SST)
The Replacements, *Let It Be* (Twin/Tone)
Hüsker Dü, *Zen Arcade* (SST)
The Minutemen, *Post Mersh, Vol. 1* (SST)
Professor Longhair, *New Orleans Piano* (Atlantic Jazz)
Van Morrison, *Astral Weeks* (Warner Bros.)
Patti Smith, *Horses* (Arista)
Ramones, *Ramones* (Sire)
The Clash, *London Calling* (Epic)
Sex Pistols, *Never Mind the Bollocks, Here's the Sex Pistols* (Warner Bros.)
Prince, *Dirty Mind* (Warner Bros.) and *1999* (Warner Bros.)
Muddy Waters, *Folk Singer* (Chess/MCA)
Flipper, *Album—Generic Flipper* (American WB): Available as an MP3 album or via Spotify.
Crime, *Murder by Guitar* (Superior Viaduct)
Sleater-Kinney, *Call the Doctor* (Sub Pop)
James Brown, *Live at the Apollo 1962* (Universal Music Group)
Talking Heads, *Talking Heads 77* (Sire/Warner Bros.)
John Fogerty/Creedence Clearwater Revival, *Chronicle: The 20 Greatest Hits* (Fantasy)
Chris Isaak, *Silvertone* (Warner Bros.) and *Heart Shaped World* (Reprise)
Townes Van Zandt, *Live at the Old Quarter, Houston, Texas* (Fat Possum/TVZ Records)
Gil Scott-Heron, *The Best of Gil Scott-Heron* (Sony Music Canada Inc.)
Jolie Holland, *Catalpa* (Anti)
Tom Waits, *Mule Variations* (Anti)
Michael Jackson, *Thriller* (Sony Legacy)
Devo, *Q: Are We Not Men? A: We Are Devo!* (Warner Bros.)
Neil Young, *Everybody Knows This Is Nowhere* (Reprise) and *Tonight's the Night* (Reprise)
Big Brother and the Holding Company, *Cheap Thrills* (Columbia)
Grateful Dead, *The Grateful Dead* (Warner Bros.) and *Live Dead* (Warner Bros.)
Country Joe & The Fish, *Electric Music for the Mind and Body* (Vanguard)
Flamin' Groovies, *Groovies Greatest Grooves* (Sire) or *Shake Some Action* (Sire)
American Music Club, *Engine* (Warner Bros.) and *Mercury* (Warner Bros.)
Laurie Anderson, *Big Science* (Nonesuch)

Lou Reed/Velvet Underground, *The Velvet Underground and Nico* (Polydor), *White Light/White Heat* (Polydor), *The Velvet Underground* (Polydor), and *Loaded* (Polydor)

Sly & The Family Stone, *Greatest Hits* (Sony Legacy) and *There's a Riot Goin' On* (Sony Legacy)

George Clinton/Funkadelic, *Maggot Brain* (Ace Records Import)

Rick James, *Street Songs* (Motown)

Dennis Wilson, *Pacific Ocean Blue* (Sony Legacy)

Brian Wilson/Beach Boys, *Pet Sounds* (Capitol) and *Sounds of Summer* (Capitol)

Captain Beefheart & His Magic Band, *Trout Mask Replica* (Zappa Records) and *Lick My Decals Off, Baby* (Rhino/Warner Bros.)

Frank Zappa/The Mothers of Invention, *Freak Out!* (Zappa Records)

Stevie Wonder, *Talking Book* (Motown) or *Innervisions* (Motown)

Richard and Linda Thompson, *Shoot out the Lights* (Hannibal)

Robbie Robertson/The Band, *Music from Big Pink* (Capitol) and *Robbie Robertson* (Universal Music Group)

Avengers, *Avengers* (Superior Viaduct) and "We Are the One" as well as their live set opening for the Sex Pistols at Winterland can be streamed on YouTube

Sleepers, *The Less an Object* (Tim Kerr)

Various, Miners' Benefit (White Noise Records) or entire album is on YouTube.

Mutants, *Fun Terminal* (White Noise) or all songs on YouTube. *New Dark Ages* EP (415 Records): "New Dark Ages" and Insect World" are on YouTube. Search on Tube for "Mutants live at Mabuhay" for entire sets.

# ACKNOWLEDGMENTS

I am grateful to Paul Krassner and Thomas Albright, both of whom are deceased, for their help in kick-starting my journalism career.

Thanks to Pat Thomas, who suggested I contact Backbeat Books and pitch this book to them. To Greil Marcus for his flattering Foreword. To Amy Rennert for her timely advice on publishing contracts and to Cory Storch of the Authors Guild for his valuable advice.

Thanks to the late Jim Henke at *Rolling Stone* who taught me plenty about reporting and writing news stories and profiles, and to Jann Wenner for letting Jim hire me. Thanks to John Goddard, who when I was a teenager owned and ran Village Music in Mill Valley. John played great records in his store and introduced me to Bessie Smith and many others. Thanks to Lester Bangs for answering a high school student's letter about writing record reviews for *Creem*. Thanks to Ed Ward and John Morthland, both now deceased, for giving me insight, as a teenager, into the world of rock criticism. Thanks to Jaan Uhelszki for interviewing Patti Smith with me and being up for having our interview be included in this book. Thanks to Toby Byron, who cofounded *Hard Road* with me when we were 17, and who was my partner in crime for many rock & roll adventures when we were teenagers. Thanks to the many editors I worked with on pieces included in this book, and pieces that aren't, including David Armstrong, Adam Moss, Pam Brunger, Nancy Friedman, Patrick Fox, David Kleinberg, Marian Zaillian, Charlie Haas, John Battelle, Ira Kamin, James Stark, Vic Gabarini, David Talbot, Andy Schwartz, Brian Wise, Simon Warner, Alan Light, Michael E. Miller, Mary Eisenhart, Ira Robbins, Susan Whitall, and the others from long, long ago whose names now escape me.

Thanks to Chester Simpson, Robert Knight, Vincent Anton Stornaiuolo, Roni Hoffman, and Charles Peterson for their wonderful photos; to Christopher Aguirre, Bill Rossi, Corin Tucker, Carrie Brownstein, Chris Lines, and Toby Silver for your help regarding the book cover; and to Steve DePace for the Flipper T-shirt art. Thanks to Frank Kozik for designing the *Addicted To Noise* logo back in 1994.

Thanks to Jeff Rosen and Mike Kappus for your help, and to Mark Mothersbaugh, David Blau, and Arthur Sadler for getting me permission to quote from the Devo song "Jocko Homo." Thanks to former Eyes singer/lyricist Alicia Pojanowski for giving me permission to quote from her songs.

Thanks to John Cerullo who was the editor at Backbeat Books who initially expressed interest in publishing this book and made me an offer I couldn't refuse; to Chris Chappell, who took over from John and has seen this book through to publication; and to Barbara Claire and Laurel Myers who dealt with much of the day-to-day of my interactions with Backbeat.

Thanks to my family: Leslie, Joe, Anne, Norah, and Sam. I love you all.

And thanks to Nici and Yuki, both dogs, who keep my days exciting.

Thanks to my best friend David Monterey, who is truly the best; thanks for your friendship and for being so supportive of my projects, including this book.

And thanks to all the artists written about in this book who made themselves available for interviews and, in some cases, let me hang around for days so I could observe them in their rock & roll world.

# PERMISSIONS

I want to thank Penguin/Random House and Bill Rossi for giving me permission to base the cover of this book on the original 1953 cover of William Burroughs' *Junkie*, a painting by Al Rossi. *Highway 61 Revisited* album cover © Sony Music Entertainment. All rights reserved. Reprinted by permission. *The Great John Lee Hooker* cover art © Ace Records. All rights reserved. Reprinted by permission. *Call the Doctor* cover art © Sleater-Kinney. All rights reserved. Reprinted by permission. Flipper logo © Flipper. All rights reserved. Reprinted by permission.

Patti Smith: Return of the "Bad Girl" © Michael Goldberg & Jaan Uhelszki. All rights reserved. Reprinted by permission.

Zappa as Reporter, Historian and Cynic © Michael & Leslie Goldberg. All rights reserved. Reprinted by permission.

Punk Lives!, James Brown: Wrestling with the Devil, John Fogerty Looks Back on the Glory Days of Creedence Clearwater Revival, Michael Jackson: The Making of The King of Pop, The Last Days of Dennis Wilson, Brian Wilson: God Only Knows, Stevie Wonder: The Timeless World of Wonder and The Second Coming of Robbie Robertson © Rolling Stone LLC. All rights reserved. Reprinted by permission of Jann Wenner/Rolling Stone LLC.

"Alley Flowers" and "All the Morning Birds" © Jolie Holland. "The Littlest Birds" © Jolie Holland and Samantha Parton. All rights reserved. Reprinted by permission.

"O Superman (For Massenet)" © Laurie Anderson/Difficult Music. All rights reserved. Reprinted by permission.

"Jocko Homo" written by Mark Mothersbaugh. Courtesy Devo. Copyright BMG Rights Management UK Ltd., a BMG Company.

"The Size of Love," "Get Up," and "The End of You" written by Carrie Brownstein and Corin Tucker of Sleater-Kinney. Copyright BMG Rights Management UK Ltd., a BMG Company. Reprinted by permission.

"'B' Movie" by Gil Scott-Heron. Copyright Brouhaha Music Inc. Reprinted by permission.

Thanks to former Eyes singer/lyricist Alicia Pojanowski for permission to quote from "Happy in the Attic," "Siren Sniper," and "Closet Queen." Pojanowski wrote the lyrics to those songs while Peggy White wrote the music. The lyrics to those songs are copyright Alicia Pojanowski.

Photographs of Frank Zappa, Bob Dylan, Ramblin' Jack Elliott, Professor Longhair, Van Morrison, Patti Smith, Muddy Waters, Crime, David Byrne, Townes Van Zandt, Jolie Holland, Tom Waits, Devo, Neil Young, Flamin' Groovies, Lou Reed, George Clinton, Captain Beefheart, The Clash, Stevie Wonder, the Ramones, the Avengers, Sam Andrews, Janis Joplin, Phil Lesh, Peter Kraemer, Jerry Garcia (*Hard Road* cover), the Sex Pistols, Robbie Robertson, and Alicia Pojanowski of Eyes © Michael Goldberg. All rights reserved. Used with permission.

Original *Addicted To Noise* logo reproduced courtesy of Frank Kozik, who designed it.

Photographs of James Brown, Prince, Rick James, Silvertone, Laurie Anderson, Michael Jackson, and Black Flag © Chester Simpson / Rock-N-RollPhotos.com. All rights reserved. Used with permission.

Photograph of John Lee Hooker © Robert Knight. All rights reserved. Used with permission.

Photograph of Prince © Daniel Gluskoter/dgpics.com All rights reserved. Used with permission.

Photograph of John Fogerty © Myriam Santos All rights reserved. Used with permission.

Photograph of Sleater-Kinney © Charles Peterson. All rights reserved. Used with permission.

Photograph of Flipper © VinceAntonPhoto. All rights reserved. Used with permission.

Photograph of Michael Goldberg © Roni Hoffman. All rights reserved. Used with permission.

"I Am Waiting" by Lawrence Ferlinghetti, from A CONEY ISLAND OF THE MIND, copyright ©1958 by Lawrence Ferlinghetti. Reprinted by permission of New Directions Publishing Corp.